D1761367

Handbook of Cultural Intelligence

Theory, Measurement, and Applications

Editors Soon Ang and Linn Van Dyne

Foreword by Harry C. Triandis

M.E.Sharpe
Armonk, New York
London, England

Library of Congress Cataloging-in-Publication Data

Handbook of cultural intelligence : theory, measurement, and applications /
edited by Soon Ang and Linn Van Dyne.
p. cm.
Includes bibliographical references and index.
ISBN 978-0-7656-2262-4 (cloth : alk. paper)
1. Diversity in the workplace. 2. Cultural awareness. 3. Social
intelligence. I. Ang, Soon. II. Van Dyne, Linn, 1949-

HF5549.5.M5H355 2008
331.2′153—dc22 2008027898

Printed in the United States of America

The paper used in this publication meets the minimum requirements of
American National Standard for Information Sciences
Permanence of Paper for Printed Library Materials,
ANSI Z 39.48-1984.

BM (c) 10 9 8 7 6 5 4 3 2

Contents

CQ as a Mediator

List of Tables and Figures

TABLES

FIGURES

Foreword
Cultural Intelligence

HARRY C. TRIANDIS

The world includes top mathematicians, pianists, statesmen, economists, educators, philosophers, athletes, and so on. All of them are intelligent; some aspects of their intelligence are the same and other aspects are different. There are also individuals who are extraordinarily effective in getting along with people from other cultures. These are the individuals who are culturally intelligent (they have high CQ).

This handbook describes CQ by examining the theory, methods, and results of the growing body of research on CQ produced in the past few years. It includes sophisticated analyses of what intelligence is and how it is conceptualized, measured, and related to its antecedents and consequences.

Sometimes one can understand a construct better by considering its opposite. Just as we can better understand "day" by considering "night," so we can understand CQ better if we consider some examples of people who are culturally unintelligent. There are cultures of honor, in the parts of the world from the Mediterranean to northwest China, as well as in parts of other regions of the world. In these cultures honor is central to the way people think about themselves and others. Women are the focus of family honor. Thus, when women do something that "dishonors" the family, according to the local norms, they must be killed. The United Nations estimates that there are 5,000 "virgin suicides" in honors cultures each year. If a girl acquires an inappropriate boyfriend, the family demands that she commit suicide. This is a major problem among Muslims in Europe, because the girls acquire Western values yet their families still hold the values of the honor cultures. The parents are culturally unintelligent and the results are terrible for the whole family.

One specific example will indicate how undesirable the concept of honor is in the context of modern Europe. The girl was Norwegian; the parents were Moroccans. The parents abducted the girl and took her to Morocco to marry a boy of their choice. Honor required that the girl obey her parents. The girl managed to get in touch with the Norwegian ambassador to Morocco and he intervened. The Norwegian government told the father that he would lose his pension if he persisted. The father had a heart attack and died. The girl was ostracized by the Norwegian Muslims. Thus, everybody lost. When there is a large cultural distance, it is necessary to train immigrants to understand the consequences of their immigration, and to become somewhat culturally intelligent. In my opinion it is irresponsible to give permanent visas to people who do not understand the local culture. It is also undesirable to use the "leave them alone" policy in "respecting" immigrant cultures. Immigrant cultures need to change, and people must become culturally intelligent or stay in the margins of society. People who are culturally intelligent zero in on aspects of culture that are different and respond appropriately.

The *Handbook of Cultural Intelligence* reviews empirical research that shows that knowing the local language, possessing cross-cultural work experience, and having lived in diverse cultural settings increase CQ. Studying abroad and taking even short trips to other cultures can also increase CQ. Interaction with unfamiliar cultures increases uncertainty about how to behave and anxiety about doing the right things, which results in cognitive simplicity. This simplicity results in behavioral inflexibility and lower-quality decisions. Cognitively simple people have a narrow framework for viewing the world that typically includes their stereotypes and prejudices and fails to appreciate the important aspects of intercultural situations. Certain personality attributes, such as openness to new experience, reduce the negative effects of interaction with strange cultures. The general beliefs that people have about the world also interact with CQ.

This book examines the content of CQ in great detail and reviews a rich literature on intercultural encounters. Correlations between CQ and personality measures, scores on different types of intelligence, as well as the antecedents and consequences of CQ result in a nomological network that is very impressive. Many findings are moderated by the extent to which cultures are different. Cultural distance can include the distance between languages (e.g., English and German are more similar than English and Mandarin), the distance in the types of family systems (patriarchal versus equal power of mother and father), and the socioeconomic level, religion, and values of the participants.

This book includes important empirical examinations of the way cultural distance and CQ interact with employee performance. Several chapters examine the way these variables impact the CEOs of global organizations. One cannot understand global leadership without the CQ construct. CQ affects expatriate adjustment, performance, retention, and career success. Personality dimensions interact with CQ to modify performance. Empirical work in the field shows how CQ mediates the relationship between personality and general adjustment.

Several authors have included suggestions for future research that are bound to be most productive. The *Handbook* shows that multicultural teams that develop a global identity (the sense of belonging to a group that is nested within a global work environment and has the expectation that one will work in such groups) and include members who are high in CQ are especially effective. The self must include roles relevant for working in such groups. Global identity and CQ are correlated. CQ attenuates the adverse effects of cultural diversity on interpersonal trust. Those high in CQ respond more effectively to changes in the external environment (e.g., a government changing a law) than those who are low in CQ. The *Handbook* also includes important discussions of the meaning of intercultural sensitivity. Those high in CQ have both verbal and nonverbal skills that enhance effective interaction in multicultural environments. English is widely used in such settings, but there are many "Englishes," and one must be able to identify which English is being used. High CQ means constructing and interpreting communications and taking their context into account.

An important strength of this book is the empirical work. A four-faceted measure of CQ was developed that has excellent psychometric attributes. This 20-item inventory was carefully developed and can be used across cultures and time. It has both self-report and observer-report items. The measure predicts many important variables, such as adjustment to different cultures, and provides a solid basis for scientific work.

The *Handbook* also discusses the use of new methods of intelligence testing, such as dynamic testing, which integrates testing and the instruction of the child. This method of testing intelligence measures the ability to learn and is a different and more effective way of measuring intelligence. It measures aspects of intelligence not tapped by conventional methods. Culture must be included in the concept of intelligence. Otherwise the concept is lacking some utility. The methods used in this book are diverse, and include the testing of large samples as well as in-depth interviews with a handful of global managers.

The work has many applications, such as to counseling, negotiations, and working as missionaries. It also has implications for human relations practitioners working on the selection, training, and promotion of individual workers and others working in global settings.

The *Handbook of Cultural Intelligence* is the beginning of a new era in the study of intercultural interaction. It provides theory and new methods for the scientific study of interactions in multicultural settings. It also describes promising empirical findings that can become the basis for future work.

Preface and Acknowledgments

SOON ANG AND LINN VAN DYNE

P. Christopher Earley and Soon Ang introduced the concept of cultural intelligence (CQ) to the social sciences and management disciplines in 2003. At that time, as now, the world was experiencing unprecedented globalization and interconnectedness prompted by advanced communication and transportation technologies. Simultaneously, the world has also been experiencing ideological clashes and cultural conflict.

Thus, although globalization may lead some to regard the world as "flattening out," cultural differences and cultural diversity present critical challenges to people all over the world. Technology and popular culture may be forces for convergence, yet deep-level cultural differences are not converging and the world is not "flat." Instead, globalization increases intercultural interactions and the probability that intercultural misunderstandings, tensions, and conflicts will occur.

CQ is defined as an individual's capability to function effectively in situations characterized by cultural diversity. Initially conceived as an individual level construct, CQ can also be applied across levels of analysis. CQ has relevance to groups, teams, organizations, and even nations.

Since 2003, the concept of CQ has attracted significant attention worldwide and across diverse disciplines. In 2004, we organized the first symposium on CQ at the Academy of Management annual meeting. In 2006, the journal *Group and Organization Management* devoted an entire special issue to CQ. In the same year, we organized the first Global Conference on Cultural Intelligence. At this conference, experts in international management, cross-cultural psychology, cross-cultural management, social psychology, and applied linguistics discussed many different perspectives on CQ and worked collaboratively to develop ideas for future CQ theory and empirical research.

Our CQ research has been presented to numerous organizations, which include the Society for Industrial and Organizational Psychology (2005); American Psychological Association (2005); International Conference in Information Systems (2005); International Academy of Intercultural Relations Conference in Taiwan (2004); the 26th International Congress of Applied Psychology in Athens, Greece (2006); the Shanghai Conference on Cultural Intelligence in China (2006); the United States Defense Advanced Research Projects Agency (DARPA) in 2007; and the International Military Testing Association (IMTA) in 2007.

We subsequently published a paper on measurement and predictive validity of CQ in *Management and Organization Review* (Ang ,Van Dyne, Koh, Ng, Templer, Tay, & Chandrasekar, 2007). The paper provided empirical evidence that the 20-item measure of CQ is stable across samples, time, and countries. More importantly, it represents a significant milestone in the research on CQ by showing that it is distinct from and has predictive validity over and above other forms of intelligence, demographic characteristics, and personality.

Since 2004, scholars from different cultures from around the world have begun to use this scale to increase understanding of predictors, consequences, mediators, and moderators in the nomological network surrounding CQ. Our objective in editing this volume was to bring together leading examples of research on CQ. Appropriately, researchers from diverse cultures, nations, and disciplines have contributed to the creation of the *Handbook of Cultural Intelligence.*

The *Handbook* is divided into six parts. Part I introduces the conceptual and empirical foundation for the concept of CQ. Chapter 1 clarifies the definition, distinctiveness, and nomological network of CQ, and Chapter 2 describes development and validation of the 20-item CQ Scale (CQS). Specifically, the epistemology and etiology for each of the four factors of CQ and evidence of the different forms of construct validity are provided.

The eight chapters in part II, "Extending the CQ Nomological Network," extend the nomological network of CQ. In Chapter 3, Shannon and Begley (Ireland) examine language skills, international work experiences, and social networks as differential predictors of CQ. In Chapter 4, Tarique and Takeuchi (a team of researchers from the United States and Hong Kong) explore the extent to which international nonwork experiences are related to CQ. In Chapter 5, Kim, Kirkman, and Chen (United States) present a rich conceptual model and preliminary findings on CQ and international assignment effectiveness. In Chapter 6, Mannor (United States) offers a formal critique of the current strategic leadership literature and proposes a new model of executive leadership that incorporates the concept of CQ. In Chapter 7, Shaffer and Miller (United States) develop testable propositions for direct and indirect effects of CQ on multiple expatriate success outcomes including expatriate adjustment, performance, retention, and career success. In Chapter 8, Tay, Westman, and Chia (a team of researchers from Singapore and Israel) examine CQ as a personal resource that alleviates short-term, international business traveler burnout, using a sample that spans Singapore, Israel, and Brazil. In Chapter 9, Oolders, Chernyshenko, and Stark (New Zealand, Singapore, and the United States) examine the complex relationship between CQ and its close personality correlate of openness to experience. In Chapter 10, Ward and Fischer (New Zealand) examine CQ as a mediator that links personality and general adjustment of international students studying in New Zealand.

The four chapters in part III, CQ Applied to Multicultural Teams," collectively explore CQ in the context of multicultural teams. In Chapter 11, Shokef and Erez (Israel) consider CQ and global identity and their differential effects on multicultural team performance. In Chapter 12, Flaherty (United States) explores the relationships between CQ and multinational team member acceptance and integration. In Chapter 13, Rocksthul and Ng (Singapore) apply social relations model methodology and demonstrate that CQ mitigates the negative effects of cultural diversity on trust. Finally, in Chapter 14, Gibson and Dibble (United States) develop the concept of collaboration external adjustment and highlight the role of CQ in increasing collaboration.

Part IV, "CQ Applied Across Disciplines," provides examples of how CQ can be applied across diverse disciplines. In Chapter 15, Rogers (United States) focuses specifically on the behavioral dimension of CQ and discusses its application to the field of cross-cultural applied linguistics. In Chapter 16, Goh, Koch, and Sanger (United States) differentiate CQ from the more general construct of multicultural counseling competence and discuss ways that CQ can be used in the field of counseling psychology. In Chapter 17, Livermore (United States) uses the CQ framework to show how CQ can be used in short-term international missions.

Part V, "CQ and Related Constructs," includes six chapters that consider similarities and differences between CQ and other related constructs. In Chapter 18, Elenkov and Pimentel (United States) discuss conceptual distinctions and similarities among cultural, social, and emotional intelligences. In Chapter 19, Sternberg (United States) offers a historical perspective on the theory of intelligences and discusses successful intelligence as a framework for understanding cultural adaptation. In Chapter 20, Klafehn, Banerjee, and Chiu (United States) explore contextualized knowledge and flexibility in switching cultural frames as mechanisms for enhancing the metacognitive dimension of CQ. In Chapter 21, Leung and Li (Hong Kong) describe the concept of social axioms—general beliefs that people have about their social world—and propose that social axioms can be integral to the cognitive dimension of CQ. In Chapter 22, Bhawuk, Sakuda, and Munusamy (United States and Singapore) introduce a model of triple-loop cultural learning with implications for CQ. Finally, in Chapter 23, Janssens and Cappellen (Belgium) consider CQ in the context of global managers who regularly work across numerous cultures without becoming experts in particular cultures.

The book concludes with a commentary (part VI) by Gelfand, Imai, and Fehr (United States). This chapter provides an integrative overview of the diverse research on CQ included in the *Handbook.* It also offers creative, innovative, and insightful suggestions for future theory development and empirical research on CQ.

ACKNOWLEDGMENTS

This project reflects the strong and ongoing collaborative efforts of the two editors (Singapore and the United States). We have been research collaborators since we attended graduate school at the University of Minnesota more than 15 years ago, and we enjoy working together despite our cultural differences, disparate geographic locations, and the 12-hour time zone difference.

The *Handbook,* however, goes well beyond our own efforts and would not have been possible without the support and contributions of others. First, we wish to thank Harry Triandis, our cultural mentor, who guided us with his wisdom and caring heart though this CQ journey.

We also acknowledge the special contributions of Ms. Wee Ling Heng and Ms. Hooi Chen Lee. We especially appreciate their gracious and tireless efforts in formatting the chapters, checking the references, and tactfully following up with contributors on missing information and deadlines.

We also thank Harry Briggs, executive editor of M.E. Sharpe, who is a sheer pleasure to work with, as well as Elizabeth Granda, associate editor, and Stacey Victor, production editor, also at M.E. Sharpe, for being on top of every detail throughout the publishing process.

Most of all, we thank the community of authors who contributed chapters to this handbook. Each contributor showed personal commitment to this new idea of CQ and invested significant time and energy in helping to increase our knowledge of CQ. In addition, we thank everyone for their timely contributions and their cooperation given the stringent deadlines for publishing this monumental book.

For updates on the latest information on Cultural Intelligence, please see the Web site: www.culturalq.com.

REFERENCES

Ang, S., Van Dyne, L., Koh, C., Ng, K.Y., Templer, K.J., Tay, C., & Chandrasekar, N.A. (2007). Cultural intelligence: Its measurement and effects on cultural judgment and decision making, cultural adaptation, and task performance. *Management and Organization Review, 3,* 335–371.

Earley, P.C., & Ang, S. (2003). *Cultural intelligence: Individual interactions across cultures.* Palo Alto, CA: Stanford University Press.

PART I

INTRODUCTION

CHAPTER 1

Conceptualization of Cultural Intelligence

Definition, Distinctiveness, and Nomological Network

SOON ANG AND LINN VAN DYNE

As organizations globalize and the workforce becomes more diverse, it is increasingly important to understand why some individuals function more effectively than others in culturally diverse situations (Erez & Earley, 1993; Gelfand, Erez, & Aycan, 2007; Triandis, 1994). Responding to this need, Earley and Ang (2003) drew on Sternberg and Detterman's (1986) multidimensional perspective of intelligence to develop a conceptual model of cultural intelligence (CQ)—defined as the capability of an individual to function effectively in situations characterized by cultural diversity. CQ research aims to provide insight into the age-old sojourner problem of why some people thrive in culturally diverse settings, but others do not.

This chapter introduces a four-factor measure of CQ, positions it in a nomological network and in the broader domain of individual differences, and concludes with a discussion of theoretical and practical implications.

THE FOUR-FACTOR MODEL OF CULTURAL INTELLIGENCE

Conceptualization of CQ

Cultural intelligence, defined as an individual's capability to function and manage effectively in culturally diverse settings, is consistent with Schmidt and Hunter's (2000, p. 3) definition of general intelligence as, "the ability to grasp and reason correctly with abstractions (concepts) and solve problems." Although early research tended to view intelligence narrowly as the ability to grasp concepts and solve problems in academic settings, there is now increasing consensus that "intelligence may be displayed in places other than the classroom" (Sternberg & Detterman, 1986). The growing interest in "real-world" intelligence has identified new types of intelligence that focus on specific content domains, such as social intelligence (Thorndike & Stein, 1937), emotional intelligence (Mayer & Salovey, 1993), and practical intelligence (Sternberg et al., 2000). CQ similarly focuses on a specific domain–intercultural settings, and is motivated by the practical reality of globalization in the workplace (Earley & Ang, 2003). Thus, following the definition of general intelligence by Schmidt and Hunter (2000), CQ is conceptualized as a specific form of intelligence focused on an individual's ability to grasp and reason correctly in situations characterized by cultural diversity. Just as emotional intelligence (EQ) complements cognitive intelligence (IQ), in that both are important for an individual to find success at work and in personal relationships in an increasingly interdependent world (Earley & Gibson, 2002), we suggest that CQ is another complementary form of intelligence that can explain variability in coping with diversity and functioning in new cultural settings. Since the norms for social interaction vary from culture to culture, it is unlikely that cognitive intelligence, EQ, or social intelligence will translate automatically into effective cross-cultural adjustment and interaction.

Cultural Intelligence as a Multidimensional Construct

Earley and Ang (2003) built on the increasing consensus that investigation of intelligence should go beyond mere cognitive abilities (Ackerman, 1996; Gardner, 1993), and theorized that CQ is a multidimensional concept that includes metacognitive, cognitive, motivational, and behavioral dimensions. CQ as a multifactor construct is based on Sternberg and Detterman's (1986) framework of the multiple foci of intelligence. Sternberg integrated the myriad views on intelligence to propose four complementary ways to conceptualize individual-level intelligence: (a) metacognitive intelligence is knowledge and control of cognition (the processes individuals use to acquire and understand knowledge); (b) cognitive intelligence is individual knowledge and knowledge structures; (c) motivational intelligence acknowledges that most cognition is motivated and thus it focuses on magnitude and direction of energy as a locus of intelligence; and (d) behavioral intelligence focuses on individual capabilities at the action level (behavior). Sternberg's framework is noteworthy because it proposes that intelligence has different "loci" within the person, i.e., metacognition, cognition, and motivation are *mental* capabilities that reside within the "head" of the person, while overt actions are *behavioral* capabilities. Metacognitive intelligence refers to the control of cognition, the processes individuals use to acquire and understand knowledge. Cognitive intelligence refers to a person's knowledge structures and is consistent with Ackerman's (1996) intelligence-as-knowledge concept, which similarly argues for the importance of knowledge as part of a person's intellect. Motivational intelligence refers to the mental capacity to direct and sustain energy on a particular task or situation, and is based on contemporary views that motivational capabilities are critical to "real-world" problem solving (Ceci, 1996). Behavioral intelligence refers to outward manifestations or overt actions—what the person does rather than what he or she thinks (Sternberg & Detterman, 1986, p. 6). Hence, unlike metacognitive, cognitive, and motivational intelligence, which involve mental functioning, behavioral intelligence refers to the capability to display actual behaviors.

The four factors of CQ mirror contemporary views of intelligence as a complex, multifactor, individual attribute that is composed of metacognitive, cognitive, motivational, and behavioral factors (see Sternberg & Detterman, 1986; Sternberg et al., 2000). Metacognitive CQ reflects the mental capability to acquire and understand cultural knowledge. Cognitive CQ reflects general knowledge and knowledge structures about culture. Motivational CQ reflects individual capability to direct energy toward learning about and functioning in intercultural situations. Behavioral CQ reflects individual capability to exhibit appropriate verbal and nonverbal actions in culturally diverse interactions.

Metacognitive CQ. The term metacognitive CQ refers to an individual's level of conscious cultural awareness during cross-cultural interactions. People with strength in metacognitive CQ consciously question their own cultural assumptions, reflect during interactions, and adjust their cultural knowledge when interacting with those from other cultures. Metacognitive CQ involves higher-level cognitive strategies that allow individuals to develop new heuristics and rules for social interaction in novel cultural environments, by promoting information processing at a deeper level (Flavell, 1979; Nelson, 1996).

For example, a Western business executive with high metacognitive CQ would be aware, vigilant, and mindful about the appropriate time to speak up during meetings with Asians. Those with high metacognitive CQ would typically observe interactions and the communication style of their Asian counterparts (such as turn-taking), and would think about what constituted appropriate behavior before speaking up.

The metacognitive factor of CQ is a critical component of CQ for a number of reasons. First, it promotes active thinking about people and situations in different cultural settings; second, it triggers active challenges to rigid reliance on culturally bounded thinking and assumptions; and third, it drives individuals to adapt and revise their strategies so that they are more culturally appropriate and more likely to achieve desired outcomes in cross-cultural encounters.

Metacognitive CQ therefore reflects mental processes that individuals use to acquire and understand cultural knowledge, including knowledge of and control over individual thought processes (Flavell, 1979) relating to culture. Relevant capabilities include planning, monitoring, and revising mental models of cultural norms for countries or groups of people. Those with high metacognitive CQ are consciously aware of the cultural preferences and norms of different societies prior to and during interactions. These individuals also question cultural assumptions and adjust their mental models during and after relevant experiences (Brislin, Worthley, & MacNab, 2006; Nelson, 1996; Triandis, 2006).

Cognitive CQ. While metacognitive CQ focuses on higher-order cognitive processes, cognitive CQ reflects knowledge of norms, practices, and conventions in different cultures that has been acquired from educational and personal experiences. The cognitive factor of CQ therefore refers to an individual's level of cultural knowledge or knowledge of the cultural environment. Cultural knowledge includes knowledge of oneself as embedded in the cultural context of the environment. Given the wide variety of cultures in the contemporary world, cognitive CQ indicates knowledge of cultural universals as well as knowledge of cultural differences.

Cultural anthropology has documented large variations in culture. Triandis (1994) and

Murdock (1987), however, suggest that at a higher level of abstraction, cultures share some common features. These are cultural universals based on fundamental needs (because all human beings have similar basic needs). Cultural universals include technological innovations (e.g., tools), methods of getting food (e.g., hunting, agriculture), economic activity (e.g., trading), patterns of social interaction (e.g., does one talk to one's mother-in-law?), child-rearing practices, beliefs and behaviors that relate humans to the universe (e.g., religion), aesthetic preferences, patterns of communication (language, gestures), and so on.

In sum, all societies possess fundamental systems to meet basic physiological needs. As a result, societies have *economic systems* to systematically produce vital commodities and distribute products and services. Societies also codify mating and child-rearing practices that create marriage, family, and other *social systems. Educational systems* enable learning and cultural transmission, while *political, legal,* and *social control systems* reduce anarchy and destruction (obedience to social norms). To facilitate interaction, societies develop language systems and *systems of communication* (verbal and nonverbal). Finally, societies have systems for explaining the unexplainable (often relying on supernatural beliefs such as religion and witchcraft), and thus have *systems of supernatural beliefs* that help to explain otherwise inexplicable phenomena.

The cognitive factor of CQ is a critical component of CQ, because knowledge of culture influences people's thoughts and behaviors. Understanding a society's culture and the components of culture allows individuals to better appreciate the systems that shape and cause specific patterns of social interaction within a culture. Consequently, those with high cognitive CQ are better able to interact with people from a culturally different society.

Motivational CQ. Motivational CQ reflects the capability to direct attention and energy toward learning about and functioning in situations characterized by cultural differences. Kanfer and Heggestad (1997, p. 39) argue that such motivational capacities "provide agentic control of affect, cognition and behavior that facilitate goal accomplishment." According to the expectancy-value theory of motivation (Eccles & Wigfield, 2002), the direction and magnitude of energy channeled toward a particular task involves two elements: the expectation of successfully accomplishing the task and the value associated with accomplishing the task. Those with high motivational CQ direct attention and energy toward cross-cultural situations based on intrinsic interest (Deci & Ryan, 1985) and confidence in cross-cultural effectiveness (Bandura, 2002).

Motivational CQ is a critical component of CQ because it is a source of drive. It triggers effort and energy directed toward functioning in novel cultural settings. For example, a Chinese executive who has a good command of Japanese and likes interacting with those from other cultures would not hesitate to initiate a conversation with a fellow colleague from Japan. In contrast, another Chinese executive who is just learning Japanese or dislikes cross-cultural encounters would be less likely to engage in such a cross-cultural interaction.

Behavioral CQ. Finally, behavioral CQ reflects the capability to exhibit appropriate verbal and nonverbal actions when interacting with people from different cultures. Behavioral CQ refers to the extent to which an individual acts appropriately (both verbally and nonverbally) in cross-cultural situations. Behavioral CQ is a critical component of CQ, because verbal and nonverbal behaviors are the most salient features of social interactions.

As Hall (1959) emphasized, mental capabilities for cultural understanding and motivation must be complemented by the ability to exhibit appropriate verbal and nonverbal actions, based on cultural values of a specific setting. When individuals initiate and maintain face-to-face interactions, they do not have access to each other's latent thoughts, feelings, or motivation. Yet they can rely on what they see and hear in the other person's vocal, facial, and other outward expressions.

The behavioral repertoires of cultures vary in three ways: (a) in the specific range of behaviors that are enacted; (b) in the display rules that govern when and under what circumstances specific nonverbal expressions are required, preferred, permitted, or prohibited; and (c) in the interpretations or meanings that are attributed to particular nonverbal behaviors (Lustig & Koester, 1999). Consequently, individuals with high behavioral CQ are flexible and can adjust their behaviors to the specifics of each cultural interaction.

In cross-cultural situations, nonverbal behaviors are especially critical, because they function as a "silent language" and impart meaning in subtle and covert ways (Hall, 1959). Because behavioral expressions are especially salient in cross-cultural encounters, the behavioral component of CQ may be the most critical factor that observers use to assess other's CQ.

CQ as an Aggregate Multidimensional Construct

Earley and Ang's (2003) theories posit that the four dimensions of CQ are qualitatively different facets of the overall capability to function and manage effectively in culturally diverse settings. Like facets of job satisfaction, the dimensions of CQ may or may not correlate with one another. This implies that the overall CQ construct may be best conceptualized as an aggregate multidimensional construct, which according to Law, Wong, and Mobley (1998) has two distinguishing features: (a) dimensions exist at the same level of conceptualization as the overall construct and (b) dimensions make up the overall construct. Accordingly, we view metacognitive, cognitive, motivational, and behavioral CQ as different types of capabilities that together form the overall CQ construct.

CONCEPTUAL DISTINCTIVENESS OF CULTURAL INTELLIGENCE

To further clarify the nature of CQ, it is important to describe what CQ is *not,* in relation to other individual differences. Specifically, we discuss the differences and similarities between CQ and personality, other intelligences (namely cognitive ability and EQ), and existing intercultural competency models.

CQ as an Individual Difference

CQ is grounded in the larger domain of individual differences. In general, the literature suggests three broad categories of individual differences: abilities or capabilities, personality, and interests (Ackerman & Humphreys, 1990; Boyle & Saklofske, 2004; Dunnette, 1976; Ilgen & Klein, 1988; Lubinski, 2000; Murphy, 1996). Conceptually anchoring CQ in the intelligence literature clearly positions it as a set of abilities or capabilities, as opposed to personality or interests. Abilities are "those personal characteristics that relate to the capability to perform the behavior of interest" (Ilgen & Klein, 1988, p. 146). Thus, we differentiate CQ conceptually from personality characteristics, interests, and outcomes (e.g., decision making, performance, and adjustment).

Individual differences vary in their specificity and stability (Ackerman & Humphreys, 1990; Chen, Gully, Whiteman & Kilcullen, 2000; Hough & Schneider, 1996). We conceptualize CQ as a *specific* individual difference construct because it focuses on culturally relevant capabilities. Thus, it is more specific than broad individual differences, such as general cognitive ability and personality (Chen et al., 2000). It is important, however, to note that CQ is not specific to a particular culture (e.g., CQ does not focus on the capability to function specifically in France or Japan as in the Culture-Specific Assimilator as described by Triandis [1995]). Thus, CQ is specific to particular types of situations (culturally diverse) and it is not culture specific.

With regard to stability over time, Chen et al. (2000) described personality as relatively stable, traitlike, individual differences, while capabilities and interests are more statelike, evolving over time. Since CQ is malleable and can be enhanced through experience, education, and training, it is a statelike individual difference. Like other forms of intelligence (Mayer, Caruso, & Salovey, 2000), CQ should increase based on multicultural and international experiences (Takeuchi, Tesluk, Yun, & Lepak, 2005). In sum, CQ is a specific, statelike, individual capability within the larger domain of individual differences.

CQ in Relation to Personality

As an ability, CQ refers to what a person can do to be effective in culturally diverse settings. Thus, it is distinct from stable personality traits, which describe what a person typically does across situations and times (Costa & McCrae, 1992). Since temperament influences choice of behaviors and experiences, some personality traits should be related to CQ. Consistent with this, Ang, Van Dyne, and Koh (2006) showed discriminant validity of the four dimensions of CQ compared to the Big Five personality traits and demonstrated meaningful relationships between specific personality characteristics and specific aspects of CQ. Notably, and as expected, openness to experience, which is the tendency to be imaginative, creative, and adventurous (Costa & McCrae, 1992), was related to all four dimensions of CQ. This makes sense since CQ is a set of capabilities targeted at novel and unfamiliar cultural situations.

CQ in Relation to Other Intelligence Constructs

CQ is similar to, yet distinct from two other forms of intelligence: general cognitive ability and EQ (Mayer & Salovey, 1993; Schutte, Malouff, Hall, Haggerty, Cooper, Golden, & Dornheim, 1998). CQ is similar to both types of intelligence because it deals with a set of abilities, rather than preferred ways of behaving (Mayer, Caruso & Salovey, 2000). CQ differs, however, from the two other intelligences in the nature of the ability examined. General cognitive ability, the ability to learn, is an important individual difference that predicts performance across many jobs and settings (Schmidt & Hunter, 1998). General cognitive ability, however, is not specific to certain contexts (Ackerman & Humphreys, 1990; Hough & Schneider, 1996), such as culturally diverse situations. In addition, general intelligence does not include behavioral or motivational aspects of intelligence.

EQ focuses on the ability to deal with personal emotions and is similar to CQ because it goes beyond academic and mental intelligence. However, EQ differs from CQ because it focuses on the general ability to perceive and manage emotions without consideration of cultural context. Given that emotional cues are symbolically constructed and historically transmitted within a culture (Fitch, 1998), the ability to encode or decode emotions in the home culture does not automatically transfer to unfamiliar cultures (Earley & Ang, 2003). Thus, EQ is culture bound, and a person who has high EQ in one cultural context may not be emotionally intelligent in another culture. In contrast, CQ is culture free and refers to a general set of capabilities with relevance to situations characterized by cultural diversity; it does not focus on capabilities in a particular culture.

CQ Scale in Relation to Other Scales of Intercultural Competencies

Paige's (2004) comprehensive review of intercultural instruments identifies ten scales that can be compared to the CQ Scale (CQS): Cross-Cultural Adaptability Inventory (CCAI) (Kelley & Meyers, 1995); Cross-Cultural World Mindedness (CCWM) (Der-Karabetian, 1992); Cultural Shock Inventory (CSI) (Reddin, 1994); Culture–General Assimilator (CGA) (Cushner & Brislin, 1996); Global Awareness Profile Test (GAPT) (Corbitt, 1998); Intercultural Development Inventory (IDI) (Hammer & Bennett, 1998); Intercultural Sensitivity Inventory (ISI) (Bhawuk & Brislin, 1992); Multicultural Awareness–Knowledge-Skills Survey (MAKSS) (D'Andrea, Daniels, & Heck, 1991); Overseas Assignment Inventory (OSI) (Tucker, 1999); and Sociocultural Adaptation Scale (SAS) (Ward & Kennedy, 1999). We also identified the Intercultural Adjustment Potential Scale (ICAPS) (Matsumoto & Associates, 2001) for comparison with the CQS.

Of these eleven cultural competency scales, two scales CCWM and ICAPS have virtually no overlap with the CQS because they focus primarily on nonability and individual differences (e.g., personality, attitudes, and values). The remaining nine scales contain ability elements that can be mapped onto our CQ framework. Three include aspects of metacognition (CCAI, IDI, MAKSS), five include cognition (CSI, CGA, GAPT, MAKSS, SAS), two include motivation (CCAI, MAKSS), and five include behavioral capabilities (CSI, IDI, ISI, OAI, SAS). None of these scales, however, is based on a multidimensional theory of intelligence. Also, seven scales (CCAI, CCWM, CSI, ICAPS, IDI, MAKSS, and OAI) include stable personality characteristics, attitudes, and values, in addition to cross-cultural capabilities (e.g., CCAI includes openness to experience and CSI includes attitudes toward other cultures and personality characteristics).

In sum, existing intercultural competency scales lack coherent theoretical foundations and often mix ability and nonability characteristics. Since this approach mixes different types of individual differences, it raises questions of construct validity. In contrast, we position CQ clearly as a set of capabilities, anchored in the multiple intelligence literature. Accordingly, CQ is a "cleaner" construct that assesses multiple aspects of intercultural competence in a single instrument, based on a theoretically grounded, comprehensive, and coherent framework.

ANTECEDENTS AND CONSEQUENCES OF CQ

Since we have conceptualized CQ as more statelike than traitlike, we expect that some personality traits will be antecedents to CQ. Research by Kanfer (1990) and Chen et al. (2000) demonstrates that traitlike individual differences predict more proximal statelike individual differences because temperament influences choice of behavior and experiences. Thus, we position more stable distal traits (e.g., Big Five) and demographic characteristics (e.g., age, experience) as antecedents to the nomological network.

To avoid tautological reasoning, we also differentiate CQ (a specific capability type of individual difference) from the consequences of CQ (such as successful functioning in international or other culturally diverse settings). This parallels similar distinctions made in other literatures that differentiate behavior and outcomes of behavior (see Miltenberger, Fuqua, & Woods, 1998). We expect that those with high CQ will have more effective performance and adjustment in multicultural work groups, study-abroad programs, and expatriate assignments (Black, Mendenhall, & Oddou, 1991; Caligiuri, Hyland, Joshi, & Bross, 1998; Kraimer, Wayne, & Jaworski, 2001; Ones & Viswesvaran, 1997; Takeuchi, Yun, & Tesluk, 2002). Thus, CQ is a capability that causes, allows, and/or facilitates outcomes such as adjustment and effective performance in culturally diverse settings.

To summarize, CQ is a specific, statelike, individual capability that should be related to other forms of intelligence and other indicators of intercultural competence, while remaining conceptually and empirically distinct. CQ should predict performance and adjustment outcomes in multicultural situations.

NOMOLOGICAL NETWORK

We propose a broader nomological network (see Figure 1.1) for understanding the role of CQ in the study of individual effectiveness.

The nomological network can be described in four major relationships. First, we propose that distal individual differences relate indirectly to individual effectiveness through statelike individual differences on the four factors of CQ. The distal individual differences include more traitlike individual differences, such as the Big Five personality (Costa & McCrae, 1992); core self-evaluation (Judge & Bono, 2001); ethnocentrism (Neuliep, 2002); need for closure (Webster & Kruglanski, 1994); and self-monitoring (Snyder, 1974). Distal antecedents also include demographic and biographical individual differences (Stokes, Mumford, & Owens 1994), such as years of intercultural education and intercultural experiences (both in work and "nonwork" contexts).

Figure 1.1 **The Nomological Network of Cultural Intelligence**

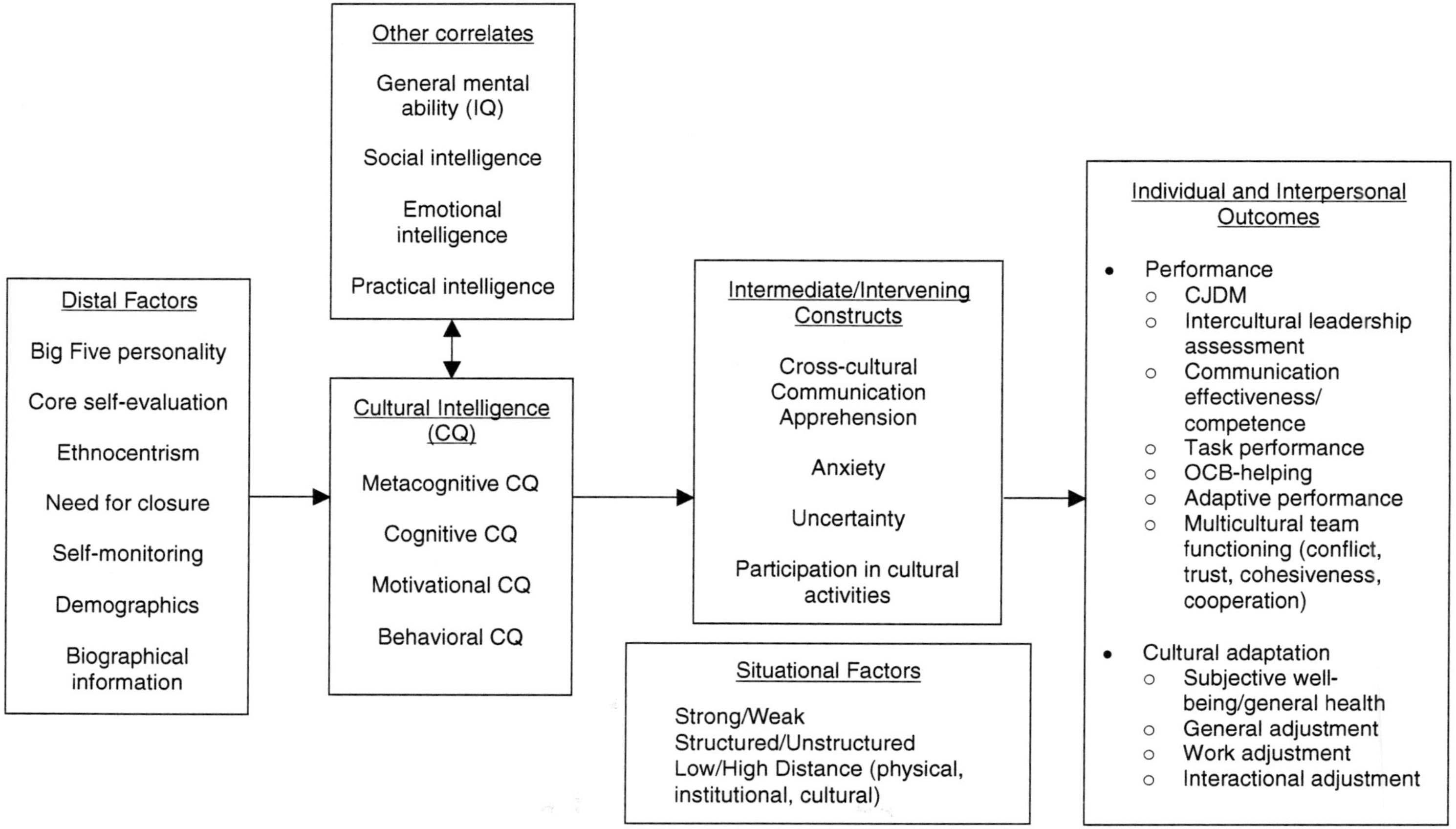

Second, the four factors of CQ affect a host of intermediate or intervening variables, such as the individual's subjective perception of cultural encounters and participation and involvement in cross-cultural roles and activities. These intermediate constructs include subjective perceptions of the uncertainty–anxiety model, which includes constructs of cross-cultural communication apprehension, uncertainty, and anxiety (Gudykunst, 2004).The four factors of CQ also relate to intermediate constructs of participation in cultural activities. Through active participation in intercultural activities, individuals acquire the requisite skills and knowledge to perform and adapt effectively in intercultural situations.

Third, the nomological network recognizes other possible contributions of an individual's cognitive ability, such as general mental ability, commonly referred to as "g," social intelligence (Thorndike, 1936; Thorndike & Stein, 1937), EQ (Mayer & Salovey, 1993); and practical intelligence (Sternberg et al., 2000), to the prediction of individual outcomes in intercultural situations.

Finally, we recognize the importance of context, which could affect the relationship between CQ and intermediate outcomes. Depending on whether the situational variables are weak or strong (Mischel, 2004), we would expect the four factors of CQ would have a stronger or weaker effect on subjective perception of the intercultural environment and participation in intercultural activities. In other words, we propose that the situational strength serves as an important moderator between the relationship of CQ and intermediate outcomes. In strong situations, where the task environment is well structured and there are clear cues for task performance, we expect CQ to play a more reduced role, since difficulties resulting from intercultural situations are attenuated as compared to weak situations. Weak situations are vague, generating mixed expectations of the desired behavior. In such situations people would have to rely much more on their CQ as guides for action (Earley & Ang, 2003; Mischel, 2004). Situational strength could also be affected by perceived cultural distance (Shenkar, 2001) of the task environment. If cultural distance is perceived to be small, we would expect that individuals share more common values and normative behaviors, and hence, CQ plays a more reduced role than in situations where cultural distance is perceived to be great.

REFERENCES

Ackerman, P.L. (1996). A theory of adult intellectual development: Process, personality, interests, and knowledge. *Intelligence, 22,* 227–257.

Ackerman, P.L., & Humphreys, L.G. (1990). Individual differences theory in industrial and organizational psychology. In M.D. Dunnette & L.M. Hough (Eds.), *Handbook of industrial and organizational psychology* (pp. 223–282). Palo Alto, CA: Consulting Psychologists Press.

Ang, S., Van Dyne, L., & Koh, C. (2006). Personality correlates of the four-factor model of cultural intelligence. *Group and Organization Management, 31,* 100–123.

Bandura, A. (2002). Social cognitive theory in cultural context. *Applied Psychology: An International Review, 51,* 269–290.

Bhawuk, D.P.S., & Brislin, R. (1992). The measurement of intercultural sensitivity using the concepts of individualism and collectivism. *International Journal of Intercultural Relations, 16,* 413–436.

Black, J.S., Mendenhall, M.E., & Oddou, G. (1991). Toward a comprehensive model of international adjustment: An integration of multiple theoretical perspectives. *Academy of Management Review, 16,* 291–317.

Brislin, R., Worthley, R., & MacNab, B. (2006). Cultural intelligence: Understanding behaviors that serve people's goals. *Group and Organization Management, 31,* 40–55.

Boyle, G.J., & Saklofske, D.H. (Eds.) (2004). Editor's introductions: Contemporary perspectives on the psychology of individual differences. In *The psychology of individual differences* (pp. xix–xvi). Thousand Oaks, CA: Sage.

Caligiuri, P.M., Hyland, M.A.M., Joshi, A., & Bross, A.S. (1998). Testing a theoretical model for examining the relationship of family adjustment and expatriate's work adjustment. *Journal of Applied Psychology, 53,* 67–88.

Ceci, S.J. (1996). *On intelligence: A bioecological treatise on intellectual development.* Cambridge, MA: Harvard University Press.

Chen, G., Gully, S.M., Whiteman, J.A., & Kilcullen, B.N. (2000). Examination of relationships among trait-like individual differences, state-like individual differences, and learning performance. *Journal of Applied Psychology, 85,* 835–847.

Costa, P.T., Jr., & McCrae, R.R. (1992). *Revised NEO personality inventory (NEO PI-R) and new five-factor inventory (NEO FFI) professional manual.* Odessa, FL: Psychological Assessment Resources.

Corbitt, J.N. (1998). *Global awareness profile (GAPtest).* Yarmouth, ME: Intercultural Press.

Cushner, K., & Brislin, R.W. (1996). *Intercultural relations: A practical guide* (2nd ed.). Thousand Oaks, CA: Sage.

D'Andrea, M., Daniels, J., & Heck, R. (1991). Evaluating the impact of multicultural counselling training. *Journal of Counseling and Development, 70,* 143–150.

Deci, E.L., & Ryan, R.M. (1985). *Intrinsic motivation and self-determination in human behavior.* New York: Plenum.

Der-Karabetian, A. (1992). World-mindedness and the nuclear threat: A multinational study. *Journal of Social Behavior and Personality, 7,* 293–308.

Dunnette, M.D. (1976). Aptitudes, abilities, and skills. In M.D. Dunnette (Ed.), *Handbook of industrial and organizational psychology* (pp. 473–520). Chicago, IL: Rand McNally.

Earley, P.C., & Ang, S. (2003). *Cultural intelligence: Individual interactions across cultures.* Palo Alto, CA: Stanford University Press.

Earley, P.C., & Gibson, C.B. (2002). *Multinational work teams: A new perspective.* Hillsdale, NJ: Lawrence Erlbaum.

Eccles, J.S., & Wigfield, A. (2002). Motivational beliefs, values, and goals. In S.T. Fiske, D.L. Schacter, & C. Zahn-Waxler (Eds.), *Annual Review of Psychology, 53* (pp. 109–132). Palo Alto, CA: Annual Reviews.

Erez, M., & Earley, P.C. (1993). *Culture, self-identity, and work.* New York: Oxford University Press.

Fitch, K. (1998). *Speaking relationally: Culture, communication and interpersonal connection.* New York: Guildford Press

Flavell, J.H.(1979). Meta-cognition and cognitive monitoring: A new area of cognitive inquiry. *American Psychologist, 34,* 906–11.

Gardner, H. (1993). *Multiple intelligence: The theory in practice.* New York: Basic Books.

Gelfand, M. J., Erez, M., & Aycan, Z. (2007). Cross-cultural organizational behavior. In S.T. Fiske, D.L. Schacter, & C. Zahn-Waxler (Eds.), *Annual Review of Psychology, 58.* (479–514). Palo Alto, CA: Annual Reviews.

Gudykunst, W.B. (2004). *Bridging differences.* Thousand Oaks, CA: Sage.

Hall, E.T. (1959). *The silent language.* New York: Doubleday.

Hammer, M.R., & Bennett, M.J. (1998). *The intercultural development inventory (IDI) manual.* Portland, OR: Intercultural Communication Institute.

Hough, L.M., & Schneider, R.J. (1996). Personality traits, taxonomies, and applications in organizations. In K.R. Murphy (Ed.), *Individual differences and behavior in organizations* (pp. 31–88). San Francisco, CA: Jossey Bass.

Ilgen, D.R., & Klein, H.J. (1988). Individual motivation and performance: Cognitive influences on effort and choice. In J.P. Campbell, R. J. Campbell, & Associates (Eds.), *Productivity in Organizations* (pp. 143–176). San Francisco, CA: Jossey-Bass.

Judge, T.A., & Bono, J.E. (2001). Relationship of core self-evaluations traits—self-esteem, generalized self-efficacy, locus of control, and emotional stability—with job satisfaction and job performance: A meta-analysis. *Journal of Applied Psychology, 86,* 80–92.

Kanfer, R. (1990). Motivation theory and industrial/organizational psychology. In M.D. Dunnette & L. Hough (Eds.), *Handbook of industrial and organizational psychology. Volume 1. Theory in industrial and organizational psychology* (pp. 75–170). Palo Alto, CA: Consulting Psychologists Press.

Kanfer, R., & Heggestad, E.D. (1997). Motivational traits and skills: A person-centered approach to work motivation. *Research in Organizational Behavior, 19,* 1–56.

Kelley, C., & Meyers, J. (1995). *The cross-cultural adaptability inventory* (manual). Minneapolis, MN: National Computer Systems.

Kraimer, M.L., Wayne, S.J., & Jaworski, R.A. (2001). Sources of support and expatriate performance: The mediating role of expatriate adjustment. *Personnel Psychology, 54,* 71–99.

Law, K.S., Wong, C.S., & Mobley, W.H. (1998). Toward a taxonomy of multidimensional constructs. *Academy of Management Review, 23,* 741–755.

Lubinksi, D. (2000). Scientific and social significance of assessing individual differences: Sinking shafts at a few critical points. *Annual Review of Psychology, 51,* 405–444.

Lustig, M.W., & Koester, J. (1999). *Intercultural competence: Interpersonal communication across cultures* (3rd ed.). New York: Addison Wesley Longman.

Matsumoto, D., LeRoux, J., Ratzlaff, C., Tatani, H., Uchida, H., Kim, C., & Araki, S. (2001). Development and validation of a measure of intercultural adjustment potential in Japanese sojourners: The Intercultural Adjustment Potential Scale (ICAPS). *International Journal of Intercultural Relations, 25,* 483–510.

Mayer, J.D., & Salovey, P. (1993) The intelligence of emotional intelligence. *Intelligence, 17,* 433–442.

Mayer, J.D., Caruso, D., & Salovey, P. (2000) Emotional intelligence meets traditional standards for an intelligence. *Intelligence, 27,* 267–298.

Miltenberger, R.G., Fuqua, W.R., & Woods, D.W. (1998). Applying behavior analysis to clinical problems: Review and analysis of habit reversal. *Journal of Applied Behavior Analysis, 31,* 447–469.

Mischel, W. (2004). Toward an integrative science of the person. *Annual Review of Psychology, 55,* 1–22.

Murdock, G.P. (1987). *Outline of cultural materials* (5th rev. ed.). New Haven, CT: HRAF.

Murphy, K.R. (1996). Individual differences and behavior in organizations: Much more than g. In K.R. Murphy (Ed.), *Individual differences and behavior in organizations* (pp. 3–30). San Francisco, CA: Jossey Bass.

Nelson, T.O. (1996). Consciousness and meta-cognition. *American Psychologist,* 51, 102–116.

Neuliep, J.W. (2002): Assessing the reliability and validity of the generalized ethnocentrism scale. *Journal of Intercultural Communication Research, 31,* 201–215

Ones, D.S., & Viswesvaran, C. (1997). Personality determinants in the prediction of aspects of expatriate job success. In Z. Aycan (Ed.), *New approaches to employee management* (pp. 63–92). Greenwich, CT: JAI Press.

Paige, R.M. (2004). Instrumentation in intercultural training. In D. Landis, J.M. Bennett, & M.J. Bennett (Eds.), *Handbook of intercultural training* (3rd ed., pp. 85–128). Thousand Oaks, CA: Sage.

Reddin, W.J. (1994). *Using tests to improve training: The complete guide to selecting, developing and using training instruments.* Englewood Cliffs: NJ: Prentice Hall.

Schmidt, F.L., & Hunter, J.E. (1998). The validity and utility of selection methods in personnel psychology: Practical and theoretical implications of 85 years of research findings. *Psychological Bulletin, 124,* 262–274.

Schmidt, F.L., & Hunter, J.E. (2000). Select on intelligence. In E.A. Locke (Ed.), *The Blackwell handbook of organizational principles* (pp. 3–14). Oxford: Blackwell.

Schutte, N.S., Malouff, J.M., Hall, L.E., Haggerty, D.J., Cooper, J.T., Golden, C.J., & Dornheim, L. (1998). Development and validation of a measure of emotional intelligence. *Personality and Individual Differences, 25,* 167–177.

Shenkar, O. (2001) Cultural distance revisited: Toward a more rigorous conceptualization and measurement of cultural differences. *Journal of International Business Studies, 32,* 519–535.

Snyder, M. 1974. The self-monitoring of expressive behavior. *Journal of Personality and Social Psychology, 30,* 526–537.

Sternberg, R.J., & Detterman, D.K. (1986). *What is intelligence? Contemporary viewpoints on its nature and definition.* Norwood, NJ: Ablex.

Sternberg, R.J., Forsythe, G.B., Hedlund, J., Horvath, J.A., Wagner, R.K., Williams, W.M., Snook, S., & Grigorenko, E.L. (2000). *Practical intelligence in everyday life.* New York: Cambridge University Press.

Stokes, G.S., Mumford, M.D., & Owens, W.A. (1994). *Biodata handbook: Theory, research, and use of biographical information in selection and performance prediction.* Palo Alto, CA: CPP Books.

Takeuchi, R., Tesluk, P.E., Yun, S., & Lepak, D.P. (2005). An integrative view of international experiences. *Academy of Management Journal, 48,* 85–100.

Takeuchi, R., Yun, S., & Tesluk, P.E. (2002). An examination of crossover and spillover effects of spouse and expatriate adjustment on expatriate outcomes. *Journal of Applied Psychology, 87,* 655–666.

Thorndike, R.L. (1936). Factor analysis of social and abstract intelligence. *Journal of Educational Psychology, 27,* 231–233.

Thorndike, R.L., & Stein, S. (1937). An evaluation of the attempts to measure social intelligence. *Psychological Bulletin, 34,* 275–285.

Triandis, H.C. (1994). *Culture and social behavior.* New York: McGraw-Hill.

Triandis, H.C. (1995). Culture specific assimilators. In S.M. Fowler (Ed.), *Intercultural sourcebook: Cross-cultural training methods* (pp. 179–186). Yarmouth, ME: Intercultural Press.

Triandis, H.C. (2006). Cultural intelligence in organizations. *Group and Organization Management, 31,* 20–26.

Tucker, M.F. (1999). Self-awareness and development using the Overseas Assignment Inventory. In S.M. Fowler & M.G. Mumford (Eds.), *Intercultural sourcebook: Cross-cultural training methods* (pp. 45–52). Yarmouth, ME: Intercultural Press.

Ward, C., & Kennedy, A. (1999). The measurement of sociocultural adaptation. *International Journal of Intercultural Relations, 23,* 659–677.

Webster, D.M., & Kruglanski, A.W. (1994). Individual differences in need for cognitive closure. *Journal of Personality and Social Psychology, 67,* 1049–1062.

CHAPTER 2

Development and Validation of the CQS
The Cultural Intelligence Scale

LINN VAN DYNE, SOON ANG, AND CHRISTINE KOH

Cultural intelligence (CQ) is a theoretical extension of contemporary approaches to understanding intelligence (Earley & Ang, 2003). CQ is defined as the capability to function effectively in culturally diverse settings. Traditionally, the study of intelligence focused mainly on "g," the academic or cognitive factor of intelligence. More recently, multiple intelligence theory (Sternberg, 1986, 1988) proposed nonacademic intelligences (Hedlund & Sternberg, 2000) that emphasize the capability to adapt to others. These newly recognized forms of intelligence include interpersonal intelligence (Gardner, 1993), emotional intelligence (Goleman, 1995; Salovey & Mayer, 1990), and social intelligence (Cantor & Kihlstrom, 1985). Each of these formulations of intelligence, however, assumes that familiarity with culture and context guides individual thoughts and social behaviors. As elaborated in Earley and Ang (2003), these relatively general capabilities may not apply when individuals have different cultural backgrounds.

DIFFERENT TYPES OF INTELLIGENCE

CQ is an important individual capability that is consistent with contemporary conceptualizations of intelligence: the ability to adapt and adjust to the environment (Cantor & Kihlstrom, 1985; Gardner, 1993; Mayer & Salovey, 1993; Sternberg, 2000). Specifically, we argue that just as nonacademic intelligences such as emotional intelligence (EQ) complement cognitive intelligence (IQ), because both are important for high-quality personal relationships and effectiveness in this increasingly interdependent world (Earley & Gibson, 2002), CQ is another complementary form of intelligence that explains adaptability to diversity and cross-cultural interactions. In sum, CQ differs from other types of intelligence, such as IQ and EQ, because it focuses specifically on settings and interactions characterized by cultural diversity. Drawing on Sternberg and Detterman's (1986) work, Earley and Ang (2003) identified three loci of individual intelligence with direct relevance to human interaction: mental (metacognition and cognition), motivational, and behavioral. For additional information on the conceptualization of CQ, see Chapter 1 in this volume and Ang, Van Dyne, Koh, Ng, Templer, Tay, and Chandrasekar (2007).

Metacognitive CQ

Metacognitive CQ is an individual's cultural consciousness and awareness during interactions with those from different cultural backgrounds. The metacognitive factor of CQ is a critical component for at least three reasons. First, it promotes active thinking about people and situations when cultural backgrounds differ. Second, it triggers critical thinking about habits, assumptions, and culturally bound thinking. Third, it allows individuals to evaluate and revise their mental maps, consequently increasing the accuracy of their understanding.

Cognitive CQ

Cognitive CQ is an individual's cultural knowledge of norms, practices, and conventions in different cultural settings. Given the wide variety of cultures in the contemporary world, cognitive CQ indicates knowledge of cultural universals as well as knowledge of cultural differences. The cognitive factor of CQ is a critical component because knowledge about cultural similarities and differences is the foundation of decision making and performance in cross-cultural situations.

Motivational CQ

Motivational CQ is an individual's capability to direct attention and energy toward cultural differences. Using the expectancy-value framework of motivation, we conceptualize motivational CQ as a special form of self-efficacy and intrinsic motivation in cross-cultural situations. Self-efficacy and intrinsic motivation play an important role in CQ because successful intercultural interaction requires a basic sense of confidence and interest in novel settings.

Behavioral CQ

Behavioral CQ is an individual's capability to exhibit appropriate verbal and nonverbal actions when interacting with people from different cultural backgrounds. Behavioral CQ is based on having and using a broad repertoire or range of behaviors. Behavioral CQ is a critical component of CQ because behavior is often the most visible characteristic of social interactions. In addition, nonverbal behaviors are especially critical because they function as a "silent language" that conveys meaning in subtle and covert ways (Hall, 1959).

EXISTING RESEARCH AND NEW CONSTRUCTS

Given the proliferation of constructs and measures in management, organizational behavior, and psychology, new theories must have a strong conceptual foundation as well as strong psychometric measures. New constructs must increase our understanding of relationships. Thus, we acknowledge the large and increasing amount of research related to CQ, with regard to culture (Adler, 2002; Erez & Earley, 1993; Hofstede, 1991; Triandis, 1994); expatriate adjustment (Bhaskar-Shrinivas, Harrison, Shaffer, & Luk, 2005; Black, Mendenhall, & Oddou, 1991; Caligiuri, Hyland, Joshi, & Bross, 1998; Mendenhall & Oddou, 1985; Shaffer, Harrison, Gregersen, Black, & Ferzandi, 2006; Takeuchi, Tesluk, Yun, & Lepak, 2005); expatriate selection and training (Spreitzer, McCall, & Mahoney, 1997); expatriate performance (Caligiuri, 2000; Kraimer, Wayne, & Jaworski, 2001; Ones & Viswesvaran, 1997; Tung, 1988); global leadership (House, Hanges, Javidan, Dorfman, & Gupta, 2004); global teams (Kirkman, Gibson, & Shapiro, 2001); cross-cultural training (Black & Mendenhall, 1990; Bhawuk & Brislin, 2000; Landis, Bennett, & Bennett, 2004; Lievens, Harris, Van Keer, & Bisqueret, 2003); and intercultural communication (Ting-Toomey, 1999; Gudykunst & Ting-Toomey, 1988).

In recognizing this research, we intend to make three key points. First, the breadth of this interdisciplinary research shows the importance of intercultural issues. Second, none of this research focuses specifically on individual capabilities to function effectively in situations characterized by cultural diversity and, therefore, CQ is unique in its conceptual focus. Third, CQ has the potential to enrich these other streams of research, just as this existing research can inform future research on CQ.

Returning to the idea that CQ must be different from existing constructs and must move beyond past research and improve our understanding of individual capabilities, we must consider whether CQ can be differentiated from cognitive ability and emotional intelligence (Mayer & Salovey, 1993), as well as adjustment and mental well-being (Black & Stephens, 1989; Ward & Kennedy, 1999). For incremental validity, we propose that CQ will make a meaningful contribution to the literature only if it increases variance above and beyond that of demographic characteristics, IQ, and EQ. For predictive validity, we examine the extent to which CQ predicts cultural judgment and decision making (CJDM), adjustment, and mental well-being.

In the next section, we report results of a series of studies that examine the construct validity of CQ. First, we describe the steps taken to define the four aspects of CQ and to develop items with which to measure these factors. Next, we describe how these items were refined and reduced to the 20-item, four-factor CQ scale (CQS) and how the stability of the scale was assessed across samples, time, countries, and methods of measurement (self-report and peer-report of CQS).

SCALE DEVELOPMENT OF THE 20-ITEM CQ SCALE

Before items were created to measure CQ, we reviewed existing intelligence and intercultural competency literatures. In addition, we interviewed eight executives with extensive global work experience. Based on these efforts, we developed operational definitions for the four theoretically based aspects of CQ: (1) Metacognitive CQ is the capability for consciousness during intercultural interactions, so we drew on educational and cognitive psychology operationalizations of metacognition (O'Neil & Abedi, 1996; Pintrich & De-

Groot, 1990) for awareness, planning, regulating, monitoring, and controlling cognitive processes of thinking and learning. (2) Cognitive CQ is the knowledge of norms, practices, and conventions in different cultural settings, so cultural knowledge domains identified by Triandis (1994) were supplemented with Murdock's (1987) Human Relations Area Files. Cultural knowledge includes knowledge of the economic, legal, and social systems in other cultures (Triandis, 1994). (3) Motivational CQ is the capability to direct attention and energy toward learning and functioning in intercultural situations, so we drew on Deci and Ryan (1985) for intrinsic satisfaction and Bandura (2002) for self-efficacy in intercultural settings. (4) Behavioral CQ is the capability to exhibit appropriate verbal and nonverbal actions when interacting with people from different cultural backgrounds, so we used intercultural communication research for verbal and nonverbal flexibility in cross-cultural interactions (Gudykunst & Ting-Toomey, 1988; Hall, 1959).

Item Pool Generation

Hinkin (1998) suggested starting with twice as many items as would be targeted in the final scale, to allow for psychometric refinement. We aimed for a parsimonious scale with four to six items for each CQ dimension to minimize response bias caused by boredom and fatigue (Schmitt & Stults, 1985), while providing adequate internal consistency reliability (Hinkin & Schriesheim, 1989). Using our operational definitions for the four CQ dimensions, we started with 53 items for the initial item pool (13–14 items per CQ dimension). Each item contained one idea, was relatively short in length, and used simple, direct language. Since negatively worded items can create artifacts (Marsh, 1996), we used positively worded items. Next, a nonoverlapping panel of three faculty and three international executives (each with significant cross-cultural expertise) independently assessed the randomly ordered 53 items for clarity, readability, and definitional fidelity (1 = very low quality; 5 = very high quality). We retained the ten best items for each dimension (40 items).

Study 1: Scale Development

Business school undergraduates (n = 576; 74 percent female; mean age 20; two years of work experience) in Singapore voluntarily completed the 40-item initial CQ questionnaire (1 = strongly disagree; 7 = strongly agree) for partial fulfillment of course requirements. In our analysis, we expected to confirm a four-factor structure since we designed the measure to reflect the four theoretical dimensions of CQ. Accordingly, we assessed dimensionality with confirmatory factor analysis (CFA) (LISREL 8: maximum likelihood estimation and correlated factors).

Starting with the initial 40 items, we conducted a comprehensive series of specification searches where we deleted items with high residuals, low factor loadings, small standard deviations or extreme means, and low item-to-total correlations. We retained 20 items with the strongest psychometric properties as the CQS: four meta-cognitive CQ, six cognitive CQ, five motivational CQ, and five behavioral CQ. Figure 2.1 lists the 20 items in the CQS. CFA demonstrated good fit of the hypothesized four-factor model to the data: χ^2

Figure 2.1 **Cultural Intelligence Scale (CQS)—Self-Report**

Read each statement and select the response that best describes your capabilities. Select the answer that BEST describes you AS YOU REALLY ARE (1 = strongly disagree; 7 = strongly agree)

CQ Factor	Questionnaire Items
Metacognitive CQ	
MC1	I am conscious of the cultural knowledge I use when interacting with people with different cultural backgrounds.
MC2	I adjust my cultural knowledge as I interact with people from a culture that is unfamiliar to me.
MC3	I am conscious of the cultural knowledge I apply to cross-cultural interactions.
MC4	I check the accuracy of my cultural knowledge as I interact with people from different cultures.
Cognitive CQ	
COG1	I know the legal and economic systems of other cultures.
COG2	I know the rules (e.g., vocabulary, grammar) of other languages.
COG3	I know the cultural values and religious beliefs of other cultures.
COG4	I know the marriage systems of other cultures.
COG5	I know the arts and crafts of other cultures.
COG6	I know the rules for expressing nonverbal behaviors in other cultures.
Motivational CQ	
MOT1	I enjoy interacting with people from different cultures.
MOT2	I am confident that I can socialize with locals in a culture that is unfamiliar to me.
MOT3	I am sure I can deal with the stresses of adjusting to a culture that is new to me.
MOT4	I enjoy living in cultures that are unfamiliar to me.
MOT5	I am confident that I can get accustomed to the shopping conditions in a different culture.
Behavioral CQ	
BEH1	I change my verbal behavior (e.g., accent, tone) when a cross-cultural interaction requires it.
BEH2	I use pause and silence differently to suit different cross-cultural situations.
BEH3	I vary the rate of my speaking when a cross-cultural situation requires it.
BEH4	I change my nonverbal behavior when a cross-cultural situation requires it.
BEH5	I alter my facial expressions when a cross-cultural interaction requires it.

(164 *df*) = 822.26, non-normed fit index (NNFI) = 0.91, comparative fit index (CFI) = 0.92, standardized root mean square residual (SRMR) = 0.06, and root mean square error of approximation (RMSEA) = 0.08 (p <0.05). Standardized factor loadings for items in the four scales (0.52–0.80) were significantly different from zero (t values: 9.30–17.51, p <0.05).

We compared this four-factor correlated model with alternate, theoretically possible models to assess relative fit compared to (1) an orthogonal four-factor model (model B), (2) three factors—metacognitive CQ and cognitive CQ combined versus motivational CQ versus behavioral CQ (model C), (3) two factors—metacognitive CQ and cognitive CQ combined versus motivational CQ and behavioral CQ combined (model D), (4) two factors—metacognitive CQ versus cognitive CQ, motivational CQ, and behavioral CQ combined (model E), and (5) one factor (model F).

Table 2.1

Comparing the Fit of Alternative Nested Models with CFA—Study 1 (n = 576)

	Model	χ^2	*df*	NNFI	CFI	SRMR	RMSEA	$\Delta\chi^2$	*p* value
A	20-item four-factor model	822.26	164	.91	.92	.06	.08		
Alternate nested models:[a]									
B	(a) Four-factor orthogonal model	1199.76	170	.87	.88	.17	.11	377.50	p <.001
C	(b) Three-factor model (metacognitive CQ and cognitive CQ combined versus motivational CQ versus behavioral CQ)	1234.17	167	.86	.88	.08	.11	411.91	p <.001
D	(c) Two-factor model (metacognitive CQ and cognitive CQ combined versus motivational CQ and behavioral CQ)	2137.25	169	.79	.81	.12	.15	1314.99	p <.001
E	(d) Two-factor model (metacognitive CQ versus the other three factors combined)	2453.43	169	.75	.77	.12	.16	1631.17	p <.001
F	(e) One-factor model with all items loading on a single factor	2753.78	170	.72	.75	.12	.17	1931.52	p <.001

[a]Compared to the hypothesized four-factor model.

Abbreviations: NNFI, non-normed fit index; CFI, comparative fit index; SRMR, standardized root mean square residual; RMSEA, root mean square error of approximation.

Nested model comparisons (see Table 2.1) demonstrate the superiority of the hypothesized four-factor model, because each of the $\Delta\chi^2$ statistics exceeds the critical value based on degrees of freedom. Model A (correlated four factors) demonstrated better fit than model B (orthogonal four factors) ($\Delta\chi^2$ [6 *df*] = 377.50, p <0.001). Model A (four factors) also had better fit than model C (three factors), which combined metacognitive CQ and cognitive CQ ($\Delta\chi^2$ [3 *df*] = 411.91, p <0.001). Likewise, model A (four factors) was a better fit than the two alternate two-factor models: model D (metacognitive CQ and cognitive CQ versus the other two factors: $\Delta\chi^2$ (5 *df*) = 1314.99, p <0.001) or model E (metacognitive CQ versus the other three factors: $\Delta\chi^2$ (5 *df*) = 1631.17, p <0.001). Finally, model A (four factors) was a better fit than model F with one factor ($\Delta\chi^2$ [6 *df*] = 1931.52, p <0.001).

In sum, the hypothesized model (model A) had the best fit. We averaged items for each factor to create scales representing each of the four CQ factors. Table 2.2 reports means, standard deviations, correlations, and Cronbach's alpha values. The four factors were moderately related (0.21–0.45), with acceptable variances (0.75–1.03). The corrected item-to-total correlations for each subscale (0.47–0.71) demonstrated strong relationships between items and their scales, supporting internal consistency. Composite reliabilities

Table 2.2

Means, Standard Deviations, Scale Reliabilities, and Intercorrelations—Study 1 (n = 576)

	MN	SD	1	2	3	4
1. Metacognitive CQ	4.71	0.75	(.71)			
2. Cognitive CQ	3.03	0.84	.39**	(.85)		
3. Motivational CQ	4.72	0.80	.45**	.33 **	(.75)	
4. Behavioral CQ	4.10	1.03	.28**	.36 **	.21**	(.83)

Note: Reliability coefficients are in parentheses along the diagonal.
$*p < .05$
$**p < .01$

Table 2.3

Means, Standard Deviations, Scale Reliabilities, and Intercorrelations—Study 2 (n = 447)

	MN	SD	1	2	3	4
1. Metacognitive CQ	4.89	0.87	(.77)			
2. Cognitive CQ	3.16	0.89	.23**	(.84)		
3. Motivational CQ	4.74	0.92	.32**	.25**	(.77)	
4. Behavioral CQ	4.22	1.05	.37**	.34**	.31**	(.84)

Note: Reliability coefficients are in parentheses along the diagonal.
$*p < .05$
$**p < .01$

exceeded 0.70 (metacognitive CQ = 0.71, cognitive CQ = 0.85, motivational CQ = 0.75, and behavioral CQ = 0.83) (Fornell & Larcker, 1981).

Study 2: Generalizability across Samples

A second, nonoverlapping sample of 447 undergraduate students in Singapore (70 percent female; mean age 20; two years of work experience) voluntarily completed the 20-item CQS for partial fulfillment of course requirements. Structrual equation modeling (SEM) analysis demonstrated good fit of the data to the hypothesized four-factor model: χ^2 (164 *df*) = 381.28, NNFI = 0.96, CFI = 0.96, SRMR = 0.04, and RMSEA = 0.05 ($p < 0.05$). Standardized loadings (0.50–0.79) were significantly different from zero (*t* values: 8.32–12.90, $p < 0.05$), with moderate correlations between factors (0.23–0.37) and acceptable variances (0.87–1.05). Corrected item-to-total correlations for each subscale (0.46–0.66) demonstrated strong relationships between items and their scales, supporting internal consistency.

Results of study 2 extend the results in study 1 and provide additional support for the four factors of CQ as measured by four items for metacognitive CQ ($\alpha = 0.77$), six for cognitive CQ ($\alpha = 0.84$), five for motivational CQ ($\alpha = 0.77$), and five for behavioral CQ ($\alpha = 0.84$). Table 2.3 reports descriptive statistics and correlations for the four factors of CQ in study 2, and Figure 2.2 reports completely standardized parameter estimates for the four-factor model.

Figure 2.2 **Confirmatory Factor Analysis of 20-Item CQ Model—Study 2 (n = 447)**

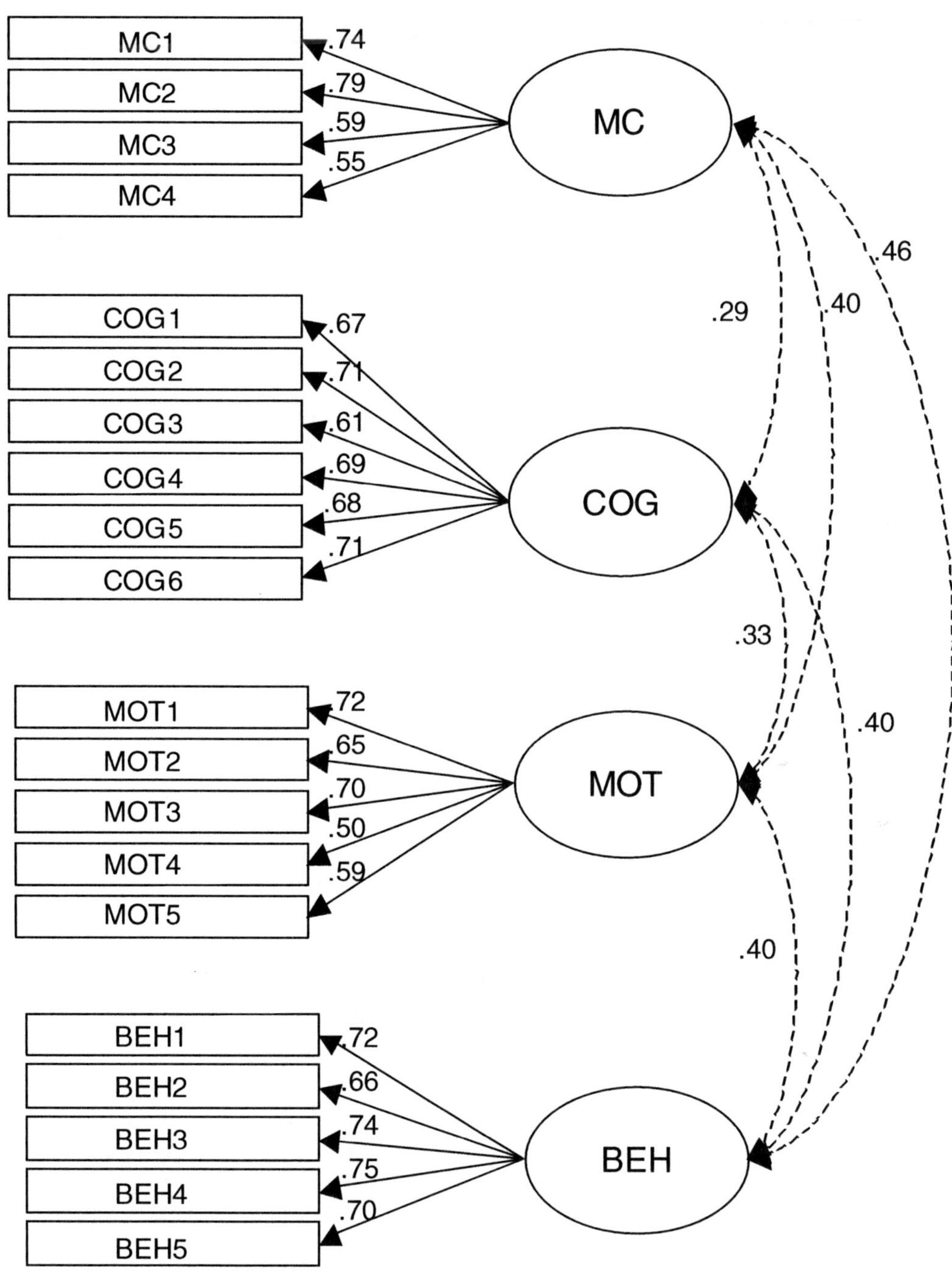

Note: x^2 (164df) = 381.28, NNFI = .96, CFI = .96, SRMR = .04, and RMSEA = .05

Table 2.4

Multiple Group CFA across Time: Comparing the Fit of Alternative Models—Study 2 (n = 204)

	Model	χ^2	*df*	NNFI	CFI	SRMR	RMSEA	$\Delta\chi^2$	*p*-value
A	Four-factor model with factor loadings freely estimated across time	981.18	692	.94	.95	.06	.04		
B	Four-factor model with invariant factor loadings across time	1003.97	708	.94	.95	.07	.05	22.79	$p > .05$
C	Four-factor model with invariant intercepts across time	1021.56	722	.94	.95	.07	.05	17.59	$p > .05$
D	Four-factor model with invariance means across time	1045.35	726	.94	.94	.07	.05	23.79	$p < .05$

Abbreviations: CFA, confirmatory factor analysis; NNFI, non-normed fit index; CFI, comparative fit index; SRMR, standardized root mean square residual; RMSEA, root mean square error of approximation.

Study 3: Generalizability across Time

A subset of respondents (n = 204; 76 percent female; mean age 20) from the Singapore cross-validation sample in study 2 completed the CQS again four months later (at the start of the next semester) in exchange for partial fulfillment of course requirements. We used these responses to analyze temporal stability of the CQS.

We examined longitudinal measurement invariance of the CQS using CFA and an augmented covariance matrix as input (rather than a multisample approach) to account for timewise correlated errors (Vandenberg & Lance, 2000). We used a 20-item by two-measurement occasion matrix and specified eight latent variables (four T1 CQ factors and four T2 CQ factors), with unique variances of identical items correlated across time (Jöreskog, 1979).

Based on procedures suggested by Vandenberg and Lance (2000), we began with a correlated four-factor model with no constraints (parameters at T1 and T2 freely estimated). Results demonstrated acceptable fit (model A: χ^2 [692 *df*] = 981.18, NNFI = 0.94, CFI = 0.95, SRMR = 0.06, RMSEA = 0.04), indicating that the four-factor model held across the two time periods (see Table 2.4). We then developed two alternative models: model B (factor loadings constrained to be invariant) and model C (item intercepts constrained to be invariant). The chi-square difference between models A and B (nested factorial invariance model) failed to reach significance ($\Delta\chi^2$ [16 *df*] = 22.79, *p* = ns), providing strong support for invariance in factor loadings across T1 and T2. The chi-square difference between models B and C (item intercepts constrained to be invariant) also failed to reach significance ($\Delta\chi^2$ [14 *df*] = 17.59, *p* = ns), supporting item intercept invariance.

We also assessed means of the four factors across time. Unlike personality charac-

Table 2.5

Means, Standard Deviations, Scale Reliabilities, and Intercorrelations—Study 4 (n = 337)

	MN	SD	1	2	3	4
1. Metacognitive CQ	4.98	0.95	(.78)			
2. Cognitive CQ	3.66	0.98	.38**	(.81)		
3. Motivational CQ	5.34	0.94	.50**	.36**	(.80)	
4. Behavioral CQ	4.20	1.14	.37**	.43**	.31**	(.81)

Note: Reliability coefficients are in parentheses along the diagonal.
*p <.05
**p <.01

teristics that are relatively stable traits, Earley and Ang (2003) conceptualized CQ as a malleable capability that may change based on cultural exposure, training, modeling, mentoring, socialization, and other experiences. Thus, we anticipated that some means for the four CQ factors could change over time, depending on experience and/or training. Comparison of model C (invariant item intercepts) with model D (invariant means) showed a decrease in fit: model C (χ^2 [722 *df*] = 1021.56) versus model D (χ^2 [726 *df*] = 1045.35), with a significant change in χ^2 ($\Delta\chi^2$ [4 *df*] = 23.79, p <0.05). Analysis of individual means demonstrated significant changes in factor means for cognitive CQ, which increased 0.33 (t = 4.87, p <0.001), and behavioral CQ, which increased 0.21 (t = 2.87, p <0.01). This makes sense because respondents studied cultural values and participated in experiential role-playing exercises during the time interval that separated T1 and T2 assessment of CQ. Neither metacognitive CQ (–0.05 [t = –0.89, p >0.05]) nor motivational CQ (0.10 [t = 1.81, p >0.05)]) changed significantly. Thus, results provide evidence of malleability as well as test–retest reliability.

Study 4: Generalizability across Countries

A fourth sample of undergraduates (n = 337; 55 percent female; mean age 22; one year of work experience) at a large school in the midwestern United States voluntarily completed the 20-item CQS for partial fulfillment of course requirements. Table 2.5 reports descriptive statistics, correlations, and reliabilities for this sample.

As recommended by Kirkman and Law (2005), we assessed equivalence of the CQS across countries and compared study 4 (U.S.) with study 2 (Singapore) (n = 447) using sequential tests of model invariance (Byrne, 1998). Model A (four factors with loadings freely estimated across samples) demonstrated good fit: χ^2 (328 *df*) = 723.23, NNFI = 0.96, CFI = 0.97, SRMR = 0.05, RMSEA = 0.05, indicating equivalence in number of factors.

We tested two alternative models: model B (four factors with loadings forced to be invariant), to test if items were interpreted equally across settings, and model C, (four factors with factor covariances forced to be invariant), to test if covariances among factors were equivalent across settings. The chi-square difference between models A and B (nested factorial invariance model) failed to reach significance ($\Delta\chi^2$ [16 *df*] = 13.74, p = ns), providing strong support for invariance in factor loadings across settings. The chi-square difference between models B and C (nested covariance invariance model) failed to reach significance ($\Delta\chi^2$ [10*df*] = 17.96, p = ns), supporting invariance in factor covariances. These multiple group tests of invariance demonstrated that the same four-factor structure holds across the two countries (Singapore and the United States).

Study 5: Generalizability across Methods

Given the self-report nature of the initial research that used the CQS, it is also important to consider observer ratings of the CQ of others. Accordingly, we developed an observer version of the CQS (Figure 2.3), which adapted each item to reflect observer ratings rather than self ratings. For example, the first item was changed from "I am conscious of the cultural knowledge I use when . . ." to "This person is conscious of the cultural knowledge he/she uses when. . . ."

We then applied multitrait multimethod (MTMM) techniques (Campbell & Fiske, 1959) to assess convergent and discriminant validity, using multiple assessors of CQ to examine generalizability across methods (self-ratings and observer ratings). If the CQS is a valid measure across methods, results for the self-report CQS should be parallel to results for the observer-report CQS. Accordingly, we used self-rated CQ to predict peer-rated interactional adjustment; and peer-rated CQ to predict self-rated interactional adjustment. Both approaches avoid common method variance because predictors (CQ) and outcomes (adjustment) are obtained from different sources (different methods of measuring CQ).

We examined these relationships with data from managers participating in an executive MBA program at a large university in the United States (n = 142; 47 percent female; average age 35). As part of a self-awareness class assignment, participants completed Web questionnaires that included self-report of CQ and interactional adjustment. In addition, each participant completed an observer questionnaire on one randomly assigned peer from their MBA team. This second Web questionnaire included a peer-report of the CQS and interactional adjustment.

We measured CQ with the 20-item CQS and interactional adjustment with three items from Black and Stephens (1989): "Rate how well you have adjusted to your current situation in terms of socializing with people, interacting with people on a day-to-day basis, getting along with people" (1 = extremely unadjusted, 7 = extremely adjusted; $\alpha = 0.91$). Respondents also provided data on sex (0 = female, 1 = male) and cross-cultural experience (number of countries lived in).

Table 2.6 reports descriptive statistics and results of the MTMM analyses, including self-report and peer-report of CQ and adjustment. Reliabilities for the two methods of self and peer ratings are shown in parentheses on the main diagonal (α = 0.79–0.95). Values of the heterotrait–monomethod triangles are shown in italics, values of the heterotrait–heteromethod triangle are underlined, and values of the monotrait–heteromethod are shown in bold.

Figure 2.3 **Cultural Intelligence Scale (CQS)—Observer Report**

Read each statement and select the response that best describes this person's capabilities. Select the answer that BEST describes this person as he/she REALLY IS (1 = strongly disagree; 7 = strongly agree)

CQ Factor	Questionnaire Items
Metacognitive CQ	
MC1	This person is conscious of the cultural knowledge he/she uses when interacting with people with different cultural backgrounds.
MC2	This person adjusts his/her cultural knowledge as he/she interacts with people from a culture that is unfamiliar.
MC3	This person is conscious of the cultural knowledge he/she applies to cross-cultural interactions.
MC4	This person checks the accuracy of his/her cultural knowledge as he/she interacts with people from different cultures.
Cognitive CQ	
COG1	This person knows the legal and economic systems of other cultures.
COG2	This person knows the rules (e.g., vocabulary, grammar) of other languages.
COG3	This person knows the cultural values and religious beliefs of other cultures.
COG4	This person knows the marriage systems of other cultures.
COG5	This person knows the arts and crafts of other cultures.
COG6	This person knows the rules for expressing nonverbal behaviors in other cultures.
Motivational CQ	
MOT1	This person enjoys interacting with people from different cultures.
MOT2	This person is confident that he/she can socialize with locals in a culture that is unfamiliar.
MOT3	This person is sure he/she can deal with the stresses of adjusting to a culture that is new.
MOT4	This person enjoys living in cultures that are unfamiliar.
MOT5	This person is confident that he/she can get accustomed to the shopping conditions in a different culture.
Behavioral CQ	
BEH1	This person changes his/her verbal behavior (e.g., accent, tone) when a cross-cultural interaction requires it.
BEH2	This person uses pause and silence differently to suit different cross-cultural situations.
BEH3	This person varies the rate of his/her speaking when a cross-cultural situation requires it.
BEH4	This person changes his/her nonverbal behavior when a cross-cultural situation requires it.
BEH5	This person alters his/her facial expressions when a cross-cultural interaction requires it.

Examination of Table 2.6 shows that results meet Campbell and Fiske's (1959) guidelines for MTMM analysis. First, the coefficients on the reliability diagonal (numbers in parentheses) are the highest in the matrix. Second, the coefficients on the validity diagonals (in bold) show the correlations between self-ratings and peer-ratings for metacognitive CQ (0.41), cognitive CQ (0.54), motivational CQ (0.50), and behavioral CQ (0.45). Each of these is significantly different from zero, indicates convergent validity, and is high enough

Table 2.6

Results of the Five Traits × Two Methods MTMM Analysis—Study 5 (n = 142)

	MN	SD	1	2	3	4	5	6	7	8	9	10
Self-Rated												
1. Metacognitive CQ	5.11	1.04	(.79)									
2. Cognitive CQ	4.14	1.53	_.76**_	(.95)								
3. Motivational CQ	5.29	1.29	_.55**_	_.56*_	(.92)							
4. Behavioral CQ	4.98	1.19	_.61**_	_.54**_	_.42**_	(.85)						
5. Interactional Adjustment	5.59	0.94	_.21*_	_.09_	_.16_	_.19*_	(.91)					
Peer-Rated												
6. Metacognitive CQ	5.11	0.94	__.41**__	.33**	.35**	.40**	.18	(.88)				
7. Cognitive CQ	4.81	1.13	.40**	__.54**__	.49**	.44**	.11	_.49**_	(.94)			
8. Motivational CQ	5.17	1.13	.37**	.48**	__.50**__	.36**	.14	_.53**_	_.61**_	(.92)		
9. Behavioral CQ	4.83	1.05	.35**	.32**	.24**	__.45**__	.27**	_.71**_	_.54**_	_.45**_	(.90)	
10. Interactional Adjustment	5.87	0.80	.26**	.23**	.31**	.34**	__.37**__	_.33**_	_.22*_	_.35**_	_.30**_	(.91)

Note: The four traits are metacognitive CQ, cognitive CQ, motivational CQ, behavioral CQ, and interactional adjustment.
The two methods are self-rating and peer-rating.
The numbers on the diagonal are the coefficient alphas.
Italic numbers are in the heterotrait-monomethod analyses.
Underlined numbers are in the heterotrait-heteromethod analyses.
Bold numbers are the results of the monotrait-heteromethod analyses.
Numbers in solid triangles are heterotrait-monomethod correlations.
Numbers in dotted triangles are heterotrait-heteromethod correlations.
*p <.05
**p <.01
Abbreviation: MTMM = multitrait-multimethod.

to warrant further investigation. Third, these validity coefficients are higher than other values in each respective column and row, providing evidence of discriminant validity.

Although the Campbell and Fiske (1959) analyses are standard, they are not sufficiently precise or normative to evaluate how well the data fit, with respect to the prescribed model (Schmitt & Stults, 1986). Therefore, as a further test, we also examined MTMM relationships with CFA, using the correlated trait-correlated method (CTCM) model (Marsh & Grayson, 1995; Widaman, 1985). The CTCM model considers each measured variable to be a function of trait, method, and error factors. Thus, it models both trait and method factors explicitly and assesses the degree of convergent and discriminant validity through variance partitioning into trait, method, and error.

For the CTCM model, we included five traits (the four CQ dimensions and interactional adjustment), each of which was measured by two methods (self-report and peer-report). The two measures of each trait load on a single trait factor, yielding five traits for this design. In addition, each item that uses the same method of measurement loads on a single factor, yielding two method factors. Thus, we specified model A as a five-trait–two-method model with a latent trait factor for each of the five traits (the four CQ dimensions and interactional adjustment) and two method factors for the traits that were assessed by self-rating and peer-rating. All of the trait factors and all of the method factors are allowed to correlate among themselves, while the trait and method factors are assumed to be uncorrelated (Widaman, 1985).

We compared results of the two-method–five-trait CFA: $\chi^2(364\ df) = 770.18$, NNFI = 0.94, CFI = 0.95, SRMR = 0.07, and RMSEA = 0.08 ($p < 0.05$) against two alternative models as recommended by Widaman (1985). Model B is a method-only model and included only two methods: $\chi^2(404\ df) = 1820.09$, NNFI = 0.82, CFI = 0.83, SRMR = 0.12, and RMSEA = 0.16. Model C is a trait-only model and included only five traits, $\chi^2(395\ df) = 2071.40$, NNFI = 0.84, CFI = 0.86, SRMR = 0.15, and RMSEA = 0.16. Comparison of model A (the two-method–five trait model) with model B (method-only) ($\Delta\chi^2\ [40\ df] = 1049.91$, $p < 0.001$) and with model C (trait-only) ($\Delta\chi^2\ [31\ df] = 1301.22$, $p < 0.001$) shows the superiority of model A, the two-method–five-trait model.

The CFA MTMM approach also allows partitioning of total observed variance of each measure into components associated with the trait and method factors (Marsh & Hocevar, 1988; Widaman, 1985). Results demonstrated that traits explained 43 percent of the total observed variance, methods explained 22 percent of the observed variance, and the remaining 35 percent was attributed to random error. In sum, the variance attributed to traits was the largest component of total observed variance, providing further convergent and discriminant validity evidence for the CQS.

To assess criterion validity of CQ, we used self-rated CQ to predict self-rated and peer-rated adjustment, controlling for sex and cross-cultural experience. We also used peer-rated CQ to predict self-rated and peer-rated adjustment. Although we examined all four possible relationships between CQ and adjustment (self-rated CQ → self-rated adjustment, peer-rated CQ → peer-rated adjustment, self-rated CQ → peer-rated adjustment, and peer-rated CQ → self-rated adjustment), we were especially interested in the relationships that involved two different sources (self-rated CQ → peer-rated adjustment

Table 2.7

Regression of Self and Peer CQ Scale on Interactional Adjustment—Study 5 (n = 142)

	Interactional Adjustment Peer-Rated				Interactional Adjustment Self-Rated			
Variable	Step 1	Step 2	Step 1	Step 2	Step 1	Step 2	Step 1	Step 2
Sex[a]	–.04	–.10	–.04	–.12	–.35***	–.40***	–.35***	–.41***
Cross-Cultural Experience	.13	–.03	.13	.05	.09	–.02	.09	.06
Self-rated								
Metacognitive CQ		.18				.13		
Cognitive CQ		.12				.06		
Motivational CQ		.27**				.22*		
Behavioral CQ		.22*				.20*		
Peer-rated								
Metacognitive CQ				.16				.03
Cognitive CQ				.05				.04
Motivational CQ				.34**				.20*
Behavioral CQ				.19*				.29**
F	0.84	2.87*	0.84	3.39**	6.69**	4.14**	6.69**	5.08***
ΔF		3.83**		4.60**		2.64*		3.88**
R^2	.02	.16	.02	.18	.12	.21	.12	.24
ΔR^2		.14		.16		.09		.12
Adjusted R^2	.00	.10	.00	.13	.10	.16	.10	.20

[a]0 = female, 1 = male
*$p < .05$
**$p < .01$
***$p < .001$

and peer-rated CQ →self-rated adjustment) because these avoid potential problems of common method bias.

Since motivational CQ and behavioral CQ focus on drive and flexibility in culturally diverse situations, we expected that each would predict interactional adjustment. In contrast, we expected that the two mental aspects of CQ (metacognitive CQ and cognitive CQ) would have less direct relevance to interactional adjustment.

Overall, hierarchical regression analysis (Table 2.7) shows CQ predicted adjustment, with increased variance ranging from 9 percent to 16 percent. In addition, and consistent with expectations, self-rated motivational CQ and self-rated behavioral CQ predicted peer-rated interactional adjustment ($\beta = 0.27$, $p < 0.01$ / $\beta = 0.22$, $p < 0.05$; 14 percent incremental explained variance; adjusted $R^2 = 0.10$). Likewise, peer-rated motivational CQ and behavioral CQ predicted self-rated interactional adjustment ($\beta = 0.20$, $p <0.05$ / $\beta = 0.29$, $p <0.01$; 12 percent incremental explained variance; adjusted $R^2 = 0.20$). We also note that self-rated motivational CQ and behavioral CQ predicted self-rated interactional adjustment ($\beta = 0.22$, $p <0.05$ / $\beta = 0.20$, $p <0.05$; 9 percent incremental variance; adjusted $R^2 = 0.16$). Finally, peer-rated motivational CQ and behavioral CQ predicted peer-rated interactional adjustment

($\beta = 0.34$, $p < 0.01$ / $\beta = 0.19$, $p < 0.05$; incremental variance 16 percent; adjusted $R^2 = 0.13$). In sum, MTMM analyses provide evidence of convergent, discriminant, and criterion validity of the CQS across self- and peer-ratings.

Study 6: Discriminant and Incremental Validity

Having assessed the psychometric characteristics of the CQS, measurement invariance of the four factors across time and across two countries, and comparability of self-report CQS compared to peer-report CQS, we now address discriminant and incremental validity of the CQS. Respondents in studies 2 and 4 completed a second questionnaire that measured cognitive ability, EQ, CJDM, interactional adjustment, and mental well-being. We obtained matched data for 251 respondents in study 2 and 249 respondents in study 4 (56 percent and 74 percent response rates respectively). Using this data, we first examined the discriminant validity of the four factors of CQ relative to cognitive ability, EQ, cultural judgment and decision making, interactional adjustment, and mental well-being. Second, we assessed incremental validity of CQ over and above demographic characteristics, cognitive ability, and EQ in predicting CJDM, interactional adjustment, and mental well-being.

Measures

For CJDM, we adapted five scenarios from Cushner and Brislin (1996). Participants read scenarios describing intercultural interactions and then selected the best response to explain the situation. We summarized each participant's correct responses (range 0–5). We measured interactional adjustment with three items from Black and Stephens (1989): "Rate how well you have adjusted to your current situation in terms of socializing with people, interacting with people on a day-to-day basis, getting along with people" (1 = extremely unadjusted, 7 = extremely adjusted; $\alpha = 0.93$). We measured mental well-being with four items from Goldberg and Williams (1988). "Rate your general well-being at this time: able to concentrate on whatever you have been doing, feel that you are playing a useful part, feel capable of making decisions, and able to face up to your responsibilities" (1 = not at all, 7 = to a very great extent; $\alpha = 0.82$).

We measured cognitive ability with the Wonderlic Personnel test (1999) of problem-solving ability. Prior research has demonstrated this scale is a reliable and valid measure of cognitive ability (e.g., see LePine, 2003). We assessed EQ with eight items from the Schutte et al. (1998) scale that is based on Salovey and Mayer's (1990) model of EQ. Items include, "I seek out activities that make me happy" and "I arrange events that others enjoy" ($\alpha = 0.80$). Participants reported their age (years) and sex (0 = female, 1 = male), and we coded each sample (0 = the United States, 1 = Singapore).

Since we previously demonstrated equivalence in number of factors, factor loadings, and structural relationships across these samples (see study 4), we combined sample 2 (n = 251) and sample 4 (n = 249) for these analyses (n = 500). Table 2.8 reports descriptive statistics, correlations, and reliabilities for the combined samples.

Table 2.8

Means, Standard Deviations, Scale Reliabilities, and Intercorrelations—Study 6 (n = 500)

	MN	SD	1	2	3	4	5	6	7	8	9	10	11	12
1. Cultural decision making	3.23	1.11												
2. Interactional adjustment	5.63	1.16	.03	(.93)										
3. Mental well-being	4.98	0.97	.01	.49**	(.82)									
4. Metacognitive CQ	4.94	0.88	.17**	.17**	.24**	(.74)								
5. Cognitive CQ	3.41	0.96	.11*	.10*	.26**	.27**	(.83)							
6. Motivational CQ	5.00	0.98	.03	.23**	.41**	.43**	.34**	(.81)						
7. Behavioral CQ	4.21	1.09	.09*	.17**	.25**	.39**	.39**	.32**	(.82)					
8. Cognitive ability	27.59	5.58	.24**	–.05	–.12**	.06	–.05	–.10*	.03					
9. Emotional intelligence	5.27	0.78	–.03	.26**	.42**	.33**	.24**	.33**	.28**	–.05	(.80)			
10. Age	21.14	2.88	.10*	.07	.17**	.05	.11*	.14**	.10*	–.14**	.05			
11. Sex[a]	0.46	0.50	.08	.02	.09*	.02	.10*	.15**	.10*	–.01	.03	.24**		
12. Sample[b]	0.50	0.50	.11*	–.19**	–.37**	–.01	–.25**	–.29**	.02	.42**	–.19**	–.29**	–.22**	

Note: Reliability coefficients are in parentheses along the diagonal.

[a]0 = female, 1 = male

[b]0 = United States, 1 = Singapore

**p* <.05

***p* <.01

Discriminant Validity

We assessed discriminant validity of the four factors of CQ relative to cognitive ability, EQ, cultural judgment and decision making, interactional adjustment, and mental well-being, using confirmatory factor analysis with study 6 data. Results demonstrated good fit for the nine-factor model (χ^2 [595 *df*] = 1303.47, NNFI = 0.95, CFI = 0.96, SRMR = 0.05, RMSEA = 0.05), supporting the distinctiveness of the four CQ factors, cognitive ability, EQ, cultural judgment and decision making, interactional adjustment, and mental well-being. All factor loadings were significant, with *t* values ranging from 8.96 to 33.07.

Incremental Validity

We tested the incremental validity of CQ with hierarchical regression. For controls, we entered age, sex (0 = female, 1 = male), and sample (0 = the United States, 1 = Singapore) in step one, and cognitive ability and EQ in step two. In step three, we added the four factors of CQ (metacognitive CQ, cognitive CQ, motivational CQ, and behavioral CQ). We used Change F statistics to assess each regression step and *t* values to assess significance of individual beta values. Table 2.9 reports results of the regression analyses for CJDM, interactional adjustment, and mental well-being.

Predictive Validity

Since metacognitive CQ and cognitive CQ represent mental capabilities, and since CJDM emphasizes analytic abilities such as deliberate reasoning and evaluation of alternative, we expected metacognitive CQ and cognitive CQ to predict CJDM. In contrast, we did not expect motivational CQ or behavioral CQ to predict CJDM, because the capabilities to direct energy (motivational CQ) or display flexible behavior (behavioral CQ) are less directly relevant to mental analysis. Consistent with the logic described in study 5, we expected motivational CQ and behavioral CQ would predict interactional adjustment. Extending this, we also expected these two factors of CQ would predict mental well-being.

Hierarchical regression results showed that age, sex, and sample explained 4 percent of the variance in CJDM, 4 percent in interactional adjustment, and 14 percent in mental well-being. The addition of cognitive ability and EQ in step 2 increased the explained variance significantly for CJDM ($\Delta F = 12.20$, $p < 0.001$), interactional adjustment ($\Delta F = 13.67$, $p < 0.001$), and mental well-being ($\Delta F = 41.83$, $p < 0.001$). Results in step 3 demonstrate the incremental validity of the four factors of CQ, over and above demographic characteristics, cognitive ability, and EQ in predicting CJDM ($\Delta F = 4.97$ $p < 0.01$), interactional adjustment ($\Delta F = 3.73$, $p < 0.01$), and well-being ($\Delta F = 10.64$, $p < 0.001$). Overall, the adjusted R^2 statistics explained 10 percent of the variance in CJDM, 10 percent of the variance in interactional adjustment, and 31 percent of the variance in mental well-being.

As expected for CJDM, results demonstrate that metacognitive CQ ($\beta = 0.16$, $p < 0.01$) and cognitive CQ ($\beta = 0.11$, $p < 0.05$) increased explained variance, over and above the

Table 2.9

Hierarchical Regression Analysis—Study 6 (n = 500)

	Cultural Decision Making			Interactional Adjustment			Mental Well-Being		
Variable	Step 1	Step 2	Step 3	Step 1	Step 2	Step 3	Step 1	Step 2	Step 3
Age	.12**	.13**	.12**	.02	.03	.01	.06	.07	.05
Sex[a]	.09	.07	.07	–.03	–.04	–.05	.00	.00	–.03
Sample[b]	.16**	.06	.07	–.19***	–.17**	–.17**	–.35***	–.30***	–.26***
Cognitive ability		.24***	.22**		.04	.04		.04	.03
Emotional intelligence		–.02	–.08		.23***	.16**		.36***	.26***
Metacognitive CQ			.16**			.05			.01
Cognitive CQ			.11*			–.06			.02
Motivational CQ			–.04			.11*			.21***
Behavioral CQ			–.01			.10*			.10*
F	6.43***	8.91***	7.32***	6.63***	9.65***	7.14***	27.04***	35.63***	26.31***
ΔF		12.20***	4.97**		13.67***	3.73**		41.83***	10.64***
R^2	.04	.08	.12	.04	.09	.12	.14	.26	.32
ΔR^2		.04	.04		.05	.03		.12	.06
Adjusted R^2	.03	.07	.10	.03	.08	.10	.14	.26	.31

[a]0 = female, 1 = male
[b]0 = the United States, 1 = Singapore
**p* <.05
***p* <.01
****p* <.001

effects of demographic characteristics, cognitive ability, and EQ. Together, metacognitive CQ and cognitive CQ increased explained variance in CJDM by 4 percent. Overall, the adjusted R^2 was 10 percent. Also as expected, results for interactional adjustment demonstrate that motivational CQ ($\beta = 0.11, p < 0.05$) and behavioral CQ ($\beta = 0.10, p < 0.05$) increased explained variance, above and beyond demographic characteristics, cognitive ability, and EQ. Incremental variance was 3 percent, and overall adjusted R^2 was 10 percent. Finally, results also demonstrated that motivational CQ ($\beta = 0.21$, $p < 0.001$) and behavioral CQ ($\beta = 0.10$, $p < 0.05$) increased explained variance in mental well-being, above and beyond demographic characteristics, cognitive ability, and EQ. Incremental variance was 6 percent, and adjusted R^2 was 31 percent.

DISCUSSION

Overall, results of these six studies allow us to draw several important conclusions. First, the sequential and systematic scale development process described in studies 1–4 provides strong evidence that the CQS has a clear, robust, and meaningful four-factor structure. In addition, results demonstrate that this structure is stable across samples (study 2), across time (study 3), and across countries (study 4). In addition, results in study 5 show the same pattern of relationships for the self-report version of the CQS (Fig. 2.1) compared to the peer-report version of the CQS (Fig. 2.3), such that self-report CQ predicted peer-report adjustment and peer-report CQ predicted self-report adjustment. Finally, results in study 6 support the discriminant validity of the CQS compared to cognitive ability, EQ, CJDM, interactional adjustment, and mental well-being. Study 6 also demonstrates that the CQS has incremental validity in predicting cultural judgment and decision making, adjustment, and mental well-being. More specifically, metacognitive CQ and cognitive CQ increased explained variance in cultural judgment and decision making by 4 percent; motivational CQ and behavioral CQ increased explained variance in adjustment by 3 percent; and motivational CQ and behavioral CQ increased explained variance in mental well-being by 6 percent

From a theoretical perspective, the findings of these six studies (n >1,500 unique respondents) indicate that the 20-item CQS holds promise as a reliable and valid measure of CQ. Potential uses of the scale in substantive research include further exploration of the nature and dimensionality of CQ. For example, future research could examine subdimensions for each factor of CQ. Additional theoretical work is also needed on the nomological network of CQ, including predictors, consequences, mediators, and moderators. Future research should also assess additional outcomes of CQ. For example, it would be interesting and useful to examine CQ as a predictor of selection into global leader positions (Lievens et al., 2003; Spreitzer et al., 1997), transfer of intercultural training (Paige, 2004; Yamazaki & Kayes, 2004), cross-cultural negotiations effectiveness (Gelfand et al., 2001), and initiative to span structural holes (Van Dyne & Ang, 2006). It also would be beneficial to examine the extent to which CQ explains job performance, contextual performance, and adaptive performance of those in domestic jobs who work in multicultural groups, those who have regular work contact with employees, suppliers, and/or customers in other countries, and those in expatriate and global leader positions (Black, Gregersen, Mendenhall, & Stroh, 1999; Gelfand, Erez, & Aycan, 2007; Shaffer et al., 2006; Tsui & Gutek, 1999).

The scale also has promising practical application. For example, it can provide important insights and personal information to individuals on their own CQ. According to Paige and Martin (1996), feedback and self-awareness are keys to enhancing intercultural effectiveness. Thus, comparison of self-report with peer-report or supervisor-report scores on the 20-item CQS should provide individuals with important insights about their personal capabilities for functioning effectively in situations characterized by cultural diversity. Accordingly, knowledge of CQ would also provide a foundation for personal self-development.

Organizations could use the CQS (both self-report and observer-report versions) to identify employees who would be particularly well-suited for overseas assignments. It also could be used to screen out those who are proficient in domestic settings but unlikely to succeed in cross-cultural settings or in jobs that require frequent and ongoing interaction with those who have other cultural backgrounds. Finally, knowledge of CQ could be used to develop corporate training and self-awareness programs or to identify employees who could serve as supportive mentors to those starting overseas assignments.

In conclusion, the results of these six studies are promising and suggest both theoretical and practical implications that warrant continued research on CQ. We hope that the CQS provides a strong foundation for future research toward significant theoretical and practical implications for self-awareness, cross-cultural interactions, corporate selection, training and development, and employee motivation, adjustment, well-being, and performance. In sum, the CQS has exciting implications for global leadership and effectiveness of individuals in work and nonwork international and domestic settings that are culturally diverse.

REFERENCES

Adler, N.J. (2002). *International dimensions of organizational behavior* (4th ed.). Cincinnati, OH: South-Western.

Ang, S., Van Dyne, L., Koh, C., Ng, K., Templer, K.J., Tay, C., & Chandrasekar, N.A. (2007). Cultural intelligence: Its measurement and effects on cultural judgment and decision making, cultural adaptation, and task performance. *Management and Organization Review, 3,* 335–371.

Bandura, A. (2002). Social cognitive theory in cultural context. *Applied Psychology: An International Review, 51,* 269–290.

Bhaskar-Shrinivas, P., Harrison, D.A., Shaffer, M.A., & Luk, D.M. (2005). Input-based and time-based models of international adjustment: Meta-analytic evidence and theoretical extensions. *Academy of Management Journal, 48,* 25–281.

Bhawuk, D.P.S., & Brislin, R.W. (2000). Cross-cultural training: A review. *Applied Psychology: An International Review, 49,* 162–191.

Black, J.S., Gregersen, H.B., Mendenhall, M.E., & Stroh, L.K. (1999). *Globalizing people through international assignments.* New York: Addison Wesley Longman.

Black, J.S., & Mendenhall, M.E. (1990). Cross-cultural training effectiveness: A review and a theoretical framework for future research. *Academy of Management Review, 15,* 113–136.

Black, J.S., Mendenhall, M.E., & Oddou, G. (1991). Toward a comprehensive model of international adjustment: An integration of multiple theoretical perspectives. *Academy of Management Review, 16,* 291–317.

Black, J.S., & Stephens, G.K. (1989). The influence of the spouse on American expatriate adjustment and intent to stay in Pacific Rim overseas assignments. *Journal of Management, 15,* 529–544.

Byrne, B.M. (1998). *Structural equation modelling with LISREL, PRELIS, and SIMPLIS: Basic concepts, applications, and programming.* Mahwah, NJ: Erlbaum.

Caligiuri, P.M. (2000). The Big Five personality characteristics as predictors of expatriate's desire to terminate the assignment and supervisor-rated performance. *Personnel Psychology, 53,* 67–88.

Caligiuri, P.M., Hyland, M.A.M., Joshi, A., & Bross, A.S. (1998). Testing a theoretical model for examining the relationship of family adjustment and expatriate's work adjustment. *Journal of Applied Psychology, 53,* 67–88.

Campbell, D.T., & Fiske, D.W. (1959). Convergent and discriminant validation by the multitrait-multimethod matrix. *Psychological Bulletin, 56,* 81–105.

Cantor, N., & Kihlstrom, J.F. (1985). Social intelligence: The cognitive basis of personality. *Review of Personality and Social Psychology, 6,* 15–33.

Cushner, K., & Brislin, R.W. (1996). *Intercultural relations: A practical guide* (2nd ed.). Thousand Oaks, CA: Sage.

Deci, E.L., & Ryan, R.M. (1985). *Intrinsic motivation and self-determination in human behavior.* New York: Plenum.

Earley, P.C., & Ang, S. (2003). *Cultural intelligence: Individual interactions across cultures.* Palo Alto, CA: Stanford University Press.

Earley, P.C., & Gibson, C.B. (2002). *Multinational work teams: A new perspective.* Hillsdale, NJ: Erlbaum.

Erez, M., & Earley, P.C. (1993). *Culture, self-identity, and work.* New York: Oxford University Press.

Fornell, C., & Larcker, D.R. (1981). Evaluating structural equation models with unobservable variables and measurement error. *Journal of Marketing Research, 18,* 39–50.

Gardner, H. (1993). *Multiple intelligence: The theory in practice.* New York: Basic Books.
Gelfand, M.J., Erez, M.E., & Aycan, Z. (2007). Cross-cultural organizational behavior. *Annual Review of Psychology, 58,* 479–514.
Gelfand, M.J., Nishii, L.H., Holcombe, K.M., Dyer, N., Ohbuchi, K., & Fukuno, M. (2001). Cultural influences on cognitive representations of conflict: Interpretations of conflict episodes in the United States and Japan. *Journal of Applied Psychology, 86,* 1059–1074.
Goldberg, D.P., & Williams, P. (1988). *A user's guide to the General Health Questionnaire.* Basingstoke: NFER-Nelson.
Goleman, D. (1995). *Emotional intelligence.* New York: Bantam Books.
Gudykunst, W.B., & Ting-Toomey, S. (1988). *Culture and interpersonal communication.* Newbury Park, CA: Sage.
Hall, E.T. (1959). *The silent language.* New York: Doubleday.
Hedlund, J., & Sternberg, R.J. (2000). Practical intelligence: Implications for human resources research. In G.R. Ferris (Ed.), *Research in personnel and human resources management* (pp. 1–52). New York: Elsevier Science.
Hinkin, T.R. (1998). A brief tutorial on the development of measures for use in survey questionnaires. *Organizational Research Methods, 1,* 104–121.
Hinkin, T.R., & Schriesheim, C.A. (1989). Development and application of new scales to measure the French and Raven (1959) bases of social power. *Journal of Applied Psychology, 74,* 561–567.
Hofstede, G. (1991). *Culture and organizations: Software of the mind.* London: McGraw-Hill.
House, R.J., Hanges, P.J., Javidan, M., Dorfman, P.W., & Gupta, V. (2004). *Culture, leadership, and organizations: A GLOBE study of 62 societies.* Thousand Oaks, CA: Sage.
Jöreskog, K.G. (1979). Statistical estimation of structural models in longitudinal-developmental investigations. In J.R. Nesselroade & P.B. Baltes (Eds.), *Longitudinal research in the study of behavior and development* (pp. 303–352). New York: Academic Press.
Kirkman, B.L., Gibson, C.B., & Shapiro, D.L. (2001). "Exporting" teams: Enhancing the implementation and effectiveness of work teams in global affiliates. *Organizational Dynamics, 30,* 12–29.
Kirkman, B.L., & Law, K.S. (2005). International management research in AMJ: Our past, present, and future. *Academy of Management Journal, 48,* 377–386.
Kraimer, M.L., Wayne, S.J., & Jaworski, R.A. (2001). Sources of support and expatriate performance: The mediating role of expatriate adjustment. *Personnel Psychology, 54,* 71–99.
Landis, D., Bennett, J.M., & Bennett, M.J. (2004). *Handbook of intercultural training* (3rd ed.). Thousand Oaks, CA: Sage.
LePine, J.A. (2003). Team adaptation and postchange performance: Effects of team composition in terms of members' cognitive ability and personality. *Journal of Applied Psychology, 88,* 27–39.
Lievens, F., Harris, M.M., Van Keer, E., & Bisqueret, C. (2003). Predicting cross-cultural training performance: The validity of personality, cognitive ability, and dimensions measured by an assessment center and a behavior description interview. *Journal of Applied Psychology, 88,* 476–489.
Marsh, H.W. (1996). Positive and negative global self-esteem: A substantively meaningful distinction or artifacts? *Journal of Personality and Social Psychology, 70,* 810–819.
Marsh, H.W., & Grayson, D. (1995). Latent variable models of multitrait-multimethod data. In R.H. Hoyle (Ed.), *Structural equation modeling: Concepts, issues, and application* (pp. 177–198). London: Sage.
Marsh, H.W., & Hocevar, D. (1988). A new, more powerful approach to multitrait-multimethods analyses: Application of second-order, confirmatory factor analysis. *Journal of Applied Psychology, 73,* 107–117.
Mayer, J.D., & Salovey, P. (1993). The intelligence of emotional intelligence. *Intelligence, 17,* 433–442.
Mendenhall, M., & Oddou, G. (1985). The dimensions of expatriate acculturation: A review. *Academy of Management Review, 10,* 39–47.
Murdock, G.P. (1987). *Outline of cultural materials* (5th rev. ed.). New Haven, CT.: HRAF Press.
O'Neil, H.E., & Abedi, J. (1996). Reliability and validity of a state metacognitive inventory: Potential for alternative assessment. *Journal of Educational Research, 89,* 234–245.

Ones, D.S., & Viswesvaran, C. (1997). Personality determinants in the prediction of aspects of expatriate job success. In Z. Aycan (Ed.), *New approaches to employee management* (pp. 63–92). Greenwich, CT: JAI Press.

Paige, R.M. (2004). Instrumentation in intercultural training. In D. Landis, J.M. Bennett, & M.J. Bennett (Eds.), *Handbook of intercultural training* (3rd ed.) (pp. 85–128). Thousand Oaks, CA: Sage.

Paige, R.M., & Martin, J.N. (1996). Ethics in intercultural training. In D. Landis & R. S. Bhagat (Eds.), *Handbook of intercultural training* (2nd ed.) (pp. 35–60). Thousand Oaks, CA: Sage.

Pintrich, P.R., & De Groot, E.V. (1990). Motivational and self-regulated learning components of classroom academic performance. *Journal of Educational Psychology, 82,* 33–40.

Salovey, P., & Mayer, J.D. (1990). Emotional intelligence. *Imagination, Cognition and Personality, 9,* 185–211.

Schmitt, N.W., & Stults, D.M. (1985). Factors defined by negatively keyed items: The results of careless respondents? *Applied Psychological Measurement, 9,* 367–373.

Schmitt, N.W., & Stults, D.M. (1986). Methodology review: Analysis of multitrait-multimethod matrices. *Applied Psychological Measurement, 10,* 1–22.

Schutte, N.S., Malouff, J.M., Hall, L.E., Haggerty, D.J., Cooper, J.T., Golden, C.J., & Dornheim, L. (1998). Development and validation of a measure of emotional intelligence. *Personality and Individual Differences, 25,* 167–177.

Shaffer, M.A., Harrison, D.A., Gregersen, H., Black, J.S., & Ferzandi, L.A. (2006). You can take it with you: Individual differences and expatriate effectiveness. *Journal of Applied Psychology, 91,* 109–125.

Spreitzer, G.M., McCall, M.W., & Mahoney, J.D. (1997). Early identification of international executives. *Journal of Applied Psychology, 82,* 6–29.

Sternberg, J.R. (1986). A framework for understanding conceptions of intelligence. In R.J. Sternberg & D.J. Detterman (Eds.), *What is intelligence? Contemporary viewpoints on its nature and definition* (pp. 3- 15). Norwood, NJ: Ablex.

Sternberg, R.J. (1988). *The triarchic mind: A new theory of human intelligence.* New York: Viking.

Sternberg, R.J. (2000). *Handbook of intelligence.* New York: Cambridge University Press.

Sternberg, R.J., & Detterman, D.J. (1986). *What is intelligence? Contemporary viewpoints on its nature and definition.* Norwood, NJ: Ablex.

Takeuchi, R., Tesluk, P.E., Yun, S., & Lepak, D.P. (2005). An integrative view of international experiences. *Academy of Management Journal, 48,* 85–100.

Ting-Toomey, S. (1999). *Communicating across cultures.* New York: Guilford Press.

Triandis, H.C. (1994). *Culture and social behavior.* New York: McGraw-Hill.

Tsui, A.S., & Gutek, B. (1999). *Demographic differences in organizations: Current research and future directions.* New York: Lexington Books/Macmillan.

Tung, R. (1988). *The new expatriates.* Cambridge, MA: Ballinger.

Vandenberg, R.J., & Lance, C.E. (2000). A review and synthesis of the measurement invariance literature: Suggestions, practices, and recommendations for organizational research. *Organization Research Methods, 3,* 4–69.

Van Dyne, L., & Ang, S. (2006). Getting more than you expect: Global leader initiative to span structural holes and reputational effectiveness. In W.H. Mobley & E.W. Weldon (Eds.), *Advances in global leadership* (pp. 101–122). New York: JAI Press.

Ward, C., & Kennedy, A. (1999). The measurement of sociocultural adaptation. *International Journal of Intercultural Relations, 23,* 659–677.

Widaman, K.F. (1985). Hierarchically nested covariance structure models for multitrait-multimethod data. *Applied Psychological Measurement, 9,* 1–26.

Wonderlic, E.F. (1999). *Wonderlic Personnel Test user's manual.* Libertyville, IL: Wonderlic Inc.

Yamazaki, Y., & Kayes, D.C. (2004). An experiential approach to cross-cultural learning: A review and integration of competencies for success expatriate adaptation. *Academy of Management Learning and Education, 3,* 362–379.

PART II

EXTENDING THE CQ NOMOLOGICAL NETWORK

CHAPTER 3

Antecedents of the Four-Factor Model of Cultural Intelligence

LU M. SHANNON AND THOMAS M. BEGLEY

With the increasing number of business organizations establishing a global presence, and the growing diversity of workplace demographics, many modern businesses require a high degree of cultural awareness in their employees. This includes the ability to work and interact with people from different cultural and ethnic backgrounds. Such interaction can be difficult for individuals and their organizations, because cultural barriers often cause misunderstandings and conflicts that detract from efficient and effective interactions (Gelfand, Nishii, Holcombe, Dyer, Ohbuchi, & Fukuno, 2001; Lievens, Harris, Van Keer, & Bisqueret, 2003; Takeuchi, Yun, & Tesluk, 2002). Interest in how organizations compete effectively when operating in a global context, and why some individuals deal more effectively than others with cultural diversity, have therefore gained increasing importance.

Responding to this need, Earley and Ang (2003) conceptualized the multifactor concept of cultural intelligence (CQ). Defined as a person's capability to deal effectively in situations characterized by cultural diversity (Earley & Ang, 2003), CQ is comprised of metacognitive, cognitive, motivational, and behavioral facets, and has specific relevance to studies in cross-cultural contexts (e.g., Triandis, 2006; Hampden-Turner & Trompenaars, 2006; Earley & Ang, 2003) and human resource management (e.g., Earley & Peterson, 2004).

The emergence of multifactor CQ measurement is nascent but promising. Ang, Van Dyne, Koh, Ng, Templer, Tay, and Chandrasekar (2007) developed a 20-item psychometric measure of Earley and Ang's (2003) four-factor model of CQ. Measurement of CQ can be conducted using psychometric as well as nonpsychometric methods. Psychometric methods focus on factor structure, reliabilities, cross-cultural equivalence, and discriminant validity of multi-item scales, while nonpsychometric approaches highlight assessment through observation and interview (Harris, Lievens, & Park, 2004). The present study has three objectives. First, we conduct confirmatory factor analyses on Ang et al.'s

(2007) psychometric measures of CQ. Second, we measure CQ using a nonpsychometric approach—peer ratings. Third, we test a set of individual differences as predictors of the four dimensions of CQ as well as overall self-reported CQ and peer-rated CQ.

OVERVIEW OF FOUR-FACTOR CQ

The special issue of the *Group and Organization Management* journal about CQ (Konrad, 2006) included articles by a range of experts on culture and intelligence. Triandis (2006) describes the ability to suspend judgment as an important element of CQ because many factors, such as situational constraints and individual personality and experiences, influence a person's thoughts and behaviors; Hampden-Turner and Trompenaars (2006) argue that CQ is the ability to see beyond value differences, and that integration of seemingly different value systems can achieve synergistic outcomes. Brislin, Worthley, and MacNab (2006) proposed a four-step process of CQ: the ability to (1) observe behaviors in a different culture, (2) introduce reasons for these behaviors, (3) consider the emotional implications and associations rising from the behavior, and (4) transfer the new knowledge acquired to other behaviors and situations. Thomas (2006) highlighted the role of mindfulness as a critical link between knowledge and behavioral ability and offered a conceptual model to develop CQ in individuals. These commentaries support the potential of CQ as a construct and its credibility as an individual capacity.

Consequences of CQ

Although CQ is a recent construct, empirical research on the concept is rapidly growing. Like any new construct, the credibility of CQ can be built by providing evidence on CQ outcomes/consequences. Ang et al. (2007) showed that CQ significantly explained variance in performance and adjustment among international executives over and above the effects of demographic characteristics and general cognitive ability. They also found that metacognitive CQ and cognitive CQ predicted outcomes that require higher level cognitive processing, such as decision making and task performance; motivational CQ and behavioral CQ predicted outcomes that represent subjective assessments of coping behaviors, such as adjustment; and behavioral CQ related to task performance in intercultural environments. In a study on motivational CQ, Templer, Tay, and Chandrasekar (2006) found that it predicted three facets of adjustment—general, work, and interaction—after controlling for relevant demographic variables, such as time in a host country and experience with international assignments.

Antecendents of CQ

In addition to examining the predictive validity of CQ, we need to understand its correlates and/or antecedents. Unlike personality, CQ is regarded as a capability that may grow and develop over time and is associated with successful cross-cultural experiences (see Earley & Ang, 2003). It is therefore important to examine antecedents of CQ in its broader nomological network (Ang, Van Dyne, & Koh, 2006). Past studies examining the antecedents of CQ have identified several possible predictive variables.

Ang et al. (2006) demonstrated differential relationships between specific Big Five personality characteristics and facets of CQ. In particular, they found that conscientiousness positively related to metacognitive CQ; agreeableness positively related to behavioral CQ; emotional stability negatively related to behavioral CQ; extraversion linked to cognitive CQ, motivational CQ, and behavioral CQ; and openness to experience related to all four facets. In another study, Tarique and Takeuchi (2006) examined the relationship between number of international nonwork experiences and length of such experiences with the four facets. They found that number of international nonwork experiences associated with all four facets, as well as length of experiences, moderated the relationship between number of experiences and metacognitive and motivational CQ. To test a wider array of possible predictors of individual CQ, we hypothesize that three individual constructs—language skill, international working experience, and social contact—will relate to CQ.

Language skills refer to the extent to which individuals can speak easily and accurately in the language that cross-cultural interactions require. Language skills serve as a fundamental instrument in acquiring cultural knowledge, such as an understanding of economic, legal, and social systems of different cultures. Earley (2002) argues that individuals who lack an aptitude for acquiring languages, at least at some reasonable level of proficiency, should have lower CQ. Research on language skills in multinational corporations (MNCs) also indicates that limited language comprehension and fluency may create a sense of remoteness and disconnectedness, which can exclude individuals from each other's view (Marschan-Piekkari, Welch, & Welch, 1999a, b). For example, in a transnational team context, team members who are fluent in the common language are likely to dominate discussion, in-group interaction, and decision making. Team members who are less able to express their opinions in the language are more likely to be excluded from group interactions and communications, and sometimes may be regarded as untalented, difficult, and best avoided (Janssens & Brett, 2006). Therefore, language acquisition skills may be a critical factor in determining CQ development.

We propose that language skills are related to the cognitive and behavioral facets of CQ. Cognitive CQ is an individual's knowledge of specific norms, practices, and conventions in different cultural settings (Earley & Ang, 2003). Given that language conveys many subtleties of a culture (Earley, 2002) and reflects its core values, such as norms, conventions, and differences in thought patterns (Nisbett, 2003), language transmits cultural knowledge. Therefore, those with high-level ability in multiple languages have a systematic mechanism for accessing the core values of different cultures and should be more knowledgeable about specific aspects of other cultures. These individuals should also be better able to validate assumptions about behaviors that reflect different cultural practices. In sum, we propose a positive relationship between language skills and cognitive CQ.

Language skills also should relate to behavioral CQ. Behavioral CQ refers to an individual's flexibility in performing appropriate verbal and nonverbal actions when interacting with people from different cultural backgrounds (Earley & Ang, 2003). Given that "people tend to restrict their communication to those who speak their own language" (Taylor & Osland, 2003, p. 221–222), verbal behaviors are highly relevant to an individual's language skills. Additionally, Triandis (1972) argues that individuals who share a common language are likely to share the same perceptions of rules and collective norms, roles, and values. So, language skills influence nonverbal behaviors through shared perceptions. Based on these shared perceptions, those who are better skilled at acquiring multiple languages are capable of recognizing situations, engaging in higher quality social interactions, and are more culturally intelligent in their verbal and nonverbal behaviors when involved in cross-cultural interactions. Multilingual people should also be better able to avoid or de-escalate social conflicts. In addition, their broad behavioral repertoire should allow them to put others at ease by exhibiting culturally appropriate verbal, vocal, facial, and other outward expressions. We predict that

H1: Language acquisition will positively relate to (a) cognitive CQ and (b) behavioral CQ.

We regard another individual variable—international experience—as a significant antecedent of CQ facets. International work experience allows individuals to obtain knowledge, skills, and behaviors that are essential for living and working in different cultural environments, such as intercultural communication skills (Gudykunst & Ting-Toomey, 1998), increased adaptability, and flexibility in volatile environments (Sambharya, 1996).

We posit that international work experience is related to metacognitive, motivational, and behavioral facets of CQ. Metacognitive CQ is an individual's cultural consciousness and awareness during interactions with those from different cultural backgrounds (Earley & Ang 2003). Individuals gain inimitable cultural consciousness, awareness, and knowledge when given the opportunity to contrast different cultural values, beliefs, and norms by working in other countries or cultures. A variety of international work experiences offers individuals the occasion to question their own cultural assumptions, think about cultural preferences, and analyze other cultural norms, before and during interactions. In addition, the global workplace offers opportunities to check and adjust mental models and to adopt metacognitive strategies when thinking about interacting with those from different cultural backgrounds.

We also expect that international work experience will relate to motivational CQ, which refers to an individual's drive and interest in adapting to cultural differences (Earley & Ang, 2003). Studies have reported that international work experience predicts expatriate success in overseas assignments because those with varied experience are likely to be inherently curious, willing to relocate to different environments (Brett & Reilly, 1988), able to work with others from different cultures (Richard, 2000), communicate well with host-country nationals (Mendenhall & Oddou, 1985), and open to experiencing new and unfamiliar environments.

Finally, we expect international work experience to positively relate to behavioral CQ. As elaborated earlier, behavioral CQ describes interpersonal skills and the ability to engage in high-quality social interactions in cross-cultural situations. Working in different cultural contexts has an observable impact on individual attitudes and behaviors (Hart, 1999). Individuals interpret and react to the information environment through a "mental template that individuals impose on an information environment to give it form and meaning" (Walsh, 1995, p. 281). As such, having international experience is likely to influence individual attitudes about foreign colleagues and subsequent behaviors toward them. In particular, intercultural sensitivity or cultural awareness may be one result of having a well-developed knowledge structure (Mendenhall & Oddou, 1985). Adaptive performance is a person's proficiency in altering his or her behavior to meet the demands of new, uncertain, and unpredictable work situations (Pulakos, Arad, Donovan, & Plamondon, 2000). Given that international work experiences and adaptive performance are closely associated, people who are open to learning new things should seek out and act on new experiences to extend their repertoire of behaviors beyond daily habits. In sum, we predict that

H2: International work experience will positively relate to (a) metacognitive CQ, (b) motivational CQ, and (c) behavioral CQ.

The degree of diversity in an individual's social contacts may also impact CQ. The contact hypothesis argues that the presence of extended contact between members of different social groups leads to a reduction of stereotyping and enhances personalization due to the frequency of counterstereotypical encounters. Social learning theory proposes that individuals develop through learning from the people around them. The social learning process involves *attention* to the situation, *retention* of the knowledge gained, *reproduction* of the behavioral skills observed, and, finally, *reinforcement* through feedback about the effectiveness of the adapted behavior. Direct experience with people who come from different cultural backgrounds should engender more positive intergroup attitudes and social acceptance.

We propose that the diversity of social contact relates to metacognitive, cognitive, and behavioral CQ. For example, individuals who have parents from different countries or cultures have greater opportunities to learn about different cultural norms, values, and practices at an early age, and to develop inherent behavioral repertoires within cross-cultural situations. Those who have spent part of their childhood in countries or cultures other than their own should be more open-minded and flexible, possess positive attitudes toward other systems and cultures, have respect for others, and exhibit tolerance of their behaviors and views. Moreover, individuals who have studied abroad as graduate and undergraduate students are expected to explore other cultures from learning perspectives and to reformulate more appreciative attitudes and behaviors toward intercultural situations. Certain significant experiences, such as an international marriage or long-term relationships might also considerably enhance CQ. Additionally, individuals who possess culturally diverse social contacts are more likely to deal with novel and unfamiliar intercultural interactions more effectively, and should display more flexible behaviors that put others at ease during intercultural encounters. These various degrees of social contact are likely to be significant factors for gaining a "global mindset," defined as a mindset "that combines an openness to and awareness of diversity across cultures and markets with a propensity and ability to synthesize across this diversity" (Gupta & Govindarajan, 2002, p. 117). Thus, we predict that

H3: Diversity of social contacts will positively relate to (a) metacognitive CQ, (b) cognitive CQ, and (c) behavioral CQ.

To date, CQ research has focused on self-report measures. This research has demonstrated that self-rated CQ predicts important outcomes, including self-reported adjustment and well-being, and observer-rated performance (Ang et al., 2007). But it is also important to ascertain whether self-rated CQ is related to observer-rated CQ. If these two operationalizations are related, we have evidence that CQ is a meaningful and useful construct. Thus, for our final hypothesis, we propose that there will be a positive relationship between self-rated and peer-rated CQ.

H4: Overall self-rated CQ will be significantly and positively related to overall peer-rated CQ.

SAMPLE, CONTEXT, AND PROCEDURE

Respondents were graduate and undergraduate business students at a large public university in Ireland. The school possesses a multicultural demographic. Respondents represented 24 nationalities, had worked in 36 countries across North and South America, Europe, the Middle East, and East and Southeast Asia, had international work experiences in an average 1.47 countries (SD = 1.2, range = from 1 to 6), and indicated a mean length of 31.47 months (SD = 51.6) of international work experience.

We collected data at two points in time. At Time 1, 333 business students provided data on demographics including age, gender, and nationality. They also indicated language ability, work experiences, and background of social contacts. We also collected self-reported CQ at Time 1. At Time 2 (9 weeks later), 245 of these students provided data on peer-rated CQ. We matched Time 1 and Time 2 responses (n = 245) for our hypothesis testing. Participants were 46.5 percent female and averaged 24.38 years of age (SD = 6.1), with a range of 18 to 48 years old.

MEASURES

Self-Reported CQ

We measured self-reported CQ with the 20-item instrument developed by Ang et al. (2007). This inventory includes four items for metacognitive, six for cognitive, five for motivational, and five for behavioral CQ. Cronbach's alphas in our study were .77 for metacognitive CQ, .82 for cognitive, .84 for motivational CQ, and .79 for behavioral CQ. These reliabilities are consistent with those reported in Ang et al. (2007). Sample

Figure 3.1 **Confirmatory Factor Analysis of 20-Item CQ model** (n=333)

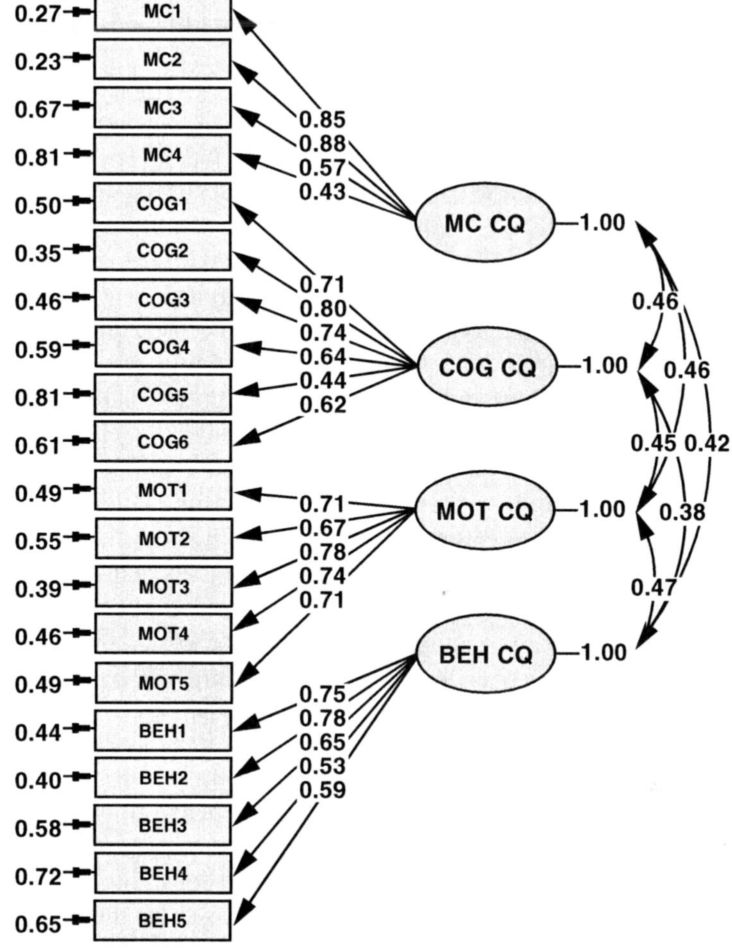

Note: x^2 *(164df) = 469.98, GFI = .88, NNFI = .93, CFI = .94, SRMR = .065, and RMSEA = .075*

items included, "I am conscious of the cultural knowledge I use when interacting with people from different cultural background," for metacognitive CQ; "I know the legal and economic systems of other cultures," for cognitive CQ; "I enjoy interacting with people from different cultures," for motivational CQ; and "I change my verbal behavior when a cross-cultural interaction requires it," for behavioral CQ.

Figure 3.1 reports standardized parameter estimates for the four-factor model. Confirmatory factor analysis (CFA) with LISREL 8 (Jöreskog & Sörbom, 1993) demonstrated a good fit of the data to a four-factor correlated model (model A): χ^2 (164 *df*) = 469.98; goodness-of-fit (GFI) = 0.88; non-normed fit index (NNFI) = 0.93; (Bentler's) comparative fit index (CFI) = 0.94; standardized root mean square residual (SRMR) = 0.065; and root mean square error of approximation (RMSEA) = 0.075. All factor loadings were significant. Although the GFI and RMSEA scores are slightly beyond optimal size, the rest of the indicators are very much within acceptable bounds. We compared relative fit of this four-factor model with alternative models, including four orthogonal factors (model B), three factors (model C), two factors (models D and E), and one factor (model F). Nested model comparisons demonstrate the superiority of the hypothesized four-factor model. Each of the $\Delta\chi^2$ statistics shows substantial differences with the hypothesized model. Model A showed better fit than model C, three factors combining metacognition with cognition, $\Delta\chi^2$ (3 *df*) = 780.28, $p < 0.001$, than two alternative two-factor models: model D (metacognition with cognition vs. motivational with behavioral): $\Delta\chi^2$ (5 *df*) = 1074.24, $p < 0.001$, or model E (metacognition vs. combining the other three facets): $\Delta\chi^2$ (5 *df*) = 1140.02, $p < 0.001$), and than model F's single factor, $\Delta\chi^2$ (6 *df*) = 1365.24, $p < 0.001$). The intercorrelations among CQ scales are sufficiently modest to indicate a good degree of independence from one another. These results replicate prior results of Ang et al. (2007) and provide additional support for the four-factor model of CQ.

Peer-rated CQ

We measured peer-rated CQ by asking peers the following question "Can this person deal effectively in multicultural contexts*?*" Respondents assessed the CQ skills of each of their classmates by using a rating from 1 to 7 (from 1 = not at all, to 7 = all the time). It was possible to ask for these ratings because respondents were in cohort groups where they took all classes together. We encoded peer-rated CQ score by averaging ratings provided by multiple peers (range from 17 to 51) for each participant. The mean score of peer-rated CQ, 3.52 (SD = 1.37), indicated a relatively modest level of assessed skills.

Language Acquisition, International Work Experience, and Social Contact

We assessed individual language acquisition with the following: "Please list your native language" and "Please list any languages you know at a proficient level." To assess international working experience, we requested respondents to list the country or countries where they had worked.

We assessed diversity of social contact with a nine-item scale. Respondents indicated diversity of their social contacts including father's birthplace, mother's birthplace, country or countries where they attended high school, and country or countries where they attended university. We summed responses, and Cronbach's alpha was 0.92. We controlled for age, gender, and nationality.

RESULTS

Table 3.1 reports descriptive statistics, correlations, and reliabilities for the variables used in the hypothesis testing. Table 3.2 presents the results from using hierarchical regressions to test the hypotheses. We entered the three control variables at step 1 and the

Table 3.1

Descriptive Statistics, Correlations, and Reliabilities (n = 245)

		M	SD	1	2	3	4	5	6	7	8	9	10	11	12
1	Age (in years)	24.38	6.05												
2	Gender (0 = female, 1 = male)	.53	.50	.21 **											
3	Nationality (0 = local, 1 = international)	.65	.48	–.06	.10										
4	Language skills	1.30	.94	–.21 **	–.18 **	–.06									
5	International work experience	1.12	1.43	.50**	.18**	.05	–.07								
6	Div. of social contact	.71	.88	.21 **	–.01	–.10	.06	.33**	(.92)						
7	Metacognitive CQ	5.21	.90	.26 **	.09	–.178	.01	.23**	.07	(.77)					
8	Cognitive CQ	3.85	1.01	.06	.02	–.15*	.24*	.12	.13	.43**	(.82)				
9	Motivational CQ	5.85	.80	.01	.00	.05	.04	.21**	.12	.42**	.37**	(.84)			
10	Behavioral CQ	5.02	.97	.22**	.05	.12	.04	.18**	.02	.43**	.33**	.38**	(.79)		
11	Composite CQ	4.98	.68	.19**	.06	–.05	.12	.25**	.12	.77**	.74**	.71**	.73**	(.73)	
12	Peer-rated CQ	3.52	1.37	.59**	.19**	.04	–.04	.47**	.35**	.20**	.05	.09	.14*	.16*	

Note: Cronbach's alpha in parentheses
*p <.05
**p <.01
Abbreviation: CQ = cultural intelligence

Table 3.2

Hierarchical Regression Analyses (n = 245)

Variable	Metacognitive CQ		Cognitive CQ		Motivational CQ		Behavioral CQ		Composite CQ		Peer-Rated CQ	
	Step 1	Step 2	Step 1	Step 2	Step 1	Step 2	Step 1	Step 2	Step 1	Step 2	Step 1	Step 2
Age (in years)	.24***	.18**	.05	.04	.01	–.12	.23***	.21**	.17**	.10	.58***	.47***
Gender (0 = female, 1 = male)	.06	.06	.03	.06	–.01	–.02	–.01	–.01	.02	.03	.06	.07
Nationality (0 = Non-Irish, 1 = Irish)	–.16**	–.17**	–.15*	–.13*	.05	.04	.14*	.13*	–.04	–.05	.06	.08
Language skills		.06		.25***		.03		.10		.17**		.08
International work experience		.15*		.09		.26***		.10		.19**		.16**
Div. of social contact		–.04		.07		.06		–.04		.02		.21***
F	8.40***	5.03***	2.09	4.56***	.20	2.71**	5.59***	3.51**	2.72	4.06***	43.77***	30.82***
ΔF		1.60		6.88***		5.21**		1.41		5.26**		11.92***
R2	.10	.11	.03	.10	.00	.06	.07	.08	.03	.09	.35	.44
ΔR2		.02		.08		.06		.02		.06		.09
Adjusted R2	.08	.09	.01	.08	–.01	.04	.07	.08	.02	.07	.34	.42

Note: Composite CQ = average of self-rated dimensions; peer-rated CQ = average of peer observers

*p <.05

**p <.01

***p <.001

three antecedent factors at step 2. Of note in the control variables is the complete lack of association between gender and CQ.

In testing the hypotheses, the set of predictors was statistically insignificant in relating to two types of CQ—metacognitive and behavioral. Hypothesis 1 predicted that language acquisition would be related to (a) cognitive CQ and (b) behavioral CQ. Results support hypothesis 1a: language acquisition related to cognitive CQ ($\beta = 0.25$, $p < 0.001$). However, results do not support hypothesis 1b. Hypothesis 2 predicted that international work experience would relate to (a) metacognitive, (b) motivational, and (c) behavioral CQ. Results support hypothesis 2b: international work experience positively related to motivational CQ ($\beta = 0.26$, $p < 0.001$). We note that although the overall equation for cognitive CQ failed to reach significance, the beta for metacognitive CQ was significant ($\beta = 0.15$, $p < 0.05$) and positive. Finally, none of the predicted relationships in hypothesis 3 received support. The diversity of individual social contacts was unrelated to any self-reported CQ dimension.

We averaged the four self-report dimensions of CQ to create an overall self-report CQ scale. As illustrated in Table 3.2, language acquisition ($\beta = 0.17$, $p < 0.01$) and international work experience ($\beta = 0.19$, $p < 0.01$) showed positive relationships. For overall peer-rated CQ, significant predictors included international work experience ($\beta = 0.16$, $p < 0.01$) and diversity of social contacts ($\beta = 0.21$, $p < 0.001$).

Finally, results support hypothesis 4. Self-rated CQ was positively and significantly related to peer-rated CQ ($r = 0.16$, $p < 0.05$).

DISCUSSION

The current study further supports the validity of Ang et al.'s (2007) 20-item four-factor measure of CQ. This sample of 333 Irish and international respondents increases the generalizability of the CQ construct beyond the studies done in Singapore and the United States. Analysis of the findings allows us to highlight several relevant points. First, in the present study, the CQ scale had strong psychometric characteristics with a stable factor structure (metacognitive, cognitive, motivational, and behavioral CQ). Second, among the antecedents of CQ, controlling for demographic characteristics, language acquisition, and international work experiences predicted overall self-reported CQ, while international work experiences and social contact predicted peer-rated CQ. Third, using multiple sources of data on CQ generated different findings compared to a single source, such as self-reports.

Our fourth finding may be the most important contribution of our study. Results supported hypothesis 4, and demonstrated a positive and significant relationship between overall self-rated CQ and peer-rated CQ. This is important because prior research has focused on self-rated CQ. Although existing research has demonstrated that self-rated CQ predicts important outcomes, including personal adjustment and well-being as well as observer-rated performance (Ang et al., 2007), it is also important to ascertain whether self and observer ratings of CQ are similar. Our results provide initial evidence that self and observer ratings of overall CQ are positively related.

The significant relationship of language acquisition with cognitive CQ supports the argument that multilingual people are capable of using language as a key instrument to obtain cultural knowledge in cross-cultural situations. The positive relationship of international work experience with motivational CQ supports the argument that those with multiple international work experiences are inherently curious, willing to work with people from different cultures, and enjoy unfamiliar and different cultural settings. Contrary to expectation, none of the antecedent variables related to behavioral CQ. Self-reported behavioral CQ might not align with behaviors observed by others. Individuals may be aware of verbal and nonverbal expressions needed in cross-cultural situations, but they may not be able to enact the most appropriate behaviors.

Antecedent factors showed different predictive ability for overall self-reported and peer-rated CQ. International work experience positively related to both self-reported and peer-rated CQ, while language acquisition did not relate to peer-rated CQ and diversity of social contact did not relate to self-reported CQ. Since the language used by our respondents was English and all foreign students were required to have English language proficiency in order to pursue daily school tasks, the non-finding between language acquisition and peer-rated CQ may be understandable. The value of language skills should be most apparent when some members of a group can converse in the native language while others cannot. Although not related to self-reported CQ, diversity of social contact had a significant positive relationship to peer-rated CQ. A diversity of social contacts encourages individuals to develop a more sophisticated behavioral repertoire about other cultures and acquire greater capabilities in putting people at ease, resulting in higher levels of peer-rated CQ.

Our results suggest that different ratings of CQ can lead to contrasting research outcomes. Including peer ratings in CQ measurement offers potentially important implications for future CQ research. Measuring CQ through multiple sources at different time points facilitates the process of overcoming single-source bias (Podsakoff & Organ 1986; Marschan-Piekkari et al., 1999a, b; Marschan & Welch, 1997).

Among the present study limitations, the sample is predominantly students, raising concerns about generalizability. And although our data were collected at different times using different scaling formats, predictors and some criterion data were collected at the same time point, which might increase the possibility of shared method variance. We believe it is not problematic here because the predictors were constructed from factual reports while the CQ measures come from subjective perceptions. Finally, peer-rated CQ was a single-item measure, which might raise a potential concern about outcome accuracy. However, each individual score was constructed from at least 17 independent observations.

THEORETICAL IMPLICATIONS

Our study on the reliability and validity of the four-factor model of CQ replicated the pioneering work of Ang et al. (2007). Although our research examined three antecedents of CQ that we considered relevant to culturally diverse settings—language acquisition, international work experiences, and diversity of social contact—additional antecedents undoubtedly exist. In addition, studies that focus on how, when, and why each CQ dimension evolves or changes would be of particular value.

To test the differences in predictive ability of self-reported CQ and peer-rated CQ, future research could focus on various consequences that CQ is most likely to influence, such as selection for cross-cultural training programs (Lievens et al., 2003), promotion to positions with international responsibilities in multinational organizations (House, Hanges, Javidan, Dorfman, & Gupta 2004), and success in international assignments (Caligiuri, 2000; Gelfand et al., 2001; Kraimer, Wayne, & Jaworski, 2001; Takeuchi, Yun, & Tesluk, 2002). In addition, given the cultural diversity within many domestic work organizations throughout the world, research is merited on the role of CQ in culturally diverse teams within particular cultural contexts (Earley & Gibson, 2002).

PRACTICAL IMPLICATIONS

If supported by future work, our findings have implications for management practice—especially for human resource professionals seeking to select, train, and develop a more culturally intelligent workforce. For example, organizations can consider recruiting individuals with language skills, international work experiences, and diversified social contacts in order to improve interactions in cross-cultural work teams. These characteristics may also help in selecting candidates for expatriation. They could be incorporated as criteria for assessing employees' cross-cultural competencies and identifying supportive mentors for those who are new to jobs with overseas responsibilities. The modest strength of the relationships indicated that these dimensions should not be used alone but rather as components of a larger set of criteria.

In conclusion, results of the current study demonstrate strong construct validity for the four-factor CQ concept and reliability of the 20-item CQ instrument (Ang et al., 2007), and show selective relationships of three antecedent factors with self-reported and peer-rated CQ. An expansion of knowledge on CQ measurement as well as its antecedents promises to deliver theoretical and practical benefits that justify further investigation into this exciting construct.

REFERENCES

Ang, S., Van Dyne, L., & Koh, C. (2006). Personality correlates of the four-factor model of cultural intelligence. *Group and Organization Management, 31,* 100–123.

Ang, S., Van Dyne, L., Koh, C., Ng, K.Y., Templer, K.J., Tay, C., & Chandrasekar, N.A. (2007). Cultural intelligence: Its measurement and effects on cultural judgment and decision making, cultural adaptation, and task performance. *Management and Organization Review, 3,* 335–371.

Brett, J. M., & Reilly, A.H. (1988). On the road again: Predicting the job transfer decision. *Journal of Applied Psychology, 73,* 614–620.

Brislin, R., Worthley, R., & MacNab, B. (2006). Cultural intelligence: Understanding behaviors that serve people's goals. *Group and Organization Management, 31,* 40–55.

Caligiuri, P.M. (2000). The Big Five personality characteristics are predictors of expatriate's desire to terminate the assignment and supervisor-rated performance. *Personal Psychology, 53,* 67–88.

Earley, P.C. (2002). Redefining interactions across cultures and organizations: Moving forward with cultural intelligence. *Research in Organizational Behavior, 24,* 271–299.

Earley, P.C., & Ang, S. (2003). *Cultural intelligence: Individual interactions across cultures.* Palo Alto, CA: Stanford University Press.

Earley, P.C., & Gibson, C.B. (2002). *Multinational work teams: A new perspective.* Mahwah, NJ: Lawrence Erlbaum Associates.

Earley, P.C., & Peterson, R.S. (2004). Elusive cultural chameleon: Cultural intelligence as a new approach to intercultural training for the global manager. *Academy of Management Learning and Education, 3,* 100–115.

Gelfand, M.J., Nishii, L.H., Holcombe, K.M., Dyer, N., Ohbuchi, K., & Fukuno, M. (2001). Cultural influences on cognitive representations of conflict: interpretations of conflict episodes in the United States and Japan. *Journal of Applied Psychology, 86,* 1059–1074.

Gudykunst, W.B., & Ting-Toomey, S. (1998). *Culture and interpersonal communication.* Newbury Park, CA: Sage.

Gupta, A.K., & Govindarajan, V. (2002). Cultivating a global mindset. *Academy of Management Executive, 16,* 116–126.

Hampden-Turner, C., & Trompenaars, F. (2006). Cultural intelligences: Is such a capacity credible? *Group and Organization Management, 31,* 56–63.

Harris, M.M., Lievens, F., & Park, S. (2004). Something old, something new, something borrowed: Methods versus constructs in measuring cultural intelligence. *The 64th Annual Meeting of the Academy of Management,* New Orleans, L.A., August, 2004.

Hart, P.M. (1999). Predicting employee life satisfaction: A coherent model of personality, work and nonwork experiences, and domain satisfaction. *Journal of Applied Psychology, 84,* 564–584.

House, R.J., Hanges, P.J., Javidan, M., Dorfman, P.W., & Gupta, V. (2004). *Culture, leadership, and organizations: The GLOBE study of 62 societies.* Thousand Oaks, CA: Sage.

Janssens, M., & Brett, J.M. (2006). Cultural intelligence in global teams: A fusion model of collaboration. *Group and Organization Management, 31,* 124–153.

Jöreskog, K.G., & Sörbom, D. (1993). *Windows LISREL 8.12.* Chicago, IL: Scientific Software.

Konrad, A.M. (2006). (Ed.) *Group and Organization Management.* Volume 31. Issue 1. Thousand Oaks, CA: Sage.

Kraimer, M.L., Wayne, S.J., & Jaworski, R.A. (2001). Sources of support and expatriate performance: The mediating role of expatriate adjustment. *Personal Psychology, 54,* 71–99.

Lievens, F., Harris, M.M., Van Keer, E., & Bisqueret, C. (2003). Predicting cross-cultural training performance: The validity of personality, cognitive ability, and dimensions measured by an assessment center and a behavior description interview. *Journal of Applied Psychology, 88,* 476–489.

Marschan, R., & Welch, D.E. (1997). Language: The forgotten factor in multinational management. *European Management Journal, 15,* 591–598.

Marschan-Piekkari, R., Welch, D.E., & Welch, L.S. (1999a). In the shadow: The impact of language on structure, power and communication in the multinational. *International Business Review, 8,* 421–440.

Marschan-Piekkari, R., Welch, D.E., & Welch, L.S. (1999b). Adopting a common corporate language. *International Journal of Human Resource Management, 10,* 377–390.

Mendenhall, M., & Oddou, G. (1985). The dimensions of expatriate acculturation: A review. *Academy of Management Review, 10,* 39–47.

Nisbett, R. (2003). *The geography of thought.* New York: Free Press.

Padsakoff, P.M., & Organ, D.W. (1986). Self-reports in organizational research: problems and prospects. *Journal of Management, 12,* 531–544.

Pulakos, E.D., Arad, S., Donovan, M.A., & Plamondon, K.E. (2000). Adaptability in the workplace: Development of a taxonomy of adaptive performance. *Journal of Applied Psychology, 85,* 612–624.

Richard, O.C. (2000). Racial diversity, business strategy, and firm performance: a resource-based view. *Academy of Management Journal, 43,* 164–177.

Sambharya, R. (1996). Foreign experience of top management teams and international diversification strategies of U.S. multinational corporations. *Strategic Management Journal, 17,* 739–746.

Takeuchi, R., Yun, S., & Tesluk, P.E. (2002). An examination of crossover and spillover effects of spouse and expatriate adjustment on expatriate outcomes. *Journal of Applied Psychology, 87,* 655–666.

Tarique, I., & Takeuchi, R. (Eds.). (2007). Developing cultural intelligence: The role of international non-work experiences. Presented at the annual meeting of the Academy of International Business, Indianapolis.

Taylor, S., & Osland, J.S. (2003). The impact of intercultural communication on global organizational learning. In M. Easterby-Smith, & M.A. Lyles (Eds.), *Handbook of organizational learning and knowledge* (pp. 212–232). Malden, MA: Blackwell Publishing.

Templer, K.J., Tay, C., & Chandrasekar, N.A. (2006). Motivational cultural intelligence, realistic job preview, realistic living conditions preview, and cross-cultural adjustment. *Group and Organization Management, 31,* 154–173.

Thomas, D.C. (2006). Domain and development of cultural intelligence: The importance of mindfulness. *Group and Organization Management, 31,* 78–99

Triandis, H.C. (1972). *The analysis of subjective culture.* New York: John Wiley & Sons.

Triandis, H.C. (2006). Cultural intelligence in organizations. *Group and Organization Management, 31,* 20–26.

Walsh, J. (1995). Managerial and organizational cognition: Notes from a trip down memory lane. *Organizational Science, 6,* 280–321.

CHAPTER 4

Developing Cultural Intelligence
The Roles of International Nonwork Experiences

IBRAIZ TARIQUE AND RIKI TAKEUCHI

In today's highly competitive global business environment, an individual's success in cross-cultural settings is greatly influenced by his or her capability to manage the challenges associated with living and working in a multicultural environment, such as managing diversity, simultaneously adjusting to multiple cultures, and being conversant in multiple languages (Briscoe & Schuler, 2004). Success in cross-cultural settings may be facilitated through the learning of cross-cultural competencies (e.g., cross-cultural knowledge, skills, and abilities). For example, knowledge of the general dimensions on which most national cultures differ and the impact of these differences on individuals (e.g., Hampden-Turner & Trompenaar, 1993) may provide the individual with some awareness regarding expected norms and behaviors in the new culture (Black & Mendenhall, 1990). This awareness may lower anxiety, reduce culture shock, and encourage appropriate behaviors when living and working in a host culture (Caligiuri & Tarique, 2006). As a result, research has been devoted to identifying and examining factors surrounding the development of cross-cultural competencies and skills (e.g., Ang, Van Dyne, & Koh, 2006; Johnson, Lenartowicz, & Apud, 2006; Shaffer, Harrison, Gregersen, Black, & Ferzandi, 2006; Yamazaki & Kayes, 2004).

Although many of these studies have focused on personality and other trait-type individual differences, we consider the amount of prior international exposure (or international experience) as another important factor in the development of cross-cultural competencies. For instance, Selmer (2002) and Takeuchi, Tesluk, Yun, and Lepak (2005) found that previous international experience of expatriates had a positive (albeit complicated) effect on their adjustment level to the host country. These studies imply that previous international experience can enhance cross-cultural competencies or cultural intelligence, which reflects a person's *capability* to gather, interpret, and act upon these radically different cues to function effectively across cultural settings or in a multicultural situation (Earley & Ang, 2003). However, to date, a majority of the existing studies that relate experience and cultural competencies has been descriptive in nature and has not been well grounded in theory (e.g., Takeuchi, Tesluk, & Marinova, 2006; Tarique, 2005), making it difficult to draw solid conclusions about the relative importance of international experiences in predicting cross-cultural competencies.

One of the main objectives of this study, therefore, is to provide an initial empirical investigation of how prior international experience is related to cultural intelligence (CQ). More specifically, we focus on two facets of nonwork prior international experiences and examine how the *number* of travel experiences is related to the four (metacognitive, cognitive, motivational, and behavioral) facets of CQ and how the *length* of travel experiences moderates these relationships. Although examining only two aspects of international experience may be considered crude, it nonetheless represents an improvement over the prior studies (cf., Takeuchi et al., 2005) and can provide additional insights into the role of international experiences.

THEORETICAL OVERVIEW OF CQ

Given that the concept of CQ has been introduced relatively recently, there are only a limited number of empirical studies that have examined this specific type of intelligence. Nevertheless research on CQ is gaining momentum and has been the focus of recent research in both the cross-cultural management (e.g., Thomas & Inkson, 2004) and international human resource management (e.g., Earley & Peterson, 2004) literature. Past studies examining the antecedents of CQ have considered several predictors. Ang, Van Dyne, and Koh (2006) demonstrated differential relationships between the Big Five personality traits (e.g., Barrick & Mount, 1991) and the four facets of CQ. More specifically, they found that conscientiousness was positively related to metacognitive CQ, agreeableness was positively related to behavioral CQ, emotional stability was negatively related to behavioral CQ; extraversion was positively related to cognitive CQ; and openness to experience was positively related to all four factors of CQ. In another study, Takeuchi et al. (2006) integrated three streams of research (work experience, adjustment, and cultural intelligence) to develop and partially test a typology of international experiences. Their study offers some preliminary evidence for the relationship between prior international experiences and CQ, but the study is limited in that CQ was not measured directly. Instead, language proficiency and previous knowledge were used as proxies of cognitive CQ, and willingness to communicate with the host country nationals was used as a proxy of motivational CQ. Studies, therefore, are needed to fill this gap, that is, to determine whether and how prior international experience relates to CQ.

PRIOR INTERNATIONAL NONWORK EXPERIENCES AND CQ

The study of international experiences has gained increasing theoretical and empirical attention during the last few years (e.g., Carpenter, Sanders, & Gregersen, 2001). Most of this literature has focused on the outcomes of international experiences at the individual (e.g., Selmer, 2002) and organizational levels (e.g., Carpenter, 2002). This stream of research has conceptualized and operationalized international experience into three categories: experience that has occurred in the past, that is currently ongoing, and that will occur in the future (Takeuchi et al., 2005). Within each category, experience is further classified as relating to either work or nonwork domains. Moreover, experience can also be classified according to its measurement mode (cf. Tesluk & Jacobs, 1998), including but not limited to the *number* of countries traveled to/worked in and *length* of time spent traveling/working in each country.

One type of experience that has not been given much attention by researchers is prior nonwork international experience (Tarique, 2005). Like work-related international experiences, international nonwork experiences such as studying abroad or short visits to foreign countries allow individuals to learn skills and behaviors important for living and working in different cultural environments (Takeuchi et al., 2005). This form of international experience has been extensively discussed in the "third country kids" (TCK) literature (e.g., Selmer & Lam, 2004). TCKs are individuals who have spent a part of their childhood in countries or cultures other than their own (Pollock & Van Reken, 1999). Research describes them as being open-minded and flexibile, with positive attitudes toward other systems and cultures, respect for others, tolerance of others' behaviors and views, and fluent in multiple languages. They tend to have distinctive characteristics in terms of stronger family and social relationships, enjoying traveling to foreign places, acceptance of foreign languages, acceptance of cultural differences, and a future orientation. As such, we argue that international nonwork experience contributes to the development of CQ. The theoretical logic behind this argument can be found in social learning theory (Bandura, 1977).

Social learning theory proposes that individuals develop through learning from other people around them. Events and consequences in the environment are cognitively processed before they are learned or before they influence behavior. The social learning process includes three components: attention, retention, and behavior reproduction. Attention occurs when the people accept the importance of new knowledge, skills, and abilities or attitudes (KSAs). These KSAs can come from another person or the participant's own observation of the results of his/her action. Retention is the processes by which the modeled behavior becomes encoded in memory by the participant and occurs when people store and remember the KSAs that have been acquired. Reproduction takes place when people use new skills and behaviors to see the consequences of using them. Reproduction of learned capability allows people to directly experience the consequences of using the new capabilities, and understand which behaviors to execute or suppress in given situations (cf. Black & Mendenhall, 1990). People are more likely to adopt a particular skill or behavior if it results in positive outcomes. That is, behaviors that are reinforced are stored in the individual's long-term memory for use in similar situations.

The process of learning described by social learning theory lends itself to the study of *how* the number of international nonwork experiences relates to CQ. We argue that when individuals travel to or study in other countries, they learn behaviors, customs, and norms of that culture through direct experience or through observations of the host nationals' behaviors (Bandura, 1997). Moreover, individuals with greater number of international nonwork experiences in other cultures are also likely to have developed more comprehensive cognitive frameworks or templates known as schemata, which are defined as sets of cognitions about people, roles, or events that govern social behavior (e.g., Fiske & Taylor, 1991) and facilitate learning of cross-cultural competencies. There are several reasons why nonwork experiences should enhance CQ. First, international experiences can affect the cognitive components of CQ by providing inimitable knowledge, worldviews, and professional ties that help them to better manage cross-cultural interactions (cf. Carpenter et al., 2001). Such knowledge, skills, and abilities may include knowing how to deal with people from different backgrounds and cultures, intercultural communication or negotiation skills (Gudykunst & Ting-Toomey, 1988), language proficiency (Mendenhall & Oddou, 1985), and increased adaptability and flexibility in volatile environments (Sambharya, 1996).

Second, international experiences can impact the motivational component of CQ. Feldman and Bolino (2000) found that for overseas interns, international experiences affected the amount of effort they exhibited. Here, a willingness to relocate (to a different environment, domestic or foreign) is also an important factor (Brett & Reilly, 1988), as is willingness to communicate with the host country nationals (Mendenhall & Oddou, 1985). From a resource-based perspective (Barney, 1991), an individual's capability to work in culturally diverse settings may be particularly important to maximally extract the benefits of diversity, such as increased creativity (Kickul & Gundry, 2001) and innovation (De Dreu & West, 2001), while minimizing the costs or "process losses" that can be associated with diversity, such as increased affective conflict (Amason, 1996), difficulty in communicating knowledge (cf. Palich & Gomez-Mejia, 1999), and distrust (Dovidio, Gaertner, Kawakami, & Hodson, 2002).

Finally, international experiences may influence behavior and the capability to display appropriate and generally expected actions across multicultural contexts. As mentioned earlier, international experiences provide knowledge and context that can affect individuals cognitively. Walsh (1995, p. 281) noted, "The cognitive structures generated from experience affect individuals' abilities to attend to, encode, and make inferences about new information." A knowledge structure, defined as a "mental template that individuals impose on an information environment to give it form and meaning" (Walsh, 1995, p. 281), affects how individuals interpret and react to the information environment. These knowledge structures may *facilitate behaviors* that are appropriate in cross-cultural settings. For instance, knowledge of the general dimensions by which most national cultures differ and the impact of these differences on individuals (e.g., Hampden-Turner & Trompenaar, 1993) may provide the individual with awareness of expected norms and behaviors in the new culture (Black & Mendenhall, 1990). This awareness may lower anxiety and encourage appropriate behaviors for those living and/or working in a new culture (Caligiuri & Tarique, 2006; Black & Mendenhall, 1990). Thus, we expect the following:

H1: Number of international nonwork experiences is positively related to metacognitive CQ (H1a), cognitive CQ (H1b), motivational CQ (H1c), and behavioral CQ (H1d).

One central thesis concerning the outcomes of international experiences is that although there is a relationship between the number of international nonwork experiences and CQ, examining the interplay between different modes of international experiences is important. Takeuchi et al. (2005) examined, among other things, the effects of expatriates' current assignment experience and past international experiences on cross-cultural adjustment. Based on the study of 243 Japanese expatriates, they found support for the unique moderating effects of past international experiences on the relationship for current assignment tenure with general and work adjustment. Similarly, Selmer (2002) examined the possibility that prior international experience moderated the relationship between current assignment tenure and adjustment among Western expatriates in Hong Kong. He found that prior Asian experience among the novice group (less than one year on an international assignment) was significantly related to adjustment while prior international experience outside Asia was not significantly related to adjustment for either group. The results of these studies support the view that prior international experience can act as a moderator in addition to an antecedent to expatriates' cross-cultural adjustment.

Building on the above two studies, we argue that the *length* of international nonwork experience is likely to influence the relationship between the number of international nonwork experiences and CQ. Particularly, we propose that the number of international nonwork experiences has a stronger influence on CQ facets when the length of international nonwork experiences is shorter. Cross-cultural adjustment theory (e.g., Black, Mendenhall, & Oddou, 1991) suggests that over time individuals change their operant frame of reference. It is possible that as time passes individuals become relatively more comfortable and familiar with the new culture. They experience the local culture and become more integrated into the host country's culture. Most importantly, these individuals adjust their attitudes and behaviors to the new environment, which limits their ability to distinguish between domestic and foreign interpersonal interactions/behaviors. Incorporating cross-cultural adjustment theory into the analysis, we suggest that, in general, for individuals with greater length of international nonwork experiences, the need to acquire and understand new cultural knowledge declines (e.g., metacognitive CQ and cognitive CQ), the magnitude and direction of an individual's energy and willingness for social discourse in new cultural settings may decrease (motivational CQ), and the capability to enact the necessary behavioral responses becomes routine or automatic (behavioral CQ). Thus we expect the following,

H2: Length of international nonwork experiences moderates the relationships between the number of international nonwork experiences and metacognitive CQ (H2a), cognitive CQ (H2b), motivational CQ (H2c), and behavioral CQ (H2d) in such a way that the number of international nonwork experiences has a stronger influence on CQ facets when the length of international nonwork experience is shorter.

METHOD

Sample

Data were collected as part of a larger project on prior international experiences. Participants were undergraduate students enrolled in management courses at a medium-sized university located in New York City. The demographics of students in the university is multicultural; undergraduate students represent 64 countries and graduate students represent 58 countries. Data were collected from students at two points in time; collected from 221 participants at time 1 and from 215 of the same participants at time 2. At time 1 (four weeks before the end of the academic semester), the first author visited each class personally and offered the students the opportunity to participate in a research project for extra credit points toward their course grade. After reading and signing the informed consent form, the participants completed the first questionnaire, which measured demographics, control variables, and prior international experiences. Three weeks later during the last week of the academic semester (time 2), participants completed the second questionnaire, which assessed the four facets of cultural intelligence. Both questionnaires were completed in class. Overall, 212 participants completed both surveys. Sixty-three percent of the sample were women, and the average age was 25 years (SD = 5.6).

Measures

Prior International Nonwork Experiences

Consistent with Takeuchi et al. (2005), participants were asked to identify the name of the countries to which they had traveled in chronological order from most recent to most distal and the length of each trip. These international nonwork histories were used to derive two forms of prior international nonwork experiences. The number of international nonwork experiences was created by counting the number of international nonwork experiences listed. The length of international nonwork experiences was created by summing each reported experience (days).

CQ

CQ was measured using the 20-item four-facet scale developed and validated by Ang, Van Dyne, Koh, Ng, Templer, Tay, and Chandrasekar (2007). (1 = strongly disagree, 7 = strongly agree). Four items measured the metacognitive facet of CQ (e.g., "I am conscious of the cultural knowledge I use when interacting with people with different cultural backgrounds"). Six items measured the cognitive facet of CQ (e.g., "I know the religious beliefs of other cultures"). Five items measured the motivational facet of CQ (e.g., "I enjoy interacting with people from different cultures"). Five items measured the behavioral facet of CQ (e.g., "I vary the rate of my speaking when a cross-cultural situation requires it"). For each facet, the items were averaged so that a higher score denoted greater amount of CQ. The reliabilities of these scales were .90, .82, .87, and .90 respectively.

Control Variables

Since we used a student sample in this study, it is possible that age and gender may affect the amount of international nonwork experiences. In general, older students could have had

Table 4.1

Means, Standard Deviations, Reliabilities, and Intercorrelations for All Variables Used in This Study (n = 212)

	M	SD	1	2	3	4	5	6	7	8
1 Gender	0.37	0.48								
2 Age	25.49	5.62	.15*							
3 The length of international nonwork experiences	499.03	1049.36	–.03	.00						
4 The number of international nonwork experiences	3.46	0.48	–.03	.04	.11					
5 Metacognitive facet of CQ	4.74	0.48	.03	–.19 **	.14*	.61**	(.90)			
6 Cognitive facet of CQ	3.65	1.31	.05	–.17*	.16*	.48**	.63**	(.82)		
7 Motivation facet of CQ	4.69	1.52	.00	–.18 **	.08	.58**	.83**	.67**	(.87)	
8 Behavioral facet of CQ	4.34	1.43	.06	–.18 **	.04	.55**	.79**	.68**	.79**	(.90)

Note: Reliabilities are noted on the diagonal.
*p <.05
**p <.01 (two-tailed tests)

more opportunities to seek out international nonwork experiences than younger students. Similarly, there may be gender differences in the amount of international nonwork experiences. Therefore, age and gender were included as control variables in the analysis.

Analytic Procedure

To test the set of hypotheses, we first standardized the variables associated with the interaction/moderating effects (i.e., the two prior international nonwork experiences) before creating the interaction terms to reduce multicollinearity problems inherent in higher order terms (Cohen & Cohen, 1983). When the beta coefficients for the interaction terms were significant, we used Aiken and West's (1991) procedure (± 1 SD) to plot the interactions. We ran four sets of moderated regression analyses: one for each facet of CQ.

RESULTS

Table 4.1 presents the descriptive statistics and correlations for all variables in this study. Unstandardized means and standard deviations are listed for informational purposes only because standardized variables were used in all the analyses. As hypothesized, the number of international nonwork experiences was positively correlated with all four facets of CQ; metacognitive CQ (r = .61, p <0.01), cognitive CQ (r = 0.48, p <0.01), motivational CQ (r = 0.58, p <0.01), and behavioral CQ (r = 0.55, p <0.01). In addition, the length of international nonwork experiences was positively correlated with metacognitive CQ ($r = .14, p < 0.05$) and cognitive CQ ($r = 0.16, p < 0.05$). Interestingly, age was negatively correlated with all four facets of CQ; metacognitive CQ ($r = -0.19$, $p < 0.01$), cognitive CQ ($r = -0.17, p < 0.05$), motivational CQ ($r = -0.18, p < 0.01$), and behavioral CQ ($r = -.18$, $p < 0.01$).

To test the hypotheses, four separate moderated regression analyses were conducted; the results are reported in Table 4.2. Models 1, 2, and 3 report results of the moderated regression for metacognitive CQ; models 4–6 present the results of the moderated regression for cognitive CQ; models 7–9 illustrate the results of the moderated regression for motivational CQ; and models 10–12 show the results of the moderated regression for behavioral CQ. In each regression analysis, predictors were entered in three steps. Step 1 included the two control variables: age and gender. Step 2 included the two independent variables: the number of international nonwork experiences and the length of international nonwork experiences. Step 3 included the interaction term: the number of international nonwork experiences multiplied by the length of international nonwork experiences. The last step for each regression indicates the incremental variance accounted for by the interaction term.

The first set of hypotheses predicted that the number of international nonwork experiences would be positively related to all four facets of CQ. The first regression analysis suggested that when entered in the second step, the number of international nonwork experiences significantly predicted metacognitive CQ ($\beta = 0.61$, $p < 0.01$) (model 2); cognitive CQ ($\beta = 0.48, p < 0.01$) (model 5); motivational CQ ($\beta = 0.53, p < 0.01$) (model 8); and behavioral CQ ($\beta = 0.56, p < 0.01$) (model 11). Similarly, the regression analysis shows that even when the interaction terms are entered in the third step, the number of international nonwork experiences remained significantly and positively related to all four facets of CQ: metacognitive CQ ($\beta = 0.60, p < 0.01$) in model 3; cognitive CQ ($\beta = 0.48$, $p < 0.01$) in model 6; motivational CQ ($\beta = 0.58$, $p < 0.01$) in model 9; and behavioral CQ ($\beta = .55, p < .01$) in model 12. These results together with the bivariate correlations provide consistent support for hypotheses 1a, 1b, 1c, and 1d.

Hypothesis 2a posited a moderating effect of the length of international nonwork experiences on the relationship between the number of international nonwork experiences and metacognitive CQ. As shown in model 3 in Table 4.2, the interaction term associated with the length of international nonwork experiences was significant and negative ($\beta = -0.14, p < 0.01$). We plotted this interaction (Aiken & West, 1991), and visual inspection of Figure 4.1 suggests that the number of international nonwork experiences had a stronger, positive effect for individuals with shorter length of international nonwork experiences, while it had a weaker effect for individuals with greater length of international nonwork experiences. These results provide support for hypothesis 2a.

Hypothesis 2b proposed a moderating effect of the length of international nonwork experiences on the relationship between the number of international nonwork experiences and cognitive CQ. However, the results indicated an insignificant interaction ($\beta = 0.01$, ns) in model 3 (Table 4.2). Thus, results do not support hypothesis 2b. For hypothesis 2c, which proposed the moderating effect of length of international nonwork experiences on the relationship between number of international nonwork experiences and motivational

Table 4.2

Results of Moderated Regression Analysis of CQ on International Nonwork Experiences (n = 212)

Variable[a]	Metacognitive CQ			Cognitive CQ			Motivational CQ			Behavioral CQ		
	Model 1	Model 2	Model 3	Model 4	Model 5	Model 6	Model 7	Model 8	Model 9	Model 10	Model 11	Model 12
Step 1: Control variables												
Gender	.05	.08	.06	.08	.09	.09	.02	.04	.03	.08	.10**	.09*
Age	–.19**	–.22***	–.22***	–.18**	–.20***	–.20***	–.18**	–.21***	–.21***	–.19**	–.21***	–.21***
Step 2: Previous international nonwork experiences												
The number of international nonwork experiences		.61***	.60***		.48***	.48***		.53***	.58***		.56***	.55***
The length of international nonwork experiences		.07	.12***		.11*	.11*		.01	.04		.01	.00
Step 3: Interactions												
(Number of international nonwork experiences) × (Length of international nonwork experiences)			–.14***			.01			–.12**			–.06
Overall F	4.07**	39.47***	33.96***	3.95**	21.25***	16.92***	3.60**	32.45***	27.35***	4.25**	28.11***	22.75***
R2	0.03	0.43	0.45	0.03	0.29	0.29	0.03	0.38	0.39	0.03	0.35	0.35
Change in F		72.10***	7.20**		37.19***	0.00		59.30***	4.64**		49.96***	1.20
Change in R2		0.39	0.01		0.25	0.00		0.35	0.01		0.31	0.00

Note: Values are standardized estimates.

[a]All standardized variables (z-score transformation)

* p <.10

** p <.05

*** p <.01 (two-tailed)

Abbreviation: CQ, cultural intelligence.

Figure 4.1 **Interaction Plot for the Moderating Effect of the Length of International Nonwork Experiences on Metacognitive CQ**

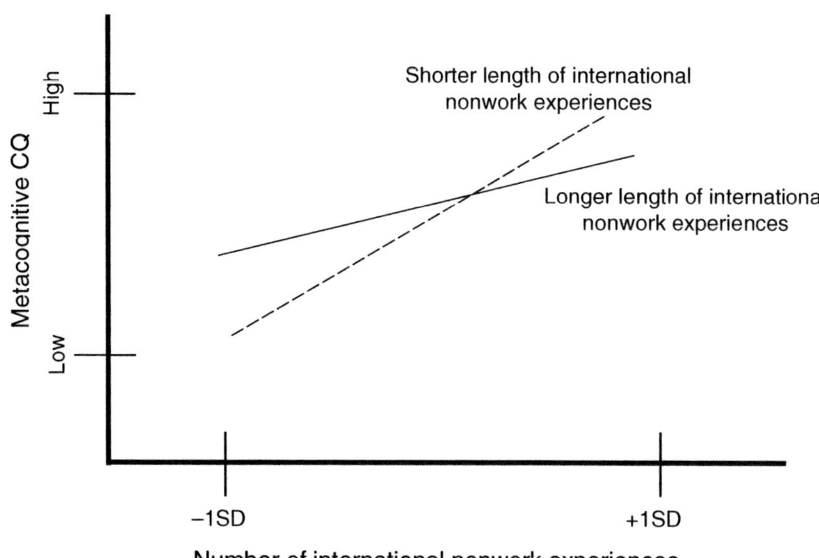

CQ, the interaction term was significant ($\beta = -0.12$, $p < 0.05$) in model 9. Visual inspection of Figure 4.2 suggests that the number of international nonwork experiences had a stronger, positive effect for individuals with shorter international nonwork experiences, while it had a weaker effect for individuals with greater length of international nonwork experiences. Thus, results provide support for hypothesis 2c.

Hypothesis 2d proposed a moderating effect of the length of international nonwork experiences on the relationship between the number of international nonwork experiences and behavioral CQ. Model 12 in Table 4.2 indicates that the interaction term was not significant ($\beta = -0.06$, ns). Therefore, results do not support hypothesis 2d.

DISCUSSION

The finding that the number of international nonwork experiences is associated with higher levels of CQ contributes to the international experience literature in two ways. First, this provides support for the conceptual models that suggest international experiences are effective in developing cross-cultural competence (cf., Johnson et al., 2006; Yamazaki & Kayes, 2004). This also extends this stream of research by illustrating that the *number* of international nonwork experiences is an important construct that influences *all four* facets of CQ. Second, this study provides one of the first empirical approaches toward a better understanding of how the *number* of international nonwork experiences influences CQ. Although the arguments put forward in this study provide an empirical basis for understanding the relationship between the number of international nonwork experiences and facets of CQ, future research needs to disentangle the mechanisms that underlie these relationships.

Figure 4.2 **Interaction Plot for the Moderating Effect of the Length of International Nonwork Experiences on Motivational CQ**

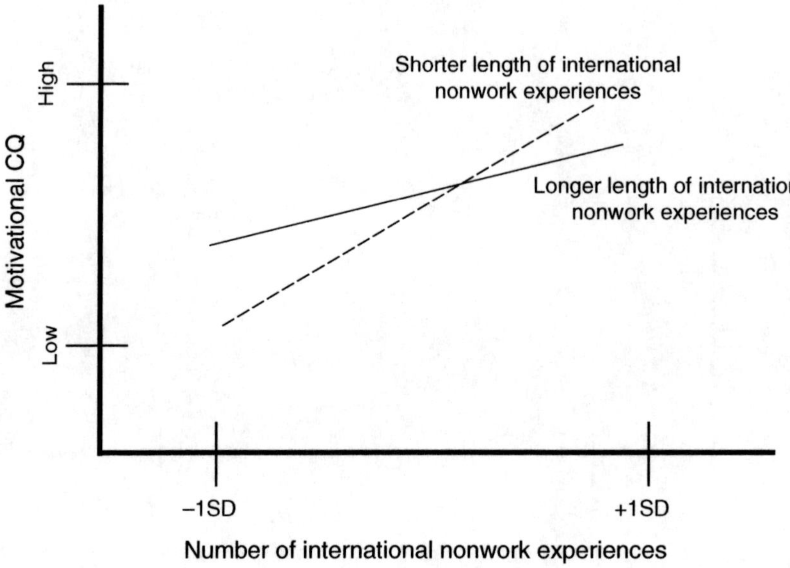

Motivational CQ
High
Low
Shorter length of international nonwork experiences
Longer length of international nonwork experiences
–1SD
+1SD
Number of international nonwork experiences

Furthermore, the finding that the length of international nonwork experiences acted as a significant moderator of the relationship between the number of international nonwork experiences and metacognitive CQ, and between the number of international nonwork experiences and motivational CQ highlights the importance of examining the interplay between different modes of international experiences. Thus, this extends the findings from two recent studies on international experiences (e.g., Selmer, 2002; Takeuchi et al., 2005). The interaction plots illustrated that when individuals had shorter international nonwork experiences, the number of international nonwork experiences had a stronger effect, while it had a weaker effect for individuals with greater length of travel experiences. Similarly to Takeuchi et al. (2005), we show different results for different "operationalizations" of international experience. This highlights the importance of including multiple measures of experience to enhance understanding of these constructs and CQ. This study also responds to the call of Bhaskar-Shrinivas et al. (2005, p. 264) who concluded that:

> Contrary to conventional wisdom and some academic arguments, the accumulated evidence shows that prior overseas assignments are only minimally helpful for present adjustment. Effect sizes for prior assignments varied slightly and were eclipsed by most of the other proposed determinants. Hence, the theoretical proposition about experience is supported, but the practical upshot of previous assignments (for adjustment, at least) is almost nil. One reason for the (practically) nonsupportive finding may lie in the conceptualization and measurement of previous overseas experience.

Thus, another important question for future researchers to address would be to extend our study to examine whether other modes of international experiences, such as variety, and other types of international experiences, such as work experiences are related to CQ and various forms of adjustment.

In addition, future research can test a more comprehensive model that includes other potential moderators, such as individual learning styles and goal orientations. Prior research has shown that individuals have a variety of learning styles such as diverger, assimilator, converger, and accommodator (see Kolb, 1984, for more information on learning styles). Knowledge of learning styles may help theorists and practitioners understand how individuals with extensive international experiences receive, process, store, and retrieve information. Moreover, researchers should also examine the moderating role of individual goal orientations (e.g., learning goal orientation vs. performance goal orientation). An understanding of goal orientation should help determine the self-efficacy and learning motivation of individuals during international encounters (cf. Gong & Fan, 2006; Wang & Takeuchi, 2007).

Perhaps, a more surprising result was that the length of international nonwork experiences did not have a significant moderating effect on the relationship between the number of international nonwork experiences and two facets (cognitive and behavioral) of CQ. It might be that the time period in which the students acquired these experiences (i.e., timing: Tesluk & Jacobs, 1998) affected the impact of the length of international nonwork experiences on these facets of CQ. As Tesluk and Jacobs' (1998) conceptualization of work experiences illustrates, the impact of international experiences on the individual is complex. Although speculative, it might be that international nonwork experiences for individuals in their low teens (who do not have a good understanding of their own culture) do not have the same positive relationship with CQ as the international nonwork experiences of individuals in their high teens (who already have a cognitive schema for their own cultures). It is also possible that the quality of these international nonwork experiences may have differed. For instance, those who experienced international nonwork experiences as a result of their parents' travel activities (taking an international trip with the family) might not have gained insights that were as valuable as those who went to different countries backpacking (on their own initiative).

LIMITATIONS

This study, like any other research, is not without limitations. First, the sample in this study is predominantly students and this raises the concern about generalizability of our findings. Future studies should test our hypotheses with samples from different populations. Second, although two measurement periods were used to obtain information about the study variables, we cannot infer causality because the time lag was primarily for convenience. Thus, future research should use theoretically based longitudinal designs to examine the effects of international experiences on CQ. Finally, common method bias may be a concern when both the criteria and predictors are from self-reports. We attempted to reduce this bias by following the procedural remedies suggested by Podsakoff, MacKenzie,

Lee, & Podsakoff (2003), such as creating a temporal separation by introducing a time lag between the measurement of the predictor and criterion variables. Furthermore, common method bias is less likely to be a plausible explanation for the significant interaction effects we found in this study (cf. Evans, 1985). However, future researchers should gather data from multiple sources to minimize shared method variance.

Despite these limitations, our findings have important implications for international human resource professionals facing staffing and training/development issues. First, given the dearth of effective global managers, organizations should consider recruiting individuals with early international experiences who may desire an international career. In addition, one of the most formidable challenges facing many multinational organizations today is the development of global managers who are well prepared for the numerous challenges of working across cultural, political, and national boundaries. Given the extraordinarily high costs of developing a cadre of global managers, IHRM professionals need data that can assist them in making informed decisions regarding the development of CQ.

In conclusion, our study adds to the growing literature on international experiences by providing an initial empirical assessment of the relationships between international nonwork experiences and CQ. The findings, however, raise additional research questions, which need to be explored. Clearly, this is an important area that will keep researchers and practitioners alike engaged for many years to come.

REFERENCES

Aiken, L., & West, S. (1991). *Multiple regression: Testing and interpreting interactions*. Thousand Oaks, CA: Sage.

Amason, A. (1996). Distinguishing the effect of functional and dysfunctional conflict on strategic decision making: Resolving a paradox for top management teams. *Academy of Management Journal, 39,* 123–148.

Ang, S., Van Dyne, L., & Koh, C. (2006). Personality correlates of the four factor model of cultural intelligence. *Group and Organization Management, 31,* 100–123.

Ang, S., Van Dyne, L., Koh, C., Ng, K.Y., Templer, K.J., Tay, C., & Chandrasekar, N.A. (2007). Cultural intelligence: Its measurement and effects on cultural judgment and decision making, cultural adaptation, and task performance. *Management and Organization Review, 3,* 335–371.

Bandura, A. (1977). *Social learning theory.* Englewood Cliffs, NJ: Prentice-Hall.

Bandura, A. (1997). *Self-efficacy: The exercise of control.* New York: Freeman.

Barney, J. (1991). Firm resources and sustained competitive advantage. *Journal of Management, 17,* 99–120.

Barrick, M., & Mount, M. (1991). The Big Five personality dimensions and job performance: A meta-analysis. *Personnel Psychology, 44,* 1–26.

Bhaskar-Shrinivas, P., Harrison, D.A., Shaffer, M.A., & Luk, D.M. (2005). Input-based and time-based models of international adjustment: Meta-analytic evidence and theoretical extensions. *Academy of Management Journal, 48,* 257–281.

Black, J., & Mendenhall, M. (1990). Cross-cultural training effectiveness: A review and theoretical framework. *Academy of Management Review, 15,* 113–136.

Black, S., Mendenhall, M., & Oddou, G. (1991). Toward a comprehensive model of international adjustment: An integration of multiple theoretical perspectives. *Academy of Management Review, 16,* 291–317.

Brett, J., & Reilly, A. (1988). On the road again: Predicting the job transfer decision. *Journal of Applied Psychology, 73,* 614–620.

Briscoe, D., & Schuler, R. (2004). *International human resource management: Policies & practices for the global enterprise* (2nd ed.). New York: Routledge.
Caligiuri, P., & Tarique, I. (2006). International assignee selection and cross-cultural training and development. In I. Björkman & G. Stahl (Eds.), *Handbook of research in international human resource management* (pp. 302–322). London: Edward Elgar Publishing.
Carpenter, M. (2002). The implications of strategy and social context for the relationship between top management team heterogeneity and firm performance. *Strategic Management Journal, 23*, 275–284.
Carpenter, M., Sanders, W., & Gregersen, H. (2001). Bundling human capital with organizational context: The impact of international assignment experience on multinational firm performance and CEO pay. *Academy of Management Journal, 44*, 493–512.
Cohen, J., & Cohen, P. (1983). *Applied multiple regression/correlation for the behavioral sciences*. Hillsdale, NJ: Lawrence Erlbaum Associates.
De Dreu, C., & West, M. (2001). Minority dissent and team innovation: The importance of participation in decision making. *Journal of Applied Psychology, 86*, 1191–1201.
Dovidio, J., Gaertner, S., Kawakami, K., & Hodson, G. (2002). Why can't we just get along? Interpersonal biases and interracial distrust. *Cultural Diversity and Ethnic Minority Psychology, 8*, 88–102.
Earley, P.C., & Ang, S. (2003). *Cultural intelligence: Individual interactions across cultures*. Palo Alto, CA: Stanford University Press.
Earley, P.C., & Peterson, R. (2004). The elusive cultural chameleon: Cultural intelligence as a new approach to intercultural training for the global manager. *Academy of Management Learning & Education, 3*, 100–16.
Evans, M. (1985). A Monte Carlo study of the effects of correlated method variance in moderated multiple regression analysis. *Organizational Behavior and Human Decision Process, 36*, 305–323.
Feldman, D., & Bolino, M. (2000). Skill utilization of overseas interns: Antecedents and consequences. *Journal of International Management, 6*, 29–47.
Fiske, S., & Taylor, S. (1991). *Social cognition* (2nd ed.). New York: McGraw-Hill.
Gong, Y., & Fan, J. (2006). Longitudinal examination of the role of goal orientation in cross-cultural adjustment. *Journal of Applied Psychology, 91*, 176–184.
Gudykunst, W., & Ting-Toomey, S. (1988). *Culture and interpersonal communication*. Newbury Park, CA: Sage.
Hampden-Turner, C., & Trompenaar, A. (1993). *The seven cultures of capitalism*. New York: Doubleday.
Johnson, J., Lenartowicz, T., & Apud, S. (2006). Cross-cultural competence in international business: Toward a definition and a model. *Journal of International Business Studies, 37*, 525–543.
Kickul, J., & Gundry, L. (2001). Breaking through boundaries for organizational innovation: New managerial roles and practices in e-commerce firms. *Journal of Management, 27*, 347–361.
Kolb, D. (1984). *Experiential learning: Experience as the source of learning and development*. Upper Saddle River, NJ: Prentice Hall.
Mendenhall, M., & Oddou, G. (1985). The dimensions of expatriate acculturation: A review. *Academy of Management Review, 10*, 39–47.
Palich, L., & Gomez-Mejia, L. (1999). A theory of global strategy and firm efficiencies: Considering the effects of cultural diversity. *Journal of Management, 25*, 587–606.
Podsakoff, P., MacKenzie, S., Lee, J., & Podsakoff, N. (2003). Common method biases in behavioral research: A critical review of the literature and recommended remedies. *Journal of Applied Psychology, 88*, 879–903.
Pollock, D., & Van Reken, R. (1999). *The third-culture kid experience: Growing up among worlds*. Yarmouth, ME: Intercultural Press.
Sambharya, R. (1996). Foreign experience of top management teams and international diversification strategies of U.S. multinational corporations. *Strategic Management Journal, 17*, 739–746.
Selmer, J. (2002). Practice makes perfect? International experience and expatriate adjustment. *Management International Review, 42*, 71–87.

Selmer, J., & Lam, H. (2004). Third-culture kids. Future business expatriates? *Personnel Review, 33*, 430–446.

Shaffer, M., Harrison, D., Gregersen, H., Black, J., & Ferzandi, L. (2006). You can take it with you: Individual differences and expatriate effectiveness. *Journal of Applied Psychology, 91*, 109–125.

Takeuchi, R., Tesluk, P., & Marinova, S. (2006). Role of international experiences in the development of cultural intelligence. In Subhendudey & V.N. Posa (Eds.), *Cultural intelligence: An introduction* (pp. 56-91). Hyderabad, India: ICFAI University Press.

Takeuchi, R., Tesluk, P., Yun, S., & Lepak, D. (2005). An integrative view of international experiences: An empirical examination. *Academy of Management Journal, 48*, 85–100.

Tarique, I. (2005). International executive development: The influence of international developmental activities, personality, and early international experience on success in global work activities. Unpublished Dissertation, Rutgers University, New Brunswick, N.J., USA.

Tesluk, P., & Jacobs, R. (1998). Toward an integrative model of work experience. *Personnel Psychology, 51*, 321–355.

Thomas, D., & Inkson, K. (2004). *Cultural intelligence: People skills for global business*. San Francisco, CA: Berrett-Koehler.

Walsh, J. (1995). Managerial and organizational cognition: Notes from a trip down memory lane. *Organization Science, 6*, 280–321.

Wang, M., & Takeuchi, R. (2007). The role of goal orientation during expatriation: A cross-sectional and longitudinal investigation. *Journal of Applied Psychology, 92*, 1437–1445.

Yamazaki, Y., & Kayes, D.C. (2004). An experiential approach to cross-cultural learning: A review and integration of competencies for successful expatriate adaptation. *Academy of Management Learning & Education, 3*, 362–379.

CHAPTER 5

Cultural Intelligence and International Assignment Effectiveness

A Conceptual Model and Preliminary Findings

KWANGHYUN KIM, BRADLEY L. KIRKMAN, AND GILAD CHEN

Ineffective international assignment causes a variety of problems for employees, their families, and companies. At an individual (expatriate) level, poor adjustment may bring loss of managerial self-confidence, and psychological stress for expatriates and their families (cf., Mendenhall & Oddou, 1985) and may affect job performance and career advancement (Foster, 1997; Hechanova, Beehr, & Christiansen, 2003). At an organizational level, companies suffer from wasteful expenditures related to expatriation and repatriation. A more serious problem may originate from the relationship with various stakeholders (i.e., local staff, customers, suppliers, government) in the host country and from potential damage to organizational reputation inflicted by less competent managers (Stroh, Black, Mendenhall, & Gregersen, 2005). For these reasons, researchers and companies have paid increasing attention to expatriate adjustment and international assignment effectiveness. Despite a growing amount of research (cf., see Bhaskar-Shrinivas, Harrison, Shaffer, & Luk, 2005; and Hechanova et al., 2003, for reviews), we still do not have sufficient knowledge about the factors affecting expatriate effectiveness.

In this chapter, we propose that cultural intelligence (CQ), defined as "a person's capability to adapt to new cultural contexts" (Earley & Ang, 2003, p. 26), is an important factor driving expatriate adjustment and effectiveness. Because individuals with a high level of CQ can more easily navigate and understand unfamiliar cultures, theoretically, they are expected to be more successful when working and managing in countries other than their own. (Ang, Van Dyne, Koh, Ng, Templer, Tay, & Chandrasekar, 2007; Earley, 2002; Earley & Ang, 2003). However, due perhaps to the relative newness of the CQ construct, there has been very little theoretical or empirical work addressing whether, how, and when CQ can enable expatriates to be more successful during international assignments.

Accordingly, the purpose of our chapter is to delineate a theoretical model of the relationship between CQ and expatriate performance, and to provide some initial validity-related evidence for the CQ construct and our model. This chapter contributes to the extant CQ literature and the research on expatriate management in several ways. First, with regard to international assignments, CQ research may provide organizations with valuable direction and tools in terms of expatriate selection, placement, and training. In particular, even though there is a large amount of research available on employee selection in the Western literature, very little research has focused on choosing *expatriates* (see Black, Mendenhall, & Oddou, 1991; Ones & Viswesvaran, 1999). Second, we propose that cross-cultural adjustment is a mediator in the relationship between CQ and expatriate performance. Previous expatriate research has shown that adjustment might mediate the relationships between various predictors and expatriate success (e.g., Kraimer, Wayne, & Jaworski, 2001; Takeuchi, Yun, & Russell, 2002a); however, to our knowledge, no one has theoretically argued that adjustment is an important mediator of CQ's effect on expatriate performance. This is important because we identify a potential *underlying theoretical mechanism* that is responsible for the link between CQ and expatriate performance. Third, we propose that cultural distance moderates the CQ–expatriate cross-cultural adjustment relationship. Rather than simply assuming that the more CQ the better, we argue for an important boundary condition that affects the impact of CQ. According to Kirkman, Lowe, and Gibson (2006), much cross-cultural research has examined the main effects of cultural distance at the country level, but its moderating effects at an individual level have not yet been examined. Thus, our model contributes to an understanding of the role of cultural distance as a moderator at the individual level of analysis. As a result, we hope to establish the conceptual uniqueness of CQ in the broader nomological network of individual difference constructs in explaining expatriates' adaptation and success.

THEORETICAL DEVELOPMENT AND PROPOSITIONS

According to Earley and colleagues (Ang et al., 2007; Earley & Ang, 2003), CQ is composed of four factors: metacognitive, cognitive, motivational, and behavioral. Metacognitive CQ refers to a person's cognitive processing to recognize and understand expectations appropriate for cultural situations, while cognitive CQ refers to cultural knowledge about economic, legal, and social aspects of different cultures. Motivational CQ refers to an individual's drive to adapt to different cultural situations; it is conceptualized as intrinsic motivation (i.e., drivers of performance that originate from within an individual) and self-efficacy (i.e., one's belief that one can be effective on a given task) in cross-cultural contexts. Lastly, behavioral CQ reflects the ability to utilize culturally sensitive communication and behavior when interacting with people from cultures different from one's own. It is still unclear whether different CQ dimensions are more or less important to the prediction of outcomes than others; therefore, we consider the specific CQ dimensions when justifying our proposed relationships involving CQ. However, since each CQ dimension adds unique information to the overall notion of CQ, we focus on CQ as a unified, multidimensional construct when building our theoretical framework and making our specific propositions (cf. Law, Wong, & Song, 2004). We have developed a

Figure 5.1 **The Effects of CQ on Expatriate Performance**

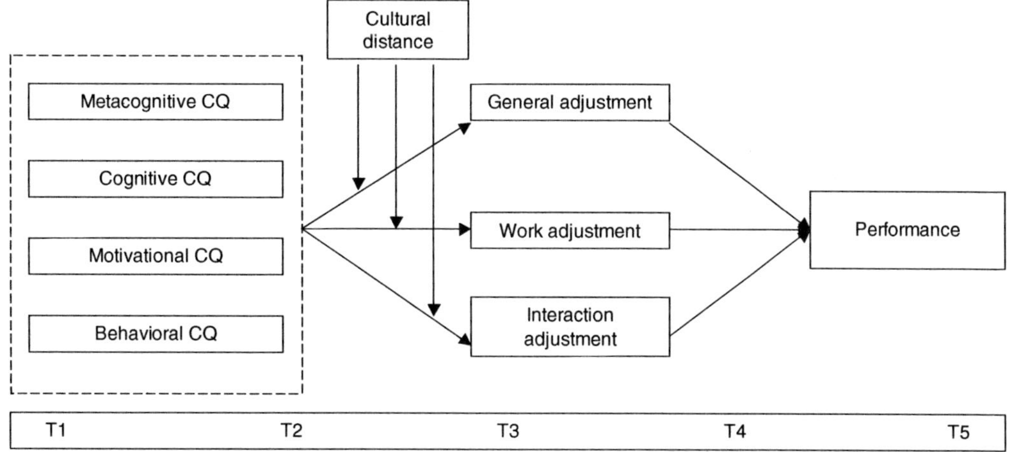

theoretical model of CQ that includes both expatriate adjustment and performance based on social learning, social support, management stress, and work-role transitions theories (see Figure 5.1). In particular, following Baron and Kenny's (1986) criteria for establishing mediation, we discuss how the relationship between CQ and expatriate performance is likely mediated by cross-cultural adjustment.

The Relationship between CQ and Expatriate Performance

It is well known in the Western-based literature that individual differences in personality and ability predict job performance (see Barrick & Mount, 1991; and Schmidt & Hunter, 1998, for reviews). Since individual expatriate performance could be one of the keys to international business success, it is therefore likely that individual differences may also explain why some expatriates are better performers in international assignments than others (e.g., see Caligiuri, 2000). While more general individual differences (e.g., openness to experience, extroversion) may affect expatriate performance, we argue that CQ will likely be a better predictor of expatriate performance in different cultural settings because it is more context- or situation-specific. This is similar to Barrick and Mount's (1991) finding that extraversion is more valid in predicting performance in sales contexts, which require interaction with others. Therefore, we argue that an individual with a higher level of CQ may manage the cultural challenges of international assignments and exhibit better performance in different cultural settings more effectively than others.

Metacognitive and cognitive CQ can influence expatriates' task performance that requires high levels of culture-related cognitive processing and knowledge about different cultures, because such performance calls for effective decision making and problem solving, which are critical aspects of expatriate performance (Earley & Ang, 2003). For example, metacognitive and cognitive CQ may have salient effects on international marketing and sales assignments, because such tasks typically require more knowledge about a host country's culture and appropriate recognition and interpretation of cultural issues in the host country (Ang et al., 2007). Next, according to theories of motivation (Eccles & Wigfield, 2002; Kanfer, 1990; Kanfer & Heggestad, 1997), motivational CQ should also influence expatriate performance because the motivational states of CQ (namely, task-specific self-efficacy and intrinsic motivation in cross-cultural settings) can enhance the strength of an individual's persistent effort toward a task. Thus, intrinsic motivation and specific self-efficacy of expatriates in different cultural contexts may increase their performance by strengthening their consistent effort. Lastly, regarding behavioral CQ, its relationship to expatriate performance can be explained by social learning theory (SLT) (Bandura, 1977). According to SLT, the content of an individual's learning may differ depending on the people with whom one interacts. In international assignment contexts, expatriates can learn appropriate norms and behaviors in host countries from their colleagues. Local coworkers provide thorough knowledge about appropriate work-related norms and behaviors, which should help expatriates to perform better. Thus, the ability to communicate in a culturally sensitive manner and display appropriate behavior when interacting with people from different cultural backgrounds should influence expatriates' ability to increase their knowledge about culturally acceptable norms and behaviors from their local coworkers (Ang et al., 2007; Templer, Tay, & Chandrasekar, 2006), and, in turn, should influence job performance. In sum, expatriates' performance can be influenced by multiple components of CQ, including being conscious of and knowledgeable about local cultures and motivated to behave suitably, and exhibiting appropriate behavior in a culturally sensitive manner within the local work environment. Thus, we propose:

P1: CQ will be positively related to expatriate performance.

The Relationship between CQ and Expatriate Adjustment

Expatriate adjustment consists of three dimensions: (1) work (e.g., meeting job responsibilities and performance expectations), (2) interaction (e.g., socializing and speaking with host country nationals), and (3) general (e.g., adjusting to housing, food, shopping, and other aspects of the foreign culture) (Black et al., 1991; Black & Stephens, 1989; Shaffer, Harrison, & Gilley, 1999). While the three dimensions of international adjustment can be influenced by a variety of individual, job, organizational, and contextual factors (see Bhaskar-Shrinivas et al., 2005 for a review), in keeping with our interest in CQ we focus on individual factors to help compensate for the lack of research attention to the effects of individual differences on expatriate adjustment and performance. The rationale for the relationship between CQ and expatriate adjustment stems from the social support literature. Social support is defined as the provision of beneficial help for an individual to buffer his or her psychological stress (Cohen & Wills, 1985; House & Kahn, 1985; Rook, 1984). The social support literature suggests that support from diverse sources (i.e., organizations, supervisors, colleagues) promotes the individual's work adjustment by reducing psychological strain and feelings of isolation (e.g., Ganster, Fusilier, & Mayes, 1986; Rook, 1984). The argument can also be applied to expatriate adjustment during international assignments, when they gain emotional, informational, and instrumental support from family, host country nationals, or peer expatriates (Caligiuri & Lazarova, 2002; Kraimer et al., 2001). According to Kraimer and colleagues (2001), emotional, informational, and instrumental support reduces expatriates' stress originating from a new cultural environment by, respectively, (a) helping them cope better with unfavorable feelings and experiences, (b) increasing their knowledge about appropriate behavioral rules and cultural norms in the host country, and (c) providing them with practical resources such as local language lessons. That is, expatriates gain feelings of reinforcement, recognition, and affirmation from this support, and these feelings may help facilitate expatriates' cross-cultural adjustment by buffering psychological stress from the new work and life environment in the host country.

In particular, interacting with host country nationals may provide expatriates with emotional support because the more interaction a person has with people from a particular culture, the more positive his or her attitudes will likely be toward those people. This, in turn, reduces psychological stress and increases psychological well-being (Church, 1982). In addition, expatriates may obtain informational support from interaction with host country nationals because they learn the way of life and the host country's social norms through such interactions. Thus, emotional and informational support will affect expatriates' adjustment in the long run, as they help expatriates to gain information about culturally suitable norms and behaviors and reduce uncertainty related to both work and nonwork environments (c.f., Aycan, 1997; Black, 1990). Accordingly, we argue that individuals having a high level of CQ will better adjust to the new work and nonwork environments in the host country, because it is likely that individuals with higher CQ gain more appropriate emotional and informational support through interactions with local people. Some individual differences (e.g., extroversion, general self-efficacy, and relational skills), which are similar to certain factors of CQ, have been found to have a positive relationship with cross-cultural adjustment in previous expatriate literature (e.g., Shaffer, Harrison, Gregersen, Black, & Ferzandi, 2006; see Bhaskar-Shrinivas et al., 2005; Hechanova et al., 2003 for reviews). Moreover, in the CQ literature, researchers have found a positive relationship between motivational CQ and cross-cultural adjustment (Templer et al., 2006) and between behavioral CQ and general adjustment (Ang et al., 2007). Based this rationale, we posit that a higher level of CQ will influence expatriates' cross-cultural adjustment:

P2: CQ will be positively related to expatriate adjustment.

The Relationship between Expatriate Adjustment and Performance

International assignments represent a considerable challenge for expatriates because they may encounter numerous cultural and instrumental barriers in different work and life environments, which may cause psychological stress. According to the stress literature, maladjustment may influence work performance by creating cognitive fatigue, thereby it may reduce the amount of energy and effort an individual exerts toward successful implementation of work (Cohen,

1980). Theories on stress can also be applied to expatriates' adjustment-performance relationship. Successful cross-cultural adjustment in host countries reduces expatriates' stress and strain, and influences their performance by helping them to expend more energy and effort on their work (cf., Feldman & Thomas, 1992; Selmer, 1999). Previous expatriate research has shown that expatriates' psychological stress caused by maladjustment negatively affects their performance (Bhaskar-Shrinivas et al., 2005; Caligiuri, 1997; Shaffer, Harrison, Gilley, & Luk, 2001). For example, expatriates who were better-adjusted at work were rated as higher performers by their supervisors (Kraimer et al., 2001).

Likewise, in jobs requiring more interaction with host country nationals, interaction and general adjustment may be positively related to performance. According to spillover theory (Bhagat, 1983), adjustment problems in nonwork domains may also create stress for an expatriate, which negatively affects his or her work-related attitudes and behaviors. Some empirical evidence suggests that cross-cultural adjustment in a nonwork domain influences adjustment in the work domain (e.g., Kraimer et al., 2001; Takeuchi, Yun, & Tesluk, 2002b; see Bhaskar-Shrinivas et al., 2005 for a review). Previous literature also supports this argument by showing that expatriate performance is greatly influenced by adjustment to the host country (see Bhaskar-Shrinivas et al., 2005 for a review; e.g., Black, 1988; Black & Mendenhall, 1990; Caligiuri, 1997; Tung, 1981). Consequently, we propose:

P3: Expatriate adjustment will be positively related to performance.

The Mediating Role of Cross-Cultural Adjustment

In the preceding discussion, we theoretically argued for three sets of relationships, shown in Figure 5.1, among CQ, expatriate adjustment, and expatriate performance. While we discussed the theoretical rationale and empirical evidence for each of these relationships, we still must discuss why we believe that CQ will work *through* cross-cultural adjustment to affect expatriate performance. The basis for our mediation logic comes from the work-role transition literature that suggests that the degree of successful adjustment to a new work situation may affect individual work outcomes (cf., Nicholson, 1984). A smooth transition across work assignments is critical to an expatriate's success because the work-role that is executed in the host country may be quite unfamiliar, even though the task is the same as it was in their home country, due to different cultural contexts. Accordingly, individuals with a higher level of CQ will perform better through a work transition to a new international assignment because they are more capable of adapting effectively to a new cultural context. If competent individuals in a domestic setting cannot make a successful work transition to an international assignment, their performance will suffer. Simply put, expatriates who have a high level of CQ, but do not effectively adjust to their new cultural environment will be less likely to reach high levels of performance compared to those who effectively adjust. Therefore, CQ is a necessary, but not sufficient, component for expatriate performance; thus, we posit that work adjustment mediates the relationship between expatriates' CQ and individual performance.

In addition, spillover effects (Bhagat, 1983) suggest that adjustment problems in nonwork domains may negatively affect expatriates' work adjustment and work-related attitudes and outcomes by creating psychological hardships. As mentioned earlier, empirical evidence in the expatriate literature demonstrates that cross-cultural adjustment in a nonwork domain influences adjustment in the work domain. For example, Takeuchi et al. (2002b) found that general adjustment was positively related to job satisfaction and Kraimer et al. (2001) found that interaction adjustment was positively related to expatriate job performance. Accordingly, even if expatriates successfully adjust to their new work assignments due to their higher level of CQ, this may not translate into high performance if they fail to adjust to interaction with host nationals and general life in the host country. Following this line of inquiry, we propose that adjustment problems in interaction and general life also mediate the relationship between expatriates' CQ and individual performance. Very few studies have proposed adjustment as a mediator (e.g., Kraimer & Wayne, 2004; Kraimer et al., 2001; Takeuchi et al., 2002b) and to our knowledge, no studies have proposed adjustment as a mediator of relationships involving CQ.

P4: The relationship between CQ and expatriate performance is mediated by cross-cultural adjustment of expatriates.

The Role of Cultural Distance in CQ–Adjustment Relationships

In the previous section, we argued that CQ influences cross-cultural adjustment. Further, we suggest that this relationship may be qualified by cultural distance between home and host country. Cultural distance refers to the extent of cultural differences between two countries on various cultural values (see Shenkar, 2001 for a review). A common approach to calculating cultural distance uses a mathematical formula that compares countries on Hofstede's (1980, 2001) cultural value dimensions including individualism–collectivism, power distance, uncertainty avoidance, and masculinity-femininity (see Kogut & Singh, 1988; Luo, Shenkar, & Nyaw, 2001). Individualism–collectivism refers to the relative societal emphasis on social ties and group affiliation as compared to reliance on oneself. Power distance is defined as the extent of a society's acceptance of unequal distribution of power in institutions and organizations. Uncertainty avoidance refers to the degree of avoidance of uncertain and ambiguous situations in society. Masculinity-femininity distinction indicates a dominant value in a society between masculinity (e.g., assertiveness, materialism, not caring for others or quality of life) and femininity (e.g., caring for others and quality of life).

An example will help clarify the argument regarding cultural distance as a moderator. According to Hofstede (1980, 2001), the United States is the most individualistic nation in the world and is ranked very low in terms of uncertainty avoidance. Canada has scores very similar to the United States on these values, whereas China is significantly more collectivistic and higher in uncertainty avoidance. Thus, using these value dimensions, China and the United States are more culturally distant, relative to the United States and Canada, because they share fewer common cultural values. For example, if expatriates whose national culture is more individualistic and has a lower level of uncertainty avoidance are dispatched to a country considerably different from their home country (i.e., U.S. expatriates in China), they may suffer more from the challenges presented by cultural differences than expatriates in countries with lesser cultural distance from the United States (i.e., U.S. expatriates in Canada), in terms of interacting with host country nationals and working and living in the new cultural environment. Stahl and Caligiuri (2005) showed the moderating effect of cultural distance in the relationship between effectiveness of problem-focused coping strategies and cross-cultural adjustment such that, for German expatriates in Japan, a relatively culturally distant country, problem-focused coping strategies were more beneficial to their adjustment in the host country. Thus, as cultural distance increases, it is expected that CQ would become more, rather than less, critical to expatriates' adjustment and success.

According to Tett and Burnett (2003), certain situations make specific individual differences more important than others. While focusing on the relationship between personality and job performance, they argue that situations both trigger manifestations of individual difference tendencies and require the behavioral manifestation of certain individual differences. Their model can be applied to the moderating effects of cultural distance on the relationship between CQ and expatriate adjustment. Because an unfamiliar cultural environment should present individuals with considerable cultural-specific challenges, individual differences in cognitive processing and knowledge about the culture, motivation to adapt, and culturally appropriate behavior may emerge as the most important individual difference within the context of cultural differences. Accordingly, high cultural distance between a home country and host country may make the variance in expatriates' CQ levels more important in relation to their adjustment. The situation also will require that expatriates have high levels of CQ in order for them to adjust well. In contrast, low cultural distance may make CQ less critical in expatriate adjustment, and the situation may not require the same levels of CQ as a situation with greater cultural distance. Thus, based on this rationale, we argue that the effect of CQ on expatriate adjustment is stronger when the cultural distance between a home country and host country is greater. Hence:

P5: Cultural distance will positively moderate the relationship between CQ and cross-cultural adjustment such that the relationship between CQ and adjustment is stronger when the cultural distance between two countries is greater.

CQ's Relationship to Other Personality Traits

While CQ may have some overlap with other related individual differences, we argue that because CQ deals specifically with cognition, motivation, and behavior *in cross-cultural contexts,* the construct is theoretically and empirically distinct from related individual differences such as openness to experience, extroversion, general self-efficacy, self-monitoring, and emotional intelligence (EQ). For example, although general self-efficacy (Chen, Gully, & Eden, 2001) may be similar to motivational CQ in that both reflect an individual's belief in his or her capabilities, general self-efficacy is a theoretically different construct from motivational CQ because it is not specific to particular tasks or situations in cultural contexts (Chen, Gully, Whiteman, & Kilcullen, 2000). Extroversion may also overlap somewhat with motivational CQ in that both characteristics are related to the willingness to interact with people from different cultural backgrounds and adjust to new cultural contexts. However, extroversion without sensitivity to cultural situations may manifest itself as aggressiveness and rudeness in some cultures, which in turn is likely to negatively impact expatriates' interaction adjustment. Lastly, metacognitive and behavioral CQ may be similar to self-monitoring (Snyder, 1974) and EQ (Law et al., 2004), in the sense that they describe individual differences about conformity and flexibility according to situational demands and social cues. Although there is similarity, individuals who are high self-monitors or are high in EQ but do not have cultural sensitivity, may suffer from cross-cultural maladjustment due to culturally inappropriate understanding and interpretation of culture-specific situational information. Thus, we propose:

P6: CQ will be distinct from, but is positively correlated with, openness to experience, extroversion, general self-efficacy, self-monitoring, and EQ.

CQ's Predictive Validity over Other Personality Traits

While the CQ construct may have some overlap with other traitlike individual differences, it will likely be a more effective indicator of differences in expatriate adjustment and the success of international assignments. While general self-efficacy (Hechanova et al., 2003; Bhaskar-Shrinivas et al., 2005), extroversion and openness (e.g., Caligiuri, 2000), and self-monitoring (e.g., Harrison, Chadwick, & Scales, 1996) are likely to have a somewhat positive relationship to adjustment and performance, we argue that these traits have relatively less to do with cross-cultural adjustment and performance than CQ, as they are more general and not sufficiently specific to cross-cultural contexts. Therefore, we argue that CQ will have more powerful and direct effects on expatriate adjustment and performance, while other personality traits will have more distal or indirect effects. Using student samples, Ang, Van Dyne, and Koh (2006) found that the Big Five personality traits correlated with some dimensions of CQ. However, to our knowledge, no study has examined the *incremental* predictive validity of CQ over and above other personality traits in expatriate research. Thus, we argue that CQ may have a better predictive validity over other personality traits (i.e., openness to experience, extroversion, general self-efficacy, self-monitoring, EQ). Accordingly, we propose:

P7: CQ will better explain the variance in cross-cultural adjustment and job performance of expatriates than other similar individual differences (e.g., self-efficacy, openness to experience, self-monitoring, and EQ).

PRELIMINARY STUDY

Based on the proposed model, we conducted a preliminary study using an undergraduate student sample to confirm the construct validity of CQ (proposition 6). We first used confirmatory analyses (CFAs) to show that CQ has four subfactors. The construct validity of CQ is further investigated by the multitrait-multimethod (MTMM) analysis with self-rating and others' ratings.

Participants and Procedures

Participants in this study were 442 undergraduate students in an introductory management class at a large southwestern U.S. university. The average age was 19, with a standard deviation of 1.44 years, 46.5 percent were male. The racial composition of the sample was 77.2 percent white/European American, 10.1 percent Latino/Hispanic, 6.9 percent Black/African American, and 5.75 percent others. The participants were asked to rate themselves on CQ, Big Five personality traits, and EQ scales on a Web-based survey, in return for extra course credit. In addition, in the student surveys, we asked for their friends' voluntary participation in a matched survey to collect the ratings of others on the students' CQ and EQ. The sample size for the matched pairs was 242, producing a response rate of 54.52 percent.

Measures

Personality

We measured participants' personalities using 40 items of the minimarkers of the Big Five scale (Saucier, 1994), which is a short version of Goldberg's unipolar Big Five markers. Participants were asked to indicate how accurately each trait described them based on a five-point Likert-type scale, ranging from 1 (very inaccurate) to 5 (very accurate). The reliabilities of all the scales were over 0.70.

EQ

The Wong and Law (2002) EQ scale was used for measuring the participants' EQ. It consists of 16 items and is divided into four subdimensions: (1) self-emotions appraisal, (2) others-emotions appraisal, (3) use of emotion, and (4) regulation of emotion. Participants were asked to read each statement concerning their emotional capabilities, and select the response (1 = strongly disagree; 5 = strongly agree) that best described their capabilities. Sample questions for each dimension included, "I have a good sense of why I have certain feelings most of the time," "I am sensitive to the feelings and emotions of others," "I always set goals for myself and then try my best to achieve them," and "I am able to control my temper so that I can handle difficulties rationally." The reliabilities of self-rating in the dimensions were over 0.70. Confirmatory factor analysis (CFA) using LISREL 8.52 (Jöreskog & Sörbom, 2002) showed a good fit of the self-rating data to a four-factor model, χ^2 (98 *df*) = 287.74, non-normed fit index (NNFI) = 0.96, comparative fit index (CFI) = 0.97, standardized root mean square residual (SRMR) = 0.049, and root mean square error of approximation (RMSEA) = 0.065. Other-ratings also had good reliabilities (0.87, 0.88, 0.80, and 0.90,

Table 5.1

Descriptive Statistics and Coefficient Alphas of Measures

Variables	No. of items	Student Sample			Friend Sample		
		M	SD	α	M	SD	α
Agreeableness	8	4.00	.52	.79			
Conscientiousness	8	3.72	.61	.81			
Emotional stability	8	3.24	.57	.73			
Extraversion	8	3.59	.65	.83			
Openness	8	3.77	.53	.72			
EQ1 (self-emotion appraisal)	4	3.84	.69	.84	4.06	.74	.87
EQ2 (others' emotion appraisal)	4	3.90	.65	.84	3.99	.77	.88
EQ3 (UOE)	4	3.93	.62	.77	4.13	.65	.80
EQ4 (ROE)	4	3.67	.76	.86	3.84	.87	.90
CQ1 (Metacognitive)	4	3.68	.67	.87	3.84	.69	.90
CQ2 (Cognitive)	6	2.68	.72	.84	3.10	.65	.82
CQ3 (Motivational)	5	3.54	.75	.84	3.67	.68	.81
CQ4 (Behavioral)	5	3.29	.71	.84	3.46	.68	.87

Note: n = 442 for all variables in student sample; n = 242 for friend sample; five-point scales are used for all variables.

Abbreviations: UOE, use of emotion; ROE, regulation of emotion.

respectively), and supported the four-factor model of EQ, χ^2 (98 *df*) = 251.95, NNFI = 0.96, CFI = 0.97, SRMR = 0.051, and RMSEA = 0.080.

CQ

CQ was measured with the 20-item four-factor CQS, the only established CQ measure to date, which was developed by Ang et al. (2007), with subfactors consisting of metacognitive, cognitive, motivational, and behavioral CQ. Participants expressed the degree to which they agreed with each statement based on a five-point Likert-type scale ranging from 1 (strongly disagree) to 5 (strongly agree). The reliabilities of self-rating in all the dimensions were over 0.80. CFA showed good fit of the self-rating data to a four-factor model, χ^2 (164 *df*) = 654.82, NNFI = 0.94, CFI = 0.95, SRMR = 0.05, and RMSEA = 0.08. Reliabilities of other-rated CQ factors were also over 0.80 for all the dimensions. CFA of the other-rating data also supported the four-factor model of CQ, χ^2 (164 *df*) = 512.22, NNFI = 0.93, CFI = 0.94, SRMR = 0.065, and RMSEA = 0.095.

Analysis and Results

Descriptive statistics, including coefficient alpha and correlations among variables, are presented in Tables 5.1 and 5.2, respectively. Results in Table 5.2 indicate that none of the correlations among self-rated personality, EQ, and CQ dimensions exceeded 0.50. However, the relationships between CQ and EQ dimensions were generally higher relative to correlations between personality traits and CQ.

Table 5.2

Correlations among Measures in Student and Friend Sample

Variables	1	2	3	4	5	6	7	8	9	10	11	12	13
1. Agreeableness	–												
2. Conscientiousness	.24	–											
3. Emotional stability	.31	.03	–										
4. Extraversion	.21	.10	.12	–									
5. Openness	.29	.26	.05	.32	–								
6. EQ: self-emotion appraisal	.19	.14	.17	.15	.19	–	.54	.42	.60	.35	.32	.36	.32
7. EQ: others' emotion appraisal	.36	.35	–.05	.18	.25	.40	–	.47	.48	.39	.27	.37	.33
8. EQ: UOE	.22	.12	.03	.26	.33	.31	.35	–	.43	.39	.27	.37	.30
9. EQ: ROE	.21	.14	.35	.15	.19	.43	.19	.35	–	.40	.30	.38	.39
10. Metacognitive CQ	.21	.14	.06	.14	.18	.15	.32	.24	.13	–	.41	.54	.43
11. Cognitive CQ	–.06	–.02	.01	.02	.22	.11	.15	.03	.10	.35	–	.48	.44
12. Motivational CQ	.19	.03	.10	.20	.21	.14	.32	.24	.17	.46	.38	–	.51
13. Behavioral CQ	.11	.10	.00	.16	.24	.17	.27	.22	.12	.49	.33	.48	–

Note: Figures on the lower triangle are correlations for self-rated measures (n = 442); numbers on the upper triangle are correlations for friend-rated measures (n = 242). Correlations greater than .10 are significant at the .05 level. Correlations greater than .12 are significant at the .01 level.

Abbreviations: UOE, use of emotion; ROE, regulation of emotion.

Table 5.3

Results of Fit Comparisons for Self- and Other-rated CQ and EQ Measures

Model	χ^2	*df*	NNFI	CFI	SRMR	RMSEA	Model Comparison Test	
							$\Delta\chi^2$	Δdf
Self-rating								
Two-factor model (CQ vs. EQ)	67.04	19	.92	.95	.053	.076		
One-factor model	228.08	20	.76	.83	.097	.154	161.04***	1
Other rating								
Two-factor model (CQ vs. EQ)	18.36	19	1.00	1.00	.030	.000		
One-factor model	105.82	20	.92	.94	.065	.133	87.46***	1

***p <.001

Abbreviations: CQ, cultural intelligence; EQ, emotional intelligence; NNFI, non-normed fit index; CFI, comparative fit index; SRMR, standardized root mean square residual; RMSEA, root mean square error of approximation.

Table 5.4

Results of the Two Traits × Two Methods MTMM Analyses

Method & Trait	M	SD	Self-rating		Friend rating	
			CQ	EQ	CQ	EQ
Self-rating						
CQ	3.23	.51	(.89)			
EQ	3.85	.48	*.30****	(.87)		
Friend rating						
CQ	3.52	.52	**.43*****	.16*	(.78)	
EQ	4.00	.60	.21**	**.26*****	*.57****	(.79)

Note: n = 242.

Coefficient alpha reliability estimates appear in parentheses. Heterotrait-monomethod correlations are italic numbers; monotrait-heteromethod correlations are numbers in boldface; heterotrait-heteromethod correlations are numbers above and under the boldface.

Abbreviations: MTMM, multitrait-multimethod; CQ, cultural intelligence; EQ, emotional intelligence.

* $p < .05$
** $p < .01$
*** $p < .001$

We conducted a CFA to assess the distinctiveness of the four factors of CQ relative to the four factors of EQ, in both the self-rating and other-rating data. Using the self-ratings and other-ratings data separately, we set the four CQ dimensions to load on one factor, and the four EQ dimensions to load on a separate factor. We then compared the fit of the two-factor measurement model against a one-factor model, in which the CQ and EQ factors were set to correlate at 1.0. As shown in Table 5.3, results supported the distinctiveness of CQ factors from EQ factors, by demonstrating a better fit for the two-factor models on both self- and other-ratings, as compared to the one-factor models.

We also utilized a MTMM approach to evaluate the convergent and discriminant validity of CQ and EQ, using matched data from students and their friends. Table 5.4 contains the results of the descriptive statistics and the MTMM analyses. The reliabilities of all measures reported by self and others are acceptable, and the requirements by Campbell and Fiske (1959) are all met: (a) reliability coefficients are the highest in the matrix; (b) the coefficients on the monotrait-heteromethod values (numbers in bold) significantly differ from zero (self-rating CQ correlates with friend-rating CQ at 0.43, whereas the correlation for EQ is 0.26); and (c) the values in bold type are higher than any other values in the column and row where it is located, providing evidence for discriminant validity. Relative to the third requirement, although the validity coefficients (numbers in bold) being smaller than the coefficients for friend-rating CQ and EQ could cause common method problems, this is common in individual difference research (Campbell & Fiske, 1959).

Consistent with Ang et al.'s (2006) study, these results confirm that CQ and Big Five personality are different, albeit related, constructs. Furthermore, the results here also indicate that CQ is related to, yet distinct from, EQ factors.

DISCUSSION

Implications for Research and Practice

With the increased reliance on cross-cultural managerial assignments and the growing implementation of multinational teams, global organizations, and international joint ventures, it is critical that we gain a better understanding of the factors that enable employees and managers to perform effectively in cross-culturally diverse contexts. Initial conceptual and empirical work on CQ by Christopher Earley, Soon Ang, Linn Van Dyne, and others has shown great promise toward gaining such understanding. Building on their initial work, our model and its eventual associated empirical support can help us to gain better knowledge of the nature and utility of CQ. This would in turn help extend our understanding of employee effectiveness across cultural contexts. In particular, our model contributes to knowledge about the underlying mechanism of the relationship between CQ and expatriate performance. Previous expatriate research notes that adjustment might mediate the relationship between various predictors and actual success (e.g., Bhaskar-Shrinivas et al., 2005; Kraimer, Wayne, & Jaworski, 2001); however, rarely have studies examined these relationships involving individual differences. Therefore, our research hopes to shed light on explaining how an individual's ability to effectively interact with people from other cultures can create enhanced performance in an international assignment.

Another theoretical contribution of our research to the cross-cultural management literature is the consideration of cultural distance as a boundary condition in the relationship between an individual difference and cross-cultural adjustment. Even though cultural distance has considerable implications in individual-level research, much cross-cultural research has examined only main effects at the country level without examining its moderating effects at the individual level (Kirkman et al., 2006). Thus, our model theoretically argues for the importance of cultural distance as a moderator at the individual level of analysis by stating that CQ's role in cross-cultural adjustment is more effective when the cultural distance between home and host country is larger, rather than smaller. Of course, one reason for the lack of research attention to examining the moderating role of cultural distance at an individual level may be a concern about creating an ecological fallacy when applying the national-level cultural distance measure to individual-level research, and the absence of a valid measure of *perceived* cultural distance. Thus, developing a perceived cultural distance scale, rather than relying on just the calculation of Hofstede's (1980, 2001) five different cultural value dimensions, should precede the testing of the moderating role of cultural distance (Kirkman et al., 2006).

Lastly, this research is one of the first to provide empirical evidence differentiating CQ's discriminant validity from a theoretically similar construct, EQ. Since EQ is also a construct concerning one's perception, assessment, and management of the emotions of oneself and others, an individual with a higher level of EQ may effectively deal with challenges in interacting with others from a different culture. However, our analysis shows that it is related to, yet different from, CQ. So it is likely that an individual with a higher level of EQ is not necessarily more effective at interacting with others from different cultures, since it does not capture the individual's appropriate *cultural* knowledge, motivation, and behavior.

Practically speaking, our research would allow multinational organizations to improve staffing and performance management systems directed at enhancing expatriate adjustment and performance. For example, providing additional validity evidence for current CQ measures would go a long way toward integrating CQ measures into expatriate selection and placement programs. We hope that field studies will increase our understanding of what organizations and managers might need to focus on in order to improve expatriate adjustment and success. This research has many applications for effectively managing multicultural teams (Earley, 2002; Earley & Gibson, 2002). For example, CQ may play an important role in multicultural work groups by influencing socialization processes, group dynamics, and teamwork, and in turn, the team's effectiveness. Another context in which CQ may be an important predictor of work outcomes is in service industries such as hospitality management and tourism. Because these industries require much interaction with customers from diverse cultural backgrounds, employee CQ will influence customer satisfaction and, in turn, the performance and effectiveness of organizations.

Limitations and Future Research

We proposed that CQ influences expatriate performance through cross-cultural adjustment and discussed the moderating role of cultural distance in the relationship between CQ and expatriate adjustment. However, our model has several limitations that will provide interesting venues for future research. First, we focused on expatriate performance, but future studies need to include other indicators of international assignment effectiveness, such as job satisfaction, organizational commitment, and premature return intention. We did not include other outcomes because individual performance may be a more effective indicator for CQ's effects on expatriate assignment effectiveness. For example, since most expatriates have a tendency to complete their assignment in an expedient manner due to the benefits of such an assignment (e.g., promotion opportunity after repatriation and international experience) and the potential damage to their career, reputation, and self-esteem if they are unsuccessful, turnover intention may not be as meaningful a consequence of expatriate adjustment (Harzing, 2002). However, regardless of such concerns, future research should address the effects of CQ on various international assignment effectiveness indicators in a more systematic way, to create a broader picture related to CQ in the expatriate assignment context. In particular, investigating whether specific dimensions of CQ predict certain kinds of international assignment effectiveness will contribute to the elaboration of CQ's effects on expatriate management.

Second, we conceptualized expatriate performance as a single construct of overall performance, but future studies may need to treat it as a multidimensional construct to better understand the relationship between CQ and expatriate performance (cf. Caligiuri, 1997). Regarding expatriate performance, the meta-analytic review by Bhaskar-Shrinivas et al. (2005) shows strong evidence for diverse dimensions of individual expatriate performance including task, relationship, and overall performance. Thus, for future research, there is a need for elaboration on the diverse dimensions of expatriate performance. For example, elaboration of the performance dimensions including technical, contextual/prosocial, contextual/managerial, and expatriate-specific performance (Caligiuri, 1997) would provide more thorough understanding of expatriate management. Such a conceptualization could assist in delineating how each factor of CQ affects different dimensions of expatriate performance.

Third, we did not consider the effects of family (or spousal) adjustment on expatriate adjustment. This topic should be addressed in future research because the existence of spouse and children can have crossover effects on an expatriate's adjustment and other work-related attitudes and outcomes by increasing psychological strain (e.g., Caligiuri, Hyland, Joshi, & Bross, 1998; Takeuchi, Wang, & Marinova, 2005). There is solid evidence that spousal adjustment affects expatriate adjustment and work-related outcomes (e.g., Black & Stephens, 1989; Caligiuri et al., 1998; Shaffer & Harrison, 1998). Thus, future studies should include the effects of family adjustment on the relationship between CQ and expatriate adjustment and other indicators of assignment effectiveness.

Another potential future research area is the examination of the effects of expatriate managers' CQ on the work attitudes and outcomes of host country national (HCN) subordinates. There is little research examining such effects, even though the roles of local workers may be important for a successful international assignment, because their satisfaction, commitment, cooperation, and support for expatriates may influence the performance of the local unit in the host country (Toh & DeNisi, 2003). Furthermore, it is well known that leaders can influence the degree of role stress and uncertainty that their subordinates experience, which in turn may affect levels of satisfaction, strain, and turnover intentions (e.g., O'Driscoll & Beehr, 1994). Therefore, examining (a) how CQ of expatriate managers influences the work attitudes and behaviors of local subordinates, and (b) how the attitudes and behaviors of HCNs affect the work attitudes and behaviors of expatriate managers will provide us with a broader and more complete picture of the effect of CQ on international assignment effectiveness. In short, the research presented here contributes to our understanding of how CQ can be integrated into the international assignment context. We conclude with the hope that this research will stimulate additional research examining various topics related to CQ for more accumulation of knowledge about cross-cultural management.

ACKNOWLEDGMENT

This research was financially supported by research grants from the Center for Leadership and CQ in Nanyang Business School at Nanyang Technological University and the Center for Human Resource Management at Mays Business School, Texas A&M University. We appreciate financial support from both centers.

REFERENCES

Ang, S., Van Dyne, L., & Koh, C. (2006). Personality correlates of the four-factor model of cultural intelligence. *Group and Organization Management, 31,* 100–123.

Ang, S., Van Dyne, L., Koh, C., Ng, K.Y., Templer, K.J., Tay, C., & Chandrasekar, N.A. (2007). Cultural intelligence: Its measurement and effects on cultural judgment and decision making, cultural adaptation, and task performance. *Management and Organization Review, 3,* 335–371.

Aycan, Z. (1997). Expatriate adjustment as a multifaceted phenomenon: Individual and organizational level predictors. *International Journal of Human Resource Management, 8,* 432–456.

Bandura, A. (1977). *Social learning theory.* Englewood Cliffs, NJ: Prentice Hall.

Baron, R.M., & Kenny, D.A. (1986). The moderator-mediator variable distinction in social psychological research: Conceptual, strategic, and statistical considerations. *Journal of Personality and Social Psychology, 6,* 1173–1182.

Barrick, M.R., & Mount, M.K. (1991). The Big Five personality dimensions and job performance: A meta-analysis. *Personnel Psychology, 44,* 1–26.

Bhagat, R.S. (1983). Effects of stressful life events on individual performance and work adjustment progress within organizational settings: A research model. *Academy of Management Review, 8,* 660–671.

Bhaskar-Shrinivas, P., Harrison, D.A., Shaffer, M.A., & Luk, D.M. (2005). Input-based and time-based models of international adjustment: Meta-analytic evidence and theoretical extensions. *Academy of Management Journal, 48,* 257–281.

Black, J.S. (1988). Work role transitions: A study of American expatriate managers in Japan. *Journal of International Business Studies, 19,* 277–294.

Black, J.S. (1990). The relationship of personal characteristics with adjustment of Japanese expatriate managers. *Management International Review, 30,* 119–134.

Black, J.S., & Mendenhall, M. (1990). Cross-cultural training effectiveness: A review and theoretical framework for future research. *Academy of Management Review, 15,* 113–136.

Black, J.S., Mendenhall, M., & Oddou, G. (1991). Toward a comprehensive model of international adjustment: An integration of multiple theoretical perspectives. *Academy of Management Review, 16,* 291–317.

Black, J.S., & Stephens, G.K. (1989). The influence of the spouse on American expatriate adjustment and intent to stay in Pacific Rim overseas assignments. *Journal of Management, 15,* 529–544.

Caligiuri, P.M. (1997). Assessing expatriate success: Beyond just "being there." In Z. Aycan (Ed.), *New approaches to employee management. Volume 4. Expatriate management: Theory and research* (pp. 117–140). Stamford, CT: JAI Press.

Caligiuri, P.M. (2000). The Big Five personality characteristics as predictors of expatriate's desire to terminate the assignment and supervisor-rated performance. *Personnel Psychology, 53,* 67–88.

Caligiuri, P.M., Hyland, M.M., Joshi, A., & Bross, A.S. (1998). Testing a theoretical model for examining the relationship between family adjustment and expatriates' work adjustment. *Journal of Applied Psychology, 83,* 598–614.

Caligiuri, P.M., & Lazarova, M. (2002). A model for the influence of social interaction and social support on female expatriates' cross-cultural adjustment. *International Journal of Human Resource Management, 13,* 761–772.

Campbell, D.T., & Fiske, D.W. (1959). Convergent and discriminant validation by the multitrait-multimethod matrix. *Psychological Bulletin, 56,* 81–105.

Chen, G., Gully, S.M., & Eden, D. (2001). Validation of a new general self-efficacy scale. *Organizational Research Methods, 4,* 62–83.

Chen, G., Gully, S.M., Whiteman, J.A., & Kilcullen, B.N. (2000). Examination of relationships among trait-like individual differences, state-like individual differences, and learning performance. *Journal of Applied Psychology, 85,* 835–847.

Church, A. (1982). Sojourner adjustment. *Psychological Bulletin, 9,* 540–572.

Cohen, S. (1980). After effects of stress on human performance and social behavior: A review of research and theory. *Psychological Bulletin, 88,* 82–108.

Cohen, S., & Wills, T.A. (1985). Stress, social support, and the buffering hypothesis. *Psychological Bulletin, 98,* 310–357.

Earley, P.C. (2002). Redefining interactions across cultures and organizations: Moving forward with cultural intelligence. In B.M. Staw & R.M. Kramer (Eds.), *Research in organizational behavior. Volume 24* (pp. 271–299). Kidlington, Oxford, UK: Elsevier.

Earley, P.C., & Ang, S. (2003). *Cultural intelligence: Individual interactions across cultures.* Palo Alto, CA: Stanford University Press.

Earley, P.C., & Gibson, C.B. (2002). *Multinational teams: A new perspective.* Mahwah, NJ: Lawrence Erlbaum Associates.

Eccles, J.S., & Wigfield, A. (2002). Motivational beliefs, values, and goals. In S.T. Fiske, D.L. Schacter, & C. Zahn-Waxler (Eds.), *Annual Review of Psychology. Volume 53* (pp. 109–132). Palo Alto, CA: Annual Reviews.

Feldman, D.C., & Thomas, D.C. (1992). Career management issues facing expatriates. *Journal of International Business Studies, 23,* 271–293.

Foster, N. (1997). The present myth of high expatriate failure rates: A reappraisal. *International Journal of Human Resource Management, 8,* 414–433.

Ganster, D.C., Fusilier, M.R., & Mayes, B.T. (1986). Role of social support in the experience of stress at work. *Journal of Applied Psychology, 71,* 102–110.

Harrison, J.K., Chadwick, M., & Scales, M. (1996). The relationship between cross-cultural adjustment and the personality variables of self-efficacy and self-monitoring. *International Journal of Intercultural Relations, 20,* 167–188.

Harzing, A. (2002). Are our referencing errors undermining our scholarship and credibility? The case of expatriate failure rates. *Journal of Organizational Behavior, 23,* 127–148.

Hechanova, R., Beehr, T.A., & Christiansen, N.D. (2003). Antecedents and consequences of employees' adjustment to overseas assignment: A meta-analytic review. *Applied Psychology: An International Review, 52,* 213–236.

Hofstede, G. (1980). *Culture's consequences: International differences in work-related values.* Beverly Hills, CA: Sage.

Hofstede, G. (2001). *Culture's consequences: Comparing values, behaviors, institutions, and organizations across nations.* Thousand Oaks, CA: Sage.

House, J.S., & Kahn, R.L. (1985). Measures and concepts of social support. In S. Cohen & L.S. Syme (Eds.), *Social support and health* (pp. 83–108). New York: Academic Press.

Jöreskog, K., & Sörbom, D. (2002). *LISREL 8.52.* Lincolnwood, IL: Scientific Software International.

Kanfer, R. (1990). Motivation theory and industrial/organizational psychology. In M.D. Dunnette & L. Hough (Eds.), *Handbook of industrial and organizational psychology. Volume 1* (pp. 75–170). Palo Alto, CA: Consulting Psychologists Press.

Kanfer, R., & Heggestad, E.D. (1997). Motivational traits and skills: A person-centered approach to work motivation. *Research in Organizational Behavior, 19,* 1–56.

Kirkman, B.L., Lowe, K.B., & Gibson, C.B. (2006). A quarter century of culture's consequences: A review of empirical research incorporating Hofstede's cultural values framework. *Journal of International Business Studies, 37,* 285–320.

Kogut, B., & Singh, H. (1998). The effect of national culture on the choice of entry mode. *Journal of International Business Studies, 19,* 411–432.

Kraimer, M.L., & Wayne, S.J. (2004). An examination of perceived organizational support as a multinational construct in the context of an expatriate assignment. *Journal of Management, 30,* 209–237.

Kraimer, M.L., Wayne, S.J., & Jaworski, R.A. (2001). Sources of support and expatriate performance: The mediating role of expatriate adjustment. *Personnel Psychology, 54,* 71–99.

Law, K.S., Wong, C.-S., & Song, L.J. (2004). The construct and criterion validity of emotional intelligence and its potential utility for management studies. *Journal of Applied Psychology, 89,* 483–496.

Luo, Y., Shenkar, O., & Nyaw, M.K. (2001). A dual parent perspective on control and performance in international joint ventures: Lessons from a developing economy. *Journal of International Business Studies, 32,* 41–58.

Mendenhall, M., & Oddou, G. (1985). The dimensions of expatriate acculturation: A review. *Academy of Management Review, 10,* 39–47.

Nicholson, N. (1984). A theory of work-role transitions. *Administrative Science Quarterly, 29,* 172–191.

O'Driscoll, M.P., & Beehr, T.A. (1994). Supervisor behaviors, role stressors and uncertainty as predictors of personal outcomes for subordinates. *Journal of Organizational Behavior, 15,* 141–155.

Ones, D.S., & Viswesvaran, C. (1999). Relative importance of personality dimensions for expatriate selection: A policy capturing policy. *Human Performance, 12,* 275–294.

Rook, K. (1984). Research on social support, loneliness and social isolation. *Review of Personality and Social Psychology, 5,* 234–364.

Saucier, G. (1994). Mini-Markers: A brief version of Goldberg's unipolar Big-Five markers. *Journal of Personality Assessment, 63,* 506–516.

Schmidt, F.L., & Hunter, J.E. (1998). The validity and utility of selection methods in personnel psychology: Practical and theoretical implications of 85 years of research findings. *Psychological Bulletin, 124,* 262–274.

Selmer, J. (1999). Effects of coping strategies on sociocultural and psychological adjustment of Western expatriate managers in the PRC. *Journal of World Business, 34,* 41–51.

Shaffer, M.A., & Harrison, D.A. (1998). Expatriates' psychological withdrawal from international assignments: Work, nonwork, and family influences. *Personnel Psychology, 51,* 87–118.

Shaffer, M.A., Harrison, D.A., & Gilley, K.M. (1999). Dimensions, determinants, and differences in the expatriate adjustment process. *Journal of International Business Studies, 30,* 557–581.

Shaffer, M.A., Harrison, D.A., Gilley, K.M., & Luk, D.M. (2001). Struggling for balance amid turbulence on international assignments: Work-family conflict, support and commitment. *Journal of Management, 27,* 99–121.

Shaffer, M.A., Harrison, D.A., Gregersen, H., Black, J.S., & Ferzandi, L.A. (2006). You can take it with you: Individual differences and expatriate effectiveness. *Journal of Applied Psychology, 91,* 109–125.

Shenkar, O. (2001). Cultural distance revisited: Toward a more rigorous conceptualization and measurement of cultural differences. *Journal of International Business Studies, 32,* 519–535.

Snyder, M. (1974). The self-monitoring of expressive behavior. *Journal of Personality and Social Psychology, 30,* 526–537.

Stahl, G.K., & Caligiuri, P. (2005). The effectiveness of expatriate coping strategies: The moderating role of cultural distance, position level, and time on the international assignment. *Journal of Applied Psychology, 90,* 603–615.

Stroh, L.K., Black, J.S., Mendenhall, M.E., & Gregersen, H.B. (2005). *International assignments: An integration of strategy, research, & practice.* Mahwah, NJ: Lawrence Erlbaum Associates.

Takeuchi, R., Wang, M., & Marinova, S.V. (2005). Antecedents and consequences of psychological workplace strain during expatriation: A cross-sectional and longitudinal investigation. *Personnel Psychology, 58,* 925–948.

Takeuchi, R., Yun, S., & Russell, E.A. (2002a). Antecedents and consequences of the perceived adjustment of Japanese expatriates in the USA. *International Journal of Human Resource Management, 13,* 1224–1244.

Takeuchi, R., Yun, S., & Tesluk, P.E. (2002b). An examination of crossover and spillover effects of spousal and expatriate cross-cultural adjustment on expatriate outcomes. *Journal of Applied Psychology, 87,* 655–666.

Templer, K.J., Tay, C., & Chandrasekar, N.A. (2006). Motivational cultural intelligence, realistic job preview, realistic living conditions preview, and cross-cultural adjustment. *Group and Organization Management, 31,* 154–173.

Tett, R.P., & Burnett, D.D. (2003). A personality trait-based interactionist model of job performance. *Journal of Applied Psychology, 88,* 500–517.

Toh, S.M., & DeNisi, A.S. (2003). Host country national reactions to expatriate pay policies: A model and implications. *Academy of Management Review, 28,* 606–621.

Tung, R.L. (1981). Selection and training of personnel for overseas assignments. *Columbia Journal of World Business, 16,* 68–78.

Wong, C-S., & Law, K.S. (2002). The effects of leader and follower emotional intelligence on performance and attitude: An exploratory study. *Leadership Quarterly, 13,* 243–274.

CHAPTER 6

Top Executives and Global Leadership

At the Intersection of Cultural Intelligence and Strategic Leadership Theory

MICHAEL J. MANNOR

Due in part to the breakdown of traditional trade barriers, advancements in worldwide transportation infrastructure, and increasing levels of wealth in developing countries, the ability of organizations to conduct business in global markets has increased exponentially in the last 50 years (MacGillivray, 2006). Areas of the world that were once cut off from capitalism are now booming markets for goods and services, and formerly developing economies are being transformed into powerful centers of cutting-edge manufacturing and production (Steger, 2003). However, along with increasing levels of access to the global business community have come new pressures for international growth and development. Businesses that were once completely comfortable doing business exclusively in their own geographic neighborhood now face intense pressure to consider the potential global possibilities for selling and producing their products (Stiglitz, 2006). The overwhelming result of all of these factors, changes, and pressures is a business environment that is much different than ever before in the historically bound domains of domestic competition.

The ramifications of the irreversible trend toward globalization are changes to nearly every dimension of business, strategy, and management. In particular, the pure technical skills for managing workforces and strategies that have traditionally been the stock and trade of top executives are now only one piece of the puzzle. Understanding the dynamics of production and demand in diverse national contexts requires an intricate understanding of culture and cultural differences, skills that until recently had only peripheral roles in business management. Modern organizations now require global leaders. Supporting this idea, Robert Nardelli, the widely admired chief executive officer (CEO) of The Home Depot and former pupil of Jack Welch, noted in a commentary that cross-cultural skills are now essential to the success of corporate executives and suggested that international experience will now be required for advancement in global organizations (Wiles, 1996). Further, a recent survey of 555 leading executives from 68 countries, conducted by the influential magazine *The Economist,* found that the greatest challenges facing top management for the next century will be understanding customer demands across cultures, managing cross-border teams, and finding cross-cultural talent (EIU, 2006). These examples suggest that the development of CEOs is no longer just about creating technical gurus or strategic wizards, but global leaders that can effectively and gracefully lead global organizations.

However, as is often the case (Barley, Meyer, & Gash, 1988), academic research on executive leadership has significantly lagged behind this trend. In fact, despite years of research on the strategic leadership of organizations, models that integrate global leadership capabilities into models of executive leadership are almost nonexistent. If this is the future of executive leadership, as the survey by *The Economist* suggests, the lack of such models represents a significant theoretical gap in the literature. Further, if the assessment of these cultural skills by *The Economist* is correct, our models of strategic leadership are missing the most important piece of the puzzle in understanding executive success and failure.

In response to this significant gap in our understanding of global leadership, this chapter builds on recent advances in the study of cultural intelligence (CQ) (e.g. Earley & Ang, 2003; Ang, Van Dyne, & Koh, 2006; Ang, Van Dyne, Koh, Ng, Templer, Tay, & Chandraseker, 2007) and integrates these ideas with traditional models from strategic leadership theory (Hambrick & Mason, 1984; Finkelstein & Hambrick, 1996) to help advance new models of global leadership. I argue that CQ research offers strong potential for providing theoretically grounded and empirically tested cultural capability research, which can in turn be integrated with traditional strategic leadership theory toward new models of global leadership.

This chapter provides a first step toward the integration of CQ with traditional models of strategic leadership theory. Although the literature on each of these constructs provides a different perspective, bridging between these knowledge domains can provide new insight into the understanding of global leadership. First, a critique of the strategic leadership literature is provided to highlight shortcomings in models that do not address dimensions of global leadership and to highlight opportunities for extending theory. Second, key potential contributions from research on CQ are reviewed, focusing on relevance for top executives. Third, propositions are developed that integrate the literature to better understand the dynamics of how CQ can influence executive information processing, decision making, and performance. Finally, I conclude with a discussion and potential agenda for future research.

SHORTCOMINGS IN TRADITIONAL STRATEGIC LEADERSHIP THEORY

Research on leadership has been building incrementally for almost 100 years, beginning with a focus on the traits of leaders and moving on to consider the behaviors and cognition of leaders and their followers (Bass, 1990; Judge, Bono, Ilies, & Gerhardt, 2002; Yukl, 1989). Although most research on leadership has been performed at the micro level of analysis, focusing on leaders regardless of their rank in an organizational hierarchy or participation in an organization, a specific stream of research has emerged over time within this literature that specifically examines the role of top executives in an organization (Carpenter, Geletkanycz, & Sanders, 2004). This work, building on the foundations of Barnard (1938), Chandler (1962, 1977), and others, primarily launched into the field of strategic management and the larger domain of macro-level research with the work of Donald Hambrick and his colleagues, notably with Hambrick and Mason's landmark work in 1984. This article argued that the upper echelons of an organization constitute a very specific and important domain in which leadership operates and has a significant influence on organizational performance. Specifically, launching a stream of work that Finkelstein and Hambrick (1996) would recast as "Strategic Leadership Theory," the key argument in this work is that the top executives, defined as the CEO of an organization and that person's direct reports, have an undue influence on the strategy and performance of a firm relative to others in the context of a firm. As a result, strategic leadership theory research has focused on how the values, biases, characteristics, and capabilities of top executives influence the strategic choices of organizations and the overall performance of such firms.

Building on this foundation, strategic leadership theory research has provided several important insights into the nature of global leadership. For example, influences of certain types of experience and demographical factors, such as executive tenure and functional background (Grimm & Smith, 1991; Miller, 1991; Wiersema & Bantel, 1992), have been fully explored. Despite the conceptual distance of such factors from outcomes, such as organizational performance (Ray, Barney, & Muhanna, 2004), empirical research has demonstrated the importance of these demographic factors for the strategic outcomes of firms (see Carpenter et al., 2004 for a review of these findings). However, in part due to data availability restrictions, the richer dimensions of executive personality, values, and capabilities (Carpenter et al., 2004), have not been thoroughly investigated. Therefore, although several executive personality dimensions, personal values, and capabilities have been proposed theoretically as being key antecedents to executive decision making (Hambrick & Mason, 1984), research has been slow to develop around these more complex constructs. Specifically, strategic leadership theory has not explored how underlying executive personality, values, or capabilities influence executive behavior in diverse contexts or what capabilities top executives need to possess in order to be effective as global leaders of multicultural organizations. Together, these issues create a significant gap in the literature on strategic leadership theory and make it difficult to use strategic leadership research to understand the nature or development of global leaders.

Research in strategic leadership has suggested that the values, personality, and capabilities of executives play a significant role in determining how executives make strategic decisions regarding their businesses (Finkelstein & Hambrick, 1996). However, scholars note that "despite the abundant literature on executive values, little theory or research has been set forth on how values are converted to action" (Finkelstein & Hambrick, 1996, p. 51). For the study of global leadership, the influence of these factors on executive behavior and actions in culturally diverse settings is of particular interest. By breaking the problem down into influences of such factors on different dimensions of executive behavior and decision making, such as information processing and specific investment decisions, it may be possible to move in new directions. Thus, extending strategic leadership theory to specifically understand how executive personality, values, and capabilities influence different strategic choices among top executives in culturally diverse settings represents an important direction for the development of more global models of executive leadership.

Furthermore, due to the increasing globalization of business, managing a large modern organization requires leadership that not only understands the technical dimensions of executing business strategies, but also has an acute understanding of the nature of international business and culture. As a result of this dramatic shift from domestic to global business, traditional models of strategic leadership that have focused primarily on the technical skills and operational capabilities of top executives have become inadequate. Despite the growing international dimensions of the position of CEO, very little research has explored how specific executive capabilities influence or prepare leaders for their global responsibilities. In fact, after almost 20 years of research on executive leadership (Hambrick & Mason, 1984), in which the roles of executive personality, values, and capabilities are of central importance, almost no research has explored which capabilities are needed for top executives to be successful in culturally diverse contexts.

These issues suggest that there is a significant need for new ideas in the strategic leadership domain that extend traditional models to better consider the culturally diverse reality faced by the next generation of global leaders. As noted earlier, advances in several areas of cultural research and international business can provide strong and proven foundations from which to extend traditional models of strategic leadership. The next section discusses how one such stream, focusing on the CQ capabilities of top executives, can be integrated with strategic leadership theory to answer some of these questions and provide direction for continuing research.

TOWARD NEW MODELS OF TOP EXECUTIVES AS GLOBAL LEADERS

Directly responding to the shortcomings in existing research, I have focused on how advances in CQ research can be leveraged to create a more complete and theoretically rich model of top executives as global leaders. Although an understanding of the importance of intercultural skills has been acknowledged in the literature for many years (Benson, 1978), CQ is a relatively new construct. However, the significance of CQ is evident in the growing literature that has developed around this construct in just the last few years (e.g. Ang et al., 2006; Ang et al., 2007; Earley & Mosakowski, 2004; Templer, Tay, & Chandrasekar, 2006). In addition, this stream of research is particularly attractive for extending models of strategic leadership because CQ has been conceptualized as a capability that is malleable and can be developed for the next generation of global leaders.

CQ is defined as a person's capability to function effectively in situations characterized by cultural diversity (Ang et al., 2006). Exploring this capability, Earley and Ang's (2003) work initially conceptualized CQ using a three-part structure. However, further research on CQ has expanded our understanding of CQ to involve four basic dimensions (Ang et al., 2006; Ang et al., 2007). The four dimensions of CQ include metacognitive CQ, cognitive CQ, motivational CQ, and behavioral CQ. Metacognitive CQ reflects the processes individuals use to acquire and understand cultural knowledge, and those with strong skills in this area are often able to anticipate what will happen in cross-cultural situations. Cognitive CQ reflects general knowledge and knowledge structures about culture, and those with higher levels of cognitive CQ tend to have a wide understanding of multicultural situations. Motivational CQ reflects the magnitude of energy applied toward learning about and functioning in cross-cultural situations, and those with strong motivational CQ tend to be confident of their capabilities and are intrinsically interested in experiencing culturally diverse settings directly. Finally, behavioral CQ reflects the ability a person has to exhibit appropriate verbal and nonverbal actions when interacting with people from different cultures, and those with strong behavioral CQ capabilities are often able to vary their verbal and nonverbal behaviors in response to the cultural characteristics of the situation (Ang et al., 2006; Van Dyne, Ang, & Nielsen, 2007).

Moving beyond these four dimensions, for this research it is helpful to identify similarities among these dimensions to understand how top executives with higher levels of CQ will think and make decisions. Both metacognitive CQ and cognitive CQ help to shape an individual's view of diverse cultural experiences by focusing on the intellectual dimension of CQ. On the other hand, both motivational CQ and behavioral CQ relate to an action orientation regarding cultural relations. Although empirical research has not directly examined these differences, it is possible that these two categories of CQ dimensions may influence executive behavior differently.

Toward this end, the four dimensions of CQ can be grouped into two categories to help with integration into strategic leadership theory. The first category examines how dimensions of CQ (metacognitive CQ and cognitive CQ) can create a cognitive lens for executive information processing. The notion of a cognitive lens traces its roots beyond the scope of CQ to the broader literature on managerial cognition (Walsh, 1995). In this tradition, an important part of managerial thought is related to the degree to which a manager's social construction of reality (Weick, 1979) can restrict a manager's vision, search for explanations, and information processing in ways that result in biased decisions. In this case, executives with higher levels of metacognitive and cognitive CQ may use these capabilities to engage in environmental information processing and scanning that differs from other managers. As the cognitive lenses through which executives see their world may result in biases (Walsh, 1988), the degree to which a leader's CQ influences executive information processing could provide interesting directions for understanding global leadership development. As a result, one extension to strategic leadership models will be the exploration of how executive CQ influences the processing of information by top executives.

The second category focuses on the role of CQ as a stimulus for action. In this perspective the motivational and behavioral dimensions of CQ are then posited to have an influence on the decision-making behavior of top executives. Each of these CQ dimensions involves evaluating an individual's willingness or comfort with engaging in culturally diverse behaviors, and as such these dimensions are likely to influence executive decision making in culturally diverse settings. This is particularly important, as understanding how executive capabilities are translated into action in culturally diverse contexts has been identified as a key shortcoming. If these two dimensions of an executive's CQ become a stimulus toward specific actions or decisions in culturally diverse settings, these dimensions of CQ may help to bridge the gap between executive capabilities and action. As a result, a second extension to strategic leadership models will be the exploration of how executive CQ influences the decision-making process of top executives.

Finally, both of these categories of CQ could also influence overall perceptions of top executive performance in culturally diverse contexts. Specifically, executives with higher levels of CQ, which influences both their cognitive approaches to culturally diverse situations and their behavioral motivations for action in such contexts, are likely to be perceived as more effective than other executives in such settings. These superior performance evaluations are likely due to the relative knowledge and decision-making advantages of culturally intelligent executives in such settings. Thus, a final extension of strategic leadership models will be to examine how the CQ of managers influences performance ratings of top executives.

INTEGRATING CQ INTO STRATEGIC LEADERSHIP THEORY

The next step is to explore how these ideas from CQ research can be brought together and integrated with the tradition of strategic leadership research to create new and richer models of global leadership. Throughout this integration, the level of analysis will remain constant to consider issues at the individual executive level of analysis. The first part of this integration builds on the argument that CQ can act as a cognitive lens for executives and influence the way they process information about the environment, which is a key task for top executives (Finkelstein & Hambrick, 1996). Specifically, information-processing factors such as environmental scanning (Sutcliffe, 1994) and the specific resources used to gather information for decisions (Daft, Sormunen, & Parks, 1988; McDonald & Westphal, 2003), are dimensions that may be influenced by the lens of CQ. However, in addition to influencing the perceptions of executives and the ways such leaders process their environment, actual decision-making behavior would also likely be influenced by the action-oriented dimensions of CQ. Thus, the second part of this section builds propositions that lead to the examination of CQ's influence on dimensions such as strategic choice and decision making, which include international investment decisions and global alliance partner selection. Finally, in the last part of this section, these ideas are brought together to examine how overall evaluations of top executive performance are likely to be impacted by executive CQ. If leaders who are more culturally intelligent are able to better scan their environment for relevant information and use this higher quality information to make better decisions and take smarter risks, such differences are inevitably going to be reflected in stakeholder evaluations of top executive performance. This analysis considers the important and diverse impacts of CQ on top executive perceptions, actions, and performance and can provide a foundation from which to further extend strategic leadership models to better consider the reality of global leadership.

CQ and Executive Information Processing

The CQ of major executives is posited to influence the way such executives process information in their environment. Specifically, CQ is argued to influence three dimensions of executive information processing—(1) the information they look at, (2) the types of informational resources they rely on for decision making, and (3) the overall quality of information that they are able to gather from the environment.

First, the breadth of executive information-scanning will likely reflect the CQ of the executive. Several theoretical and empirical findings support this conclusion. Specifically, Sutcliffe and colleagues (Sutcliffe, 1994; Sutcliffe & Huber, 1998; Sutcliffe & Weber, 2003) have suggested that the way managers scan their environments is significantly dependent on their personal experiences and values. In this sense, managers who come from an engineering background tend to focus more on the technical dimensions of their environment, while executives from a sales and marketing background tend to focus on the consumer-centered dimensions of their environment. These ideas are rooted in Dearborn and Simon's (1958) work on managerial values in which lab experiments were conducted to assess the degree to which managerial values influenced scanning behavior and decision making. This work was extended by Walsh (1988) who also found that belief structures had a significant influence on the decision-making behavior of executives.

Extending this logic, and focusing specifically on the context of global leadership, managerial capabilities for understanding cultural differences are likely to influence how executives search for information in culturally diverse environments. In particular, executives who are less comfortable and familiar with cultures different from their own (i.e., possess lower CQ) are less likely to engage in wide intercultural search or scanning behaviors that would require them to explore many unfamiliar information environments. However, executives who are strong in these areas (i.e., possess higher CQ) are very likely to draw on their knowledge of different cultures when engaging in scanning, as people tend to search for information in locations that are familiar and comfortable to them (Stuart & Podolny, 1996; Rosenkopf & Nerkar, 2001). Because executives with higher levels of CQ have specific knowledge and structures for understanding culturally diverse settings (based on the cognitive lens dimensions of CQ) they are more likely to search through a wider range of information-rich and culturally diverse locations for information. The result is a broader and more extensive search of the information environment.

P1: Executive CQ is positively related to breadth of the information-scanning behaviors of top executives in culturally diverse settings.

A second factor of executive information processing that is likely to be influenced by the CQ of top managers is the specific resources that executives utilize in their attempts to process information. These information sources are likely to differ depending on the CQ of managers. The discrepancy between information sources arises for several reasons. More culturally intelligent managers are likely to have knowledge of informational resources that less culturally intelligent executives do not. Specifically, one component of CQ is specific knowledge of diverse cultural norms, values, traditions, and religious and legal systems (Ang et al., 2007). This knowledge of potentially valuable sources of information makes it easier and more likely that executives with higher CQ would use informational resources generated from within a culture, rather than descriptions of cultural phenomena that originate from outside the culture. Knowledge of the information context is half the battle in finding good informational resources (Brucks, 1985).

Stronger motivational CQ indicates that executives are confident of their capabilities and are intrinsically interested in experiencing culturally diverse settings (Templer et al., 2006). This suggests that such executives would be more willing to search out direct and embedded sources of culture-specific information than other managers. For example, in cases of international product market expansions, culturally intelligent executives would be more likely to find better and more culturally specific sources of local information than their colleagues. The costs of a so-called in-culture search are therefore lower for executives with higher CQ, both in terms of time and energy. These executives are intrinsically interested in encountering diverse cultures head-on and have the knowledge to do so effectively. Finding local taste experts and fashion trendsetters requires knowledge and motivation, so those with stronger CQ are likely to seek out firsthand information from local sources due to their internal drive to experience other cultures personally. As a result, I propose that CQ positively influences top executives toward the use of more direct and proximal sources of information.

P2: Executive CQ influences the selection of more direct and proximal sources of information in culturally diverse settings.

Finally, CQ not only influences what top executives look for in an information environment and which information resources these executives use, but also affects the quality of information they receive. Specifically, it is argued that top executives with higher levels of CQ gain access to higher quality information relative to their peers. The relationship between CQ and quality of information is proposed for several reasons. First, research on knowledge search processes has consistently demonstrated that a broader search brings in better information (Stuart & Podolny, 1996; Ahuja & Lampert, 2001). Most of this research has occurred in the context of patent citation analysis, where scientists who cite a wider range of knowledge domains as inspiration for their innovation are found to realize improved innovation performance (Rosenkopf & Nerkar, 2001). These ideas are also supported by research in information processing as well (Ungson, Braunstein, & Hall, 1981; Vandenbosch & Huff, 1997). Second, building on proposition 2, executives with higher levels of CQ are likely to find more direct and proximal information sources, which can provide better information. Specifically, getting access to firsthand knowledge of a culture provides a deep and rich understanding of the complexity of a culture that more distant information sources simply cannot provide (Eriksson, Johanson, Majkgard, & Sharma, 1997; Denis & Depelteau, 1985). Third, better knowledge of cultural differences allows top executives to better sort through and identify high-quality information. When processing large amounts of information, as is often the case when making decisions in a culturally diverse setting that is full of distant norms, values, and traditions, having higher levels of knowledge and a better sense of the culture can make such sorting more effective. As more culturally intelligent executives have both better knowledge and meta-structuring skills for dealing with diverse cultures (Earley & Ang, 2003), they should be much better at such sorting than their peers. Finally, culturally intelligent executives are more likely to persist in information search efforts to find high-quality information, due to their high levels of motivation for engaging with diverse cultures. Taking these ideas together, I propose that more culturally intelligent top executives will achieve higher levels of information quality when processing information in culturally diverse contexts.

P3: Executive CQ is positively related to the quality of information top executives are able to gather when making decisions in culturally diverse contexts.

CQ and Top Executive Decision Making

In addition to the proposed influences of CQ on executive information processing, this capability is also likely to influence executive decision making. As strategic decision making is a key element in strategic leadership theory, these propositions are being developed to help extend existing models to better consider the global component of such decisions. Two CQ influences on executive decision making are proposed, an influence on international investment behavior and a bias in alliance partner selection decisions.

First, executives with higher levels of CQ are argued to provide foreign partners with higher levels of equity in joint ventures than other executives. This influence on international investment behavior is posited for several reasons. To begin with, higher levels of top executive CQ make it easier to build quality relationships with foreign partners despite partner differences. Although extensions into culturally unfamiliar territories are risky for any organization, such risks are mitigated to a large degree by the CQ of the executive. Specifically, these risks are reduced because more culturally intelligent top executives have greater knowledge of cultural differences, are more adept at engaging in behavioral flexibility, and have the intrinsic motivation to fully engage with culturally distant partners. These factors come together to make foreign partnerships higher quality, and more likely to be based on trust than risk reduction. As research in the supply chain literature has found, when partners build collaborative alliances based on trust, the partnership becomes a relationship that benefits both parties (Aulakh, Kotabe, & Sahay, 1996; Sahay, 2003; Hoyt & Huq, 2000). When the top executives who build such partnerships with foreign counterparts have weak CQ capabilities, their ability to communicate effectively and understand their partners is reduced. Further, such executives have less common ground to build upon with their new colleagues, and the cultural distance between the partners may become magnified. In these situations, instead of building trust-based relationships with these partners, the focus may become more on skeptical business arrangements with high degrees of contractual focus. In this case, rather than concentrating on the relationship that is being built, the transaction can focus on risk or hazard, with a constant fear of opportunism clouding judgment.

This schism between trust-focused and hazard-focused business relationships is likely to play out in top executive decision making. Building on these ideas, executives with higher levels of CQ are then posited to provide larger equity (ownership) stakes to foreign partners than less culturally intelligent executives. Equity sharing in partnerships reflects, to a large extent, the quality of a relationship. In cases where two partners are unable to communicate effectively and are consistently monitoring each other for signs of opportunism, equity sharing becomes problematic. When these difficulties are magnified an organization is less likely to provide large equity stakes to foreign partners (or any equity at all) and focus on licensing and distribution relationships rather than equity-based joint ventures. However, when the partnership is built on a trust-based relationship, providing equity stakes can make a great deal of sense for top executives who can then draw on the local expertise of their foreign partners and hedge overall business risks without fear of opportunistic behavior. As a result, due to the fact that top executives with higher levels of CQ are more likely to engage in true partnerships (trust-focused) rather than skeptical business arrangements with high degrees of contractual focus (risk- or hazard-focused), such executives should be expected to provide larger equity stakes to their foreign partners than other executives.

P4: Executives with higher levels of CQ will provide larger equity stakes to foreign partners than other executives when working with partners in culturally diverse contexts.

In addition to the posited relationship to investment decision making, CQ is also argued to influence alliance partner selection decisions in culturally diverse contexts. Specifically, executives who have stronger CQ capabilities are more likely to engage in alliances and joint ventures with partners who are culturally distant from their own organization. Although most situations in which an organization partners with another organization to work together toward joint goals constitute potentially risky endeavors, working with partners who are culturally distant represents a particularly risky situation (Shenkar, 2001; Pothukuchi, Damanpour, Choi, Chen, & Park, 2002). Further, for many executives, fears of strategic misunderstandings or concerns about miscommunication (Carté & Fox, 2004) may lead them to avoid such arrangements altogether. However, for more culturally intelligent individuals such risks are reduced because of their specific skills in engaging successfully with individuals from different cultures, which results in lowered costs of engagement in such alliances. As executive values and potential cultural distance with partners significantly influence how managers go about choosing potential partners (Tihanyi, Griffith, & Russell, 2005; Park & Ungson, 1997), which in many cases can become a personal decision for top leaders, the specialized skills of culturally intelligent managers are likely to influence alliance partner selection decisions.

P5: Executives with higher levels of CQ will engage in alliances with strategically valuable foreign partners that are more culturally distant than other executives when working with partners in culturally diverse contexts.

CQ and Top Executive Performance

CQ influences the actual performance of top executives in addition to their information processing and strategic decision-making behaviors. Executives with higher levels of CQ are argued to make, on average, smarter decisions in terms of overall investment decisions in culturally diverse contexts. Support for this improved decision making comes in large part from the cumulative effects of the previous five propositions. To begin with, if top executives with higher levels of CQ engage in broader environmental scanning, they are likely to encounter a more diverse range of potential investments than other executives (Sutcliffe, 1994). A larger selection of potential investments increases the likelihood of finding better opportunities, helping to improve overall decision making by providing better strategic opportunities and better potential investments from which to pick. Further, in making each of these investment decisions from an improved pool of potential options, executives with higher levels of CQ have been argued to gather higher quality information. This high-quality information then helps such executives to make decisions more accurately than other executives who have inferior information (Sutcliffe & Weber, 2003). In addition, when relationships with foreign partners are built on trust rather than skepticism, communication is improved and investment decision making throughout the course of cross-cultural ventures is improved. For example, decisions about when to expand operations, launch new products, or pull out stakes in a foreign context are all important investment decisions in culturally diverse contexts. When these decisions are made in ventures with trusted partners they are likely to be of higher quality than decisions made by executives in lower trust relationships. Finally, if executives with higher CQ are able to take smarter risks with potentially culturally distant but more strategically valuable partners, such risks should pay off with higher levels of performance. Thus, overall, executives with higher levels of CQ should be able to use their capabilities to pick "smart" investments and make better strategic decisions throughout the course of these investments, due to their superior knowledge of real differences, opportunities, and higher quality relationships in diverse contexts.

P6: Executive CQ is positively related to the quality of investment decisions made by top executives in culturally diverse contexts.

Finally, it is also argued that CQ will positively influence stakeholder evaluations of executive performance in global firms. This is posited for several reasons. First, the improved quality of the information gathered as a result of executive information processing advantages (as described in proposition 3) is likely to improve overall managerial performance. In fact, a great deal of research has argued that although good information has a high cost (Sutcliffe & Weber, 2003), such information is critical for executive performance. As a result, the improved information quality that is achieved by culturally intelligent executives relative to their peers is likely to improve evaluations of their performance. Second, traditional research on risk has suggested that risk and return are positively related such that higher levels of risk should be rewarded with higher potential for return (Bowman,

1980). However, not all risks are equal, and the degree to which executives can use their unique skills to take on better risks should help to improve their ability to make better investment decisions. In other words, because culturally intelligent leaders are better able to understand the dynamics of culturally diverse settings in which their organizations are considering investments, such managers will be better able to choose good risk situations from bad risk situations. As many investments and international joint ventures are ultimately failures due specifically to miscommunications and misunderstandings between firms and their culturally distant partners, suppliers, or customers (Hambrick, Li, Xin, & Tsui, 2001), the ability of executives to overcome these factors should allow them to achieve higher levels of performance. As these types of investments are critical to the success of global organizations (Oviatt & McDougall, 1994; Reuer & Koza, 2000), and therefore global leaders, the overall managerial performance of more culturally intelligent executives should be significantly higher than that of their peers.

P7: Executive CQ is positively related to overall ratings of managerial performance in global firms.

DISCUSSION AND FUTURE DIRECTIONS

The overall message of this chapter is simple. Traditional models of strategic leadership can be significantly improved by better considering the factors that influence global leadership. To promote such development, I have provided a critique of strategic leadership theory, highlighting the shortcomings of traditional research. I have also proposed that advances in research on CQ provide a strong foundation from which to build new and more complex models of global leadership that specifically explore the influences of these capabilities on executive information processing, decision making, and performance. These ideas provide a myriad of interesting new directions for future research. To help further motivate such research, I have outlined a few of these potential research directions.

This chapter has highlighted the opportunity for future research to explore how other dimensions of executive values influence strategic scanning, decision making, and performance. Specifically, although research has touched the surface of such factors by examining executive locus of control and some dimensions of personality, a wide range of personality factors and cultural values are also likely to underlie executive decision-making practices and prejudices. For example, direct research on Hofstede's (1980) or Trompenaars' (1993) dimensions of cultural differences may also help to understand how leaders from different cultural traditions approach and solve organizational problems.

Another potential area for additional research would be the extension of research on strategic leadership to examine cross-national contexts (e.g. Elenkov, Judge, & Wright, 2005). Such research could help to explore whether or not executive values and capabilities exert different influences on behavior and performance in different cultures, and how such differences might be managed by multinational organizations. In particular, although the relationships posited in this chapter proposed positive relationships between top executive CQ and a variety of strategic factors and outcomes, such relationships may be moderated in specific international settings. Exploring these boundaries holds significant promise for ongoing research.

This research also highlights the fact that further investigation is needed into the development of global leaders and, specifically, the development of global leadership skills among aspiring top managers who may not possess the capability set they need to perform at top levels in the global arena. Although business schools and executive training centers abound, developing knowledge about how to train aspiring leaders to be prepared for culturally diverse leadership positions in a multicultural world remains a key priority and challenge that is not being fully addressed. In part, by leveraging the ideas in this research and the broader research on CQ, training programs and capability development systems may be possible to meet the growing demand for such global leaders.

Interesting avenues for additional theoretical and empirical research remain for work on how leaders who lack CQ capabilities may harm organizational progress or growth. In fact, it is possible that due to their inhibitions in international contexts, brashness in sensitive culturally diverse settings, or poor information quality due to inferior environmental scanning abilities, such capability deficiencies may significantly impede progress toward organizational goals and in some ways highlight the dark side of executive leadership.

Finally, there is certainly a need to empirically evaluate the ideas advanced in this chapter to understand how the executive dynamics explored here actually play out in longitudinal field settings.

CONCLUSION

In conclusion, although this chapter takes steps toward extending models of leadership to better capture the dynamics of globalization by integrating CQ and strategic leadership theory, much work remains to be done. The continued extension of traditional leadership models to consider how executives shape and are shaped by the culturally diverse settings where they do business will continue to provide research opportunities for years to come. Further, how these factors come together to influence the behavior of global organizations has important implications, both for organizations and for the culturally diverse contexts in which they do business. We are entering into a new era of global business, and our research is struggling to catch up. Although the strategic leadership and CQ literatures provide different starting points, bridging between these knowledge domains holds the promise of providing new insight into the understanding of global leadership.

REFERENCES

Ahuja, G., & Lampert, C.M. (2001). Entrepreneurship in the large corporation: A longitudinal study of how established firms create breakthrough inventions. *Strategic Management Journal, 22,* 521–543.

Ang, S., Van Dyne, L., & Koh, C. (2006). Personality correlates of the four-factor model of cultural intelligence. *Groups and Organization Management, 31,* 100–123.

Ang, S., Van Dyne, L., Koh, C., Ng, K.Y., Templer, K.J., Tay, C., & Chandrasekar, N.A. (2007). Cultural intelligence: Its measurement and effects on cultural judgment and decision making, cultural adaptation, and task performance. *Management and Organization Review, 3,* 335–371.

Aulakh, P.S., Kotabe, M., & Sahay, A. (1996). Trust and performance in cross-border marketing partnerships: A behavioral approach. *Journal of International Business Studies, 27,* 1005–32.

Barley, S.R., Meyer, G.W., & Gash, D.C. (1988). Cultures of culture—Academics, practitioners and the pragmatics of normative control. *Administrative Science Quarterly, 33,* 24–60.

Barnard, C.I. (1938). *The functions of the executive.* Cambridge, MA: Harvard University Press.

Bass, B. (1990). *Bass & Stogdill's handbook of leadership.* New York: Free Press.

Benson, P.G. (1978). Measuring cross-cultural adjustments: The problem of criteria. *International Journal of Intercultural Relations, 2,* 21–36.

Bowman, E.H. (1980). A risk-return paradox for strategic management. *Sloan Management Review, 21,* 17–31.

Brucks, M. (1985). The effects of product class knowledge on information search behavior. *Journal of Consumer Research, 12,* 1–16.

Carpenter, M.A., Geletkanycz, M.A., & Sanders, W.G. (2004). Upper echelons research revisited: Antecedents, elements, and consequences of top management team composition. *Journal of Management, 30,* 749–778.

Carté, P. & Fox, C. (2004). *Bridging the culture gap: A practical guide to international business communication.* London: Kogan Page.

Chandler, A.D. (1962). *Strategy and structure: Chapters in the history of the industrial enterprise.* Cambridge, MA: The MIT Press.

Chandler, A.D. (1977). *The visible hand: The managerial revolution in American business.* Cambridge, MA: Belknap Press.

Daft, R.L., Sormunen, J., & Parks, D. (1988). Chief executive scanning, environmental characteristics, and company performance—An empirical study. *Strategic Management Journal, 9,* 123–139.

Dearborn, D.C., & Simon, H.A. (1958). Selective perception—A note on the departmental identifications of executives. *Sociometry, 21,* 140–144.

Denis, J.E., & Depelteau, D. (1985). Market knowledge, diversification and export expansion. *Journal of International Business Studies, 16,* 77–89.

Earley, P., & Ang, S. (2003). *Cultural intelligence: Individual interactions across cultures.* Palo Alto, CA: Stanford University Press.

Earley, P., & Mosakowski, E. (2004). Cultural intelligence. *Harvard Business Review, 82,* 139–146.

Economist Intelligence Unit. (2006). CEO Briefing: Corporate priorities for 2006 and beyond. *The Economist:* Economic Intelligence Unit (EIU). http://a330.g.akamai.net/7/330/2540/20060213185601/graphics.eiu.com/files/ad_pdfs/ceo_Briefing_UKTI_wp.pdf. Accessed February 16, 2007.

Elenkov, D.S., Judge, W., & Wright, P. (2005). Strategic leadership and executive innovation influence: An international multi-cluster comparative study. *Strategic Management Journal, 26,* 665–682.

Eriksson, K., Johanson, J., Majkgard, A., & Sharma, D.D. (1997). Experiential knowledge and cost in the internationalization process. *Journal of International Business Studies, 28,* 337–360.

Finkelstein, S., & Hambrick, D.C. (1996). *Strategic leadership: Top executives and their effects on organizations.* Minneapolis, MN: West Publishing.

Grimm, C.M., & Smith, K.G. (1991). Management and organizational change—A note on the railroad industry. *Strategic Management Journal, 12,* 557–562.

Hambrick, D.C., Li, J.T., Xin, K., & Tsui, A.S. (2001). Compositional gaps and downward spirals in international JV management groups. *Strategic Management Journal, 22,* 1033–1053.

Hambrick, D.C., & Mason, P.A. (1984). Upper echelons—The organization as a reflection of its top managers. *Academy of Management Review, 9,* 193–206.

Hofstede, G. (1980). *Culture's consequences: International differences in work-related values.* Newbury Park, CA: Sage.

Hoyt, J., & Huq, F. (2000). From arms-length to collaborative relationships in the supply chain: An evolutionary process. *International Journal of Physical Distribution & Logistics Management, 30,* 750–764.

Judge, T.A., Bono, J.E., Ilies, R., & Gerhardt, M.W. (2002). Personality and leadership: A qualitative and quantitative review. *Journal of Applied Psychology, 87,* 765–780.

MacGillivray, A. (2006). *A brief history of globalization: The untold story of our incredible shrinking planet.* New York: Carroll & Graf.

McDonald, M.L., & Westphal, J.D. (2003). Getting by with the advice of their friends: CEO advice networks and firms' strategic responses to poor performance. *Administrative Science Quarterly, 48,* 1–32.

Miller, D. (1991). Stale in the saddle—CEO tenure and the match between organization and environment. *Management Science, 37,* 34–52.

Oviatt, B.M., & McDougall, P.P. (1994). Toward a theory of international new ventures. *Journal of International Business Studies, 25,* 45–64.

Park, S.H., & Ungson, G.R. (1997). The effect of national culture, organizational complementarity, and economic motivation on joint venture dissolution. *Academy of Management Journal, 40,* 279–307.

Pothukuchi, V., Damanpour, F., Choi, J., Chen, C.C., & Park, S.H. (2002). National and organizational culture differences and international joint venture performance. *Journal of International Business Studies, 33,* 243–265.

Ray, G., Barney, J.B., & Muhanna, W.A. (2004). Capabilities, business processes, and competitive advantage: Choosing the dependent variable in empirical tests of the resource-based view. *Strategic Management Journal, 25,* 23–37.

Reuer, J.J., & Koza, M.P. (2000). Asymmetric information and joint venture performance: Theory and evidence for domestic and international joint ventures. *Strategic Management Journal, 21,* 81–88.

Rosenkopf, L., & Nerkar, A. (2001). Beyond local search: Boundary-spanning, exploration, and impact in the optical disk industry. *Strategic Management Journal, 22,* 287–306.

Sahay, B.S. (2003). Understanding trust in supply chain relationships. *Industrial Management & Data Systems, 103,* 553–563.

Shenkar, O. (2001). Cultural distance revisited: Towards a more rigorous conceptualization and measurement of cultural differences. *Journal of International Business Studies, 32,* 519–535.

Steger, M.B. (2003). *Globalization: A very short introduction.* Oxford: Oxford University Press.

Stiglitz, J.E. (2006). *Making globalization work.* New York: W.W. Norton.

Stuart, T.E., & Podolny, J.M. (1996). Local search and the evolution of technological capabilities. *Strategic Management Journal, 17,* 21–38.

Sutcliffe, K.M. (1994). What executives notice—Accurate perceptions in top management teams. *Academy of Management Journal, 37,* 1360–1378.

Sutcliffe, K.M., & Huber, G.P. (1998). Firm and industry as determinants of executive perceptions of the environment. *Strategic Management Journal, 19,* 793–807.

Sutcliffe, K.M., & Weber, K. (2003). The high cost of accurate knowledge. *Harvard Business Review, 81,* 74–84.

Templer, K.J., Tay, C., & Chandrasekar, A. (2006). Motivational cultural intelligence, realistic job preview, realistic living conditions preview, and cross-cultural adjustment. *Group and Organization Management, 31,* 154–173.

Tihanyi, L., Griffith, D.A., & Russell, C.J. (2005). The effect of cultural distance on entry mode choice, international diversification, and MNE performance: a meta-analysis. *Journal of International Business Studies, 36,* 270–283.

Trompenaars, F. (1993). *Riding the waves of culture: Understanding cultural diversity in business.* London: The Economist Press.

Ungson, G.R., Braunstein, D.N., & Hall, P.D. (1981). Managerial information-processing—A research review. *Administrative Science Quarterly, 26,* 116–134.

Van Dyne, L., Ang, S., & Nielsen, T.M. (2007). Cultural intelligence. In S. Clegg, & J. Bailey (Eds.), *International encyclopedia of organization studies* (pp. 345–350). Thousand Oaks, CA: Sage.

Vandenbosch, B., & Huff, S.L. (1997). Searching and scanning: How executives obtain information from executive information systems. *MIS Quarterly, 21,* 81–107.
Walsh, J.P. (1988). Selectivity and selective perception—An investigation of manager belief structures and information-processing. *Academy of Management Journal, 31,* 873–896.
Walsh, J.P. (1995). Managerial and organizational cognition—Notes from a trip down memory lane. *Organization Science, 6,* 280–321.
Weick, K. (1979). *The social psychology of organizing* (2nd ed.). Reading, MA: Addison-Wesley.
Wiersema, M.F., & Bantel, K.A. (1992). Top management team demography and corporate strategic change. *Academy of Management Journal, 35,* 91–121.
Wiles, M.M. (1996). GE seeks employees with international experience. *The Business Review,* October.
Yukl, G. (1989). Managerial leadership—A review of theory and research. *Journal of Management, 15,* 251–289.

CHAPTER 7

Cultural Intelligence
A Key Success Factor for Expatriates

MARGARET SHAFFER AND GLORIA MILLER

Pat, a successful manager in JKL Corporation, is worried. He has just been offered the opportunity to transfer to the JKL plant in China for 18 months. He has been told that his success in the U.S. plant, especially his ability to turn around his department from a mediocre function to a highly profitable one, is the main reason for this decision. He also knows that managers are expected to accept these opportunities as they are presented. Although he's concerned that he does not know Chinese, nor has he had any contact with Chinese businessmen in the past, he thinks this experience will be a good career move. He now has to convince his wife to agree to the transfer and move their two preschool children to another country. They have moved twice within the United States for company assignments; he assures her that this move will be similar to those. Although he has never liked change, he and his wife were able to adapt to two new U.S. communities. How different could this be? Six months after the move, Pat is even more worried. He and his wife still do not speak any of the language, they are not comfortable with the food or public transportation, and his wife feels she needs to stay home with their children rather than place them in an international preschool where they would need to deal with many different languages and cultural practices. Their social life consists of dining out alone as neither has made friends—either local or other expatriates. Pat's attempts to replicate his previously successful work tasks have not been successful. He is angry at his new assignment, his coworkers, the country in general, and his inability to understand why everything is so different. He wants to return to the United States, but he is fearful that asking to end his assignment early will negatively impact his future at the global firm. He decides to stick it out, dreading the many months stretching in front of him and his family. He has another concern now; will his second-rate performance in this country due to lack of motivation and satisfaction also hurt his future career? His anger and resentment grow.

With globalization growing at an ever-increasing pace, Pat's opportunities and challenges are being duplicated many times in many countries and are growing in importance in the eyes of individual employees and global organizations. Globalization has led to expatriate, or international, assignments for a rising number of employees. In the 1990s, the United States alone had more than 3,400 multinational companies, 25,000 companies with overseas affiliates or branches, and about 40,000 companies doing business abroad (Ones & Viswesvaran, 1997). Although the exact size of the expatriate population is unknown, evidence suggests that the number of expatriates is increasing. According to a recent survey by Mercer Human Resource Consulting (Mercer, 2006), 44 percent of multinational corporations increased their international assignments during the last two years. Organizations are also increasingly recognizing the value of such assignments. In a survey by the Employee Relocation Council/Worldwide ERC, 24 percent of participating firms reported that senior managers had completed international assignments, and 50 percent expected this number to increase by 50 percent over the next five years (Worldwide ERC, 2007).

An expatriate assignment brings extra challenges to the individual and the organization, as well as additional costs, as the expatriate attempts to adjust to life and work in a new country and culture. Unfortunately, failure rates of expatriate placements remain high. The cost of an expatriate in a four-year assignment in a host country can be as high as US $2 million (Klaff, 2002; O'Connor, 2002). The common failure rate (the rate of early return) of expatriates is up to 40 percent for assignments to developed countries, and 70 percent when the assignment is in an underdeveloped country (Andreason, 2003). Twenty years ago, estimates of the costs incurred when an expatriate failed to adjust exceeded $200,000, depending on moving expenses (Copeland & Griggs, 1985). Today's costs are probably much higher. In addition to financial costs, failed expatriate assignments result in career costs for the firm or for the individual who is affected by the early return (Briscoe, 1995). There are also opportunity costs that arise from failed expatriate assignments, in that the high level of domestic competence is lost at home while the employee is abroad (Earley & Ang, 2003). With the numbers of expatriates expected to continue to expand, increasing the success of these assignments is a great concern to organizations around the world.

Expatriate success has been defined differently by researchers, organizations, and individual expatriates themselves. Historically, researchers of expatriates have looked at the end results of placements, including adjustment (Black, 1988; Black, Mendenhall, & Oddou, 1991), retention (Black & Gregersen, 1991; Naumann, 1992; Takeuchi, Yun, & Tesluk, 2002), and performance (Arthur & Bennett, 1995). At the organizational level, performance in the new job is often the main component of success that is measured by the home office (Earley & Ang, 2003). Although it is usually not tracked, retention is also of great concern to organizations. Individual expatriates tend to look mainly at career progress when determining the level of success of their expatriate assignment. All of these perspectives on the success of international assignments are illustrated in our initial story about Pat, whose concern about his future career will probably cause him to remain in the host country and continue the negative experience until the organization determines the assignment is complete.

Efforts to understand what contributes to a successful international assignment have

Table 7.1

Definitions of Cultural Intelligence

Reference	Definition	Focus
Brislin et al., 2006	People's success (or lack thereof) when adjusting to another culture, for example, on an overseas business assignment.	Outcomes
Earley & Ang, 2003	A person's ability to adapt effectively to new cultural contexts.	Capabilities
Earley & Mosakowski, 2004	Seemingly natural ability to interpret someone's unfamiliar and ambiguous gestures in just the way that person's compatriots and colleagues would, even to mirror them.	Capabilities
Johnson et al., 2006	An individual's effectiveness in drawing upon a set of knowledge, skills, and personal attributes in order to work successfully with people from different national cultural backgrounds at home or abroad.	Outcomes
Ng & Earley, 2006	Capability to be effective across cultural settings.	Capabilities
Thomas, 2006	The ability to interact effectively with people who are culturally different.	Capabilities
Thomas & Inkson, 2005	Being skilled and flexible about understanding a culture, learning increasingly more about it, and gradually shaping one's thinking to be more sympathetic to the culture and one's behavior to be more fine-tuned and appropriate when interacting with others from the culture.	Capabilities

coalesced to form a strong body of theoretical and empirical research (see Harrison, Shaffer, & Bhaskar-Shrinivas, 2004; Mendenhall, Kuhlman, Stahl, & Osland, 2002). Based on a recent meta-analysis of relationships initially proposed by Black, Mendenhall, and Oddou (1991), several inputs to success have been confirmed (Bhaskar-Shrinivas, Harrison, Shaffer, & Luk, 2005). These inputs include anticipatory factors (previous experience and language ability), individual factors (self-efficacy and relational skills), job factors (role clarity, role discretion, role novelty, and role conflict), organizational factors (coworker support and logistical support), and nonwork factors (spouse adjustment and cultural novelty). For the most part, these influences have differentially affected the various indicators of expatriate success, but inputs common across success criteria remain elusive. We believe that cultural intelligence (CQ) may provide insights into general predictors of success across a range of criteria.

CQ is distinct from general intelligence (IQ) and emotional intelligence (EQ) (Alon & Higgins, 2005). IQ refers to rational and logic-based verbal and quantitative intelligence. EQ reflects a person's ability to understand and convey human emotion (Earley & Peterson, 2004). As CQ is a fairly new construct, there is no clear consensus about how to define it. The definitions offered by various scholars (see Table 7.1) generally refer to CQ as a capability to interact effectively with others from different cultural backgrounds, or the outcome of these interactions. The focus is on intercultural interactions and behaviors rather than on rationality or emotions. Conceptually, CQ is the same as what Johnson and colleagues refer to as cross-cultural competence (Johnson, Lenartowicz, & Apud, 2006).

The three facets of CQ are cognitive, motivational, and behavioral. Some researchers (Ang, Van Dyne, & Koh, 2006; Earley & Peterson, 2004; Templer, Tay, & Chandrasekar, 2006) consider metacognitive CQ, or the processes that individuals use to gain and understand cultural knowledge, as a separate dimension; others (Earley & Mosakowski, 2004; Thomas, 2006) subsume it under the cognitive dimension. While some researchers have studied CQ specifically in these three (or four) dimensions, we will limit our study here to an overall concept of CQ. Although later we specifically refer to one or more of the dimensions when discussing relationships throughout the chapter for clarification of understanding, we do not intend to infer that dimensions not utilized are not related.

Our main purpose in this chapter is to consider how CQ will directly and indirectly affect various aspects of expatriate success. With socioanalytic theory and self-efficacy theory as a foundation, we develop propositions for various roles that CQ might play in the expatriation process. We begin by looking at possible direct effects of CQ on multiple success criteria, including expatriate adjustment, performance, retention, and career success. Proposing that CQ also has indirect effects on expatriate success, we consider both moderating and mediating roles. We believe our contribution to the expatriate and CQ literature is the provision of theoretical arguments for the proposed relationships. By understanding how CQ influences the experiences of expatriates, organizations will be able to develop appropriate selection and training mechanisms that build and reinforce the competitive advantage that expatriates represent. To stimulate future research in this area, we provide a discussion of methodological issues associated with testing the propositions offered in this chapter.

A MODEL OF CQ AND EXPATRIATE SUCCESS

As illustrated in the opening vignette, expatriation is a complex process that has important consequences for individuals and organizations. Reflecting the complexity of this process is a wide array of personal, job, and cultural inputs to various forms of expatriate success such as adjustment, performance, retention, and career success (Bhaskar-Shrinivas et al., 2005). Although these outcomes share the same criterion space, established predictors are differentially related to them (see Harrison et al., 2004), and much of the variance in these outcomes remains unexplained.

In this chapter, we consider the role of CQ in expatriate success. As depicted in Figure 7.1, we believe that CQ is directly relevant to all success criteria. We also envision it in complex relationships with established predictors. We think that CQ as a moderator will interact with various personal, job, and cultural factors to influence expatriate effectiveness. As a mediator, CQ will intervene in the influence of anticipatory factors on expatriate adjustment. Drawing on the extant expatriate literature, including the few empirical assessments involving CQ (Ang et al., 2006; Ang, Van Dyne, Koh, Ng, Templer, Tay, & Chandrasekar, 2007; Osland & Osland, 2005; Templer et al., 2006), we develop propositions for the direct and indirect effects of CQ.

Figure 7.1 **The Role of Cultural Intelligence on Expatriate Success**

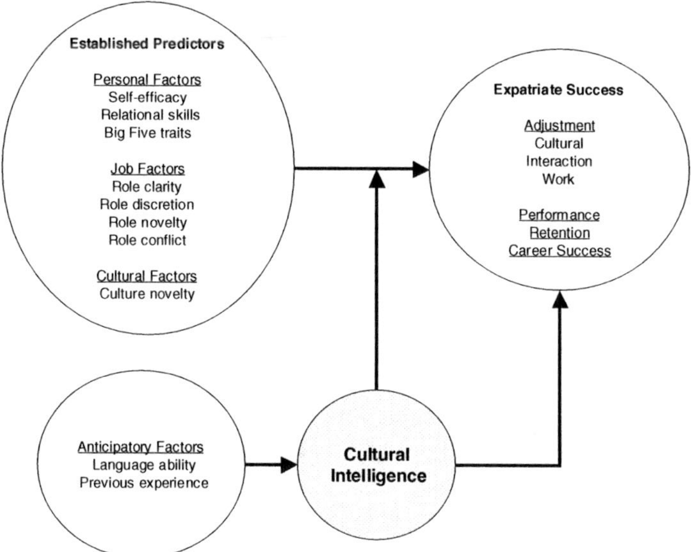

Direct Effects of CQ on Expatriate Success

In this section, we develop propositions for the direct effects of CQ on several important indicators of expatriate success, including adjustment, performance, retention, and overall career success. The underlying theoretical rationale for the influence of CQ on these outcomes stems from socioanalytic theory (Hogan, 1983, 1991, 1996; Hogan & Roberts, 2000), which explains how individual differences, such as personality, affect outcomes, such as career success and performance. According to this theory, individuals have three basic needs: those for (1) acceptance and approval, which translates into behaviors designed for getting along with other group members; (2) status, power, and the control of resources, which translates into behaviors toward getting ahead in terms of achieving status; and (3) predictability and order, which translates into behaviors designed to make sense of the world (Hogan & Shelton, 1998). Individual differences represent personal resources that enable individuals to satisfy these basic needs. For example, extraversion facilitates behaviors that are associated with getting along with others. Similarly, we contend that CQ will fulfill the need for expatriates to get along with others, to achieve, and to make sense of their new (foreign) world; by doing so, CQ will contribute directly to various forms of expatriate success.

CQ and Expatriate Adjustment

Adjustment has been defined in terms of well-being or interaction effectiveness, but most researchers have adopted the definition offered by Black and colleagues, which states that expatriate adjustment is a multidimensional construct that refers to psychological (dis)comfort associated with various aspects of the international assignment, including the general cultural environment, interactions with host country nationals (HCNs), and the work itself (Black et al., 1991). An extensive body of research has been devoted to understanding expatriate adjustment, and various personal, work, organizational, and environmental antecedents have been identified (see Harrison et al., 2004, for a review). However, only recently have researchers begun to consider the effects of CQ on expatriate adjustment (Osland & Osland, 2005; Templer et al., 2006). To assist in these endeavors, we offer theoretically based arguments for the influence of CQ on the three realms of adjustment: cultural, interactional, and work adjustment.

In our opening vignette, Pat and his family clearly had difficulty with general adjustment as they struggled with daily challenges in a foreign country. This form of adjustment includes various aspects of everyday life in a new culture, including general living conditions, local food, transportation, entertainment, and health care services (Black et al., 1991). From a socioanalytic perspective (Hogan & Shelton, 1998), cultural adjustment is affected by the cognitive, motivational, and behavioral domains of CQ; these domains of CQ facilitate expatriates' need for predictability and order, allow them to make sense of their foreign experience, and allow them to exhibit appropriate actions and, thus, fit in better. The cognitive domain of CQ encompasses one's knowledge of what culture is, how cultures vary, and how a culture affects behaviors of those living within it (Thomas & Inkson, 2005). This knowledge directly influences cultural adjustment as a new expatriate begins to learn the "lay of the land" in the host country. Predeparture knowledge regarding the new country and expatriate experiences in general have been found to be related to general adjustment (Black, 1988). Motivational factors of CQ also strongly affect cultural adjustment. Motivation in this context includes an individual's interest in new cultural surroundings and the initiative to embrace them (Ang et al., 2007). Expatriates with high motivational CQ are more open to different experiences and also enjoy attempting new things. Such individuals are more likely to persist in adapting to different cultural situations and living conditions, thus attaining higher cultural adjustment (Templer et al., 2006). Indeed, Ang and colleagues (2007) recently found that motivational and behavioral CQ related positively to cultural adjustment. Pat's eventual resignation to his assignment and his desire to "just get through it" show low motivation toward adapting to the new environment, much less thrive in it.

Pat also struggled to make friends in the host country, limiting his social activities to his wife and children. This suggests that he had problems with interaction adjustment, which refers to an expatriate's ability to relate to HCNs in both work and nonwork situations (Black et al., 1991). From a socioanalytic theory (Hogan & Shelton, 1998) perspective, expatriates who are driven by a strong need for acceptance and approval will engage in more effective interactions with HCNs. The cognitive and behavioral facets of CQ join here to enable an expatriate to consider a well-developed repertoire of behaviors that have been found to be correct for different intercultural situations and then extrapolate that knowledge to generate appropriate behavior in a new cultural interaction (Thomas, 2006). Motivational CQ also contributes to effective interactions because it includes the individual's basic sense of confidence for social interactions in novel settings, confidence in the ability to relate to those from different cultures, and interest in developing relationships with culturally different persons (Earley & Ang, 2003). CQ has been found to positively relate to interaction adjustment (Templer et al., 2006); individuals with high CQ are therefore expected to adjust well in their interactions with people from different cultural backgrounds.

Work adjustment, which refers to the expatriate's ability to adjust to the new job itself, including its roles and tasks (Black et al., 1991), is assisted by the fact that most organizations use somewhat uniform work policies and procedures globally (Harrison et al., 2004). As Pat found, however, procedures that work in one's home country are not necessarily effective in another culture. From a socioanalytic perspective (Hogan & Shelton, 1998), Pat was not able to make sense out of his new world, nor was he able to achieve his personal goals or those of his firm. These difficulties could have been avoided if Pat had higher CQ. The behavioral and motivational factors of CQ are especially relevant to work adjustment. Persons with high CQ would be expected to detect the tacit nuances of the salient contextual activities required in the host country (Earley & Ang, 2003). The behaviors exhibited by expatriates with high CQ will assist them in "fitting in" better with HCNs within the new work environment, thereby reducing uncertainty and stress associated with work. However, the effect of behavioral differences depends on the nature of the job and the level of interaction with HCNs. Individuals with high motivational CQ are motivated intrinsically and by their efficient beliefs of adaptive capabilities to properly deal with new cultural situations (Templer et al., 2006). Indeed, in one study, motivational CQ was found to be positively related to work adjustment of expatriates (Templer et al., 2006). The above findings lead us to offer:

P1a–c: CQ will relate positively to the three realms of adjustment: (a) general, (b) interactional, and (c) work.

CQ and Expatriate Retention

Pat's conflicting desires to return home early and to avoid the stigma of a failed assignment are typical among expatriates. Retention, or remaining on the international assignment through the original deadline or until the company decides to bring one home, increases an expatriate's effectiveness as perceived by the company. However, as we noted in the introduction, retention of poor performers may result if expatriates transfer their frustrations with the international assignment to the job, possibly damaging relationships with host nationals and failing to fulfill assignment objectives. Expatriates with high CQ are better able to conform to necessary cultural differences in their assignments, easing stress levels, and finding more enjoyment with the overseas experience. From a socioanalytic perspective, this fulfills their need to make sense of their "new" world (Hogan & Shelton, 1998). Cognitive and behavioral CQ come into play here as the ability to accurately predict and interpret the behavior of HCNs increases the likelihood of completing an expatriate assignment (Ones & Viswesvaran, 1997). In addition, those with high levels of CQ will be less ethnocentric; instead of viewing their own cultural behaviors and traditions as correct and differing cultural behaviors and traditions as wrong, they will be motivated to learn about and engage in interactions with host nationals. The negative relationship between ethnocentrism and withdrawal cognitions (Shaffer, Harrison, Gregersen, Black, & Ferzandi, 2006) suggests that CQ will result in greater retention of expatriates. Thus, we propose:

P2: CQ will relate positively to expatriate retention.

CQ and Expatriate Performance

Despite Pat's recognition that his performance is second rate, he seems to be more concerned about "surviving" his assignment rather than improving his effectiveness in the workplace. For expatriates in particular, work performance is more than the fulfillment of specific task requirements. It also includes a strong contextual or relational dimension because of the emphasis on developing and maintaining relationships with HCNs (Ones & Viswesvaran, 1997). Overall performance includes an individual's organizational contributions and productivity and the extent and quality of his or her execution of assigned duties, including relationship and task maintenance (Bhaskar-Shrinivas et al., 2005). Such performance is often the main component of expatriate success as measured by the home office (Earley & Ang, 2003). Insofar as high levels of CQ help to fulfill the need for achievement as well as the need to get along with others (Hogan & Shelton, 1998), expatriates who are culturally intelligent will be more effective in carrying out their tasks and in maintaining relationships with HCNs. Cognitive forms of CQ enable expatriates to acquire the knowledge needed to accomplish tasks and to work with others in a new cultural context. Motivational CQ focuses the energies of the expatriate on the tasks at hand and on the interactions necessary to complete them. Behavioral CQ manifests itself in verbal and nonverbal actions that are appropriate in the foreign culture. Both metacognitive and behavioral CQ have been empirically found to predict task performance (Ang et al., 2007). Together, these facets of CQ relieve overall stress for the expatriate, making the individual more able to properly attend to the job at hand. Thus, we propose:

P3: CQ will relate positively to expatriate task and contextual performance.

CQ and Career Success

Pat's concerns about his career prospects are echoed throughout the expatriate community. For many individuals, especially those within large organizations, career success is defined by whether an individual is able to retain a position and continue to achieve even higher-level positions (Callanan, 2003). This knowledge is part of the reason that Pat accepted his expatriate assignment and that he felt the need to remain in the position, even though he was struggling with it daily. An American expatriate that we interviewed and who had returned from an assignment in Venezuela stated that in his organization, it was very clear that, "you're offered the position, you turn it down, that's the end of your career." He further stated that "you were sent to Venezuela for two to four years, if you did well there, [the company] considered that you would do well anywhere, so if you didn't do well there, you were put on the slow track. Several companies looked at it that way."

Career success from the organizational point of view is based on one's ability to perform in a present sense while meeting the dictates of the organization's culture and internal control systems (Callanan, 2003). For individuals, career success is often equated with promotions. In global organizations, the ability to move up within the organization requires CQ (Alon & Higgins, 2005). Evidence shows that organizations leverage individuals with CQ to achieve their goals and strategies (Tan, 2004). These practices increase the value of employees who possess CQ to their global employers and raise their career success, thus fulfilling their need for achievement as well as getting along (Hogan & Shelton, 1998). Tan states that "cultural thinking and learning and acquiring cultural knowledge are both critical to success" (2004, p. 20). There is also a relationship between international experience and promotions that suggests that successful global assignments might help aspirant executives succeed in their ascent of the corporate ladder (Judge, Cable, Boudreau, & Bretz, 1995). Thus, we propose:

P4: CQ will relate positively to the career success of expatriates.

Indirect Effects of CQ on Expatriate Success

From the opening vignette, it is obvious that taking on an international assignment involves a complex set of decisions and behaviors. In the previous section, we developed arguments for the direct effects of CQ on expatriate success. Recognizing the complexity of the process, however, we now consider possible indirect effects—both moderating and mediating. With CQ as a moderator, we propose that the relationships between various personal, job, and cultural factors and expatriate success will differ across different levels of CQ. As a mediator, we predict that CQ will clarify the causal process between anticipatory factors and expatriate effectiveness. In the next sections, we draw upon relevant theory to develop propositions for the moderating and mediating roles of CQ in relation to expatriate success.

CQ as a Moderator

Insofar as CQ refers to the ability to interact effectively with others from different cultural backgrounds, we conceptualize it as a social skill. According to socioanalytic theory, social skills facilitate the attainment of goals to achieve, to get along with others, and to find meaning by translating individuals' identities into actions (Hogan & Shelton, 1998). Although socioanalytic theory focuses on personal forms of identity (i.e., personality), we extend this conceptualization to include other sources of identity, such as interactions with others and the situational context (Ogden, 1995). Thus, based on socioanalytic theory (Hogan & Shelton, 1998), we contend that CQ as a social skill will moderate the relationships involving personal, job, and cultural factors and various forms of expatriate success. As illustrated in the opening story, Pat suffered a crisis of identity when he encountered difficulties in the new environment. With CQ, we believe that he would have been better able to cope with the challenges that faced him.

CQ and Personal Identity Factors. Personal identity factors include basic psychological and behavioral attributes (Tajfel, 1982; Tajfel & Turner, 1985) that expatriates carry with them to an international assignment. The influence of these factors on expatriate effectiveness has been extensively studied. In particular, researchers have looked at the effects of the Big Five personality traits (conscientiousness, extraversion, emotional stability, openness to experience, and agreeableness) on various expatriate outcomes. They have found that all of the Big Five traits differentially influenced expatriate adjustment, performance, and retention (Shaffer et al., 2006). Also, various forms of CQ have been associated with the Big Five traits (Ang et al., 2006), with CQ as a more proximal input to adjustment because of its malleability. The combined effects of CQ and personality, however, have not been tested. From a socioanalytic perspective, an individual must have some ability to express a personality trait. For example, someone with an extraverted personality must have the ability to select appropriate expressive behaviors. In interactions with those from other cultures, CQ provides the ability to select appropriate behaviors that lead to effective exchanges. Therefore, we propose the following:

P5: CQ will strengthen the positive relationships between the Big Five personality traits and the expatriate effectiveness criteria of adjustment, performance, retention, and career success.

CQ and Job Identity Factors. Within the expatriate literature, the four job-related factors of role clarity, role discretion, role novelty, and role conflict have been related to expatriate work adjustment (see Harrison et al., 2004). Role clarity refers to an exact understanding of the position requirements. It is important because it reduces the amount of uncertainty associated with the work situation (Black & Gregersen, 1991). Role discretion (or decision-making autonomy) is the expatriate's flexibility to determine how work should be accomplished (Earley & Ang, 2003). High role discretion can facilitate work adjustment as it allows the expatriate to adapt to the work role and setting rather than needing to wholly adjust to the new situation (Black & Gregersen, 1991). Role novelty is the perceived difference in job duties and requirements between the expatriate's former native assignment and the new overseas assignment (Nicholson, 1984). Higher role novelty causes increased stress in the average expatriate and decreases the ability to make sense of the situation. Role conflict is caused when the expatriate is torn between the two roles, where the home office is expecting certain actions while the local environment requires different actions. Role conflict requires the expatriate to comprehend conflicting signals, filter the relevant ones, and ultimately execute appropriate conduct (Bhaskar-Shrinivas et al., 2005).

From a socioanalytic perspective (Hogan & Shelton, 1998), role clarity and role discretion satisfy the needs to find meaning in the world and achieve; the result of fulfilling these needs is greater success at work (Bhaskar-Shrinivas et al., 2005). In contrast, role novelty and role conflict inhibit the expatriate's ability to achieve and to make sense of the new environment, making it more difficult to be effective within the work domain. With CQ, however, we expect expatriates to capitalize on the advantages of role clarity and role discretion and to attenuate the disadvantages of role novelty and role conflict. Expatriates with high CQ will be in tune with cultural differences and will, therefore, be better able to deal with poor role clarity and role novelty. With high CQ, expatriates who have low role discretion will be able to decipher the issues that are important and that need to be conceded in the local culture. Expatriates with high CQ will be more likely than those with low CQ to know which of their decisions will be accepted by HCNs. They will also be more adept at reading signals of the host country and deciding which of those signals are important, thus making sense of their new work environment and avoiding conflicting situations. Thus, we offer the following:

P6: CQ will strengthen (weaken) the positive (negative) relationships between the job factors and the expatriate effectiveness criteria of work adjustment, task performance, and contextual performance.

CQ and Cultural Identity Factors. An individual's identity stems not only from within, but also from interactions with others and with the external environment in general (Ogden, 1995). A cultural factor that is especially relevant to expatriates is cultural novelty, which is the perceived difference between the home situation and the host country in terms of living conditions, general environment, weather, norms, values, and beliefs. Insofar as qualities of the local environment affect one's identification with a particular place (Cuba & Hummon, 1993), greater perceived discrepancies between the native and host cultures create greater doubts and often more serious adjustment difficulties. Negative and significant relationships have been found between cultural novelty and all levels of adjustment (Bhaskar-Shrinivas et al., 2005). CQ, however, has the potential to weaken these negative effects. The cognitive and behavioral domains of CQ strengthen the expatriate's ability to more rationally examine cultural novelty by building the knowledge of different cultures and the repertoire of possible actions one can take in unknown situations. Consequently, for expatriates with high CQ, cultural novelty will have a less adverse effect on their successful adjustment, retention, and performance. Thus, we offer the following.

P7: CQ will weaken the negative relationships between cultural novelty and all three dimensions of expatriate adjustment, both forms of expatriate performance, and expatriate retention.

CQ as a Mediator

In addition to the direct and moderating relationships, we believe that CQ may also play a mediating role, especially with respect to the relationships between anticipatory factors and expatriate effectiveness. Anticipatory variables are the initial set of inputs to expatriate adjustment and refer to expectations and groundwork that an expatriate experiences prior to an upcoming assignment (Black et al., 1991). Language ability and previous international experience are two personal anticipatory variables that have been empirically found to predict expatriate adjustment (Bhaskar-Shrinivas et al., 2005). Just as personality is strongly associated with performance through mediating variables such as contextual skill and knowledge (Motowidlo, Borman, & Schmit, 1997), we argue that CQ is the conduit through which these personal anticipatory factors influence all forms of expatriate effectiveness.

Self-efficacy theory, which explains the conviction that one can successfully execute a given behavior required to produce certain outcomes (Bandura, 1977), has been linked to CQ (Earley & Ang, 2003). Self-efficacy is an important part of CQ because success in intercultural interaction is anchored in a person's general sense of confidence for social conversation in a novel setting. This confidence is enhanced when expatriates acquire culture-specific knowledge about the foreign assignment. A wide body of management research has demonstrated that cultural sensitivity and cultural savvy affect self-efficacy (Brislin, Worthley, & MacNab, 2006). Prior research on cross-cultural adjustment has shown that factors on an individual level, including self-efficacy, are important predictors of cross-cultural adjustment (Templer et al., 2006). These findings indicate that CQ includes perceptions of self-efficacy and that these feelings of confidence enable expatriates to succeed in international assignments.

The first anticipatory variable we consider here is language ability, or fluency in the host country language (Bhaskar-Shrinivas et al., 2005). Although many countries do use English as a second language, fluency in the local language eases an expatriate's transition. In fact, knowledge of the host language contributes to all aspects of an expatriate's environment (Mendenhall & Oddou, 1986). Indeed, ability to converse in the local language will contribute to the development of CQ, making interactions with HCNs less difficult, both in work and nonwork situations. One American wife of an expatriate who had been sent to Italy stated that "language was a struggle . . . I managed by learning enough to get by." However, when asked if anything made it difficult for her to adjust to Italy, she said that the language was the key problem. She stated, "You can't just go into a store and expect them to speak English." So, although she originally felt she knew enough language to get by, it was still an issue in her adjustment to the host country. Likewise, in Pat's story, the language barrier became an obstacle to obtaining food, transportation, and his children's educational opportunities.

Self-efficacy theory helps us to understand the link between language fluency and expatriate effectiveness. Success in intercultural interactions is anchored in a person's general sense of confidence for social conversation in a novel setting (Earley & Ang, 2003), which is the essence of actually speaking a foreign language in a foreign land. However, knowledge of the language itself does not guarantee expatriate success. An example of this is the concept of *guanxi* in Chinese society (Alon & Higgins, 2005). The word translates simply to connections, while the concept in society is much deeper. For example, an American colleague of one of the authors who had moved to and worked in Shanghai stated, "Reading about it is one thing. Living it is totally different" (Alon & Higgins, 2005, p. 509). A deeper understanding of language, beyond what is offered by a Chinese/English dictionary, is needed to truly understand the concept of *guanxi*. CQ, strengthened by language ability, provides a deeper understanding, including the motivation needed to dig deeper than the simple dictionary translation. A culturally intelligent individual portrays an effective intercultural communicator (Berry & Ward, 2006). Indeed, several other researchers state that to be culturally competent one must be able to communicate clearly in the host language (LaFromboise, Coleman, & Gerton, 1993). Knowledge of the host language strengthens one's CQ, which in turn leads to greater success.

Another personal anticipatory factor is previous international experience. Such experience contributes to attributional knowledge, which is defined as a heightened awareness of appropriate behavior, building upon conceptual and factual knowledge in order to correctly ascribe an individual's behavior in the target culture (Johnson et al., 2006). Attributional knowledge can be learned through socialization, including frequent exposures to other cultures through visits or overseas postings (Johnson et al., 2006). In this way, CQ may also intervene in the relationship between previous international experience and expatriate effectiveness. Previous experience gives an expatriate knowledge of dealing with different culture(s), and that experience often eases dealings with yet another culture. Indeed, an expatriate on a second foreign assignment said that the company "was more willing to give second assignments to those who had had successful prior assignments, because they know that they will not have problems with them." Black and colleagues suggested that prior experience allows an expatriate to anticipate problems more clearly, leading to easier adjustment (Black et al., 1991). Although experience itself has been found to be somewhat helpful in adjusting to a new assignment (Bhaskar-Shrinivas et al., 2005), CQ adds another dimension to that knowledge and memory. Previous overseas experience generally adds to CQ (Osland & Osland, 2005), which often makes the new experience more positive. Past international experience also provides an individual with a history of dealing with new situations. Making correct judgments often requires a very large amount of information (Triandis, 2006). Two important skills of CQ include knowing how to suspend judgment until enough information becomes available (Earley & Mosakowski, 2004) and the expectation for misunderstanding, or confusion acceptance (Brislin et al., 2006). Experience in previous overseas assignments builds these skills in an expatriate. The experiences will be used in conjunction with CQ to read new situations and decide which actions to follow in the new assignment. Thus, we offer the following:

> **P8a–b:** CQ mediates the relationship between (a) language fluency and (b) previous overseas experience, and expatriate effectiveness criteria of adjustment, performance, retention, and career success.

IMPLICATIONS AND FUTURE DIRECTIONS

We have suggested how CQ could help Pat and other expatriates to have more successful international assignments for themselves and for their organizations. Drawing upon socioanalytic theory (Hogan & Shelton, 1998) and self-efficacy theory (Bandura, 1977), we have incorporated CQ into a model that includes established predictors of multiple forms of expatriate success, including adjustment, performance, retention, and career success. We believe that CQ has the potential to explain a significant amount of variance in these effectiveness criteria via both direct and indirect effects. We also believe that CQ represents an important link between established personal, job, and cultural factors and success. One role that we have proposed for CQ is that of a moderator. In this role, we envision CQ as strengthening the positive inputs to success and mitigating the negative inputs. For example, an expatriate with a high level of openness to experience and a high level of CQ will be more effective than one with the same level of openness but a low level of CQ. We also contend that CQ, in an intervening role, will elucidate the influence of anticipatory factors (i.e., language fluency and previous international experience) on expatriate success. This somewhat ubiquitous nature of CQ portends several practical implications for the management of expatriates. In the next section, we elaborate on these and discuss some implications for continued research in this area.

Managerial Implications

Recalling the opening vignette, it seems that Pat's frustrations and lackluster performance could have been avoided if CQ had been taken into consideration when deciding to send him to China. Indeed, we believe that CQ is relevant to various areas of international human resource management, particularly job analysis and design, assessment and selection, performance appraisal, training, and career planning. Had CQ been taken into consideration when making decisions in each of these areas, Pat could have enjoyed a positive, successful assignment. Below, we offer some suggestions for how organizations can integrate CQ into their human resource (HR) systems.

Many expatriate assignments are made to solve a particular problem or meet a technological need, often with little consideration given to adaptation skills, international experience, or training (Shaffer et al., 2006). A thorough job analysis would ensure that all aspects of the assignment are assessed, providing a valid and reliable basis for expatriate selection and training. The job analysis of international assignments could be strengthened by the inclusion of CQ as a competency or even a requirement. Examining those tasks and relationships that could be affected by CQ might enrich the job analysis process, making the final product a fuller description of the total position. Job design processes could also benefit from the knowledge and use of CQ. Including tasks or structuring roles that either include or increase an individual's CQ may benefit the organization through higher employee satisfaction or increased CQ of employees.

Armed with a thorough job analysis, it is incumbent upon organizations to select someone who is a good fit for the international position. Doing so remains a major challenge for global firms (GMAC, 2001). As stated earlier, placement of employees into expatriate assignments that ultimately fail is expensive for the organization as well as the employee. As we understand more about how CQ fits into expatriate success, it may aid organizations in selecting appropriate persons for expatriate assignments. Self-report assessments are available that would enable firms to gauge the CQ levels of their employees, such as the CQ scale (Ang et al., 2007). CQ scores could inform expatriate selection decisions as well as the design and implementation of training and development programs.

CQ might also be added to performance appraisals in those organizations where the value of international experience is recognized. Knowing the CQ levels of employees will assist international HR managers in deciding the future value of these employees, as the upcoming need for expatriate assignments may be unknown at present but can be expected to become more and more important. In an organization where CQ is a part of the performance appraisal, employees who are evaluated with such appraisals will recognize the importance of CQ as well as their ranking in that area. Insofar as employees with CQ provide a source of competitive advantage for global companies (Tan, 2004), this competitive advantage must be acknowledged, quantified, and recorded for its full usefulness. Incorporating CQ into written performance appraisals would serve this purpose.

CQ can be developed through training (Earley & Peterson, 2004), and this may be especially important for expatriates who have relatively low levels of CQ but who meet other selection criteria that are important to the particular industry or organization. Training can incorporate all areas of CQ, including cognitive, motivational, and behavioral components, and training programs can be adapted to meet the needs of individuals with different levels of CQ (Earley & Peterson, 2004). According to Earley and Peterson (2004), the existing training assumption that all individuals should be trained alike is false. For example, an employee with low levels of CQ may need more predeparture training to develop his or her knowledge of the foreign culture and to build effective interpersonal skills needed to interact with HCNs. Such training may preempt potential adjustment problems that those with low levels of CQ are likely to encounter.

Career planning processes may also benefit from the inclusion of CQ. In many organizations, expatriate assignments are considered part of career development and expatriates understand the value of these career experiences (Mervosh, 1997). Management in global organizations may well encourage employees to acknowledge and build their level of CQ in order to show their value, both present and future, to their employers. Those with high levels of CQ may be groomed for global roles within the organization.

Implications for Research

Although our focus in this chapter has been on understanding how CQ influences expatriate success within the context of established predictors, we encourage researchers to examine how CQ operates in the presence of other forms of intelligence, such as EQ and IQ. While all three (CQ, EQ, and IQ) are separate facets of intelligence within an individual (Alon & Higgins, 2005), they likely build upon each other to some extent. Future researchers might examine whether high levels of one of the intelligence measures is needed for another type of intelligence, as well as the possible relationships between all three types of intelligence within one person.

Further development of the proposed model through empirical study would also be helpful. One challenge in this area, however, has to do with the assessment of CQ. Most tests of CQ, including the 20-item four-factor model initiated and validated by Ang and colleagues (2007) are self-reports. We encourage the development of an abilities-based measurement tool of CQ similar to the Mayer-Salovey-Caruso Emotional Intelligence Test (2000). Such an instrument would allow future researchers to better compare and contrast EQ and CQ within individuals. Another challenge has to do with collecting longitudinal data. Ideally, CQ would be assessed before an employee takes an international assignment, as well as during the assignment. This would allow for a more rigorous assessment of the effects of CQ on expatriate success and an examination of the developmental potential of CQ over time.

Designing an empirical study of the propositions offered in this chapter could include several methods. Other than the often-used method of surveying individuals, one could conduct a field study including direct employee observation and examination of archival records. This type of study may give insight to potential behavioral differences between those with high and low levels of CQ. It might be possible to design a lab experiment to test some of the relationships of CQ with the proposed variables, perhaps presenting the same situation to those with high CQ and those with low CQ and documenting the responses. A field experiment, where a researcher is actually able to manipulate conditions within an existing global organization, might yield interesting and more generalizable results. This type of study could include providing CQ training to a randomly selected group of possible future expatriates, then comparing their success levels with another group that did not receive the training.

In addition to examining CQ with respect to expatriates, as much of the literature has done in the past, future researchers may develop new insights as they study the influence of CQ on diverse groups of individuals. Studying immigrants as they strive to adapt permanently to a novel culture could give us some important insights into CQ. Another group of individuals where CQ is likely significant would be so-called third-culture kids. These are children, often adolescents, who have spent at least one of their formative years in a country other than their home country (Lam & Selmer, 2004). CQ may also be relevant to domestic employees within diverse organizations where interactions with coworkers from different cultural backgrounds are commonplace. Additionally, CQ levels of workers that are involved in cross-cultural teams, either face-to-face or virtual, could be studied and tested.

Understanding the relationship of CQ to expatriate success is a promising and exciting area for future research. We hope that the model and propositions developed in this chapter will help guide that research in the area of expatriates and beyond, both theoretically and empirically. Hopefully, with continued study and use of CQ in expatriate assignments, the Pats of the future will have more successful experiences that will benefit both employee and organization.

REFERENCES

Alon, I., & Higgins, J.M. (2005). Global leadership success through emotional and cultural intelligences. *Business Horizons, 48,* 501–512.

Andreason, A.W. (2003). Expatriate adjustments to foreign assignments. *International Journal of Commerce and Management, 13,* 42–60.

Ang, S., Van Dyne, L., & Koh, C. (2006). Personality correlates of the four-factor model of cultural intelligence. *Group and Organization Management, 31,* 100–123.

Ang, S., Van Dyne, L., Koh, C., Ng, K.Y., Templer, K.J., Tay, C., & Chandrasekar, N.A. (2007). Cultural intelligence: Its measurement and effects on cultural judgment and decision making, cultural adaptation, and task performance. *Management and Organization Review, 3,* 335–371.

Arthur, W., Jr., & Bennett, W., Jr. (1995). The international assignee: The relative importance of factors perceived to contribute to success. *Personnel Psychology, 48,* 99–114.

Bandura, A. (1977). Self-efficacy: Toward a unifying theory of behavioral change. *Psychological Review, 84,* 191–215.

Berry, J.W., & Ward, C. (2006). Commentary on "Redefining interactions across cultures and organizations." *Group and Organization Management, 31,* 64–77.

Bhaskar-Shrinivas, P., Harrison, D.A., Shaffer, M.A., & Luk, D.M. (2005). Input-based and time-based models of international adjustment: Meta-analytic evidence and theoretical extensions. *Academy of Management Journal, 48,* 257–281.

Black, J.S. (1988). Work role transitions: A study of American expatriate managers in Japan. *Journal of International Business Studies, 19,* 277–294.

Black, J.S., & Gregersen, H. (1991). Antecedents to cross-cultural adjustment for expatriates in Pacific Rim assignments. *Human Relations, 44,* 497–515.

Black, J.S., Mendenhall, M., & Oddou, G. (1991). Toward a comprehensive model of international adjustment: An integration of multiple theoretical perspectives. *Academy of Management Review, 16,* 291–317

Briscoe, D.R. (1995). *International human resource management.* Englewood Cliffs, NJ: Prentice Hall.

Brislin, R., Worthley, R., and MacNab, B. (2006). Cultural intelligence: Understanding behaviors that serve people's goals. *Group and Organization Management, 31,* 40–55

Callanan, G.A. (2003). What price career success? *Career Development International, 8,* 126–133.

Copeland, L., & Griggs, L. (1985). *Going international: How to make friends and deal effectively in the global marketplace* (1st ed.). New York: Random House.

Cuba, L., & Hummon, D.M. (1993). A place to call home: Identification with dwelling, community, and region. *The Sociological Quarterly, 34,* 111–131.

Earley, P.C., & Ang, S. (2003). *Cultural intelligence: Individual interactions across cultures.* Palo Alto, CA: Stanford University Press.

Earley, P.C., & Mosakowski, C. (2004). Cultural intelligence. *Harvard Business Review, 82*(10), 139–146.

Earley, P.C., & Peterson, R.S. (2004). The elusive cultural chameleon: Cultural intelligence as a new approach to intercultural training for the global manager. *Academy of Management Learning & Education, 3,* 100–115.

GMAC Global Relocation Services. (2001). Global relocation trends survey. http://www.gmacglobalrelocation.com/insight_support/global_relocation.asp, accessed March 1, 2007.

Harrison, D.A., Shaffer, M.A., & Bhaskar-Shrinivas, P. (2004). Going places: Roads more and less traveled in research on expatriate experiences. In J.J. Martocchio (Ed.), *Research in personnel and human resources management 23* (pp. 199–247). Oxford: Elsevier.

Hogan, R. (1983). A socioanalytic theory of personality. In M.M. Page (Ed.), *1982 Nebraska symposium on motivation* (pp. 55–89). Lincoln: University of Nebraska Press.

Hogan, R. (1991). Personality and personality measurement. In D.L.M. Hough (Ed.), *Handbook of industrial and organizational psychology.* Volume 2 (2nd ed.) (pp. 327–396). Palo Alto, CA: Consulting Psychologists Press.

Hogan, R. (1996). A socioanalytic perspective on the five-factor model. In J.S. Wiggins (Ed.), *The five-factor model of personality* (pp. 163–179). New York: Guilford Press.

Hogan, R., & Roberts, B.W. (2000). A socioanalytic perspective on person-environment interaction. In W.B. Walsh, K.H. Craik & R.H. Price (Eds.), *Person-environment psychology: New directions and perspectives* (2nd ed.) (pp. 1–23). Mahwah, NJ: Lawrence Erlbaum Associates.

Hogan, R., & Shelton, D. (1998). A socioanalytic perspective on job performance. *Human Performance, 11,* 129–144.

Johnson, J.P., Lenartowicz, T., & Apud, S. (2006). Cross-cultural competence in international business: Toward a definition and a model. *Journal of International Business Studies, 37,* 525–543.

Judge, T.A., Cable, D.M., Boudreau, J.W., & Bretz, R.D., Jr. (1995). An empirical investigation of the predictors of executive career success. *Personnel Psychology, 48,* 485–519.

Klaff, L.G. (2002). The right way to bring expats home. *Workforce, 81*(7), 40–44.

LaFromboise, T., Coleman, H.L.K., & Gerton, J. (1993). Psychological impact of biculturalism: Evidence and theory. *Psychological Bulletin, 114,* 395–412.

Lam, H., & Selmer, J. (2004). Are former "third-culture kids" the ideal business expatriates? *Career Development International, 9,* 109–122.

Mayer, J.D., Caruso, D., & Salovey, P. (2000). Selecting a measure of emotional intelligence: The case for ability scales. In R. Bar-On & J. D. Parker (Eds.), *Handbook of emotional intelligence* (pp. 320–342). New York: Jossey-Bass.

Mendenhall, M., & Oddou, G. (1986). Acculturation profiles of expatriate managers: implications for cross-cultural training programs. *Columbia Journal of World Business, 21*(4), 73–79.

Mendenhall, M., Kuhlman, T.M., Stahl, G.K., & Osland, J.S. (2002). Employee development and expatriate assignments. In M. Gannon & F. Newman (Eds.), *Handbook of cross-cultural management* (pp. 155–183). Oxford: Blackwell Publishers.

Mercer. (2006). International assignments increasing, Mercer survey finds. http://www.mercerhr.com/summary.jhtml?idContent=1222700, accessed May 8, 2007.

Mervosh, E.M. (1997). Managing expatriate compensation. *Industry Week, 246*(14), 13–16.

Motowidlo, S.J., Borman, W.C., & Schmit, M.J. (1997). A theory of individual differences in task and contextual performance. *Human Performance, 10*(2), 71–83.

Naumann, E. (1992). A conceptual model of expatriate turnover. *Journal of International Business Studies, 23*(3), 499–531.

Ng, K.-Y., & Earley, P. C. (2006). Culture + intelligence: Old constructs, new frontiers. *Group and Organizational Management, 31* (1), 4.

Nicholson, N. (1984). A theory of work role transitions. *Administrative Science Quarterly, 29,* 172–191.

O'Connor, R. (2002). Plug the expat knowledge drain. *HR Magazine, 47*(10), 101–107.

Ogden, J. (1995). Psychosocial theory and the creation of the risky self. *Social Science Medicine, 40,* 409–415.

Ones, D.S., & Viswesvaran, C. (1997). Personality determinants in the prediction of aspects of expatriate job success. *New Approaches to Employee Management, 4,* 63–92.

Osland, J., & Osland, A. (2005). Expatriate paradoxes and cultural involvement. *International Studies of Management & Organization, 35*(4), 91–114.

Shaffer, M.A., Harrison, D.A., Gregersen, H., Black, J.S., & Ferzandi, L.A. (2006). You can take it with you: Individual differences and expatriate effectiveness. *Journal of Applied Psychology, 91,* 109–125.

Tajfel, H. (1982). Instrumentality, identity and social comparisons. In H. Tajfel (Ed.), *Social identity and intergroup relations* (pp. 483–507). Cambridge: Cambridge University Press.

Tajfel, H., & Turner, J.C. (1985). The social identity theory of intergroup behavior. In S. Worchel & W.G. Austin (Eds.), *Psychology of intergroup relations* (2nd ed.) (pp. 7–24). Chicago, IL: Nelson-Hall.

Takeuchi, R., Yun, S., & Tesluk, P.E. (2002). An examination of crossover and spillover effects of spousal and expatriate cross-cultural adjustment on expatriate outcomes. *Journal of Applied Psychology, 87,* 655–666.

Tan, J.-S. (2004). Cultural intelligence and the global economy. *Leadership in Action, 24*(5), 19–21.

Templer, K.J., Tay, C., & Chandrasekar, N.A. (2006). Motivational cultural intelligence, realistic job preview, realistic living conditions preview, and cross-cultural adjustment. *Group and Organization Management, 31,* 154–173.

Thomas, D.C. (2006). Domain and development of cultural intelligence: The importance of mindfulness. *Group and Organization Management, 31,* 78–99.

Thomas, D.C., & Inkson, K. (2005). People skills for a global workplace. *Consulting to Management, 16*(1), 5–10.

Triandis, H.C. (2006). Cultural intelligence in organizations. *Group and Organization Management, 31,* 20–26.

Worldwide ERC, T.E.R.C.W. (2007). Workforce mobility facts page. http://www.erc.org/who_is_ERC/facts.shtml, accessed August 11, 2007.

——CQ as a Mediator——

CHAPTER 8

Antecedents and Consequences of Cultural Intelligence Among Short-Term Business Travelers

CHERYL TAY, MINA WESTMAN, AND AUDREY CHIA

This chapter examines factors that can potentially influence the development of cultural intelligence (CQ) among short-term business travelers and the effects of travelers' CQ on travel outcomes, specifically, perceived travel flexibility or autonomy and burnout. To set the context for the study, we first provide the conceptual background on short-term business travelers and present the multidimensional concept of CQ: "an individual's capability to function and manage effectively in culturally diverse settings" (Ang et al., 2007). We then propose that within the context of short-term business travelers, individual factor (need for control) and job-related factor (multicultural experiences [MCEs]) are potential antecedents to travelers' CQ. Additionally, we investigate whether a person-by-situation interaction, i.e., need for control and MCEs, explains variance in travelers' CQ beyond what could be attributed to either factor alone. Finally, we propose that business travelers' CQ alleviates burnout and promotes perception of control over their travel schedule.

CONCEPTUAL BACKGROUND ON SHORT-TERM BUSINESS TRAVELERS

Despite technological advances and rapid growth in electronic communications, global managers recognize the significance of face-to-face interactions to close deals, solve problems, negotiate contracts, and develop mutual trust and respect (Govindarajan & Gupta, 2001; Ivancevich, Konopaske, & DeFrank, 2003). Consequently, with increasing globalization and growing economic pressures, life in the twenty-first century is characterized by increases in the incidence of short business trips. Defined in the current study as traveling for the organization for periods of a week or so while crossing international borders, business trips are generally regarded as a source of stress to the travelers and their families (e.g., DeFrank, Konopaske, & Ivancevich, 2000; Dimberg et al., 2002). Dimberg et al. (2002) found that the physical and psychological impact on the traveler is especially substantial when traveling is frequent, as this prevents easy adaptation and opportunities to settle in to new routines. However, more recent studies have recognized that short business trips can bring about positive impact, e.g., insight into new business practices and productive ideas, individual growth, and respite from routine work demands (Welch & Worm, 2006). In this study, we focus on the positive impact of short business trips, i.e., the MCEs gained from the business trips on travelers' CQ. We present briefly the multidimensional concepts of CQ followed by our proposal on antecedents to travelers' CQ.

THE MULTIDIMENSIONAL CONCEPT OF CQ

CQ is a theoretical extension of contemporary approaches to understanding intelligences, defined as "a person's capability for successful adaptation to new cultural settings" (Earley & Ang, 2003, p. 59). CQ is conceptualized as a complex, multifactor individual attribute that is composed of four factors: cognitive, metacognitive, motivational, and behavioral components.

The cognitive factor of CQ refers to an individual's level of cultural knowledge or knowledge of the cultural environment. Metacognitive CQ refers to individuals' mental processes used to acquire and understand cultural knowledge and encompasses an individual's cultural consciousness and awareness during cross-cultural interactions. Motivational CQ refers to an individual's interest and drive to learn and adapt to new cultural surroundings. Finally, behavioral CQ refers to the extent to which individuals act appropriately (both verbally and nonverbally), are flexible, and adjust their behaviors to the specifics of each cultural interaction (Ang, Van Dyne, Koh, Ng, Templer, Tay, & Chandrasekar, 2007; Earley & Ang, 2003).

ANTECEDENTS TO BUSINESS TRAVELERS' CQ

Multicultural Experiences

We define MCEs as the amount of cultural exposure short-term business travelers experience on business trips. In this context, MCEs can be reflected by frequency and length of trips, number of different destinations, and intensity of exposure to different cultures. MCEs provide opportunities for business travelers to increase their knowledge of specific cultural environments (i.e., their cognitive CQ). For example, a greater number of trips abroad to different destinations expands knowledge about different business and social cultural norms. Travelers with more MCEs should have more opportunities to acquire and cultivate metacognitive strategies and interaction models, such as greater cultural sensitivities to and awareness of cultural differences and norms. However, in the context of short business trips, more MCEs may not translate into higher metacognitive CQ. The negative physical and psychological impact of short, frequent trips that focus on accomplishing specific business objectives may prevent travelers from processing and adapting cultural experiences at a deeper level, which would promote metacognitive CQ.

Greater cross-cultural experiences should build travelers' confidence in their ability to function in different cultures. That is, we expect MCEs to be a source of efficacious beliefs on a traveler's capability to interact and work with business partners from different cultures. Thus, we expect MCEs to enhance travelers' motivational CQ. A greater number of trips abroad should also expose travelers to wider repertoires and deeper understanding of behavioral norms. However, knowledge or understanding of acceptable behaviors need not necessarily translate into actual enacted behaviors on the part of the traveler. Particularly when the trips are short term in nature as in this context, MCEs may not provide travelers adequate opportunities to practice and develop verbal and nonverbal repertoires of acceptable behaviors at their business destinations.

Therefore, we do not propose any associations between MCEs and metacognitive CQ or behavioral CQ. We will however test the relationships in our analyses. In sum, we hypothesize the following:

> **H1:** Business travelers' MCEs will be positively associated with their (a) cognitive CQ and (b) motivational CQ.

Need for Control

Need for control is conceptualized as an individual disposition, defined as an individual's desire and intent to exert influence over the situations in which the person operates (see Burger, 1995). Need for control is basic and universal. The strength of this need varies from person to person (Gebhardt & Brosschot, 2002). DeCharms (1968) suggested that people need to feel a sense of mastery and personal competence in their environments. Indeed, Sutton and Kahn (1986) noted that the importance of control in organizational settings is "a persistent theme in the behavioral sciences" (p. 276). Thus, the greater the individual's desire to control, the greater is the desire to take action to understand the cultural environment. We suggest that this desire translates to greater development of CQ.

Compared to travelers who have little desire to control their environment, those with high need for control are likely to research the destination, engage in serious planning of business trips, and be more motivated to learn about international business partners and their cultures. In other words, we expect travelers with greater need for control to have a larger store of cultural information (cognitive CQ), to be more conscious and mindful of environmental changes including cultures in different travel destinations (metacognitive CQ), and to be more confident in and interested to learn about effective interactions at different destinations (motivational CQ).

Similarly, travelers who have greater need for control may consciously monitor and adjust their verbal and nonverbal behaviors to align them with the cultural expectations of their business partners when they visit their partners' host organization and country. To minimize negative and unexpected outcomes that may arise from erroneous behavioral gaffes, travelers with high need for control over their environment are more likely to develop broad and enhanced behavioral repertoires that match different cultural situations than those with lower need for control. In sum, we hypothesize as follows:

H2: Business travelers' need for control will be positively associated with their (a) cognitive CQ, (b) metacognitive CQ, (c) motivational CQ, and (d) behavioral CQ.

Moderated Relationships

Within the business traveler context, the individual's need for control is expected to moderate the MCEs-to-CQ relationship. This is because an individual's need for control suggests a desire to minimize uncertainties, plan for contingences, and influence outcomes or situations. Moreover, high need for control tends to increase an individual's responsiveness or attentiveness to available resources, including their prior travel experiences, to their advantage. Thus, when travelers have a high need for control, the effects of MCEs on development of CQ may be heightened. For instance, travelers with high need for control should be more sensitive to and should draw more from MCEs that enhance mental processing of cultural information and insight (cognitive CQ), as well as development of cultural competencies and efficacies (motivational CQ). Conversely, those who have low need for control are less likely to seek direct control of their work situations or consciously draw from their MCEs to develop and build on their cognitive or motivational CQ capabilities. Thus, we hypothesize the following:

H3: Business travelers' need for control will moderate the relationships between MCEs and (a) cognitive CQ and (b) motivational CQ such that the relationships between MCEs and CQ facets will be stronger among travelers' with higher need for control than those with lower need for control.

CONSEQUENCES OF BUSINESS TRAVELERS' CQ

In this section, we discuss the concept of burnout and present our conceptual arguments linking CQ dimensions to burnout. Thereafter, we discuss the concept of travelers' perceived travel schedule autonomy and our proposed link between travelers' CQ to schedule autonomy.

Burnout

Burnout is a unique affective response to stress. Literature on burnout regards it as an affective response to continuous and prolonged exposure to work-related stress. The most influential and widely used model of burnout was initially posed by Maslach (1982, 1993), and consists of three core components. The first component, emotional exhaustion, refers to feeling "drained and used up" due to work demands and interactions with people that deplete emotional resources. The second, depersonalization, refers to feeling detached from the job and is often characterized by cynicism toward clients or coworkers. Reduced personal accomplishment, the third component, is characterized by an internal sense of failure and inability to perform at work.

"Exhaustion is the central quality of burnout" (Maslach, Schaufeli & Leiter, 2001, p. 402) and best captures the "core meaning" of the burnout phenomenon (Shirom, 1989). This component has received the most attention in empirical studies (see Cordes & Dougherty, 1993). Research also suggests that the effects of emotional exhaustion on work-related outcomes may be stronger than other components of burnout (Lee & Ashforth, 1996). Accordingly, we focus on the emotional exhaustion component of burnout within the context of business travelers.

We propose that short-term business travelers who exhibit greater cognitive, metacognitive, motivational, and behavioral CQ should have lower levels of burnout. This is consistent with Hobfoll's (1989) Conservation of Resource (COR) theory in which personal attributes of CQ would serve as resources, defined as "those objects, personal characteristics, conditions, or energies that are valued by the individual" (Hobfoll 1989, p. 516). In the COR theory, resources are used to prevent resource loss, which is the principal ingredient in the stress burnout process (Hobfoll, 1989). Business travelers who have greater cognitive and metacognitive CQ (i.e., are better informed and more aware of the cultural environment in different travel destinations) should be in a better position to cognitively plan and manage the stress that arises from interacting in the different cultural contexts during business travel.

In the same way, business travelers who feel more efficacious, have greater motivation and drive to interact, and work with others in different cultures (i.e., high motivational CQ) have more psychological resources at their disposal to address emotional demands and the stress of adjusting and making deals with people of different cultures. Motivation serves as an energy resource and is valued for its ability to add to the acquisition of other kinds of resources (Hobfoll, 1998). We suggest that business travelers who are high in motivational CQ would have greater drive and desire to develop personal and work resources to facilitate their intercultural business tasks and interactions that help ease work stress. In contrast, those who are low in motivational CQ may lack the confidence and energy resources to invest in establishing necessary intercultural networks to facilitate work relations in their business travels.

Similarly, we propose that travelers with higher behavioral CQ, i.e., those who can display a wide repertoire of verbal and nonverbal behaviors, possess more personal resources that will prevent threatened loss of other resources needed to address issues that arise due to different cultural interactions. We expect business travelers with higher behavioral CQ to have lower levels of burnout than those who struggle with limited behavioral repertoires. Travelers who need to interact and work with business partners and associates from different cultures feel more stressed if they lack the resources and capabilities that would allow them to display appropriate and expected social behaviors during their trips, in order to avoid offending others and successfully adapt to the norms of other cultures (i.e., behavioral CQ). In sum, we propose the following:

H4: Business travelers' (a) cognitive, (b) metacognitive, (c) motivational, and (d) behavioral CQ will be negatively associated with burnout (emotional exhaustion).

Schedule Autonomy

Schedule autonomy in this study refers to travelers' perceived ability to influence and/or make changes to their business trip schedules. Similar to job autonomy, we suggest that for short-term business travelers, schedule autonomy represents a precondition to an extended array of individual and work-related outcomes (e.g., psychological and physical well-being, family conflicts, job performance and withdrawal behaviors). It is thus of interest to investigate the antecedents to schedule autonomy.

We propose that business travelers' CQ can affect travelers' appraisals of schedule autonomy. Travelers who are high in cognitive CQ have rich, complex, and well-organized knowledge structures, and possess increased repertoire of specific and universal cultural norms, practices, and conventions in different settings. Those with high metacognitive CQ are better able to monitor, analyze, and adjust their behaviors in different cultural settings (Ang et al., 2007; Earley & Ang, 2003). As such, these travelers are more likely to conclude that they are better able to manage and exert influence over their business trip schedule in culturally relevant and acceptable ways than those with low cognitive and/or metacognitive CQ.

Travelers with high motivational CQ enjoy and are motivated to learn and adapt to new and diverse cultural situations. Their confidence in their adaptive capabilities (Earley & Ang, 2003) is likely to influence their assessment of their ability to exert influence over business scheduling in different cultural destinations. Travelers with high behavioral CQ are also expected to favorably assess their ability to control their business schedules. Travelers with high behavioral CQ possess a broad repertoire of adaptive and communicative behaviors, which they can use depending on the cultural sensitivities of those with whom they interact. The ability to communicate effectively and to enact appropriate behaviors should aid these individuals in persuading international business partners to accept their suggested schedule changes and thus provide a basis for greater autonomy perception. Thus, we propose that

H5: Business travelers' (a) cognitive CQ, (b) metacognitive CQ, (c) motivational CQ, and (d) behavioral CQ will be positively associated with perceived schedule autonomy.

METHOD

Data Collection

Data were collected from business travelers working in large multinational corporations in Singapore, Israel, and Brazil. In Singapore and Israel, respondents filled out questionnaires in English. In Brazil, the English questionnaire was translated into Portuguese and then back into English (Brislin, 1970).

A total of 300 questionnaires were distributed and 70 were completed and returned in Singapore, giving a response rate of 23 percent. In Israel, a total of 120 questionnaires were distributed and 98 returned, giving a response rate of 82 percent. In Brazil, 420 questionnaires were distributed and 328 returned, for a response rate of 78 percent. Of the total sample of 496, we dropped three cases where respondents indicated that they had not spent any work time outside their home country in the past year and another two that had missing data. The final sample of 491 short-term business travelers was analyzed, 61.5 percent of these were males and 61.7 percent were married. On average, respondents had been with their current employer for 9.83 years (SD = 7.94) and were well educated, with 75.1 percent holding at least a bachelor's degree. Almost 92 percent of the respondents had made trips that lasted one week or less and had made an average of 9.25 (SD = 9.7) trips in the last year.

Measures

Burnout was measured with five items that tap into the emotional exhaustion component (Maslach, Jackson & Leiter, 1996). A seven-point scale ranging from 0 = never to 6 = every day was used. Coefficient alpha reliability was 0.90.

Schedule autonomy was measured with three items that assessed the extent to which respondents perceived (1) they had control over their travel schedule, (2) that it was not a problem if they were unable to go on a scheduled trip because of personal reasons, and (3) that their travel agendas were flexible. Responses were made on a seven-point scale (1 = strongly agree and 7 = strongly agree). Coefficient alpha reliability was 0.66.

CQ was measured with eight items from the cultural intelligence scale CQS (Ang et al., 2007) on cognitive (two items), metacognitve (one item), motivational (three items), and behavioral (two items) components of CQ. We selected items that were most relevant to business travelers, such as, "I am confident that I can socialize with locals in a culture that is unfamiliar to me" and "I change my nonverbal behavior when a cross-cultural situation requires it." Items were measured on a seven-point scale (1 = strongly disagree and 7 = strongly agree). Coefficient alpha reliability for cognitive CQ was 0.67, motivational CQ was 0.77, and behavioral CQ also 0.77.

MCEs was measured by the average of two items: (1) the proportion of work time spent outside of home country, and (2) the product of the number of business trips and average duration of business trips made in the year. Coefficient alpha reliability was 0.66.

Need for control was measured with five items, which were adapted from Kushnir and Melamed (1991). An example was, "To what extent is it important for you to determine the way your work is done?" Items were measured on a five-point scale (1 = very important and 5 = very unimportant). Coefficient alpha reliability was 0.85.

Control Variables

We controlled for several factors that could potentially affect our outcome variables in the analyses. Specifically, we controlled for gender (female = 1, male = 2), marital status (others = 1, married = 2), educational level (0 = below degree education, 1 = degree and above), tenure with current company (in years), and location (dummy coded).

Researchers have demonstrated that work-family and family-work conflicts are related to burnout and autonomy and are more pronounced among business travelers (Westman, Etzion, & Gortler, 2004). To control for their effects when analyzing CQ on burnout and schedule autonomy, we added Frone, Russell, and Cooper's (1992) work-family conflict items, where two items measured the extent to which work interfered with family (WIF), and two items measured the extent to which family interfered with work (FIW). Items were on a five-point frequency response scale (1 = almost never/never to 5 = almost always/always). Coefficient alpha reliability for WIF was 0.65, and 0.77 for FIW.

Prior to testing our hypotheses, confirmatory factor analysis (CFA) established discriminant and convergent validity of the constructs (including WIF and FIW). All items loaded significantly on the intended factors (loadings exceed 0.51). The overall goodness-of-fit statistics indicated that the data fitted the factor structure reasonably well: χ^2 (280, n = 491) = 698.20, root mean square error of approximation (RMSEA) = 0.054, goodness-of-fit (GFI) = 0.91, comparative fit index (CFI) = 0.95, non-normed fit index (NNFI) = 0.94.

RESULTS

Table 8.1 reports means, standard deviations, intercorrelations, and Cronbach alphas.

We tested hypotheses 1 and 2 with hierarchical regression analyses. We entered control variables (tenure with current company, gender, marital status, educational level, and location) in step 1, followed by the proposed CQ antecedents, MCEs, and need for control in step 2. These steps were conducted for each of the four CQ dimensions.

We predicted in hypothesis 1 that MCEs would positively relate to (a) cognitive CQ and (b) motivational CQ. Results in Table 8.2 show that MCEs were significantly related to cognitive CQ (β = .13, p <0.001) but not motivational CQ (β = 0.06, ns) over and above the control variables, supporting hypotheses 1(a) but not 1(b). MCEs were not significantly related to metacognitive (β = 0.04, ns) or behavioral CQ (β = 0.04, ns).

In hypothesis 2, we predicted that travelers' need for control would be positively related to all four CQ dimensions. Results support our hypothesis (see Table 8.2). After accounting for the control factors, need for control was significantly related to (a) cognitive CQ (β = 0.16, p <0.001), (b) metacognitive CQ (β = 0.19, p <0.001), (c) motivational CQ (β = 0.21, p <.001), and (d) behavioral CQ (β = 0.16, p <0.001).

We tested hypothesis 3 with moderated hierarchical regressions (Cohen, Cohen, West, & Aiken, 2003) by adding the interaction term between MCEs and need for control to the equation after both these predictors were included. All CQ factors were examined. Predictors were mean centered as recommended by Aiken and West (1991). Results (see Table 8.2, step 3) show a significant MCEs × need-for-control interaction, and incremental variance explained over-and-above controls and the two predictors on cognitive CQ (β = −0.11, p <0.01), ΔR^2 = 0.01, ΔF (9, 481) = 5.74, p <0.05, and motivational CQ (β = −0.09, p <0.05), ΔR^2 = 0.01, ΔF (9, 481) = 4.14, p <0.05. However, contrary to our prediction, the positive MCEs–cognitive CQ and MCEs–motivational CQ relationships were stronger (steeper slope) when need for control was lower than when it was higher. Figures 8.1 and 8.2 illustrate the significant MCEs × need-for-control interactions (+1.0 SD and −1.0 SD from the mean) (Aiken & West, 1991; Cohen et al., 2003). Although not

Table 8.1

Means, Standard Deviations, Correlations, and Cronbach's Alphas

	Mean	SD	1	2	3	4	5	6	7	8	9	10	11	12	13	14	15	16	17
Burnout (emotional exhaustion)	2.46	1.41	(.90)																
Schedule autonomy	4.34	1.51	–.32	(.66)															
Cognitive CQ	4.93	1.36	–.12	.22	(.67)														
Metacognitive CQ	5.81	1.21	–.11	.19	.48	(–)													
Motivational CQ	5.78	0.97	–.19	.20	.55	.48	(.77)												
Behavioral CQ	5.42	1.19	–.14	.20	.46	.45	.53	(.77)											
Multicultural experiences [a]	23.82	19.11	–.02	.07	.15	.06	.08	.05	(.66)										
Need for control	4.51	0.60	–.15	.19	.17	.20	.22	.17	–.02	(.85)									
Family interfering with work	1.99	0.88	.27	–.08	–.04	–.10	–.20	–.09	.03	–.04	(.77)								
Work interfering with family	2.91	1.02	.37	–.05	–.05	.15	.08	.10	.14	–.04	.22	(.65)							
Tenure with current company	9.83	7.94	–.09	.05	.07	–.03	.03	.00	.00	.11	–.01	–.02	(–)						
Gender[b]	1.61	0.49	.09	.02	–.07	.05	.08	.04	–.04	.05	–.07	.19	–.17	(–)					
Marital status[c]	1.62	0.49	–.04	.00	.04	.03	.03	.06	–.01	.03	–.01	.09	.11	–.02	(–)				
Educational level[d]	0.75	0.43	.02	–.05	.13	.11	.11	.10	–.01	.11	–.03	.08	.01	–.02	.00	(–)			
Singapore (dummy-coded)	0.14	0.34	–.10	.18	.14	.15	.13	.08	.15	.00	–.13	–.07	–.03	.01	.11	–.14	(–)		
Israel (dummy-coded)	0.20	0.40	–.09	–.16	.03	–.05	.08	–.03	–.02	–.08	–.20	.13	.09	.03	.17	.12	–.20	(–)	
Brazil (dummy-coded)	0.67	0.47	.15	.01	–.12	–.07	–.16	–.04	–.10	.07	.26	–.06	–.05	–.04	–.22	.00	–.56	–.70	(–)

Note: n = 491 for all variables. Cronbach's alpha (in parentheses). Correlations between .08 and .09 are significant at p <.05; between .10 and .13 are significant at p <.01, above .13 are significant at p <.001, one-tailed

[a]Mean of (No. of business trips × length of business trip expressed as proportion) and proportion of work time outside country

[b]1 = female, 2 = male

[c]1 = others, 2 = married

[d]0 = below degree education, 1 = degree and above

Table 8.2

Hierarchical Regression Analyses on CQ Dimensions

	Cognitive CQ				Metacognitive CQ				Motivational CQ				Behavioral CQ			
	Step 1	Step 2a	Step 2b	Step 3	Step 1	Step 2a	Step 2b	Step 3	Step 1	Step 2a	Step 2b	Step 3	Step 1	Step 2a	Step 2b	Step 3
Tenure with current company	.06	.06	.04	.03	–.01	–.01	–.04	–.05	.04	.04	.01	.00	.01	.01	–.01	–.01
Gender[a]	–.06	–.06	–.08*	–.08*	.06	.06	.04	.03	.08	.08*	.06	.06	.05	.05	.04	.03
Marital status[b]	.01	.01	.00	.01	.02	.02	.02	.02	.00	.00	–.01	–.01	.05	.05	.04	.05
Educational level[c]	.15***	.15***	.13***	.14***	.14***	.14***	.11**	.13***	.12	.12***	.09*	.10*	.12**	.12***	.10**	.11**
Singapore	.17***	.15***	.17***	.15***	.16***	.15***	.16***	.16***	.16***	.15***	.16***	.16***	.09*	.08*	.09*	.09*
Israel	.04	.06	.06	.06	–.04	–.04	–.02	–.02	.09	.09*	.12**	.12	–.03	–.03	–.02	–.01
Multicultural experiences (A)[d]		.13***		.12***		.04		.04		.06		.06		.04		.03
Need for control (B)			.16***	.20***			.19***	.23***			.21***	.24***			.16***	.18***
A × B				–.11**				–.12**				–.09*				–.06
ΔF		8.23*	12.41***	5.74*		.78^{ns}	17.62***	6.42**		1.96^{ns}	23.20***	4.14*		.60^{ns}	11.92***	1.78^{ns}
ΔR^2		.02	.03	.01		.00	.03	.01		.00	.04	.01		.00	.02	.00
R^2	.05	.07	.08	.10	.05	.05	.08	.09	.05	.05	.09	.11	.03	.03	.05	.05
Adjusted R^2	.04	.06	.07	.09	.03	.03	.06	.08	.04	.04	.08	.09	.01	.01	.03	.03
df	(6,484)	(7,483)	(7,483)	(9,481)	(6,484)	(7,483)	(7,483)	(9,481)	(6,484)	(7,483)	(7,483)	(9,481)	(6,484)	(7,483)	(7,483)	(9,481)
F	4.47***	5.07***	5.70***	6.18***	3.84***	3.40***	5.92***	5.48***	4.04***	3.75***	6.94***	6.17***	2.12*	1.90*	3.56***	3.05***

Note: n = 491 for all variables.

* $p < .05$; ** $p < .01$; *** $p < .001$, one-tailed

[a]1 = female, 2 = male

[b]1 = others, 2 = married

[c]0 = below degree education, 1 = degree and above

[d]Mean of (No. of business trips × length of business trip expressed as proportion) and proportion of work time outside country

Figure 8.1 **Interaction between Multicultural Experiences and Need for Control in Predicting Cognitive CQ**

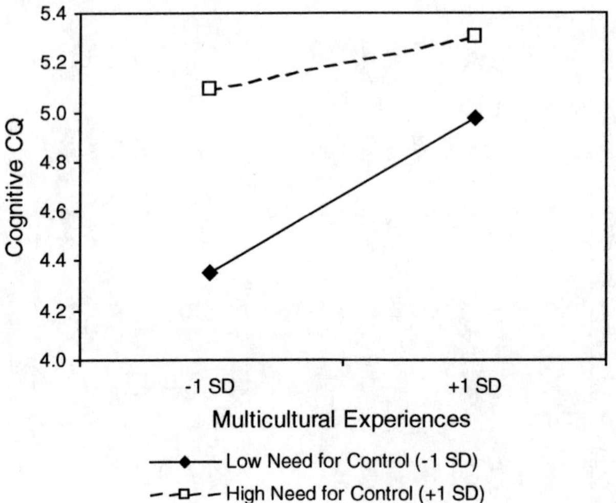

Figure 8.2 **Interaction between Multicultural Experiences and Need for Control in Predicting Motivational CQ**

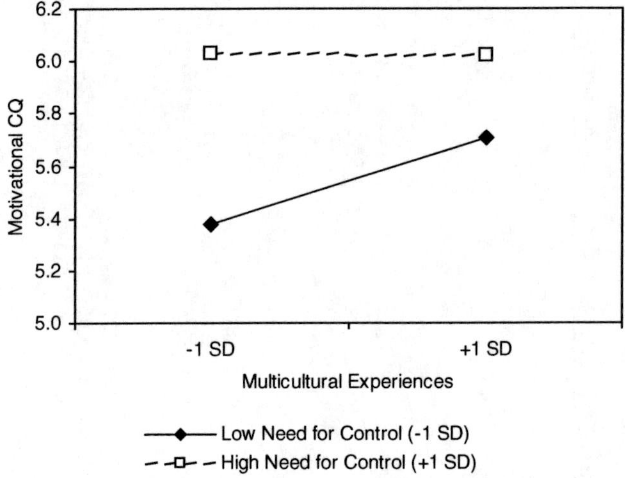

hypothesized, we found significant MCEs × need-for-control interaction on metacognitive CQ ($\beta = -0.12$, $p < 0.01$), $\Delta R^2 = 0.01$, $\Delta F\ (9, 481) = 6.42$, $p < 0.001$. The significant interaction in Figure 8.3 also shows that travelers with low rather than high need of control experienced higher levels of metacognitive CQ when exposed to more MCEs.

In hypotheses 4 and 5, we proposed that all four CQ factors would negatively relate to burnout and positively relate to schedule autonomy respectively. Results in Table 8.3 show that even after controlling for family-to-work, work-to-family interference and control

Figure 8.3 **Interaction between Multicultural Experiences and Need for Control in Predicting Metacognitive CQ**

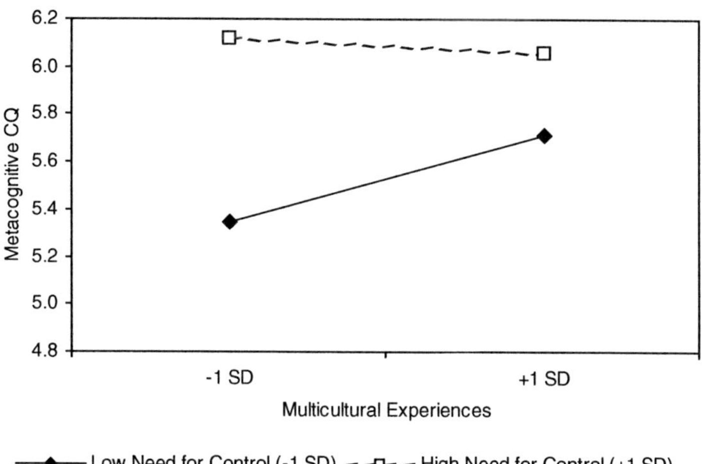

factors, metacognitive ($\beta = -0.13$, $p < 0.001$), motivational ($\beta = -0.16$, $p < 0.001$), and behavioral CQ ($\beta = -0.14$, $p < 0.001$) were significantly and negatively related to burnout. However, contrary to our prediction, cognitive CQ was not related to burnout ($\beta = -0.05$, ns). Thus, hypotheses 4(b)–4(d) are supported, but hypothesis 4(a) is not. Results in Table 8.4 support hypothesis 5. All CQ factors—cognitive ($\beta = 0.18$, $p < 0.001$), metacognitive ($\beta = 0.14$, $p < 0.001$), motivational ($\beta = 0.16$, $p < 0.001$), and behavioral CQ ($\beta = 0.16$, $p < 0.001$)—were significantly and positively related to schedule autonomy.

Post hoc analyses following Baron and Kenny's (1986) procedures suggest that schedule autonomy partially mediates each CQ factor to burnout relationship. In each instance, predictor–mediator, predictor–outcome, and mediator–outcome conditions were satisfied (see Table 8.3). Finally, for the predictor–mediator–outcome condition, results demonstrate that the respective CQ factor to burnout relationship was weakened when schedule autonomy was included in the equation (Table 8.3). Sobel tests support that autonomy is a partial mediator for the metacognitive ($Z = -2.85$, $p < 0.001$), motivational ($Z = -3.09$, $p < 0.001$), and behavioral CQ ($Z = -3.19$, $p < 0.001$) to burnout relationship.

DISCUSSION

The aims of the study were twofold; first, to examine the antecedents of CQ among business travelers, and, second, to investigate the effects of CQ on travel outcomes, i.e., burnout and schedule autonomy. Below we discuss our findings and their implications.

Antecedents of CQ

We established two antecedents to CQ that have not yet been examined in the CQ literature: MCEs, a job-related factor, and need for control, an individual factor. As proposed,

Table 8.3

Hierarchical Regression Analyses on Burnout

	Step 1	Step 2a	Step 3a	Step 2b	Step 3b	Step 2c	Step 3c	Step 2d	Step 3d
Tenure with current company	–.05	–.04	–.03	–.05	–.03	–.04	–.03	–.05	–.03
Gender[a]	.03	.03	.04	.03	.04	.04	.05	.04	.04
Marital status[b]	–.03	–.03	–.03	–.03	–.03	–.03	–.03	–.02	–.03
Educational level[c]	.02	.02	.01	.03	.02	.03	.02	.03	.02
Singapore (dummy-coded)	–.07*	–.06	–.03	–.05	–.02	–.05	–.02	–.06	–.03
Israel (dummy-coded)	–.13***	–.12**	–.17***	–.13***	–.17***	–.12**	–.16***	–.13***	–.17***
Multicultural experiences[d]	–.07*	–.06	–.05	–.07	–.05	–.06	–.05	–.06	–.05
Need for control	–.14***	–.13***	–.08*	–.11*	–.07	–.10*	–.06	–.11*	–.07
Family interfering with work	.16***	.16***	.14***	.15***	.13**	.14***	.12*	.15***	.13**
Work interfering with family	.34***	.34***	.34***	.37***	.36***	.36***	.35***	.36***	.35***
Cognitive CQ		–.05	.00						
Metacognitive CQ				–.13***	–.09*				
Motivational CQ						–.16***	–.11*		
Behavioral CQ								–.14***	–.09*
Schedule autonomy			–.30***		–.28***		–.28***		–.28***
ΔF		1.55^{ns}	52.98***	9.85***	49.59***	13.61***	48.12***	13.61***	48.45***
ΔR^2		.00	.08	.02	.07	.02	.07	.02	.07
R_2	.22	.22	.30	.24	.31	.24	.31	.24	.31
Adjusted R2	.20	.20	.28	.22	.29	.22	.29	.22	.29
df	(10,480)	(11,479)	(12,478)	(11,479)	(12,478)	(11,479)	(12,478)	(11,479)	(12,478)
F	13.58***	12.50***	17.11***	13.46***	17.73***	13.90***	18.01***	13.63***	17.77***

Note: n = 491 for all variables.
* p <.05; * p <.01; *** p <.001, one-tailed
[a]1 = female, 2 = male
[b]1 = others, 2 = married
[c]0 = below degree education, 1 = degree and above
[d]Mean of (No. of business trips × length of business trip expressed as proportion) and proportion of work time outside country

Table 8.4

Hierarchical Regression Analyses on Schedule Autonomy

	Step 1	Step 2a	Step 2b	Step 2c	Step 2d
Tenure with current company	.05	.05	.06	.05	.06
Gender[a]	.03	.04	.03	.02	.02
Marital status[b]	–.01	–.01	–.01	.00	–.01
Educational level[c]	–.03	–.06	–.05	–.04	–.05
Singapore (dummy-coded)	.13***	.10**	.11**	.11**	.12**
Israel (dummy-coded)	–.14***	–.15***	–.13**	–.15***	–.13**
Multicultural experiences[d]	.05	.03	.05	.05	.05
Need for control	.18***	.15***	.15***	.14***	.15***
Family interfering with work	–.08*	–.08*	–.06	–.05	–.06
Work interfering with family	–.01	.01	–.03	–.02	–.03
Cognitive CQ		.18***			
Metacognitive CQ			.14***		
Motivational CQ				.16***	
Behavioral CQ					.16***
ΔF		16.32***	9.71***	11.89***	12.89***
ΔR^2		.03	.02	.02	.02
R^2	.10	.13	.12	.12	.12
Adjusted R^2	.08	.11	.10	.10	.10
df	(10,480)	(11,479)	(11,479)	(11,479)	(11,479)
F	5.06***	6.23***	5.57***	5.79***	5.89***

Note: n = 491 for all variables.
* *p* <.05; ** *p* <.01; *** *p* <.001, one-tailed
[a]1 = female, 2 = male
[b]1 = others, 2 = married
[c]0 = below degree education, 1 = degree and above
[d]Mean of (No. of business trips × length of business trip expressed as proportion) and proportion of work time outside country

results show that after accounting for tenure, gender, marital status, educational level, and location, MCEs were positively associated with cognitive CQ, i.e., MCEs build and expand travelers' cultural knowledge. However, contrary to our prediction, MCEs were not related to motivational CQ. It could be that the business travels were too short and task-focused to afford travelers the opportunity to interact sufficiently and build confidence and efficacy for intercultural interactions. Results also support our expectation that in the context of short-term trips, travelers do not have adequate time to reflect, adapt, and develop the more complex CQ capabilities, i.e., metacognitive and behavioral CQ.

Results demonstrate that need for control is positively associated with and thus an important antecedent to all four CQ dimensions (cognitive, metacognitive, motivational, and behavioral). This makes sense, as individuals who have a greater need to control their environment seek more cultural information, plan more, are more motivated to learn and interact, and develop a communication repertoire for socializing and networking with people in new cultural settings. Thus, the inclusion of need for control in the current study is an important contribution to CQ research.

We further investigated whether a person-by-situation interaction, i.e., need for control and MCEs together, explain variance in travelers' CQ beyond what could be attributed to either factor alone. Results demonstrate a significant interaction of MCEs with need for control on cognitive, metacognitive, and motivational CQ. But, contrary to our prediction, the positive relationships between MCEs and the respective CQ dimensions were stronger when need for control was lower than when it was higher.

The graphical illustrations in Figures 8.1–8.3 show that across different levels of MCEs, travelers with high need for control have higher cognitive, metacognitive, and motivational CQ than those who have a low need for control. However, travelers with low need for control were better able to capitalize on their MCEs to gain and develop their CQ, such that they have a higher rate of CQ when MCEs increase than those with high need for control. We speculate that travelers with different levels of need for control apply different strategies to cope with business travels. Perhaps, those with high need for control are more proactive prior to leaving for their trips and may thus seek and rely more on pre-trip learning, planned searches of the cultural and business destination and less on actual on-site experiences. This is consistent with Westman and Etzion's (2004) finding that managers with high need for control used proactive coping before business travels. On the other hand, those with low need for control should have less pre-trip preparations, not needing to have a strong control over the environment. Without preconceived notions, they may be more responsive to cultural cues during the trips. As such, on-site MCEs may have a greater impact on these travelers' CQ.

Consequences of CQ

Results demonstrate that all but cognitive CQ alleviate burnout. The significant relationships are made more significant when the effects of controls (tenure, gender, marital status, educational level, and location) and FIW and WIF were taken into account. The finding that metacognitive, motivational, and behavioral CQ decreased travelers' burnout is consistent with COR theory, which states that such personal capabilities prevent and/or lower burnout (Hobfoll & Shirom, 2000). Contrary to our expectations, cognitive CQ did not significantly contribute to lower levels of burnout. We suspect that cognitive knowledge alone, without the capability and desire to apply this knowledge during intercultural interactions, may not constitute resources that combat stress.

As expected, all four CQ factors promote perceptions of schedule autonomy over and above controls, FIW, WIF, and CQ antecedents. Travelers' perceptions could be bolstered by high levels of CQ to believe that their cultural knowledge and adaptive capabilities can help them better negotiate, persuade, and elicit agreements with intercultural business partners with regard to their schedules. Our findings indicate that CQ is part of the process of decreasing travel stress and burnout directly through travelers' CQ capabilities and indirectly through perceived schedule autonomy. Additionally, since both CQ and autonomy are personal resources (Hobfoll, 1989), this may trigger a positive spiral where possession of CQ resources enables travelers to gain another important resource, vis-à-vis schedule autonomy, to combat burnout.

CONTRIBUTIONS AND IMPLICATIONS

This study has several key contributions and strengths. We investigated CQ in a unique situation of short-term business travel. To the best of our knowledge, this is the first study to examine CQ in this area. Recent conceptual and empirical work on multidimensional CQ suggests that CQ dimensions are capabilities that can be developed. Here, we add to the growing body of literature to suggest that MCEs, an environmental factor, and, particularly, need for control, an individual factor, can potentially develop an individual's CQ dimensions. We incorporated COR theory into the CQ phenomenon. CQ dimensions as personal resources have significant effects on perceived schedule autonomy, another personal resource, and burnout, an individual psychological outcome.

Our study also has important implications for practicing managers. As short business trips can be a source of stress for both traveler and traveler's family, developing CQ capabilities and promoting a sense of autonomy can alleviate burnout, which is a major threat to the health of the individual as well as the organization in today's fast-paced world. Interestingly, our findings provide initial evidence that MCEs in the context of frequent, short-term trips develop only the cognitive aspect of CQ. And it is the other aspects of CQ, i.e., metacognitive, motivational, and behavioral, that alleviate travelers' burnout. Cognitive CQ was not related to burnout. One implication of this is that even more experienced travelers, who have more knowledge of other cultures, may still be vulnerable to burnout if their metacognitive, motivational, and behavioral CQ do not rise in tandem with their cognitive CQ. Additionally, results suggest that these CQ dimensions are part of a gain spiral in combating burnout. This has important implications for employees and managers because most cross-cultural training emphasizes primarily the development of the cognitive aspect of CQ (Templer, Tay & Chandrasekar, 2006). Our findings suggest that it is more sensible to develop travelers' metacognitive, motivational, and behavioral CQ rather than focus on cognitive CQ alone. Training may also include other family members so that they can be more knowledgeable of the travel process and be better able to give informational, evaluative, and instrumental support to those who travel on business.

LIMITATIONS AND FUTURE RESEARCH

Our study used cross-sectional data, so the usual cautions about drawing causal relationships from cross-sectional data apply. We also used a single data source, relying on self-reports from travelers. However, as far as possible, we asked for objective data, e.g., number and duration of trips; used different scale endpoints and anchors; and assured respondents of confidentiality so that they would answer the questions as truthfully as possible. We suggest that future research should employ longitudinal design to better capture the potential mediating linkages as indicated in our post hoc analyses, as well as test for our notion of a gain spiral. Additionally, episodic or event analyses may be conducted to better examine the developmental effects of CQ dimensions. The use of interviews and/ or other qualitative methodology may also prove fruitful in providing greater depth and understanding of travelers' CQ development before, during, and after each business trip episode. An intensive case study approach with grounded theory is also likely to identify additional factors that facilitate CQ development. This approach also provides deeper insight into the developmental processes of the CQ dimensions and how they differentially affect outcomes for individual travelers and their organizations.

In this study, we used only eight items from the 20-item CQS to safeguard against respondent fatigue. However, this approach does not do justice in capturing the various nuances in the construct, particularly for metacognitive CQ that was measured with only one item. Still, the one measure was strong enough to produce significant results attesting to the efficacy of the construct. We suggest that in future CQ studies, the full 20-item scale be used in order to provide a more comprehensive understanding of the antecedents to and consequences of the four CQ dimensions, as well as allow consolidation of research results across studies that use the same instrument.

The business travelers in our study came from three different countries—Singapore, Israel, and Brazil. Brazil had the highest ratio of respondents in the sample and results may be skewed toward the population in Brazil. We have controlled for location effects and, since we are not primarily interested in country effects, the uneven number of respondents from each country is not deleterious to our study. However, it might be interesting to examine whether the same patterns of results would emerge from a larger Singaporean sample of travelers as well as travelers from different countries. Finally, future research should further investigate the nature of MCEs, e.g., whether it is a neutral variable and under what circumstances MCEs can contribute to travelers' developmental gain or loss.

In conclusion, this study presents intriguing findings that further our understanding of the potential antecedents of the CQ dimensions and their effects on short-term business travel. Our study provides initial evidence of individual and environmental factors and their interacting effects on the development of cognitive CQ, a potentially important resource in facilitating and negotiating business trip schedules and combating burnout. Findings suggest that CQ plays an important role in business travel processes. Travelers' CQ capabilities are strong resources that can prevent the loss of resources, which leads to travel stress. CQ plays an important role in business travel processes. We recommend continued research through alternative and innovative research designs to further explicate the development of CQ dimensions and investigate their effects on a wider set of traveler outcomes.

REFERENCES

Aiken, L.S., & West, S.G. (1991). *Multiple regression: Testing and interpreting interactions*. Newbury Park, CA: Sage.

Ang, S., Van Dyne, L., Koh, C., Ng, K., Templer, K.J., Tay, C., & Chandrasekar, N.A. (2007). Cultural intelligence: Its measurement and effects on cultural judgment and decision making, cultural adaptation, and task performance. *Management and Organization Review*, *3*, 335–371.

Baron, R.M., & Kenny, D.A. (1986). The moderator-mediator variable distinction in social psychological research: Conceptual, strategic, and statistical considerations. *Journal of Personality and Social Psychology, 51*, 1173–1182.

Brislin, R.W. (1970). Back-translation for cross-cultural research. *Journal of Cross-Cultural Psychology, 1*, 185–216.

Burger, J.M. (1995). Need for control and self-esteem: Two routes to a high desire for control. In M.H. Kernis (Ed.), *Efficacy, agency, and self-esteem* (pp. 217–233). New York: Plenum Press.

Cohen, J., Cohen, P., West, S.G., & Aiken, L.S. (2003). *Applied multiple regression/correlation analysis for the behavioral sciences* (3rd ed.). Hillsdale, NJ: Lawrence Erlbaum Associates.

Cordes, C.L., & Dougherty, T.W. (1993). A review and integration of research on job burnout. *Academy of Management Review, 18*, 621–656.

DeCharms, R. (1968). *Personal causation: The internal affective determinants of behavior.* New York: Academic Press.

DeFrank, R.S., Konopaske, R., & Ivancevich, J.M. (2000). Executive travel stress: Perils of the road warrior. *The Academy of Management Executive, 14*, 58–71.

Dimberg, L.A., Striker, J., Nordanlycke-Yoo, C., Nagy, L., Mundt, K.A., & Sulsky, S.I. (2002). Mental health insurance claims among spouses of frequent business travelers. *Occupational and Environmental Medicine, 59*, 175–181.

Earley, P.C., & Ang, S. (2003). *Cultural Intelligence: Individual interactions across cultures.* Palo Alto, CA: Stanford University Press.

Frone, M.R., Russell, M., & Cooper, M.L. (1992). Antecedents and outcomes of work-family conflict: Testing a model of the work-family interface. *Journal of Applied Psychology, 77*, 65–78.

Gebhardt, W.A., & Brosschot, J.F. (2002). Desirability of control: Psychometric properties and relationships with locus of control, personality, coping, and mental and somatic complaints in three Dutch samples. *European Journal of Personality, 16*, 423–438.

Govindarajan, V., & Gupta, A.K. (2001). *The quest for global dominance.* San Francisco, CA: Jossey-Bass.

Hobfoll, S.E. (1989). Conservation of resources: A new attempt at conceptualizing stress. *American Psychologist, 44*, 513–524.

Hobfoll, S.E. (1998). *Stress, culture, and community.* New York: Plenum Press.

Hobfoll, S.E., & Shirom, A. (2000). Conservation of resources theory: Applications to stress and management in the workplace. In R.T. Golembiewski (Ed.), *Handbook of organization behavior* (pp. 57–81). New York: Dekker.

Ivancevich, J.M., Konopaske, R., & DeFrank, R.S. (2003). Business travel stress: A model, propositions and managerial implications. *Work & Stress, 17*, 138–157.

Kushnir, T., & Melamed, S. (1991). Work-load, perceived control, and psychological distress in Type A/B industrial workers. *Journal of Organizational Behavior, 12*, 155–168.

Lee, R.T., & Ashforth, B.E. (1996). A meta-analytic examination of the correlates of the three dimensions of job burnout. *Journal of Applied Psychology, 81*, 123–133.

Maslach, C. (1982). *Burnout: The cost of caring.* Englewood Cliffs, NJ: Prentice Hall.

Maslach, C. (1993). Burnout: A multi-dimensional perspective. In W.B. Schaufeli, C. Maslach, & T. Marek (Eds.), *Professional burnout: Recent developments in theory and research* (pp. 19–32). Washington, DC: Taylor & Francis.

Maslach, C., Jackson, S.E., & Leiter, M.P. (1996). *Maslach burnout inventory manual* (3rd ed.). Palo Alto, CA: Consulting Psychologists Press.

Maslach, C., Schaufeli, W.B., & Leiter, M.P. (2001). Job burnout. *Annual Review of Psychology, 52*, 397–422.

Shirom, A. (1989). Burnout in work organizations. In C.L. Cooper & I. Robertson (Eds.), *International review of industrial and organizational psychology* (pp. 25–48). New York: John Wiley & Sons.

Sutton, R.I., & Kahn, R.L. (1986). Prediction, understanding and control as anecdotes to organizational stress. In J. Lorsch (Ed.), *Handbook of organizational behavior* (pp. 272–285). Englewood Cliffs, NJ: Prentice Hall.

Templer, K.J., Tay, C., & Chandrasekar, N.A. (2006). Motivational cultural intelligence, realistic job preview, realistic living conditions preview, and cross-cultural adjustment. *Group and Organization Management, 31*, 154–173.

Welch, D.E., & Worm, V. (2006). International business travelers: A challenge for IHRM. In G.K. Stahl & I. Björkman (Eds.), *Handbook of research in international human resource management* (pp. 283–301). Northampton, MA: Edward Elgar Publishing.

Westman, M., & Etzion, D. (2004). Characteristics of business trips and their consequences: A summary of recent findings. Working Paper No. 13/2004. The Israel Institute of Business Research, Tel Aviv University.

Westman, M., Etzion, D., & Gortler, E. (2004). The work-family interface and burnout. *International Journal of Stress Management, 11*, 413–428.

CHAPTER 9

Cultural Intelligence as a Mediator of Relationships Between Openness to Experience and Adaptive Performance

TANIA OOLDERS, OLEKSANDR S. CHERNYSHENKO, AND STEPHEN STARK

Recent research demonstrates that the four factors of cultural intelligence (CQ)—metacognition, cognition, behavior, and motivation—are strongly related to the personality trait referred to as openness to experience (Ang, Van Dyne, & Koh, 2006). In addition, significant links between CQ and criteria such as task performance, cultural decision making, well-being, and adjustment in expatriate samples suggest that CQ may have considerable utility in performance prediction (Ang, Van Dyne, Koh, Ng, Templer, Tay & Chandrasekar, 2007; Templer, Tay, & Chandrasekar, 2006). Yet while CQ has a keen following in management circles (Ang et al., 2006; Earley & Ang, 2003; Peterson, 2004), it is almost unknown in the organizational psychology literature. A search of the psych-info and psych-article databases (September 2007) using the keywords "cultural intelligence" produced no journal articles on this construct. Although articles and books referred to related concepts, such as intercultural effectiveness (Leong, 2007), sociocultural adjustment (Wang & Takeuchi, 2007), cultural competence (Gong & Fan, 2006), and intercultural competence (Sternberg & Grigorenko, 2004), nowhere was CQ (as used in this study) referenced in the psychological literature. In contrast, the management journal *Group and Organization Management* has recently published an entire special edition focusing on CQ (Konrad, 2006). A recent review on cross-cultural organizational behavior attests that interest is clearly increasing in how culture impacts management and organizational behavior (Gelfand, Erez, & Aycan, 2007). We believe organizational psychologists may have paid little attention to CQ to date because its relationship to performance is relatively unexplored. This chapter attempts to address this deficiency by establishing the position of the CQ construct within the predictor-criterion network commonly studied by organizational psychologists, namely, the theory of job performance.

THE THEORY OF JOB PERFORMANCE

Performance is the central construct in organizational psychology, as it subsumes all work behaviors that make a difference to accomplishing organizational goals (Campbell, 1990). One of the key tasks for psychologists is to "establish the causal pattern of relations between antecedents of job performance and its various dimensional components" (Motowidlo, Borman, & Schmitt, 1997), thus clarifying constructs that may be used in selection or organizational development.

According to Campbell, almost all individual differences in performance are assumed to be a function of three classes of determinants: declarative knowledge (DK), procedural knowledge (PKS) and skill, and motivation. DK is the knowledge of facts, principles, and goals, among other things. When DK is combined with knowledge of how to do things, PKS results, which includes various perceptual, cognitive, interpersonal, and self-management skills. Motivation is the third determinant and is perhaps the most important, because performance does not occur unless an individual decides to exert focused effort for a period of time. Furthermore, researchers have postulated that these determinants or characteristic adaptations (McCrae & Costa, 1996) act as mediators of relationships between a number of innate basic tendencies (e.g., personality, cognitive ability) and various performance dimensions (Campbell, McCloy, Oppler, & Sager, 1993; Motowidlo et al., 1997). Taken together, this interplay between basic tendencies, characteristic adaptations, and performance behaviors forms the basis of the theory of individual differences in job performance. The theory is useful from an applied perspective, because it specifies the mechanism by which predictors, commonly used in selection, exert their influence on work behaviors. It is also general enough to allow new predictors and criteria to be added, as our understanding of employee behavior changes in response to globalization and technological innovations.

CQ AND THE THEORY OF JOB PERFORMANCE

To map CQ onto this framework, it is necessary to establish at which level it fits: basic tendency, characteristic adaptation, or performance domain. Both Templer et al. (2006) and Ang et al. (2007) maintain that CQ is an antecedent of performance. It then follows that CQ is either an innate tendency or a mediator—a characteristic adaptation. We believe it is the latter, for the following two reasons. First, the construct's four factors are conceptually similar to the characteristic adaptations described by Campbell and McCrae and Costa. For instance, items designed to measure the cognitive factor of CQ include, "I know the religious beliefs of other cultures" and "I know the rules of other languages." These constitute DK. Further, items measuring the metacognitive and behavioral CQ factors involve procedural skills ("I adjust my cultural knowledge as I interact with people from an unfamiliar culture" and "I use pause and silence differently to suit different cross-cultural situations"). Moreover, the items designed to measure motivation in a cross-cultural context relate to Campbell's motivation determinant as well as to McCrae and Costa's "habits." Second, characteristic adaptations, which consist of competencies, attitudes, beliefs, and behaviors, are acquired as individuals interact with the environment, unlike personality traits, which endure independent of context (McCrae & Costa, 1996). Therefore if CQ *was* a characteristic adaptation, it would be a dynamic construct, subject to change as an individual accumulated experience over a lifetime. The fact that courses on intercultural skills and CQ have been run for more than 20 years, successfully enhancing the skills of expatriate workers, supports the idea that it is indeed a trainable competency or characteristic adaptation (Earley, 1987; Thomas & Inkson, 2004).

We also note that, while this was not our aim, locating CQ as a mediator within the theory of job performance is conceptually convenient. If CQ is not a basic, intrinsic quality, it does not need to "fit" existing models of intelligence. This obviates problems similar to those faced by researchers in the emotional intelligence (EQ) domain who have had considerable difficulty establishing the discriminant validity of the EQ construct (Landy, 2005; Locke, 2005; Roberts, Zeidner, & Matthews, 2001). Questions over CQ's capacity to add incremental validity to either cognitive ability or personality in the prediction of performance also become irrelevant.

RELATING CQ TO PERSONALITY AND PERFORMANCE

With CQ positioned as a mediator within the theory of performance, our next step was to match it with relevant constructs in the personality and performance domains, bearing in mind the precondition for mediation that all three constructs correlate significantly with one another (Jose, 2003). Of the Big Five factors, openness to experience appeared to be most relevant. Recall that a culturally intelligent individual is able to switch between cultural settings with relative ease and accurately interpret social signals that are embedded in cultural context. It seems logical that one of the raw ingredients for acquiring these skills would be openness, a trait that carries with it relatively high levels of intellectual efficiency, tolerance, curiosity, flexibility, depth, and ingenuity. Existing research supports this association. It has been shown that open individuals more readily accept differences between various cultures, compared with individuals who are not open (Bhagat & Prien, 1996); they are also less likely to adopt racial stereotypes and other biases (Flynn, 2005). Ang et al. (2006) found CQ to have stronger relationship with openness than with other Big Five factors.

However, knowing that openness to experience, of all the Big Five personality factors, had consistently demonstrated the lowest meta-analytic correlations with overall performance (ranging between –0.02 and 0.06 [Barrick & Mount, 1991; Salgado, 1997]) we needed to expand the criterion domain to find a performance dimension that would correlate significantly to both openness to experience and CQ. One promising development has been the suggested addition of adaptive performance to the existing task and contextual model of performance (Ones & Viswesvaran, 1999; Griffin & Hesketh, 2003; Allworth & Hesketh, 1999).

LINKING ADAPTIVE PERFORMANCE, OPENNESS TO EXPERIENCE, AND CQ

Adaptive performance has been defined as the proficiency with which people alter their behavior to meet the demands of the environment, an event, or a new situation (Pulakos, Arad, Donovan, & Plamondon, 2000). Not only has it been persuasively argued that an individual's level of openness is likely to predict adaptive performance (Allworth & Hesketh, 1999; Pulakos, Schmitt, Dorsey, Arad, Hedge, & Borman, 2002), a number of recent studies have found significant links between openness and adaptive criteria. For example, openness was found to be the only personality factor to predict self-rated contextual and task performance for a group of 155 expatriates from 20 countries (Shaffer, Harrison, Gregersen, Black, & Ferzandi, 2006). Another study on expatriates working in Korea found narrow facets of openness predicted performance (Ones & Viswesvaran, 1999). Openness therefore appears to be most relevant to performance when situations are novel, transitional, or complex. If one takes the view that in novel environments *all* performance is essentially adaptive—that getting a job done in unpredictable conditions constitutes a different output to completing a routine task—then the previously mentioned studies indicate that openness and adaptive performance are indeed significantly correlated.

Adaptive performance also seems conceptually relevant to CQ. Both constructs are measured by behaviors that require individuals to operate across a variety of complex and novel environments. We would expect certain behaviors from an individual who had the ability to adjust their strategies for interaction with others (as required in the metacognitive and behavioral factors of CQ). For example, such an individual would be able to learn the rules of other cultures (the cognitive factor of CQ), be motivated in approaching the unfamiliar (the motivation factor of CQ), and show a greater range of adaptive performance behaviors than individuals who are low in CQ. Although links between CQ and adaptive performance have not specifically been tested, the results of studies using expatriate workers show that, in these samples and these environments, CQ correlates significantly with task performance (Ang et al., 2007; Earley & Ang, 2003; Templer et al., 2006). Once again, if one conceives of task performance in a culturally novel environment as substantially adaptive, it follows that CQ and adaptive performance are likely to be significantly related.

The model we propose is shown in Figure 9.1. In essence, it suggests that openness to experience leads an individual to develop CQ and CQ, in turn, enables an individual to perform adequately in novel environments. If possessing CQ were the *only* way in which an open individual could achieve such performance, the relationship would be described as fully mediated. However, if characteristic adaptations other than CQ are likely to influence adaptive performance, full mediation is not expected.

The main hypothesis of this study was:

H1: CQ will mediate the relationship between openness to experience and adaptive performance.

Figure 9.1 **Cultural Intelligence as a Mediator between Openness to Experience and Adaptive Performance**

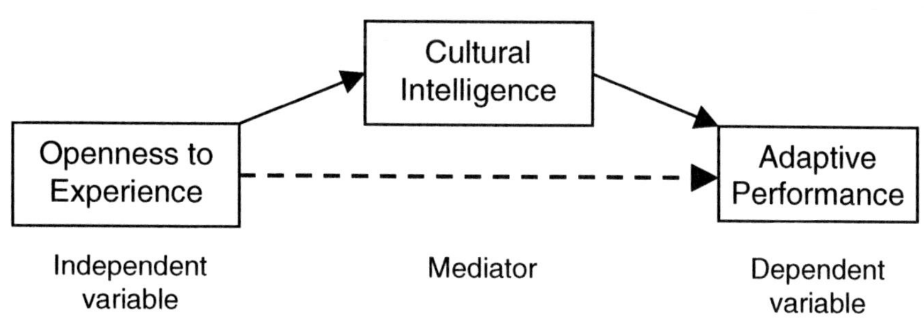

A more detailed version of the above hypothesis should, in our view, focus on narrow facets of openness. Although research to date has concentrated on relationships between broad factors, the role of CQ in predicting performance criteria will become clearer once we know which facets of openness align most closely with CQ, and also the extent to which CQ mediates the variance associated with each openness facet. Research involving openness facets has been relatively limited, however, because there has been a divergence of views among researchers about the precise structure of the openness construct. Even at the broadest level, there is a disagreement as to whether openness to experience should be viewed solely as intellect (ability to efficiently process information or create new ideas) or whether it should also include other, less intellectualized behaviors, such as tolerance, fantasy, and interest in artistic experiences. In this study, we used the six-facet structure of openness proposed by Chernyshenko, Stark, Sang, Longley, Fay, and Koncz (2007). By factor analyzing responses to 34 scales from seven widely used personality inventories and later replicating the results involving a different set of measures and respondents, Chernyshenko et al. (2007) found a much broader configuration of the openness construct involving three intellectual facets (intellectual efficiency, ingenuity, curiosity) and three nonintellectual facets (aesthetics, tolerance, depth). Importantly, the six facets showed only moderate interfacet correlations, suggesting that considerable amounts of facet-specific variance were present.

For the study, each individual's adaptive performance score was operationalized in terms of successful adaptation by incoming first-year students to a wider university culture. Such adaptation is likely to be determined not only by CQ, but also other important competencies, many of which may be dependent on intellectual facets of openness. For example, the development of successful study habits among new university entrants should help with better transition from school to university environment. If we assume that the rate with which such study habits are acquired is likely to be dependent on an individual's curiosity, ingenuity, and intellectual efficiency levels, then the relationships between intellectual aspects of openness and adaptive performance should not be fully mediated by CQ. On the other hand, nonintellectual openness facets (i.e., tolerance, depth, and aesthetics) are less likely to affect development of study habits or other relevant competencies, so their influence on adaptive performance should be primarily through CQ. Hence, we predicted tolerance, depth, and aesthetics to be fully mediated by CQ.

Our facet-level hypotheses are therefore:

H2: CQ will partially mediate the relationship between intellectual facets of openness (intellectual efficiency, curiosity, and ingenuity) and adaptive performance.
H3: CQ factors will fully mediate the relationship between nonintellectual facets of openness (aesthetics, tolerance, and depth) and adaptive performance

METHOD

Participants and Procedure

Participants consisted of 311 volunteers who were each paid NZ$20 in retail or gasoline vouchers for completing a questionnaire comprising several self-rating measurement scales. All were first- and-second year undergraduate students studying in New Zealand. Participants' ages ranged from 17 to 57 years with a mean age of 24 (SD = 7). All participants had jobs, either full time or part time, and all spoke English as their first language. Seventy-one percent were female and 29 percent were male. The questionnaire was administered to respondents in proctored groups that ranged in number from two to twenty individuals.

Measures

Openness to Experience

A 120-item measure was used in the study to measure six facets of openness: intellectual efficiency, ingenuity, curiosity, tolerance, aesthetics, and depth (Chernyshenko et al., 2007). Intellectual efficiency refers to an individual's preference to process information quickly and efficiently. Ingenuity deals with one's capacity to generate new ideas or to make improvements to the existing information or products. Individuals with high scores on the curiosity facet are characterized as inquisitive and perceptive; they read popular science/mechanics magazines and like experimentation. Individuals scoring high on the aesthetics facet genuinely enjoy acquiring, participating in, or creating various forms of artistic, musical, or architectural outputs. Unlike individuals high on the curiosity facet, they are not necessarily interested in understanding how or why the things they enjoy are created; instead, they are more interested in the experiential component of the behavior. Tolerance deals with one's typical behavior toward strangers and, more generally, toward novel stimuli. The final openness facet, depth, involves mainly "within person" experiences, such as understanding self and/or facilitating self-improvement and self-actualization.

Each facet was measured using 20 items. Examples of items included: "I feel at ease working on more difficult tasks" to measure intellectual efficiency; "I can be quite inventive at times" to measure ingenuity; "In a quiz I like to know what the answers are if I get the questions wrong" for curiosity; "I learn a great deal from people with differing beliefs" for tolerance; "I see the beauty in art when others do not" for aesthetics; and "It is important for me to be in touch with my inner feelings" for depth. All items were in a four-point Likert format, ranging from 1 (strongly disagree) to 4 (strongly agree). To produce facet scores, item scores for that facet were added together and then divided by the number of items; to produce an overall openness to experience score, scores on all 120 items were averaged.

Sang, Zhang, Chiu, Chernyshenko, and Longley (2008) conducted a series of confirmatory factor analyses involving this measure and showed support for the six-facet structure. The six facets of openness, in turn, were best represented by a hierarchical factor model having one general factor and two specific factors: namely, intellectual openness (i.e., "intellect") and nonintellectual openness (i.e., "culture"). In this model, each facet is specified to load on a general factor and on one of two specific factors; the general and specific factors are uncorrelated. The hierarchical factor model fit considerably better than a competing single-factor model

Extroversion, Agreeableness, Emotional Stability, and Conscientiousness

The remaining four broad personality factors were measured using a shortened version of Goldberg's (1992) adjective markers. Each scale consisted of seven bipolar markers presented in a nine-point Likert format. For example, extraversion was measured by such adjectives as silent-talkative, timid-bold, inactive-active.

Cultural Intelligence

The 20-item self-rating CQ measure (Ang et al., 2007) is based on four components: metacognition; cognition, motivation, and behavior. An example of one item from each of the above components is, respectively: "I am conscious of the cultural knowledge I apply to cross-cultural interactions"; "I know the legal and economic systems of other cultures"; "I am confident that I can socialize with locals in a culture that is unfamiliar to me"; and, "I alter my facial expressions when a cross-cultural interaction requires it." The scale is based on an extension of the CQ conceptualization in Earley and Ang (2003). Respondents were required to indicate a score from 1 (disagree strongly) to 5 (agree strongly) for each item. CQ factor scores were the average of item scores from that factor; the average of all items served as an overall CQ score.

Adaptive Performance

Building on the work of Pulakos et al. (2000, 2002) and Johnson (2003), we designed a measure of adaptive performance specific to the sample. Questions about feelings and attitudes were deliberately excluded to avoid possible overlaps with other measures when developing the pool of items. The survey consisted of eight performance-like questions about behaviors that indicate a student's successful adjustment to the new environment. Examples included, "I belong or have belonged to a university club or society," "I could show a visitor where these four campus facilities are: the physical sciences library, Bentley's bar, the recreation center, and the Reboot Café," "I know how to do a thorough literature search by computer," and "I attend talks by visiting lecturers that are not part of my coursework." All items were dichotomous, with participants given the option of either "yes" (coded as 1) or "no" (coded as 0) response. These scores were then added to produce the adaptive performance score. The eight-item self-rating measure was derived by exploratory factor analysis using principal axis factoring with an oblique rotation (direct oblimin). The coefficient alpha was 0.51, which appears low. However, because this study aimed mainly to investigate relationships between variables and not to make evaluative judgments about respondents' performance, the reliability of the adaptive performance scale was not a critical concern. Due to the high amount of random error in the adaptive performance scores, we expected the magnitude of observed correlations with this criterion to be modest. We also note that dichotomous response formats impose a significant range restriction on variability of item scores and that alpha represents the lower boundary to reliability of a scale of items.

Analyses

The study's hypotheses were tested using mediated regression (Baron & Kenny, 1986). The extent of mediation (partial, full, or nonsignificant) was determined using the Sobel test (Sobel, 1982). Generally speaking, "full" mediation is deemed to occur when the effect of the independent variable on the dependent variable becomes insignificant once the mediator is included in the regression.

RESULTS

Table 9.1 presents the means, standard deviations, reliabilities, and intercorrelations among all study variables: adaptive performance, CQ and its four factors, openness to experience and its six facets, and the four remaining Big Five factors. Note that a strong positive association between the broad measure of CQ and openness to experience ($r = 0.49$) replicated findings by Ang et al. (2006). Moreover, CQ correlations with the other four broad personality factors were considerably smaller, reinforcing the idea that openness, rather than the other Big Five factors, is likely to be responsible for the development of CQ competencies. Adaptive performance significantly correlated with CQ and openness to experience, showing the precondition for mediation was met. No other Big Five personality factor correlated significantly with adaptive performance.

Examination of the facet-level correlations showed that all openness facets significantly correlated with CQ. Importantly, although the tolerance and intellectual efficiency facets had similar correlations with CQ (0.44 and 0.38 respectively), their intercorrelation was only 0.25, suggesting that not all observed relations to CQ could be explained by the effects of the higher-order openness factor.

Regression results for openness and its six facets are presented in Table 9.2. For each personality variable, we show regression results when it is the only predictor of adaptive performance (row 1) and when it is paired with CQ (rows 2 and 3). Column 2 shows standardized regression weights for each predictor, column 3 presents Sobel test results,

Table 9.1

Means, Standard Deviations, Reliabilities, and Intercorrelations among Study Variables (n = 311)

Variable	M	SD	1	2	3	4	5	6	7	8	9	10	11	12	13	14	15	16	17
1. Adaptive Performance	4.51	1.81	**.51**																
2. Cultural Intelligence	3.37	0.43	.26	**.82**															
3. Metacognitive CQ	3.51	0.62	.13	.61	**.73**														
4. Cognitive CQ	2.71	0.70	.22	.73	.22	**.80**													
5. Motivational CQ	3.85	0.67	.20	.69	.22	.33	**.84**												
6. Behavioral CQ	3.58	0.57	.10	.59	.38	.12	.21	**.75**											
7. Openness to Experience	2.90	0.28	.22	.49	.32	.31	.43	.23	**.96**										
8. Intellectual Efficiency	2.80	0.38	.25	.38	.23	.28	.27	.22	.65	**.90**									
9. Ingenuity	2.87	0.41	.15	.30	.14	.23	.28	.12	.74	.58	**.93**								
10. Curiosity	3.10	0.33	.23	.39	.28	.16	.36	.25	.79	.59	.60	**.87**							
11. Aesthetics	2.83	0.53	.11	.29	.24	.20	.21	.11	.71	.21	.35	.33	**.94**						
12. Tolerance	2.98	0.36	.15	.44	.24	.23	.54	.13	.68	.22	.30	.47	.46	**.87**					
13. Depth	2.84	0.37	.06	.33	.27	.19	.23	.19	.72	.25	.35	.53	.48	.49	**.86**				
14. Extraversion	6.62	1.18	.09	.22	.09	.02	.33	.15	.31	.30	.39	.29	.08	.20	.13	**.84**			
15. Neuroticism	6.34	1.16	.05	.12	.06	.04	.22	–.01	.18	.23	.22	.15	.06	.17	–.06	.29	**.83**		
16. Conscientiousness	6.97	1.01	.08	.09	.10	–.03	.10	.11	.04	.09	.03	.06	–.01	.02	–.02	.21	.18	**.80**	
17. Agreeableness	7.28	0.92	–.03	–.03	.02	–.10	.09	–.06	.13	–.05	.04	.09	.15	.23	.10	.21	.36	.33	**.84**

Note: Alphas are in bold along the diagonal; correlations equal or higher than .11 are significant ($p = .05$).

Table 9.2

Regression Results for Openness to Experience and Its Six Facets, Mediated by Cultural Intelligence (n = 311)

Variable	ß	Sobel Z	% of I.V. effect mediated	Mediation	ΔR²	Total R²
Broad Factor Model						
Openness to experience	.22*					.047*
Openness (mediated by)	.12					
Cultural intelligence	.20*	2.45*	45	Partial	.03*	.077*
Openness Facets						
Intellectual efficiency	.25*					.063*
Intellectual efficiency (mediated by)	.18*					
Cultural intelligence	.19*	2.61*	28	Partial	.03*	.093*
Ingenuity	.15***					.022*
Ingenuity (mediated by)	.08					
Cultural intelligence	.23***	2.22*	47	Full	.049*	.071*
Curiosity	.23***					.054*
Curiosity (mediated by)	.16***					
Cultural intelligence	.20***	2.60*	30	Partial	.032*	.086*
Tolerance	.15*					.022*
Tolerance (mediated by)	.05					
Cultural intelligence	.24*	2.19*	70	Full	.045***	.067*
Aesthetics	.11*					.013*
Aesthetics (mediated by)	.04					
Cultural intelligence	.24*	1.81*	62	Full	.054***	.067*
Depth	.06					.003
Depth (mediated by)	–					
Cultural intelligence	–					

Note: Adaptive performance is the dependent variable in all regressions. The mediational hypothesis for the depth facet was not tested as depth was not significantly correlated with adaptive performance.

* = one-tailed, p =.05

*** = one-tailed, p =.005

Abbreviation: I.V. = Independent Variable

column 4 computes the percentage of the original effect being mediated by CQ, column 5 indicates whether mediation was full or partial, and columns 6 and 7 show R^2 results.

It can be seen in Table 9.2 that CQ partially mediated the relationship between openness to experience and adaptive performance. In the general model, the standardized regression coefficient for openness shrank by more than a third (39%) when the mediator was included in the regression calculation; however, the relationship between openness and adaptive performance remained significant, indicating partial rather than full mediation. Hence, hypothesis 1 was supported.

The regression results for the six narrow facets of openness showed that CQ mediated all but one relationship. The only exception was the depth facet, which had an insignificant correlation with adaptive performance and, thus, did not qualify for the test of mediation. As predicted by hypothesis 2, CQ partially mediated both the relationships between adaptive performance and the intellectual efficiency and curiosity facets of openness. In these two cases, CQ added incremental validity to predicting performance, but the effects of personality variables remained significant. In contrast, and as hypothesis 3 predicted, CQ fully mediated the effects of the tolerance and aesthetics facets of openness. In the case of the tolerance facet, CQ mediated as much as 70 percent of the original effect. However, contrary to hypothesis 2, relationships between ingenuity and adaptive performance were fully, rather than partially, mediated by CQ. It appears that, for this undergraduate sample, CQ is the only competency affecting relationships between ingenuity and adaptation to the new university environment.

DISCUSSION

At the outset, we noted that CQ—the skills required to function effectively in diverse cultural environments—is relatively understudied by organizational psychologists. Yet the effects of globalization and information technology mean that organizations increasingly require people with CQ capabilities. In order to command more research attention from psychologists, the new CQ construct needs to be placed within a widely accepted network of predictor–criterion variables, namely, the theory of individual differences in job performance. In this chapter, we therefore proposed the idea that patterns of behavior and cognitions representing CQ and its subcomponents should be viewed as performance determinants (also known as DK, procedural skills, and motivation); and furthermore, that these determinants act as mediators of the relationships between basic tendencies (personality) and job performance. To support our argument empirically, we conducted a study investigating CQ as a mediator of the relationship between openness to experience and adaptive performance.

The results demonstrated that CQ indeed mediated the relationship between openness and adaptive performance. At the broad factor level, 45 percent of the effect of openness was mediated. Thus, it appears that open individuals will tend to be high in CQ; in turn, they will tend to perform more effectively in transitional or novel environments.

At the narrow trait level, the mediating role of CQ was greater for nonintellectual facets of openness (tolerance and aesthetics facets were fully mediated by CQ) than for intellectual facets (intellectual efficiency and curiosity facets were only partially mediated by CQ). We expected this pattern because we believe intellectual aspects of openness are likely to be instrumental in the development of other important competencies that facilitate adaptive performance abilities, such as study habits or those tested in team adaptation exercises (LePine, 2005).

LIMITATIONS AND FUTURE DIRECTIONS

Conceptualizing adaptive performance and devising an appropriate measure for the target sample presented the biggest challenge in the present study. Although adaptive performance was first suggested as an addition to the task and contextual performance domain more than a decade ago (Allworth & Hesketh, 1999), a clear theoretical framework and research-validated taxonomy has not yet emerged. For example, the eight-dimensional framework proposed by Pulakos et al. (2000) has yielded conflicting data with regard to the number of factors in the construct (Pulakos et al., 2002; Griffin & Hesketh, 2003). In this study, we approached the task of constructing adaptive performance measures pragmatically, focusing on concrete behavioral outcomes that new students are expected to acquire in order to successfully adapt to the university culture. We did not want to develop another self-report measure about one's intentions or cognitions, because such a measure would inevitably contain overlapping content with either the openness or CQ measures, and would likely inflate the observed relationships between these variables. Our resulting dichotomously scored measure was a relatively short scale of eight items and therefore had a rather low reliability. Further research involving improved adaptive performance measures, designed for student or other target populations, would undoubtedly help to strengthen the findings of this study.

Another potential limitation was the target sample: first- and-second year undergraduate university students studying in their home country. The CQ measure was principally devised for use by individuals facing cross-cultural demands in their jobs. With a mean age of 24 years, these individuals have had less opportunity to develop CQ competencies than most expatriate executives. We believe, however, that an intensive learning environment is, to a large extent, an unfamiliar and fluid environment, in which unexpected demands frequently arise. Further, we suggest that successful adaptation to such an environment requires the development of skills similar to those of the culturally intelligent individual. Therefore, we expected and confirmed that CQ skills were relevant to those entering a novel academic setting. To generalize these findings to job performance settings, we recommend future research on employees working in novel and unfamiliar environments.

REFERENCES

Allworth, E. & Hesketh, B. (1999). Construct-oriented biodata: Capturing change-related and contextually relevant future performance. *International Journal of Selection and Assessment, 7*(2).

Ang, S., Van Dyne, L., & Koh, C. (2006). Personality correlates of the four-factor model of cultural intelligence. *Group and Organization Management, 31,* 100–123.

Ang, S., Van Dyne, L., Koh, C., Ng, K.Y., Templer, K.J., Tay, C., & Chandrasekar, N.A. (2007). Cultural intelligence: Its measurement and effects on cultural judgment and decision making, cultural adaptation, and task performance. *Management and Organization Review, 3,* 335–371.

Baron, R.M., & Kenny, D.A. 1986. The moderator-mediator variable distinction in social psychological research: Conceptual, strategic, and statistical considerations. *Journal of Personality and Social Psychology, 51,* 1173–1182.

Barrick, M.R., & Mount, M.K. (1991). The Big Five personality dimensions and job performance: A meta-analysis. *Personnel Psychology, 44,* 1–26.

Bhagat, R.S., & Prien, K.O. (1996). Cross-cultural training in organizational contexts. In D. Landis & R.S. Bhagat (Eds.), *Handbook of intercultural training* (pp. 216–230). Thousand Oaks, CA: Sage.

Campbell, J.P. (1990). Modeling the performance prediction problem in industrial and organizational psychology. In M.D. Dunnette & L.M. Hough (Eds.), *Handbook of industrial and organizational psychology. Volume 1* (2nd ed.) (pp. 687–732). Palo Alto, CA: Consulting Psychologists Press.

Campbell, J.P., McCloy, R.A., Oppler, S.H., & Sager, C.E. (1993). A theory of performance. In N. Schmit & W.C. Borman (Eds.), *Personnel selection in organizations* (pp. 35–70). San Francisco, CA: Jossey-Bass.

Chernyshenko, O.S., Stark, S., Sang, W., Longley, A., Fay, A., & Koncz, G. (2007). Openness to experience: Its facet structure, measurement, and usefulness in predicting important organizational outcomes. Working paper, Nanyang Business School, Nanyang Technological University, Singapore.

Earley, P.C. (1987). Intercultural training for managers: A comparison of documentary and interpersonal methods. *Academy of Management Journal, 30,* 685–698.

Earley, P.C., & Ang, S. (2003). *Cultural intelligence: Individual interactions across cultures.* Palo Alto, CA: Stanford University Press.

Flynn, F.J. (2005). Having an open mind: The impact of openness to experience on interracial attitudes and impression formation. *Journal of Personality and Social Psychology, 88,* 816–826.

Gelfand, M.J., Erez, M., & Aycan, Z. (2007). Cross-cultural organizational behavior. *Annual Review of Psychology, 58,* 479–514.

Goldberg, L.R. (1992). The development of markers for the Big-Five Factor Structure. *Psychological Assessment, 4,* 26–42.

Gong, Y., & Fan, J. (2006). Longitudinal examination of the role of goal orientation in cross-cultural adjustment. *Journal of Applied Psychology, 91,* 176–184.

Griffin, B., & Hesketh, B. (2003). Adaptable behaviours for successful work and career adjustment. *Australian Journal of Psychology, 55,* 65–73.

Johnson, J.W. (2003). Toward a better understanding of the relationship between personality and individual job performance. In M.R. Barrick & A.M. Ryan (Eds.), *Personality and work: Reconsidering the role of personality in organizations.* San Francisco, CA: Jossey-Bass.

Jose, P.E. (2003). MedGraph-I: A programme to graphically depict mediation among three variables. http://www.vuw.ac.nz/psyc/staff/paul-jose/files/medgraph. Accessed April 18, 2007.

Konrad, A.M. (Ed.) (2006). Editorial comment. *Group and Organization Management, 31*(1), 627.

Landy, F.J. (2005). Some historical and scientific issues related to research on emotional intelligence. *Journal of Organizational Behavior, 26,* 411–424.

LePine, J.A. (2005). Adaptation of teams in response to unforeseen change: Effects of goal difficulty and team composition in terms of cognitive ability and goal orientation. *Journal of Applied Psychology, 90,* 1153–1167.

Leong, C-H. (2007). Predictive validity of the Multicultural Personality Questionnaire: A longitudinal study on the socio-psychological adaptation of Asian undergraduates who took part in a study-abroad program. *International Journal of Intercultural Relations, 31,* 545–559.

Locke, E.A. (2005). Why emotional intelligence is an invalid concept. *Journal of Organizational Behavior, 26,* 425–431.

McCrae, R.R., & Costa, P.T. (1996). Toward a new generation of personality theories: Theoretical contexts for the five-factor model. In J.S. Wiggins (Ed.), *The five-factor model of personality* (pp. 51–87). New York: Guilford.

Motowidlo, S.J., Borman, W.C., & Schmitt, M.J. (1997). A theory of individual differences in task and contextual performance. *Human Performance, 10,* 71–83.

Ones, D.S., & Viswesvaran, C. (1999). Relative importance of personality dimensions for expatriate selection: A policy capturing study. *Human Performance, 12,* 275–294.

Peterson, B. (2004). *Cultural intelligence: A guide to working with people from other cultures.* Yarmouth, ME: Intercultural Press.

Pulakos, E.D., Arad, S., Donovan, M.A., & Plamondon, K.E. (2000). Adaptability in the workplace: Development of a taxonomy of adaptive performance. *Journal of Applied Psychology, 85,* 612–624.

Pulakos, E.D., Schmitt, N., Dorsey, D.W., Arad, S., Hedge, J.W., & Borman, W.C. (2002). Predicting adaptive performance: further tests of a model of adaptability. *Human Performance, 15,* 299–323.

Roberts, R.D., Zeidner, M., & Matthews, G. (2001). Does emotional intelligence meet traditional standards for an intelligence? Some new data and conclusions. *Emotion, 1,* 196–231.

Salgado, J.F. (1997). The five-factor model of personality and job performance in the European Community. *Journal of Applied Psychology, 82,* 30–43.

Sang, E.W., Zhang, Z., Chiu, C.Y., Chernyshenko, O.S., & Longley, A. (2008). The six-faceted measure of openness to experience: Its construct validity and measurement invariance across three cultures. Working paper. University of Illinois at Urbana-Champaign.

Shaffer, M.A., Harrison, D.A., Gregersen, H., Black, J.S., & Ferzandi, L.A. (2006). You can take it with you: Individual differences and expatriate effectiveness. *Journal of Applied Psychology, 91,* 109–125.

Sobel, M.E. (1982). Asymptotic intervals for indirect effects in structural equations models. In S. Leinhart (Ed.), *Sociological methodology* (pp. 290–312). San Francisco, CA: Jossey-Bass.

Sternberg, R.J., & Grigorenko, E.L. (2004). *Culture and competence: Contexts of life success.* Washington, DC: American Psychological Association.

Templer, K.J., Tay, C., & Chandrasekar, A. (2006). Motivational cultural intelligence, realistic job preview, realistic living conditions preview, and cross-cultural adjustment. *Group and Organization Management, 31,* 154–173.

Thomas, D.C., & Inkson, K. (2004). *Cultural intelligence: People skills for global business.* San Francisco, CA: Berrett-Koehler Publishers.

Wang, M., & Takeuchi, R. (2007). The role of goal orientation during expatriation: A cross-sectional and longitudinal investigation. *Journal of Applied Psychology, 92,* 1437–1445.

CHAPTER 10

Personality, Cultural Intelligence, and Cross-Cultural Adaptation

A Test of the Mediation Hypothesis

COLLEEN WARD AND RONALD FISCHER

For more than three decades the advancement of psychological research on cross-cultural transition and adaptation has been largely guided by theories grounded in social and health psychology (Ward, Bochner, & Furnham, 2001). Two major conceptual frameworks have been used to understand, explain, and predict cross-cultural adaptation. The first, culture learning, has arisen from Argyle's (1969) work on social skills and interpersonal behaviors and focuses on the social psychology of intercultural interactions. This approach is based on the assumption that cross-cultural problems arise because cultural novices have difficulty managing everyday social encounters. Adaptation, therefore, comes in the form of learning the culture-specific skills that are required to negotiate the new cultural milieu (Bochner, 1986; Masgoret & Ward, 2006). From this perspective, empirical research investigating the predictors of adaptive outcomes has highlighted the importance of factors such as length of residence in a new culture, culture-specific knowledge, cultural distance, interactions with host nationals, and acculturation strategies (Furnham & Bochner, 1982; Kurman & Ronen-Eilon, 2004; Searle & Ward, 1990). The second conceptual framework has been strongly influenced by Lazarus and Folkman's (1984) work on stress, appraisal, and coping. This approach conceptualizes cross-cultural transition as a series of stress-provoking life changes that tax resources used in adjustment and require coping responses. From this perspective, adaptation is reflected in psychological well-being, and its predictors have been linked to life changes, personality, stress appraisal, coping styles, and acculturation strategies (Berry, 2006; Berry & Sam, 1997; Ward & Kennedy, 2001).

More recently, Earley and Ang (2003) introduced a new perspective on cross-cultural transition and adaptation that arose from contemporary work on intelligence (Sternberg, 1988, 2000) and is situated in the literature on expatriate effectiveness (e.g., Aycan, 1997; Black, Gregersen, & Mendenhall, 1992). Their approach emphasizes interindividual differences in the ability to adapt to novel cultural settings and the influences of these differences on the success in global work assignments (GWAs). More specifically, they have highlighted the importance of cultural intelligence (CQ), defined as "a person's capability to adapt effectively to new cultural contexts" (Earley & Ang, 2003, p. 59). Earley and Ang's multilevel model specifies that CQ leads to success in global work assignments, including general adjustment and work performance, but that the relationships between CQ and the adaptive outcomes are affected by individual factors such as personality and technical competence, familial factors, job and organizational factors, and characteristics of the host culture.

CQ represents a multidimensional construct of intelligence based on four components—cognitive, metacognitive, motivational, and behavioral—giving the construct both process and content features (Earley & Ang, 2003). The cognitive component of CQ relates to an individual's knowledge of specific norms, practices, and conventions in new cultural settings. Metacognitive CQ is defined as an individual's cultural awareness during interactions with people from different cultural backgrounds. Motivational CQ is conceptualized as a person's drive to learn more about and function effectively in culturally varied situations. Finally, behavioral CQ is defined as an individual's flexibility in demonstrating appropriate actions when interacting with people from different cultural backgrounds. Ang, Van Dyne, Koh, and Ng (2004) have advanced research on CQ with the construction and validation of a scale for its measurement confirming the four-factor structure based on data from Singapore and the United States. More recently, Ward, Fischer, Lam, and Hall (in press) corroborated the structure with a sample of international students in New Zealand.

As CQ is a relatively new construct, there has been limited empirical research published on its predictive validity. Preliminary evidence from Ang and colleagues, however, appears promising. Over a series of studies, the researchers reported that metacognitive CQ was related to performance on a cultural judgement and a decision-making task; motivational CQ was linked to general adjustment; behavioral CQ predicted both task performance and general adjustment; and the four CQ factors explained variance in general adjustment and task performance over and above that accounted for by a test of cognitive ability (Ang et al., 2004). More recent research has confirmed that motivational CQ predicts work and general adjustment (Templer, Tay, & Chandrasekar, 2006). None of these studies, however, has addressed the complex relationship between personality, CQ, and adaptive outcomes.

In their seminal work on cultural intelligence Earley and Ang (2003) advanced two suppositions about the relationship between personality, CQ, and success on global assignments. First, they stated that "personality characteristics are conceptualized as antecedents or causal agents of cultural intelligence" (p. 160). However, they later posited that personality "can moderate the relationship between CQ and adjustment in GWA" (p. 218). More specifically, they suggested that the Big Five personality factors may only engender expatriate success for those who are high in CQ.

Ang et al. (2006) examined the first of these propositions in their study of CQ and the Big Five personality factors. Using hierarchical regression to control for age, gender, and cross-cultural experience, they demonstrated that metacognitive CQ was predicted by openness and conscientiousness; cognitive and motivational CQ were predicted by extraversion and openness; and behavioral CQ was predicted by agreeableness, extraversion, openness, and neuroticism. Although the research did not examine the links between personality and CQ to adaptive outcomes, Ang et al. suggested that "trait-like" individual differences, such as personality characteristics, are more distal to performance outcomes than are "state-like" individual differences, such as CQ, and that the former exerts indirect effects on outcomes through the intervening, more malleable "state-like" qualities.

The first study to link CQ, personality, and cross-cultural adaptation was conducted by Ward et al. (in press) with international students in New Zealand. This earlier research used van der Zee and van Oudenhoven's (2000) multicultural personality questionnaire, Ang et al.'s (2004) measure of cultural intelligence, and Raven's advanced progressive matrices (Raven, 1998) as a test of cognitive ability and assessments of psychological, sociocultural, and academic adaptation in a sample of 102 international students. Hierarchical regression analyses failed to document the incremental validity of the four CQ subscales in the prediction of psychological, sociocultural, and academic adaptation over and above the variance explained by demographic variables (age, gender, and English language proficiency), cognitive ability, and personality. In each adaptation domain, however, the emotional stability subscale of the multicultural personality questionnaire (MPQ) remained a significant predictor of the outcome in the final step of the analysis.

The failure of CQ to demonstrate incremental validity in this study tacitly undermines the mediation hypothesis. Despite the initial results, however, we believe that the mediation model deserves further attention for at least two reasons. First, in our original study, both the CQ and MPQ domains were combined for analysis; that is, the five MPQ factors and the four CQ subscales were entered in blocks on respective steps in the regression analyses. The block entry, particularly with the strong effects of emotional stability, may have obscured more subtle influences of specific CQ domains on specific MPQ factors. Exploration of these links warrants more refined theorizing about the specific relationships among CQ and MPQ factors and their influences on cross-cultural adaptation. Second, more sophisticated theorizing about the relationship between CQ and MPQ domains should be accompanied by more precise statistical analyses. More specifically, a test of the mediation hypothesis might be better achieved with causal modeling. Accordingly, this study aims to test an integrated model of general adjustment linking personality and CQ using structural equation modeling.

PERSONALITY, CQ, AND CROSS-CULTURAL ADAPTATION

Personality has traditionally occupied a central role in studies of cross-cultural transition and adaptation. Research has shown that an internal locus of control (Neto, 1995; Ward & Kennedy, 1993), hardiness (Ataca, 1996), mastery (Sam, 1998), curiosity (Ones & Viswesvaran, 1997), and low levels of authoritarianism and dogmatism (Taft & Steinkalk, 1985) predict cross-cultural adaptation in sojourners and immigrants. More recent studies with the Big Five have reported that extraversion, agreeableness, conscientiousness, and emotional stability are associated with psychological and sociocultural adaptation in international students and expatriate businesspeople (Ward, Leong, & Low, 2004), that extraversion and agreeableness are related to a reduced likelihood of terminating an expatriate posting, and that conscientiousness is positively related to supervisory ratings of job performance (Caligiuri, 2000). Selection and training instruments (e.g., Cross-Cultural Adaptability Inventory, Kelley & Meyers, 1989; Intercultural Adaptation Potential Scale, Matsumoto & Le Roux, 2003; Multicultural Personality Questionnaire, van der Zee & van Oudenhoven, 2000) designed to predict or enhance intercultural effectiveness have further substantiated the importance of personality, linking emotional resilience and stability, flexibility, openness, perceptual acuity, social initiative, and cultural empathy to psychological, social, and work adjustment across groups of expatriate employees, expatriate spouses, and international students (Ali, van der Zee, & Sanders, 2003; van Oudenhoven, Mol, & van der Zee, 2003; Ward, Berno, & Main, 2002).

Although there is a range of assessment instruments that might be used to investigate the relationship between CQ, personality, and cross-cultural adaptation, we believe the MPQ is best suited to this objective. The MPQ is a 91-item instrument composed of five subscales: cultural empathy, openmindedness, emotional stability, social initiative, and flexibility. Cultural empathy refers to the ability to empathize with the feelings, thoughts, and behaviors of members of different cultural groups. Openmindedness is defined as a nonjudgmental attitude toward different cultural groups, norms, and practices. Emotional stability reflects an ability to remain composed in stressful situations while social initiative refers to the tendency to approach social situations in a proactive manner. Finally, flexibility represents a tendency to adjust behaviors to changing circumstances. The MPQ has been widely used in research on cross-cultural transition and adaptation and has demonstrated good reliability and validity with a range of cross-cultural and international samples of both expatriates on overseas assignments and international students; it has also been recommended as a selection tool for global work assignments and as a diagnostic tool for assessing training needs (Ali et al., 2003; Leone, van der Zee, van Oudenhoven, Perugini, & Ercolani, 2005; van der Zee & van Oudenhoven, 2000, 2001; van Oudenhoven et al., 2003; van Oudenhoven & van der Zee, 2002). More importantly, the MPQ has demonstrated incremental validity over and above the Big Five in predicting an international orientation, aspiration for an international career in students (van der Zee & van Oudenhoven, 2000), and behavioral competence in job applicants (van der Zee, Zaal & Piekstra, 2003).

Cultural intelligence has cognitive, behavioral, and motivational components that may mediate the relationship between personality and cross-cultural adaptation. Theoretical and empirical factors have led us to hypothesize that motivational CQ is the most promising component to investigate in a parsimonious mediation model. First, motivational domains have been relatively neglected in research on cross-cultural transition and adaptation (Berry & Ward, 2006). Although the importance of motivational factors has been highlighted in the literature on expatriate effectiveness, their "discussion has been generally atheoretical and lacking a coherent structure" (Earley & Ang, 2003, p.

128). The definition, measurement, and situation of motivational CQ in Earley and Ang's (2003) model of success in global work assignments constitute the most original aspects of their contribution to the study of cross-cultural transition and adaptation. Cognitive and behavioral elements have traditionally occupied a significant position and have been extensively investigated, albeit not with specific reference to intelligence, in the culture learning framework (Ward, 2004). Second, it is easy to see how motivational factors may act as effective mediators of personality dispositions. Individuals with greater perceived flexibility, cultural empathy, openmindedness, or social initiative are likely to feel more motivated to engage in intercultural interactions, due to a greater perceived efficacy (Bandura, 1977, 1986). Third, from a statistical perspective, a number of empirical relationships need to be found. In the traditional regression model, mediation is said to occur if the mediator is related to both the predictor and the criterion variable and if the path from the predictor variable to the criterion becomes insignificant (full mediation) or reduced in strength (partial mediation) when the mediator is introduced in the regression model (Baron & Kenny, 1986).

Motivational CQ has already emerged as a significant predictor of general adjustment in studies of international executives by Ang et al. (2004) and Templer et al. (2006). Our previous research on CQ, personality, and adaptation also showed that each of the MPQ subscales correlated significantly with general adjustment and moderate correlations (r's = 0.20–0.30) were found among the MPQ and CQ subscales. Furthermore, motivational CQ showed the most consistent relationship to the MPQ and was significantly related to flexibility, openmindedness, cultural empathy, and social initiative. These findings converge to suggest that motivational CQ is a good candidate for a mediator. In addition, as previously mentioned, emotional stability was the only one of the nine CQ and MPQ factors to remain a significant predictor of adaptation on the final step of a series of hierarchical regression analyses, suggesting a direct and unmediated path from this factor to general adjustment.

Based on a theoretical and empirical rationale, our proposed model is presented in Figure 10.1. The model proposes a direct link between emotional stability and general adjustment. Furthermore, it proposes that the effects of social initiative, openmindedness, flexibility, and cultural empathy on general adjustment are mediated by motivational CQ.

METHOD

Participants and Procedure

Three hundred and forty-six international students (65 percent females) recruited through a New Zealand university's international orientation program participated in the research. Participation was anonymous and voluntary.

Students originated from 30 countries with the largest groups coming from the United States (38.6 percent), Malaysia (16 percent), and the People's Republic of China (15.4 percent). Their ages ranged from 17 to 38 years (M = 21.14, SD = 2.63), and length of residence in New Zealand varied from one day to 15 years (M = 227 days; SD = 511.7

Figure 10.1 **The Proposed Model**

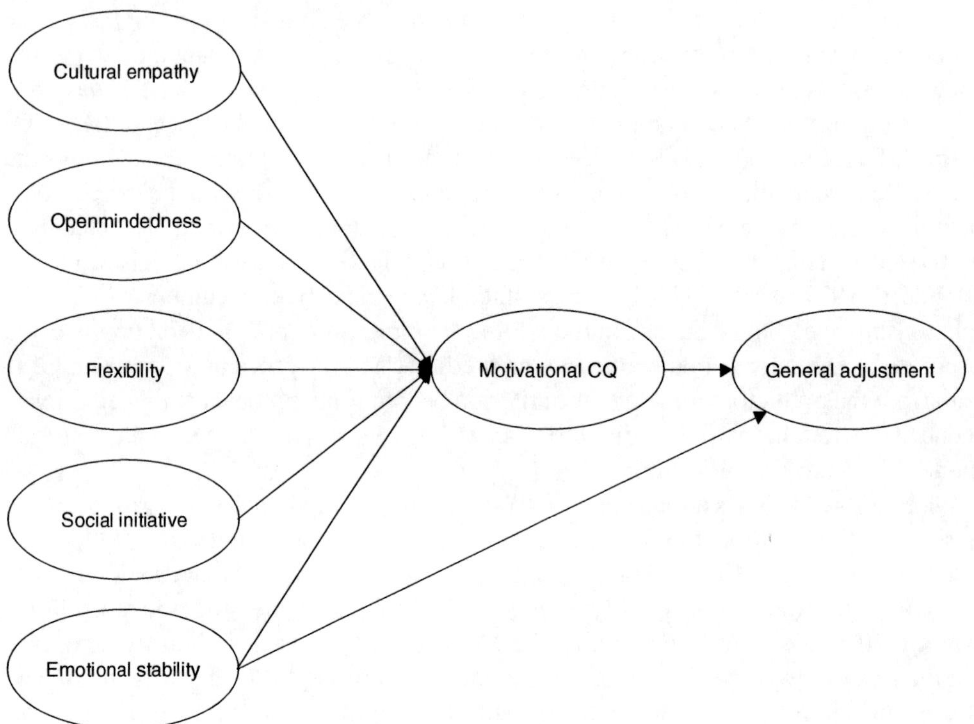

days). Almost half of the respondents (48.9 percent) were self-rated fluent English speakers, with a further 19 percent nearly fluent; 16.7 percent indicated that they did not speak English very well.

Materials

The survey included personal background information (e.g., age, gender, nationality, English proficiency, and length of residence in New Zealand) and assessments of CQ, personality, using MPQ, and general adjustment, using the sociocultural adaptation scale (SCAS).

Participants completed the five-item motivational subscale of CQ (Ang et al., 2004; Ang et al., 2007). Responses were made on five-point "agree-disagree" scales with higher scores reflecting greater CQ. A sample item is, "I enjoy interacting with people from different cultures." Ang and colleagues (2004, 2006, 2007) have produced convincing evidence of the measure's reliability and validity.

The MPQ consists of 91 items measuring five factors: flexibility (18 items), cultural empathy (18 items), social initiative (17 items), openmindedness (18 items), and emotional stability (20 items). All statements are rated on a six-point dimension of applicability ranging from "totally not applicable" to "completely applicable." For the most part, the items reflect generic statements, such as, "I avoid surprises" or "I take the lead" with only four of the 91 items explicitly mentioning culture, e.g., "I feel uncomfortable in a different culture." Past research has shown the MPQ to be a valid and reliable instrument for international and multicultural samples (Leone et al., 2005; van der Zee & van Oudenhoven, 2000, 2001; van Oudenhoven et al., 2003; van Oudenhoven & van der Zee, 2002).

General adjustment was assessed using the SCAS, a 23-item measure that taps the amount of difficulty experienced negotiating everyday situations in a new cultural milieu (e.g., shopping, making oneself understood). Five-point rating scales (endpoints: no difficulty/extreme difficulty) are used with higher scores indicating greater adaptation problems. The SCAS has been used extensively in sojourner research and has demonstrated good reliability and validity with a wide variety of cross-cultural samples (Ward & Kennedy, 1999). The scale is most commonly used in acculturation research to tap the construct of sociocultural adaptation as distinct from psychological well-being. However, the SCAS incorporates all of the domains included in Black's (1988) measure of general adjustment, which also forms the basis of the general adjustment measures used in CQ research (Ang et al., 2004, 2007; Templer et al., 2006). As this construct is more commonly discussed in the expatriate effectiveness literature in which the CQ research has been situated, the SCAS is referred to as *general adjustment* in this study.

RESULTS

Initial Analyses

We conducted a confirmatory factor analysis using LISREL 8.71 and maximum likelihood (ML) estimation. For the MPQ and SCAS we used item parcels (using four-item parcels with randomly allocated items for each of the MPQ dimensions and the SCAS). The fit for this seven-factor model was acceptable: χ^2 (356) = 857.65, Tucker Lewis Index (TLI) = 0.96, comparative fit index (CFI) = 0.97, root mean square error of approximation (RMSEA) = 0.066. A model in which we forced all the MPQ dimensions and motivational CQ to load on a single factor did not fit as well: χ^2 (376) = 2154.49, TLI = 0.91, CFI = 0.92, RMSEA = 0.12. Since two of the MPQ dimensions (cultural empathy and openmindedness) correlated quite highly (see Table 10.1), we also tested a model in which we combined these two dimensions. This model did fit significantly worse: $\Delta \chi^2$ (5) = 50.55, p <0.01. Therefore, our measures show discriminant validity. Cronbach's alphas were calculated to check scalar reliability of measures, and all scales demonstrated good internal consistency (see Table 10.1).

Model Testing

The purpose of this study is to assess the adequacy of a model of cross-cultural adaptation that proposes a mediating role of motivational CQ in determining general adjustment.

A model was tested that proposed direct and indirect links between the five subscales of the MPQ and general adjustment. Figure 10.1 presents this model showing the relationships of the indicator variables to the latent variables, as well as the functional relationships

Table 10.1

Descriptive Statistics

	Mean	SD	1	2	3	4	5	6	7
1. Motivational CQ	5.08	.92	(.82)						
2. Cultural Empathy	4.42	.62	.54**	(.82)					
3. Openmindedness	4.32	.59	.57**	.72**	(.76)				
4. Social Initiative	3.96	.57	.44**	.57**	.59**	(.84)			
5. Emotional Stability	3.67	.49	.37**	.28**	.33**	.46**	(.80)		
6. Flexibility	3.82	.51	.51**	.41**	.47**	.50**	.45**	(.76)	
7. General Adjustment	4.00	.57	.46**	.42**	.44**	.44**	.36**	.34**	(.87)

**p <.001. Cronbach's alpha is printed on the diagonal.

among the latent variables. A path model was adopted, as this is superior to traditional tests of mediation (Iacobucci, Saldanha & Deng, 2007).

A single indicator model incorporating random measurement error was specified. Williams and Hazer (1986) suggested fixing the loadings from indicator to constructs to the square root of the coefficient alpha estimate for each construct, and to fix the error variance to the product of the variance of the observed indicator multiplied by the quantity one minus the estimated reliability of each construct. This approach has been frequently used in applied psychological research (e.g., Clugston, 2000; Frone, Russell, & Cooper, 1992; Moorman, 1991) and has been shown to yield identical results to latent model estimates (Netemeyer, Johnston, & Burton, 1990). This procedure is appropriate if the number of indicators is large.

The proposed model was tested using the LISREL 8.71, and the data provided mixed support for the model (Figure. 10.2). The fit indices for CFI was 0.99, and for the Tucker-Lewis index 0.95, which is excellent (Hu & Bentler, 1999; Marsh, Balla, & McDonald, 1988). However, the RMSEA was 0.10, which is above the traditionally recommended level of 0.08 or more recent recommendations of 0.06 (Browne & Cudeck, 1993; Hu & Bentler, 1999; Marsh et al., 1988). Furthermore, modification indices suggested that the model was not fitting very well. Examining residuals and modification indices for this model, direct paths from the MPQ dimensions to the outcome measure seemed appropriate. More specifically, the residuals between cultural empathy, openmindedness, and social initiative on one hand and adaptation on the other were all larger than 3.4 and the modification indices were all in the range between 15.6 and 16.6 (which is substantial considering the overall chi square of 22.2). We therefore decided to free the direct path between social initiative and adaptation since this pair showed the highest standardized residual (3.75). We also removed the direct path between social initiative and motivational CQ since the completely standardized path between the two constructs was negative, not significant and close to zero (–0.08). This revised model provided excellent fit: χ^2 (5) = 8.01, p = 0.16, TLI = 0.99. CFI = 1.00, RMSEA = 0.043. This revised model is shown in Figure 10.3. The indirect effect of flexibility on general adjustment was significant (z = 3.7, p <0.01), but not the effects of cultural empathy and openmindedness (z <1.5).

Figure 10.2 **Test of the Proposed Model**

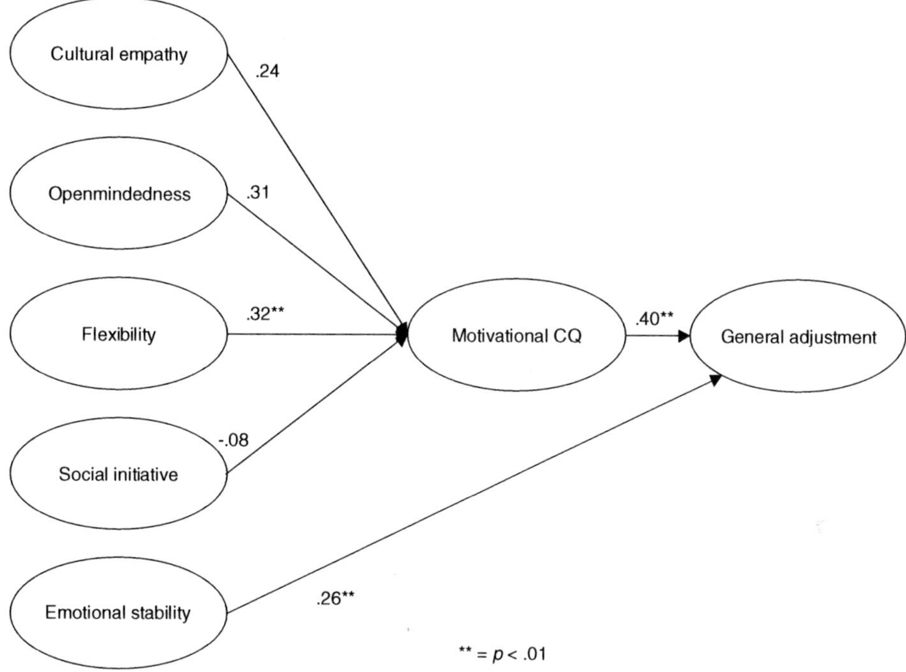

Figure 10.3 **The Revised Model**

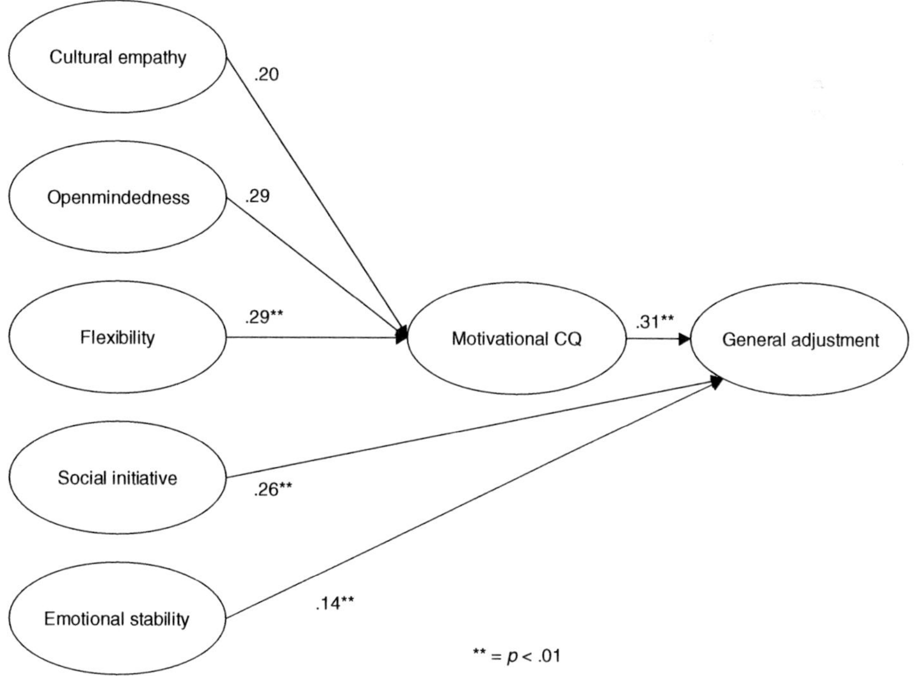

DISCUSSION

The relationship between CQ and personality, and their influences on adaptive outcomes, are core issues for the theoretical and empirical precision of CQ research. Arising from theorizing by Ang et al. (2004) and guided by empirical research by Ward et al. (in press), the research tested a structural model of cross-cultural adaptation with a direct path from emotional stability to general adjustment and mediated paths from cultural empathy, flexibility, openmindedness, and social initiative through motivational CQ. The data did not provide a strong fit to the model, and modification indices suggested direct paths from the MPQ subscales to the outcome measure. A modified model with a direct path from social initiative to general adjustment provided an excellent fit to the data; however, the results indicated that flexibility alone was mediated by motivational CQ. As such, the findings provide limited support for Ang et al.'s (2004) mediation model of personality, CQ and cross-cultural adaptation.

Motivational CQ has been described as a drive and interest in learning about and functioning in new and different cultural settings (Ang et al., 2004). Individuals with high motivational CQ have a strong desire to experience cultural novelty; they enjoy interacting with people from diverse backgrounds, and they have a strong sense of self-efficacy in cross-cultural contexts. Templer at al. (2006) propose that motivational CQ "stimulates and channels an individual's knowledge and strategies into guided action in novel cultural experiences" (p. 157). Our findings suggest that motivational CQ may "channel" flexibility to enhance general adjustment.

At the most basic level, Earley and Ang (2003) acknowledged the importance of flexibility in their theory of CQ, noting that constant reshaping and adaptation are required to operate effectively in a new cultural milieu. They also postulate that a consistency motive is negatively related to CQ. From this perspective, then, the personality trait of flexibility may be seen as a prerequisite of motivational CQ. Motivational CQ, in turn, leads to better cross-cultural adaptation. Such an interpretation is consistent with theorizing by Earley and Ang (2003) and Ang et al.'s (2004) proposed mediation model.

In addition to the mediated influence of flexibility on general adjustment, social initiative and emotional stability exerted direct effects on the adaptation outcome. Social initiative refers to the tendency to approach social situations in a proactive manner and to take initiative. Research has previously demonstrated a link between social initiative and peer support and psychological well-being, both of which are associated with general adjustment (van Oudenhoven et al., 2003; van Oudenhoven & van der Zee, 2002). Emotional stability reflects the tendency to remain calm in stressful situations. Research with the MPQ has revealed that emotion stability is the most robust predictor of adaptive outcomes, including expatriates' personal, professional, and social adjustment, and international students' psychological, sociocultural, and academic adaptation (van Oudenhoven et al., 2003; Ward et al., in press).

Cultural empathy and openmindedness were positively correlated with motivational CQ but did not significantly relate to CQ after controlling for flexibility. This is to be expected given the relatively larger intercorrelations among the MPQ dimensions, especially openmindedness and cultural empathy. Both domains share common characteristics of being open, transcending one's own perspective, and remaining nonjudgmental in intercultural interactions. Although both dimensions are associated with an increase in motivation to engage in intercultural encounters, the unique effect of each dimension controlling for the other is not significant.

The main objective of the current research was to test a mediation model of personality, CQ, and cross-cultural adaptation. Two of our studies have now directly or indirectly examined this proposition. The first produced no evidence of mediation in that CQ failed to explain any additional variance in psychological, sociocultural, and academic adaptation in international students above and beyond that accounted for by the MPQ (Ward et al., in press). The second study, reported here, found only partial support for a mediation model with motivational CQ mediating the influence of flexibility on general adjustment. In both studies, personality factors appeared to be strong predictors of adaptation outcomes.

Recently, Ang et al. (2007) have advanced more sophisticated theorizing about the four CQ domains and their influences on specific adaptive outcomes. In particular, they have hypothesized and confirmed that motivational CQ is related to cultural adaptation in both affective and behavioral domains. Motivational CQ predicted interaction adjustment and well-being, and demonstrated incremental validity over and above either the Big Five personality traits or the four domains (emotional resilience, perceptual acuity, autonomy, and flexibility) of the Cross-Cultural Adaptability Inventory (Kelly & Meyers, 1989). However, in all of these cases personality factors remained significant predictors of the adaptive outcomes, again undermining the proposed mediational role of CQ. The relative and specific influences of personality and CQ require further research.

In the broader context, however, there are a number of issues that must be considered before firm conclusions can be drawn about the relative roles and influences of personality and CQ on cross-cultural adaptation. One issue that deserves serious attention is the relationship between theory and measurement. In their discussion of the measurement of cultural intelligence, Lee and Templer (2003) noted that various approaches may be adopted: surveys, interviews, observations, computer simulations, critical incidents, cultural assimilators, and assessment centers. The self-report survey method in current use has obvious limitations. It shares the same weaknesses of other self-report instruments (e.g., response biases) and has particular limitations with respect to the measurement of intelligence. More specifically, the CQ measure asks respondents to describe aspects of their CQ rather than to demonstrate it objectively. This is problematic. A more valid test of intelligence would not ask respondents if they have the knowledge or ability to solve a problem, it would require respondents to engage in problem solving! The development of alternative measurement techniques should be considered in future research.

The limitations of self-report measures raise additional issues for our research. The sole reliance on this format may increase the problem of common method variance and lead to inflated correlations. Despite research showing constructs that can be verified externally (e.g., through observer reports on personality and adjustment) are less prone to common method variance problems (Crampton & Wagner, 1994), this is an issue that deserves further attention.

A notable weakness of our current study is the cross-sectional design; testing mediation using measurements at only one point in time is problematic as it does not adequately address the mechanism of causality inherent in mediation models. Mediation theoretically involves one variable affecting another variable, which then leads to changes in a third variable. To test the causality of any mediation model properly, longitudinal designs would be needed. It would be necessary to measure personality dimensions at time 1, which would then predict changes in CQ at time 2, which, in turn, are associated with increased adjustment at time 3. It would also be worthwhile to measure both predictor and criterion variables at all time points to establish more firmly which are the causal variables. This is currently being undertaken in our research program. Alternatively, experimental designs could be used to test the causal mediation path more directly. If CQ is state-like, as maintained by Ang et al. (2006, 2007), it may be possible to manipulate its salience in experimental settings.

In conclusion, the theory and measurement of cultural intelligence is in its infancy. It holds promise for the future in offering a novel perspective on cross-cultural transition and adaptation, one that can potentially complement existing stress and coping and culture learning perspectives. It also potentially has strong areas of application in relation to selection and training of expatriate employees and international students. However, before the potential and promise can be realized, there are a number of obstacles to overcome and goals to be achieved. First, more sophisticated designs in CQ research should be undertaken. This refers particularly to longitudinal research to assess causal relationships and experimental studies with training interventions and the assessment of adaptation outcomes. Second, translating theory into measurement is a major challenge. The current measurement has demonstrated a robust structure and some evidence of predictive and incremental validity; however, it is subject to the same criticisms as other self-report measures of intelligence and may not always be sufficiently sensitive to test for complex relationships among key predictor and outcome variables. Finally, a critical mass of CQ research is needed, conducted by international scholars and collaborative teams, using a wide range of sojourning samples in diverse cultural settings. This chapter and others in the *Handbook on Cultural Intelligence* take one step toward achieving those goals.

REFERENCES

Ali, A., van der Zee, K.I., & Sanders, G. (2003). Determinants of intercultural adjustment among expatriates. *International Journal of Intercultural Relations, 27,* 563–580.

Ang, S., Van Dyne, L., & Koh, C. (2006). Personality correlates of the four-factor model of cultural intelligence. *Group and Organization Management, 31,* 100–123.

Ang, S., Van Dyne, L., Koh, C., & Ng, K.Y. (2004). The measurement of cultural intelligence. Working paper, presented at the Academy of Management Symposium on Cultural Intelligence in the 21st Century, New Orleans, LA.

Ang, S., Van Dyne, L., Koh, C., Ng, K., Templer, K.J., Tay, C., & Chandrasekar, N.A. (2007). Cultural intelligence: Its measurement and effects on cultural judgment and decision making, cultural adaptation, and task performance. *Management and Organization Review, 3,* 335–371.

Argyle, M. (1969). *Social interaction.* London: Methuen.

Ataca, B. (1996). Psychological and sociocultural adaptation of Turkish immigrants, Canadians and

Turks. Working paper, presented at the XIII Congress of the International Association for Cross-cultural Psychology, Montreal, Canada.

Aycan, Z. (1997). Expatriate adjustment as a multifaceted phenomenon: Individual and organizational level predictors. *International Journal of Human Resource Management, 8,* 434–456.

Bandura, A. (1977). *Social learning theory.* Englewood Cliffs, NJ: Prentice Hall.

Bandura, A. (1986). *Social foundations of thought and action: A social cognitive theory.* Englewood Cliffs, NJ: Prentice Hall.

Baron, R.M., & Kenny, D.A. (1986). The moderator-mediator distinction in social psychological research. *Journal of Personality and Social Psychology, 51,* 1173–1182.

Berry, J.W. (2006). Stress perspectives on acculturation. In D.L. Sam & J.W. Berry (Eds.), *Cambridge handbook of acculturation psychology* (pp. 43–57). Cambridge: Cambridge University Press.

Berry, J.W., & Sam, D.L. (1997). Acculturation and adaptation. In J.W. Berry, M.H. Segall, & C. Kagitçibasi (Eds.), *Handbook of cross-cultural psychology. Volume 3. Social behavior and applications* (pp. 291–326). Boston, MA: Allyn & Bacon.

Berry, J.W., & Ward, C. (2006). Commentary on "Redefining interactions across cultures and organizations." *Group and Organization Management, 31,* 64–77.

Black, J.S. (1988). Work role transitions: A study of American expatriate managers in Japan. *Journal of International Business Studies, 19,* 533–546.

Black, J.S., Gregersen, H.B., & Mendenhall, M. (1992). *Global assignments.* San Francisco, CA: Jossey-Bass.

Bochner, S. (1986). Coping with unfamiliar cultures: Adjustment or culture learning? *Australian Journal of Psychology, 38,* 347–358.

Browne, M.W., & Cudeck, R. (1993). Alternative ways of assessing model fit. In K.A. Boleen & J.S. Long (Eds.), *Testing structural equation models* (pp. 136–162). Newbury Park, CA: Sage.

Caligiuri, P. (2000). The Big Five personality characteristics as predictors of expatriate's desire to terminate the assignment and supervisor-rated performance. *Personnel Psychology, 53,* 67–88.

Clugston, M. (2000). The mediating effects of multidimensional commitment of job satisfaction and intent to leave. *Journal of Organizational Behavior, 21,* 477–486.

Crampton, S.M., & Wagner, J.A. (1994). Percept-percept inflation in micro-organizational research: An investigation on prevalence and effect. *Journal of Applied Psychology, 79,* 67–76.

Earley, P.C., & Ang, S. (2003). *Cultural intelligence: Individual interactions across cultures.* Stanford, CA: Stanford University Press.

Frone, M.R., Russell, M., & Cooper, M.L. (1992). Antecedents and outcomes of work-family conflict: Testing a model of the work-family interface. *Journal of Applied Psychology, 77,* 65–78.

Furnham, A., & Bochner, S. (1982). Social difficulty in a foreign culture. In S. Bochner (Ed.), *Cultures in contact: Studies in cross-cultural interactions* (pp. 161–198). Oxford: Pergamon Press.

Hu, L.T., & Bentler, P.M. (1999). Cut-off criteria for fit indexes in covariance structure analysis: Conventional criteria versus new alternatives. *Structural Equation Modeling, 6,* 1–55.

Iacobucci, D., Saldanha, N., & Deng, Z. (2007). A meditation on mediation: Evidence that structural equations models perform better than regressions. *Journal of Consumer Psychology, 17,* 139–153.

Kelley, C., & Meyers, J.E. (1989). *The Cross-Cultural Adaptability Inventory.* Minneapolis, MN: National Computer Systems.

Kurman, J., & Ronen-Eilon, C. (2004). Lack of knowledge of a culture's social axioms and adaptation difficulties among immigrants. *Journal of Cross-Cultural Psychology, 35,* 192–208.

Lazarus, R.S., & Folkman, S. (1984). *Stress, coping and appraisal.* New York: Springer.

Lee, C.-H., & Templer, K.J. (2003). Cultural intelligence assessment and measurement. In P.C. Earley & S. Ang (Eds.), *Cultural intelligence: Individual interactions across cultures* (pp. 185–208). Stanford, CA: Stanford University Press.

Leone, L., van der Zee, K.I., van Oudenhoven, J.P., Perugini, M., & Ercolani, A.P. (2005). The cross-cultural generalizability and validity of the Multicultural Personality Questionnaire. *Personality and Individual Differences, 38,* 1449–1462.

Marsh, H.W., Balla, J.R., & McDonald, R.P. (1988). Goodness of fit indexes in confirmatory factor analysis: The effect of sample size. *Psychological Bulletin, 103,* 391–410.

Masgoret, A.-M., & Ward, C. (2006). Culture learning approach to acculturation. In D.L. Sam & J.W. Berry (Eds.), *Cambridge handbook of acculturation psychology* (pp. 58–77). Cambridge: Cambridge University Press.

Matsumoto, D., & LeRoux, J.A. (2003). Measuring the psychological engine of intercultural adjustment: The intercultural adjustment potential scale (ICAPS). *International Journal of Intercultural Relations, 36,* 37–52.

Moorman, R.H. (1991). Relationship between organizational justice and organizational citizenship behaviors: Do fairness perceptions influence employee citizenship? *Journal of Applied Psychology, 76,* 845–855.

Netemeyer, R.G., Johnston, M.W., & Burton, S. (1990). Analysis of role conflict and role ambiguity in a structural equations framework. *Journal of Applied Psychology, 75,* 148–157.

Neto, F. (1995). Predictors of life satisfaction among second generation migrants. *Social Indicators Research, 35,* 93–116.

Ones, D.S., & Viswesvaran, C. (1997). Personality determinants in the prediction of aspects of expatriate job success. *New Approaches to Employee Management, 4,* 63–92.

Raven, J.C. (1998). *Raven's advanced progressive matrices manual.* London: Harcourt Assessment.

Sam, D.L. (1998). Predicting life satisfaction among adolescents from immigrant families in Norway. *Ethnicity and Health, 3,* 5–18.

Searle, W., & Ward, C. (1990). The prediction of psychological and sociocultural adjustment. *International Journal of Intercultural Relations, 14,* 449–464.

Sternberg, R.J. (1988). *The triarchic mind: A new theory of human intelligence.* New York: Cambridge University Press.

Sternberg, R. (2000). The concept of intelligence. In R.J. Sternberg (Ed.), *Handbook of intelligence* (pp. 3–15). New York: Cambridge University Press.

Taft, R., & Steinkalk, E. (1985). The adaptation of recent Soviet immigrants in Australia. In I. Reyes Lagunes & Y.H. Poortinga (Eds.), *From a different perspective: Studies of behavior across cultures* (pp. 19–28). Lisse, the Netherlands: Swets & Zeitlinger.

Templer, K., Tay, C., & Chandrasekar, N.A. (2006). Motivational cultural intelligence, realistic job preview, realistic living conditions preview and cross-cultural adjustment. *Group and Organization Management, 31,* 154–171.

van der Zee, K.I., & van Oudenhoven, J.P. (2000). The Multicultural Personality Questionnaire: A multidimensional instrument of multicultural effectiveness. *European Journal of Personality, 14,* 291–309.

van der Zee, K.I., & van Oudenhoven, J.P. (2001). The Multicultural Personality Questionnaire: Reliability and validity of self and other ratings of multicultural effectiveness. *Journal of Research in Personality, 35,* 278–288.

van der Zee, K.I., Zaal, J.N., & Piekstra, J. (2003). Validation of the Multicultural Personality Questionnaire in the context of personnel selection. *European Journal of Personality, 17,* 77–100.

van Oudenhoven, J.P., Mol, S., & van der Zee, K.I. (2003). A study of the adjustment of Western expatriates in Taiwan ROC with the Multicultural Personality Questionnaire. *Asian Journal of Social Psychology, 6,* 159–170.

van Oudenhoven, J.P., & van der Zee, K.I. (2002). Predicting multicultural effectiveness of international students: The Multicultural Personality Questionnaire. *International Journal of Intercultural Relations, 26,* 679–694.

Ward, C. (2004).Theories of culture contact and their implications for intercultural training and interventions. In D. Landis, J.M. Bennett & M.J. Bennett (Eds.), *Handbook of intercultural training* (3rd ed.) (pp. 185–216). Thousand Oaks, CA: Sage.

Ward, C., Berno, T., & Main, A. (2002). Can the CCAI predict sojourner adjustment? In P. Boski, F.J.R. van de Vijver, & A.M. Chodynicka (Eds). *New directions in cross-cultural psychology* (pp. 409–424). Warsaw, Poland: Polish Academy of Sciences.

Ward, C., Bochner, S., & Furnham, A. (2001). *The psychology of culture shock.* London: Routledge.
Ward, C., Fischer, R., Lam, F.S.Z., & Hall, L. (in press). The convergent, discriminant and incremental validity of the scores of a self-report measure of cultural intelligence. *Educational and Psychological Measurement.*
Ward, C., & Kennedy, A. (1993). Where's the culture in cross-cultural transition? Comparative studies of sojourner adjustment. *Journal of Cross-Cultural Psychology, 24,* 221–249.
Ward, C., & Kennedy, A. (1999). The measurement of sociocultural adaptation. *International Journal of Intercultural Relations, 23,* 659–677.
Ward, C., & Kennedy, A. (2001). Coping with cross-cultural transition. *Journal of Cross-Cultural Psychology, 32,* 636–642.
Ward, C., Leong, C.-H., & Low, M. (2004). Personality and sojourner adjustment: An exploration of the "Big Five" and the cultural fit proposition. *Journal of Cross-Cultural Psychology, 35,* 137–151.
Williams, L.J., & Hazer, J.T. (1986). Antecedents and consequences of satisfaction and commitment in turnover models: A reanalysis using latent variable structural equation methods. *Journal of Applied Psychology, 71,* 219–231.

PART III

CQ APPLIED TO MULTICULTURAL TEAMS

CHAPTER 11

Cultural Intelligence and Global Identity in Multicultural Teams

EFRAT SHOKEF AND MIRIAM EREZ

As part of the globalizing work environment, new forms of organizations have emerged, ranging from international to transnational organizations. These organizations require high levels of cross-national interdependence, and often the formation of multicultural teams (MCTs), nested within them. Members of MCTs hold diverse cultural identities, affecting their understanding, interpretation, and manner of responding to various situations (Erez & Earley, 1993). Employees who operate in this global multinational context are expected to develop shared common meanings, values, and codes of behaviors in order to effectively communicate with each other and coordinate their activities.

What helps global MCT members create the social cohesiveness that connects them together beyond the national cultures to which they belong? We focus on two possible factors that may facilitate team members' adaptation to MCTs and enhance MCT performance: (1) *Global identity,* defined as "an individual's sense of belonging to groups nested within the global work environment of multinational organizations (i.e., MCTs), and the expectations associated with the roles of working in such groups" (Shokef & Erez, 2006), and (2) *cultural intelligence* (CQ), defined as "a person's capability to deal effectively in situations characterized by cultural diversity" (Earley & Ang, 2003).

Both global identity and CQ aim at improving our understanding of the factors that can explain why some people succeed better than others in coping with situations involving cultural diversity. The objective of this chapter is to explore the relationship between global identity and CQ and their possible roles in MCTs. We begin with a brief discussion of the context of MCTs and a description of CQ and global identity. Then, we discuss their relationships and their possible contribution to team performance and present some preliminary results supporting our conceptual model.

MULTICULTURAL TEAMS

MCTs consist of "individuals from different cultures working together on activities that span national borders" (Snell, Snow, Davidson, & Hambrick, 1998). Multinational organizations recognize the need to leverage the diversity of their employees in order to sustain their competitive advantage in the global marketplace (Ely, 2004; Jehn & Bezrukova, 2004). Accordingly, they establish MCTs that pool global talents to meet organizational goals (Joshi, Labianca, & Caligiuri, 2002). MCTs are typically formed when specialized skills are possessed by experts who are situated in different places (Prieto & Arias, 1997). One advantage of MCTs is that they can be rearranged and reassigned to respond to shifting opportunities in global markets (Solomon, 1995) in order to meet ever-changing task requirements in the highly turbulent and dynamic global business environment (Jarvenpaa & Leidner, 1999; Mowshowitz, 1997).

Although MCTs and traditional teams share many characteristics, their team composition and communication patterns differ. MCTs must cope with additional challenges. An in-depth study of the challenges faced by 40 managers working in MCTs conducted by Behfar, Kern, and Brett (2006) revealed that, similar to any other team, MCTs cope with interpersonal tensions and disagreements about work pace, fairness in the workload distribution, and procedures for getting the work done. However, other issues related to cultural diversity, such as differences in work norms and behaviors, violation of respect and hierarchy, lack of common ground, language fluency, and ways of communicating, whether implicit or explicit, emerge. These additional challenges underscore the importance of knowing how to deal effectively with situations characterized by cultural diversity.

CULTURAL INTELLIGENCE

CQ is an individual's capability to deal effectively with situations characterized by cultural diversity (Earley & Ang, 2003). Individuals with high levels of CQ are expected to work more effectively on multinational workforces, and to adjust successfully to overseas assignments. CQ is a multidimensional concept comprising three dimensions: (1) mental—both metacognitive and cognitive; (2) motivational; and (3) behavioral. CQ is considered a malleable state that may change, as a result of cultural exposure, during training, modeling, mentoring, socialization, and other multicultural experiences (Earley & Ang, 2003). Indeed, Moynihan, Peterson, and Earley (2006) demonstrated a change in CQ over time in MCTs. In their study, conducted on 48 MCTs of MBA students who worked together on various assignments over a year, they showed that individuals' CQ levels were significantly higher after four months of working in MCTs compared to the members' initial CQ levels.

GLOBAL IDENTITY

Fundamental questions such as "Who am I?" and "Where do I belong?" reflect an individual's self-identity (Stryker & Burke, 2000; Tajfel, 1981; Triandis, 1989). This identity is composed of the personal and social selves, and conveys the individual's awareness of both entities (Stryker & Burke, 2000; Tajfel, 1981). The personal self contains notions about one's own attitudes, traits, feelings, and behaviors, while the social self contains affiliations and group memberships (Trafimow, Triandis, & Goto, 1991; Triandis, 1989). Selves are created within contexts and take into account the values and norms of the others likely to participate in these contexts (Oyserman, 2004).

Working in the global work environment provides individuals with additional answers to these questions of "Who am I?" For example, people may define themselves as "an employee of multinational organization X," "a world traveler," "a cosmopolitan," "a member of multicultural team Y," and so on. These possible answers and internalized meanings and expectations associated with being members of various groups operating in the global work environment (such as working in a multinational organization or in MCTs nested within them) create an identity related to this group membership. Hence, global identity is defined as the individual's sense of belonging to, and identification with, groups (such as MCTs) operating in the global work environment of multinational organizations (Shokef & Erez, 2006).

In order for an individual to develop a social identity, such as a global identity, related to a specific group, this group should have a psychological meaning to the individual (Tajfel, 1978). This meaning does not necessarily have to include physical interaction with any of its members. In a study conducted on virtual groups, McKenna and Bargh (1998) showed that participation in a virtual newsgroup had significant effects on the transformation of an individual's social identity. Increased involvement led to increased salience of the virtual group, followed by increased self-acceptance of the group identity. Thus, membership in MCTs, which are often to some extent virtual (Jarvenpaa & Leidner, 1999), can provide a group identity.

Being part of a global work team with team members of diverse cultural backgrounds is different from being a member of a culturally homogeneous team to which most people belong in their local cultural settings. A person may hold multiple identities that reflect membership in multiple groups (Stryker & Burke, 2000; Tajfel & Turner, 1979). Individuals in the global work environment often develop a bicultural identity that combines a local identity with a global identity, but the two identities do not necessarily compete with each other (Arnett, 2002). Rather, individuals assume the relevant identity depending on the situation.

A person's global identity, local identity, and other forms of identity become salient in different situations depending on the level of commitment to a particular social group instigated by the situation. Once affiliation with a particular group becomes salient, the corresponding identity, whether global or local, dominates the other identities (Stryker, 1980). Level of commitment is influenced by the cost of not expressing identity-based roles and behaviors relevant to the salient social network (Stryker & Burke, 2000). In the work environment, employees respond to role expectations in line with the most salient identity in a given situation. When a work situation stimulates two identities that compete with each other, the one with the stronger commitment determines the behavioral responses (Stryker & Burke, 2000). In homogenous, same-culture teams, a local identity is more likely to be dominant while, in contrast, working in an MCT should evoke global identity.

Recent empirical studies repeatedly find global identity and local identity to be independent of each other (Cohavi, Erez, & Shokef, 2007; Shokef & Erez, 2006; Shokef, Erez, & De-Haan, 2007). The development of global identity is related to a number of factors (Cohavi et al., 2007). First, global identity is related to the individual's level of involvement in both global work activities, such as working with others from different cultures, and in global nonwork activities, such as having friends from different cultural backgrounds and leisure travel to other countries. Second, similar to Ang, Van Dyne, and Koh (2006), who found that openness to experience was a crucial personality characteristic for functioning in culturally diverse environments, global identity is also related to the individual's level of "openness" as a personal disposition (Cohavi et al., 2007). This relationship was mediated by personal involvement in nonwork-related global activities, such as surfing the Internet. Finally, global identity is related to two biographic characteristics: the number of languages spoken by an individual and the number of countries lived in for more than one year. Local identity is not related to any of the above characteristics. Yet, local identity is related to the individual's level of embeddedness, reflecting the extent to which individuals become part of their work surroundings and their community (Mitchel, Holtom, Lee, Sablynski, & Erez, 2001), which supports the differentiation between global and local identities (Cohavi et al., 2007). These findings suggest that the sense of global identity can develop not only in relation to work-related experiences, but also on the basis of personal dispositions and life experiences with regard to being part of the global environment.

Global identity is stronger for individuals working in global organizations, compared to those working in international organizations and local, domestic organizations (Cohavi et al., 2007). Furthermore, employees working for multinational organizations who had strong global identities attributed greater importance to global work values than others (Shokef et al., 2007). Most likely, this relationship between global identity and global work values is reciprocal: global identity influences acceptance of global work values, which reciprocally strengthens global identity. Employees working in multinational organizations and MCTs develop a sense of belonging to these groups and learn their role expectations from members operating in the global work environment and from the cultural values that dominate the global work environment. Reciprocally, individuals endorsing the values of the global work culture, such as openness to diversity, are more likely to feel at ease in multicultural groups, and to develop a sense of a global identity. Findings from a study conducted on 69 MCTs of MBA students who participated in a four-week joint virtual project showed that working in MCTs increased the level of participants' global identity over time. Nonetheless, it did not lead to any change in the individuals' local identities (Shokef & Erez, 2006).

THE RELATIONSHIP BETWEEN INDIVIDUAL GLOBAL IDENTITY AND CQ IN MCTS

It is often suggested that familiarity or experiences with other cultures may temper misunderstandings (Martin & Hammer, 1989). Indeed, personal involvement in both work and nonwork global activities has been found to be related to global identity (Cohavi et al., 2007). Moynihan, Peterson, and Earley (2006) demonstrated that the individual's level of CQ increases over time; Shokef and Erez (2006) showed that global identity increases over time. These findings suggest that exposure to the global work environment, with its multicultural nature, enhances the development of individual CQ and global identity. They also indicate that both global identity and CQ are shaped by social learning processes and by the opportunity to form a shared meaning system for understanding and overcoming cultural differences. Therefore, we propose:

P1: Working in MCTs enhances the development of CQ and global identity.

What type of relationship exists between global identity and CQ? We refer to global identity and CQ as independent constructs. While global identity focuses on the sense of belonging to groups nested within the global work environment (Shokef & Erez, 2006), CQ is the individual's capability to deal with situations characterized by cultural diversity (Earley & Ang, 2003). According to social identity theory, the individual's identity affects the way he or she thinks, feels, and behaves in all social domains (Meal & Ashforth, 1992; Tajfel & Turner, 1979). One belongs to specific groups prior to accepting the groups' common behaviors, norms, and values, and before developing the ability to deal with these groups. Yet other theories suggest that acceptance of a group's values influences identification with this group (O'Reilly, Chatman, & Caldwell, 1991), and that, through a process of socialization, the group's values are internalized and represented in the self (Erez & Earley, 1993). Once the group values are represented in the self, the individual develops a sense of belonging to the group and identifies with it. These two approaches can represent a reciprocal relationship. When employees work in MCTs, which are groups nested within the global work environment, they develop a sense of belonging to the MCT and learn what is expected of them as part of their role as employees in a particular global environment. Since the global work environment is multicultural in nature (Miroshnik, 2002; Trefry, 2006), individuals who develop a sense of global identity reflecting their belongingness to the MCT are likely to encounter multicultural situations that lead to the development of CQ. Reciprocally, individuals experienced in dealing effectively in multicultural situations are more likely to join multicultural groups. Becoming part of such groups leads to the development of a sense of belonging to these groups, that is, a global identity. The sense of belonging to an MCT may facilitate the development of CQ. In turn, knowing how to effectively deal with others from various cultures enhances one's global identity. Therefore, we propose:

P2: The relationship between CQ and global identity is reciprocal: Individuals with high CQ are more likely to develop a global identity when working in MCTs. Reciprocally, individuals with a strong global identity are more likely to develop CQ when working in MCTs.

While global identity should be related to all four facets of CQ, we expect stronger relations between global identity and motivational CQ, compared to the other CQ dimensions. Motivational CQ refers to an individual's drive, interest, and competence in learning about and functioning in a situation characterized by cultural differences (Ang, Van Dyne, Koh, Ng, Templer, Tay, & Chandrasekar, 2007; Earley & Ang, 2003). Those with high motivational CQ are expected to be confident in their ability to engage in cross-cultural interactions and should experience intrinsic satisfaction from involvement in culturally diverse settings (Ang et al., 2007; Earley & Ang, 2003). Motivational CQ has been conceptualized as a specific form of self-efficacy and intrinsic motivation in cross-cultural situations (Ang et al., 2007, Bandura, 2002; Earley & Ang, 2003). In terms of the relationship between motivational CQ and global identity, once an individual feels confident about the ability to engage in cross-cultural interactions, he or she should experience intrinsic satisfaction from being in culturally diverse settings. This will increase the opportunities of being a member of groups operating in the global environment, such as MCTs, and developing a sense of belongingness to these groups—a global identity.

Reciprocally, social identities, such as a global identity, provide meaningful and significant self-references through which individuals perceive themselves and the world around them (Bar-Tal, 1998). Individuals' initial motivation is to enhance their own self-esteem and positive self-concept. Thus they wish to belong to groups that compare favorably with and are distinct from other groups (Tajfel & Turner, 1979). Hence, individuals who have a global identity are more likely to be interested in learning about and functioning in situations characterized by cultural differences. They seek and enjoy situations that are culturally different, as defined by motivational CQ. While high metacognitive CQ conveys awareness and knowledge, high motivational CQ is defined in dynamic terms of willingness and intentions, congruent with the meaning of global identity as the readiness to belong to a global multicultural work group. The behavioral dimension of CQ is the outcome of the willingness to be part of the multicultural group. Therefore, we propose:

P3: Global identity will be more strongly related to motivational CQ, compared to the other CQ dimensions.

GLOBAL IDENTITY AND CQ AT THE TEAM LEVEL: CAN THEY ENHANCE MCT PERFORMANCE?

One of the challenges faced by organizations operating in the global environment is the creation of MCTs that work effectively (Montoya-Weiss, Massey, & Song, 2001). The highly diverse nature of MCTs may either facilitate or inhibit group performance. On the one hand, the MCTs' cultural diversity enables a broad range of perspectives, skills, and insights, which can increase the group's creativity and problem-solving capabilities, thereby enhancing performance (Cox & Blake, 1991). On the other hand, MCTs can also have high levels of conflict and misunderstanding (Armstrong & Cole, 1995; Behfar et al., 2006; Jehn, Northcraft, & Neale, 1999; Joshi et al., 2002; Salk & Brannen, 2000).

A number of recent studies support the notion that both global identity and CQ can enhance performance at the individual level. Ang et al. (2007) found that among international executives and foreign professionals, CQ significantly explained performance and adjustment, beyond the effects of demographic characteristics and general cognitive ability. In their findings, high mental CQ (metacognitive and cognitive) predicted cultural judgment and decision making, high motivational CQ and behavioral CQ predicted cultural adaptation, and high metacognitive CQ and behavioral CQ predicted task performance in intercultural settings. Templer, Tay, and Chandrasekar (2006) found that high motivational CQ predicted cross-cultural adjustment of foreign professionals, over and above pre–job assignment interventions, such as realistic job previews and realistic living condition previews.

At the team level, Moynihan et al. (2006) showed that the mean CQ level of MCTs composed of MBA students, measured at the formation of the MCTs, was positively correlated with the levels of group cohesion and trust, and with the team's performance, three months into the joint project. A study conducted on MBA students from seven different countries who worked in virtual MCTs on a joint class project resulted in similar findings (Shokef & Erez, 2006). Specifically, the mean level of global identity prior to working in virtual MCTs affected (a) team performance, (b) satisfaction from working with the team, and (c) degree of learning from the experience of working in an MCT. These empirical findings suggest that CQ was related to global identity, and therefore indicated that both high levels of CQ and a strong global identity shared by the MCT members can increase MCT effectiveness.

P4: High mean team CQ and mean team global identity will enhance the performance of MCTs.

AN EMPIRICAL ILLUSTRATION

A recent study conducted by the authors aimed at examining the effects of working in MCTs on global identity and CQ, and the relationship between them. Participants in this study were 191 MBA students from five countries: Israel (n = 35), Hong Kong (n = 35), Spain (n = 27), South Korea (n = 24), and the United States (n = 70). These students participated in a cross-school academic project in which they worked in 55 virtual MCTs on a joint project for four weeks. The project assigned to all teams was to develop guidelines for an expatriate visiting a host country selected by the team members. In addition to the guidelines, the teams were also asked to analyze the difficulties that managers from their own countries might encounter while visiting the host country, to compare the challenges faced by each of them as a native of his/her own culture, and reflect on their team processes. As each team member was located in a different country, they communicated using computer mediated tools, such as e-mails and chats. The final product of each team was a PowerPoint presentation. The average mean evaluation score served as the team performance measure. Data on team members' characteristics, including global identity and CQ, were collected by means of electronic questionnaires that were administered twice—before and after the beginning of the project. Here, we present some initial findings at the individual level of analysis that relate to some of our propositions.

Global and local identities were measured using an eight-item measure developed by Erez and Gati (2004; see also Cohavi et al., 2007). Each scale included four items, for example: global identity, "I see myself as part of the global international community," local identity, "I see myself as part of my society (Israeli, American, Korean, etc.)." These were developed to be parallel in content, each referring to the global/local environment. Confirmatory factor analysis (CFA) confirmed that global and local identities are independent factors: Time 1: $\chi^2(16) = 34.44$, $p < 0.01$; root mean square error of approximation (RMSEA) = 0.077; non-normed fit index (NNFI) = 0.97; comparative fit index (CFI) = 0.98. The internal consistency reliability estimate for global identity was 0.88 at time 1, and 0.90 at time 2, and for local identity 0.88 at time 1, and 0.90 at time 2. CQ was measured using Ang et al.'s (2007) CQ scale (CQS), which includes 20 items. CFA, conducted using LISREL 8.8, confirmed the four CQ factors with acceptable fit levels at both measurement points: Time 1: $\chi^2(161) = 282.31$, $p < 0.001$; RMSEA = 0.062; NNFI = 0.98; CFI = 0.98). The internal consistency reliability estimates of the four factors at time 1 were 0.91, 0.91, 0.91, 0.90, and at time 2 were, 0.89, 0.90, 0.89, 0.91 for metacognitive, cognitive, motivational, and behavioral CQ, respectively.

Table 11.1 summarizes the means and standard deviations for the four CQ factors, global identity, local identity, and the correlations among them, at both time points. As can be observed based on the correlations in Table 11.1, and further confirmed by CFA analysis, global identity, local identity, and the four CQ factors clearly emerged as distinct factors at both time points: Time 1: $\chi^2(328) = 524.99$, $p < 0.001$; RMSEA = 0.056; NNFI = 0.97; CFI = 0.98; Time 2: $\chi^2(328) = 554.88$, $p < 0.001$; RMSEA = 0.060; NNFI = 0.97; CFI = 0.97).

Results of Hierarchical Linear Modeling (HLM) analysis, with "team" as the random effect while controlling for pre-project individual levels of global identity and CQ, provide initial support for the first proposition. As can be seen in Table 11.1, and illustrated in Figure 11.1, there was a significant increase in participants' level of global identity, metacognitive CQ, motivational CQ, and behavioral CQ as a result of their experience in working on their multicultural projects in the MCTs. No changes were observed for local identity and cognitive CQ. Local identity was already high when the students began working on the MCTs. Furthermore, a consistent level of local identity is to be expected, since working on an MCT does not evoke one's local identity. The relatively low and stable scores of cognitive CQ at Times 1 and 2 may be partially explained by the content of items that focus on knowledge about economic systems, religion, and rules of languages, and not on managerial practices that were the focus of the multicultural team project. The type of cultural knowledge measured by Ang et al.'s (2007) cognitive CQ scale was not familiar to most of the students participating in our short academic program and for some of them this was their first experience working in MCTs.

Preliminary results based on HLM analysis, with "team" as the random effect, provide initial support for the second proposition. They show that global identity measured at time 1 affects all four CQ factors as measured at time 2, and that reciprocally, all four CQ factors as measured at time 1 affect individual global identity as measured at time 2. Finally, the correlations between the six factors provide initial support for the third

Table 11.1

Means, Standard Deviations, and Correlations

	Time 1		Time 2							
	Mean	SD	Mean	SD	1	2	3	4	5	6
1. Global identity	4.72	1.24	5.14	1.14		.08	.37***	.34***	.43***	.24**
2. Local identity	5.19	1.18	5.15	1.24	.10		.30***	.02	.12*	.10
3. Metacognitive CQ	4.95	0.99	5.19	0.93	.44***	.03		.38***	.59***	.52***
4. Cognitive CQ	3.85	1.17	3.74	1.14	.40***	−.02	.53***		.40***	.39***
5. Motivational CQ	5.24	1.06	5.32	1.00	.55***	.13*	.55***	.51***		.53***
6. Behavioral CQ	4.73	1.13	4.86	1.15	.27***	.06	.63***	.49***	.45***	

Note: Correlations between variables at time 1 are below the diagonal; correlations at time 2 are above the diagonal.

**p* <.10; ***p* <.05; ****p* <.01

Figure 11.1 **Change in Levels of Global Identity and Cultural Intelligence during the Project**

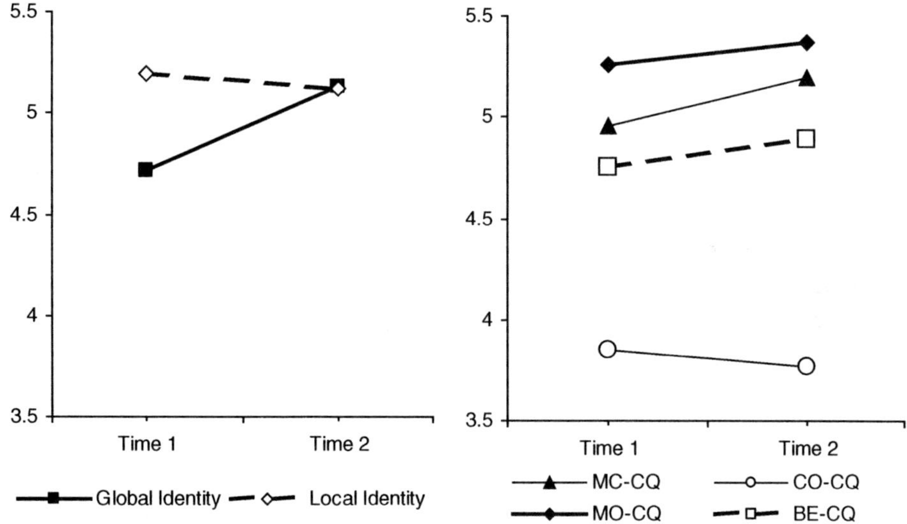

Abbreviations: MC-CQ, metacognitive CQ; CO-CQ, cognitive CQ; MO-CQ, motivational CQ; BE-CQ, behavioral CQ.

proposition according to which the relationship between global identity and motivational CQ (time 1 pre-project, r = 0.55; time 2 post-project, r = 0.43) is stronger compared to the relationship between global identity and the other CQ factors. Nonetheless, further examination is needed to determine whether the effect of global identity and CQ is reciprocal or whether there is one dominant causal path.

We have yet to test our fourth proposition concerning the relation of global identity and CQ at the team level and MCT performance. Conceptualizing both global identity and CQ at the team level is not trivial and requires further thought and examination (Ng & Earley, 2006). Both concepts were developed at the individual level and aggregation as a mean score may not be appropriate for conceptualizing them at a higher level of analysis.

SUMMARY

The objective of this chapter was to take an initial step in exploring the relationship between the constructs of CQ and global identity. Both concepts have emerged from the global multicultural work environment and are being used to gain a better understanding of why some people are more successful than others in coping with situations involving cultural diversity. This chapter provides an initial step in the examination of the relationship between these constructs and MCTs as well as their relevance to each other. Global identity, local identity, and the four CQ factors emerged as distinct factors supporting the notion that global identity and CQ are different yet related concepts. The strongest link between the two concepts at the individual level appears to be between global identity and motivational CQ. The important finding of a significant increase in participants' level of global identity, metacognitive CQ, motivational CQ, and behavioral CQ as a result of their experience working together in MCTs, demonstrates the benefits of getting involved in a multicultural team context for development of global identity and CQ. This suggests that adaptation to the global work context is a matter of learning and that opportunities to work in interdependent multicultural teams that have a common goal can overcome or reduce cross-cultural differences in norms and behaviors. Hence, facilitating the development of employee's global identity and CQ may help them adapt to work in global work environments.

FUTURE DIRECTIONS

The appropriate way to conceptualize both global identity and CQ at the team level is not yet clear. Often, team-level characteristics are an emergent phenomenon that originates in the characteristics of individuals, amplified by their interactions and manifested as a higher level collective phenomenon (Klein & Kozlowski, 2000). As previously discussed in relation to CQ (Moynihan et al., 2006), there are two major concerns when conceptualizing individual level constructs at the team level: (1) whether it is appropriate to conceptualize the individual-level constructs at the team level and if so, (2) what is the appropriate approach for conceptualizing and operationalizing CQ and global identity at the team level? One possibility is the *composition* model according to which each of the individual team members contributes to the collective pool of resources in proportion to the strength of his or her particular attribute (LePine, 2003, 2005; Klein & Kozlowski, 2000). In these cases, the team-level characteristic is typically represented by the mean score of all team members on a specific attribute (LePine, 2003). The disadvantage of the composition model is that it may mask the effect of the most competent team members (Arbel, Erez, Weiss, & Kroll, 2005; Miron-Spektor, Erez, & Naveh, 2006). Both Moynihan et al. (2006) and Shokef and Erez (2006) in their studies of CQ and global identity relative to team performance used the composition model, testing the effect of mean CQ and mean global identity, respectively, on performance. An alternative model to the composition model is the *compilation* approach, which views a higher-level phenomenon as a complex combination of diverse lower-level contributions (Klein & Kozlowski, 2000). In this case, the scores of the most capable team members may better capture the competence of the team (Barrick, Stewart, Neubert, & Mount, 1998), assuming that this leading member can carry the team to its highest performance level (Arbel et al., 2005; Barry & Stewart, 1997; West & Anderson, 1996).

Based on the definition of CQ and global identity, we suggest that the composition approach may be more appropriate for conceptualizing global identity at the team level, while the compilation approach may be more appropriate for conceptualizing CQ at the team level. Our reasons are as follows: CQ is the individual's capability to cope with situations characterized by cultural diversity (Earley & Ang, 2003). In the context of MCTs and especially newly formed ones, team members can vary greatly in their level of CQ. In such a case, we suggest that the members with the knowledge, motivation, and behavioral repertoire of coping with cross-cultural and multicultural situations can help the team rise above possible misunderstandings and miscommunications. Naturally, even a few MCT members who have high CQ can contribute significantly to a MCT performance, and the more members with high CQ, the better the team performance will be.

Global identity is derived from a sense of belonging to an MCT, and the individual's identity is based on social identification. Similarly to CQ, a small number of team members with a strong global identity may enhance team performance. Yet we suggest that perhaps the more appropriate way to conceptualize global identity at the team level is through the composition model, because if only a small number of team members have a sense of group belongingness the rest of the team members may not share the same understanding needed for effective team performance. A shared team global identity may help overcome barriers rising from cultural diversity by creating the common ground for a shared understanding. We differentiate between individual global identity and a shared team global identity. Individual global identity may enhance team performance by evoking cognitions, motivations, and behaviors adaptive to cross-cultural and multicultural situations, as captured by CQ. Yet a team global identity can enhance team performance by providing the team with a shared sense of belonging that facilitates the emergence of a shared meaning system and the formation of a common foundation of values, norms, and appropriate behaviors necessary for effective team performance. A shared meaning system is an important factor in overcoming many challenges in MCTs, allowing team members to understand each other and interpret each other's intentions and behaviors (Earley & Gibson, 2002). For example, Klimoski and Mohammed (1994) found that developing a team-shared mental model, which is a shared psychological representation of the team's environment, increased the propensity of members to trust each other and therefore improved team performance.

Members of MCTs have three cultural systems (Shokef & Erez, 2006): (1) a global work culture, (2) a hybrid culture, and (3) a national culture. The global work culture (Erez & Shokef, 2008; Shokef & Erez, 2006; Shokef et al., 2007) represents the most macro level of culture formed above and beyond national cultures, and is represented by shared team global identity (Erez & Gati, 2004). It is defined as the shared understanding of the visible rules, regulations, and behaviors, and the deeper values and ethics of the global work context (Shokef & Erez, 2006). Individuals with a strong global identity attribute greater importance to global work values such as "competitive performance orientation," "customer orientation," and "openness to cultural diversity," compared to individuals with a weaker global identity (Shokef et al., 2007). The second cultural system that MCT members have is that of a hybrid culture, often referred to as team synergy (Adler, 1991) or a third culture (Casmir, 1992). A hybrid culture emerges on the basis of shared and enacted mutual interactions among team members (Earley & Gibson, 2002). It serves as the immediate social glue, enabling team interdependence (Earley & Gibson, 2002; Earley & Mosakowski, 2000). The formation of a third culture seems to be instrumental to within-group adaptation, but it does not replace the need to adapt to the external global work context, outside the team boundaries. Finally, the national culture of each team member conveys the differences rather than the similarities among team members. However, with the support of the global value of "openness to cultural diversity," group members' identification with their respective national cultures enables them to preserve their self-definition beyond their MCT work context (Shokef & Erez, 2006).

CQ and global identity are conceptualized using the etic approach, applying across specific cultural circumstances (Ng & Earley, 2006) and providing a sense of belonging to diverse cultural environments. Nevertheless, as such, their application and examination in MCTs is yet to be elucidated. The meaning of CQ (Ang et al., 2007; Berry & Ward, 2006; Brislin, Worthley, & MacNab, 2006) and of global identity may very well differ across different cultures. Therefore, there is a need to validate the measurement equivalence of global identity and of the four factors of CQ across different cultures. This may have methodological implications for the applicability of aggregating these constructs to the team level beyond culturally diverse members. Finally, further complications that need to be considered when studying global identity and CQ are introduced by the structure of most MCTs, which are geographically dispersed and use virtual communication and computer-mediated technologies.

ACKNOWLEDGMENT

This research was supported by a grant from the Center of Cultural Intelligence at the Nanyang Business School, Singapore. We thank Alon Lisak for his help in data collection. We thank Simon Dolan, Mannsso Shin, Leigh Thompson, Linn Van Dyne, and Jane Yang for their participation in the multicultural team project in which the empirical data were collected and which provided the basis for our theory development.

REFERENCES

Adler, N.J. (1991). *International dimensions of organizational behavior* (2nd ed.). Boston, MA: PWS-Kent.

Ang, S., Van Dyne, L., & Koh, C. (2006). Personality correlates of the four-factor model of cultural intelligence. *Group and Organization Management, 31,* 100–123.

Ang, S., Van Dyne, L., Koh, C., Ng, K.Y., Templer, K.J., Tay, C., & Chandrasekar, N.A. (2007). Cultural intelligence: Its measurement and effects on cultural judgment and decision making, cultural adaptation, and task performance. *Management and Organization Review, 3,* 335–371.

Arbel, I., Erez, M., Weiss, M.P., & Kroll, E. (2005). Effects of team composition and team processes on the conceptual design of new products. Working paper, presented as part of a symposium on "Team innovation: effects of leadership, team composition, structure and processes" at the 2005 Academy of Management Annual Meeting, Hawaii.

Armstrong, D.J., & Cole, P. (1995). Managing distance and differences in geographically distributed work groups. In S.E. Jackson & M.N. Ruderman (Eds.), *Diversity in work teams: Research paradigms for changing work place* (pp. 187–215). Washington, DC: American Psychological Association.

Arnett, J.J. (2002). The psychology of globalization. *American Psychologist, 57,* 774–783.

Bandura, A. (2002). Social cognitive theory in cultural context. *Applied Psychology: An International Review, 51,* 269–290.

Bar-Tal, D. (1998). *Societal beliefs of ethos: A social psychological analysis of society.* London: Sage.

Barrick, M.R., Stewart, G.L., Neubert, M.J., & Mount, M.K. (1998). Relating member ability and personality to work-team processes and team effectiveness. *Journal of Applied Psychology, 83,* 377–391.

Barry, B., & Stewart, G.L. (1997). Composition, process, and performance in self-managed groups: The role of personality. *Journal of Applied Psychology, 82,* 62–78.

Behfar, K., Kern, M., & Brett, J. (2006). Managing challenges in multicultural teams. In E.A.M. Mannix, M. Neale, & Y. Chen (Eds.), *Research on managing groups and teams: National culture and groups. Volume 9* (pp. 239–269). Oxford: Elsevier Science Press.

Berry, J.W., and Ward, C. (2006). Commentary on "Refining interactions across cultures and organizations." *Group and Organization Management, 31,* 64–77.

Brislin, R., Worthley, R., and MacNab, B. (2006). Cultural intelligence: Understanding behaviors that serve people's goals. *Group and Organization Management, 31,* 40–55.

Casmir, R. (1992). Third culture building: A paradigm shift for international and intercultural communication. *Communication Yearbook, 16,* 407–428.

Cohavi, I., Erez, M., & Shokef, E. (2007). Antecedents to the development of a global identity. Working paper, Technion, Haifa, Israel.

Cox, T.H. Jr., & Blake, S. (1991). Managing cultural diversity: Implications for organizational competitiveness. *Academy of Management Executive, 5,* 45–56.

Earley, P.C., & Ang, S. (2003). *Cultural intelligence: Individual interactions across cultures.* Palo Alto, CA: Stanford University Press.

Earley, P.C., & Gibson, C.B. (2002). *Multinational work teams: A new perspective.* Mahwah, NJ: Lawrence Erlbaum Associates.

Earley, P.C., & Mosakowski, E. (2000). Creating hybrid team cultures: An empirical test of transnational team functioning. *Academy of Management Journal, 43,* 26–49.

Ely, R.J. (2004). A field study of group diversity, participation in diversity education programs, and performance. *Journal of Organizational Behavior, 25,* 755–780.

Erez, M., & Earley, P.C. (1993). *Culture, self-identity, and work.* Oxford: Oxford University Press.

Erez, M., & Gati, E. (2004). A dynamic, multi-level model of culture: From the micro-level of the individual to the macro-level of a global culture. *Applied Psychology: An International Review, 53,* 583–598.

Erez, M., & Shokef, E. (2008). The culture of global organizations. In P. Smith, M. Peterson, & D. Thomas (Eds), *Handbook of cross-cultural management research.* Thousand Oaks, CA: Sage.

Jarvenpaa, S.L., & Leidner, D.E. (1999). Communication and trust in global virtual teams. *Organization Science, 10,* 791–815.

Jehn, K.A., & Bezrukova, K. (2004). A field study of group diversity. Workgroup context, and performance. *Journal of Organizational Behavior, 25,* 703–729.

Jehn, K.A., Northcraft G.B., & Neale, M.A. (1999). Why differences make a difference: A field study of diversity, conflict, and performance in workgroups. *Administrative Science Quarterly, 44,* 741–763.

Joshi, A., Labianca, G., & Caligiuri, P.M. (2002). Getting along long distance: Understanding conflict in a multinational team through network analysis. *Journal of World Business, 37,* 277–284.

Klein, K.J. & Kozlowski, S.W.J. (2000). *Multilevel theory, research, and methods in organizations: Foundations, extensions and new directions.* San Francisco, CA: Jossey-Bass.

Klimoski, R., & Mohammed, S. (1994). Team mental models: Construct or metaphor? *Journal of Management, 20,* 403–437.

LePine, J.A. (2003). Team adaptation and postchange performance: Effects of team composition in terms of members' cognitive ability and personality. *Journal of Applied Psychology, 88,* 27–39.

LePine, J.A. (2005). Adaptation of teams in response to unforeseen change: Effects of goal difficulty and team composition in terms of cognitive ability and goal orientation. *Journal of Applied Psychology, 90,* 1153–1167.

Martin, J.N., & Hammer, M.R. (1989). Behavioral categories of intercultural communication competences: Everyday communicators' perceptions. *International Journal of Intercultural Relations, 13,* 303–332.

McKenna, K.Y.A., & Bargh, J.A. (1998). Interpersonal relations and group processes: Coming out in the age of the Internet: Identity demarginalization through virtual group participation. *Journal of Personality and Social Psychology, 75,* 681–698.

Meal, F.A., & Ashforth, B.E. (1992). Alumni and their alma mater: A partial test of the reformulated model of organizational identification. *Journal of Organizational Behavior, 13,* 103–123.

Miron-Spektor, E., Erez, M., & Naveh, E. (2006). The personal attributes that enhance individual versus team innovation. Presented at the Academy of Management Annual Meeting. Atlanta, GA.

Miroshnik, V. (2002). Culture and international management: A review. *The Journal of Management Development, 21,* 521–544.

Mitchel, T.R., Holtom, B.C., Lee, W.T., Sablynski, J.S., & Erez, M. (2001). Why people stay: Using job embeddedness to predict voluntary turnover. *Academy of Management Journal, 44,* 1102–1122.

Montoya-Weiss, M.M., Massey, A.P., & Song, M. (2001). Getting it together: Temporal coordination and conflict management in global virtual teams. *Academy of Management Journal, 44,* 1251–1262.

Mowshowitz, A. (1997). Virtual organization. *Communications of the ACM, 40* (9), 30–37.

Moynihan, L.M., Peterson, R.S., & Earley, P.C. (2006). Cultural intelligence and the multicultural team experience: Does the experience of working in a multinational team improve cultural intelligence? In E.A.M. Mannix, M. Neale, & Y. Chen (Eds.), *Research on managing groups and teams: National culture and groups. Volume 9* (pp. 279–304). Oxford: Elsevier Science Press.

Ng, K.Y., & Earley, P.C. (2006). Culture + intelligence: Old constructs, new frontiers. *Group and Organization Management, 31,* 4–19.

O'Reilly, C.A., Chatman, J., & Caldwell, D.F. (1991). People and organizational culture: A profile comparison approach to assessing person-organization fit. *Academy of Management Journal, 14,* 487–516.

Oyserman, D. (2004). Self concept and identity. In M.B. Brewer, & M. Hewstone (Eds.), *Self and social identity* (pp. 5–24). Boston, MA: Blackwell Publishing.

Prieto, J.M., & Arias, R.M. (1997). Those things yonder are no giants, but decision makers in international teams. In P.C. Earley & M. Erez (Eds.), *New perspectives on industrial/organizational psychology* (pp. 410–445). San Francisco, CA: The New Lexington Press.

Salk, J.E., & Brannen, M.Y. (2000). National culture, networks, and individual influence in a multinational management team. *Academy of Management Journal, 43,* 191–202.

Shokef, E., & Erez, M. (2006). Global work culture and global identity, as a platform for a shared understanding in multicultural teams. In E.A.M Mannix, M. Neale, & Y. Chen (Eds.), *Research in managing groups and teams: National culture and groups. Volume 9* (pp. 325–352). Oxford: Elsevier Science Press.

Shokef, E., Erez, M., & De-Haan, U. (2007). Global work culture: Developing a new measure of organizational culture of multinational organizations. Working paper, Technion, Haifa, Israel.

Snell, S.A., Snow, C.C., Davidson, S., & Hambrick D.C. (1998). Designing and supporting transnational teams: The human resource agenda. *Human Resource Management, 37,* 147–158

Solomon, C.M. (1995). Global teams: The ultimate collaboration. *Personnel Journal, 74(9),* 49–58.

Stryker, S. (1980). *Symbolic interactionism: A social structural version.* Palo Alto, CA: Benjamin/Cummings.

Stryker, S., & Burke, P.J. (2000). The past, present, and future of an identity theory. *Social Psychology Quarterly, 63,* 284–297.

Tajfel, H. (1978). *Differentiation between social groups.* London: Academic Press.

Tajfel, H. (1981). *Human groups and social categories: Studies in social psychology.* Cambridge: Cambridge University Press.

Tajfel, H., & Turner, J.C. (1979). An integrative theory of intergroup conflict. In W.G. Austin & S. Worchel (Eds.), *The social psychology of group relations* (pp. 33–47). Monterey, CA: Brooks-Cole.

Templer, K.J., Tay, C., & Chandrasekar, N.A. (2006). Motivational cultural intelligence, realistic job preview, realistic living conditions preview, and cross-cultural adjustment. *Group and Organization Management, 31,* 154–173.

Trafimow, D., Triandis, H.C., & Goto, S.G. (1991). Some tests of the distinction between the private and the collective self. *Journal of Personality and Social Psychology, 60,* 649–655.

Trefry, M.G. (2006). A double-edged sword: Organizational culture in multicultural organizations. *International Journal of Management, 23,* 563–575.

Triandis, H.C. (1989). The self and social behavior in differing cultural contexts. *Psychological Review, 96,* 506–520.

West, M.A., & Anderson, N.R. (1996). Innovation in top management teams. *Journal of Applied Psychology, 6,* 680–693.

CHAPTER 12

The Effects of Cultural Intelligence on Team Member Acceptance and Integration in Multinational Teams

JANE E. FLAHERTY

At the end of World War II the global business economy shifted. Companies expanded beyond their national boundaries and international organizations were created. Industrial organizations led the way as more companies transformed into multinational corporations (Galbraith, 1978).

"Now it seems the rule of the day is that businesses (and the people who run them) have to go global or go broke" (Peterson, 2004, p. 77). Though somewhat true, the idea of a global village "where a common culture of management unifies the practice of business around the world" (Kanter, 1991, p. 4) is not realistic. Cultural differences preclude this from happening because management and working styles that stand out in some cultures are expected behaviors in others.

Increased globalization combined with modern management theories has resulted in a new type of work group called the multinational team (MNT). "The importance of multinational teams is evidenced not by well-developed research programs advocated by scholars but by the dominance of MNTs in the attention of global businesses" (Earley & Gibson, 2002, p. 50). This new type of team reinforces the need to understand how diverse individuals interact in a group.

"Groups do not begin to function instantaneously" (Thomas & Inkson, 2004, p. 158). Tuckman contends that groups evolve through a five-step process called "forming, storming, norming, performing, and adjourning" (2001, p. 66). Diverse expectations of group interactions are a factor that potentially delays MNTs from progressing through these processes. However, "research shows that newly formed culturally diverse groups reduce their process losses over time by finding ways of working together better" (Thomas & Inkson, 2004, p. 159).

Thus, individuals seeking success in MNTs must begin to recognize and understand national cultural differences and incorporate this knowledge into future cross-cultural interactions (Earley & Ang, 2003; Trompenaars & Hampden-Turner, 1998). Cultural intelligence (CQ), defined as "an individual's capability to deal effectively in situations characterized by cultural diversity" (Earley & Ang, 2003, p. 9) is one construct that can be used to help individuals in these efforts.

Earley and Ang developed the first CQ framework "to understand why people vary so dramatically in their capacity to adjust to new cultures" (2003, p. xii). Their model explained how CQ worked in three specific dimensions: cognitive CQ, motivational CQ, and behavioral CQ. Ang, Van Dyne, Koh, Ng, Templer, Tay, and Chandrasekar (2007) further developed this model and added a fourth dimension: metacognitive CQ. Metacognitive CQ is the higher-order mental capability to think about personal thought processes, anticipate cultural preferences of others, and adjust mental models during and after intercultural experiences. Cognitive CQ is the knowledge of norms, practices, and conventions in different cultures acquired through education and personal experiences. Motivational CQ is the capability to direct attention and energy toward learning about and functioning in situations characterized by cultural differences. Behavioral CQ is the capability to exhibit appropriate verbal and nonverbal actions when interacting with people from different cultures.

Multicultural teams are more creative, innovative, and effective in understanding diverse needs than single-culture teams (Francesco & Gold, 1998). This is often offset by a diverse team's increased probability for failure (Thomas & Inkson, 2004) and lack of cohesion (Wright & Drewery, 2006). Multicultural teams can experience difficulties with integration that keep them from reaching their potential. "To achieve high performance, members need a knowledge base to anticipate likely differences and similarities among themselves. They need to use the similarities to bridge the differences. They need to learn from the available multiple perspectives" (Maznevski & Peterson 1997, p. 62).

Today, it is fairly safe to assume that most teams have some sort of diversity, be it age, race, tenure, function, gender, education, or cultural background. Laboratory and field research supports the conclusion that team dynamics are positively impacted through effective diversity management (Jackson, Stone, & Alvarez, 1993). The challenge is to create an environment that encourages team cohesion while honoring the unique contributions that people from diverse backgrounds can offer (Jackson et al., 1993; Thomas & Inkson, 2004).

Jackson et al. (1993) suggest that teams undergo a transition each time a new member joins. They found that newcomers seeking integration use the culture of the new team as well as their own culture as behavioral guides. They proposed that new and existing group members are attracted to each other based on demographic similarities; however, this transition time is "characterized by somewhat lower cohesiveness for all teams, regardless of the degree of similarity between old timers and newcomers" (p. 91). They contend there is a "need for theoretical models that explain why and how diversity impacts team dynamics and performance outcomes" (p. 66).

Triandis stated that "a culturally intelligent person suspends judgment until information becomes available beyond the ethnicity of the other person" (2006, p. 21). Earley and Mosakowski added, "Only when conduct you have actually observed begins to settle into patterns can you safely begin to anticipate how these people will react in the next situation" (2004, p. 2).

While evidence suggests that aspects of CQ support effective adjustment for expatriate work (Ang et al., 2007; Thomas & Inkson, 2004), there has been little research conducted on the effects of CQ on team dynamics in cross-cultural settings. This multiple case study begins to fill that gap by exploring the effects of CQ on team member acceptance and integration (defined as the threshold at which an individual feels part of the team and when the team feels the individual is part of their group, characterized by mutual attraction and respect for the individual being inducted into the team) in MNTs. Data were collected based on surveys and interviews from 51 individuals representing 27 nationalities, 6 MNTs, and 3 companies.

TEAM BACKGROUND INFORMATION

To qualify for the study, each team had to utilize English as their primary business language and have members from at least three different countries.

Company 1 is a world supplier of technology, project management, and information solutions to the oil and gas industry. It employs more than 60,000 people from more than 140 nationalities and has operations in more than 80 countries. Company 1 supplied two software engineering development teams for this research. One team was located in the United Kingdom and the other was in the United States.

Company 2 is a global leader in power and automation technologies that enable utility and industry customers to improve performance while lowering environmental impact. It employs 104,000 people and has operations in 100 countries. Company 2 provided three teams for this research: a human resource and development team, a financial services team, and a research and development team. All three teams were located in Switzerland.

Company 3 is a global, market-leading software sales, marketing, and technical organization. It employs close to 60,000 people in more than 90 countries. Company 3 supplied one team for this research. This was a regional leadership team with its members geographically dispersed across Europe and the United Kingdom.

PARTICIPANT DEMOGRAPHIC INFORMATION

The participating teams were diverse in terms of gender, age, nationality, company tenure, and team tenure. In addition, participants varied in number of language fluencies and amount of international experience. Detailed demographic information follows.

On an aggregate level, 76 percent of the participants were male. Individual teams were either predominantly male or they had close to a 50–50 gender split.

Overall, 23.5 percent of the participants were age 20–30; 39.2 percent were 31–40; 27.4 percent were 41–50; and 9.8 percent were over 51. With the exception of one team, each team had representatives from at least two of the age categories.

The participating teams were highly diverse from a nationality perspective: participants represented at least 27 different nationalities (two respondents did not disclose their nationality). Team 1B had the largest single national contingent on one team with three participants or 27 percent of the team composed of individuals from the United States. Team 2A had the second largest national contingent with three participants or 25 percent of the team composed of individuals from Switzerland. Table 12.1 provides team nationality composition details.

Eighty percent of the participants were fluent in more than one language with 33 percent fluent in three languages and 14 percent fluent in four or more languages. Of the participants, 94 percent had experience working in more than one country, 30 percent had worked in two countries, 45 percent had worked in three, and 20 percent had worked in four or more countries.

Of the participants, 14 percent had worked for their respective companies for one to three years, 49 percent had been there four to six years, and 37 percent had worked for their companies more than seven years. Additionally, 12 percent had joined their respective teams within the last six months; 8 percent had joined within the last six to twelve months; 63 percent had been on their team for one to three years; and the remaining 18 percent had been on their team for more than four years.

RESEARCH RESULTS

CQ Survey Findings

Table 12.2 reports the CQ descriptive statistics.

Team Member Acceptance and Integration Results

Team member acceptance and integration time frames were captured in individual follow-up interviews. The mean time of self-reported feelings of acceptance and integration was 2.61 months with a range of 0.05 to 14 months (standard deviation = 3.12). The mean time of team acceptance and integration of new members was 2.94 months with a range of 0.09 to 24 (standard deviation = 3.96).

Spearman's Rho (r_s) was used to explore the correlations between variables. The r_s calculations were generated for each of the four factors and both self-reported acceptance and integration times and acceptance and integration times for new members. Table 12.3 summarizes r_s for team level CQ with acceptance and integration times. The only statistically significant finding was the positive correlation ($r_s = 0.943$ at $p < 0.01$) between team motivational CQ and team acceptance and integration times for new members. In other words, as team levels of motivational CQ went up, so did the time for that team to accept and integrate new members.

Table 12.4 reports r_s for individual CQ with team acceptance and integration times. There were two statistically significant findings among these calculations. First, there was a positive correlation ($r_s = 0.417$ at $p < 0.01$) for individual motivational CQ with team acceptance and integration times for new members. In other words, as individual moti-

Table 12.1

Team Nationality Composition

Team 1A	Team 1B	Team 2A	Team 2B	Team 2C	Team 3A
Czech Republic	China	Australia	Colombia	Germany	Spain
France (2)	France	Finland	Italy	Hong Kong	Switzerland
Germany	Iran	Germany	Malaysia	Montenegro	Sweden (2)
India	Nigeria	India	Pakistan	Sweden	United Kingdom
Ivory Coast	Pakistan	Norway	Switzerland	Did not disclose (1)	United Kingdom and ex-Kenyan
Nigeria	Switzerland and United States	Switzerland (3)	United States		United States
Poland	Taiwan	Switzerland and Australia			
Spain (2)	United States (3)	United Kingdom (2)			
	Did not disclose (1)	United States			

Table 12.2

Cultural Intelligence Descriptive Statistics

	Mean	Range	SD
Metacognitive CQ	5.70	3.25–6.75	0.74
Cognitive CQ	4.69	1.67–5.83	0.99
Motivational CQ	5.98	3.20–7.00	0.66
Behavioral CQ	5.16	2.00–7.00	0.96

Table 12.3

Spearman's Rho: Team Cultural Intelligence—Team Acceptance and Integration Times (n = 6)

	Team Self-Reported Acceptance and Integration Time	Team Acceptance and Integration Time for New Members
Metacognitive CQ	0.486	0.257
Cognitive CQ	0.776	0.000
Motivational CQ	–0.200	0.943***
Behavioral CQ	0.689	0.632

***p <0.01

Table 12.4

Spearman's Rho: Individual Cultural Intelligence—Team Acceptance and Integration Times (n = 51)

	Team Self-Reported Acceptance and Integration Time	Team Acceptance and Integration Time for New Members
Metacognitive CQ	0.025	0.229
Cognitive CQ	0.322*	0.061
Motivational CQ	–0.162	0.417***
Behavioral CQ	0.215	0.259

*p <0.05; ***p <0.01

vational CQ went up, so did the amount of time for that team to accept and integrate new members onto the team. Second, there was a positive correlation ($r_s = 0.322$ at $p < 0.05$) for individual cognitive CQ with team self-reported acceptance and integration times. In other words, as individual cognitive CQ went up, so did the amount of time for the average member of that person's team to feel accepted and integrated onto the team.

Interview Results

I explored the dynamics of acceptance and integration in individual interviews as summarized on the following pages.

Team 1A

Team 1A is a software engineering group in the United Kingdom. Socializing is a big part of their dynamics. They play team sports together and socialize on the weekend. In their hiring practices, social skills are valued over technical proficiency. Other factors impacting acceptance and integration include prior relationships with people on the team, a shared expatriate experience, technical competence, and team dynamics such as personality, age, and member motivations.

Most of the participants thought cultural diversity impacted the team's dynamics through varied perspectives, increased adaptability, and enhanced learning opportunities. One participant said, "It makes things unpredictable, in the good sense. When ideas are needed late in the project, we can't assume where the good ideas will come from or what they will be."

Team 1B

Team 1B is a software engineering team in the United States. Most participants said their team's cultural diversity had little or no impact on their dynamics or they mentioned the expanded perspective of having different points of view. Respondents reported having better communication on single-culture teams since they had to be selective of their language in a multicultural setting. One member stated, "It is harder to predict behavior on a multicultural team as you are less likely to be able to assume what will happen."

Teams in this company normally disband after two to three years, so one participant felt acceptance and integration had to be fast or the team would not function. Others factors impacting this team's acceptance and integration of new members include knowing people on the team prior to joining and an individual's technical competence.

Team 2A

Team 2A is a global human resource management and development team in Switzerland. When asked how the team's cultural diversity impacted team dynamics, responses ranged from "I can't think of anything special that is occurring just because we are multicultural" to "it is significant." Several responses listed a broader view of the world and an openness to diverse thinking, and some responses identified the misunderstandings and barriers created by cultural differences. One respondent felt there was more clarity and a higher level of understanding on a single-culture team. Another said, "It is more interesting and enjoyable to work on a multinational team. However, you have to pay attention to the dynamics as different people respond in different ways based on their cultural background." A third participant stated "it can be used to manipulate others. For instance, if I know this culture won't weigh in against something, I can use that to further my interests."

Factors other than CQ impacting team 2A's acceptance and integration included knowing people prior to joining the team and the degree to which the new team was welcoming and supportive. Due to a previous team downsize, one member thought he felt accepted and integrated because 80 percent of his previous team had lost their jobs. Another member said that finally being in the same physical office made him feel a part of the team and not "just remembered when I was in the office."

Team 2B

Team 2B is a financial consolidation and reporting team in Switzerland. One member spoke of the challenges different work ethics can cause and added that this team is flexible in taking the different cultures into account and respecting them. Another stated, "While being on a multicultural team can slow down decision making, the quality is far higher."

The factors other than CQ that impact team 2B's acceptance and integration were events, technical competence, prior knowledge of team members, seniority levels, social activities, team dispersion, and team dynamics. One respondent said, "It took a while to meet everyone because we aren't always here at the same time."

Team 2C

Team 2C is a research and development team in Switzerland. Everyone on this team has their own office. This proved to be a disadvantage at first as it does not allow for natural conversations to occur during the workday. However, when someone new joins the team, he or she is assigned a mentor for the first couple of months.

Members felt that the team's diversity made their work more interesting because of the varied ideas, perspectives, and backgrounds. One member added, "I don't think where you are from impacts how you work. It may give it more richness, but it doesn't impact how the work is completed." Other factors impacting team member acceptance and integration include an individual's education and seniority level, whether they know someone on the team prior to joining, and team dynamics issues such as communication levels and member personalities.

Team 3A

Team 3A is a regional leadership team with members in the United Kingdom, France, Switzerland, and Italy. Team 3A was the only team that was permanently geographically dispersed in this study. One member addressed this dispersion, saying, "There is an understanding that we are working on a team that isn't together a lot so there has to be a willingness to make that work."

The team felt their cultural diversity helped them to build relationships faster and expand their knowledge of cultures including their own. Conversely, it has slowed their communication as they work harder to ensure mutual understanding. One participant said, "It is how we work, deliver, and plan. It opens our scope to think broader in how to service our customers and our subsidiaries."

Other factors impacting team 3A's acceptance and integration include how well they knew members of the team prior to joining, team and member seniority, and team environmental factors such as whether there was a team leader when they joined and if that leader had clarity of focus and mission. One member added, "If I'm working closely with one person for two weeks, then acceptance comes much quicker than if I am only working with someone twice a month."

DISCUSSION AND RECOMMENDATIONS

The purpose of this research was to explore the effects of CQ on team member acceptance and integration in MNTs. This section discusses what these multiple case study findings mean and how they relate to existing literature. In addition, I recommend a future research agenda and consider implications for practitioners as well as limitations of the study.

Discussion

Using Spearman's Rho (r_s), I examined the correlation of CQ with acceptance and integration times. Three of these r_s calculations showed statistical significance. Two pertained to motivational CQ and the third dealt with cognitive CQ.

There was a positive correlation ($r_s = 0.943$ at $p < 0.01$) for team motivational CQ with acceptance and integration times for new members and a positive correlation ($r_s = 0.417$ at $p < 0.01$) for individual motivational CQ with team acceptance and integration times for new members. These correlations indicate that as levels of motivational CQ or "the capability to direct attention and energy toward learning about and functioning in situations characterized by cultural differences" (Ang et al., 2007, p 338) rose (whether on the individual or team level), so did the amount of time for a team to accept and integrate new members. These positive correlations might suggest that individuals and teams with a stronger desire to interact with others from differing cultures may have higher thresholds of acceptance and integration and may be more cautious and conscientious in their interactions. These behaviors may have impacted the perceived acceptance and integration times for new members joining the team.

The three companies chosen valued multinational diversity, and many of the interviewed individuals indicated a preference for working in MNTs, which is consistent with the quantitative findings of motivational CQ as the highest scored factor across each team. This indicates that these team members, at a minimum, were interested in learning about each other and their representative cultures. One team 2B member stated "I've gotten to know my teammates better personally on this team. Since we are all foreigners we share experiences, tell each other problems, and become close. I have friends (in my home country) but there is more of a defined line between work and friends there."

A positive correlation was also found for individual cognitive CQ with team levels of self-reported acceptance and integration times ($r_s = 0.322$ at $p < 0.05$). Stated another way, as an individual's cognitive CQ or "knowledge of norms, practices, and conventions in different cultures acquired from education and personal experiences" (Ang et al., 2007, p. 338) went up, so did the team's average time for self-reported feelings of acceptance and integration. This correlation might suggest that the more an individual knows about the cultural differences among members on their team, the higher their threshold of feeling accepted and integrated onto the team. For instance, one member of team 2A stated, "We are more careful in an international environment. We know that people are different and we work to find out different in what ways." A member of team 3A added, "In all relations and groups there are misunderstandings. I have found that multicultural teams are more aware of the fact that they will happen. Single-culture teams, on the other hand, seem to be shocked when it happens."

While culturally intelligent individuals understand that differences exist between individuals based on their cultural backgrounds, they are able to suspend the tendency to base their interactions on stereotypes associated with these differences (Thomas & Inkson, 2004; Triandis, 2006). Instead, they use this knowledge and their experiences to form behavioral patterns that allow them to more effectively interact with culturally diverse individuals (Earley & Ang, 2003; Maznevski & Peterson, 1997).

It is important to remember that correlations do not indicate cause-and-effect relationships. As such, the effects of cultural diversity on each team's dynamics were specifically addressed in the interviews. Answers varied from no impact at all to a significant impact. There were positive effects of the diversity mentioned, such as building relationships faster, opening the scope of the team to better understand their international customers, increased adaptability, and expanded learning opportunities. Also mentioned were challenges associated with differing ethic backgrounds and barriers to mutual understanding. These results are consistent with Maznevski and Peterson's (1997) view of the difficulties multicultural teams can face with integration.

Cumulatively, these findings demonstrated that these teams experienced a diversity impact on their team dynamics and had a positive correlation for some of the CQ factors with acceptance and integration times. When the remaining interview results were added to these findings, it became evident that team member acceptance and integration were impacted by many things, CQ among them. Other items mentioned included prior knowledge of team members, job or technical competence, team dispersion, events, and team dynamics.

Specifically, teams with the opportunity to socialize and play team sports together formed friendships that resulted in stronger team cohesion levels. A person's competence and job skills decreased his or her time to acceptance and integration on teams that were more technical in nature. A few teams mentioned how the physical location of individual team members impacted their acceptance and integration times, with those in the same location having, on average, shorter acceptance and integration times. While each group had different rituals for inducting a new member, nothing in their welcoming process significantly impacted team member acceptance and integration times.

Openness was the most frequently listed item when the characteristics of new members easily fitting on each team were explored. Other characteristics mentioned included adaptability, competence, and honesty. This supports Triandis's statement that "people who are culturally intelligent are also more flexible than the average person and thus able to adjust to different organizational environments" (2006, p. 24).

Ng and Earley contend that "CQ is a capability that is posited to predict, but is distinct from, the actual outcome arising from a specific situation or episode of interaction" (2006, p. 8). They added, "we expect that, in general, individuals with high CQ are likely to adapt faster and more effectively, although the presence (or absence) of other factors may alter this relationship" (p. 8). Conversely, this study found that the higher the motivational CQ and/or cognitive CQ the longer the acceptance and integration time. However, it also demonstrated results consistent with the idea of other factors having an impact. Further research on this topic is warranted to test whether the positive correlations found in this small sample are true in the general population.

Recommendations for Future Research

Being motivated to recognize and understand cultural differences and similarities and then modifying one's behavior is the basis of CQ. As the number of MNTs grows, so does the potential impact of understanding and using CQ to one's advantage. This research continued the CQ foundation work of Earley and Ang. In addition, it provided results that warrant further investigation into the effects of CQ on team member acceptance and integration in MNTs. As the companies used in this study were all global organizations that valued national diversity and the teams chosen were broadly multicultural, future research on this topic should include less diverse teams to provide a more complete perspective.

The CQ instrument's authors do not calculate an overall CQ value. Instead, they look at the values of the individual four factors and their respective antecedents and consequences. While I agree that the individual CQ factors have their place in research, I also contend that overall CQ is a construct worth future investigation because the interaction of the four factors may provide more insight into a person's cultural adaptation as well as the team dynamics. For this work to be completed, a new framework needs to be developed and validated that assesses the interplay between the four factors.

Another area worth future investigation would be to explore experiential factors that result in higher levels of CQ. For instance, what is the impact on CQ of having immediate family members from different nationalities? Also, how does the amount of time an individual has spent working on multicultural teams in the past affect his or her CQ score? These are but two examples of the type of research possible here.

While not statistically significant, the only negative correlation results of this study were for motivational CQ (both individual and team levels) with self-reported feelings of acceptance and integration onto the team. Conversely, two of the statistically significant positive correlations were for motivational CQ with the acceptance and integration times of others. Thus, an additional area of research could focus on whether there is a difference in self-reported feelings of acceptance and integration compared to perceptions of the team's acceptance and integration of new members based on individual or team level of motivational CQ.

Further research on team dynamics should include looking at it through a CQ lens. For instance, how does each individual's CQ impact the team's dynamics? What impact does an individual with higher CQ have versus one with lower CQ? How does the team leader's CQ impact the team? There are countless opportunities here; however, the idea behind this line of research is to gain a better understanding of how MNT members impact each other.

A final area of recommended future investigation deals with teams made up of either all or a majority of expatriates. Comments made during the interviews indicated that working outside of one's home country and physically away from family and friends can result in more socialization within the team. An exploration of how this increased social level impacts team dynamics is worth further investigation.

As this section indicates, there are various potential areas for future research in the areas of CQ and team dynamics. This research study indicated a value in pursuing future research on the effects of CQ on team member acceptance and integration within MNTs. In addition, it has implications for practitioners that are explored in the next section.

Implications for Practitioners

As globalization and MNTs grow in popularity, understanding diversity's impact on team dynamics becomes increasingly important. CQ is one construct that helps us understand why some people adjust more easily to cross-cultural situations than others. As the prevalence of global organizations and MNTs increases, this level of understanding will help consultants and team members better identify the dynamics they encounter.

In addition, CQ has a role in international training and preparation programs. Instead of focusing only on the cognitive aspects such as cultural differences based on frameworks developed by Hofstede (2001), House, Javidan, Hanges, and Dorfman (2002), and Trompenaars and Hampden-Turner (1998), CQ training can be used to teach individuals how to raise their cultural awareness, increase motivation, and evolve behavior. This four-factor–based evolution will allow individuals to more effectively interact with people from different cultures. CQ training curriculums that involve customizing the training based on the individual's current CQ level and intended cultural interaction are in the early development stage. They utilize methods such as role play, simulation, experiential learning, goal setting, and drama techniques similar to method acting (Tan & Chua, 2003).

Limitations of the Study

As is common, this study has limitations. First, this is a multiple case study of six multicultural teams within three separate organizations. As it is not possible to draw absolute conclusions from an exploratory case study or a sample size this small in relation to the population, further research in this area may be warranted.

Second, while the official business language of each of these teams was English, it should be noted that, due to the nature of an MNT, working with individuals whose native language was not English called for identifying miscommunications, misunderstandings, and questions to eliminate errors whenever possible.

And finally, all three participating companies valued diversity as evidenced by their global focus, practice, and workforce and their individual mission, vision, and value statements. In addition, all six teams were broadly multicultural. This organizational emphasis on diversity and the high level of team diversity may not accurately reflect general MNT compositions. Future research may need to be conducted with less diverse teams to provide a more complete perspective.

CONCLUSION

MNTs have become more prevalent as organizations throughout the world have crossed national boundaries. This prevalence has led to a widespread need to understand how to interact with individuals from other countries. Earley and Ang (2003) developed the CQ construct to help explain why individuals adapt differently to new cultural interactions and settings. Diversity literature has shown a lack of cohesion in multicultural teams (Wright & Drewery, 2006) and integration difficulties among MNTs (Maznevski & Peterson, 1997).

The purpose of this research was to tie these constructs together and explore the relationship of CQ to team member acceptance and integration in MNTs, using an exploratory case study with members of six teams from three global organizations.

Data were collected through an online survey and individual follow-up interviews. Descriptive statistics were calculated for CQ, acceptance and integration times, and participant demographic information. In addition, Spearman's Rho (r_s) was calculated to explore linear relationships for CQ with acceptance and integration times. Aggregate and team levels of the qualitative interview data were summarized and presented.

Positive relationships were found between the aggregate team and individual motivational CQ or "the capability to direct attention and energy toward learning about and functioning in situations characterized by cultural differences" (Ang et al., 2007, p 338) with acceptance and integration times for new members. In addition, a positive relationship was found between individual cognitive CQ or "knowledge of norms, practices, and conventions in different cultures acquired from education and personal experiences" (Ang et al., 2007, p. 338) with his or her team's self-reported acceptance and integration times.

The quantitative and qualitative findings together show that team member acceptance and integration were related to many things, including CQ. Other factors include prior knowledge of team members, job or technical competence, team dispersion, events, and team dynamics.

As the number of MNTs grows, so does the potential benefits of understanding and using CQ. This research continued the CQ foundation work of Earley and Ang (2003) and reports results that warrant further investigation into the relationship between CQ and team member acceptance and integration in MNTs. These findings have implications for practitioners focused on understanding MNT dynamics and for those who help individuals prepare for MNT assignments.

REFERENCES

Ang, S., Van Dyne, L., Koh, C., Ng, K.Y., Templer, K.J., Tay, C., & Chandrasekar, N.A. (2007). Cultural intelligence: Its measurement and effects on cultural judgment and decision making, cultural adaptation, and task performance. *Management and Organization Review, 3,* 335–371.

Earley, P.C., & Ang, S. (2003). *Cultural intelligence: Individual interactions across cultures.* Palo Alto, CA: Stanford University Press.

Earley, P.C., & Gibson, C.B. (2002). *Multinational work teams: A new perspective.* Mahwah, NJ: Lawrence Erlbaum Associates.

Earley, P.C., & Mosakowski, E. (2004). Cultural intelligence. *Harvard Business Review, 82*(10), 1–9.

Francesco, A.M., & Gold, B.A. (1998). *International organizational behavior: Text, readings, cases, and skills.* Upper Saddle River, NJ: Prentice Hall.

Galbraith, J.K. (1978). The defense of the multinational company. *Harvard Business Review, 56*(2), 83–93.

Hofstede, G. (2001). *Culture's consequences: Comparing values, behaviors, institutions, and organizations across nations* (2nd ed.). Thousand Oaks, CA: Sage Publications.

House, R., Javidan, M., Hanges, P., & Dorfman, P. (2002). Understanding cultures and implicit leadership theories across the globe: An introduction to project GLOBE. *Journal of World Business, 37*(1), 3–10.

Jackson, S.E., Stone, V.K., & Alvarez, E.B. (1993). Socialization amidst diversity: The impact of demographics on work team old timers and newcomers. *Research in Organizational Behavior, 15,* 45–109.

Kanter, R.M. (1991). Transcending business boundaries: 12,000 world managers view change. *Harvard Business Review, 69*(3), 3–16.

Maznevski, M., & Peterson, M.F. (1997). Societal values, social interpretation, and multinational teams. In C.S. Granrose & S. Oskamp (Eds.), *Cross-cultural work groups* (pp. 61–89). Thousand Oaks, CA: Sage Publications.

Ng, K.Y., & Earley, P.C. (2006). Culture + intelligence: Old constructs, new frontiers. *Group and Organization Management, 31,* 4–19.

Peterson, B. (2004). *Cultural intelligence: A guide to working with people from other cultures.* Yarmouth, ME: Intercultural Press.

Tan, J.S., & Chua, R.Y. (2003). Training and developing cultural intelligence. In P.C. Earley & S. Ang (Eds.), *Cultural intelligence: Individual interactions across cultures* (pp. 258–303). Palo Alto, CA: Stanford University Press.

Thomas, D.C., & Inkson, K. (2004). *Cultural intelligence: People skills for global business.* San Francisco, CA: Berrett-Koehler Publishers.

Triandis, H.C. (2006). Cultural intelligence in organizations. *Group and Organization Management, 31,* 20–26.

Trompenaars, F., & Hampden-Turner, C. (1998). *Riding the waves of culture: Understanding diversity in global business* (2nd ed.). New York: McGraw-Hill

Tuckman, B.W. (2001). Developmental sequence in small groups. *Group Facilitation: A Research and Applications Journal, 3,* 66–81.

Wright, N.S., & Drewery, G.P. (2006). Forming cohesion in culturally heterogeneous teams: Differences in Japanese, Pacific Islander and Anglo experiences. *Cross Cultural Management, 13,* 43–53.

CHAPTER 13

The Effects of Cultural Intelligence on Interpersonal Trust in Multicultural Teams

THOMAS ROCKSTUHL AND KOK-YEE NG

With increasing globalization, growing diversity in workforce demography, and the popular use of team-based organizational structures (Ilgen & Pulakos, 1999), multicultural teams (MCTs) are a central feature in organizations today. As employees are increasingly required to work interdependently with team members that have different culturally significant affiliations (Cox, 1995), understanding the effective functioning of members in MCTs is a rising concern of organizations and their employees.

A critical challenge faced by members of MCTs is the development of interpersonal trust. Trust is particularly difficult to foster in MCTs because members with different cultural values and perspectives may have different understandings of the goals, roles, and rules for the team (Gibson & Zellmer-Bruhn, 2001), which can result in reduced understanding and, hence, predictability of the other team members' intentions and actions (Child, 2001; Earley & Mosakowski, 2000). Moreover, social categorization theory (Tajfel, 1981; Turner, 1987) suggests that members of MCTs are less likely to trust one another because of the human tendency to classify those who are different as members of the out-group, as opposed to in-group members.

Gaining trust is a key intervening process in culturally diverse teams that influences their effectiveness (Earley & Mosakowski, 2000). Therefore, understanding factors that alleviate the negative consequences of cultural diversity on interpersonal trust has immense implications for MCTs. In this study, we examine how differences in ethnicity—a salient surface-level attribute that engenders social categorization—affect team members' trust in each other. More importantly, we investigate whether the negative effect of cultural diversity on trust between members in MCTs differs across individuals. Here, we advance the notion that a relevant and timely individual difference construct that can yield important insights to our research question is the construct of cultural intelligence (CQ).

Although an increasing body of research has demonstrated the importance of CQ for a range of intercultural effectiveness outcomes (e.g., Ang, Van Dyne, Koh, Ng, Templer, Tay, & Chandrasekar, 2007; Templer, Tay, & Chandrasekar, 2006), research has yet to examine how CQ affects interpersonal trust in the context of MCTs. Specifically, our study examines how CQ affects the level of interpersonal trust a member has in another member of a multicultural project team. Thus, our focus is on the dyadic level (between any pair of members within the team) because social categorization, the common theoretical perspective for explaining the detrimental effects of diversity, is fundamentally an interpersonal phenomenon. Our key research objective is to examine whether the effect of dyadic-level cultural diversity on interpersonal trust is moderated by the level of CQ that members in the dyad possess.

Our findings contribute to two streams of research. First, we expand our current understanding of the nomological network of CQ by extending its application to trust and MCTs. By examining group members' CQ, we highlight the importance of individuals' cross-cultural capabilities in MCTs, and attempt to provide insight into how such capabilities may influence members' experiences in culturally diverse teams.

Second, we delineate dyadic-level and group-level cultural diversity by focusing on the dyadic level, in order to highlight the importance of precise theorizing and adoption of the correct level of analysis for research on group diversity. Although much research has been done in recent years to understand how cultural diversity in teams affects team functioning and member experiences (for reviews, see Jackson, May, & Whitney, 1995; Stewart, 2006; Williams & O'Reilly, 1998), most of these studies have examined diversity at the group level. We suggest that a reason for the many inconsistent findings reported in the field is the lack of attention paid to interpersonal dynamics within the team (Jackson et al., 1995). This omission results in an underspecified model that fails to account more fully for the effects of diversity on the outcomes of interest, thus impeding the field's advancement.

We tested our hypotheses using data collected from 40 project teams comprising 259 team members. Data were analyzed using the social relations model (Kenny, 1994) to segregate variance at the appropriate level of analysis. Finally, we discuss our results and implications for future research as well as for practice.

THEORY DEVELOPMENT

In this section, we review the literature and research on interpersonal trust, group diversity and social categorization theory, followed by the development of our hypotheses.

Interpersonal Trust

Trust involves the willingness to make oneself vulnerable to another person despite uncertainty regarding motives, intentions, and prospective actions (Kramer, 1999; Mayer, Davis, & Schoorman, 1995). Mayer et al. (1995, p. 712), for example, defined trust as "the willingness to be vulnerable to the actions of another party based on the expectation that the other will perform a particular action important to the trustor, irrespective of the ability to monitor or control that other party." Underlying these notions of trust is an individual's confidence in the goodwill of others and the expectation that others will act in beneficial ways (e.g., Pruitt, 1983).

Trust is a complex, multidimensional construct that operates on different bases (Lewicki & Bunker, 1996; Lewis & Weigert, 1985; McAllister, 1995). One common distinction is that of affect-based versus cognition-based trust. Building on the work of Lewis and Weigert (1985), McAllister (1995) proposed that affect-based trust is founded on the emotional bonds between individuals, where individuals express care and concern for the welfare of their partners, believe in the intrinsic virtue of such relationships, and believe that these sentiments are reciprocated (Rempel, Holmes, & Zanna, 1985). On the other hand, cognition-based trust hinges on an appraisal of the other's track record—the competence and reliability this person has demonstrated in the past. Thus, cognition-based trust provides a rational basis upon which individuals develop confidence in the other party.

In this study, we focus on affect-based trust to be consistent with the nature of diversity that is examined. According to Jackson et al.'s (1995) diversity framework, ethnicity is a relations-oriented characteristic that is more likely to invoke affect-based responses through social cognitive processes such as social categorization. Thus, examining affect-based trust as the criterion outcome is more conceptually aligned with our focus on ethnic diversity.

Social Categorization Theory and Diversity

Social categorization theory (Tajfel, 1981; Turner, 1987) argues that individuals frequently classify themselves and others into social categories using salient characteristics such as age, race, status, and organizational membership. Based on these classifications, individuals who perceive themselves as similar to others are more likely to view these others as common in-group members, while those who perceive differences are likely to view others as out-group members. This in-group versus out-group categorization in turn brings about important consequences. For example, to maintain a positive social identity, individuals often demonstrate favoritism toward in-group members, and derogation toward out-group members.

Many diversity studies have relied on social categorization theory to explain why diverse groups are more likely to experience problems such as lower cohesion (Smith, Smith, Olian, Sims, O'Bannon, & Scully, 1994), greater conflict (Pelled, Eisenhardt, & Xin, 1999), and poorer performance (Pelled, 1996). The argument is that compared to homogeneous groups, members in diverse groups are more likely to classify other members as in-group or out-group, leading to negative behaviors toward out-group members that, in turn, disrupt the group's functioning.

In these studies, diversity is typically operationalized at the group level, which can mask important dynamics of interpersonal interactions within the team. We contend that examining group-level diversity based on social categorization theory is imprecise, because the target of social comparison is not specified at this level of analysis. In a completely homogeneous group, the group as the target is of less importance since everyone shares the same characteristics. In diverse groups however, treating the group as the target assumes that the degree of interpersonal attraction within each dyad is similar across all dyads (cf. Klein & Dansereau, 1994). This however, is a questionable assumption because whether one arrives at an in-group or out-group classification depends very much on the targets being compared. For example, in a bicultural team where a strong faultline divides the team into two dominant subgroups, specifying the target of comparison is critical since the interactions between members belonging to the same subgroup should differ quite considerably from interactions between members across the two subgroups (Dreachslin, Hunt, & Sprainer, 2000; Lau & Murnighan, 1998).

We therefore propose that examining diversity of dyads *within* the team is more appropriate when social categorization theory is used to explain effects of diversity on outcomes such as trust and commitment. This is because at the dyadic level of analysis, a specific target in the group is identified. Hence, based on social categorization theory and prior research that has shown that people often view in-group members as more trustworthy than out-group members (Brewer, 1981), we expect that a member (focal individual) will develop lower trust in a target team member (partner) if they do not share the same ethnic cultural background because of the out-group characterization processes than if they both have the same ethnic cultural background.

H1: A focal member's trust in his/her partner team member will be lower if the two do not share the same ethnic cultural background than if they do.

Cultural Intelligence

More importantly, our major research interest is to examine how CQ moderates the negative relationship between cultural diversity and interpersonal trust as proposed in hypothesis 1. Specifically, we argue that the CQ capabilities of both the focal member and the partner play an important role in attenuating the negative impact of cultural diversity on the level of interpersonal trust. However, different CQ capabilities operate for the focal and partner members, as depicted in our model presented in Figure 13.1.

The general underlying mechanism for the role of CQ in our model is that it reduces the tendency of focal members to view partners with different ethnic cultural backgrounds as out-group members. Hence, we expect focal members' capabilities in metacognitive CQ, cognitive CQ, and motivational CQ to enable them to develop a more accurate understanding of their partners' cultural background, thus helping them to overcome negative reactions and misunderstandings that arise from social categorization processes. Although partners' CQ capabilities also play an important part in enhancing the quality of interactions, we propose that it is essentially only the partners' capability to demonstrate appropriate behaviors (behavioral CQ) that will be most directly observed by the focal members. This, in turn, will help focal members dampen out-group classifications based on ethnic differences, which in turn, promotes greater trust in their partners. We elaborate on our arguments for each of our hypotheses below.

Metacognitive CQ is the capability for consciousness and awareness during intercultural interactions, and includes the mental capabilities to plan, monitor, and check the

Figure 13.1 **Theoretical Model and Hypotheses**

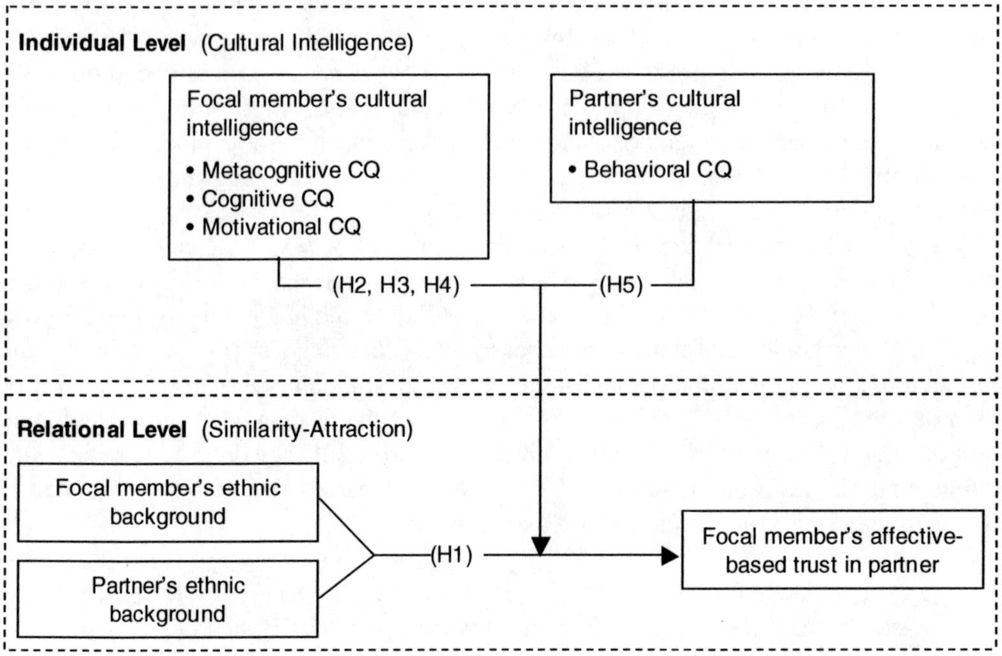

Individual Level (Cultural Intelligence)

Focal member's cultural intelligence
• Metacognitive CQ
• Cognitive CQ
• Motivational CQ

Partner's cultural intelligence
• Behavioral CQ

(H2, H3, H4) (H5)

Relational Level (Similarity-Attraction)

Focal member's ethnic background

Partner's ethnic background

(H1)

Focal member's affective-based trust in partner

accuracy of cultural assumptions (Ang et al., 2007; Earley & Ang, 2003). We propose that focal members' metacognitive CQ will attenuate the negative impact of diversity on their trust in their partners. This is because focal members with greater metacognitive CQ are more conscious of the cultural differences and influences present in their interactions with partners from different cultural backgrounds, and, hence, are less likely to make superficial and inaccurate judgments based on salient ethnic differences. They are also better at checking the accuracy of cultural assumptions and adjusting their mental models during and after interactions (Brislin, Worthley, and MacNab, 2006; Triandis, 2006), thus enabling them to develop a more accurate and deeper understanding of partners from different cultural backgrounds. We argue that the metacognitive CQ of focal members in culturally diverse dyads will enable them to counter the negative effects of social categorization on interpersonal trust (Gaertner & Dovidio, 2000).

On the other hand, focal members' CQ should be less relevant for interpersonal trust in culturally homogeneous dyads, because a common ethnic cultural background mitigates social categorization processes based on cultural identity and therefore negates the need for cross-cultural capabilities.

H2: In culturally diverse dyads, focal members with higher metacognitive CQ should report greater trust in their partners than those with lower metacognitive CQ, whereas in homogeneous dyads, metacognitive CQ of focal members should not have an effect on trust ratings.

Cognitive CQ focuses on knowledge of norms, practices, and conventions in different cultural settings acquired from education and personal experiences (Ang et al., 2007; Earley & Ang, 2003). Likewise, we argue that focal members' cognitive CQ will attenuate the negative impact of diversity on their trust in their partners. This is because focal members with good knowledge of culture should have a more in-depth understanding and accurate attribution of cross-cultural similarities and differences (Brislin et al., 2006). Intergroup contact theory (Allport, 1954; Pettigrew, 1998) also posits that one reason that contact reduces intergroup prejudice is the development of more accurate knowledge about the out-group. As such, individuals with high cognitive CQ are less likely to form negative stereotypes based on superficial cultural characteristics such as ethnicity (Abreu, 2001).

We therefore argue that when interacting with other members from a different cultural ethnic background, focal members with higher cognitive CQ should develop greater trust because of a more accurate understanding of the cultural norms and preferences of their partners. On the other hand, cognitive CQ has less relevance and effect on the development of trust with members from a similar cultural ethnic background.

H3: In culturally diverse dyads, focal members with higher cognitive CQ should report greater trust in their partners than those with lower cognitive CQ, whereas in homogeneous dyads, cognitive CQ of focal members should not have an effect on trust ratings.

Motivational CQ is the capability to direct attention and energy toward learning about and functioning in situations characterized by cultural differences (Ang et al., 2007; Earley & Ang, 2003). Since individuals with high motivational CQ have a strong desire and a high self-efficacy to communicate with people from different cultural backgrounds (Earley & Ang, 2003), we argue that they are less likely to maintain a strong in-group–out-group distinction when interacting with different ethnic members in the group (Reynolds & Oakes, 2000). In fact, these individuals may actively look for opportunities to interact with group members of different cultural backgrounds. Thus, we propose that focal members' motivational CQ will attenuate the negative impact of diversity on their trust in their partners, such that those with higher motivational CQ will develop greater trust in partners from different cultural ethnic backgrounds. Conversely, motivational CQ should be less relevant for the trust development between two culturally similar team members.

H4: In culturally diverse dyads, focal members with higher motivational CQ should report greater trust in their partners than those with lower motivational CQ, whereas in homogeneous dyads, motivational CQ should not have an effect on trust ratings.

Behavioral CQ is the capability to exhibit situationally appropriate behaviors from a broad repertoire of verbal and nonverbal behaviors (Ang et al., 2007; Earley & Ang, 2003). Here, we argue that it is the partner's behavioral CQ, rather than the focal member's behavioral CQ, that will enhance interpersonal trust. This is because partners who possess the flexibility to adapt behaviors in their interactions to suit team members from different cultural ethnic background will enhance the sense of familiarity and similarity in the relationships (Earley & Mosakowski, 2004; Gudykunst, Ting-Toomey, & Chua, 1998), weaken perceptions of salient cultural differences, and increase predictability of behaviors, thereby building the focal members' trust in them. Conversely, the focal member's behavioral CQ should also affect the partner's trust in him or her, rather than affect trust in the partner.

H5: In culturally diverse dyads, focal members should report greater trust in their partners who have higher behavioral CQ than in partners with lower behavioral CQ, whereas in homogeneous dyads, behavioral CQ of the partners should not have an effect on focal member's trust ratings.

METHODS

Sample and Procedures

Data for the study were collected from 259 participants from 40 project teams in a large business school in Singapore. The average age was 22 years (SD = 1.9), and 75 percent were female. A total of 197 were local Singaporean students. The remaining were exchange students from 19 countries, including the United States, United Kingdom, Canada, New Zealand, Finland, Norway, Sweden, Holland, and Germany. In terms of ethnic background, 190 participants were Chinese, 62 were Caucasian, 4 were Indian, and 3 were Malay.

Students were enrolled in a four-month international organizational behavior class, where they were assigned by the course instructor to culturally diverse teams at the beginning of the course. A major task for each team was to make a 45-minute presentation to the class on an international management topic. The presentation was evaluated by both the instructor and other students in the class, and constituted 20 percent of the course grade.

We collected data on CQ and demographics at the beginning of the semester, and data on members' trust ratings at the end of the semester. In the second data collection, we employed a round-robin design (Kenny, 1994) in which every participant had to rate his or her trust level in each group member. We emphasized to participants that the data collected was strictly for research purposes and would not influence their grades, and that participation was voluntary.

Measures

Trust

We assessed focal members' trust in their partner group members with three items from McAllister's (1995) affect-based trust measure. A sample item was, "I feel that I can freely share my ideas, feelings and hopes with this person." All items were rated on a five-point Likert scale (1 = strongly disagree to 5 = strongly agree). Cronbach's alpha was 0.89.

Dyad-Level Cultural Diversity

Within each group, we coded for the cultural diversity of every possible pair of group members. In total, 623 dyads from the 40 groups were coded. A dyad was coded 1 when the two members had different ethnic backgrounds, and 0 when they had the same ethnic background. In total, 32 percent (199) of the dyads were cross-cultural.

Group-Level Cultural Diversity

We control for group-level diversity to partial out group-level dynamics that may affect interpersonal trust. For instance, Earley and Mosakowski (2000) found that bicultural groups (groups with two subgroups) are less likely to develop a "hybrid team culture" than more culturally diverse groups, which in turn, could affect the predictability of team members' behavior via shared group norms. As such, controlling for group-level diversity allows us to partial out group-level effects that may otherwise affect interpersonal trust in the dyads.

We used Blau's (1977) index to compute the cultural diversity of the 40 groups based on four ethnic categories: Chinese, Caucasian, Malay, and Indian. Because the numerical value for the maximum of Blau's index is dependent on the number of categories used in its calculation, we standardized it by dividing it with its theoretical maximum (see Agresti & Agresti, 1978). This index therefore has a minimum of zero, and a maximum of 1 (M = 0.37, SD = 0.26).

Cultural Intelligence

We assessed CQ with Ang and colleagues' (2007) 20-item cultural intelligence scale. Metacognitive CQ was assessed using four items (e.g., "I adjust my cultural knowledge as I interact with people from a culture that is unfamiliar to me"; Cronbach's alpha = 0.77); cognitive CQ was assessed using six items (e.g., "I know the religious beliefs of other cultures"; Cronbach's alpha = 0.87), motivational CQ was measured with five items (e.g., "I enjoy interacting with people from different cultures"; Cronbach's alpha = 0.85); and behavioral CQ was assessed with five items (e.g., "I change my verbal behavior [e.g., accent, tone] when a cross-cultural interaction requires it"; Cronbach's alpha = 0.81). All items were rated on a seven-point Likert scale (1 = strongly disagree and 7 = strongly agree).

Data Analytic Strategy

Our data analytic strategy was based on Kenny's (1994) social relations model, which is particularly well-suited for a round-robin design in which one person rates every other person in the group on a particular measure. In its most basic form, the social relations model describes a dyadic variable as the sum of four components: a constant, an actor effect, a partner effect, and a relationship effect.

The *actor effect* represents an individual's tendency to generally trust other people. The *partner effect* represents an individual's tendency to be generally trusted by other people. Both actor effect and partner effect are individual-level effects that refer to a person. Neither of these effects is relational. The *relationship effect* represents one individual's unique tendency to trust in a particular individual. The *constant* represents the mean rating across all actors, partners, and relationships, and across multiple groups it can be understood as measuring the mean level of trust in each group. These effects in the social relations model are conceived as random effects to be estimated. For the testing of our hypotheses, fixed effects are added to the model after establishing random effects.

The model essentially treats dyadic ratings as nested within raters and ratees, which in turn are crossed factors nested within groups. We used the proc-mixed procedure in SAS 9.1 for the estimation of the model and the testing of our hypotheses. Based on the social relations model methodology (Kenny, 1994), the first step in the analysis was to estimate a model with no predictor variables. This model separates the variance in trust ratings into the following: groups, dyads, actor, partner, and error.

To test hypothesis 1 (H1), we added group-level diversity as the control variable, followed by the dummy variable assessing cultural diversity of the dyad. To test hypotheses 2 through 5 (H2–H5) on the moderating role of CQ, we entered the four dimensions of CQ followed with one product term (cultural diversity × one CQ dimension) at a time to avoid multicollinearity between multiple product terms.

RESULTS

Results for the variance partitioning of interpersonal trust demonstrate that there was significant variance at the level of the self, partner, and the dyad, but not at the group level. According to Kenny (1996), we fixed the group variance estimate to zero for more efficient parameter estimation in all our subsequent analyses, while still including cultural diversity at the group level for control purposes.

Table 13.1 presents the multilevel regression results for our hypotheses. Our first hypothesis proposes that culturally diverse dyads will show lower levels of affect-based trust than monocultural dyads. Our results supported this hypothesis ($\beta = -0.21, p < 0.01$), after controlling for group-level diversity. Cohen's d, as an estimate for the effect size of cross-cultural dyads on relationship-specific affect-based trust, is –0.91, indicating a rather large effect.

Hypotheses 2 through 4 proposed that focal members' CQ in the dyad would attenuate the negative effect of cultural diversity on trust. For metacognitive CQ (H2), results show a significant interaction between metacognitive CQ of the focal individual and dyadic diversity ($\beta = 0.24, p < 0.11$) in predicting trust. For cognitive CQ (H3), the interaction between cognitive CQ of the focal individual and diversity of dyad was also significant ($\beta = 0.09, p < 0.06$). For motivational CQ (H4), the interaction term was not significant. For behavioral CQ (H5), we proposed that the behavioral CQ of the partner would moderate

Table 13.1

Results for Hypotheses 1–5

		cc-dyad	Focal Individual's CQ			Partner's CQ
	Empty model	(H1)	(H2)	(H3)	(H4)	(H5)
Intercept	4.13**	4.35**	3.81**	3.83**	3.82**	4.46**
Cultural diversity (group)		–.41*	–.39*	–.37*	–.39*	–.36*
Cross-cultural dyad		–.21**	–.24**	–.25**	–.24**	–.27**
Metacognitive CQ			.16*	.16**	.17**	–.05†
Cognitive CQ			.04	.04	.04	–.02
Motivational CQ			–.04	–.04	–.04	.02
Behavioral CQ			–.05	–.05	–.06	.03
Metacognitive CQ * cross-cultural dyad			**.11***			
Cognitive CQ * cross-cultural dyad				**.08†**		
Motivational CQ * cross-cultural dyad					.03	
Behavioral CQ * cross-cultural dyad						**.08†**

†p <0.1
*p <0.05
**p <0.01
Note: coefficients are unstandardized parameters.

the negative effect of cultural diversity. As expected, results show that behavioral CQ of the partner interacted with dyadic diversity to predict trust ratings ($\beta = 0.08$, $p < 0.06$). Thus H2, H3, and H5 received support, but not H4.

We also conducted two sets of post hoc analyses to further illuminate our findings. First, we ran a set of analyses with the subsample of monocultural dyads to examine whether the four CQ factors affected trust when cultural diversity was absent. As expected, none of the CQ factors affected affect-based trust in monocultural dyads. Given that approximately 70 percent of our dyads are monocultural, suggesting that statistical power is generally not an issue, these nonsignificant results provide further evidence to support the notion that CQ is a set of capabilities targeted at culturally diverse settings and interactions.

Second, we tested for interactions between group-level diversity and individuals' CQ to examine whether diversity at the group level exerts similar effects as diversity at the dyadic level. As expected, none of these moderation effects was significant, suggesting that individuals' CQ operates more at the dyadic rather than the group level of diversity.

DISCUSSION

Fostering trust between culturally dissimilar individuals constitutes a major challenge for MCTs. In this study, we examine how individuals' CQ alleviates the detrimental effect of cultural diversity on interpersonal trust, thereby demonstrating the relevance of CQ for MCTs. Further, our study highlights the importance of paying attention to cultural diversity at the dyadic level of analysis, rather than solely at the group level. Disentangling dyadic- and group-level diversity offers a more precise approach to understanding interpersonal dynamics within the team, and also facilitates a better understanding of the importance of an individual's CQ in MCTs.

Our study yields two major findings. First, our results demonstrate that dyadic- and group-level diversity exert a unique impact on group members' trust for each other, confirming the importance and utility of segregating the two levels in examining cultural diversity effects. Not surprisingly, our results show that dyadic-level diversity ($\beta = -0.21$, $p < 0.01$) had a stronger effect on members' trust for the other member in the dyad than group-level diversity ($\beta = -0.41$, $p < 0.05$), supporting our contention that social categorization and interpersonal trust are more appropriately examined at the dyadic level.

Second, our results demonstrate that CQ is an important capability for MCT members. In particular, we found that in cross-cultural dyads, focal members with higher metacognitive CQ and cognitive CQ reported greater trust in their culturally different partners. Behavioral CQ, as we expected, operated from the partner's perspective because partners who were able to demonstrate appropriate behaviors were more likely to weaken focal members' perceptions of salient cultural differences that could lead to out-group classification. Taken together, these results suggest that the negative effects of social categorization on cross-cultural interactions within the MCT can be reduced by increasing the CQ of both parties in the interactions.

Surprisingly, motivational CQ did not affect trust in the dyad. A possible reason was the ceiling and restriction of range observed in the motivational CQ scores in the sample. The mean level of motivational CQ was 5.14 (SD = 0.93) and, although not significantly higher than the mean level of metacognitive CQ, was significantly higher than the mean level of cognitive CQ ($t = 20.12$; $p < 0.01$) and behavioral CQ ($t = 2.63$; $p < 0.01$).

Theoretical Implications

Findings in this study have three major implications for existing research. First, this study offers important support to the construct validity of CQ. Although prior research (Ang et al., 2007) has demonstrated the importance of CQ in predicting outcomes in culturally diverse settings, our research extends these efforts by showing that CQ affects the interpersonal trust in cross-cultural dyads but not in monocultural dyads where cultural diversity is absent.

Second, our findings that the various CQ factors attenuate the negative effect of diversity on trust offer new insight to social categorization theory (Fiske, 1998). Specifically, our results suggest that the effect of social categorization may depend on individual characteristics. Social categorization research has shown that automatic biases can be influenced by knowledge about the attitude object (Fiske, 1998). Our findings confirm existing research by demonstrating the positive impact of knowledge (cognitive CQ) on trust, and offer further insight by demonstrating the importance of metacognitive capabilities and behavioral flexibility for overcoming the potential negative consequences of social categorization between two culturally different individuals.

Third, our study highlights the importance of an appropriate specification of levels of analysis in group diversity research. We contend that although research on group diversity has offered theoretical mechanisms for explaining the negative effects of diversity on group processes at both the group level (Earley & Mosakowski, 2000; Lau & Murnighan, 1998) and the dyadic level (Tajfel, 1981; Turner, 1987), empirical research has often not been specific in aligning the level of analysis of the theoretical mechanism with the level of analysis of the empirical constructs. This omission in existing research results in underspecified models that fail to account more fully for the effects of diversity on outcomes of interest. For instance, recall that our post hoc analyses did not yield any significant interactions between group-level diversity and members' CQ. Thus, had we only examined the interaction between group-level diversity and individuals' CQ, we would have concluded that CQ had no effects on group-level trust. However, by segregating group- and dyadic-level effects, we were able to demonstrate that CQ had an important role in enhancing interpersonal dynamics within the team. Hence, the present research extends prior research by showing that both group-level and dyadic-level dynamics independently contribute to the formation of trust in MCTs, and an accurate specification of the level of analysis is critical.

Managerial Implications

The results of this study suggest several important lessons for MCTs. First, selection of members based on CQ capabilities, in addition to technical qualifications, is important to help reduce the negative effects of diversity on team functioning.

Second, training that targets the different facets of CQ should be considered for MCT members. We suggest that existing diversity programs may focus too narrowly on the knowledge component, since they are typically designed to sensitize employees to the impact of stereotypes on their own and others' behaviors (Ely, 2004). Hence, these programs seem to focus more on increasing employees' knowledge about accurate "cultural explanations" of behavior, or cognitive CQ, and less on metacognitive or behavioral facets. As discussions in the area of expatriates' cultural awareness training suggest, while being a necessary first step, such a focus also faces the danger of replacing simple stereotypes with "sophisticated stereotypes" (Bird, Osland, Mendenhall, & Schneider, 1999). Diversity programs that focus too superficially on communicating diversity as a company value rather than giving people concrete skills for using diversity as a resource and managing conflict constructively may fall short of their intentions.

Future Research

Our findings in this study suggest several interesting areas for future research. We focus on three areas that will yield further insights into CQ and MCTs. First, we have examined cultural diversity as a "surface-level" characteristic, given that visible differences in ethnicity are more likely to activate social categorization processes. Future research however, can examine the role of CQ in mitigating effects of "deep-level" diversity on trust. This is because research shows that as teams mature, team performance is affected more by deep-level, rather than surface-level diversity (Harrison, Price, & Bell, 1998; Harrison, Price, Gavin, & Florey, 2002). An example of a "deep-level" characteristic is that of cultural values (Kirkman & Shapiro, 2005), since research has demonstrated how such cultural value differences lead to different behaviors (Adler, 2002; Elron, 1997).

Second, our research has focused on the relationship between cultural diversity and CQ from a social categorization perspective. Future research might also investigate the role of CQ in culturally diverse teams from an information and decision-making perspective. Although cognitive resource theory (Cox & Blake, 1991) generally proposes that diversity has positive impact on group performance because of increased breadth in the skills, abilities, information, and knowledge that diverse team members bring, recent research suggests that these advantages can only be realized if a psychologically safe communication climate exists (Gibson & Gibbs, 2006). Since trust among team members is important in fostering a psychologically safe communication climate, we expect trust to accentuate the informational benefits of MCTs. In light of our current results, future research could investigate whether MCTs with higher CQ are more likely to benefit from the diverse perspectives as suggested by the information perspective.

Third, even though our model is multilevel in nature, we have focused on the dyadic level of analysis (controlling for group-level diversity), given our interest in interpersonal trust. Future research could examine group and dyadic effects simultaneously in greater depth, to arrive at a more fully specified model that considers both interpersonal and team dynamics within MCTs. For instance, in addition to the dyadic model examined in this study, future research could also examine compositional models of CQ and group-level trust, to better understand group-level dynamics. This would require careful design considerations, such as measures of trust that are conceptualized at the appropriate level of analysis. In our study, we measured trust at the dyadic level. While we are confident that the average level of interpersonal trust in a group is an important conceptualization of trust at the group level, it is clearly not the only one. Trust at the group level could also be understood as trust *in* the group, which will then require a shift to the group as the reference (Chan, 1998).

CONCLUSION

In conclusion, we agree with Jackson and Joshi (2004, p. 697) that "multilevel and cross-level investigations offer some potential for improving our understanding of diversity dynamics within organizations." Our study builds on this recommendation by highlighting the importance of aligning theoretical mechanisms with the appropriate level of empirical analysis. Our study also highlights the importance of members' CQ in ameliorating the negative effects of diversity on team and member experiences in MCTs.

REFERENCES

Abreu, J.M. (2001). Theory and research on stereotypes and perceptual bias: A resource guide for multicultural counseling trainers. *The Counseling Psychologist, 29,* 487–512.

Adler, N.J. (2002). *International dimensions of organizational behavior* (4th ed.). Cincinnati, OH: South-Western.

Agresti, A., & Agresti, B.F. (1978). Statistical analysis of qualitative variation. In K.F. Schuessler (Ed.), *Sociological methodology* (pp. 204–237). San Francisco, CA: Jossey-Bass.

Allport, G.W. (1954). *The nature of prejudice.* Reading, MA: Addison-Wesley.

Ang, S., Van Dyne, L., Koh, C., Ng, K.Y., Templer, K.J., Tay, C., & Chandrasekar, N.A. (2007). Cultural intelligence: Its measurement and effects on cultural judgment and decision making, cultural adaptation, and task performance. *Management and Organization Review, 3,* 335–371.

Bird, A., Osland, J.S., Mendenhall, M., & Schneider, S.C. (1999). Adapting and adjusting to other cultures. What we know but don't always tell. *Journal of Management Inquiry, 8,* 152–165.

Blau, P.M. (1977). *Inequality and composition: A primitive theory of social structure.* New York: Free Press.

Brewer, M.B. (1981). Ethnocentrism and its role in interpersonal trust. In M.B. Brewer & J.E. Collins (Eds.), *Scientific inquiry and the social sciences* (pp. 345–360). San Francisco, CA: Jossey-Bass.

Brislin, R., Worthley, R., & MacNab, B. (2006). Cultural intelligence: Understanding behaviors that serve people's goals. *Group and Organization Management, 31,* 40–55.

Chan, D. (1998). Functional relations among constructs in the same content domain at different levels of analysis: A typology of composition models. *Journal of Applied Psychology, 83,* 234–246.

Child, J. (2001). Trust: The fundamental bond in global collaboration. *Organizational Dynamics, 29,* 45–64.

Cox, T.J. (1995). The complexity of diversity: Challenges and directions for future research. In S.E. Jackson & M.N. Ruderman (Eds.), *Diversity in work teams: Research paradigms for a changing workplace* (pp. 235–246). Washington, DC: American Psychological Association.

Cox, T.J., & Blake, S. (1991). Managing cultural diversity: Implications for organizational competitiveness. *Academy of Management Executive, 5,* 45–56.

Dreachslin, J.L., Hunt, P.L., & Sprainer, E. (2000). Workforce diversity: Implications for the effectiveness of health care delivery teams. *Social Science & Medicine, 50,* 1403–1414.

Earley, P.C., & Ang, S. (2003). *Cultural intelligence: Individual interactions across cultures.* Palo Alto, CA: Stanford University Press.

Earley, P.C., & Mosakowski, E. (2000). Creating hybrid team cultures: An empirical test of transnational team functioning. *Academy of Management Journal, 43,* 26–49.

Earley, P.C., & Mosakowski, E. (2004). Cultural intelligence. *Harvard Business Review, 82,* 139–146.

Elron, E. (1997). Top management teams within multinational corporations: Effects of cultural heterogeneity. *Leadership Quarterly, 8,* 393–412.

Ely, R.J. (2004). A field study of group diversity, participation in diversity education programs, and performance. *Journal of Organizational Behavior, 25,* 755–780.

Fiske, S.T. (1998). Stereotyping, prejudice, and discrimination. In S.T. Fiske & D.T. Gilbert (Eds.), *The handbook of social psychology. Volume 2* (4th ed.) (pp. 357–411). New York: McGraw-Hill.

Gaertner, S.L., & Dovidio, J.F. (2000). *Reducing intergroup bias: The common ingroup identity model.* Philadelphia, PA: Brunner/Mazel.

Gibson, C.B., & Gibbs, J.L. (2006). Unpacking the concept of virtuality: The effects of geographic dispersion, electronic dependence, dynamic structure, and national diversity on team innovation. *Administrative Science Quarterly, 51,* 451–495.

Gibson, C.B., & Zellmer-Bruhn, M. (2001). Metaphor and meaning: An intercultural analysis of the concept of teamwork. *Administrative Science Quarterly, 46,* 274–303.

Gudykunst, W.B., Ting-Toomey, S., & Chua, E. (1998). *Culture and interpersonal communication.* Newbury Park, CA: Sage.

Harrison, D.A., Price, K.H., & Bell, M.P. (1998). Beyond relational demography: Time and the effects of surface- and deep-level diversity on work group cohesion. *Academy of Management Journal, 41,* 96–107.

Harrison, D.A., Price, K.H., Gavin, J.H., & Florey, A.T. (2002). Time, teams, and task performance: Changing effects of surface- and deep-level diversity on group functioning. *Academy of Management Journal, 45,* 1029–1045.

Ilgen, D.R., & Pulakos, E.D. (1999). *The changing nature of performance: Implications for staffing, motivation, and development.* San Francisco, CA: Jossey-Bass.

Jackson, S.E., & Joshi, A. (2004). Diversity in social context: A multi-attribute, multilevel analysis of team diversity and sales performance. *Journal of Organizational Behavior, 25,* 675–702.

Jackson, S.E., May, K.E., & Whitney, K. (1995). Understanding the dynamics of diversity in decision making teams. In R.A. Guzzo & E. Salas (Eds.), *Team effectiveness and decision making in organizations* (pp. 204–261). San Francisco, CA: Jossey-Bass.

Kenny, D.A. (1994). *Interpersonal perception: A social relations analysis.* New York: Guilford Press.

Kenny, D.A. (1996). The design and analysis of social interaction research. *Annual Review of Psychology, 47,* 59–86.

Kirkman, B.L., & Shapiro, D.L. (2005). The impact of cultural value diversity on multicultural team performance. *Advances in International Management, 8,* 33–67.

Klein, K.J., & Dansereau, F. (1994). Levels issues in theory development, data collection, and analysis. *Academy of Management Review, 19,* 195–229.

Kramer, R.M. (1999). Trust and distrust in organizations: Emerging perspectives, enduring questions. *Annual Review of Psychology, 50,* 569–598.

Lau, D.C., & Murnighan, J.K. (1998). Demographic diversity and faultlines: The compositional dynamics of organizational groups. *Academy of Management Review, 23,* 325–340.

Lewicki, R.J., & Bunker, B.B. (1996). Developing and maintaining trust in work relationships. In R.M. Kramer & T.R. Tyler (Eds.), *Trust in organizations: Frontiers of theory and research* (pp. 114–139). Thousand Oaks, CA: Sage.

Lewis, J.D., & Weigert, A. (1985). Trust as a social reality. *Social Forces, 63,* 967–985.

Mayer, R.C., Davis, J.H., & Schoorman, F.D. (1995). An integrative model of organizational trust. *Academy of Management Review, 20,* 709–734.

McAllister, D.J. (1995). Affect- and cognition-based trust as foundations of interpersonal cooperation in organizations. *Academy of Management Journal, 38,* 24–59.

Pelled, L.H. (1996). Demographic diversity, conflict, and work group outcomes: An intervening process theory. *Organization Science, 7,* 615–631.

Pelled, L.H., Eisenhardt, K.M., & Xin, K.R. (1999). Exploring the black box: An analysis of work group diversity, conflict, and performance. *Administrative Science Quarterly, 44,* 1–28.

Pettigrew, T.F. (1998). Intergroup contact theory. *Annual Review of Psychology, 49,* 65–85.

Pruitt, D.G. (1983). Experimental gaming and the goal/expectation hypothesis. *Small Groups and Social Interaction, 2,* 107–121.

Rempel, J.K., Holmes, J.G., & Zanna, M.D. (1985). Trust in close relationships. *Journal of Personality and Social Psychology, 49,* 95–112.

Reynolds, K.J., & Oakes, P.J. (2000). Variability in impression formation: Investigating the role of motivation, capacity, and the categorization process, *Personality & Social Psychology Bulletin, 26,* 355–373.

Smith, K.G., Smith, K.A., Olian, J.D., Sims, H.P., O'Bannon, D.P., & Scully, J.A. (1994). Top management team demography and process: The role of social integration and communication. *Administrative Science Quarterly, 39,* 412–438.

Stewart, G.L. (2006). A meta-analytic review of relationships between team design features and team performance. *Journal of Management, 32,* 29–55.

Tajfel, H. (1981). *Human groups and social categories: Studies in social psychology.* Cambridge: Cambridge University Press.

Templer, K.J., Tay, C., & Chandrasekar, N.A. (2006). Motivational cultural intelligence, realistic job preview, realistic living conditions preview, and cross-cultural adjustment. *Group and Organization Management, 31,* 154–174.

Triandis, H.C. (2006). Cultural intelligence in organizations. *Group and Organization Management, 31,* 20–26.

Turner, J.C. (1987). *Rediscovering the social group: A self-categorization theory.* Oxford: Basil Blackwell.

Williams, K.Y., & O'Reilly, C.A.I. (1998). Demography and diversity in organizations: A review of 40 years of research. In L.L. Cummings & B.M. Staw (Eds.), *Research in organizational behavior. Volume 20* (pp. 77–140). Greenwich, CT: JAI.

CHAPTER 14

Culture Inside and Out

Developing a Collaboration's Capacity to Externally Adjust

CRISTINA B. GIBSON AND REBEKAH DIBBLE

How does a multicultural team harness cultural differences to innovate successfully? In many ways, the answer may involve looking outward to the external environment (rather than inward to the organization) and adjusting expediently. For example, in the world of technology design, says John Thackara of the Netherlands Design Institute, "Too much industrial research development is driven by a frantic scampering after technological Holy Grails—not by an exploration of changing social needs" (Hofmeester, 1999). For two years, John served as Chair of the Steering Group for the Maypole Project, a multinational collaboration among sociologists, psychologists, interaction designers, and electronics engineers across Europe.

Maypole conducted research into the communicative behavior of the family and developed new applications for communication technology. The project was part of the European Network for Intelligent Information Interfaces (i^3), which was formed with funding from the European Commission to look into the role of new media in social renewal. Maypole was deemed an overwhelming success, not just because of the technology concepts developed, but due to their unique ability to scan the target market and environment, comprehensively understand the changes occurring in the way families interact with technology, and adjust their team objectives and processes accordingly. This same capability may be the key to success in many other types of collaborations, as broad-ranging as multinational outsourcing, disaster relief, filmmaking, or health care.

In this chapter we explore this idea by developing the concept of *collaboration external adjustment,* defined as the capability of a collaboration to adapt to challenges in the external environment. The chapter is organized into four sections. First, we address the nature of the capability, further refining our definition, elaborating on the types of challenges many multicultural collaborations face, and the ways in which they adapt. Second, we discuss why external adjustment is important, proposing a set of outcomes it predicts for multicultural collaborations. Third, we review previously developed concepts such as team reflexivity, establishment of external ties and networks, expatriate adjustment and repatriation, and adaptation in the context of joint ventures, identifying commonalities, and drawing critical distinctions between these concepts and collaboration external adjustment. Finally, we conclude with a discussion of antecedents to the capability, describing how it forms, and proposing several features of collaborations that help to develop the capability. In this final section we highlight the important role of cultural intelligence (CQ) as an individual level antecedent to collaboration external adjustment. We argue that when individual members of a collaboration possess CQ, this increases the ability of the collaboration as a whole to cope with and respond to changes in the external environment.

THE NATURE OF COLLABORATION EXTERNAL ADJUSTMENT

Partners in three countries participating in an outsourcing agreement must renegotiate their contracts due to a new regulation imposed by a local government. A multinational group of documentary filmmakers must change locations and replace equipment because a mudslide has obliterated their film set at a remote site. Humanitarian aid workers are forced out of a specific region due to political uncertainty and military unrest and must gain permission to enter a new region to refocus their efforts. The funding for a team of doctors developing a medical device has suddenly become available, enabling the addition of new staff, and a broader and more ambitious development trajectory. In the first three examples, participants in a collaboration have experienced a negative change (i.e., a threat) in the external environment in which they operate and must make fundamental adjustments in their collaborative behavior to succeed or simply survive. However, external adjustment need not always be an adaptation to a negative phenomenon. In the last example, we see a situation where external adjustment entails taking advantage of an opportunity that presents itself in the form of a "positive" environmental challenge. In this section, we elaborate on the types of challenges collaborations such as these might face and the ways in which they can adapt to these challenges.

Challenges in Multicultural Collaborations

Multicultural collaborations are time limited, multiparty efforts to produce an explicit product or service with cooperative action involving participants from more than one cultural group. We use the term *collaboration* rather than *team,* because many of the concerted efforts we have seen around the globe do not fit the most common definition of a team found in the organizational behavior literature (e.g., Cohen & Bailey, 1997; Earley & Gibson, 2002). Specifically, participants in a collaboration may come together on a one-time basis, without anticipating continued interaction. A core set of members may remain involved for an extended period of time, but other participants may float on and off the effort, working only on an "as needed" sporadic basis. Further, collaborations may have periods of intensely interdependent interaction, but may otherwise consist of quite independent actors. Many are not embedded in a single organizational context, but rather represent either cross-organizational cooperation or participants may not have any organizational affiliation at all. Participants may feel as though they share a common purpose for the duration of a given project, yet may not view themselves as a "team." Collaborators may never meet face-to-face, may be geographically dispersed, and may be primarily connected by communication technology (Gibson & Gibbs, 2006). Thus, collaborations are more loosely structured, more temporary, more fluid, and often more electronically enabled than traditional teams (Gibson, 2006).

Multicultural collaborations are formed for many reasons. They may enable bringing together the best minds, skills, and knowledge, without heavy administrative, relocation, or travel costs. Participants bring with them local knowledge, skills, resources, and institutional connections that become important assets in many projects. As a result, multicultural collaborations are not limited to any given industry or project type. They may occur in settings as diverse as new product development in the pharmaceutical industry, in the procurement function in the automotive industry, in delivery of services in the travel and hospitality industry, or in humanitarian aid efforts. In addition to the collaboration we described in the opening paragraph involving concept development in the information technology domain, we have systematically observed successful multicultural collaborations in consulting and professional services, filmmaking, human resource management, peacekeeping forces, educational services, emergency health care, scientific research, and training and development efforts.

A variety of challenges are experienced through multicultural collaborations. Many of these have in common the occurrence of rapid change. That is, changes in the external environment create challenges for the collaboration by changing the way a collaboration experiences and interacts with its environment. We have witnessed challenges related to external environmental change that fall into five broad categories, which are not intended to be exhaustive: (1) economic (e.g., devaluation or stabilization of currency, inflation), political (e.g., regime change, public unrest, military action, transition to a more market-friendly environment), and regulatory challenges and opportunities (e.g., trade barriers, taxation, imposition or relaxation of legal restrictions); (2) technological (e.g., technical failure, new technologies to incorporate, new enabling technologies) and human resource challenges and opportunities (e.g., labor disputes, access to skilled workforce at lower wages); (3) financial (e.g., lack of funding, increased resource needs, increased funding, decreased resource needs) and time pressure challenges and opportunities (e.g., increased urgency of deadlines, delays, relaxation of timelines, innovations enabling more efficient processes); (4) physical environment adversity (e.g., natural disaster, weather hazards, access to locations with ideal weather conditions); and (5) cultural challenges and opportunities (e.g., differing values or ways of viewing the world, stereotypes, prejudice, cultural development). Due to the theme of this book, we focus here on this last set of challenges, hence the notion that external adjustment incorporates culture "inside and out." In particular, we note the important connections between the skills and abilities of collaboration members, such as CQ, and the ability of the collaboration to adjust.

The Maypole Project, for example, involved participants from Austria, Germany, the United Kingdom, the Netherlands, Finland, and India. These nations are char-

Figure 14.1 **Forms of Collaboration External Adjustment**

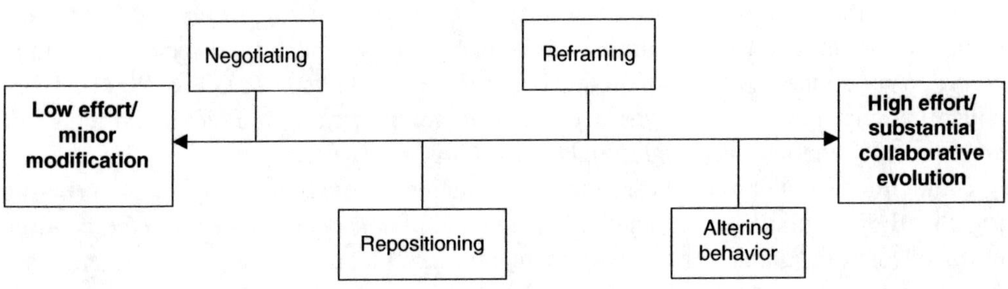

acterized by very different cultural values, cognitive styles, and work preferences. The participants viewed these differences as a strength of the collaboration, because it allowed them to draw upon a variety of knowledge, experiences, and perceptions. More challenging than the cultural differences internal to the collaboration were the changes in the external environment that evolved as the collaboration progressed. The European Union (EU) expanded to include new member nations during the course of the project, changing the national profiles of the target end users. Sociocultural trends toward greater technological proficiency, particularly among children, accelerated during the course of the collaboration. Cooperation (and animosity) across national borders waxed and waned. These shifts in the external environment necessitated ongoing reinterpretation of the project's core objective: designing technology that enabled social renewal.

In another case, a multinational documentary film team reported having encountered a great deal of cultural adversity, in the form of stereotypes and prejudice, in addition to significant amounts of political and economic challenges, in the process of making their film in Baghdad, Iraq. The cultural challenges were the most difficult to overcome, creating barriers to access in certain areas of the city, reluctance to share information, and concerns over personal safety. The multicultural composition of the team and the CQ of the collaboration allowed the members to successfully adapt to these challenges and complete the film, in spite of the difficulties they faced.

Forms of Adaptation

When an external environmental challenge is experienced, how might a multicultural collaboration adjust? Recognizing that the nature of external adjustment is likely to be very complex and perhaps as diverse as the many different types of collaborations that exist, we have begun to identify four broad categories of external adjustments: *negotiating, repositioning, reframing,* and *altering behavior* (see Figure. 14.1). These categories represent a continuum from low effort and minor modification to high effort and substantial evolution in the collaboration. We elaborate on these below with the caveat that systematic empirical assessment and exploration of these and other potential forms of adjustment are critical next steps in this research domain.

Negotiating

Participants in a multicultural collaboration may adjust by focusing efforts outside the collaboration, attempting to bargain with key parties to entice them to change so that the collaboration itself does not have to explicitly change. Although it does not involve substantial modification of processes, negotiating with the external environment requires effort, hence we view it as a type of adjustment. For example, consider a hypothetical new product development project called Europe Connect which may have received funding under the same program as the Maypole Project, and has similar objectives focused on development of technology concepts. Participants in Europe Connect may have attempted to convince those outside the collaboration that new member nations who happen to join the EU during the project share many of the same cultural values that pertain to their domain as existing members. By "explaining away" any differences, they could curtail any dramatic changes in their own work. Or, members of Europe Connect could attempt to promote awareness and adoption of these sociocultural trends in the new member nations, such that they are aligned with existing member nations, again reducing the degree to which they have to adjust their own work. Additionally, consider the example of humanitarian aid collaborations working in societies plagued by war and where conflicting political and cultural factions are less than supportive of humanitarian norms. One of the momentous challenges facing humanitarian relief groups is safeguarding the residents of these locations and providing necessary assistance. Adjustment to this type of hostile context could involve negotiations with the relevant political and cultural groups to explain and justify the humanitarian aid effort. Without such negotiations, it is doubtful that the collaboration could fulfill its mission.

Repositioning

When negotiating with parties who are external to the collaboration does not provide for a smooth path forward, participants in a multicultural collaboration may reposition themselves vis-à-vis the external environment, essentially carving out a new market, or niche, or redefining the constituents, stakeholders, and end users. For example, although new member nations may have been added to the EU, and the EU may have been the ultimate source of funding for a project such as Europe Connect, collaborators may have negotiated with the specific program (e.g., the i^3 initiative) to maintain a focus on the original EU member nations that had joined prior to project launch. This would mean "ignoring" the cultural needs of the new member nations, but would simplify the degree to which the collaboration would need to make adjustments.

This adjustment is basically a tightening and refining of the constituents, or a process of making the target constituents more explicit. Another example of repositioning in order to adjust to external challenges might be a documentary film team that learns they have carved out too broad a niche for their film. As a result, they might reposition their film, redefining their audience as a particular activist or interest group that they anticipate will be particularly receptive to the film.

Reframing

While repositioning maintains an outward focus and requires relatively minor changes, collaborators who engage in reframing to adjust to external challenges are beginning to address more fundamental changes in the nature of their work together. Reframing involves a shift in the objectives, goals, or mission of the collaboration to maintain alignment with the change in the external environment. Again, drawing on the Maypole Project as an example, given the increasingly common trend for children to interact with (and own!) their own technology, the participants likely had to gradually reframe their objectives as enabling the sharing of information between adults and children and among children via communication technology. This focus on children and the family unit corresponded to the sociocultural trends that their research uncovered. Without such an adjustment, their objectives would have been obsolete.

Another hypothetical example of reframing might be a group of humanitarians that embarks on a recovery effort with a specific set of objectives, such as rebuilding housing destroyed by a flood within a given region. However, upon arrival at the scene of the crisis, interaction with the local population as well as initial assessments of the environment might reveal a need to reframe their objectives to include a broader geographic area. The same set of basic activities would be conducted, just expanded to include a larger region. If they continued to pursue their original objective, the urgent needs of the constituents would not be met, and the collaboration would have less impact.

Altering Behavior

Finally, the most effortful adjustment entails substantial changes in participants' behavior in their interaction with the collaboration's external environment. There are a whole host of changes that a collaboration might make internally among the participants (without interfacing with the external environment); however, we view these internal adjustments as comprising other collaborative concepts (such as reflexivity). Examples of external adjustments that involve altering behavior include adapting work processes to better fit a change that occurred in a location, changing the style in which collaborators work with those outside the collaboration, developing new roles on the collaboration to liaise with the external environment, or altering the time frame, production schedule, or delivery schedule for the collaboration to better fit the external environment. On a technology development project such as Europe Connect, an example of altering behavior might involve adding a position dedicated to media relations if it became clear that the media would play an important role in securing samples needed for feasibility studies in the new member nations.

As another example, consider a documentary film team conducting its work in multiple countries. As it moves from one location to the next, the manner in which participants collaborate with local officials will likely need to be adjusted. However, if they find that certain issues are more salient in some locations than in others, they may need to alter the very content of their film, in order to most effectively educate viewers and disseminate the most pertinent knowledge. External adjustment for this collaboration requires modifying their basic work processes to incorporate the cultural differences they encounter in each location.

THE IMPORTANCE OF COLLABORATION EXTERNAL ADJUSTMENT

In the preceding section, we emphasized the types of challenges that multicultural collaborations often face and the manner in which they may adjust to them. We now make a case for the importance of collaboration external adjustment by discussing the evolution in the nature of collaborative environments that necessitates external adjustment, as well as the potential outcomes that can be achieved through the external adjustment process.

The Evolving Nature of Collaborative Environments

We have found that collaborations are becoming more and more common, while traditional teams are less common (Gibson & Cohen, 2003). This is because work and organizations themselves are being transformed by globalization, communication technology, and political and economic reform. Many traditional organizational models assume that work processes are best proactively mapped according to milestones and concrete deadlines, with extraneous factors managed to buffer progress (Bluedorn & Denhardt, 1988; McDonough & Leifer, 1983). In many work settings today, however, participants operate in crisis mode, necessitated by urgent constituent needs and extraordinary environmental volatility. Witness the cardiac surgery team that must prepare on a moment's notice, and change course when technology fails or risk losing the life of a patient (Edmondson, Bohmer, & Pisano, 2001). These circumstances are equally relevant in a complex collaboration such as a disaster relief project. Volunteers, independent contractors, and local vendors collaborate to provide relief in a compressed time frame and very turbulent physical environments (e.g., earthquake aftershocks), with substantial loss occurring due to delayed reactions. Models are needed that capture the features of a collaboration that are necessary to face such urgent needs and volatility in the physical and constituent environment.

Innovation as a Critical Success Factor

As collaboration has evolved, innovation has become most often the key outcome that many collaborators hope to achieve. Innovation is the collective process of incorporating knowledge into new methodologies, products, and services (Nonaka & Takeuchi, 1995; Dougherty, 2001; Leonard-Barton, 1995; Mohrman, Klein, & Finegold, 2003). Innovation is important because, even more than other competitive moves such as merger or acquisition, it is a critical means by which members of organizations diversify and reinvent themselves to match evolving market and technical conditions (Schoonhoven, Eisenhardt & Lyman, 1990). This has been demonstrated in single industry studies, including technology (Vessey, 1991; Eisenhardt & Tabrizi, 1995; Galunic & Eisenhardt, 2001), pharmaceuticals (Zellmer-Bruhn & Gibson, 2006), and automotive settings (Clark & Fujimoto, 1991; Obstfeld, 2005), as well as in multi-industry studies, which often control for industry effects across industries such as agriculture, aerospace, retail, professional services, medical products, chemicals, telecommunications, and consumer electronics (Hargadon & Sutton, 1997; Gatignon et al., 2002).

Researchers have also documented the relationship between innovation and effectiveness at the team level (Gibson & Vermeulen, 2003; Gibson & Birkinshaw, 2004; Bain, Mann, & Pirola-Merlo, 2001; Edmondson et al., 2001). This is also true of the type of multicultural collaborations we address here. Yet, innovation is impossible if collaborations cannot make use of contextual knowledge (Davenport, De Long, & Beers, 1998; Gibson & Gibbs, 2006) and translate it into effective behavior. Collaboration external adjustment is a critical component in this process, and hence has the power to enable innovation.

Outcomes of Collaboration External Adjustment

Innovation is not the only outcome that multicultural collaborations often experience when they externally adjust. The Maypole Project is an example of a collaboration that experienced innovation as well as efficiency, productivity, and effectiveness, and was deemed a success by the i^3 initiative as well as the EU because it achieved its multifaceted objectives. Perhaps equally important, participants were satisfied with their work in the collaboration, felt that they personally gained from their involvement, and were eager and enthusiastic about participating in a similar collaboration in the future, involving some of the same participants.

Beyond these important indicators of performance, we have also observed that those collaborations that fail to adjust may in fact fail to survive. An information technology collaboration that does not negotiate well with investors when they show cultural proclivities toward certain sociocultural trends, may see their funding dry up and be forced to close up shop. Filmmaking teams who cannot position their films so that they will be well received by the audiences that view their films may find it impossible to get their films screened or distributed. Humanitarian aid workers that do not develop work processes that incorporate the cultural values of their constituents may see the aid go unused or misapplied. All of these examples underscore the fundamental nature of collaboration external adjustment, and provide insight into which collaborations will be most successful in the future.

DISTINGUISHING COLLABORATION EXTERNAL ADJUSTMENT FROM OTHER CONSTRUCTS

We have defined collaboration external adjustment as the ability of a collaboration to adapt to challenges in the external environment. Concepts and processes such as team reflexivity, establishment of external ties and networks, expatriate adjustment and repatriation, and adaptation in the context of joint ventures share some notable similarities with our construct of collaboration external adjustment, but nevertheless are critically distinct. In the section that follows we draw upon the literature in order to underscore commonalities and draw critical distinctions between collaboration external adjustment and other similar constructs.

Team Reflexivity

Team reflexivity is one of several concepts that bear some resemblance to collaboration external adjustment. Team reflexivity has been defined as the "extent to which group members overtly reflect upon and communicate about the group's objectives, strategies (e.g., decision making), and processes (e.g., communication), and adapt them to current or anticipated circumstances" (Schippers, Den Hartog, Koopman, & Wienk, 2003). Other scholars have cited process assessment as a key to avoiding the obsolescence that can occur with environmental change and have noted that reflexivity is particularly critical in environments characterized by complexity and uncertainty (Schippers et al., 2003).

The concept of reflexivity is similar to the concept of collaboration external adjustment in the sense that both are focused on changes necessary to bring processes into alignment with goals. The most notable difference between the concept of reflexivity and collaboration external adjustment is that reflexivity is centered on the monitoring and adjustment of *internal* team processes, including evaluation of the appropriateness of their objectives and the effectiveness of their methods and processes (Schippers et al., 2003), while collaboration external adjustment involves the evaluation of *external* environmental conditions and the collaboration's ability to adjust its interactions with external constituents appropriately to changes in the external environment to achieve its objectives.

Establishment of External Ties and Networks

Collaboration external adjustment is also distinct from two concepts that address external relationships formed by social entities: external ties and external networks. External ties are "linkages between a pair of actors" (Wasserman & Faust, 1994, p. 18) where the actors are embedded in two different contexts. The combined set of external ties that team members have established with individuals outside the team comprise a team's external network (Ancona & Caldwell, 2000). Scholars have emphasized the importance of developing external relationships in order to share knowledge and facilitate political tactics, especially under conditions of complexity and high interdependence with other teams. Evidence has been found that a team's interaction with external ties and networks can impact performance (e.g., Ancona, 1990; Ancona & Caldwell, 1992; Peng & Luo, 2000; Joshi, 2006). External relationships have also been found to impact organizational performance (Rowley, Behrens, & Krackhardt, 2000).

There are several important distinctions to be made between our concept of collaboration external adjustment and the establishment of external ties or networks. First, although external ties and networks may be utilized to address challenges that arise in the environment outside a collaboration, they are not always formed in response to change and may exist in a steady state, which is maintained for months or even years without representing specific adaptation to a challenge or problem. Our concept of collaboration external adjustment, however, specifically represents dynamic change processes in a collaboration that may be necessary for survival and are brought about as a result of some occurrence in the collaboration's environment. Second, while the development of external ties and networks are essential ways collaborations adapt to external challenges, external adjustment is inclusive of strategies other than those related to the development of relationships. Hence, the establishment of external ties and networks is only one mechanism for collaboration external adjustment.

Expatriate Adjustment

The international management literature has examined adjustment processes in the context of expatriation and repatriation. When employees accept an overseas assignment, they are often faced with a very challenging new environment, consisting of different norms, values, rules, culture, business practices, daily customs, and living conditions than what they are accustomed to at home (Black, Mendenhall, & Oddou, 1991). For example, an expatriate working in Indonesia might need to adapt to a new level of pollution, heat, traffic, or different standards of productivity in the work environment. There is evidence to suggest that expatriates who adjust experience performance gains (Bhaskar-Shrinivas et al., 2005; Takeuchi Wang, & Marinova, 2005). Repatriation also involves significant adjustments including adapting to interaction with home country nationals and to the general environment and culture of the home country following an overseas assignment (Black, Gregersen, & Mendenhall, 1992).

A key difference between collaboration external adjustment and expatriate or repatriate adjustment is the level of analysis at which each is most commonly examined. While we locate our analysis of external adjustment at the collaboration level, most expatriation and repatriation literature is situated at the individual level of analysis, with implications at the organizational level. Furthermore, collaboration external adjustment may involve adjusting to external challenges posed by the local environment while expatriate adjustment involves adaptation to cultural differences on an international assignment. Additionally, while expatriate and repatriate adjustment involves fitting into an international subsidiary organization or back into the home office organization, a collaboration as we have defined it is less likely to be subject to this type of adjustment.

Adaptation in Joint Ventures

The literature on joint ventures also addresses external adjustment. When two organizations form an alliance, there is often the need for each to adjust their processes and policies (Buckley, Glaister & Husan; 2002, Inkpen & Currall, 2004), and those that do so have been found to be more effective (e.g., Fu, Peng, Kennedy, & Yukl, 2004; Szymanski, 1998). Nokia provides a recent example of the need for joint ventures to adjust. Due to

Figure 14.2 **Framework for Collaboration External Adjustment**

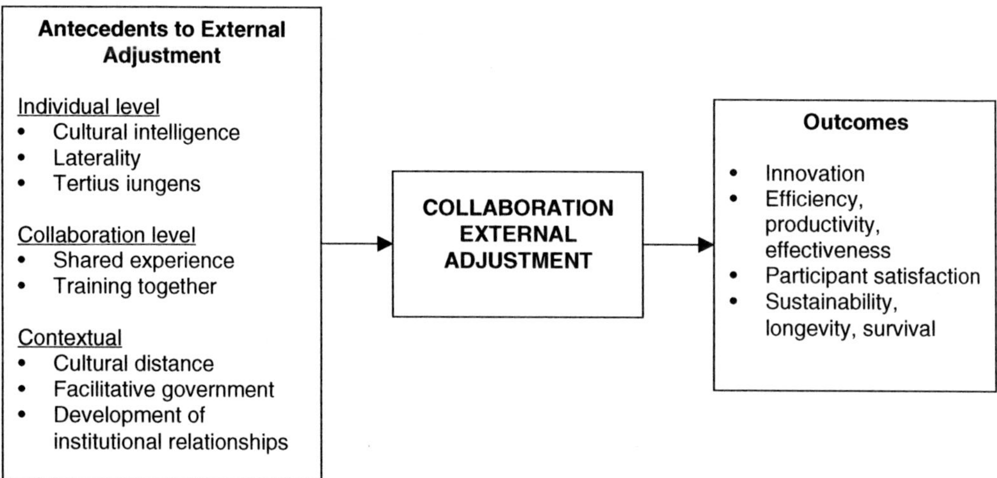

policy restrictions, Nokia entered the market in China via the establishment of four joint ventures with Chinese partners. However, due to fierce competition in the communications industry, it became necessary to adjust and combine the four joint ventures into one new company. The general manager of the new company noted that integrating the joint ventures would allow Nokia to optimize resource allocation among their companies in China (SinoCast China IT Watch, 2005).

Again, there are several important distinctions between establishing a joint venture and collaboration external adjustment. First, collaboration external adjustment involves formulating a solution on behalf of a time-limited endeavor, whereas a joint venture may be a permanent solution. Second, collaboration external adjustment is initiated by a small social entity that may involve as few as three people, whereas joint ventures take place at the firm or business unit level. Third, while the forging of new ties may be one tool by which a collaboration externally adjusts, no new, independent organizational entities (as with a joint venture) are formed. Finally, there are many other motivations (other than adjusting to unplanned circumstances) for establishing joint ventures (Inkpen & Beamish, 1997; Makino & Delios, 1996, Wong & Ellis, 2002).

DEVELOPING THE CAPABILITY TO EXTERNALLY ADJUST

Having addressed the defining features of collaboration external adjustment, including why collaborations adjust and how they might adjust, as well as how external adjustment is distinct from other concepts, we now identify several possible antecedents to collaboration external adjustment. We consider antecedents at three levels: the individual level, the collaboration level, and the larger external context outside the collaboration. Together, factors at each of these levels represent potential points of leverage for multicultural collaborations desiring to develop the capability to externally adjust. These are summarized in Figure 14.2.

Individual Level Antecedents

External adjustment may be enabled by the strategic composition of collaboration members who possess particular skills. Although choice of collaborators is not always within the discretion of participants, leaders may be charged with the responsibility of assembling the contributors. We anticipate that three individual characteristics enable the development of external adjustment: CQ, laterality, and tertius iungens. Each of these has received attention in the recent literature and all hold great promise in terms of bolstering the effectiveness of multicultural collaborations (perhaps directly and) through their effect on external adjustment.

Cultural Intelligence

The subject of much of this book, CQ is an aptitude and skill that enables someone from outside a culture to interpret unfamiliar gestures and actions as though they were insiders to that culture. According to Earley and Ang (2003), those with CQ are able to separate out three features of other people's behavior: those that are universally human, those that are idiosyncratically personal, and those that are rooted in culture. Further, in the Earley and Ang (2003) framework, there are cognitive (e.g., the structure and interrelatedness of cognitions relevant for comprehending and functioning within a culturally dissimilar context), motivational (e.g., willingness to stay engaged in the process of making sense of unfamiliar situations), and behavioral (e.g., linguistic behaviors including facial expression and proxemics) components of CQ. We anticipate that all three of these components may enable external adjustment in multicultural collaborations. The cognitive component will be useful in recognizing the need for adjustment, the motivational component will encourage persistence in the adjustment process in the face of setbacks or particularly enduring challenges, and the behavioral component will contribute to the most intensive adjustment processes which require the entire collaboration to alter their functioning, vis-à-vis the external environment.

Laterality

The second individual characteristic that we argue can enable collaboration external adjustment is laterality, defined as the ability to cut across boundaries and relate to others from different areas (Gibson & Cohen, 2003). Laterality is a communication skill that overlaps to some degree with the behavioral component of CQ (Gibson, 2006). People with laterality are able to act as a bridge and interpreter between different functional or cultural areas, can rapidly learn the basic language and conceptual framework of their collaborators, are confident but not egotistical about what they know, and are not defensive about their lack of knowledge in other areas. Scholars have argued that to take maximum advantage of the innovation-creating capabilities of a global collaboration, participants must be aware of and connected to the larger system, and the larger system must be responsive to and able to incorporate the knowledge that is generated in its various subunits

(Mohrman et al., 2003). Laterality is likely the key to establishing these connections. For example, in defense industry collaborations, systems engineering integration specialists play key roles in linking across customer needs, firms, and subdisciplines (Fallows, 2002). Laterality enables individuals in these roles to create such links. When participants in a multicultural collaboration have laterality, it is likely they will be better able to contribute to collaboration external adjustment through negotiation, repositioning, and reframing, since each of these forms of adjustment are communication intensive.

Tertius Iungens

Finally, the individual characteristic known as *tertius iungens* represents a strategic, behavioral orientation toward connecting people in one's social network by either introducing disconnected individuals or facilitating new coordination between connected individuals (*tertius iungens* is Latin for "the third who joins") (Obstfeld, 2005). A person with a tertius iungens orientation is similar to Simmel's concept of a third party that acts as a mediator or nonpartisan to create or preserve group unity (Simmel, 1950). Recent empirical evidence demonstrates that those with a tertius iungens orientation are more involved in innovation than those without such an orientation (Obstfeld, 2005). They orchestrate and alter social networks, enlisting and introducing those that can be of assistance to each other. In multicultural collaborations, tertius iungens may be particularly useful in enabling external adjustment through behavioral alterations. In both of the examples of behavioral alterations we presented earlier, which involved adding a new position to liase with the media and collaborating with government officials to gain access to certain geographical areas, the ability to connect two unconnected parties is essential. Having more individuals on the collaboration with this skill would facilitate such adjustments.

Collaboration Level Antecedents

In addition to antecedents at the individual level, we argue that the level of experience and training together at the collaboration level are likely to impact the capability to externally adjust. Each of these factors constitutes strategic decisions regarding the management of the collaboration as a whole—and each of these factors can be carefully designed to enhance external adjustment.

Experience

Collaboration experience, in the form of previous collaborative work experience, likely contributes to the capability to externally adjust. When participants work together over time, perhaps across numerous collaborations or within the context of simulated activities during training, they create a shared history (Earley & Gibson, 2002). Shared history allows for the development of patterns of responses to external challenges and a common behavioral repertoire (Gibson, 2001; Zellmer-Bruhn, 2003). Although previous actions may not always fit novel circumstances, they do provide a basis from which to start, increasing the efficiency of external adjustment. Equally important are shared experiences, which are a basis for common understanding of identity (Stryker, 1980), strengthening each member's commitment to the collaboration and their role in the collaboration (Maznevski, 1994; Turner, 1987), and developing myths and rituals that reinforce membership with a community (Rosaldo, 1989). All of these features can help a multicultural collaboration to persist even in the face of substantial environmental challenges.

Training

In a similar vein, scholars have argued that training that increases isomorphic attributions, appropriate affect, synergistic information extraction, and decision making can increase effective use of CQ (Janssens & Brett, 2006; Triandis, 2006). The expatriation literature also suggests that there is a learned component of successful cultural adaptation at the individual level, and that organizations may assist with individual adjustment through training programs, standardization of organizational culture across locations, and providing social and logistical support to individuals in transition (Black & Gregersen, 2000). Hence, the extent to which collaborators develop a set of common experiences and shared history, either through working together over time or through training, may also enable external adjustment.

Contextual Antecedents

Successful adjustment to the external environment in which a collaboration operates may include the ability to deal with political instability, currency fluctuation, national or regional cultural differences, language barriers, unfavorable weather conditions, difficulty accessing critical resources, or opposition from various special interest groups. Given that not all locations hold similar probabilities for encountering these and other types of environmental adversity, it follows that features of the context (i.e., the location in which collaborations occur) are critical antecedents for external adjustment. Some locations will enhance and others exacerbate the external adjustment process. Joshi argues that "along with the demographics of the team, the demography of the embedding context will shape the nature and extent of external team networks" (Joshi, 2006, p. 583), which in turn have a direct impact on team performance. Katz et al. (2004) also acknowledge the importance of understanding the context in which a team is embedded in order to understand the way a team functions. We too argue that there is a critical relationship between the nature of the location or embedding context and the performance of a collaboration. In their research on local knowledge transfer, Makino and Delios (1996) refer to the problem of "location-based disadvantage," which they define as a foreign firm's disadvantage due to comparatively less knowledge about political, economic, and social situations than their local counterparts. Similarly, Inkpen and Beamish (1997) cite market uncertainties as a type of external challenge and note that the acquisition of local knowledge, consisting of critical information about "cultural traditions, norms, values, and institutional differences" (Inkpen & Beamish, 1997, p. 181) is an important means of adjusting. When those leading a collaboration select a location so that "location-based disadvantages" are minimized, chances for successful adjustment should improve. Three contextual features likely to be particularly salient influences on external adjustment include national cultural distance, facilitative government, and institutional relationships.

Cultural Distance

Cultural distance is a concept that has been utilized by multiple scholars as a means of quantifying differences between national cultures that influence managerial decisions. Kogut and Singh (1988) argue that the greater the cultural distance between two countries, the more distinct their organizational characteristics will be. Cultural distance represents "a proxy for disadvantages a firm faces when it establishes operations in a host country outside of its home country" (Mezias et al., 2002, p. 408). Kostova and Zaheer (1999) suggest that where there are greater institutional differences between the native environment of a multinational enterprise (MNE) and the host country in which its subunit operates, the MNE subunit will face more challenges establishing and maintaining legitimacy in the host country (Kostova & Zaheer, 1999). We argue that in a multicultural collaboration, one way of potentially minimizing a "location-based disadvantage" is selecting a location such that cultural distance is minimized between the native and host environments of the collaboration. The United States and Australia are examples of countries where cultural distance is low. That is, they are relatively similar on key cultural dimensions (Hofstede, 1980). The cultural distance between Pakistan and the United States, on the other hand, would be much higher, indicating significant differences in cultural values and norms. We argue that when it is within the control of the collaboration, location selection based on consideration of cultural distance will have an impact on a collaboration's ability to externally adjust.

Facilitative Government

In addition to cultural distance, facilitative government is a characteristic of collaboration context likely to impact external adjustment. While some political contexts provide a safe haven for organizations, others are much less "facilitative," making external adjustment more difficult. Facilitating governments are supportive and seek to provide predictable laws and regulations that they are capable of enforcing. As governments become less facilitative, the less supportive they are of organizations, and the more unpredictable they are (Pearce, 2001). Nonfacilitative governments are hostile to independent organization, and have weak or nonexistent legal regulation. Symptoms of these governmental ills are manifest in organizational maladies such as distrust, fear, cheating, exploitation, and rule breaking (Pearce, 2001). As an example, in their study of entrepreneurial ventures in Russia during the 1990s, Puffer and McCarthy (2001) provide examples of the ways that nonfacilitative governments threaten an organization's ability to externally adjust. They note that a hostile environment characterized by an unstable government, an underdeveloped legal system, overregulation, a virtually unfathomable taxation system, a pervasive mafia, and an inadequate business infrastructure pervaded the environmental context in Russia during this time period (Puffer & McCarthy, 2001). Accordingly, entrepreneurs were faced with the thorny task of adjusting to hostile legislation, currency devaluation, exposure to mafia, and shifting tax laws—adjustments that would have been far less complex in a more facilitative environment. An understanding of the role that facilitative governments play in the external adjustment of a collaboration may allow collaborators to make more informed decisions when entering foreign locations. It may also permit them to develop realistic expectations about critical success factors in various political and cultural settings.

Institutional Relationships

A final potential antecedent to external adjustment is the development of relationships with institutional interfaces. Gibson (2006) has argued that establishing relationships with local business and government organizations will contribute to the ability of collaborations to adjust to environmental adversity. By institutional relationships, we refer to relationships that are forged between members of a collaboration and the business, municipal, or national government leaders of the host country in which they work. While little if any has been written to date about the relationship between the development of institutional relationships and the ability to externally adjust at the collaboration level of analysis, the literature on networks and on joint ventures suggests that establishing such ties increases the performance of teams and organizations (Joshi, 2006; Makino & Delios, 1996).

We argue that the development of institutional relationships allows collaborations to externally adjust by providing them with legitimacy and resources. Organizational legitimacy is the acceptance by the host country's industrial and institutional environment (Luo, Shenkar, & Nyaw, 2002). The establishment of institutional relationships is a key mechanism by which collaborations may gain institutional legitimacy in a local context. Furthermore, institutional relationships can provide access to critical physical and informational resources. Through such relationships a collaboration can gain information on government policy regarding future economic development, taxation, and import and export regulations. Similarly, partnerships with financial institutions can provide a firm with a competitive edge in obtaining benefits such as low interest rate loans (Wu & Choi, 2004). With added legitimacy and resources, multicultural collaborations that develop institutional relationships are more likely to be able to externally adjust.

CONCLUSION

Multicultural collaborations, in contrast to traditional teams or permanent organizations, are becoming increasingly salient in the current business environment. Such collaborations often face economic, political, regulatory, technological, financial, or human resource challenges, or may encounter time-related pressure, change in their natural physical environment, or cultural challenges. In order to remain competitive in a market economy, the ability to adapt to these external environmental conditions (both favorable and unfavorable) is a critical capability for multicultural collaborations. In this chapter, we have refined the concept of collaboration external adjustment and explained how it differs from other similar constructs, noting that it bears some resemblance to the concepts of reflexivity, external ties and networks, expatriate and repatriate adjustment, and adjustment in joint ventures, yet is nevertheless distinct. We have discussed four forms of external adjustment, including negotiation, repositioning, reframing, and altering behavior, and we have highlighted important outcomes such as innovation, efficiency, and sustainability associated with collaboration external adjustment. Finally, we propose that certain key characteristics of a collaboration will facilitate the capability to externally adjust, including individual characteristics such as CQ, collaboration characteristics such as prior experience together, and contextual characteristics such as institutional relationships.

Awareness of these antecedents to adjustment enables collaborations to identify opportunities for improvement in their capability to externally adjust. Due to the complexity, urgency, and volatility common in the environments in which multicultural collaborations typically operate, failure to adjust may mean a failure to survive.

REFERENCES

Ancona, D.G. (1990). Outward bound: Strategies for team survival in an organization. *Academy of Management Journal, 33,* 334–365.

Ancona, D.G., & Caldwell, D.F. (1992). Bridging the boundary: External activity and performance in organizational teams. *Administrative Science Quarterly, 37,* 634–665.

Ancona, D.G., & Caldwell, D.F. (2000). Compose teams to assure successful boundary activity. In E.A. Locke (Ed.), *Handbook of principles of organizational behavior.* Oxford: Blackwell Publishers.

Bain, P.G., Mann, L., & Pirola-Merlo, A. (2001). The innovation imperative. *Small Group Research, 32,* 55–73.

Bhaskar-Shrinivas, P., Harrison, D.A., Shaffer, M.A., & Luk, D.M. (2005). Input-based and time-based models of international adjustment: Meta-analytic evidence and theoretical extensions. *Academy of Management Journal, 48,* 257–281.

Black, J.S., & Gregersen, H.B. (2000). High impact training: Forging leaders for the global frontier. *Human Resource Management, 39,* 173–184.

Black, J.S., Gregersen, H.B., & Mendenhall, M.E. (1992). Toward a theoretical framework of repatriation adjustment. *Journal of International Business Studies, 23,* 737–760.

Black, J.S., Mendenhall, M., & Oddou, G. (1991). Toward a comprehensive model of international adjustment: An integration of multiple theoretical perspectives. *Academy of Management Review, 16,* 291–317.

Bluedorn, A.C., & Denhardt, R.B. (1988). Time and organization. *Journal of Management, 14,* 299–320.

Buckley, P.J., Glaister, K.W., & Husan, R. (2002). International joint ventures: Partnering skills and cross-cultural issues. *Long Range Planning, 35,* 113–134.

Clark, K.B., & Fujimoto, T. (1991). *Product development performance: Strategy, organization and management in the world automotive industry.* Boston, MA: Harvard Business School Press.

Cohen, S.G., & Bailey, D.E. (1997). What makes teams work: Group effectiveness research from the shop floor to the executive suite. *Journal of Management, 23,* 239–290.

Davenport, T.H., De Long, D.W., & Beers, M.C. (1998). Successful knowledge management projects. *Sloan Management Review, 39,* 43–59.

Dougherty, D. (2001). Re-imagining the differentiation and integration of work for sustained product innovation. *Organization Science, 12,* 612–631.

Earley, P.C., & Ang, S. (2003). *Cultural intelligence: Individual interactions across cultures.* Palo Alto, CA: Stanford University Press.
Earley, P.C., & Gibson, C.B. (2002). *Multinational teams: A new perspective.* Mahwah, NJ: Lawrence Erlbaum Associates.
Edmondson, A.C., Bohmer, R.M.J., & Pisano, G. (2001). Disrupted routines: Team learning and new technology adaptation. *Administrative Science Quarterly, 46,* 685–716.
Eisenhardt, K.M., & Tabrizi, B.N. (1995). Accelerating adaptive processes: Product innovation in the global computer industry. *Administrative Science Quarterly, 40,* 84–110.
Fallows, J. (2002). Uncle Sam buys an airplane. *Atlantic Monthly,* June, 62–74.
Fu, P.P., Peng, T.K., Kennedy, J.C., & Yukl, G. (2004). Examining the preferences of influence tactics in Chinese societies: A comparison of Chinese managers in Hong Kong, Taiwan and Mainland China. *Organizational Dynamics, 33,* 32–46.
Galunic, D.C., & Eisenhardt, K.M. (2001). Architectural innovation and modular corporate forms. *Academy of Management Journal, 44,* 1229–1249.
Gatignon H., Tushman M.L., Smith W., & Anderson P. (2002). A structural approach to assessing innovation: Construct development of innovation locus, type, and characteristics. *Management Science, 48,* 1103–1122
Gibson, C.B. (2001). From accumulation to accommodation: The chemistry of collective cognition in work groups. *Journal of Organizational Behavior, 22,* 121–134.
Gibson, C.B. (2006). The art and science of global team-based collaboration. Working paper, University of California, Irvine.
Gibson, C.B., & Birkinshaw, J. (2004). The antecedents, consequences, and mediating role of organizational ambidexterity. *Academy of Management Journal, 47,* 209–226.
Gibson, C.B., & Cohen, S.G. (2003). *Virtual teams that work: Creating conditions for virtual team effectiveness.* San Francisco, CA: Jossey-Bass.
Gibson, C.B., & Gibbs, J. (2006). Unpacking the concept of virtuality: The effects of geographic dispersion, electronic dependence, dynamic structure and national diversity on team innovation. *Administrative Science Quarterly, 51,* 451–495.
Gibson, C., & Vermeulen, F. (2003). A healthy divide: Subgroups as a stimulus for team learning behavior. *Administrative Science Quarterly, 48,* 202–239.
Hargadon, A., & Sutton, R.I. (1997). Technology brokering and innovation in a product development firm. *Administrative Science Quarterly, 42,* 716–749.
Hofmeester, K. (1999). A look at Maypole's work, aims and methods. *Interactions, 6,* 8–12.
Hofstede, G. (1980). *Culture's consequences.* Newbury Park, CA: Sage.
Inkpen, A.C., & Beamish, P.W. (1997). Knowledge, bargaining power, and the instability of international joint ventures. *Academy of Management Review, 22,* 177–202.
Inkpen, A.C., & Currall, S.C. (2004). The coevolution of trust, control, and learning in joint ventures. *Organization Science, 15,* 586–599.
Janssens, M., & Brett, J.M. (2006). Cultural intelligence in global teams: A fusion model of collaboration. *Group and Organization Management, 31,* 124–153.
Joshi, A. (2006). The influence of organizational demography on the external networking behavior of teams. *Academy of Management Review, 31,* 583–595.
Katz, L., Lazer, D., Arrow, H., & Contractor, N. (2004). Network theory and small groups. *Small Group Research, 35,* 307–332.
Kogut, B., & Singh, H. (1988). The effect of national culture on the choice of entry mode. *Journal of International Business Studies, 19,* 411–432.
Kostova, T., & Zaheer, S. (1999). Organizational legitimacy under conditions of complexity: The case of the multinational enterprise. *Academy of Management Review, 24,* 64–81.
Leonard-Barton, D. (1995). *Wellsprings of knowledge: Building and sustaining the sources of innovation.* Boston, MA: Harvard Business School Press.

Luo, Y., Shenkar, O., & Nyaw, M. (2002). Mitigating liabilities of foreignness: Defensive versus offensive approaches. *Journal of International Management, 8,* 283–300.
Makino, S., & Delios, A. (1996). Local knowledge transfer and performance: Implications for alliance formation in Asia. *Journal of International Business Studies, 27,* Global Perspectives on Cooperative Strategies, 905–927.
Maznevski, M. (1994). Understanding our differences: Performance in decision-making groups with diverse members. *Human Relations, 47,* 531–552.
McDonough, E., & Leifer, R. (1983). Using simultaneous structures to cope with uncertainty. *Academy of Management Journal, 26,* 727–735.
Mezias, S.J., Chen, Y., Murphy, P., Biaggio, A., Chuawanlee, W., Hui, H., Okamura, T., & Starr, S. (2002). National cultural distance as liability of foreignness: The issue of level of analysis. *Journal of International Management, 8,* 407–421.
Mohrman, S.A., Klein, J.A., & Finegold, D. (2003). Managing the global new product development network: A sense-making perspective. In C.B. Gibson & S.G. Cohen (Eds.), *Virtual teams that work: Creating conditions for virtual team effectiveness* (pp. 37–58). San Francisco, CA: Jossey-Bass.
Nonaka, I., & Takeuchi, H. (1995). *The knowledge creating company.* New York: Oxford University Press.
Obstfeld, D. (2005). Social networks, the tertius iungens orientation, and involvement in innovation. *Administrative Science Quarterly, 50,* 100–130.
Pearce, J.L. (2001). *Organization and management in the embrace of government.* Mahwah, NJ: Lawrence Erlbaum Associates.
Peng, M.W., & Luo, Y. (2000). Managerial ties and firm performance in a transition economy: The nature of a micro-macro link. *Academy of Management Journal, 43,* 486–501.
Puffer, S.M., & McCarthy, D.J. (2001). Navigating the hostile maze: A framework for Russian entrepreneurship. *Academy of Management Executive, 15,* 24–36.
Rosaldo, R. (1989). *Culture and truth.* Boston, MA: Beacon Press.
Rowley, T., Behrens, D., & Krackhardt, D. (2000). Redundant governance structures: An analysis of structural and relational embeddedness in the steel and semiconductor industries. *Strategic Management Journal, 21,* 369–386.
Schippers, M.C., Den Hartog, D.N., Koopman, P.L., & Wienk, J.A. (2003). Diversity and team outcomes: The moderating effects of outcome interdependence and group longevity and the mediating effect of reflexivity. *Journal of Organizational Behavior, 24,* 779–802.
Schoonhoven, C.B., Eisenhardt, K.M., & Lyman, K. (1990). Speeding products to market: Waiting time to first product introduction in new firms. *Administrative Science Quarterly, 35,* 177–207.
Simmel, G. (1950). *The sociology of George Simmel.* Translated by K.H. Wolff. Glencoe, IL: Free Press.
SinoCast China IT Watch. (2005). Nokia integrates joint ventures in China. *SinoCast China IT Watch,* June 29, 2005.
Stryker, S. (1980). *Symbolic interactionism: A social structural version.* Menlo Park, CA: Benjamin/Cummings.
Szymanski, S. (1998). Joint ventures in Russia: The view from the Russians. *Business Strategy Review, 8,* 7–14.
Takeuchi, R., Wang, M., & Marinova, S.V. (2005). Antecedents and consequences of psychological workplace strain during expatriation: A cross-sectional and longitudinal investigation. *Personnel Psychology, 58,* 925–948.
Triandis, H.C. (2006). Cultural intelligence in organizations. *Group and Organization Management, 32,* 20–26.
Turner, J.C. (1987). *Rediscovering the social group.* Oxford: Basil Blackwell.
Vessey, J.T. (1991). The new competitors: They think in terms of speed to market. *Academy of Management Executive, 5,* 23–33.

Wasserman, S., & Faust, K. (1994). *Social network analysis: Methods and applications.* New York: Cambridge University Press.

Wong, P.L., & Ellis, P. (2002). Social ties and partner identification in Sino-Hong Kong international joint ventures. *Journal of International Business Studies, 33,* 267–289.

Wu, W., & Choi, W.L. (2004). Transaction cost, social capital and firms' synergy creation in Chinese business networks: An integrative approach. *Asia Pacific Journal of Management, 21,* 325–343.

Zellmer-Bruhn, M.E. (2003). Interruptive events and team knowledge acquisition, *Management Science, 49,* 514–528.

Zellmer-Bruhn, M., & Gibson, C.B. (2006). Team strategic context: Implications for process and performance. *Academy of Management Journal, 49,* 501–518.

PART IV

CQ APPLIED ACROSS DISCIPLINES

CHAPTER 15

The Challenge of Behavioral Cultural Intelligence
What Might Dialogue Tell Us?

PRISCILLA S. ROGERS

Earley and Ang's (2003) interest in enabling the individual to navigate across cultures resonates with business, management, and professional communication (hereafter called professional communication). These sister fields have long sought to equip individuals to communicate effectively within and across professional contexts, including intercultural contexts. In research and teaching, considerable attention is devoted to verbal and nonverbal communication skills.

Ang, Van Dyne, Koh, Ng, Templer, Tay, and Chandrasekar (2007), and Earley and Ang (2003) refer to these verbal and nonverbal skills as behaviors. In their model, individuals with high cultural intelligence (CQ) are capable of acquiring and enacting verbal and nonverbal behaviors that are appropriate for different cultural contexts. High CQ individuals are also mindful of the impressions their behaviors make (self-presentation) and how their behaviors may affect the perceptions and responses of counterparties from other cultures.

This chapter identifies ways in which CQ challenges professional communication and proposes "CQ talk," or the deliberate use of evolving interactive dialogue, as one vehicle for addressing these challenges. Motivating questions are: What do these challenges suggest for training and the necessary research to support such training? How can individual CQ be improved given these challenges? What can dialogue teach us? The focus in this chapter is professional, day-to-day interactions in English; the theoretical perspective is externalist and dialogic. After describing the perspective, four challenges are presented followed by an introduction to CQ talk and examples showing how to make it work.

EXTERNALIST PERSPECTIVE

"The *internalist* says that the contents of our thoughts . . . are determined wholly by what is in the head" (Kent, 1993a, p. 6). This prevailing and useful paradigm is evident in Beamer's

(1992, 1995) intercultural communication model of "matching schemata." Beamer outlines five levels of learning: (1) acknowledging diversity, (2) organizing by drawing on stereotypes, (3) challenging stereotypes, (4) analyzing the communication episode, and (5) generating messages reflective of the other culture. Along similar lines, Earley and Ang explain that "CQ requires knowing what to do and how to do it (cognitive CQ)," having the "wherewithal to persevere and exert effort (motivational CQ)," and a repertoire of responses to choose from for a given situation (behavioral CQ) (2003, p. 81; p. 83). In these studies, attention is given to behavior as the product of cognition and motivation.

The *externalist* turns this around, looking from the outside world so that the communicative act itself is the point of departure. "[Y]ou can't have a thought about an apple if you haven't had at some point in your life some contact—indirect or direct—with apples" (Kent, 1993a, p. 6). Externalism is associated with the "writing to learn" movement—the external act of writing enabling us "to find out what we know—and what we don't know—about whatever we're trying to learn" (Zinsser, 1988, p. 16).

The externalist believes that internal cognitive processes and conceptual schemes do not recreate an external world; rather, the external world creates our sense of an internal one (Kent, 1993b; Couture, 1998; Davidson, 1984). Interaction itself and its allied behaviors form the basis for thought, rather than the other way around. Earley and Ang's conceptualization of CQ seems to accommodate this idea when they explain that it is "not enough that a person is an effective actor able to control personal displays and actions; she must be able to use the various behavioral cues provided by others to interpret their actions and underlying motives" (2003, p. 85).

While this chapter views CQ from an externalist perspective, beginning with behavior and working in to cognition, it should be noted that CQ requires a blend of both. The intent here is to illustrate behavior as an effective starting point.

DIALOGIC PERSPECTIVE

The *dialogic* perspective focuses on the discourse produced by interacting individuals or the collaborative performance itself. Traits, categorizations, and systems associated with different cultural groups by Hall (1976), Hofstede (1984), and subsequent researchers, including many in professional communication, are viewed as potentially useful background (Scollon & Scollon, 2001; Starke-Meyerring, 2005). But affixing categorical cultural expectations onto individuals' interactions is inadequate and may impede cultural understanding rather than enabling it. Individuals may too quickly assume that they know with whom they speak, for example, "He's Russian, so. . . ."

According to the dialogic perspective, predeterminations get in the way. As Yoshikawa (1987) describes it, if communicator "A perceives B only in A's own frame of reference . . . B is a mere shadow of A [and the] integrity of B's culture, its uniqueness, and differences are simply ignored" (1987, p. 320; see also Yuan, 1997). However, if A and B's cultural characterizations and models are tempered by a willingness to let the interactive behaviors speak for themselves, then the individuals may remain sufficiently receptive to learning something of their cultural differences and similarities.

CHALLENGES

Four challenges that behavioral CQ presents for professional communication were identified via a review of the literature in this field, particularly the last decade of work in the periodicals *Business Communication Quarterly, Journal of Business Communication, Journal of Business and Technical Communication,* and *Management Communication Quarterly.* The challenges are as follows: (1) verbal and nonverbal behaviors are intertwined and differ from individual to individual, (2) cultural identities overlap, (3) English language usage and proficiency comprise a moving target, and (4) environments in which business English is used may mask cultural differences that matter.

Verbal and Nonverbal Behaviors Are Intertwined and Individual

Earley and Ang (2003) posit that an individual with high CQ is capable of acquiring and enacting appropriate verbal and nonverbal behaviors. Nonverbal behaviors include silence, space (proxemics), time (chronemics), body movements and facial expressions (kinetics), eye contact (oculesics), touch (haptics), paralanguage (vocalics), physical appearance, emblems, tokens, signs, smell (olfactics), and color (chromatics). Verbal behaviors of interest to professional communication researchers include language issues, degree of fluency, genre use, content development (use of themes and appreciation of data types), topic management, level of formality, patterns of organization (both direct and indirect receive great attention), speech acts, amount of detail, pronoun usage, self-revelation, storytelling, and turn-taking tendencies. The challenge for CQ in professional communication is the fact that nonverbal and verbal behaviors are highly interdependent and individualized.

The idea of verbal and nonverbal interdependency is not new. Van Dijk and Kintsch's (1983) discourse comprehension model views the nonverbal-verbal interface as necessary for discourse production and comprehension (see also Burgoon, 1985). Scherer and Wallbott (1985) see nonverbals serving a semantic function, amplifying, modifying, or even contradicting discourse. And although Chapel, like many others, sees nonverbal behavior as the major source of information, he believes it must "be learned alongside verbal language to acquire the knowledge and skills to manage successfully in the global marketplace" (1997, p. 287).

To the idea that cultural awareness requires an integrated view of verbal and nonverbal behaviors, one readily responds, "of course." But in practice, verbal and nonverbal have been treated separately. Consider the "debate" about which plays the greater role as an example. Compared to words, nonverbal cues have been said to carry from 65 up to 93 percent of the meaning in social interactions (Birdwhistell, 1970; Neuliep, 2000). Scollon and Scollon (2001) call this "intercultural folklore," which may be traced back to Hall's enthusiastic estimate that, according to Scollon and Scollon, is based on faulty analysis that has never been substantiated (2001, p. 16). Seeing such claims as "wildly exaggerated," Scollon and Scollon attribute a greater role to language and discourse. No matter which side of the argument one takes, the fact that this discussion exists suggests that verbal and nonverbal behaviors are regarded as separate.

A second aspect of this challenge stems from the individualized nature of behaviors. With its focus on the sojourner, CQ challenges us to put more attention on the individual's unique mix of cultural identities—national heritage, disciplinary training, professional—and the impact of these on behaviors during encounters with others. An individual's cultural identity and associated behaviors are also "intertwined with power and privilege, affected by close relationships, and negotiated through communication" (Jameson, 2007, p. 199). Physical attributes and upbringing come into play as well. No two individuals are exactly alike, nor are their interactions with others. When person A meets with person B, their synergistic behaviors will be different than when B interacts with person C.

If individuals are to become more culturally aware, they must learn to see some of the reality that is interaction—along with its messy, amorphous, complex of intertwined and individual verbal and nonverbal behaviors.

Cultural Identities Overlap

Starke-Meyerring earmarks the diversity resulting from "pluralized identities and blurred cultural boundaries" as one of the core challenges for professional communicators (2005, p. 474) and, we might add, for CQ. Consider identity first. According to the United Nations *Human Development Report,* "people do not have single, fixed identities. They have multiple and often changing identities and loyalties" (2004, p. 100). The report concludes that one contributor is that the number of people moving outside their country of birth has doubled since 1970. What is the culture from which they are made? Study after study confirms the answer—this culture, that culture, and yet another culture. For example, Alkhazraji, Gardner, Martin, and Paolillo's (1997) survey of Muslim immigrants shows that those who were more accepting of U.S. national culture were also highly allegiant to their original culture. Alkhazraji and collaborators concluded that any study failing to recognize "the extent to which individualism and collectivism vary across *individuals within cultures*" is deficient (1997, p. 225, emphasis mine). Individuals hold multiple citizenships, were educated in different countries, and speak from diverse disciplines (e.g., clinical researchers, regulatory professionals, and chemists). It is simplistic to assume that an individual fully conforms to the practices of the cultural groups to which they are said to belong, i.e., an American businessperson communicates like a "typical American" and a Japanese like a "typical Japanese" (Zaidman, 2001, p. 410).

Likewise, fixed boundaries cannot be ascribed to entire groups of people and their communications (Starke-Meyerring, 2005). Some scholars have suggested that rather than attributing linguistic and rhetorical attributes to national groups, we need to analyze differences among discourse systems, including *within groups* (Jameson, 2007; Zaidman, 2001). For example, Hagen found a "dual-cultural orientation that defies easy classification" (1998, p. 121). The Russian "culture of the state," with a highly developed system of informers and strict adherence to policy, fostered a genre with detailed information (low context). Operating simultaneously was a distinct "culture of personal life," with communications lacking in details (high context). Hall's distinction between high-context and low-context cultures may describe "unified cultures with stable traditions that have evolved over the years," Hagen concludes, but not the Russian communicative environment (1998, p. 120).

An organizational example of blurred cultural boundaries within a country is Hong and Engestrom's (2004) study of communications in two Chinese companies. They observed both "Confucian authority," with its emphasis on governance by those higher in the chain of command, and *guanxi,* which appreciates reciprocity and mutual respect, operating side-by-side. Meetings might be authoritarian in structure, disallowing feedback from participants and including formalities to elevate the manager, but the manager's tone might suggest a spirit of negotiation via the absence of imperatives (e.g., "this is not allowed") and use of the conditional "if." Hong and Engestrom conclude "Both systems play an important role in the accomplishment and development of middle managers' activity" (2004, p. 577). It is this global working environment with its mix of overlapping cultural identities and systems that individuals must navigate to be culturally intelligent.

English Is a Moving Target

Language acquisition, which Earley and Ang see as important for high CQ, is increasingly pressing for effective intercultural professional communication. Professionals may have functioned adequately in the early stages of globalization after World War II when communication technology was in its infancy and messages tended to be channeled through fully bilingual translators (Babcock & Du-Babcock, 2001). But today, individual personal encounters (e.g., e-mail) are the norm and English competency the expectation. "English has emerged as the world's prominent linking language in international business communication and individuals from around the world are learning English in order to fulfill this linking role" wrote Babcock and Du-Babcock (2001, p. 377; see also Crystal, 1997; Kameda, 1996). But as Gilsdorf (2002) suggests, English is a moving target. Consider usage and proficiency.

We use various "Englishes," not plain English, when communicating across cultures; even across English-speaking countries. The question for interlocutors then is "which English?" The different spellings for the same words in American and British English comprise just one example. Some spelling forms reoccur, making it easier for the learner, such as the suffix -er versus–re, as in center/centre; -or versus -our as in color/colour; and -og versus -ogue as in dialog/dialogue. Idiosyncratic differences prove more challenging: Americans use check, plow, specialty, story, and learned; British use cheque, plough, speciality, storey, and learnt (Scott, 2004). Vocabulary differences provide another challenge. Scott (2000) observed usage of the same expression with differences in connotation, the same expression with one or more different or shared meanings, the same expression with very different meanings, and different expressions with the same shared meaning.

In professional communication the accepted principle is "to accommodate toward the practices of other cultures whenever feasible" (Scott, 2004, p. 161; Beamer & Varner, 2008; Victor, 1992). Indeed, individuals with higher proficiency have been observed simplifying their usage to a level that their less proficient interlocutors may more readily understand (Babcock & Du-Babcock, 2001). Green and Scott (1992) found that professionals in the 100 largest companies in the United States and the United Kingdom thought it was critically important to be sensitive to differences in English language, including spelling. However, there may be less tolerance than one might hope. Students in these countries responded strongly to words they perceived to be spelled wrong (Scott, 2004).

Even if one wants to be accommodating, it is not always easily managed. It has been estimated that non-native speakers of English comprise 80 percent of its user population (Crystal, 1997; Lesznyak, 2002; Charles, 2007). Individuals writing and speaking to each other have varying levels of language proficiency and this makes a difference. Some research indicates that individuals less competent in the language-in-use will assume a less active role and contribute fewer ideas in intercultural interactions (Du-Babcock, 1999). The point is that high CQ for professional communication involves not only knowing English, but also being cognizant of others' usage and proficiency.

Business English Lingua Franca May Mask Differences

CQ involves recognizing both similarities and differences. Failure to recognize differences may become an issue in the use of English as a globally shared language. While some say that a common language, or Business English Lingua Franca (BELF), is in its early stages of development, there is considerable evidence that Business English has been developing for some time (Louhiala-Salminen, Charles, & Kankaanranta, 2005). For example, Park, Dillon, and Mitchell's (1998) study of complaint letters written in English showed U.S. managers using a direct pattern and Koreans an indirect one. But in the same year, Thomas found directness was the norm in the persuasive writing of both groups. And Beamer's study of nineteenth-century extant English-language business letters revealed that Chinese writers followed a fairly direct, straightforward delivery, perhaps to signal power differences deliberately (2003; Zhu, 2000, 2005). This suggests that the style now often associated with BELF has been around for some time in cultures said to communicate differently.

BELF has been described as a practical discourse system with common communicative standards and practices in the areas of purpose, organization, and style (Zaidman, 2001; Ortiz, 2005). For example, observing business communications in Mexico, Tebeaux (1999) noted a shift to a homogenized style with formatting devices rather than paragraphs, conciseness, and substance, that were dictated by the company's chosen software, rather than traditional, local practices. Conaway and Wardrope's (2004) study of Spanish-language letters written by managers in Guatemalan firms revealed the use of the formal convention typical of those used in the United States, for example, an absence of buffers when presenting bad news.

Given its generic nature, some have argued that BELF is a "cultureless" language. For example, Louhiala-Salminen found that English was regarded as "just a code I use" by employees in a Finnish export company (1997, p. 317). Seidlhofer (2004) characterizes it as a language that is nobody's and everybody's. Others contend that BELF creates a culture all its own, an operational discourse community bent on getting work done across cultural boundaries (Charles, 2007). Research shows that despite frequent lexical and syntactic anomalies, BELF users have few misunderstandings related to the language itself as would be expected of individuals in a shared culture (Charles, 2007; Nikko, 2007; Poncini, 2004).

But in both positions lurk the danger—and thus the challenge—of ignoring the fact that users of BELF do have diverse cultural orientations. Sometimes in professional communication these differences matter, but they may be overlooked in the relative comfort of a communal business language (Meierkord, 2002). Panning (1986) called this group homophility, or shared views among group members resulting from their frequent contact and collaborative activities. Homophility, he argued, can foster overconfidence and redundancy recalling Janis's (1972) groupthink. Auer-Rizzi and Berry (2000) saw homophility operating when groups of Austrian, Finnish, and Swedish students worked on business problems. "[H]omogeneity in terms of shared business frames of reference was such a strong antecedent condition that national culture played no role in making the group decision even if it did influence students' communication styles" (2000, p. 282). They concluded that cultural diversity was underexplored, as were opportunities for innovation.

On one hand, it could be posited that the existence of BELF demonstrates some measure of cultural adaptation in global business environments. On the other hand, if the use of BELF prompts acquiescence or masks differences, the value of diversity could be lost.

ADDRESSING THE CHALLENGES

So what do these challenges mean for training and the necessary research to support it? CQ cognition and motivation have been explored in some detail (e.g., Ang et al., 2007). Emphasizing the development of cultural knowledge (cognition) and consciousness-raising (motivation), Tan and Chua (2003) suggest using role-playing situations to better acquaint trainees with the nonverbal and verbal aspects of behavior as listed earlier. They encourage awareness training to help individuals evaluate their behavioral capabilities and acquire "the requisite *repertoire* of behavior skills and impression management tactics to adapt to alternative cultural settings" (Earley & Ang, 2003, p. 165, emphasis mine).

Studies have suggested what might be included in a rich personal repertoire. For example, Rogers, Ho, Thomas, Wong, and Cheng (2004) analyzed graduating Singaporean and U.S. business student (soon-to-be-new hires) responses to scenarios, such as reporting bad news to the boss, and identified linguistic and rhetorical strategies that would help or hinder successful communication in such situations. For example, hedging and using soft modal verbs and the conditional "if" might be selected to show deference in some environments with some bosses. In contrast, use of the absolute verb "to be," strong modal verbs (must, should, will), imperatives, and challenging questions might hinder success. Identifying many of the same features, Thomas's (1998) analysis of American and Korean business letters surfaced significant direct, modified direct, and indirect structures; implicit and explicit approaches; and linear and recursive reasoning patterns (see also Morand, 2000; Scollon & Scollon, 2001). More extensive studies that may prove useful for repertoire building include Yli-Jokipii's *Requests in Professional Discourse:*

A Cross-Cultural Study of British, American, and Finnish Business Writing (1994); Spencer-Oatey's *Culturally Speaking: Managing Rapport Through Talk Across Cultures* (2000); Poncini's *Discursive Strategies in Multicultural Business Meetings* (2004); and Zhu's *Written Communication across Cultures* (2005). Studies like these could provide a basis for an intercultural repertoire catalogue for research and teaching.

CQ TALK

CQ talk is proposed as another vehicle for addressing the communication challenges. As an initial definition, CQ talk is an individual's deliberate verbal and nonverbal behavior during an evolving intercultural interaction that allows the individual to find out what needs to be learned. Responsive in nature, CQ talk is dependent upon the dialogue that emerges when individuals interact. For example, individual A observes B's nod of approval but fidgets uneasily and responds "I'm sorry. My experience working in Thailand is very limited. You grew up there and know intimately how things are done. Please let me defer to you." To this B responds and, hopefully, an informative interplay will ensue.

CQ talk is envisioned as an active rather than a passive endeavor. Consider for a moment that dialogue is like a crossword puzzle (Scollon & Scollon, 2001). "When we communicate, we make guesses about the meaning of others' utterances, and we, in turn, guess about the interpretations that others will give our utterances" (Kent, 1993b, p. 5). A few guesses seem to fit, leading to more, and more again. As the dialogue evolves, there are times of uncertainty, confusion, correction, and clarity. But ultimately it is a matter of considering possibilities, initiating, and responding in ways that are both appropriate and exploratory. "People having high CQ use the cues that they gain from others to infer accurately [others'] states and views," Earley and Ang explain (2003, p. 84). "The professional communicator today must learn to be a better . . . interpreter of signs and a [better] *formulator of messages that construct meaning in different cultural contexts*" (Weiss, 1997, p. 322, emphasis mine).

CQ talk is about becoming a skilled puzzle solver. It is "talk about talk" in an effort to fill in the blanks. This requires a conscious effort to see what is being conveyed or could be conveyed verbally and nonverbally. In this effort, CQ talk intermingles with cognition and motivation. Knowledge of behaviors that might meaningfully be observed in different situations, possession of a repertoire of various responses, and having the persistence to follow up on leads given by the other facilitate the use of CQ talk. However, CQ talk is *guided* by what the dialogue itself is revealing and requires a willingness to be directed by it rather than dominated by preconceptions, trained responses, and expectations based on book learning, classroom exercises, and past experience. One who practices CQ talk is a *participant* observer, involved in the dialogue and appropriating it organically, not prescriptively.

Observing managers' intercultural interactions over many years and drawing on interpersonal strategies and linguistic knowledge, several types of responses are suggested here as potentially useful for CQ talk: inquiry/checking, self-revelation, correction/alternative, and building. *Inquiry/checking* is proposed as talk for the purpose of either finding out more about the interlocutor's knowledge, experience, intention, and meaning, or determining if interpretation of the interlocutor's behavior has any validity, e.g., "Have you experienced this kind of conflict in the Bangalore office? Do they expect that meetings follow an agenda?" or "What do you mean by hot?" Conversely, *self-revelation* is volunteering information about oneself, e.g., "Unfortunately, I've not worked in another culture before," or "In working with colleagues from the States, Asia, and Europe, I can't feel any differences between them; we had a clear goal and an objective to work together."

Providing *correction/alternatives* in talk might involve rephrasing a misstatement or suggesting a different possible interpretation or approach. Corrections or suggested alternatives may come in response to an interlocutor's negative response, hesitation, or lack of expression, e.g., "I apologize for talking so much. Would it work better if we took turns? Or perhaps we could write each other about these issues and then meet for discussion?" Such talk may stem from self-monitoring, a cognitive activity that Earley and Ang discuss in some detail. For example, an individual may say something like, "The Dutch are very open-minded; I think his nationality is already an advantage. Dutch people like traveling. He should easily get accustomed to another place." Recognizing that the statement is simplistic or unhelpful interculturally ("Stereotypes don't hold. I should consider the individual here") correction may follow: "To put it more specifically, Hein is Dutch and has traveled all over Europe and lived in Turkey. Given his international experience suggests that he might adjust more quickly to relocation."

CQ talk that *builds* stems from the idea that dialogue is a means for collaborative learning. The external act of dialoguing (like writing) enables "us to find out what we know—and what we don't know—about whatever we're trying to learn" (Zinsser, 1988, p. 16). Consider what might be learned if the interlocutors discussed the following statement in some detail: "One reason they're so successful is that they focus on Asia and they use the Asian way. This gives them a cultural advantage." Building talk treats such comments as an invitation to explore what the interlocutor means by "the Asian way" and its cultural advantages.

CQ Talk to Address Challenges

To move a step further, with the caution that this concept is very preliminary, consider how CQ talk might be appropriated to address the challenges presented here. For example, notice how individual B's talk below reflects some understanding that *verbal and nonverbal behaviors are interrelated and individual.*

Individual A: smiles a lot, nods his head in agreement, and says very little, but fidgets quite a bit and seems somewhat uneasy about making a decision.
Individual B: using *inquiry:* "Might you have a different view?"
Individual A: smiling and nodding as if there's no dissent: "No, it's okay."
Individual B: using *indirect inquiry* and suggesting an *alternative* that removes the pressure to respond and relocates the decision to a potentially less threatening situation: "Why don't we think about this in the next day or two? I could follow up with you later."

Here CQ talk in the form of inquiry and alternative posing is used in response to conflicting nonverbal cues.

Or the fact that *cultural identities overlap* may prompt an individual to recover from a simplistic statement, such as "We can reach the same conclusion very easily because we are both Japanese." A *corrective* follow-up might be, "I mean we're likely to have some things in common that could help us be more efficient, but I know our training is quite different so I might need you to explain sometimes." Or consider the potential of *self-revelation:*

Individual A: "I've got a pretty good grasp of Mandarin even though I grew up in Penang and never really used it."
Individual B: "I'm Singaporean, but I did my graduate work at the IESE Business School in Barcelona and learned Spanish well enough to stay on several years for work."
Individual C: "So I'm the only one who doesn't speak a second language. Sorry. I bring some product experience that might help us. We're missing expertise on the South America market though, aren't we?"

Here *inquiry builds* on the round of *self-revelation.* CQ talk invites exploration of team competences as well as what may be missing.

Or, since *English is a moving target,* it makes sense to ask how a word might be appropriately spelled or interpreted—"Is it 'call centre' or 'call center?'" or "What do you mean by hot?" Inquiry might be coupled with the suggestion of an alternative, for example, "Since the presentation is at the Royal Bank in Toronto, should we pronounce 'schedule' the Canadian way?" Here, the culturally experienced individual is asked about the appropriateness of another way of doing it.

Knowing that *BELF may mask differences* could encourage individuals to watch for situations where surfacing cultural diversity may contribute to a better understanding and decision making. For example, consider how *building* and *inquiry* are used for CQ talk in the following exchange:

Individual A: "Han has more technical expertise and should manage the team."
Individual B: "But an older person supporting a younger person in a management role is a little extraordinary in Korea."
Individual C: "That's true, but this division is very Westernized. So is this a problem?
Individual B: "I know seniority has not been an issue before in this group, but it would really break with tradition in this case since this project manager reports directly to the board of directors."

Here, CQ talk involves actively looking for opportunities to make meaning with the other person by together finding out what is known and not known.

Making CQ Talk Work

Making CQ talk work requires appropriate curiosity and, always, charity. Individuals may initially engage in CQ talk because they are curious. But expressions of curiosity must remain within the bounds of cultural acceptability and they should be mindful of "face" concerns. CQ talk is itself a behavior and we know that "behaviors deemed appropriate in one culture may not naturally reflect the same meaning or level of propriety in another" (Earley & Ang, 2003, p. 164). For example, asking questions may be considered rude or embarrassing. Questions may readily be taken as cross examination, even in cultures where individuals are accustomed to inquiry. Making it safe not to answer is one reason for talk.

Charity is also involved. Employing the "principle of charity means that when we communicate we have no choice but to minimize error and to maximize agreement concerning the meaning of another's utterances" (Kent, 1992, p. 63). Charity seeks commonality in an effort to establish a shared world (Yuan, 1997). Its focus is not on English-language errors, for example, but rather on communication. The only errors that really matter are those that might interfere with understanding (Rogers & Rymer, 2001). Firth (1996) called this the "let-it-pass" principle when characterizing the cooperative and supportive language he heard in phone conversations between sellers and buyers. Nikko (2007) observed charity in internal business meetings during which Swedish and Finnish participants helped each other with tricky bits of language.

CONCLUSION

Talk is puzzling, but also revealing. The notion of CQ talk asks us to consider how CQ might improve if individuals become more skilled in using their intercultural interactions to actively find out what they do and do not know. With CQ talk in mind, cataloging past discoveries about verbal and nonverbal behaviors—which might apply to the individual sojourner apart from global cultural categories—could prove useful. CQ talk can also be considered as a teaching and navigational tool. For example, the challenges presented here might provide a useful framework for analyzing writing samples and transcriptions of dialogues in professional communication classes. There is a long way to go. For the sojourner in us and in those we train, the question remains, "What might the dialogue tell us?

ACKNOWLEDGMENT

This chapter benefited greatly from discussions with Joo Seng Tan, my collaborator on related projects.

REFERENCES

Alkhazraji, K.M., Gardner III, W.L., Martin, J.S., & Paolillo, J.G.P. (1997). The acculturation of immigrants to U.S. organizations: The case of Muslim employees. *Management Communication Quarterly, 11,* 217–265.

Ang, S., Van Dyne, L., Koh, C., Ng, K., Templer, K.J., Tay, C., & Chandrasekar, N.A. (2007). Cultural intelligence: Its measurement and effects on cultural judgment and decision making, cultural adaptation, and task performance. *Management and Organization Review, 3,* 335–371.

Auer-Rizzi, W., & Berry, M. (2000). Business vs. cultural frames of reference in group decision making: Interactions among Austrian, Finnish, and Swedish business students. *The Journal of Business Communication, 37,* 264–292.

Babcock, R.D., & Du-Babcock, B. (2001). Language-based communication zones in international business communication. *The Journal of Business Communication, 38,* 372–412.

Beamer, L. (1992). Learning intercultural communication competence. *Journal of Business Communication, 29,* 285–303.

Beamer, L. (1995). A schematic model for intercultural encounters and case study: The emperor and the envoy. *Journal of Business Communication, 32,* 141–161.

Beamer, L. (2003). Directness in Chinese business correspondence of the nineteenth century. *Journal of Business and Technical Communication, 17,* 201–237.

Beamer, L., & Varner, I. (2008). *Intercultural communication in the global workplace* (4th ed.). Boston, MA: McGraw-Hill/Irwin.

Birdwhistell, R.L. (1970). *Kinesics and context: Essays on body motion communication.* Philadelphia, PA: University of Pennsylvania Press.

Burgoon, J.K. (1985). Nonverbal signals. In M.L. Knapp & G.R. Miller (Eds.), *Handbook of interpersonal communication* (pp. 344–390). Beverly Hills, CA: Sage.

Chapel, W.B. (1997). Developing international management communication competence. *Journal of Business and Technical Communication, 11,* 281–296.

Charles, M. (2007). Language matters in global communication. *The Journal of Business Communication, 44,* 260–282.

Conaway, R.N., & Wardrope, W.J. (2004). Communication in Latin America: An analysis of Guatemalan business letters. *Business Communication Quarterly, 67,* 465–474.

Couture, B. (1998). *Toward a phenomenological rhetoric: Writing, profession, and altruism.* Carbondale and Edwardsville, IL: Southern Illinois University Press.

Crystal, D. (1997). *English as a global language.* Cambridge: Cambridge University Press.

Davidson, D. (1984). *Inquiries into truth and interpretation.* Oxford: Clarendon.

Du-Babcock, B. (1999). Topic management and turn taking in professional communication: First- versus second-language strategies. *Management Communication Quarterly, 12,* 544–574.

Earley, P.C., & Ang, S. (2003). *Cultural intelligence: Individual interaction across cultures.* Palo Alto, CA: Stanford Business Books.

Firth, A. (1996). The discursive accomplishment of normality: On "lingua franca" English and conversation analysis. *Journal of Pragmatics, 26,* 237–259.

Gilsdorf, J. (2002). Standard Englishes and world Englishes: Living with a polymorph business language. *The Journal of Business Communication, 39,* 364–378.

Green, D.J., & Scott, J.C. (1992). International business correspondence: Perceptives of major U.S. companies with related implications for business education. *NABTE Review, 19,* 39–43.

Hagen, P. (1998). Teaching American business writing in Russia: Cross-cultures/cross-purposes. *Journal of Business and Technical Communication, 12,* 109–126.

Hall, E.T. (1976). *Beyond culture.* New York: Anchor.

Hofstede, G. (1984). *Culture's consequences: International differences in work related values.* Beverly Hills, CA: Sage.

Hong J., & Engestrom, Y. (2004). Changing principles of communication between Chinese managers and workers. *Management Communication Quarterly, 17,* 552–585.

Jameson, D.A. (2007). Reconceptualizing cultural identity and its role in intercultural business communication. *The Journal of Business Communication, 44,* 199–235.

Janis, I.L. (1972). *Victims of groupthink: A psychological study of foreign-policy decisions and fiascoes.* Boston, MA: Houghton Mifflin.

Kameda, N. (1996). *Business communication toward transnationalism: The significance of cross-cultural business English and its role.* Tokyo: Kindaibungeishai.

Kent, T. (1992). Externalism and the production of discourse. *Journal of Advanced Composition, 12,* 57–74.

Kent, T. (1993a). Language philosophy, writing, and reading: A conversation with Donald Davidson. *Journal of Advanced Composition, 13,* 1–17.

Kent, T. (1993b). *Paralogic rhetoric: A theory of communicative interaction.* Lewisburg, PA: Bucknell University Press.

Lesznyak, A. (2002). From chaos to the smallest common denominator: Topic management in English lingua franca communication. In K. Knapp & C. Meierkord (Eds.), *Lingua Franca communication* (pp. 163–194). Frankfurt: Peter Lang.

Louhiala-Salminen, L. (1997). Investigating the genre of a business fax: A Finnish case study. *Journal of Business Communication, 34,* 316–333.

Louhiala-Salminen, L., Charles, M., & Kankaanranta, A. (2005). English as a lingua franca in Nordic corporate mergers: Two case companies. *English for Specific Purposes, 24,* 401–421.

Meierkord, C. (2002). "Language stripped bare" or "linguistic masala"? Culture in lingua franca communication. In K. Karpp & C. Meierkord (Eds.), *Lingua Franca communication* (pp.109–134). Frankfurt: Peter Lang.

Morand, D.A. (2000). Language and power: An empirical analysis of linguistic strategies used in superior-subordinate communication. *Journal of Organizational Behavior, 21,* 235–248.

Neuliep, J.W. (2000). *Intercultural communication: A contextual approach.* Boston, MA: Houghton Mifflin.

Nikko, T. (2007). Co-constructing meaning in international work place meetings: A dialogical approach to communicational understanding in face-to-face interaction. Working paper, Helsinki School of Economics, Finland.

Ortiz, L.A. (2005). The emerging hybrid discourse of business communication in a Mexican-U.S. border region. *The Journal of Business Communication, 42,* 28–50.

Panning, W.H. (1986). Information pooling and group decisions in nonexperimental settings. In B. Grofman & G. Owen (Eds.), *Proceedings of the second University of California, Irvine, conference on political economy* (pp. 159–166). Greenwich, CT: JAI Press.

Park, M.Y., Dillon, W.T., & Mitchell, K.L. (1998). Korean business letters: Strategies for effective complaints in cross-cultural communication. *The Journal of Business Communication, 35,* 328–345.

Poncini, G. (2004). Communicating local elements to diverse audiences: Promotional materials for wineries. In M. Gotti (Ed.), *Intercultural aspects of specialized communication: Linguistic insights. Volume 14.* New York: Peter Lang.

Rogers, P.S., & Rymer, J. (2001). Analytical tools from a communicative perspective facilitate transition into new writing context. *Journal of Business Communication, 38,* 112–152.

Rogers, P.S., Ho, M., Thomas, J., Wong, F.H., & Cheng, C.O.L. (2004). Preparing new entrants for subordinate reporting: A decision-making framework. *Journal of Business Communication, 41*(2), 1–32.

Scherer, K.R., & Wallbott, H.G. (1985). Analysis of nonverbal behavior. In A.T.A. van Dijk (Ed.), *Handbook of discourse analysis* (pp. 199–230). London: Academic Press.

Scollon, R., & Scollon, S.W. (2001). *Intercultural communication: A discourse approach* (2nd ed.). Malden, MA: Blackwell Publishing.

Scott, J.C. (2000). Differences in American and British vocabulary: Implications for international business communication. *Business Communication Quarterly, 63*(4), 27–39.

Scott, J.C. (2004). American and British business-related spelling differences. *Business Communication Quarterly, 67*(2), 153–167.

Seidlhofer, B. (2004). Research perspectives on teaching English as a lingua franca. *Annual Review of Applied Linguistics, 24,* 209–239.

Spencer-Oatey, H. (2000). *Culturally speaking: Managing rapport through talk across cultures.* New York: Continuum.

Starke-Meyerring, D. (2005). The rhetoric of the Internet in higher education policy: A cross-cultural study. *Business Communication Quarterly, 67*(2), 468–499.

Tan, J.S., & Chua, R.Y.J. (2003). Training and developing cultural intelligence. In P.C. Earley & S. Ang, *Cultural intelligence: Individual interactions across cultures* (pp. 258–303). Palo Alto, CA: Stanford Business Books.

Tebeaux, E. (1999). Designing written business communication along the shifting cultural continuum: The new face of Mexico. *Journal of Business and Technical Communication, 13,* 49–85.

Thomas, J. (1998). Contexting Koreans: Does the high/low model work? *Business Communication Quarterly, 61(4), 9–22.*

United Nations Development Program. (2004). *Human development report 2004: Cultural liberty in today's diverse world.* New York: United Nations. Available at http://hdr.undp.org/reports/global/2004/pdf/hdr04_complete.pdf. Accessed Jan 5, 2005.

van Dijk, T.A., & Kintsch, W. (1983). *Strategies of discourse comprehension.* Orlando, FL: Academic Press.

Victor, D.A. (1992). *International business communication.* New York: HarperCollins.

Weiss, T. (1997). Reading culture: Professional communication as translation. *Journal of Business and Technical Communication, 11,* 321–338.

Yli-Jokipii, H. (1994). *Resquests in professional discourse: A cross-cultural study of British, American, and Finnish business writing.* Helsinki: Suomalainen Tiedeakatemia.

Yoshikawa, M.J. (1987). The double-swing model of intercultural communication between the East and the West. In D.L. Kincaid (Eds.), *Communication theory: Eastern and Western perspectives* (pp. 319–329). San Diego, CA: Academic Press.

Yuan, R. (1997). Yin/yang principal and the relevance of externalism and paralogic rhetoric to intercultural communication. *Journal of Business and Technical Communication, 11,* 297–320.

Zaidman, N. (2001). Cultural codes and language strategies in business communication: Interactions between Israeli and Indian businesspeople. *Management Communication Quarterly, 14,* 408–441.

Zhu, Y. (2000). Rhetorical moves in Chinese sales genres, 1949 to the present. *Journal of Business Communication, 37,* 156–172.

Zhu, Y. (2005). *Written communication across cultures: A sociocognitive perspective on business genres.* Amsterdam, PA: John Benjamins Publishing.

Zinsser, W. (1988). *Writing to learn.* New York: Harper & Row, Publishers.

CHAPTER 16

Cultural Intelligence in Counseling Psychology

Applications for Multicultural Counseling Competence

MICHAEL GOH, JULIE M. KOCH, AND SANDRA SANGER

Cultural intelligence (CQ) (Earley and Ang, 2003) is a well-conceptualized and rigorously researched concept that offers a stimulating perspective for psychologists and other mental health practitioners who strive to provide culturally competent care for their clients. More importantly, it has the potential to bring focus to longstanding efforts to educate and consequently train psychologists to be culturally competent (S. Sue, 1998). In this chapter, we use the term *counseling* as having relevance to psychological counseling, psychotherapy, therapy, and mental health counseling. The goals of this chapter are to (a) define and clarify how terms regarding cultural competence are used in counseling, (b) provide a brief overview of efforts to define and measure cultural competence in mental health, (c) discuss how CQ can be applied in counseling psychology and related fields, and (d) conclude with ideas for possible research to further the role of CQ in multicultural counseling competence.

DEFINITIONS

Counseling psychology is a specialty area that involves training practitioners to work with clients in addressing personal, interpersonal, career, and educational issues on a psychological wellness continuum that ranges from mental health to mental illness.

S. Sue (1998) defines cultural competence in counseling as "the belief that people should not only appreciate and recognize other cultural groups but also be able to work effectively with them" (p. 440). The term *multicultural counseling competence* has been traditionally defined as a counselor's knowledge, awareness, and skills that relate to working with culturally diverse clients (D. W. Sue et al., 1998). Knowledge typically refers to content knowledge about various cultures; awareness refers to the counselor's own preconceived notions or biases that he or she brings into the counseling relationship; and skills refers to actual behaviors in which the counselor engages. Another definition describes multicultural counseling as "preparation and practices that integrate multicultural and culture-specific awareness, knowledge and skills into counseling interactions" (Arredondo et al., 1996, p. 43), hence, adding the dynamic relationship between client and counselor. A more recent definition by Sue and Torino (2005) adds a critical component to cultural competence whereby individuals have an impact at organizational and systemic levels resulting in culturally responsive theories, policies, and organizations.

In the field of counseling psychology, definitions of culture are often inclusive of gender, ability/disability, age, socioeconomic status, and sexual orientation, and deal with a broader diversity than just purely race and ethnicity (D. W. Sue, 2001).

MULTICULTURAL COUNSELING COMPETENCE IN COUNSELING PSYCHOLOGY

Training culturally competent counselors to work effectively with the increasing diversity in schools, higher education, the workplace, families, and communities is an urgent need now more than ever (Sue & Sue, 2003). The report titled "Mental Health: Culture, Race, and Ethnicity" noted discrepancies in the delivery of mental health services to ethnic minority populations in the United States (U.S. Department of Health and Human Services, 2001). Culture, it was concluded, matters when explaining why ethnic minorities fail to access mental health services. The report found that "major disparities exist in the access, utility, and quality of mental health services for racial minorities" (p. 163). It is also increasingly recognized that cultural factors such as race, gender, sexual orientation, national origin, ability/disability, and so on play a role in the therapist-client relationship and effectiveness of therapy (Pope-Davis, Coleman, Liu, & Toporek, 2003). Ridley, Baker, and Hill (2001) consider cultural competence to be "one of the most important considerations facing applied psychology" (p. 822). There is little disagreement that determining whether counselors are capable of providing culturally competent counseling services is paramount. However, complicating this task is the fact that cultural competence is multifaceted and complex (Reynolds, 2001; D. W. Sue, 2001).

In an effort to assess the cultural competence of mental health practitioners and counseling students, a number of self-report instruments have been developed in counseling psychology. However, even though the various instruments share common theoretical models of cultural competence that comprise awareness, knowledge, and skills, there is, in fact, divergence regarding what the instruments actually measure (Constantine & Ladany, 2001). Furthermore, scholars and practitioners alike often speculate that there are other salient factors critical to multicultural counseling competence that these instruments fail to measure or take into account. S. Sue (1998) noted that a primary obstacle preventing a successful search for cultural competence has been a weak theoretical research base. Ridley et al. (2001) have reasoned that cultural competence is elusive due to a lack of consensus about the nature of the construct.

We therefore present in this chapter the compelling and well-researched framework offered by CQ and its potential to inform our understanding, training, and practice of multicultural counseling competence.

INTEGRATING CULTURAL INTELLIGENCE IN COUNSELING PSYCHOLOGY

CQ provides a conceptual framework for understanding multicultural counseling competence that encompasses and expands upon previous definitions offered in the counseling literature. Applying CQ to the mental health profession expands and elucidates our conceptualization of multicultural counseling competence beyond the essentially unchallenged three-factor model described earlier, which focuses on knowledge, awareness, and skills. These previous definitions are limiting and do not take into account other factors that may affect counselors' ability to work with people who are culturally different from themselves. These factors include metacognition and the ability to mentally strategize and the role of motivation in the ability to interact with people of different cultures.

CQ is defined as an individual's ability to deal effectively with people from different cultural backgrounds (Earley & Ang, 2003) and is a theoretical extension of contemporary approaches to understanding intelligences. Traditionally, the study of intelligence focused mainly on *g*, the academic or cognitive facets or types of intelligence. More recently, multiple intelligence theory (Gardner, 1993; Sternberg, 2000) proposed other dimensions or types of intelligence, such as emotional intelligence and social intelligence (Ford & Tisak, 1983; Goleman, 1995). Consistent with this trend, Earley and Ang have focused on CQ, which is an individual's ability to adapt effectively to new cultural contexts. They view CQ as an emerging and important type of intelligence that is consistent with contemporary conceptualizations of intelligence as the ability to adapt and adjust to the environment (Gardner, 1993; Mayer & Salovey, 1993; Sternberg, 2000). Thus, the four dimensions of CQ mirror contemporary views of intelligence as a complex, multifaceted individual attribute, and include metacognitive CQ, cognitive CQ, motivational CQ, and behavioral CQ components (see Sternberg, 2000). Just as emotional intelligence (EQ) complements cognitive intelligence (IQ) as important for work effectiveness and positive personal relationships in this increasingly interdependent world (Earley & Gibson, 2002), Earley and Ang (2003) suggest that CQ is another complementary form of intelligence that can explain variability in coping with diversity and new cultural settings. However, since the norms for social interaction vary from culture to culture, it is unlikely that IQ, EQ, or social intelligence will translate automatically into effective cross-cultural adjustment and interaction.

Counselors are usually well-versed in IQ, EQ, and social intelligence. These types of intelligence are often coupled with the practitioner's reasons and motivations for choosing counseling as a vocation and they are often developed through counselor training programs. For example, the analytic ability needed to develop accurate and cogent case conceptualizations is related to the concept of IQ. EQ and social intelligence are also essential to the process of creating and maintaining a solid therapeutic alliance (or bond between counselor and client), which has long been noted as a cornerstone for effective counseling practice (Norcross, 2002). Although these types of intelligence are necessary components of a counselor's repertoire, by themselves they are not sufficient to ensure ethical and effective dealings with an increasingly diverse population of clients.

CQ thus complements the broad array of types of intelligence that are integral to sound mental health practice. In the absence of an adequate framework in counseling psychology for explaining the complexities in multicultural counseling competence, we believe that CQ offers a robustly researched theoretical framework with an ability to predict effective cultural judgment, decision making, adjustment, and performance (Ang, Van Dyne, Koh, Ng, Templer, Tay, & Chandrasekar, 2007). Applying CQ to couneling psychology is therefore a significant step in our search for cultural competence in mental health practice.

In the next section, we address each facet of CQ by defining it with counseling examples and then relating each facet to existing counseling literature to illustrate how counselors can develop and apply their CQ toward multicultural counseling competence.

Metacognitive CQ

Metacognitive CQ refers to an individual's capability for actively monitoring behaviors, cultural assumptions, and knowledge during cross-cultural interactions (Ang, Van Dyne, Koh, Ng, Templer, Tay, and Chandrasekar, 2007). When applied to counseling psychology, metacognitive CQ may be described as a counselor's level of cultural strategizing during cross-cultural counseling interactions. For example, Carrie is a psychologist at a small urban elementary school. She is a European-American female and many of her students are children of immigrants from Honduras, Mexico, Guatemala, Nicaragua, and other Central American countries. As Carrie works with one family, she wonders whether she should address her concerns to the father, as he is sometimes the most powerful member of a Latin American family. Metacognitively, Carrie considers the following: Are all fathers at the top of the Latin American family's hierarchy? Does this mean that she should not give as much weight to her interactions with the mother? She plans to have an interpreter available, as she assumes the child's family is fairly uneducated and does not speak English. Again, she starts to question this assumption: Why would she assume the family is uneducated? And what does the situation have to do with a working knowledge of English? What if the father speaks Spanish and French? These questions represent a lively cognitive strategizing process indicated by the metacognitive facet of CQ.

Those with high metacognitive CQ plan and reflect in every counseling interaction, and, as a result, they are able to modify their understanding of and behavior in cross-cultural interactions as called upon by shifting information and circumstances. As a trait, metacognitive CQ shares characteristics with Sue and Torino's (2005) conceptualization of multicultural awareness. In the mental health professions, an awareness of one's own cultural biases is essential in shedding light on the precipitants and consequences of one's interaction dynamics with culturally diverse individuals. It is the combination of continued reflection upon this awareness, along with the ability and willingness to alter behaviors as needed to fit the demands of cross-cultural interactions, which allows for culturally competent practice. In two recent studies of exemplars of culturally competent psychological practice (Goh & Yang 2007; Goh, Starkey, Skovholt, & Jennings, 2007), culturally competent practitioners consistently demonstrated the ability to be cognitively lithe and adaptable and to perpetually strategize for better ways to communicate and relate across cultures.

That such metacognitive dialogue exists in counseling interactions was recognized by Pedersen (1994), who developed the Triad model as a counseling skills training simulation designed to make explicit the client's internal dialogue. In a simulated counseling interview, a counseling trainee is matched with three individuals of a similar cultural background to act as client, anticounselor, and procounselor. The anticounselor's role is to express and exaggerate negative messages that the client is likely to be thinking but not saying in the counseling process. The procounselor's role is to express positive internal messages that a client may be thinking but not saying. The videotaping, briefing, and debriefing within this process help counselors to become more familiar with such messages that arise when working with culturally diverse clients, so that they can effectively incorporate such messages in the therapeutic relationship.

S. Sue (1998) noted that understanding client expectations and counselors' cognitive styles were more potentially important than matching counselor and client ethnicity in cross-cultural counseling situations. Sue compared a computer science term, "dynamic sizing," used to describe a fluctuating computer cache size, to the kind of metacognitive flexibility required on the part of culturally competent counselors. Such flexibility helps counselors know when culturally specific knowledge may be generalized to a particular client and when it may not. Similarly, López (1997) described cultural competence as a counselor's ability to navigate contrasting cultural perspectives in order to decipher culturally based meaning from clients' perspectives. This description indicates the importance of the culturally competent counselor's perspective-taking ability, cognitive flexibility, and problem-solving ability. A good example of such strategizing is Leong and Lee's (2006) cultural accommodation approach, which offers three steps for adjusting a theoretical method to a different cultural context: (a) identifying the cultural gaps or cultural blind spots in an existing theory that restricts its cultural validity, (b) selecting current culturally specific concepts and models from cross-cultural and ethnic minority psychology to fill in these missing components and increase the existing theory's effective application to the group in question, and (c) testing the culturally accommodated theory to determine if it has incremental validity above and beyond the culturally unaccommodated theory (p. 414).

The *Diagnostic and Statistical Manual of Mental Disorders* (American Psychiatric Association, 2000) provides a concise strategy for making culturally relevant cognitive adjustments when assessing psychological manifestations in clients. In discerning what is described to be the client's "cultural idioms of distress," counselors have to (a) understand the cultural identity of the individual, (b) explore cultural explanations of the individual's illness, (c) elicit cultural factors related to the psychosocial environment and levels of functioning, (d) navigate cultural elements of the relationship between the individual and the clinician, and (e) make an overall cultural assessment for diagnosis and care (pp. 843–844). This cultural formulation of a client's psychological presentation grew out of a classic strategy of using eight questions (Kleinman, Eisenberg, & Good, 1978) to gain cultural understanding of a client's psychological issues from the client's cultural frame of reference.

More recently, Hays (2001) proposed the acronym ADDRESSING as a broader framework to help culturally responsive therapists avoid making inaccurate generalizations based on a client's appearance, language abilities, or even family name. Hays suggested that when counselors hold metacognitions that conceptualize clients as potentially having multiple group memberships and identities, the potential for counselor prejudice is diminished. Hays's framework encourages counselors to (a) take into account **a**ge-related issues, (b) consider **d**evelopmental and acquired **d**isability, (c) understand client's **r**eligious beliefs and practices, if relevant, (d) reflect on the client's **e**thnic identity and **s**ocioeconomic status, (e) deliberate **s**exual orientation issues where relevant, (f) delve into **i**ndigenous heritage and **n**ational identity, and (g) contemplate **g**ender-related roles and expectations (ADDRESSING).

The above examples are important metacognitive strategies for counselors to develop when working with culturally diverse clients. As a core counseling skill, being able to recognize and strategize within and across complex cultural contexts is fundamental to effective communication in counseling (Johnson, 2005). More importantly, it helps counselors who practice in diverse societies to develop an understanding of how race, racism, and racial identity have considerable relevance to the experiences of clients they work with and inherent biases that dominate the sociopolitical climates in diverse societies such as North America (Carter & Pieterse, 2005; Ponterotto, Utsey, & Pedersen, 2006; D. W. Sue, 2003).

Cognitive CQ

Cognitive CQ is defined as knowledge about the cultural aspects of the environment and one's place within it, and broadly encompasses both cultural universals and cultural differences (Ang et al., 2007). When applied to counseling psychology, cognitive CQ may be defined as a counselor's level of knowledge about the client's culture, including but not limited to values, norms, and environment. An example of cognitive CQ in counseling: Brian is a male psychologist of African descent at a college counseling center. He meets with a new client, who is a Native American woman. As she discusses her difficulties in getting a job, Brian considers a number of variables that make her job search more formidable. He is aware, for example, that although many companies purport to be equal opportunity employers, there is still much discrimination against Native Americans as well as women in hiring practices. He is aware of his own educational background and cultural values as he asks her to share her experiences in order to learn about her educational background and cultural values. He asks for her opinion about how her culture may or may not play a role in her career choices thus far.

As such, cognitive CQ bears similarities to the knowledge component in the Sue and Sue (2003) tripartite model of cultural competence. This cognitive aspect of CQ is important in understanding the dynamics of social interaction with individuals of a particular culture. It is operationalized as including knowledge about the economic, marriage, and legal systems, as well as common religious beliefs, rules of languages, arts and crafts, cultural values, and nonverbal behavior patterns of other cultures. This factor incorporates both notions of *etic* (culturally universal) and *emic* (culturally specific) perspectives in counseling psychology (Sue & Sue, 2003). While etic perspectives argue that some concepts of psychology can be applied across cultures, emic perspectives emphasize how "culture and life experiences affect the expression of . . . behavior" and propose that "culture-specific strategies" should be used in counseling (p. 5). Sue and Sue state that it is crucial that counselors be familiar with the cultural backgrounds of their clients. They propose that counselors form a sense of "cognitive empathy" with their clients in order to "see and accept other worldviews in a nonjudgmental manner" (Sue & Sue, 2003, p. 20).

Pedersen (2005) suggests that cultural complexity does not have to mean cultural chaos and a lack of direction for counselors. Citing the multicultural theory presented in Sue, Ivey, and Pedersen (1996), Pedersen emphasized six propositions for developing a culture-centered cognitive perspective. These propositions highlight the counselor's ability to consider alternative worldviews, alternative ways of relating and helping, and adopting a systemic approach to conceptualizing and working with clients.

Cognitive CQ provides a flexible, overarching umbrella under which these competencies may be organized, and mirrors the traditional knowledge component of applied multicultural counseling theory. In addition to the above factors, it is necessary for counselors to have knowledge of communication styles; family dynamics and systems; racial/cultural/ethnic minority identity development models and theories; worldviews, including locus of control, locus of responsibility, and values; and factors that are specific to unique cultural groups. For example, in work with Asian Americans, Sue and Sue (2003) emphasize the "model minority" myth, collectivistic orientation and hierarchical relationships, holistic view of mind and body, and academic/occupational goals. In work with Hispanic/Latino Americans, there are other areas of focus: family values and structure; sex/gender roles; and spirituality and religiosity. For clients of both cultural backgrounds, acculturation issues are addressed.

One question that remains is, to what extent does one's cultural knowledge need to be specific? In other words, is it enough to be familiar with traditional Asian-American family systems, or does one need more specific knowledge to differentiate between patterns seen in Japanese-American households versus Filipino-American households? We argue that to the extent possible, counselors should become familiar with the specific practices and customs of their clients. Without this contextual knowledge, mental health professionals are more likely to practice ethnocentrically and attempt to treat all clients in a universal manner, ignoring salient differences and possibly doing more harm than good.

Motivational CQ

Motivational CQ is an individual's capability to direct attention and energy toward learning and functioning in culturally diverse situations. It refers to the extent to which individuals are confident about their ability to engage in cross-cultural interactions and find intrinsic satisfaction in these interactions (Ang et al., 2007). When applied to counseling psychology, motivational CQ may be defined as the extent to which a counselor has the intrinsic drive to learn, perceive, and adapt to culturally diverse clientele and their culturally complex circumstances. For example, Harma is a psychologist who works at a small private hospital in a suburban area. She is European-American and upper-middle-class. She has traveled with her family throughout Europe and Asia and particularly enjoyed traveling to Africa. When Harma hears of a job opening in a new wing of a large urban hospital that is designed specifically to target ethnically diverse women in the community, she does not listen to her parents' concerns for her safety at working in that neighborhood and applies for the job. She is thrilled when she gets the offer, even though it means less pay than her other job, because she considers it gratifying to be able to serve as well as learn from diverse clients.

Motivational CQ therefore reflects an individual's intrinsic drive to seek out and enjoy interactions with culturally diverse persons on a consistent basis. Motivation to engage in cross-cultural counseling is not explicitly addressed by Sue et al.'s (1982) model of multicultural counseling competence. The increasingly frequent need for mental health professionals to competently treat individuals from diverse populations obviously does not translate directly into increased motivation to work with these clients. In other words, the fact that counselors are forced to work with increasingly diverse clientele does not reveal how motivated they are to interact with such clients in a multiculturally competent manner. Attitudinal differences among counselors as to the importance of working with diverse individuals, as well as variations in their confidence about their abilities to effectively treat clients from different cultures, may thus be significant in differentiating levels of multicultural counseling competence above and beyond the traditional three-factor model.

While counseling psychology does not explicitly address motivational CQ, there are several concepts in applied psychology that overlap. In describing the overarching concept of human motivation, Deci and Ryan's (1985) self-determination theory focuses on the influence of the social context on either supporting or inhibiting individuals' assumed innate tendencies toward psychological growth. Within self-determination theory, cognitive evaluation theory speaks to the effects of social environments on intrinsic motivation. The interaction between individuals and their environments subsequently provides the basis for predictions about behaviors, experience, and development. Thus, it is expected that counselors' intrinsic motivation for seeking out cross-cultural interactions would be influenced not only by personal factors, but also by their social contexts. Referring to our earlier example of Harma, counselors who have had many positive cross-cultural experiences would be expected to have the potential for higher motivational CQ.

Bandura's (1997) concept of self-efficacy, or the belief that one has the capacity for success in a given situation, may also be important in shaping individuals' motivational CQ. Counselors are more likely to seek out cross-cultural counseling interactions if they believe they have a high potential for effecting change. Implied in multicultural counseling competency is one's belief in said competencies. Similar to self-determination theory, Bandura posits that both individual and social/contextual factors, such as previous experience, modeling, amount of encouragement, and attributions, may change individuals' confidence in their ability to successfully navigate cross-cultural interactions.

Other factors potentially contributing to counselors' motivational CQ include a social justice orientation and racial/cultural identity development status. Constantine, Hage,

Kindaichi, and Bryant (2007) described social justice as the pursuit of fairness and equity for all individuals in society. Historically, counseling psychology has aligned with the social justice movement through counselors' attempts to actively "change social institutions, political and economic systems, and governmental structures that perpetuate unfair practices, structures, and policies in terms of accessibility, resource distribution, and human rights" (Fouad, Gerstein, & Toporek, 2006, p. 1). As a field, counseling psychology has thus garnered strong impetus toward effecting change in multicultural contexts. Training within this historical context provides counseling psychologists with an institutional starting point for developing motivational CQ.

Finally, counselors may be more or less prone to seek out cross-cultural counseling interactions based upon their level of racial/cultural identity development. Models of racial identity development have been proposed for individuals belonging to minority and mainstream cultures (e.g., Sue & Sue, 2003; Helms, 1990; Cross, 1995). Earlier levels of development tend to be characterized by little understanding of the impact of race and acceptance of mainstream culture (Sue & Sue, 2003). At these "color blind" stages, counselors are unlikely to have high intrinsic motivation to interact with individuals different from themselves, as they may not perceive racial and ethnic differences as important influences in the counselor-client partnership. Counselors who have progressed toward later stages of development, characterized by the integration of multicultural "ways of knowing" (Sue & Sue, 2003), are more likely to choose to work with culturally different individuals.

Our attempt to illustrate counselors with high motivational CQ also brings to mind Ramirez's (1991) concept of the multicultural personality. Ramirez defined the multicultural person as a "synthesis and amalgamation of resources learned from different peoples and cultures to create multicultural coping styles, thinking styles, perceptions of the world (world views) and multicultural identities" (p. 26). As cited by Ponterotto, Utsey, and Pedersen (2006), Ramirez (1999) describes someone as having a multicultural worldview on life when the person voluntarily and intentionally seeks diverse experiences and environments as well as leadership opportunities within that diversity. Among the characteristics describing the multicultural personality in Ponterotto (2006) is the attribute of one who actively pursues opportunities to learn about other cultures as well as to interact with people of different cultural origins.

Behavioral CQ

Behavioral CQ, the final dimension of CQ, refers to the capability to use a flexible behavioral repertoire based on specifics of a given cultural situation, that is, the capability to enact both appropriate verbal and nonverbal behaviors in specific cross-cultural situations (Ang et al., 2007). When applied to counseling psychology, behavioral CQ may be defined as the extent to which a counselor acts appropriately in cross-cultural counseling situations. For example, Joseph is a second-generation Chinese-American psychologist in San Francisco, California. He speaks a little Mandarin. His coworkers tease him because they say that with the parents of Chinese-American students, he acts polite, nice, and deferential. He always calls parents "Mr. So-and-So or Mrs. So-and-So." With parents of white students, though, he is more casual and sometimes even jokes with them. Those parents all call him "Joe." His coworkers call him "Mr. Split Personality" because it is as if he has two personalities, "The Chinese-American one and the white one." What Joseph is, in fact, demonstrating, is his ability to behaviorally adapt to culturally different situations as the occasion requires.

While latent thoughts, feelings, and motivation are not readily apparent in face-to-face interactions, an individual's verbal and nonverbal communications are an immediate source of information in judging cultural competency. In a broad conceptual sense, behavioral CQ reflects the skills component of multicultural counseling competence.

Sue and Sue (2003) describe essential multicultural counseling skills as incorporating culturally appropriate verbal and nonverbal responses, supporting institutional change on clients' behalf, and adapting to the clients' role expectations.

In this realm, the counselor applies the other factors of CQ in a fashion that is observable and measurable. Counseling is essentially based on a verbal currency of exchange; without the appropriate use of words, as well as silence, mental health professionals are unlikely to reach clients. Given that communication styles tend to vary across cultures, it is also important for counselors to adopt a flexible style with respect to communicating with others in culturally complex situations.

For counselors to successfully negotiate culturally complex situations, Pedersen (1997) described ten behavioral examples: (a) clear and separate identification of multiple but conflicting culturally learned viewpoints *between* persons; (b) clear and separate identification of multiple but conflicting culturally learned viewpoints *within* persons; (c) ability to accurately relate the actions of different persons in ways that would explain their behavior from their own cultural perspective; (d) ability to listen and store information without interruption, when culturally appropriate, for introduction later; (e) ability to shift topics in culturally appropriate ways; (f) accurate labeling of culturally appropriate feelings in specific rather than general terms; (g) identification of culturally defined multiple support systems for the client; (h) ability to identify alternative solutions and anticipate the consequences of each solution; (i) ability to identify the culturally learned criteria being used to evaluate alternative solutions; and (j) ability to generate insights about specific situations based on that person's culturally learned perspective(s)

Saldaña (2001), in noting the fundamental importance of communication in multicultural counseling competence, suggested that counselors should pay attention to (a) different preferences for personal space, (b) appropriateness of eye contact and feedback behavior, (c) different rules for turn-taking and interrupting speech, (d) variations in gesturing, (e) interpretation of facial expressions, (f) use of silence, (g) deciphering assertiveness and aggressiveness, (h) modifying volume as appropriate, and (i) differences in amount of touch expected. In order to establish rapport, Saldaña believes that learning how to pronounce a client's name correctly, determining if other family members should be involved, describing the therapeutic process, and clarifying relationships, roles, and expectations are critical ingredients for therapeutic success.

In an excellent analysis of issues confronting cultural competence- and evidence-based practices, Whaley and Davis (2007) noted the increasing role of cultural adaptations in explaining what effective treatment is. They defined cultural adaptation as "any modification to an evidence-based treatment that involves changes in the approach to service delivery, in the nature of the therapeutic relationship, or in components of the treatment itself to accommodate the cultural beliefs, attitudes, and behaviors of the target population. Under this definition, the translation of a treatment protocol into the native language of a non–English-speaking population would fall under the rubric of changing the approach to service" (pp. 570–571). In this regard, Goh, Dunnigan, and McGraw Schuchman (2004) offer specific guidelines for using mental health interpreters before, at the beginning, during, and after each clinical session. Most important in communicating with English language learners is to ensure that what a speaker intends to say is what is heard by the listener.

CONCLUSION

Ang et al. (2007) demonstrate that CQ is a key individual characteristic that predicts success in overseas assignments, positive and constructive working relationships with a wide variety of people, and adaptability when traveling or working in different cultural settings. In this chapter, we presented definitions of multicultural counseling competence and counseling examples similar to those encountered in the cross-cultural management contexts where the use of CQ is most prevalent. The similar nuances and complexities represented in global management and multicultural counseling suggest that CQ provides a unique and refreshing contribution to our search for a more comprehensive and coherent definition of cultural competence for counseling psychology and related fields.

The rigor of the theory and research findings (e.g., Ang et al., 2007) raises hope and promise for the study and measure of CQ within counseling psychology and related fields to inform such areas as evidence-based practices (Whaley & Davis, 2007), Ponterotto's (2006) notion of the multicultural personality, or the application of the multicultural counseling guidelines (American Psychological Association, 2003), to name a few examples. Extremely attractive is CQ's ability to predict effective cross-cultural outcomes (Ang et al., 2007), which is highly desirable in our study of multicultural counseling competence.

In this chapter, we described the potential of CQ to be a useful concept and framework for the development of culturally competent mental health counselors by drawing from the existing counseling literature. While we can be encouraged by the breadth and depth of how counseling psychology has addressed multicultural counseling competence in many ways similar to CQ, we look forward to moving beyond our initial attempt to articulate CQ dimensions in counseling language and terms and moving toward research that demonstrates CQ as a comprehensive concept for describing multicultural counseling competence. Our intention in this chapter was to introduce the notion of CQ to the field. There is yet a lot of work to be done. We anticipate an ongoing research program of CQ in counseling psychology and related mental health fields that will include but not be limited to the following: ways in which CQ is related to other proposed dimensions of multicultural counseling competencies (such as knowledge, awareness, and skills) and the client-counselor relationship; outcome studies in cross-cultural counseling interactions using CQ versus traditional conceptualizations; and contextualizing the CQ measure to reflect counseling more specifically.

If CQ is to help reduce biases and barriers in how mental health services are delivered and whether counseling is culturally relevant and appropriate, an important next step is to delineate ways that counselors can develop CQ and grow in all dimensions of CQ. Carter (2005) notes that such training is never easy and is often fraught with conflict as experienced in his racial-cultural counseling training laboratory. Anecdotally, our professional experience of introducing the CQ concept to the mental health community and counseling psychology students has been tremendously positive. Particularly beneficial and illuminating is the 360-degree perspective provided by raters familiar with the student who complete the CQ measure about the student. Presently, we are working on a training model for using CQ within Carter's (2005) exemplary training model as well as developing guidelines that provide concrete steps that counseling students can take to develop their CQ. We invite psychologists and other related applied psychology and human services scientists and practitioners to join us in investigating the promotion and practice of CQ in multicultural counseling competence.

REFERENCES

American Psychiatric Association. (2000). *Diagnostic and statistical manual of mental disorders* (4th ed.). Text Revision. Washington, DC: American Psychiatric Association.

American Psychological Association. (2003). Guidelines on multicultural education, training, research, practice, and organizational change for psychologists. *American Psychologist, 58,* 377–402.

Ang, S., Van Dyne, L., Koh, C., Ng, K.Y., Templer, J.K., Tay, C., & Chandrasekar, N.A. (2007). Cultural intelligence: Its measurement and effects on cultural judgment and decision making. *Management and Organization Review, 3,* 335–371.

Arredondo, P., Toporek, R., Brown, S., et al. (1996). Operationalization of the multicultural counseling competencies. *Journal of Multicultural Counseling and Development, 24,* 42–78.

Bandura, A. (1997). *Self-efficacy: The exercise of control.* New York: WH Freeman and Company.

Carter, R.T. (2005). Teaching racial-cultural competence: A racially-inclusive model. In R.T. Carter (Ed.), *Handbook of racial-cultural psychology and counseling. Volume 2. Training and practice* (pp. 36–56). Hoboken, NJ: John Wiley & Sons.

Carter, R.T., & Pieterse, A.L. (2005). Race: A social and psychological analysis of the term and its meaning. In R.T. Carter (Ed.), *Handbook of racial-cultural psychology and counseling. Volume 1. Theory and research* (pp. 41–63). Hoboken, NJ: John Wiley & Sons.

Constantine, M.G., Hage, S.M., Kindaichi, M.M., & Bryant, R.M. (2007). Social justice and multicultural issues: Implications for practice and training of counselors and counseling psychologists. *Journal of Counseling & Development, 85,* 24–29.

Constantine, M.G., & Ladany, N. (2001). New visions for defining and assessing multicultural counseling competence. In J.G. Ponterotto, J.M. Casas, L.A. Suzuki, & C.M. Alexander (Eds.), *Handbook of multicultural counseling* (2nd ed.) (pp. 482–498). Thousand Oaks, CA: Sage.

Cross, W.E., Jr. (1995). The psychology of nigrescence: Revising the Cross model. In J.G. Ponterotto, J.M. Casas, L.A. Suzuki, & C.M. Alexander (Eds.), *Handbook of multicultural counseling* (2nd ed.) (pp. 93–122). Thousand Oaks, CA: Sage.

Deci, E.L., & Ryan, R.M. (1985). *Intrinsic motivation and self-determination in human behavior.* New York: Plenum Press.

Earley, P.C., & Ang, S. (2003). *Cultural intelligence: Individual interactions across cultures*. Palo Alto, CA: Stanford University Press.

Earley, P.C., & Gibson, C.B. (2002). *Multinational teams: New perspectives*. Mahwah, NJ: Lawrence Erlbaum Associates.

Ford, M., & Tisak, M. (1983). A further search for social intelligence. *Journal of Educational Psychology, 75*, 196–206.

Fouad, N.A., Gerstein, L.H., & Toporek, R.L. (2006). Social justice and counseling psychology in context. In R.L. Toporek, L.H. Gerstein, N.A. Fouad, G. Roysircar, & T. Israel (Eds.), *Handbook for social justice in counseling psychology* (pp.1–16). Thousands Oaks, CA: Sage.

Gardner, H. (1993). *Multiple intelligence: The theory in practice*. New York: Basic Books.

Goh, M., Dunnigan, T., & McGraw Schuchman, K. (2004). Bias in counseling Hmong clients with limited English proficiency. In J.L. Chin (Ed.), *The psychology of prejudice and discrimination. Volume 2: Ethnicity and multiracial identity* (pp. 109–136). Westport, CT: Praeger.

Goh, M., Starkey, M., Skovholt, T.M., & Jennings, L. (2007). In search of cultural competence in mental health practice: A study of expert multicultural counseling therapists. Paper presented at the 115th annual convention of the American Psychological Association, San Francisco, CA.

Goh, M., & Yang, A. (2007). The developmental model of intercultural sensitivity: A study of culturally competent exemplars. Paper presented at the 115th annual convention of the American Psychological Association, San Francisco, CA.

Goleman, D. (1995). *Emotional intelligence*. New York: Bantam Books.

Hays, P.A. (2001). *Addressing cultural complexities in practice: A framework for clinicians and counselors*. Washington, DC: American Psychological Association.

Helms, J.E. (1990). *Black and white racial identity: Theory, research, and practice*. Westport, CT: Greenwood Press.

Johnson, S.D. (2005). Culture, context, and counseling. In R.T. Carter (Ed.), *Handbook of racial-cultural psychology and counseling. Volume 1. Theory and research* (pp. 17–25). Hoboken, NJ: John Wiley & Sons.

Kleinman, A., Eisenberg, L., & Good, B. (1978). Culture, illness, and care: Clinical lessons from anthropologic and cross-cultural research. *Annals of Internal Medicine, 88*, 83–93.

Leong, F.T.L., & Lee, S.H. (2006). A cultural accommodation model for cross-cultural psychotherapy: Illustrated with the case of Asian Americans. *Psychotherapy: Theory, Research, Practice, Training, 43*, 410–423.

López, S.R. (1997). Cultural competence in psychotherapy: A guide for clinicians and their supervisors. In C.E. Watkins (Ed.), *Handbook of psychotherapy and supervision* (pp. 570–588). New York: John Wiley & Sons.

Mayer, J.D., & Salovey, P. (1993). The intelligence of emotional intelligence. *Intelligence, 17*, 433–442.

Norcross, J.C. (2002). *Psychotherapy relationships that work: Therapist contributions and responsiveness to patient needs*. New York: Oxford University Press.

Pedersen, P. (1994). *Handbook for developing multicultural awareness* (2nd ed.). Alexandria, VA: American Counseling Association.

Pedersen, P.B. (1997). *Culture-centered counseling interventions: Striving for accuracy*. Thousand Oaks, CA: Sage.

Pedersen, P.B. (2005). The importance of cultural psychology theory for multicultural counselors. In R.T. Carter (Ed.), *Handbook of racial-cultural psychology and counseling. Volume 1. Theory and research* (pp. 3–16). Hoboken, NJ: John Wiley & Sons.

Ponterotto, J.G. (2006). Multicultural personality. In Y. Jackson (Ed.), *Encyclopedia of multicultural psychology*. Thousand Oaks, CA: Sage.

Ponterotto, J.G., Utsey, S.O., & Pedersen, P.B. (2006). *Preventing prejudice: A guide for counselors, educators, and parents* (2nd ed.). Thousand Oaks, CA: Sage.

Pope-Davis, D.B., Coleman, H.L.K., Liu, W.M., & Toporek, R.L. (2003). *Handbook of multicultural competencies in counseling and psychology*. Thousand Oaks, CA: Sage.

Ramirez, M., III. (1991). *Psychotherapy and counseling with minorities: A cognitive approach to individual and cultural differences.* New York: Pergamon Press.

Ramirez, M., III. (1999). *Multicultural psychotherapy: An approach to individual and cultural differences* (2nd ed.). New York: Pergamon Press.

Reynolds, A.L. (2001). Multidimensional cultural competence: Providing tools for transforming psychology. *The Counseling Psychologist, 29,* 822–832.

Ridley, C.R., Baker, D.M., & Hill, C.L. (2001). Critical issues concerning cultural competence. *The Counseling Psychologist, 29,* 822–832.

Saldaña, D. (2001). *Cultural competency: A practical guide for mental health service providers.* Austin, TX: Hogg Foundation for Mental Health.

Sternberg, R.J. (2000). *Handbook of intelligence.* New York: Cambridge University Press.

Sue, D.W. (2001). Multidimensional facets of cultural competence. *The Counseling Psychologist, 29,* 790–821.

Sue, D.W. (2003). *Overcoming our racism: The journey to liberation.* New York: John Wiley & Sons.

Sue, D.W., Carter, R.T., Casas, J.M., et al. (1998). *Multicultural counseling competencies: Individual and organizational development.* Thousand Oaks, CA: Sage.

Sue, D.W., Ivey, A.E., & Pedersen, P.B. (1996). *Multicultural counseling theory.* Pacific Grove, CA: Brooks/Cole.

Sue, D.W., & Sue, S. (2003). *Counseling the culturally diverse: Theory and practice* (4th ed.). New York: John Wiley & Sons.

Sue, D.W., & Torino, G.C. (2005). Racial-cultural competence: Awareness, knowledge, and skills. In R.T. Carter (Ed.), *Handbook of racial-cultural psychology and counseling. Volume 2. Training and Practice* (pp. 3–18). Hoboken, NJ: Wiley & Sons.

Sue, D.W., Bernier, J.E., Durran, A., et al. (1982). Position paper: Cross-cultural counseling competencies. *The Counseling Psychologist, 10,* 45–52.

Sue, S. (1998). In search of cultural competence in psychotherapy and counseling. *American Psychologist, 53,* 440–448.

U.S. Department of Health and Human Services. (2001). *Mental health: Culture, race, and ethnicity—A supplement to mental health: A report of the surgeon general.* Rockville, MD: U.S. Department of Health and Human Services.

Whaley, A.L., & Davis, K.E. (2007). Cultural competence and evidence-based practice in mental health services: A complementary perspective. *American Psychologist, 62,* 563–574.

CHAPTER 17

Cultural Intelligence and Short-Term Missions

The Phenomenon of the Fifteen-Year-Old Missionary

DAVID LIVERMORE

Long before Starbucks was selling lattes in Bangkok and centuries before one could fly to virtually anywhere in the world within 24 hours, Christian missionaries and the locals they encountered engaged in cross-cultural interaction. Missionaries have been leaving their homelands to do the work of Jesus for nearly 2,000 years. In fact, some of the earliest research on intercultural relationships originated in studying missionary activity.

However, as globalization is transforming the way nearly every profession does its work, the "missionary profession" is undergoing a major shift. Throughout most of the history of Christian missions, the vast majority of missionaries have been lifelong "professionals" who raised financial support, studied local languages and customs, and packed all their earthly belongings in a coffin to take to the mission field. Though those kinds of lifelong missionary professionals still exist (referred to as "long-term missionaries" hereon) far more common today are "short-term missionaries," who serve as missionaries for two weeks at a time or less.

A typical American missionary today is a 15-year-old who sends out a few letters seeking financial support, gets a passport and plane ticket, and goes to serve as a "missionary" for ten days to two weeks. Nearly one-third of all American high school students participate in some kind of religious cross-cultural experience before they graduate. In fact, church ministries for youth have to run a full-fledged, short-term missions program in order to be considered legitimate. In his book *Soul Searching,* Smith (2005) reports more than 5.5 million American youths between the ages of 13 and 17 have cumulatively participated in more than 11.5 million missions trips. This involves more than 2 million trips a year just for this age bracket.

Though these kinds of "missionaries" are most often high school and college students, more and more families, adults, and senior citizens are participating as well. According to Robert Wuthnow, professor of sociology of religion at Princeton, an additional 1.6

million American church members (Protestant and Catholic adults, aged 18 and older) participated in short-term missions trips outside the United States during the year 2005. An additional, unknown number traveled within the United States doing similar kinds of work in cross-cultural contexts (e.g., rebuilding efforts in New Orleans, development work in West Virginia, or evangelistic outreach in New York City). Most of these trips last two weeks at most, a length of time that fits well into school holidays or annual vacations. In contrast to the millions of short-term missionaries traveling annually, there are about 60,000 American long-term missionaries serving overseas.

Though the short-term missionary phenomenon seems to have the most momentum in the United States, it has parallel movements in other parts of the world. Christians in the United Kingdom, Australia, South Korea, Singapore, and even in places like Russia, Uganda, and Guatemala are also traveling around the world on short-term missions trips. For example, between January and September of 2005, 22,000 Koreans went on two-week short-term missions trips to Mongolia, typically in groups of 30–80 people at a time.

The cost of these short-term missions sojourns now outpaces what American Christians spend supporting the more traditional, long-term missions efforts of their churches and denominations. Hundreds of organizations have been started simply to organize and coordinate these trips. The short-term missionary movement is primarily a grassroots and populist phenomenon. Short-term missions, work moves ahead in a way that it is almost completely divorced from scholarship, missiology, and seminary education. Most youth ministers are expected to lead groups of young people on these kinds of cross-cultural encounters but receive little, if any training (Priest, Dischinger, Rasumssen, & Brown, 2006).

I am part of a small but growing research community that has been gathering data and assessing the efficacy of short-term missions. The motivation behind why many trips happen, the paternalistic interactions that often occur, and the growing amounts of money spent are a cause for concern. Many studies raise questions about whether there are positive results for the local communities that receive the missionaries. Some even question whether the trips are having the transformative impact upon the participants that they are alleged to have. It is impossible to fairly assess the efficacy of short-term missions without a framework from which to measure effectiveness. In order to address the objectives of this book, I have made evaluative judgments about short-term missions based upon the cultural intelligence (CQ) framework and by analyzing whether the actual outcomes of short-term missions trips align with the outcomes espoused by short-term missions proponents. In particular, my interest has been in exploring the nature of the cross-cultural interactions that occurred between short-term missionaries and locals.

METHOD

The findings reported in this chapter are themes drawn from three studies conducted that compared the experiences of North American short-term missionaries with the experiences of the locals who hosted those short-term missionaries. The subjects were 630 North American missionaries (95 percent from the United States, 5 percent from Canada) and 380 locals from 23 different countries. These studies were intended to be descriptive in nature. A grounded theory approach was used, which included interviews, research in journals written by the North American subjects, surveys, and on-site observation. Discussion from a subset of these findings was published in the book *Serving with Eyes Wide Open: Doing Short-Term Missions with Cultural Intelligence* (Livermore, 2006).

Many of the discoveries found in this research on short-term missions parallel findings from research done on more traditional missionary efforts. Similar data surface in research on study-abroad programs sponsored by higher educational institutions throughout the United States. In fact, it is noteworthy that the growth in short-term missions activity among American Christians mirrors the rapid growth occurring in study-abroad programs at universities across the United States. Between 1985 and 2000, enrollment by American students in study-abroad programs more than tripled. The dominant major of the students enrolled in these programs shifted from humanities and social sciences to more professionally oriented studies such as business and education (Dolby, 2005). More comparative work is needed to look at the similarities and differences between educational short-term study-abroad programs and religiously motivated short-term missions trips.

Researchers and practitioners from missiology assert that the most important research questions related to short-term missions lie in finding ways to ensure that these religious pilgrimages produce self-transformation among participants as well as bringing about positive change in the communities they serve. The interdisciplinary, meta-model of CQ and its distinctive nature as a transformative model for cross-cultural interaction uniquely positions CQ as a lens through which short-term missions can be viewed. In addition to providing a helpful framework for researching the effectiveness of short-term missions, CQ provides a research-based approach to developing more effective interventions to improve short-term missionary practice.

The following section, "Findings," describes four key themes that emerged in studying the cross-cultural behavior and thinking among American short-term missionaries. The findings are presented in light of the concepts of CQ. The final section, "Culturally Intelligent Missions," looks more specifically at how the four factors of CQ come to bear on short-term missions work.

FINDINGS: THEMES FROM THE CROSS-CULTURAL BEHAVIOR OF SHORT-TERM MISSIONARIES

I have been researching the phenomenon of short-term missions for nearly a decade, giving primary attention to the comparison between how North American short-term missionaries describe their experiences and how the locals who hosted them described the same experiences. While the American participants typically assessed their trips as successful, most of the local perspectives challenged that perception. Looking across the three studies, and further corroborating those findings with the research of others, four key themes emerged as recurring descriptions of many American short-term missionaries' cross-cultural practice: ethnocentrism, "bounded-set thinking," the money factor, and category width. The following material briefly overviews those four themes and suggests the connection of these themes to CQ.

Ethnocentrism

Proponents of short-term missions often defend these experiences as being less colonialist and ethnocentric than long-term missions. The argument is that at least short-term missions do not depend upon white men pastoring white churches with white steeples and white pews. Yet ethnocentrism and paternalism permeated the sentiments and behaviors of the North American subjects studied. From references to "weird" food, a desire to fix the inefficiency of the "chaos" observed, and an overall ignorance about the unique strengths and dynamics of the citizens and Christians encountered, ethnocentrism was abundant.

One study measured short-term participants' ethnocentrism before they went on a trip and again when they returned. The study indicated participants' ethnocentrism was found to be significantly lower at the end of the trip than it was at the beginning. However, when tested more longitudinally, the lowered ethnocentrism was not sustained. Participants reverted to their original ethnocentric perspectives. In some cases, the cross-cultural experience actually worsened ethnocentrism by perpetuating stereotypes of the seemingly barbaric, uncivilized lives of people living outside of Western society (Priest et al., 2006).

On the whole, short-term missionaries were largely unaware of how culture shaped the behavior of themselves and the "Other." CQ is needed in order for short-term missionaries to understand the interplay between cultural values in the place visited and those in their own cultural context. Equally important is drawing upon CQ to better understand the stereotypes the locals may have of the short-term missionaries, who are oftentimes uninvited guests. Greater cognitive and metacognitive CQ would have likely yielded greater understanding and awareness of the powerful influence of culture upon the self and the Other.

The ethnocentric behavior and thinking demonstrated by short-term missionaries was not significantly different from the typical behavior seen in American travelers as a whole. It was noteworthy however, that most of the short-term missionaries examined espoused strong apprehension about being ethnocentric and described their desire to behave in ways that would defy the "ugly American" image. However, the ensuing behavior and thinking demonstrated that most of the individuals resorted back to the very kind of ethnocentrism they sought to avoid. The North American participants did as anthropologists have often noted of tourists—they fled from social Others at home and simultaneously exoticized those that lived in distant lands. American students gushed about the Mexicans they spent ten days with, yet returned home to prejudiced relationships with Latino classmates. CQ helps to grasp the complexities of the discrepancies that occur between espoused perspectives and what is revealed in actual practice.

The CQ framework can result in the creative development of interventions that challenge the ethnocentrism of short-term missions participants. The most effective plans employ the use of these kinds of interventions before, during, and after the cross-cultural sojourns of short-term missionaries. The ubiquitous presence of ethnocentrism among short-term missionaries thwarts the transformative potential that exists in the altruistic intentions of the travelers. Given that CQ draws from multiple disciplines, it is uniquely suited to speak to the complexities of what goes on personally, socially, and missiologically in short-term missions.

Bounded-Set Thinking

Ethnocentrism was further exacerbated by the missionaries' so-called bounded-set thinking—a type of reasoning that simplifies things into either/or categories. For example, despite the profound differences that existed in the worlds encountered by most of the short-term missionaries studied, almost every North American subject talked first about the similarities they observed rather than the differences. For example, one subject said, "I wish I had spent less time studying about the culture and the differences because I was really more struck by the similarities than the differences."

The tendency to look for similarities in an unfamiliar context is a typical coping strategy for cross-cultural travelers. The *awareness* that is needed to be effective cross-culturally, as described in literature about metacognitive CQ, would help short-term missionaries more carefully interpret what they observed on their sojourns. Subjects assumed smiling, nodding, and silence all meant the same things for all people. For example, North American ministers who went on short-term missions trips to train other ministers assumed they were teaching effectively because their local counterparts appeared captivated by the teaching and never left the room other than at formal break times. However, the local students said things such as, "I'm glad the teachers felt respected. They should. What they need to realize however, is that we would never think about talking or getting up to leave in the middle of their lecture. It would be repulsive to do that to a teacher in our culture."

There was little evidence that short-term missionaries were prepared to look beyond the artifacts of culture to explore the deeper values and assumptions at work. Part of this simplistic observation and interpretation seemed to be a result of placing complex issues into simple either/or categories. This categorization is described by anthropologist Paul Hiebert (1994) as bounded-set thinking, which is directly related to metacognitive CQ because it gets at how culture shapes the way individuals think about thinking.

Bounded-set thinking, which is most typical among people of Western cultures, refers to drawing clear boundaries around those things believed to share intrinsic characteristics. For example, an apple may be red or green, it may be a variety of shapes and sizes, but everyone agrees it is an apple and not an orange. Bounded-set thinking defines an apple based on its fitting within the boundaries that make something an "apple." Things are identified based on clear boundaries. The logical inference is that there can be no crossing of the boundary. Something cannot be partially an apple. It is either an apple or it is not. The bud and blossom that precede the tangible fruit are not considered apples in a bounded-set world.

In contrast, many cultures organize their cognitive thinking using centered-set logic. A centered set is not determined by its boundary, though it may have one. It is determined by its center. If the objects to be organized are moving toward the center, they are considered to be in the set. In this case, anything moving toward becoming an apple, such as an apple bud or blossom, can easily be considered an apple, even though it looks nothing like the "boundaries" Westerners use to define an apple. Objects, which in some sense may be considered near the center but moving away from it, are seen to be outside the set. Thus, the boundary is determined by the relation of the objects to the center and not by essential characteristics of the objects themselves. A magnetic field is an example of a centered set, the pole being the center. Some particles are drawn toward the center and others are repelled by it (Hiebert, 1994, pp. 110–36).

There are other cognitive sets identified by analysts, but these two—bounded-set and centered-set—describe how different cognitive processes shape an individual's cross-cultural practice. The thoughts and behaviors of short-term missionaries might be influenced when they try to determine whether someone is a Christian. Using bounded-set thinking, most American short-term missionaries have clear definitions of what makes someone a Christian as compared to what keeps someone *out* of that set. In contrast, many Eastern Christians are less concerned about identifying what boundaries characterize someone as being a Christian. Instead, the focus is on the center, so they would consider someone who is moving toward Jesus and the values represented by Christ to be a Christian, rather than focusing on the boundaries established around a prescribed set of doctrines or "Christian" behaviors.

Much more needs to be explored about the implications of cognitive processing for how the individual behaves and relates cross-culturally. The anthropological and psychological underpinnings of CQ provide a helpful connection to this area. In particular, the metacognitive CQ dimension is particularly helpful in gaining a better understanding of this finding.

The Money Factor

Few things are as complicated in cross-cultural interactions as the issues related to money and economics between different cultural groups. The disparity in income levels between short-term participants and locals, the power issues associated with giving money, and the tension created by returning to "life at home" after encountering poverty firsthand are all among the complexities associated with money and short-term missions. In particular, the behavior and conversation of short-term participants varies between charitable sympathies for the poverty of those they encounter versus seeing the locals as quite happy without the "trappings" of materialistic gain. Both ends of this continuum are complex and require a heightened degree of CQ.

Most short-term missionaries travel to places where they face the issue of poverty head-on. The predominant topic of conversation as short-term missionaries describe their experiences is the issue of poverty. The participants feel sympathetic toward what appear to be substandard living situations and talk about the desire to see something done to give people a better quality of life. The participants frequently talk about how blessed they are to have been born in the United States and cannot imagine what it would have been like to be born as a Mexican or Rwandan. While the poverty, illiteracy, and disease throughout places such as Africa are devastating, Africa is also a place where many people are thriving. Democracy has begun to take hold in many of its nations and Africans are grappling with answers to their own problems. Not all Rwandans, Mexicans, or Sri Lankans are sitting back waiting to be rescued by heroic short-term missionaries (or Hollywood stars for that matter).

The recipients of the missionaries' generosity, while grateful, often describe feeling dehumanized. One Ugandan church leader said it this way, "We did not know we were poor until someone from the outside told us" (Schwartz, 2004, p. 32). The local communities visited by short-term missionaries have abundant wealth of a different kind. In a spirit of mutuality, short-term teams need to learn to give in ways that do not perpetuate the tired power structures of colonialism while also learning to receive from the plenty that exists in the communities they visit.

Ironically, there is no evidence that encountering poverty on a short-term missions trip provides lasting results on participants' philanthropic giving or on how they personally spend money once they return home. On one hand, short-term missionaries might be too quick to view locals in a dehumanizing way by seeing them in light of their poverty and living conditions. On the other hand, due to limited CQ, short-term participants often conclude locals in the developing world are quite happy the way they are. The most frequent statement made by hundreds of short-term missionaries interviewed was "They're so happy!" The assumption was that, despite having little material wealth, the locals are quite content the way they are.

Much more needs to be studied to understand how inexperienced, uneducated (as it relates to development and economics) short-term missionaries can and should interact with local communities. A great deal of the CQ framework will enhance the ability to think through these complex issues. In particular, the novel aspects of motivational CQ, which seeks to understand what it is that drives individuals to behave as they do cross-culturally, will especially enrich the ability to address the economic issues related to short-term missions work.

Category Width

The literature describing the cross-cultural behavior of business professionals, students who study abroad, and military personnel cites themes that are similar to the findings described here. However, an additional theme that is directly related to short-term missionary work is the way the missionary views morality and, specifically, the way he or she views the teachings of Jesus and the Bible.

Christianity, like many other faiths, espouses some universal morals, regardless of cultural variance and preference. There is wide agreement among Christians worldwide that there are some defined categories of right versus wrong. Most Christians agree that it is wrong to abuse wealth and power. And Christianity is opposed to women being dehumanized by men, governments, and religions. It holds that it is not simply the option of a culture to socially construct a moral code that allows for these kinds of oppressive practices. Instead, Christians believe that the moral code taught and characterized by Christ and the Bible supersedes cultural notions of morality.

Figure 17.1 **Category Width**

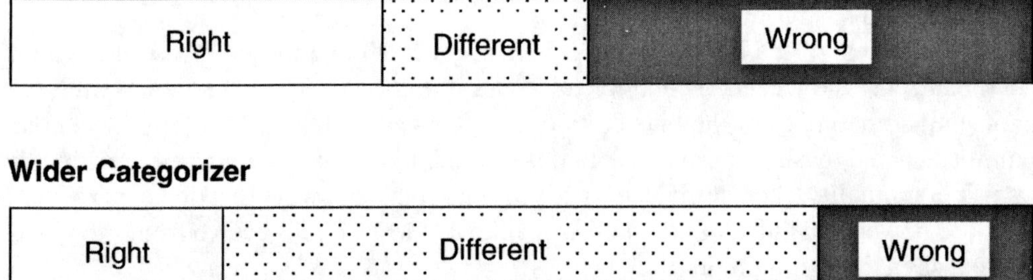

American short-term missionaries often combine their universalist perspectives with bounded-set thinking. The work of Pettigrew (1958) and Detwiler (1978) on "category width" is a helpful way of thinking about this. The subjects studied tended to be narrow categorizers (see Figure 17.1, *top*) and, as a result, they placed most issues into categories of right versus wrong with a very small category for things that are simply different. Short-term training programs should explore how to help participants widen their categories of difference (see Figure 17.1, *bottom*) while still respecting their personal convictions of right versus wrong.

Further, findings from my research on American missionaries (Livermore, 2006) show limited awareness of how significantly culture shapes the way one reads the Bible and therefore views morality. Most subjects missed out on the rich hermeneutical treasure that exists in encountering fellow Christians in other parts of the world, who hold to some similar presuppositions of Jesus' moral teaching but often interpret its application in very different ways. Again, the cultural understanding that is gained through cognitive and metacognitive CQ would likely have tempered some of the dogmatism demonstrated in seeing only one right way to interpret the teachings of the Bible.

In my study that looked at North American ministers who went on short-term missions trips to train ministers in other parts of the world (Livermore, 2006), the American pastors spoke of the importance of teaching only biblical principles. In their minds, as long as they exclusively taught principles rather than describing specific programs in their churches, the teaching would be transcultural. Subjects frequently said things such as, "We teach timeless, transferable principles therefore our biblical teaching applies worldwide, whatever the context." There was limited CQ evident in that the American pastors failed to see the ways the principles they taught were embedded in cultural narratives.

More study is needed that explores how to reconcile a commitment to universal morals alongside an equally ruthless commitment to constructivist notions of knowledge and mutuality. Behavioral CQ examines how being flexible in displaying verbal and nonverbal behaviors can be helpful in exploring this tension. Knowing how to be true to oneself while respecting the Other is essential for everyone engaged in cross-cultural work.

These four themes—ethnocentrism, bounded-set thinking, the money factor, and category width—were the most consistent themes found in examining the cross-cultural behavior and thinking among short-term missionaries. The qualitative design that was utilized allowed for a rich description of what was occurring in these brief missional sojourns. While sample sizes were often limited, cross examination of these findings with a growing number of other qualitative and quantitative studies that explore short-term missions work will further validate the findings. In addition, much of the literature regarding service learning and study-abroad initiatives further supports the findings of this study.

CULTURALLY INTELLIGENT MISSIONS

As described throughout the preceding findings, the CQ framework is uniquely suited to address future research and resulting effectiveness of short-term missions. This final section will more specifically address the relevance of the four factors of CQ to short-term missions study and practice. Many of these implications are also germane to short-term study-abroad programs employed by colleges and universities. I have engaged in research that explicitly tests the relationship between CQ and itinerant mission work.

Cognitive CQ

Cognitive CQ, the measurement of an individual's understanding about cross-cultural issues and differences, is the dimension of CQ emphasized most in short-term missions preparation. Many short-term missions initiatives include some cross-cultural training before the trip. The predeparture training usually emphasizes a brief history about the destination and some culturally specific behaviors of which participants should be mindful.

Upon encountering the culture, however, participants typically disregarded the information they received beforehand. In the face of dissonance, they resorted to values and behaviors that were most comfortable and familiar. Furthermore, some of the locals who received the short-term missionaries expressed concern that pre-trip training gave the missionaries just enough cultural knowledge to make them "dangerous." Local subjects recounted illustrations of missionaries who acted like experts about the local region because they had completed some pre-trip training.

Research related to CQ accounts for the potential danger of predeparture training by demonstrating the limitations of addressing one factor of CQ without the other three factors. The four factors of CQ interact symbiotically. With this in mind, the ideal situation is a short-term missionary who *does* go through predeparture training that combines all four factors of CQ.

Many missions mishaps could be avoided or at least mitigated if short-term missionaries simply learned more about cultural values in general and how those play out in the locales that they visit. Cultural-general understanding will be most helpful given the brevity of these encounters. Instead of trying to master cognitive CQ, participants should be encouraged to use the upcoming trip as an ideal way to enhance their cultural understanding without feeling like they must become experts in the said culture. When combined with training—both formal and informal—short-term missions sojourns have the potential to help participants become constructive global citizens. By tapping into some of the suggestions included in the other three dimensions of CQ, short-term missions experience can be a meaningful way for individuals to reflect more broadly on how culture in general shapes people's perceptions of the world, not the least of which is their own. These trips can also channel the zeal and compassion of well-intentioned missionaries into service that is truly empowering and mutually beneficial.

Metacognitive CQ

The importance of metacognitive CQ was continually seen in the discussion of the four themes, which emerged in the cross-cultural behavior of short-term missionaries. The American missions movement was founded upon zeal and action, so it is not surprising that metacognitive CQ is the factor most absent among the subjects' observed. Reflection and contemplation are not practices that are highly valued among American Christians. More often than not, subjects engaged in conversations and observed situations without demonstrating an understanding that a different cultural script was at work behind the behavior and circumstances. Whether it was an inability to see their ethnocentrism, the surface-level observations, or the simplistic tendencies that were apparent in the ways they talked about economics, short-term missionaries did not demonstrate an ongoing awareness of cultural surroundings and social cues. They remained on autopilot and interpreted events in the same way they would have if they saw those same things in their home cultures.

There is a great deal to be gained by looking for connections between transformative, experiential learning theories and metacognitive CQ. The potential of these connections goes far beyond short-term missions. Some preliminary work has been done exploring the relationship between Kolb's model of experiential learning and CQ (Yamazaki & Kayes 2004). Additional work has been begun that views the connections between Joplin's (1995) five-stage model of experiential learning, which was based largely upon Kolb's work, and CQ. A small group of researchers recently convened exemplars of effective short-term missions practice to conduct focus group research. Joplin's model of transformative learning as adapted by Linhart (2006) and CQ were the theoretical frameworks that guided the data collection (see Figure 17.2).

Stage One: Focus

An important starting point for enhancing the transformative nature of cross-cultural pilgrimages lies in helping participants focus on their upcoming experiences. Prepara-

Figure 17.2 **A Model for Transformational Learning**

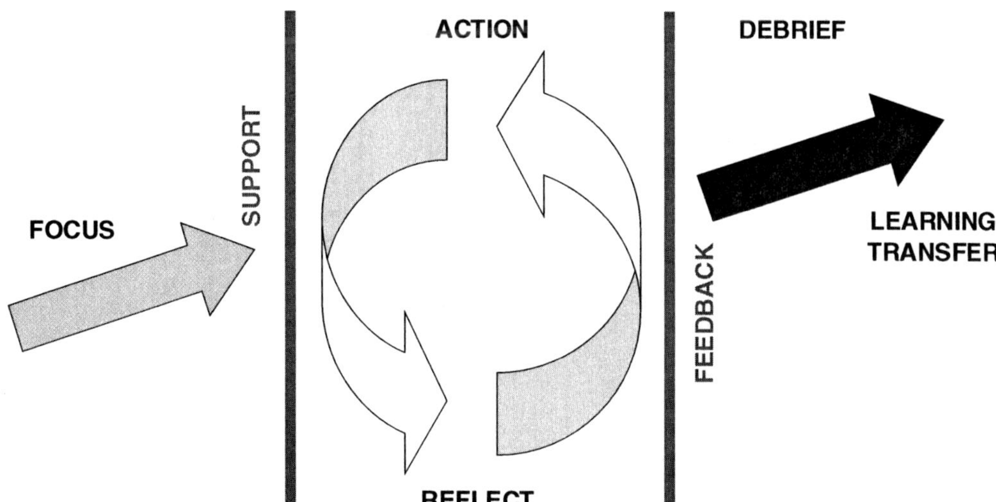

tion and planning are consistent themes in Joplin's model as well as in the metacognitive factor of CQ. The focus stage is designed to help participants anticipate potential areas of awareness.

Stage Two: Action–Reflection

The main component in nurturing metacognitive CQ during the trip is the action–reflection process. In this ongoing cycle, participants are placed in a situation in which they are purposefully stretched. The action is an opportunity to engage with familiar skills in an unfamiliar environment.

Consciously or not, participants are constantly making meaning out of their actions. They are continually engaged in a highly personal, ongoing "conversation" in their own minds about who they are in relation to what they are encountering. Since this is generally internal, participants may draw conclusions from their experiences that do not reflect reality. Facilitators are needed who can stand alongside participants in the midst of the provocative encounters that occur in these cross-cultural situations. Facilitators need to ask questions that help participants decipher the meaning behind what they experience.

Stage Three: Support and Feedback

To facilitate the action–reflection cycle, Joplin recommends surrounding the discussions and experiences with walls of support and feedback. The support usually comes from others who shared the experience, such as other participants, trip leaders, and locals from within the communities being visited. However, support can also include the encouragement that comes from helpful relational networks at home. Research shows a strong correlation between an individual's success in a cross-cultural experience and the emotional and tangible support they have from friends and family.

As the action–reflection cycle continues throughout the learning process, facilitators must intervene with participants and help them talk about the meanings participants are creating from their experiences. Many groups share daily in small "debriefing" sessions, but the size of the group and the limited time often limit feedback to simply reviewing the activities of the day rather than effectively directing reflection that stimulates transformation. Because cross-cultural encounters often bring about so many new experiences in a short, rapid amount of time, participants often feel pressured to label or make sense of each moment too quickly. In doing so, they resort to the kinds of things described in the themes section of this chapter.

Stage Four: Debrief

When the action component is completed, participants begin the process of leaving, and enter into a stage described as the "debrief." Different from the reflection process, the debrief stage is the organized process of identifying learning that has occurred, discussing it with others, and evaluating it. This debrief process can be undertaken individually but is most effectively done with others. The most helpful debriefs often include a rereading of journals where reflections have been recorded.

Stage Five: Learning Transfer

The final stage is the learning transfer. Most short-term missions participants invest little time in transferring the learning from their cross-cultural sojourn. Two realities fight against effective learning transfer. First, most of the significant learning on a short-term trip takes place in an environment very different from the home communities of participants. Second, the participants themselves do not know how to transfer the learning to their own lives. Short-term missions experiences need to be woven into the year-round life of the parish and individual. This correlates positively with the literature that refers to CQ as a malleable, ongoing growth process.

Much more needs to be examined about the connections between metacognitive CQ and short-term missions work. In helping short-term missionaries to carefully view what is going on below the surface within themselves and the Other, participants can reach across the chasm of cultural difference in ways that reflect mutuality and dignity.

Motivational CQ

Cognitive and metacognitive CQ cannot be sustained without continual motivation to be culturally adaptive. Short-term missionaries typically manifest little desire to slog through the complex cultural differences that exist in the communities they visit. The brief duration of the trips makes it difficult to engage in a highly motivated adaptation to the local context. Though the issues related to perseverance and culture shock are different for expatriates on long-term assignments, there are certain motivational dynamics at play for those who engage in brief cross-cultural sojourns. The tasks performed by short-term missionaries include teaching, constructing buildings, and running medical clinics. Participants appear to be highly motivated to perform those tasks well. However, the motivation to acculturate beyond the immediate task is generally abysmal. Participants rarely see the need to immerse themselves in eating local foods or learning about local customs. In their minds, "We're headed home in another week so it's better to stay healthy by eating familiar foods, getting a good night of rest, and keeping focused on our real task here."

Participants often reported profound, affect-laden experiences of confusion and resistance to some local cultural rituals, while others described a strong sense of connection and were deeply moved by their experiences. Even during these brief encounters, some profound affective experiences occurred, which clearly overshadowed the more cognitive outcomes. Much further exploration is required to understand the emotional and affective dimensions of these kinds of short-term experiences. CQ combined with literature from the field of psychodynamic cultural psychology could yield access to hidden aspects of how these experiences affect the construction of oneself. In addition, more correlation should be made between the literature on culture shock and the affective, motivational dynamics that result from short-term missionaries' experiences with cultural differences.

Behavioral CQ

Most of the findings reported in this chapter reflect the behavioral CQ of short-term missionaries. One of the most helpful ways to see the need for CQ in this group is through a description of the behavior represented by the existing studies. Coordinators of these trips need to be cautioned, however, against placing primary energy toward intervening in the behavior aspect itself. Clearly there are some appropriate behaviors that need to be learned to avoid offending the locals encountered. However, far more effective in altering one's behavior in these kinds of trips is to give attention to the other three dimensions of CQ.

Behavioral CQ is not unimportant however. Ultimately, short-term missionaries will be judged by locals based on their behavior. Given the brevity of the encounters, participants will be best served by strategies that help them develop a repertoire of behaviors from which to draw whenever they encounter someone from another culture. This is a distinctive advantage of the CQ framework over many other cross-cultural competency theories, many of which lean toward behavior modification rather than truly nurturing transformation.

As the world becomes increasingly multicultural, culturally intelligent behavior is an essential skill. This is true in the short-term missionary's hometown and workplace as much as it is on a two-week sojourn abroad. Studies and training need to be developed to help missionaries discern when it is appropriate to adapt to the behaviors of locals and when it is inappropriate to do so. Increasingly, short-term missionaries need to become multicultural individuals, not simply people who learn to "navigate cultural differences." As compared to theories of cross-cultural competency that depend upon cognitive information to transform behavior, CQ is uniquely suited to serve American Christians. CQ is a more authentic, transformative approach to interacting with human beings from various cultures in mutually enriching ways.

Finally, while most of the findings reported have emphasized the cross-cultural behavior and thinking of American short-term missionaries, much needs to be done to view the cross-cultural behavior and thinking of the locals who receive these missionaries. CQ is needed on both sides of the cultural chasm. However, as the guests in local communities, the onus is on the short-term missionaries to take the initiative to grow in CQ.

CONCLUSION

Just as transcontinental travel among business professionals is no longer exclusive to senior-level executives, transcontinental mission work no longer reserved for those traditionally referred to as "missionaries." Lay people, old and young, are traversing the planet on spiritual pilgrimages where sacred goals are pursued, normal structures are dissolved, and personal transformation is assumed. This transformation ideally produces new selves to be reintegrated into everyday life at home as well as serving and helping others in distant places. "That is, they aim not only for self-transformation, but for change in the places to which they go" (Priest, et al., 2006).

More research is needed to examine short-term missions in light of CQ. For example, there is a need to develop interventions and assessment tools based on CQ that can be used to make short-term missions trips more mutually beneficial to participants and to the local communities that they visit. The research design and methodology must be informed by CQ, particularly as data are collected from locals in receiving communities. For example, many of the potential informants operate from cultural perspectives where "saving face" is highly valued. Consequently, creative, thoughtful methodology must be employed to gather accurate data.

The increased presence of cross-cultural service and mission as a result of globalization holds great potential for responding to the injustices of our day and for acceptance of the Other. Rather than simply objectifying the peoples of the world as a potential market for goods, services, or religion, short-term missions undertaken with CQ can be a vehicle for greater good in the world. CQ provides a way to help direct the growing phenomenon of short-term missions toward truly exercising kindness as the highest form of wisdom.

REFERENCES

Detwiler, R. (1978). Culture, category width, and attributions. *Journal of Cross-Cultural Psychology, 9,* 259–284.

Dolby, N. (2005). Encountering an American self: Study abroad and national identity. *Comparative Education Review, 48,* 150–174.

Hiebert, P. (1994). *Anthropological reflections on missiological issues.* Grand Rapids, MI: Baker Books.

Joplin, L. (1995). On defining experiential education. In K. Warren, M. Sakofs, & J.S. Hunt Jr. (Eds.), *The theory of experiential education* (pp. 15–22). Dubuque, IA: Kendall/Hunt.

Linhart, T. (2006). Planting seeds: The curricular hope of short-term mission experiences in youth ministry. *Christian Education Journal, 3,* 256–272.

Livermore, D. (2006). *Serving with eyes wide open: Doing short-term missions with cultural intelligence.* Grand Rapids, MI: Baker Books.

Pettigrew, T.F. (1958). The measurement and correlates of category width as a cognitive variable. *Journal of Personality, 26,* 532–44.

Priest, R.J., Dischinger, T., Rasmussen, S., & Brown, C.M. (2006). Researching the short-term mission movement. *Missiology, 34,* 431–450.

Schwartz, G. (2004). Two awesome problems: How short-term missions can go wrong. *International Journal of Frontier Missions, 20,* 4, 28–33.

Smith, C. (2005). *Soul searching: The religious and spiritual lives of American teenagers.* New York: Oxford University Press.

Yamazaki, Y. & Kayes, D.C. (2004). An experiential approach to cross-cultural learning: A review and integration of competences for successful expatriate adaptation. *Academy of Management Learning & Education, 3,* 362–379.

PART V

CQ AND RELATED CONSTRUCTS

CHAPTER 18

Social Intelligence, Emotional Intelligence, and Cultural Intelligence

An Integrative Perspective

DETELIN S. ELENKOV AND JOANA R.C. PIMENTEL

Intelligence represents one of the most elusive constructs in the psychology field. From the psychometric "g" (Spearman, 1927) to the multifaceted perspective of intelligence offered by Gardner (1999), the existing literature reports numerous attempts at defining and measuring the construct. A plausible reason for the absence of a unitary definition of intelligence lies in the intricacies of the relationship between individuals and their surrounding environment. In this sense, explaining the connection between individuals in their complex functioning and the equally complex external environment demands an all-encompassing framework integrating the versatile response mechanisms that individuals activate in the presence of different stimuli.

This chapter offers an integrative perspective on intra- and interpersonal intelligences—social, emotional, and cultural—and considers the relationship between these three constructs and the psychometric *g*, or general intelligence factor. The practical implications of considering alternative intelligences in the work setting are also examined.

Howard Gardner is widely recognized as an expert in the multiple intelligence field of research. While acknowledging their interdependence, Gardner (2006) defined multiple intelligences as "computational capacities" that enable area-specific information processing and problem solving. This definition reveals an underlying acceptance that some individuals are better able to take advantage of a broader array of intelligences, or to capitalize on a specific group of intelligences, than others. Decades of research on the subject of intelligence culminated with the categorization of seven intelligences: linguistic, musical, spatial, logical-mathematical, bodily kinesthetic, intrapersonal (possessing an effective working model of oneself, the capacity to understand personal feelings), and interpersonal (capacity to accurately read the feelings and motivations of others) (Gardner, 1999). The theory defends that each individual possesses all of these intelligences to some degree.

The optimism surrounding the concept of *g* may have been the principal source of skepticism within the academic field concerning Gardner's theory of multiple intelligences. Nonetheless, the theory's applicability to practical settings, in particular the school system, popularized Gardner's view of intelligence(s) and stimulated the interest of researchers and practitioners. As a result, research on multiple intelligences was extended to contemplate individual and group-level variables such as gender and national origin (Furnham & Mottabu, 2004). This research clarified the role of individual differences on levels of intelligence and provided insight regarding differential valuation of types of intelligence across cultures. Reflecting on the possibility that there are different types of intelligence and that valuations of intelligence are specific to context, Gardner (2006) criticized *g* on its two major limitations. First, *g* is merely a function of the measures used and their conditions of application, and is therefore expected to vary across measurement instruments and populations. Second, *g* is a measure of scholastic aptitude inspired by Western learning systems that emphasize linguistic and logical mathematical abilities, so its values are typically higher among individuals accustomed to materials and methods found in academic settings. One of Gardner's most compelling arguments denouncing *g* involved the measures and methods used and their basis in spatial intelligence measures. According to Gardner (2006), spatial aptitude measured with vision-based tests may actually be tapping into visual acuity to a large extent, since blind individuals display considerable spatial intelligence but are unable to successfully complete the measures.

The concept of *g* had also been criticized by Thorndike in his earlier research on human intelligence (Thorndike, 1921, 1924). One of his main criticisms regarding the definition and measurement of intelligence concerned the fact that there was not a unitary concept of intelligence that could be measured using a single instrument and method. Thorndike's (1924) argument stated that while the existing intelligence measures assumed an absolute zero point of the construct, intelligence scores varied within individuals as a function of the type of intelligence measured (e.g., spatial, verbal) and of the type of measurement tool applied (e.g., speed-based, memory-based). Hence, changes in the zero point of intelligence within and across individuals as a function of measurement tools and intelligence types logically implied that the construct of intelligence was ill-defined. Moreover, different instruments to measure intelligence might assess different forms of intelligence beyond the theorized general factor.

Recent contributions to the study of intelligence (Gardner, 1999; Goleman, 2006) have demonstrated that there are facets of intelligence beyond *g* that explain individual differences in ways of functioning, and suggested that other disciplines, such as neuroscience, and different areas of the social sciences should be integrated to illuminate research in the field. It is based on these contributions that we provide an overview of three of the alternative facets of intelligence—social, emotional, and cultural. The following sections will highlight the extent to which these intelligences are related to but still distinguishable from *g*. In addition, we propose an overview of the existing literature that focuses on dimensionality, measurement issues, and practical implications.

SOCIAL INTELLIGENCE

Construct Definition, Dimensionality, and Measurement

For almost nine decades, researchers have struggled with the convoluted construct definition and dimensionality of social intelligence (SI). The notion of SI was initially of particular interest to researchers who attempted to determine how individuals made judgments regarding themselves and others. Those researchers tended to conceptualize and measure that intelligence type in accordance with particular subjects of interest. As a result, SI has been approached from different standpoints (e.g., cognitive focus vs. communication and interactive processes), and has been investigated using various methodologies (e.g., psychometric, social psychological). That resulted in a loss of focus in SI research and contributed to the liberal adoption of concepts and measurement instruments from alternative research fields.

Originally, SI was seen as the cognitive ability to understand others and to get along with those others, but that definition evolved to a more encompassing notion involving an adaptive behavioral component, whereby the individual was able to act in accordance with the specificity of a situation. Walker and Foley (1973) suggested that there are three recurring conceptual approaches to defining the construct. The first approach considers SI as the ability to accurately decode social information; a second approach views SI as the effectiveness and adaptability to improve social performance; and the third framework regards SI as the performance on any test that contains a component that represents social skills.

A number of frameworks have been offered in an attempt to capture the dimensionality of SI in view of these individual and contextual determinants. For example, Scott's (1974) research on social cognitive functioning provided a checklist of certain aspects that an individual should be aware of in order to successfully engage in interactions with others. These included recognition of the existence of different perceptions and feelings regarding a situation, and the recognition of the importance of analyzing others' perspectives to enrich one's own knowledge of the situation. The most commonly adopted definition and dimension categorization of SI was offered by Marlowe (1986), who described SI as the ability to understand the feelings, thoughts, and behaviors of self and others in interpersonal situations and to act appropriately upon that understanding. Marlowe decomposed the construct of SI into five distinct areas: (1) motivation, which emphasized an individual's capacity for developing goals and initiating goal-directed activities, (2) self-efficacy in a social context, associated with an expectation of personal mastery and success, (3) social skills were conceptualized as the ability act in ways that led to positive reinforcements and eliminated negative reinforcements, (4) performance, which defined a socially competent individual as capable of achieving personal objectives, and (5) traits related to SI were conceptually organized in patterns of cognitive, affective, and behavioral nature. Consequently, a number of researchers agreed that SI should be investigated as a multidimensional construct, comprised of cognitive, emotional, and behavioral components. A later categorization by Kosmitzki and John (1993) organized components of SI into three broad dimensions: cognitive (perspective taking, understanding people, knowing social rules, and openness to others), behavioral (good at dealing with people, social adaptability, and interpersonal warmth), and a separate motivational dimension (manipulating, leading, and motivating others).

The main obstacles to the existence of good SI measures have stemmed from the complexity of the construct's definition, the resulting extension of the core construct into alternative definitions of interpersonal intelligence requiring different measurement tools, and the lack of a systematic method that would enable the development and validation of a broadly accepted instrument. In practice, numerous studies claiming to use SI as one of the variables of interest provide different definitions for the construct, offer dissimilar explanations for the interpersonal phenomena, and utilize different measurement tools, most of which were developed for use in each particular study.

Several authors noted that SI might overlap with cognitive abilities (e.g., verbal ability) because the measurement techniques are confounded (Frederiksen, Carlson, & Ward, 1984; Riggio, Messamer, & Throckmorton, 1991). Empirical evidence suggests that the contradictory results found in SI research may be attributed not only to the use of different measurement tools and techniques to determine the same construct, but also to the fact that similar methods are utilized in the assessment of SI and of alternative constructs (Marlowe, 1986). The absence of a sound definition of what the construct should entail leads to an uncoordinated choice of methods adopted to determine its dimensions and related variables. In practice, the manner in which researchers conceptualize the SI construct leads to the adoption of different methods in different studies, which in turn determines the dimensions of SI that are identified as well as the results that are found. For example, Lowman and Leeman (1985) used four distinct instruments in an attempt to establish the dimensionality of SI: (1) an interpersonal problem-solving assessment, (2) a self-directed search survey, (3) the fundamental interpersonal relations orientation behavior survey, and (4) a leaderless group discussion. Since the choice of measures was based on the premise that SI is comprised of basic social and interpersonal skills, social abilities, and personality variables, the measurement instruments merely confirmed the dimensions suggested. It is expected that other multimethod approaches would have elicited different dimensions and results.

SI and Job Performance

Although the definition and dimensionality of SI have been widely discussed in the extant literature, there has been little investigation of its criteria in the workplace. Still, it is possible to identify several criteria variables from the existing studies on construct definition, validation, and dimensionality. Leadership effectiveness and motivating capacity attracted the most attention as likely outcomes of SI. Based on the common dimensions of SI, several authors agree that when the ability to understand others, to use techniques to manipulate others, and to motivate others toward a personal or institutional goal are inherent in socially intelligent individuals, they can potentially enhance leadership skills (Kosmitzki & John, 1993; Marlowe, 1986; Zaccaro, Gilbert, Thor & Mumford, 1991).

Other likely SI criteria in organizational settings are the capacity for analysis and problem solving, and effective communication skills (Zaccaro et al., 1991).

In an attempt to provide an encompassing approach of the social attributes related to leadership, Zaccaro et al., (1991) postulated a series of characteristics associated with SI of leaders. The authors argued that leaders with a high level of SI demonstrated complex knowledge structures regarding people and situations, rapid understanding of critical aspects of situations, understanding of implications of a situation at various levels, access to a vast range of adequate responses, and appropriateness of the provided responses. However, these characteristics were integrated in a complex network with diverse implications and multiple levels of analysis. Researchers have also examined the extent to which socially intelligent individuals have more career success, as suggested by Mayer and Salovey (1995). Although the concept of career success linked to interpersonal intelligence was borrowed from research on emotional intelligence (EQ), it is plausible that socially intelligent individuals have the capacity for insight regarding their career goals and direction. More research is needed to examine criterion variables that will further contribute to advances in SI research.

SI and *g*

Although the discussion surrounding the distinction between SI and *g* parallels early SI studies, the specific characteristics of SI differentiating it from *g* have only recently been substantiated by research. Multitrait, multimethod studies investigating the dimensionality and validity of SI, as well as its distinction from *g* (Lee, Wong, Day, Maxwell, & Thorpe, 2000; Weis & Sub, 2007; Wong, Day, Maxwell, & Meara, 1995) are unanimous in their conclusion that there is in fact a higher order SI factor that differs from *g*. Furthermore, SI appears to be a multidimensional construct consisting of social perception, or the extent to which individuals make sense of others in the course of social interactions; social knowledge, or the general understanding of the social norms and expectations that guide interactions; and social behavior, which involves the capacity to adequately respond to social demands based on accurate perceptions of others and on social knowledge (Wong et al., 1995). These three dimensions reflect awareness of others' emotions, needs, and motives, the ability to learn and integrate basic and complex social rules, and the motivation to act in accordance with these perceptions and knowledge.

Even though the majority of research on *g* and SI has focused on the attempt to demonstrate that the two constructs represent distinct domains, recent studies have taken this assumption further and investigated the dynamics within SI dimensions. Results reported in Lee et al.'s (2000) study on the dimensions of fluid intelligence (based on social inference) and crystallized intelligence (based on social knowledge) clarify the relationship between academic and social intelligences. First, academic and social intelligences represent different domains. Second, the findings regarding fluid and crystallized dimensions of intelligence seem to imply interdependence between SI and academic intelligence. Crystallized academic intelligence is closely related to the social knowledge dimension of SI, suggesting that academic intelligence might be a necessary albeit not sufficient prerequisite of SI. Reinforcing this premise, results also show that the exercise of social inference requires both crystallized and fluid intelligences.

At present, there is general consensus among researchers investigating SI that socially intelligent behaviors can be observed at different levels in different people, and that the construct is unique in relation to academic intelligence. The latter statement has found considerable support in the neuroscience field, with study findings identifying different areas of the brain that are responsible for different components of intelligence. Although a connectionist perspective explaining the existing relationship between social and academic intelligences is still accepted, it is becoming increasingly evident that logical reasoning and language typically associated with *g* occur in the cortical structures, whereas the limbic neural system is responsible for emotional responsiveness and other relational SI components (Mutsuo, 2004). Recent research findings also confirm Gardner's argument that *g* is to a large extent contingent upon measures and methods, and that its capacity to subsume other intelligences is due to the fact that the measures used to assess these alternative intelligences are linguistic and logical in nature (Legree, 1995). The high correlations between *g* and SI found in past studies are now attributed to the use of methods adapted from academic settings to measure SI (Lee et al., 2000).

Considering that the SI dimension "social knowledge" is founded on the individual's capacity for knowledge acquisition, thus based on cognitive ability, *g* measures and methods to assess SI are merely identifying one facet of the construct. Future research would benefit from a better understanding of the relationship between social and academic intelligences, in particular that of causality. It is quite plausible that the full expression of SI (i.e., perceptual, knowledge-based, motivational, and behavioral) can only be achieved if a certain level of cognitive ability is present. Moreover, it is conceivable that *g* affects different dimensions of SI to different degrees (e.g., has a greater impact on the knowledge dimension).

EMOTIONAL INTELLIGENCE

Construct Definition, Dimensionality, and Measurement

The term *emotional intelligence* was introduced in an unpublished paper by Payne (1986; cited by Ashkansy & Daus, 2005) and defined as an ability to perceive, understand, and manage emotion in oneself and others. This construct appears to have the same bases as SI, with the addition of a self-regulation component that fits into specific developmental periods of one's life cycle. Until the mid-1990s, the topic of EQ had attracted attention only from researchers in the clinical and educational fields. The recent interest from organizational practitioners arose from findings by a group of researchers that suggested that EQ might be a developable and measurable quality of significant relevance to the effective functioning of organizational systems (Dulewicz & Higgs, 2000).

Despite its popularity among researchers and practitioners, recent empirical research on EQ has raised a number of concerns regarding the construct's definition, dimensionality, and measurement (Brackett, Rivers, Shiffman, Lerner, & Salovey, 2006; Livingstone & Day, 2005;

Roberts, Schulze, O'Brien, MacCann, Reid, & Maul, 2006; Tett & Fox, 2006). Similar to SI, construct definition and measurement appear to represent the Achilles' heel of EQ research.

With respect to construct definition, the existing literature offers several alternatives, according to the specific framework from which the concept of EQ is derived. Mayer and Salovey (1997) described EQ as the ability to perceive emotions and to use them to improve performance on cognitive tasks, to make sense of emotions, and to effectively regulate these emotions. Mayer and Salovey's definition illustrates an ability model of EQ, while their earlier work (Salovey & Mayer, 1990) and the framework proposed by Bar-On and Parker (2000) describe a mixed or trait approach. Martinez-Pons's (1997) definition of EQ also entails the exercise of noncognitive skills advanced in the trait approach. According to Martinez-Pons (1997), a higher or lower development of these skills explains individual differences in the ability to cope with environmental demands and pressures. As expected, the methods and measures that have been developed based on the distinct ability and trait conceptual models exhibit different relationships with individual and organizational variables of interest (Brackett et al., 2006; Livingstone & Day, 2005) and therefore fail to contribute to the clarification and validation of the EQ construct. For example, Mayer and Salovey's original trait-based model of EQ included three main dimensions and a total of 10 components (Tett & Fox, 2006).

These dimensions included the appraisal and expression of emotions (including verbal and nonverbal emotions in the self, nonverbal emotions in others, and empathy), regulation of emotion (including the components of regulation of emotion in self and in others), and utilization of emotions (including flexible planning, creative thinking, mood redirected attention, and motivating emotions). Tett and Fox's (2006) recent evaluation of the model's factor structure provided a reconceptualization of the original framework, suggesting three main dimensions of EQ: self orientation, other orientation, and emotional sharing. Bar-On and Parker (2000) proposed an alternative approach to EQ, the EQi, comprised of five factors: intrapersonal functioning, interpersonal skills, adaptability, general mood, and stress management. This approach included both trait and ability dimensions, providing a more comprehensive framework. Finally, the Mayer Salovey Caruso Emotional Intelligence Test (MSCEIT) provided an ability-based measure of EQ that was comprised of four factors: emotional management, emotional understanding, emotional facilitation, and emotional perception (Livingstone & Day, 2005).

Several researchers conducted empirical research on the most popular EQ tests—the MSCEIT and the EQi—in an attempt to examine their validity (Brackett et al., 2006; Livingstone & Day, 2005; Roberts et al., 2006). Findings of these studies suggest that each test measures a distinct construct or facet of EQ. This is attributed not only to the specific dimensions present in each framework, with differential emphasis on traits, abilities, or personality characteristics, but also to the methodology adopted and to the properties of the used measure (e.g., type of stimuli, scoring system) (Roberts et al., 2006). Moreover, most studies conducted in the field of EQ have relied on the analysis of facial expressions, the Myers-Briggs test, and other self-report measures to draw conclusions regarding the extent to which individuals are more or less emotionally intelligent. These methods have proven to be fairly unreliable and invalid.

EQ and Job Performance

Bar-On and Parker (2000), Goleman (1995), Mayer and Salovey (1995), and Sosik and Megerian (1999) have contended that EQ is fundamental to career success, leadership effectiveness, and organizational performance. In a study using multisource feedback data in an organizational setting, Shipper, Kincaid, Rotondo, and Hoffman (2003) found that a managers' self-awareness of strengths and weaknesses was conducive to an effective optimization of their employees' competencies, had a positive impact on relationships through open communication, and elicited an increase in motivation to perform well. These results suggest that the study of EQ should be conducted at multiple levels that consider the individual, the group, and the intraorganizational and environmental outcomes.

Despite the encouraging findings, EQ has been challenged as a sound construct with significant impact on organizational variables. Landy (2005) criticized the refusal by some researchers to make their data and methods public, which impedes any independent validation attempts and further delays the construct's development. He has also asserted that the construct emerged out of theoretical misunderstanding and was fed by sensationalist researchers. Another issue that has been brought forth concerns the direction of causality. Specifically, it is unclear whether EQ is responsible for organizational success or vice versa. On the same note, Locke (2005) argued that EQ should not be taken as a prerequisite for effective leadership since leadership mainly involves situational knowledge and rational thinking regarding interpersonal, organizational, and environmental events. In practice, motivation to engage others in action and behavioral manifestations that adequately integrate needs of subordinates and organizational goals are essential components of leadership. EQ in isolation is insufficient to ensure effective leadership behaviors. Alternative interpersonal intelligence constructs that rely on continuous environmental learning and adequate responsiveness to the environment might constitute more cogent prerequisites to managerial effectiveness, especially in novel or changing settings and situations.

CULTURAL INTELLIGENCE

Construct Definition, Dimensionality, and Measurement

Cultural intelligence (CQ) can be defined as a capability that allows for an accurate interpretation of unfamiliar verbal and nonverbal cues in different cultural situations. According to Earley and Ang (2003), a culturally intelligent individual will (a) exhibit impression awareness, that is, knowledge that provides a basis for people to know how others form impressions and an ability to predict them, (b) possess knowledge of cultural differences, that is, anticipate cause-effect social relationships and social rules across cultures, and (c) have the ability to successfully translate intentions to perform and produce a particular behavior. Knowing how others form impressions is largely contingent upon acknowledging that individuals in different cultures have different experiences of the self and of others. For example, individuals immersed in Eastern cultures typically define the "self" as a function of the relationships established with others, whereas individuals from Western cultures tend to value independence, self-reliance, and focus on individual growth (Markus & Kitayama, 1991).

A recent study by Chua, Leu, and Nisbett (2005) further confirms these different experiences of the self and others. When asked to interpret a given set of social events about others, U.S. respondents perceived actions as a result of social intentions and focused on the main personality characteristics. Conversely, Chinese respondents focused on peripheral characteristics and attributed social events to emotions and changes to the context. The conclusion was twofold. First, one's situational perception cannot be dissociated from the cultural context, since the valued behaviors and perception mechanisms inherent in each culture are dissimilar (Sternberg & Grigorenko, 2006). Second, CQ requires awareness of cultural patterns that bound one's situational perception, and expectation or knowledge that others' perceptions will be equally contingent upon their cultural background.

Three perspectives on CQ measurement are dominant within the CQ research. According to Earley and Ang (2003), CQ consists of three key structural components: cognitive, motivational, and behavioral. Another perspective on the analysis of CQ, advanced by Thomas and Inkson (2004), involves three major interlocking components of cultural knowledge, mindfulness, and behavioral skills. Finally, Ang, Van Dyne, Koh, Ng, Templer, Tay and Chandrasekar (2007) proposed a four-factor model of CQ based on Earley and Ang's (2003) conceptualization, comprised of cognitive, metacognitive, motivational, and behavioral dimensions. According to Ang et al.'s framework, individuals with high cognitive CQ have a working knowledge of themselves and of the social environment. These individuals expect cultural differences to emerge in the course of social interactions and are able to communicate in multicultural settings keeping these differences in mind. Individuals with high metacognitive CQ understand processes and conduct business transactions more effectively because they track their progression, identify potential cultural misunderstandings, and modify their behavior according to the cultural setting.

Another necessary condition for the development of CQ is the desire to gain understanding and knowledge of how to effectively communicate with individuals from diverse cultural backgrounds and adapt behaviors accordingly, defined as motivational CQ. Motivational CQ triggers attention and effort, and channels individuals' cultural knowledge and strategies into effective behavior (Templer, Tay, & Chandrasekar, 2006). Finally, behavioral CQ involves choosing the appropriate behavior based on knowledge of a series of acceptable behaviors for varying cultural situations. Overall, culturally intelligent individuals possess the ability and motivation to broaden their wealth of behavioral responses, and to appropriately select among those responses given the situation. In this sense, the dimensions of CQ are interwoven.

A recent study (Ang, Van Dyne, & Koh, 2006), which examined relationships between Ang et al.'s (2006) CQ framework and the Big Five personality factors, found that specific personality factors are differentially related to particular CQ dimensions. While it is unclear whether similar results would be found for the alternative CQ frameworks, future research should advance a nomological framework for the study of CQ, considering antecedents, moderators, and criterion variables.

CQ and Job Performance

Few studies have investigated the practical applications and implications of CQ for managers in organizations. Most of the empirical research has focused on job performance of expatriate managers and cultural adjustment as criteria for CQ (Chen, 1992; Goldstein & Smith, 1999). Still, the existing research on the application of CQ to organizational settings provides valuable insight. In a recent study, Templer et al. (2006) examined the influence of motivational CQ on cross-cultural adjustment, controlling for realistic job previews and realistic living conditions preview. Results indicate that motivational CQ is positively related to work adjustment beyond realistic job previews and realistic living conditions preview. An important advancement provided by this study was the demonstration of the generalizability, validity, and applicability of CQ to organizational settings. In addition, the increase of overseas assignments and information-sharing across cultures promoted by a global economy demands new and enhanced selection tools that can predict adjustment to new cultural settings and work modes. In practice, a growing demand for cross-cultural savvy and capacity for behavioral adjustment are expected in multinational organizations, as research shows that different cultures value different managerial behaviors (Shipper et al., 2003).

CQ research may also challenge the present cross-cultural research paradigm. The extant literature offers numerous frameworks of cultural dimensions for each country or cluster of countries (Hofstede, Neuijen, Ohayv, & Sanders, 1990; Hofstede & McRae, 2004; Smith, Dugan, & Trompenaars, 1996). These frameworks provide limited information that reflects trends at the country level and is not explicative of individual differences. In addition, such categorizations tend to reinforce cultural stereotypes that may be detrimental to the quality of cross-cultural interactions. Hence, there are several benefits in investigating CQ at the individual level of analysis, and of having a measurement system in place to examine it.

First, a notion of CQ relies on the basic premise that within a culture with specific characteristics (e.g., individualistic) it is possible to find individuals of different cultural orientations (e.g., collectivistic). This reduces the detrimental effects of overgeneralization and stereotypical beliefs. Second, although some individuals may have their beliefs and typical behaviors rooted on a particular cultural frame, it is possible that these individuals are able to understand and respond to unfamiliar behavioral manifestations in an effective manner. It would be unrealistic to assume that cultural background does not bound culturally intelligent individuals to some extent, but it is equally improbable that the cultural frames in which people are inevitably immersed hinder their capacity to effectively respond to individuals of different backgrounds.

INTEGRATING SI, EQ, AND CQ

SI and EQ

In addition to the definition, dimensionality, and measurement issues that permeate EQ research, the greatest argument in opposition to the use of EQ measures in work settings is the fact that SI is believed to subsume EQ (Brackett et al., 2006; Kobe, Reiter, & Rickers, 2001; Mayer & Salovey, 1993; Roberts et al., 2006). SI accounts for variance in leadership above and beyond EQ (Kobe et al., 2001). Brackett et al. (2006) further posited that the generalizability of empirical research on EQ might be compromised given its insulation from social and cultural factors. In particular, some of the differences in EQ test results are likely the outcome of societal norms. These patterns are noticeable both across individuals of different cultural background and within natural and societal groups.

Recent EQ frameworks have broadened the scope of the construct to include interaction-based skills. Kunnanat's (2004) view of EQ expands on the classical individual-centered notion of understanding the self and others, and offers a description of EQ as the regulation system where social attraction and repulsion determine the instrumental value of current interactions and the quality of subsequent exchanges. According to this framework, EQ competencies entail personal competence, similar to dimensions found in classical EQ theories, and social competence, where the connection between EQ and SI becomes more evident. Personal competence includes self-awareness and self-regulation, whereas social competence involves social awareness, and a dimension of social influence, defined as the capacity to influence and effect positive changes in others. The latter dimension of social competence suggests the positive and proactive venue of interpersonal intelligence, beyond reactive awareness, regulation, and understanding of self and others in specific contexts.

The social psychology perspective on SI in relation to self-esteem emerges as a parallel theory that relates self- and other-awareness, borrowed from EQ, to SI. According to this view, self-representation mediates the organization of other-perceptions, of the assimilation of social experiences, and of behavioral responses (Oubrayrie, Safont, & Tap, 1991). Furthermore, self-esteem becomes increasingly positive and self-awareness increasingly coherent when individuals feel accepted by others. Considering that positive responses from others are simultaneously a reflection and a cause of social savvy, we might infer that individual input on broader social change requires a baseline level of EQ, but it ultimately calls for socially intelligent behaviors that positively change the social environment. These changes perceived as positive by others will enhance self- and other-awareness, which in turn will simultaneously develop EQ and SI.

SI and CQ

The CQ construct has been far less challenged than SI has been in current literature. Yet, there are a few theoretical and methodological questions that deserve a more cautious analysis, namely the level of analysis in which CQ should be examined and the construct's dimensionality. With respect to the level of analysis, there is still some skepticism surrounding the value of measuring CQ from an individual standpoint instead of considering it a group phenomenon. In a recent theoretical paper, Hampden-Turner and Trompenaars (2006) advance three hypotheses that are considered to be fundamental in framing the concept of CQ. The gist of their propositions is that every culture possesses the capacity to manifest both ends of a value dimension (e.g., individualism/collectivism) and that culturally intelligent cultures are able to accept and effectively make use of their latent or less dominant values.

Although theoretically sound, the concept of CQ as a societal phenomenon has very little utility for practical purposes for two reasons. First, CQ at this level of analysis cannot be easily manipulated or enhanced, and any verifiable changes will likely be a product of sociopolitical transformations that occur over time. Second, the acceptance of a culture's latent values does not necessarily mean that the same society is able to make the most effective and positive use of the characteristics inherent in its dominant value dimensions. However, CQ examined at the individual level of analysis is trainable, more easily measured, and its outcomes are readily verifiable. Unlike CQ at a societal level of analysis, CQ examined from an individual standpoint allows for understanding and acceptance of unfamiliar cultural manifestations (i.e., the acceptance of one's latent value dimension), and for an integration of this expression of CQ with the capacity to effectively operate within one's cultural frame, or SI. Culturally intelligent individuals refrain from making judgments and evaluations regarding others until information beyond ethnic characteristics are made available (Triandis, 2006).

Although other constructs such as EQ and SI also refer to a capacity for reading interpersonal actions and acting in an appropriate manner, emotionally and socially intelligent individuals are not necessarily culturally intelligent (Earley & Ang, 2003). CQ requires an ability to categorize behavioral manifestations into universal behaviors (e.g., basic facial expressions of joy and fear), idiosyncratic behaviors specific to individuals, and behaviors that are culturally determined. While socially and emotionally intelligent individuals are able to interpret the first two behavioral categories, only culturally intelligent individuals are aware that a number of behaviors are rooted in culture. From a practical standpoint, Earley and Ang (2003) argue that it is possible for managers to be socially intelligent within their own cultural frame, but to engage in ineffective exchanges when faced with a culturally unfamiliar setting. Conversely, a culturally intelligent individual might possess a high ability to read and adjust to situations in unfamiliar settings (outward cultural perspective) but have a relatively small capacity to look inward and to be equally aware of other sources of interpersonal influences. Triandis (2006) argues that culturally intelligent individuals are attentive to the situation or context in which the behavior takes place, which puts less emphasis on the personal basis for that behavioral manifestation. In view of these shortcomings for each construct, a comprehensive construct encompassing SI and CQ would provide a broader definition of the individual ability to understand social and cultural cues and subsequently respond accordingly.

Different cognitive and noncognitive mechanisms are involved in manifestations of EQ and SI. On the one hand, SI is expected to encompass a balanced amount of cognitive and noncognitive mechanisms. From a noncognitive standpoint, SI is largely dependent on specific physiological structures that evolve following human stages of development and allow for self- and other-awareness. From a cognitive standpoint, SI is also an expression of the adequate use of socially learned responses that determine social adaptation to a particular environment. On the other hand, CQ stems from the motivation and ability to be aware of and to learn novel social codes. Learning social rules that are culturally determined is, in essence, a cognitive task. The ability to quickly grasp the intricacies and subtleties of social interactions is founded on noncognitive processes, but the understanding of individual reactions across cultural settings is cognitive- or knowledge-based. For example, the capacity to accurately read facial expressions originates in noncognitive mechanisms similar to those that explain EQ and SI, but the ability to make sense of those facial expressions within specific cultural contexts is learned, and, therefore, cognitive.

SI and CQ also differ with respect to their motivational bases. The manifestation of SI is less likely affected by motivation than manifestations of CQ. In practice, socially intelligent behaviors serve immediate social needs of affect and affiliation. Hence, it is expected that the baseline motivation to display these behaviors will show little variation across individuals. Conversely, the need to display culturally intelligent behaviors is typically less pressing, and so individuals with similar knowledge of cultural norms might display dissimilar levels of culturally intelligent behavior by virtue of their varying motivation to do so.

As mentioned previously, the capacity to respond to social demands is widely dependent on what those demands are, in particular the ability to identify valued behaviors within a specific setting. As a result, culture determines socially endorsed behaviors. With this in mind, recent research has investigated the role of national culture on perceptions of intelligence. Findings of a study conducted using two samples of students from different countries (Italy and Portugal) corroborated the belief that the culturally determined concept that individuals have of intelligence will impact and be affected by the behaviors endorsed in different cultural settings (Faria, Pepi, & Alesi, 2006). Culture shapes the concept of SI or of what is considered socially intelligent behavior, but individual SI is not contingent upon any specific cultural characteristics. Manifestations of SI depend on individual levels of ability and EQ, and on specific cultural constraints that define social demands to which individuals must adequately respond.

Higher levels of SI allow individuals to see beyond culturally determined paradigms and promote positive changes in social interactions. Hence, the development of a measure of sociocultural intelligence appears to be plausible and intellectually appealing. It should avoid culture-specific items to determine SI, but include these content-particular items in a section evaluating cross-cultural capacity. In brief, there is apparently a need for a new methodology for examining sociocultural intelligence. Following the work of Goleman (2006), that methodology should involve not only the role of overt cognitions, but should also take into account subconscious, noncognitive capacity.

Measuring Sociocultural Intelligence

There is already a long history of objective testing in relation to an individual's responses to social stimuli. The traditional paper-and-pencil testing methodologies that have been presented earlier in this chapter have, for many years, provided a good indication of an individual's conscious response to social stimuli. What has been missing is the testing of the subconscious responses to social stimuli that inform, and in some cases even define, individual responses to those stimuli. If only conscious responses are tested, then a significant portion of an individual's sociocultural intelligence is being left unexamined, and the same is true if only the subconscious is tested at the expense of measuring an individual's cognitive capacity. To develop an accurate picture of sociocultural intelligence, both the conscious and subconscious responses to stimuli must be tested.

Two of the tests for the evaluation of subconscious responses to social stimuli currently in use, and cited by Goleman (2006), are the Profile of Nonverbal Sensitivity (PONS) and the Ekman test. The PONS test is based on the assessment of a predefined set of nonverbal prompts presented via facial expression, body language, or voice tone. This measure requires the test respondents to utilize their subconscious reactions to stimuli, versus their conscious and pondered reaction to a situation. Testing an individual's response to these nonverbal stimuli provides an opportunity to evaluate the specific representations of subconscious perceptions. Paul Ekman's Web-based test measures the capacity of a person to detect so-called microemotions. It is a novel means for assessing someone's ability to empathize at a noncognitive level, a prerequisite for emotional attunement. Encouragingly, Ekman's assessment also reveals the social brain to be an eager learner for reading microemotions (Goleman, 2006, p. 669), suggesting that some key aspects of sociocultural intelligence can be strengthened through training via electronic media and other similar developmental approaches. While there is obviously a place in the assessment process for analyzing an individual's conscious reactions to stimuli, it is becoming increasingly clear that an individual's ability to operate successfully in different sociocultural situations is associated with one's subconscious reactions and noncognitive capacity. By adding similar measures to the array of assessment instruments, it should be possible for evaluators to better discern an individual's sociocultural skills and abilities for a given work environment.

CONCLUSION

The purpose of this chapter was to systematize the extant literature on emotional, social, and cultural intelligence, bringing forth dissimilarities and commonalities with regard to construct, dimensionality, and measurement, and highlighting the positive features of each construct to be incorporated into a sound and applicable framework. Recent efforts to measure subconscious perceptions of social events and the identified need for means to assess interpersonal competence in organizations beyond cognitive ability suggest that an integrative construct of sociocultural intelligence, encompassing both cognitive and noncognitive manifestations, is essential to provide a competitive edge. In today's organizations, where individuals must skillfully interact with or manage others with diverse perspectives and cultural backgrounds, a well-defined construct and measure of sociocultural intelligence would undoubtedly improve leadership techniques, selection systems, and training interventions.

REFERENCES

Ang, S., Van Dyne, L., & Koh, C. (2006). Personality correlates of the four-factor model of cultural intelligence. *Group and Organization Management, 31,* 100–123.

Ang, S., Van Dyne, L., Koh, C., Ng, K., Templer, K.J., Tay, C., & Chandrasekar, N.A. (2007). Cultural intelligence: Its measurement and effects on cultural judgment and decision making, cultural adaptation, and task performance. *Management and Organization Review, 3,* 335–371.

Ashkansy, N.M., & Daus, C.S. (2005). Rumors of the death of emotional intelligence in organizational behaviors are vastly exaggerated. *Journal of Organizational Behavior, 26,* 441–452.

Bar-On, R., & Parker, J.D.A. (2000). *The handbook of emotional intelligence: Theory, development, assessment, and application at home, school, and in the workplace.* San Francisco, CA: Jossey-Bass.

Brackett, M.A., Rivers, S.E., Shiffman, S., Lerner, N., & Salovey, P. (2006). Relating emotional abilities to social functioning: A comparison of self-report and performance measures of emotional intelligence. *Journal of Personality and Social Psychology, 91,* 780–795.

Chen, G.M. (1992). Communication adaptability and interaction involvement as predictors of cross-cultural adjustment. *Communication Research Reports (June),* 33–41.

Chua, H.F., Leu, J., & Nisbett, R.E. (2005). Culture and diverging views of social events. *Personality and Social Psychology Bulletin, 31,* 925–934.

Dulewicz, V., & Higgs, M. (2000). Emotional intelligence: A review and evaluation study. *Journal of Managerial Psychology, 15,* 341–372.

Earley, C., & Ang, S. (2003). *Cultural intelligence: Individual interactions across cultures.* Stanford, CA: Stanford Business Books.

Faria, L., Pepi, A., & Alesi, M. (2006). Personal conceptions of intelligence: Cross-cultural comparisons between Portuguese and Italian students. *Social Behavior and Personality, 34,* 815–826.

Frederiksen, N., Carlson, S., & Ward, W.C. (1984). The place of social intelligence in a taxonomy of cognitive abilities. *Intelligence, 8,* 315–337.

Furnham, A., & Mottabu, R. (2004). Sex and culture differences in the estimates of general and multiple intelligence: A study comparing British and Egyptian students. *Individual Differences Research, 2,* 82–96.

Gardner, H. (1999). *Intelligences reframed: Multiple intelligences in the 21st century.* New York: Basic Books.

Gardner, H. (2006). On failing to grasp the core of MI theory: A response to Visser et al. *Intelligence, 34,* 503–505.

Goldstein, D.L., & Smith, D.H. (1999). The analysis of the effects of experimental training on sojourners' cross-cultural adaptability. *International Journal of Intercultural Relations, 23,* 157–173.

Goleman, D. (1995). *Emotional intelligence.* New York: Bantam Books.

Goleman, D. (2006). *Social intelligence: The new science of human relationships.* New York: Random House.

Hampden-Turner, C., & Trompenaars, F. (2006). Cultural intelligence: Is such a capacity credible? *Group and Organization Management, 31,* 56–63.

Hofstede, G., & McRae, R.R. (2004). Personality and culture revisited: Linking traits and dimensions of culture. *Cross-Cultural Research: The Journal of Comparative Social Science, 38,* 52–88.

Hofstede, G., Neuijen, B., Ohayv, D.D., & Sanders, G. (1990). Measuring organizational cultures: A qualitative and quantitative study across twenty cases. *Administrative Science, 35,* 286–316.

Kobe, L.M., Reiter, P.R., & Rickers, J.D. (2001). Self-reported leadership experiences in relation to inventoried social and emotional intelligence. *Current Psychology: Developmental, Learning, Personality, Social, 20,* 154–163.

Kosmitzki, C., & John, O.P. (1993). The implicit use of explicit conceptions of social intelligence. *Personality and Individual Differences, 15,* 11–23.

Kunnanat, J.T. (2004). Emotional intelligence: The new science of interpersonal effectiveness. *Human Resource Development Quarterly, 15,* 489–495.

Landy, F. (2005). Some historical and scientific issues related to research on emotional intelligence. *Journal of Organizational Behavior, 26,* 411–424.

Lee, J., Wong, C.T., Day, J.D., Maxwell, S.E., & Thorpe, P. (2000). Social and academic intelligences:

A multitrait-multimethod study of their crystallized and fluid characteristics. *Personality and Individual Differences, 29,* 539–553.

Legree, P.J. (1995). Evidence for an oblique social intelligence factor established with a Likert-based testing procedure. *Intelligence, 21,* 247–266.

Livingstone, H.A., & Day, A.L. (2005). Comparing the construct and criterion-related validity of ability-based and mixed-model measures of emotional intelligence. *Educational and Psychological Measurement, 65,* 757–779.

Locke, E.A. (2005). Why emotional intelligence is an invalid concept. *Journal of Organizational Behavior, 26,* 425–431.

Lowman, R.L., & Leeman, G.E. (1985). The dimensionality of social intelligence: Social abilities, interests, and needs. *The Journal of Psychology, 122,* 279–290.

Markus, H.R., & Kitayama, S. (1991). Culture and the self: Implications for cognition, emotion, and motivation. *Psychological Review, 98,* 224–253.

Marlowe, H.A. (1986). Social intelligence: Evidence of multidimensionality and construct independence. *Journal of Educational Psychology, 78,* 52–58.

Martinez-Pons, M. (1997). The relation of emotional intelligence with selected areas of personal functioning. *Imagination, Cognition, and Personality, 17,* 3–13.

Mayer, J.D., & Salovey, P. (1993). The intelligence of emotional intelligence. *Intelligence, 17,* 433–442.

Mayer, J.D., & Salovey, P. (1995). Emotional intelligence and the construction and regulation of feelings. *Applied and Preventive Psychology, 4,* 197–208.

Mayer, J.D., & Salovey, P. (1997). What is emotional intelligence? In P. Salovey & D. Sluyter (Eds.), *Emotional development and emotional intelligence: Educational implications* (pp. 3–34). New York: Basic Books.

Mutsuo, S. (2004). Different roles of left and right frontal lobes for cognitive versus emotional and social intelligence. *Tohoku Psychologica Folia, 63,* 73–83.

Oubrayrie, N., Safont, C., & Tap, P. (1991). Identite personnelle et intelligence sociale: A propos de l'estime de soi. *Les Cahiers Internationaux de Psychologie Sociale, 9*(10), 63–76.

Payne,W. L. (1986). A study of emotion, developing emotional intelligence: self-integration; relating to fear, pain, and desire. *Dissertation Abstracts International, 47,* 203A.

Riggio, R.E., Messamer, J., & Throckmorton, B. (1991). Social and academic intelligence: Conceptually distinct but overlapping constructs. *Personality and Individual Differences, 12,* 695–702.

Roberts, R.D., Schulze, R., O'Brien, K., MacCann, C., Reid, J., & Maul, A. (2006). Exploring the validity of the Mayer-Salovey-Caruso Emotional Intelligence Test (MSCEIT) with established emotions measures. *Emotion, 6,* 663–669.

Salovey, P., & Mayer, J.D. (1990). Emotional intelligence. *Imagination, Cognition, and Personality, 9,* 185–211.

Scott, W.A. (1974). Varieties of cognitive integration. *Journal of Personality and Social Psychology, 30,* 563–578.

Shipper, F., Kincaid, J., Rotondo, D.M., & Hoffman, R.C. (2003). A cross-cultural exploratory study of the linkage between emotional intelligence and managerial effectiveness. *The International Journal of Organizational Analysis, 11,* 171–191.

Smith, P.B., Dugan, S., & Trompenaars, F. (1996). National culture and the values of organizational employees: A dimensional analysis across 43 nations. *Journal of Cross-Cultural Psychology, 27,* 231–264.

Sosik, J.J., & Megerian, L.E. (1999). Understanding leader emotional intelligence and performance: The role of self-other agreement on transformational leadership perceptions. *Group and Organization Management, 24,* 367–390.

Spearman, C. (1927). *The abilities of man.* Oxford: Macmillan.

Sternberg, R.J., & Grigorenko, E.L. (2006). Cultural intelligence and successful intelligence. *Group and Organization Management, 31,* 27–39.

Templer, K.J., Tay, C., & Chandrasekar, N.A. (2006). Motivational cultural intelligence, realistic job preview, realistic living conditions preview, and cross-cultural adjustment. *Group and Organization Management, 31,* 154–173.
Tett, R.P., & Fox, K.E. (2006). Confirmatory factor structure of trait emotional intelligence in student and worker samples. *Personality and Individual Differences, 41,* 1155–1168.
Thomas, D., & Inkson, K. (2004). *Cultural intelligence: People skills for global business.* San Francisco, CA: Berrett-Koehler Publishers.
Thorndike, E.L. (1921). On the organization of intellect. *Psychological Review, 28,* 141–151.
Thorndike, E.L. (1924). Measurement of intelligence. *Psychological Review, 31,* 219–252.
Triandis, H.C. (2006). Cultural intelligence in organizations. *Group and Organization Management, 31,* 20–26.
Walker, R.E., & Foley, J.M. (1973). Social intelligence: Its history and measurement. *Psychological Reports, 33,* 839–864.
Weis, S., & Sub, H. (2007). Reviving the search for social intelligence: A multitrait multimethod study of its structure and construct validity. *Personality and Individual Differences, 42,* 3–14.
Wong, C.T., Day, J.D., Maxwell, S.E., & Meara, N.M. (1995). A multitrait-multimethod study of academic and social intelligence in college students. *Journal of Educational Psychology, 87,* 117–133.
Zaccaro, S.J, Gilbert, J.A., Thor, K.K., & Mumford, M.D. (1991). Leadership and social intelligence: Linking social perspectiveness and behavioral flexibility to leader effectiveness. *Leadership Quarterly, 2,* 317–342.

CHAPTER 19

Successful Intelligence as a Framework for Understanding Cultural Adaptation

ROBERT J. STERNBERG

Not long ago I was in Manchester, England, and was beginning to cross the street. As I started to cross, a bus swooped in front of me and came within inches of mowing me down. It was not the bus driver's fault. I had looked for traffic when I crossed the street, but I had looked to my left, the direction from which traffic in my own country normally would have been coming. The bus, of course, came from the right.

This example of cultural maladaptation might seem small, but unfortunately, it is easy to find rather large examples. What is considered intelligent clearly differs from one place to the next (Sternberg, 2004a, 2004b). Is it smart or fatally stupid to drive on the left side, to cross the street during the day (in war zones of Iraq), or to criticize the existing regime publicly, for example? Yet researchers often do their research as though culture does not matter. This research continues despite pervasive evidence that people in different cultures think and act differently (e.g., Greenfield, 1997; Sternberg, 1982; Nisbett, 2003; Serpell, 2000; Super & Harkness, 1986; see essays in Sternberg & Grigorenko, 2004).

Earley and Ang (2003; Ang, Van Dyne, Koh, Ng, Templer, Tay, & Chandrasekar, 2007) have proposed a distinct *cultural intelligence* (CQ) as people's ability to function effectively in different cultures. Here I seek to account for these differences in terms of a theory of "successful intelligence" (Sternberg, 1997). But I also consider what is the same across cultures. The theory considers both implicit and explicit theories of intelligence. I describe each of these kinds of theories in turn, and then specifically discuss assessment and instruction.

LAY IMPLICIT THEORIES OF INTELLIGENCE AROUND THE WORLD

In some cases, Western notions about intelligence are not shared by other cultures. For example, at the mental level, the Western emphasis on speed of mental processing (Sternberg, Conway, Ketron, & Bernstein, 1981) is not shared in many cultures. Other cultures may even be suspicious of the quality of work that is done very quickly. Even in cultures that emphasize speed, such as in North America, speed is not always valued. If a jury has to make a decision as to whether an accused is innocent or guilty, no one would properly encourage the members to rush their decision.

Yang and Sternberg (1997a) reviewed Chinese philosophical conceptions of intelligence. The Confucian perspective emphasizes the characteristic of benevolence and of doing what is right. As in the Western notion, the intelligent person spends a great deal of effort in learning, enjoys learning, and persists in lifelong learning with a great deal of enthusiasm. The Taoist tradition, in contrast, emphasizes the importance of humility, freedom from conventional standards of judgment, and full knowledge of oneself as well as of external conditions.

The difference between Eastern and Western conceptions of intelligence may persist even in the present day. Yang and Sternberg (1997b) studied contemporary Taiwanese Chinese conceptions of intelligence, and found five factors underlying these conceptions: (a) a general cognitive factor, much like the *g* factor in conventional Western tests; (b) interpersonal intelligence (i.e., social competence); (c) intrapersonal intelligence; (d) intellectual self-assertion; and (d) intellectual self-effacement.

The factors uncovered in Taiwan differ substantially from those identified by Sternberg et al. (1981) in the conceptions about intelligence of people from the United States: (a) practical problem solving, (b) verbal ability, and (c) social competence. In both cases, however, people's implicit theories of intelligence seem to go quite far beyond what conventional psychometric intelligence tests measure.

Studies in Africa provide another window on the substantial differences. Ruzgis and Grigorenko (1994) argued that, in Africa, conceptions of intelligence revolve largely around skills that help to facilitate and maintain harmonious and stable intergroup relations; intragroup relations are probably equally important and at times more important. The emphasis on the social aspects of intelligence is not limited to African cultures. Notions of intelligence in many Asian cultures also emphasize the social aspect of intelligence more than does the conventional Western or IQ-based notion (Azuma & Kashiwagi, 1987; Lutz, 1985; Poole, 1985; White, 1985). The Sternberg et al. (1981) study showed that social intelligence is considered important in the United States (Goleman, 1995, 2006). It should be noted that neither African nor Asian conceptions emphasize exclusively social notions of intelligence. These conceptions of intelligence emphasize social skills much more than conventional U.S. conceptions of intelligence do and also recognize the importance of cognitive aspects of intelligence.

In a study of Kenyan conceptions of intelligence (Grigorenko et al., 2001), it was found that there are four distinct terms constituting conceptions of intelligence among rural Kenyans: *rieko* (knowledge and skills), *luoro* (respect), *winjo* (comprehension of how to handle real-life problems), *paro* (initiative). Only the first directly refers to knowledge-based skills (including but not limited to the academic). These skills go well beyond the cognitive and include social and practical aspects of intelligence.

There is no single, overall U.S. conception of intelligence. Indeed, Okagaki and

Sternberg (1993) found that different ethnic groups in San Jose, California, had rather different conceptions of what it means to be intelligent. For example, Latino parents of schoolchildren tended to emphasize the importance of social-competence skills in their conceptions of intelligence, whereas Asian parents tended rather heavily to emphasize the importance of cognitive skills. Anglo parents also emphasized cognitive skills. Teachers, representing the dominant culture, placed more emphasis on cognitive skills than on social-competence skills. The rank order of the performance by children from various groups (including subgroups within the Latino and Asian groups) could be perfectly predicted by the extent to which their parents shared the teachers' conception of intelligence. In other words, teachers tended to reward those children who were socialized into a view of intelligence that happened to correspond to the teachers' own. Yet, as we argue later, social aspects of intelligence, broadly defined, may be as important as or even more important than cognitive aspects of intelligence in later life. Some, however, prefer to study intelligence not in its social aspects rather than cognitive aspect.

One can conclude that CQ lies in a person's flexibility in alternating among these different conceptions of intelligence. To be smart requires different skills in different cultures, and the culturally intelligent person calls upon these skills as necessary.

EXPLICIT-THEORETICAL INVESTIGATIONS OF INTELLIGENCE AROUND THE WORLD

Many times, investigations of intelligence conducted in settings outside the developed world can yield a picture of intelligence that is quite at variance with the picture one would obtain from studies conducted only in the developed world. In a study in Usenge, Kenya, near the town of Kisumu, Sternberg and colleagues were interested in school-age children's ability to adapt to their indigenous environment. They devised a test of practical intelligence for adaptation to the environment (see Sternberg & Grigorenko, 1997, 2002b; Sternberg et al., 2001). The test of practical intelligence measured children's informal tacit knowledge for natural herbal medicines that the villagers believe can be used to fight various types of infections. At least some of these medicines appear to be effective, and most villagers certainly believe in their efficacy, as shown by the fact that children in the villages use their knowledge of these medicines an average of once a week in medicating themselves and others. Thus, tests of how to use these medicines constitute effective measures of one aspect of practical intelligence as defined by the villagers as well as their life circumstances in their environmental contexts. Middle-class Westerners might find it quite a challenge to thrive or even survive in these contexts, or, for that matter, in the contexts of urban ghettos often not distant from their comfortable homes.

The Kenya Study

The researchers measured the Kenyan children's ability to identify the medicines, where they come from, what they are used for, and how they are dosed. Based on work the researchers had done elsewhere, they expected that scores on this test would not correlate with scores on conventional tests of intelligence. In order to test this hypothesis, they also administered to the 85 children the Raven Colored Progressive Matrices Test (Raven, Court, & Raven, 1992), which is a measure of fluid or abstract-reasoning-based abilities, as well as the Mill Hill Vocabulary Scale (Raven et al., 1992), which is a measure of crystallized or formal-knowledge-based abilities. In addition, they gave the children a comparable test of vocabulary in their own Dholuo language. The Dholuo language is spoken in the home, and English is spoken in the schools.

The researchers found no correlation between the test of indigenous tacit knowledge and scores on the fluid ability tests. But to their surprise, they found statistically significant correlations of the tacit-knowledge tests with the tests of crystallized abilities. The correlations, however, were *negative.* In other words, the higher the children scored on the test of tacit knowledge, the lower they scored, on average, on the tests of crystallized abilities. This surprising result can be interpreted in various ways, but based on the ethnographic observations of the anthropologists on the team, Geissler and Prince, the researchers concluded that a plausible scenario takes into account the expectations of families for their children.

Many children in Usenge drop out of school before graduation, for financial or other reasons, and many families in the village do not particularly value formal Western schooling. There is no reason they should, as the children of many families will for the most part spend their lives farming or engaged in other occupations that make little or no use of Western schooling. These families emphasize teaching their children the indigenous informal knowledge that will lead to successful adaptation in the environments in which they will live. Children who spend their time learning the indigenous practical knowledge of the community generally do not invest themselves heavily in doing well in school, whereas children who do well in school generally do not invest themselves as heavily in learning the indigenous knowledge—hence the negative correlations.

The Kenya study suggests that the identification of a general factor of human intelligence may tell us more about how abilities interact with patterns of schooling and especially Western patterns of schooling than it does about the structure of human abilities. In Western schooling, children typically study a variety of subject matter from an early age and thus develop skills in several areas. This kind of schooling prepares the children to take a test of intelligence, which typically measures skills in a variety of areas. Often, intelligence tests measure skills that children were expected to acquire a few years before taking the intelligence test. But as Rogoff (1990) and others have noted, this pattern of schooling is not universal and has not even been common for much of the history of humankind. Throughout history and in many places still, schooling takes the form of apprenticeships in which children learn a craft from an early age.

Intelligence and Developing Expertise

We have found related although certainly not identical results in a study we have done among Yup'ik Eskimo children in southwestern Alaska (Grigorenko, Meier, Lipka, Mohatt, Yanez, & Sternberg, 2004). We assessed the importance of academic and practical intelligence in rural and urban Alaskan communities. A total of 261 children were rated for practical skills by adults or peers in the study: 69 in grade 9, 69 in grade 10, 45 in grade 11, and 37 in grade 12. Of these children, 145 were females and 116 were males, and they were from 7 different communities, 6 rural and 1 relatively urban. We measured academic intelligence with conventional measures of fluid and crystallized intelligence. We measured practical intelligence with a test of tacit knowledge as acquired in rural Alaskan Yup'ik communities. The urban children generally outperformed the rural children on a measure of crystallized intelligence, but the rural children generally outperformed the urban children on the measure of Yup'ik tacit knowledge. The test of tacit knowledge was superior to the tests of academic intelligence in predicting practical skills of the rural children but not of the urban ones.

The test of practical intelligence developed for use in Kenya, as well as some of the other practically based tests described in this chapter, may seem more like tests of achievement or of developing expertise (see Ericsson, 1996) than of intelligence. But it can be argued that intelligence is itself a form of developing expertise—that there is no clear-cut distinction between the two constructs (Sternberg, 1998, 1999). Indeed, all measures of intelligence, one might argue, measure a form of developing expertise.

An example of how tests of intelligence measure developing expertise rather than some fixed quantity emanates from work Sternberg, Grigorenko, and their colleagues have done in Tanzania. One study done in Tanzania (see Sternberg & Grigorenko, 1997, 2002a; Sternberg et al., 2002) points out the risks of giving tests, scoring them, and interpreting the results as measures of some latent intellectual ability or abilities. The investigators administered to 358 school children between the ages of 11 and 13 years near Bagamoyo, Tanzania, tests including a form-board classification test, a linear syllogisms test, and a Twenty Questions test, which measure the kinds of skills required on conventional tests of intelligence. Of course, the investigators obtained scores that they could analyze and evaluate, ranking the children in terms of their supposed general or other abilities. However, they administered the tests dynamically rather than statically (Grigorenko & Sternberg, 1998; Sternberg & Grigorenko, 2002a; Tzuriel, 1995; Vygotsky, 1978).

Dynamic Testing

Dynamic testing is like conventional static testing in that individuals are tested and inferences about their abilities are made. But dynamic tests differ in that children are given some kind of feedback in order to help them improve their scores. Vygotsky (1978) suggested that the children's ability to profit from the guided instruction they received during the testing session could serve as a measure of children's zone of proximal development, or the difference between their developed abilities and their latent capacities. In other words, testing and instruction are treated as being of one piece rather than as being distinct processes. This integration makes sense in terms of traditional definitions of intelligence as the ability to learn (Sternberg & Detterman, 1986; Thurstone, 1921). What a dynamic test does is directly measure processes of learning in the context of testing rather than measuring these processes indirectly as the product of past learning. Such measurement is especially important when not all children have had equal opportunities to learn in the past.

In the assessments, children were first given the ability tests. Then they were given a brief period of instruction in which they were able to learn skills that would potentially enable them to improve their scores. Then they were tested again. Because the instruction for each test lasted only about 5–10 minutes, one would not expect dramatic gains. Yet, on average, the gains were statistically significant. More importantly, scores on the pretest showed only weak although significant correlations with scores on the post-test. These correlations, at about the 0.3 level, suggested that when tests are administered statically to children in developing countries, they may be rather unstable and easily subject to influences of training. The reason could be that the children are not accustomed to taking Western-style tests, and so profit quickly even from small amounts of instruction as to what is expected of them. Of course, the more important question is not whether the scores changed or even correlated with each other, but rather how they correlated with other cognitive measures. In other words, which test was a better predictor of transfer to other cognitive performance, the pretest score or the post-test score? The investigators found the post-test score to be the better predictor.

In interpreting results, whether from developed or developing cultures, it is always important to take into account the physical health of the participants one is testing. In a study we did in Jamaica (Sternberg, Powell, McGrane, & McGregor, 1997), we found that Jamaican schoolchildren who suffered from parasitic illnesses (for the most part, whipworm or Ascaris) did more poorly on higher level cognitive tests (such as of working memory and reasoning) than did children who did not suffer from these illnesses, even after controlling for socioeconomic status. Why might such a physical illness cause a deficit in higher level cognitive skills?

Ceci (1996) has shown that increased levels of schooling are associated with higher IQ. Why would there by such a relation? Presumably, in part, because schooling helps children develop the kinds of skills that are measured by IQ tests, and that are important in turn for survival in school. Children with whipworm-induced illnesses and related illnesses are less able to profit from school than are children without these illnesses. Every day they go to school, they are likely to be experiencing symptoms such as listlessness, stomachache, and difficulty concentrating. These symptoms reduce the extent to which they are able to profit from instruction and in turn reduce their ultimate performance on higher level cognitive tests.

A Russian Study

The ideas studied in Kenya can be extended elsewhere. In one set of studies, Grigorenko and Sternberg (2001) tested 511 Russian schoolchildren (ranging in age from 8 to 17 years) as well as 490 mothers and 328 fathers of these children. They used entirely distinct measures of analytical, creative, and practical intelligence. Consider, for example, the tests used for adults. Similar tests were used for children.

Fluid analytical intelligence was measured by two subtests of a test of nonverbal intelligence. The "Test of *g:* Culture Fair, Level II" (Cattell & Cattell, 1973) is a test of fluid intelligence designed to reduce, as much as possible, the influence of verbal comprehension, culture, and educational level, although no test eliminates such influences. The test of crystallized intelligence was adapted from existing traditional tests of analogies and synonyms/antonyms used in Russia. The measure of creative intelligence also comprised two parts. The first part asked the participants to describe the world through the eyes of insects. The second part asked participants to describe who might live and what might happen on a planet called "Priumliava."

The measure of practical intelligence was self-report and also comprised two parts. The first part was designed as a 20-item, self-report instrument, assessing practical skills in the social domain (e.g., effective and successful communication with other people), in the family domain (e.g., how to fix household items, how to run the family budget), and in the domain of effective resolution of sudden problems (e.g., organizing something that has become chaotic). The second part had four vignettes, based on themes that appeared in popular Russian magazines in the context of discussion of adaptive skills in the current society. Each vignette was accompanied by five choices and participants had to select the best one. Obviously, there is no one "right" answer in this type of situation. Hence, Grigorenko and Sternberg used the most frequently chosen response as the keyed answer.

In this study, exploratory principal-component analysis for both children and adults yielded very similar factor structures. Both varimax and oblimin rotations yielded clear-cut analytical, creative, and practical factors for the tests. Thus, with a sample of a different nationality (Russian), a different set of tests, and a different method of analysis (exploratory rather than confirmatory analysis) again supported the theory of successful intelligence.

In this same study, the analytical, creative, and practical tests the investigators employed were used to predict mental and physical health among the Russian adults. Mental health was measured by widely used paper-and-pencil tests of depression and anxiety and physical health was measured by self-report. The best predictor of mental and physical health was the practical-intelligence measure. (Or, because the data are correlational, it may be that health predicts practical intelligence, although the connection here is less clear). Analytical intelligence came second and creative intelligence came third. All three contributed to prediction, however. Thus, the researchers again concluded that a theory of intelligence encompassing all three elements provides better prediction of success in life than does a theory comprising just the analytical element.

The studies of explicit theories show, much as do the implicit theories, that CQ requires a broad array of skills that is brought to bear as one moves across cultures. A narrow set of skills, as measured by traditional tests, does not suffice.

A UNIFIED ASSESSMENT EFFORT

Assessment, in general, should take into account cultural context (Sternberg, 2007a, in press). Through our most recent venture, the Rainbow Project (Sternberg & the Rainbow Project Collaborators, 2005, 2006), we have developed a test for high school students that can be used for college admissions, called the Rainbow Assessment. The project has been tested on roughly 1,000 ethnically diverse U.S. students of high school and college age.

The Rainbow measures are designed to assess analytical, creative, and practical abilities along the lines specified by the theory of successful intelligence. The instruments consisted of both multiple-choice tests (the Sternberg Triarchic Abilities Test, STAT) and performance measures of creative and practical skills. They were thus designed to sample across ability domains as well as methods of assessment.

What did we find? We found that by using the Rainbow measures to augment the STAT, we could roughly double prediction of first-year academic performance across 13 different colleges and universities. Moreover, we found that differences between ethnic groups—white Americans, African Americans, Latino Americans, Native Americans—were reduced quite substantially. In other words, the tests measure skills that are important for college success that are not measured by conventional tests. At the same time, they decrease differences across members of different ethnic groups. These results show that it is possible, in the context of a single test, to assess abilities across an ethnically/culturally diverse constituency. Children of different groups are socialized to develop different intellectual skills, best assessed by a broad battery.

The Rainbow Project was oriented at college admissions. In another project oriented toward business school admissions (Hedlund, Wilt, Nebel, Ashford, & Sternberg, 2006), we showed that we could reduce cultural and ethnic differences in comparison with a test commonly used for business school admissions (the GMAT) by a measure of practical intelligence. In a third study of achievement testing for college-level work done by high schoolers (Stemler, Grigorenko, Jarvin, & Sternberg, 2006), we found that we could substantially reduce ethnic/cultural differences relative to scores on advanced placement achievement tests in psychology and, to a lesser extent, statistics, by the use of creative and practical items to supplement the conventionally used standardized tests.

The principles we brought to bear in these studies could be used in any culture. What is creative or practical differs from one culture to another, and the culturally intelligent person, as noted earlier, has the flexibility of repertoire to learn what is creative or practical, and then apply these skills in a fashion that is culturally appropriate.

CULTURE AND INSTRUCTION

Culture must be taken into account in instruction (Sternberg, 2007b). We have shown that when children are taught in a way that better matches their culturally acquired knowledge, their school performance improves (Sternberg, Lipka, Newman, Wildfeuer, & Grigorenko, 2007). Grade 6 students from seven communities in three school districts in Alaska participated in a mathematics curriculum project. Eight classes of students containing a total of 196 students were taught the concepts of area and perimeter using an Alaskan culturally based, triarchic curriculum and 5 classes containing 55 students were taught the same subject matter using conventional textbook-based curriculum. Both groups contained students from rural regions with a population that was almost 100 percent Alaskan Native (predominantly Yup'ik) and urban regions with a population that was approximately 71 percent ethnically white and 12 percent Alaskan Native.

Due to absenteeism a total of 17 students did not complete the pretest and 30 students did not complete the post-test. This resulted in a total of 158 students (35 rural and 123 urban) in the culturally based triarchic curriculum group and 46 students (29 rural and 17 urban) in the conventional curriculum group being included in the analysis. Pre- and post-test measures of the "area and perimeter curriculum" were collected for all the students. Only students who completed both the pre- and post-test measures were included in the study sample.

Teachers in the culturally-based curriculum group received a math unit devised by Jerry Lipka, called "Fish Racks," as part of the curriculum sponsored by the National Science Federation, "Adapting Yup'ik Elders' Knowledge." The unit addressed the National Council of Teachers of Mathematics standards for the topics of area and perimeter using both native content (building of fish racks) and native teaching strategies (demonstrations by Yup'ik elders). The building of fish racks is a native tradition and requires everyday, practical mathematics to build racks that will be stable, strong, and have sufficient area for placing salmon on them. The math unit comprised two complex problems, each involving a number of different activities revolving around the building of fish racks and the concepts of area and perimeter.

Teachers in the control group used their mathematics textbooks to teach the concepts of perimeter and area. The approach used in these textbooks is a procedurally based approach for teaching perimeter and a formula-based approach for teaching area. The perimeter and area unit covered approximately the same material and began and ended at approximately the same time as the treatment group.

Prior to and following the intervention, students completed tests designed to capture their knowledge of area and perimeter concepts. The tests were each composed of 15 questions involving a combination of multiple choice, short answer, and open-ended items. The intervention for students lasted between three and four weeks; approximate time for instruction was an hour a day. The training session for teachers lasted two days.

The results were simple. There were no pretest differences. At the post-test, the treatment group outperformed the control group on all indicators. In other words, teaching in ways that capitalized on cultural knowledge enhanced student performance. This would be true for any culture one might choose to examine.

CONCLUSION

Intelligence cannot be understood outside its cultural context. CQ is a matter of learning the tacit knowledge of a culture and applying a broad repertoire of skills relevant in a given cultural setting. It is largely a matter of mental flexibility. A culturally intelligent person understands that the skills needed for adaptive performance differ across cultures. So he or she must learn what these skills are, and then apply them in a practical way in everyday life. In a sense, then, CQ is practical intelligence flexibly applied across cultural settings.

People from developed countries, and especially Western ones, can show and have shown a certain kind of arrogance in assuming that concepts (such as implicit theories of intelligence) or results (such as of studies based on explicit theories of intelligence) obtained in one culture—usually, *their culture*—apply anywhere. In all likelihood, they do not. Or at least, it cannot be assumed they do until this assumption is tested.

Many of the results we have described here are at variance with results typically obtained in Western countries. Other investigators as well have obtained results that differ dramatically from those obtained in the developed West. Cultural views of intelligence help us to understand intelligence in a broad, rather than narrow, way.

Earley and Ang (2003) pointed out the necessity of a concept of CQ. Consistent with this notion, the studies described in this essay show that what constitutes intelligence somewhat differs across cultures. But there are certain things that are constant. In every culture, people need to recognize when they have problems, define what these problems are, figure out how to solve the problems, and then monitor and evaluate their problem solving. Across cultures, people also need to adapt to, shape, and select environments. So there are universal common processes of intelligence (Sternberg, 2003, 2004a). What differs across cultures is the content to which these processes are applied, and the behavioral consequences of the content that is considered "intelligent." Thus intelligence is partly culturally relative and partly culturally universal. Someone who has well-developed abilities to define and solve problems will be at an advantage in any culture. But whether he or she will have the knowledge base—both explicit and implicit or tacit (Sternberg et al., 2000)—to adapt successfully will depend on the kinds of experiences he or she has had. Adaptation will also depend on the person recognizing that what is adaptive in one culture is not necessarily adaptive in another culture. To a large extent, one becomes culturally intelligent because one recognizes that the skills one needs to adapt differ from one culture to another. Those who do not realize this, no matter how intelligent they are in one culture, may fail to adapt in other cultures.

REFERENCES

Ang, S., Van Dyne, L., Koh, C., Ng, K.Y., Templer, K.J., Tay, C., & Chandrasekar, N.A. (2007). Cultural intelligence: Its measurement and effects on cultural judgment and decision making, cultural adaptation, and task performance. *Management and Organization Review, 3,* 335–371.

Azuma, H., & Kashiwagi, K. (1987). Descriptions for an intelligent person: A Japanese study. *Japanese Psychological Research, 29,* 17–26.

Cattell, R.B., & Cattell, H.E.P. (1973). *Measuring intelligence with the Culture Fair tests.* Champaign, IL: Institute for Personality and Ability Testing.

Ceci, S.J. (1996). *On intelligence . . . more or less* (ex. ed.). Cambridge, MA: Harvard University Press.

Earley, P.C., & Ang, S. (2003). *Cultural intelligence: Individual interactions across cultures.* Stanford, CA: Stanford University Press.

Ericsson, K.A. (1996). *The road to excellence.* Mahwah, NJ: Lawrence Erlbaum Associates.

Goleman, D. (1995). *Emotional intelligence.* New York: Bantam.

Goleman, D. (2006). *Social intelligence.* New York: Bantam.

Greenfield, P.M. (1997). You can't take it with you: Why abilities assessments don't cross cultures. *American Psychologist, 52,* 1115–1124.

Grigorenko, E.L., Geissler, P.W., Prince, R., Okatcha, F., Nokes, C., Kenny, D.A., Bundy, D.A., &

Sternberg, R.J. (2001). The organization of Luo conceptions of intelligence: A study of implicit theories in a Kenyan village. *International Journal of Behavioral Development, 25,* 367–378.

Grigorenko, E.L., Meier, E., Lipka, J., Mohatt, G., Yanez, E., & Sternberg, R.J. (2004). Academic and practical intelligence: A case study of the Yup'ik in Alaska. *Learning and Individual Differences, 14,* 183–207.

Grigorenko, E.L., & Sternberg, R.J. (1998). Dynamic testing. *Psychological Bulletin, 124,* 75–111.

Grigorenko, E.L., & Sternberg, R.J. (2001). Analytical, creative, and practical intelligence as predictors of self-reported adaptive functioning: A case study in Russia. *Intelligence, 29,* 57–73.

Hedlund, J., Wilt, J.M., Nebel, K.R., Ashford, S.J., & Sternberg, R.J. (2006). Assessing practical intelligence in business school admissions: A supplement to the graduate management admissions test. *Learning and Individual Differences, 16,* 101–127.

Laboratory of comparative human cognition (1982). Culture and intelligence. In R. J. Sternberg (Ed.), *Handbook of human intelligence* (pp. 642–719). New York: Cambridge University Press.

Lutz, C. (1985). Ethnopsychology compared to what? Explaining behavior and consciousness among the Ifaluk. In G.M. White & J. Kirkpatrick (Eds.), *Person, self, and experience: Exploring Pacific ethnopsychologies* (pp. 35–79). Berkeley, CA: University of California Press.

Nisbett, R.E. (2003). *The geography of thought: Why we think the way we do.* New York: The Free Press.

Okagaki, L., & Sternberg, R.J. (1993). Parental beliefs and children's school performance. *Child Development, 64,* 36–56.

Poole, F.J.P. (1985). Coming into social being: Cultural images of infants in Bimin-Kuskusmin folk psychology. In G.M. White & J. Kirkpatrick (Eds.), *Person, self, and experience: Exploring Pacific ethnopsychologies* (pp. 183–244). Berkeley, CA: University of California Press.

Raven, J.C., Court, J.H., & Raven, J. (1992). *Manual for Raven's Progressive Matrices and Mill Hill Vocabulary Scales.* Oxford: Oxford Psychologists Press.

Rogoff, B. (1990). *Apprenticeship in thinking. Cognitive development in social context.* New York: Oxford University Press.

Ruzgis, P.M., & Grigorenko, E.L. (1994). Cultural meaning systems, intelligence and personality. In R.J. Sternberg & P. Ruzgis (Eds.), *Personality and intelligence* (pp. 248–270). New York: Cambridge.

Serpell, R. (2000). Intelligence and culture. In R.J. Sternberg (Ed.), *Handbook of intelligence* (pp. 549–580). New York: Cambridge University Press.

Stemler, S.E., Grigorenko, E.L., Jarvin, L., & Sternberg, R.J. (2006). Using the theory of successful intelligence as a basis for augmenting AP exams in psychology and statistics. *Contemporary Educational Psychology, 31,* 344–376.

Sternberg, R.J. (1997). *Successful intelligence.* New York: Plume.

Sternberg, R.J. (1998). Abilities are forms of developing expertise. *Educational Researcher, 27,* 11–20.

Sternberg, R.J. (1999). Intelligence as developing expertise. *Contemporary Educational Psychology, 24,* 359–375.

Sternberg, R.J. (2003). *Wisdom, intelligence, and creativity synthesized.* New York: Cambridge University Press.

Sternberg, R.J. (2004a). Culture and intelligence. *American Psychologist, 59,* 325–338.

Sternberg, R.J. (2004b). *International handbook of intelligence.* New York: Cambridge University Press.

Sternberg, R.J. (2007a). Culture, instruction, assessment. *Comparative Education, 43,* 5–22.

Sternberg, R.J. (2007b). Who are the bright children? The cultural context of being and acting intelligent. *Educational Researcher, 36,* 148–155.

Sternberg, R.J. (in press). Culture and measurement. *Measurement: Interdisciplinary Research and Perspectives.*

Sternberg, R.J., Conway, B.E., Ketron, J.L., & Bernstein, M. (1981). People's conceptions of intelligence. *Journal of Personality and Social Psychology, 41,* 37–55

Sternberg, R.J., & Detterman, D.K. (Eds.) (1986). *What is intelligence?* Norwood, NJ: Ablex Publishing.

Sternberg, R.J., Forsythe, G.B., Hedlund, J., Horvath, J., Snook, S., Williams, W.M., Wagner, R.K., & Grigorenko, E.L. (2000). *Practical intelligence in everyday life.* New York: Cambridge University Press.

Sternberg, R.J., & Grigorenko, E.L. (Eds.) (1997). The cognitive costs of physical and mental ill health: Applying the psychology of the developed world to the problems of the developing world. *Eye on Psi Chi, 2,* 20–27.

Sternberg, R.J., & Grigorenko, E.L. (2002a). *Dynamic testing.* New York: Cambridge University Press.

Sternberg, R.J., & Grigorenko, E.L. (2002b). Just because we "know" it's true doesn't mean it's really true: A case study in Kenya. *Psychological Science Agenda, 15,* 8–10.

Sternberg, R.J., & Grigorenko, E.L. (2004). *Culture and competence.* Washington, DC: American Psychological Association.

Sternberg, R.J., Grigorenko, E.L., Ngrosho, D., Tantufuye, E., Mbise, A., Nokes, C., Jukes, M., & Bundy, D.A. (2002). Assessing intellectual potential in rural Tanzanian school children. *Intelligence, 30,* 141–162.

Sternberg, R.J., Lipka, J., Newman, T., Wildfeuer, S., & Grigorenko, E.L. (2007). Triarchically based instruction and assessment of sixth-grade mathematics in a Yup'ik cultural setting in Alaska. *International Journal of Giftedness and Creativity, 21,* 6–19.

Sternberg, R.J., Nokes, K., Geissler, P.W., Prince, R., Okatcha, F., Bundy, D.A., & Grigorenko, E.L. (2001). The relationship between academic and practical intelligence: A case study in Kenya. *Intelligence, 29,* 401–418.

Sternberg, R.J., Powell, C., McGrane, P.A., & McGregor, S. (1997). Effects of a parasitic infection on cognitive functioning. *Journal of Experimental Psychology: Applied, 3,* 67–76.

Sternberg, R.J., & The Rainbow Project Collaborators (2005). Augmenting the SAT through assessments of analytical, practical, and creative skills. In W. Camara & E. Kimmel (Eds.), *Choosing students: Higher education admission tools for the 21st century* (pp. 159–176). Mahwah, NJ: Lawrence Erlbaum Associates.

Sternberg, R.J., & The Rainbow Project Collaborators (2006). The Rainbow Project: Enhancing the SAT through assessments of analytical, practical and creative skills. *Intelligence, 34,* 321–350.

Super, C.M., & Harkness, S. (1986). The developmental niche: A conceptualization at the interface of child and culture. *International Journal of Behavioral Development, 9,* 545–569.

Thurstone, L.L. (1921). Intelligence and its measurement. *Journal of Educational Psychology 16,* 201–207.

Tzuriel, D. (1995). Dynamic-interactive assessment: The legacy of L. S. Vygotsky and current developments. Unpublished manuscript.

Vygotsky, L.S. (1978). *Mind in society: The development of higher psychological processes.* Cambridge, MA: Harvard University Press.

White, G.M. (1985). Premises and purposes in a Solomon Islands ethnopsychology. In G.M. White & J. Kirkpatrick (Eds.), *Person, self, and experience: Exploring Pacific ethnopsychologies* (pp. 328–366). Berkeley, CA: University of California Press.

Yang, S., & Sternberg, R.J. (1997a). Conceptions of intelligence in ancient Chinese philosophy. *Journal of Theoretical and Philosophical Psychology, 17,* 101–119.

Yang, S., & Sternberg, R.J. (1997b). Taiwanese Chinese people's conceptions of intelligence. *Intelligence, 25,* 21–36.

CHAPTER 20

Navigating Cultures

The Role of Metacognitive Cultural Intelligence

JENNIFER KLAFEHN, PREETA M. BANERJEE, AND CHI-YUE CHIU

"An American manager was sent to Malaysia to close a major deal. While there, he was introduced to someone he thought was named Roger so he proceeded to call him 'Rog' several times during the negotiations. Unfortunately, this important potential client was a *rajah,* which is an important Malaysian title of nobility. The U.S. tendency to use first names, and even more familiar abbreviated names, was the cause of the serious error in this case. Rather than showing respect, the American appeared disrespectful and insensitive. When the error was discovered, the damage had been done" (Ricks, 1999, p. 98).

In this anecdote, the American manager failed to capitalize on what might have been a very lucrative business venture due simply to the fact that he was undereducated with regard to the cultural norms and customs governing the Malaysian lifestyle. So-called cultural blunders like the one described above occur more frequently than anyone would care to admit. Given the speed with which today's organizational playground is becoming increasingly diverse and globalized, these cross-cultural interactions are not only here to stay, but may one day come to characterize the majority of business transactions that occur around the world. It is no surprise, then, that individuals adept at dealing effectively with these kinds of intercultural situations are extremely coveted by today's organizations. Also high in demand is the psychological research aimed at identifying the specific blend of personality traits, experiential knowledge, and interpersonal skills that best characterize these unique, *culturally intelligent* individuals.

Cultural intelligence (CQ) refers to an individual's ability to engage successfully in diverse cultural environments or settings (Ang, Van Dyne, Koh, Ng, Templer, Tay, & Chandrasekar, 2007; Earley & Ang, 2003). According to Ang and colleagues (2007), CQ is a multidimensional construct comprised of four distinct facets (i.e., metacognitive CQ, cognitive CQ, motivational CQ, and behavioral CQ). Each facet is thought to capture a different ability or type of CQ that helps individuals deal with cross-cultural situations in different ways. In this chapter, we focus on the metacognitive facet, which refers to the mental processes directed at acquiring, comprehending, and calibrating cultural knowledge (Ang et al., 2007). These metacognitive processes improve performance in diverse cultural settings by enhancing (a) contextualized (vs. abstract) thinking: a thinking style characterized by high degrees of sensitivity to the cultural embeddedness of human motivations and actions, and (b) cognitive flexibility: the discriminative use of normative schemas and behavioral scripts in response to the shifting cultural expectations in the environment. As stated by Ang et al. (2007), "those with high metacognitive CQ are consciously aware of others' cultural preferences before and during interactions. They also question cultural assumptions and adjust their mental models during and after interactions."

In this chapter, we discuss metacognitive capability from the perspective of its antecedents, that is, the psychological mechanisms responsible for its development. Specifically, we examine the experiential factors that differentially contribute to contextualized thinking and cognitive flexibility. For example, we posit that exposure to multicultural experiences increases cognitive flexibility and contextualized thinking by providing individuals with a broader set of cultural knowledge on which to base their thoughts, feelings, and actions (or cognitive CQ, see Ang et al., 2007). However, exposure to diverse cultures can also increase intercultural uncertainty, leading to lower levels of cognitive flexibility and a higher reliance on abstract, decontextualized thinking. We also hypothesize that openness to experience, one of the Big Five personality factors (McCrae & Costa, 1997), moderates the link between multicultural experiences and these two metacognitive capabilities, such that more open individuals respond in a more culturally intelligent manner as their multicultural experiences grow. In this chapter, we elucidate the propositions of this metacognitive model of CQ and review the research evidence for each of them.

A METACOGNITIVE MODEL OF CQ

For ease of interpretation, the model can be broken down into three distinct parts, each of which represents a different stage in the development of the metacognitive capability underlying CQ. The first part, exposure to multicultural experiences, is crucial to metacognitive CQ because it provides the basis for which individuals can make culturally appropriate judgments and decisions.

The second part of the model relates to the effects of multicultural experiences. Oftentimes, exposure to an unfamiliar culture will lead individuals to feel a sense of uncertainty toward that particular culture. This uncertainty increases as the perceived distance between the individuals' own culture and the foreign culture increases. When the distance between the two cultures is quite large, the resultant uncertainty can manifest itself in several ways. First, individuals will tend to think less flexibly in the face of novel ideas. Second, they will employ the use of stereotypes as shortcuts to explain novel behaviors in the other culture. In essence, the greater the distance (uncertainty) an individual perceives to exist between two cultures, the greater the chance that individual will rely on abstract thinking to guide his or her judgment and decision-making processes.

Certain personality traits, such as openness to experience, determine whether the effects of multicultural experiences are beneficial or detrimental to an individuals' level of metacognitive CQ. Thus, openness composes the third and final part of our model. Individuals who are higher in openness are less negatively affected by intercultural uncertainty and use multicultural experiences to their benefit. In response to an unfamiliar culture, these individuals apply cultural knowledge flexibly to their environment in a manner that capitalizes on the context of the situation. In essence, openness to experience moderates the impact of multicultural experiences, and ultimately distinguishes between those who have high or low levels of metacognitive CQ.

In short, our model emphasizes that metacognitive CQ is jointly determined by individuals' multicultural experiences and psychological propensities. Although we recognize that a variety of other factors and/or facets may also contribute to the development of metacognitive CQ (e.g., cultural identity management, Benet-Martínez, Leu, Lee, & Morris, 2002), we chose to limit our review to the factors most pertinent to our proposed model.

Cognitive Flexibility

In the context of metacognitive CQ, cognitive flexibility refers to the ability to deploy cultural knowledge flexibly so that an individual may meet shifting cultural demands and achieve his or her valued goal in the intercultural environment. Two examples of cognitive flexibility are cultural frame switching and the generation of culturally integrative ideas.

Cultural frames are cognitive reflections of how different cultures interpret the world around them. In order to switch cultural frames, individuals must be sufficiently well versed in a culture outside their own so that they are capable of adopting either the native or foreign cultural frame when interpreting their experiences. The most widely studied population in this domain of investigation is that of the bicultural. Biculturals are unique in that they embody more than one cultural identity. As such, they are able to think, act, and behave as members of two distinct cultures, making them extremely good candidates for research on frame switching.

Some of the most frequently studied biculturals are Chinese Americans, Chinese Canadians, highly Westernized Hong Kong Chinese, and Beijing Chinese university students. In these studies, situations signaling greater appropriateness of the Chinese cultural frame prompt bicultural individuals to display responses characteristic of Chinese culture—they explain behaviors in terms of situational press or group pressure (Hong, Morris, Chiu, & Benet-Martínez, 2000), describe themselves in a more humble and interdependent manner (Ross, Xun, & Wilson, 2002; Sui, Zhu, & Chiu, 2007), and engage in more cooperative behaviors when working with their friends (Wong & Hong, 2005). In contrast, when the situation signals greater appropriateness of the American cultural frame, these individuals will display behaviors characteristic of American culture—they explain behaviors in terms of personal qualities (Hong et al., 2000), describe themselves in primarily independent and positive terms (Ross et al., 2002; Sui et al., 2007), and display more competitive behaviors when working with others (Wong & Hong, 2005). In short, when the situation calls for Chinese responses, bicultural individuals downplay the positive distinctiveness of the self, preferring behavioral strategies that promote in-group harmony. When the situation calls for American responses, however, these individuals become more aware of their positive distinctiveness, and prefer behavioral strategies that reveal personal competitiveness.

Individuals with high metacognitive CQ are thought to behave much as bicultural individuals do. For example, a cognitively flexible American expatriate in Beijing may choose to interpret an event he or she encounters from an American perspective or from a Chinese perspective, depending on which interpretation is most appropriate for the situation. Similarly, a cognitively flexible Chinese student in America might choose to behave differently around American students as opposed to Chinese students in an effort to better blend in with his or her peers. In both cases, cognitive flexibility characterizes culturally intelligent individuals' discriminative facility by emphasizing their ability to react in response to changing environmental demands.

The ability to integrate ideas from diverse cultural sources is another hallmark of culturally intelligent individuals that results from cognitive flexibility. Instead of compartmentalizing ideas by their cultural origins, cognitive flexibility allows individuals to place seemingly nonoverlapping, even contradictory, ideas from two cultures in cognitive juxtaposition and integrate them to form a creative idea (Chiu & Hong, 2005). McDonald's rice burger, for example, is a creative integration of Asian rice-based cuisine and the traditional North American hamburger. Shanghai Tang fashion is another example of creative integration that was formed by synthesizing traditional Chinese costumes with Western fashion design.

The Role of Multicultural Experiences

The extent to which one can engage in cognitively flexible behaviors is related to the degree to which one can be immersed in a variety of multicultural experiences. Individuals with extensive exposure in a second culture, for example, often acquire insider expertise in that second culture. As a result, they can spontaneously and effortlessly switch between cultural frames as the situation demands, thereby maintaining cognitive and behavioral congruence with the culture that is being cued at that time. Take, for example, the interpretation of written text. When encountering a text in our native culture, we, as members of that culture, are naturally able to decode the nuanced cultural meanings in the text. When presented with text from a foreign culture, however, only those individuals with extensive experience in that culture can switch to the foreign cultural frame and decode similar nuances in the text. Such flexibility in cultural frame switching has not been found among individuals with limited exposure to a second culture (Fu, Chiu, Morris, & Young, 2007).

Extensiveness of multicultural experiences also plays a significant role in developing the ability to integrate nonoverlapping ideas from different cultural sources. There are several research findings to support this contention. First, individuals with extensive exposure to other cultures tend to have higher levels of cognitive complexity (Benet-Martínez, Lee, & Leu, 2006). For example, when asked to perform a creativity task, individuals with more extensive multicultural experiences are more likely to consult ideas from diverse cultural sources to expand an initial rough idea (Leung & Chiu, in press-a).

Second, a number of studies have shown that individuals who engage in multicultural activities or who have had a variety of multicultural experiences across the course of their lives are, in general, more creative than those who have not. Some of the experiences examined by these studies include studying abroad (Schuster, Zimmerman, Schertzer, & Beamish, 1998) and participating in diverse groups (Guimerà, Uzzi, Spiro, & Amaral, 2005). One limitation of these studies is that their findings are correlational. Hence, it is unclear whether multicultural experiences contribute to cognitive flexibility or whether cognitively flexible individuals tend to seek out multicultural experiences. Recently, however, Leung and Chiu (in press-a) found that exposing participants to various multicultural events in a controlled setting increased their creative performance when assessed both immediately after exposure and after a week had passed. Such findings lend support to the positive effects of multicultural experiences on creativity.

The Moderating Role of Openness

The results reviewed here indicate that exposure to multicultural experiences is necessary for the development of cognitive flexibility, a metacognitive component of CQ. As mentioned earlier, however, mere immersion in multicultural experiences does not guarantee a higher level of metacognitive CQ. Case in point: investigators studying Chinese Americans have found that, despite their extensive exposure to Chinese and American cultures, some participants have tremendous difficulty shifting between cultural frames (Benet-Martínez et al., 2002). These individuals, unlike their proficient, frame-switching counterparts, tend to cling to their heritage culture and exhibit heightened physiological reactivity when cultural demands in the environment change (Chao, Chen, Roisman, & Hong, 2007; Hong, Wan, No, & Chiu, 2007). Studies conducted on immigrant populations have also revealed that, when encountering a new mainstream culture, instead of assimilating into the new culture, some immigrants become gradually encapsulated within the norms and values of an earlier era in their homeland, and thus adhere more strongly to their heritage culture than do members of their home country (Kim, Yang, Atkinson, Wolfe, & Hong, 2001). For instance, some Chinatown Chinese Americans adhere more strongly to traditional Chinese values and beliefs than do native Chinese in major cities in China. These results suggest that the cognitive benefits of multicultural experiences are not as straightforward as one would think. Rather, it appears that such effects are contingent on some other moderating variables.

One such moderator is the level of openness to experience. Openness to experience has long held a place in the cross-cultural literature. Generally speaking, individuals high in openness are more worldly, innovative, spontaneous, and diplomatic than their low-openness counterparts (George & Zhou, 2001; Hofstede, de Raad, & Goldberg, 1992). Furthermore, high-openness individuals are not only more likely to be accepting of new ideas and ways of thinking, but they are also more likely to act empathically toward members of another culture. For example, rather than refusing to follow a set of non-native norms, individuals high in openness will be more willing to adapt their thoughts and actions to those of another culture than will individuals low in openness.

In contrast, individuals who are low in openness remain very intolerant of uncertainty. They crave predictability, order, and firm answers (Kruglanski & Webster, 1996). These individuals also tend to display a rigid adherence to the norms, values, and beliefs of their native culture, as they often provide consensually validated answers to questions. When retrieving ideas from memory to solve problems, for example, they are likely to retrieve conventional ideas instead of novel ones (Ip, Chen, & Chiu, 2006). Research has provided clear support for the hypothesis that less open individuals tend to adhere rigidly to the dominant interpretive frame in their own culture. For example, compared to close-minded Americans, close-minded Chinese are more likely to explain everyday events in terms of group factors rather than personal factors. Close-minded Americans, on the other hand, are more likely to explain the same events in terms of personal factors rather than group factors. When comparing Americans and Chinese who are high in openness, however, no cultural differences in causal interpretation are found (Chiu, Morris, Hong, & Menon, 2000).

Close-minded individuals are also less likely to benefit from the ideas gained through multicultural experiences than are individuals who are high in openness. Thus, it is not surprising that studies have found close-mindedness to moderate the tendency of immigrants to become culturally encapsulated. When individuals migrate to a new country, those who are more (versus less) close-minded adhere more strongly to the norms, beliefs, and practices of their heritage culture. This is particularly true when people migrate to a new country with their co-nationals, presumably because living together with their co-nationals affords more opportunities for them to practice and hence preserve their heritage culture (Kashima & Loh, 2006; Kosic, Kruglanski, Pierro, & Mannetti, 2004).

While the majority of studies examining openness to experience have been limited to cross-cultural contexts, other areas of research have begun to realize its significance, as well. One area in which openness has received a lot of attention is organizational psychology. Studies examining everything from team dynamics to expatriate assignments have shown that individuals high in openness perform substantially better on tasks measuring levels of creative ability and divergent thinking than do individuals low in openness (Huang, Chi, & Lawler, 2005; King, Walker, & Broyles, 1996). Their wide acceptance of new ideas and unique approaches to problem solving also help make difficult situations more readily navigable, particularly when those situations involve negotiating with people from different organizations or cultural backgrounds (Ang, Van Dyne, & Koh, 2006). Consistent with this idea, high-openness individuals are particularly likely to benefit from multicultural experiences. Recall that individuals with more extensive multicultural experiences tend to perform better on creativity tasks (Leung & Chiu, in press-a). Openness to experience has been shown to moderate this relationship, such that extensive exposure to multicultural experiences predicts better creative performance only among high-openness individuals (Leung & Chiu, in press-b). There is also evidence that individuals with higher levels of personality flexibility (a major component of openness) perform better in a culturally diverse work group (van der Zee, Atsma, & Brodbeck, 2004).

In summary, extensive exposure to multicultural experiences affords more opportunities for gaining insider expertise in other cultures, and therefore increases an individual's ability to accumulate resources from multiple cultures to respond discriminatively and appropriately to changing environmental demands. It is the level of openness to experience, however, that ultimately determines how much an individual will benefit from multicultural experiences, and, more importantly, whether those experiences will be parlayed into CQ. Those with high levels of openness behave more flexibly with more exposure to multicultural experiences and develop higher levels of metacognitive CQ. Those who are close-minded, however, tend to adhere rigidly to the norms and practices of their native culture, independent of their amount of exposure to other cultures.

Contextualized versus Abstract Cultural Reasoning

Socially intelligent individuals encode social information in a contextualized manner (Cheng, Chiu, Hong, & Cheung, 2001; Chiu, Hong, Mischel, & Shoda, 1995). In other words, they tend to encode situations in "if–then," conditional terms (i.e., *if* a certain environmental or psychological condition is present, *then* a certain behavior will follow). In contrast, socially incompetent individuals tend to encode social situations in abstract, decontextualized terms (i.e., a certain behavior occurs because the actor possesses a certain disposition or is a certain kind of person).

Extending this idea to intercultural interactions, individuals with high levels of metacognitive CQ behave similarly to socially intelligent individuals, in that they tend to encode behaviors of people from foreign cultures contextually. They are sensitive to the distribution of ideas and goals in the foreign culture and the applicability of these goals in the culture. For example, Americans high in metacognitive CQ know that Americans are generally reluctant to punish a group for an individual member's misconduct, but they will do so when the salient goal in the situation is to increase group cohesion. They also know that Chinese are more inclined to punish the group, and are particularly likely to do so when the dominant goal is to ensure that no group members will perform similar misconduct in the future (see Chao, Zhang, & Chiu, 2006a). In contrast, Americans with lower levels of metacognitive CQ do not possess such nuanced cultural knowledge and tend to predict behaviors on the basis of broad, decontextualized cultural stereotypes (e.g., Americans are individualistic and Chinese are collectivistic).

Much like cognitive flexibility, the tendency to engage in contextualized versus abstract cultural reasoning is also related to the kind of multicultural experiences an individual encounters. As noted, not all individuals will benefit from multicultural experiences. Furthermore, some multicultural experiences may actually *hurt* an individual's performance on future culturally related tasks. Culture shock is one phenomenon through which these negative effects are often observed. Despite using cultural training programs as intercultural "buffers" for their employees, organizations still face an alarming number of failed expatriate assignments each year, due mainly to problems associated with culture shock (Kaye & Taylor, 1997; Ward, Bochner, & Furnham, 2001).

Studies have shown, for example, that, while abroad, expatriates report feeling more depressed, anxious, and angry than when they were in their home country (Sussman, 2000). They also report having increasingly negative feelings toward the local culture, such that they became irritable, close-minded, and impatient with the people of their host country. Although it can be said that the psychological costs associated with expatriate culture shock are quite substantial, it is also important to recognize that the financial costs associated with a failed assignment can be just as great. For example, it has been estimated that a single failed expatriate assignment can cost an organization up to five times the executive's salary, which, depending on the individual and his or her assignment, could mean a potential loss of millions of dollars.

Multicultural experiences can negatively influence areas outside of expatriate performance, as well. Other studies examining group performance, for example, have shown that working in a multicultural team often causes more conflict between group members than working in a team whose members are of the same culture (Adler, 2002; Jentsch, Hoeft, Fiore, & Bowers, 2004; Maznevski, 1994). This is due to the fact that heterogeneous group members lack a common ground. Instead of working together to fulfill the purpose for which the group was initially formed, they become overwhelmed by others' stylistic differences and interpersonal approaches to solving group problems. As a result of this cultural discord, individuals' own cultures begin to feel threatened and their levels of intercultural uncertainty increase. Abstract, decontextualized reasoning, however, can reduce this uncertainty by attributing cross-situational consistency and temporal stability to the structure of the cultural group's behaviors. Therefore, as individuals' uncertainty increases, so too will their reliance on abstract, top-down processing, leading them to more frequently engage in the use of heuristics and stereotypes, as opposed to hard facts, when making cultural assessments (Kruglanski, Pierro, Mannetti, & DeGrada, 2005).

The Role of Intercultural Distance

The preceding analysis implies that culture shock increases the likelihood of engaging in decontextualized cultural thinking. People are more likely to experience culture shock when they encounter a culture very different from their own. Indeed, there is some preliminary evidence for this hypothesized link. In one study, Chao and Chiu (2007) applied multidimensional scaling to determine the perceived similarity between different cultures among American university students. These investigators found that American students perceived Australian culture as very similar to their own culture, whereas Brazilian culture was seen as very dissimilar to American culture. Next, another group of American university students was asked to imagine having to spend a few months in either Australia or Brazil. Participants who imagined having to live in Brazil reported higher levels of uncertainty and anxiety than did participants who imagined having to live in Australia. More importantly, on a subsequent unrelated task, compared to those in the Australia condition, participants in the Brazil condition displayed more abstract thinking; that is, they believed more strongly that a person's dispositions determined his or her behaviors in concrete situations. This result indicates that even imagining the self living in an unfamiliar culture can evoke feelings of uncertainty and anxiety and strengthen a *generalized* tendency to engage in decontextualized thinking.

The Moderating Role of Openness

As we have seen, encountering an unfamiliar culture elicits feelings of uncertainty. Because uncertainty is a cognitively uncomfortable state, people engage in abstract social reasoning to reduce feelings of uncertainty. However, individuals differ in the amount of uncertainty they feel should be reduced. Close-minded individuals, for example, crave sureness and predictability and therefore have lower tolerance for ambiguity and uncertainty. These individuals, when placed in an unfamiliar culture, are particularly likely to experience difficulty in managing the uncertainty in this setting. As such, they are likely to apply cultural stereotypes to guide their decision.

In support of this hypothesis, Chao, Zhang, and Chiu (2006b) found that when American university students were asked to manage a conflict in China (an unfamiliar cultural setting), they were more close-minded and more likely to be influenced by their stereotypes of Chinese conflict management styles. Likewise, when Beijing Chinese were asked to allocate a reward between two coworkers in the United States (also an unfamiliar cultural setting), the more close-minded they were, the more closely their allocation would follow their stereotypes of Chinese distributive preferences.

In short, encountering an unfamiliar cultural setting elicits uncertainty and decreases contextualized thinking. However, being open-minded can increase tolerance of uncertainty and hence reduce an individual's vulnerability to the negative effects of unfamiliar experiences.

In summary, the evidence reviewed in this section supports five fundamental propositions in the model: (1) cognitive flexibility and contextualized thinking are metacognitive processes underlying CQ; (2) exposure to multicultural experiences can promote cognitive flexibility and contextualized thinking by providing individuals with insider knowledge of diverse cultures (cognitive CQ); (3) exposure to experiences with an unfamiliar culture can hinder the development of cognitive flexibility and contextualized thinking by eliciting intercultural uncertainty; (4) having high (vs. low) levels of openness to experience tends to enhance the facilitative effects of multicultural experiences on cognitive flexibility and contextualized thinking; and (5) at the same time, openness reduces the negative impact of intercultural uncertainty on cognitive flexibility and contextualized thinking. In the next section, we discuss the implications of our model within an organizational context.

IMPLICATIONS FOR ORGANIZATIONS

Over the course of the last decade, businesses have found themselves increasingly at the mercy of the global market. This emphasis on international boundary-spanning has gained so much momentum in recent years that it has become one of the main determining factors of a company's competitiveness and overall success (Cox, Lobel, & McLeod, 1991). For example, not only are four out of every five new U.S. jobs said to be generated due to increases in international commerce, but a full 33 percent of U.S. corporate profits can be attributed to growth in international trade, as well (Ting-Toomey, 2001). Organizations are also finding it increasingly necessary to send their workers overseas to perform various job-related tasks. Such tasks may include opening foreign branches, filling managerial positions, selecting new employees for hire, or negotiating the terms of a joint venture. Whatever the situation may be, today's employees are participating in multicultural contexts at rates far surpassing those of our predecessors.

Despite these advantages, however, the situation facing today's organizations is still paradoxical: while it certainly remains in an organization's best interest to increase its opportunities for worldwide business ventures, doing so also increases that organization's opportunity for falling victim to messy and potentially detrimental interpersonal transactions. One of the most widely known and commonly frequented transactions of this sort is the cross-cultural negotiation. Cross-cultural negotiation is, by nature, a fastidious and difficult process. In a cross-cultural negotiation, not only are negotiators expected to manage obstacles associated with negotiations in general, but they must do so while interacting on a culturally uneven playing field. For this reason, negotiators who possess business savvy as well as CQ are in high demand among top organizations.

Given this demand, how can an organization increase its cultural capital? One straightforward answer is to enhance employees' CQ by enriching their multicultural experiences. Not surprisingly, there has been a great deal of emphasis in the organizational literature on the role of cultural experience and its differential effects on the development of CQ (Anderson, Lawton, Rexeisen, & Hubbard, 2006; Gibson & Zhong, 2005; Magala, 2006; Masgoret, 2006). Meanwhile, many American universities, inspired by the idea that multicultural experiences enhance CQ, have begun instituting study-abroad programs to better prepare students for entry into the global business environment. These programs allow participants to immerse themselves in a new cultural lifestyle, while giving them an opportunity to earn credit toward their degree at the same time. This experience may include engaging in anything from dining on local cuisine or visiting popular museums to living with a host family or learning the country's native language.

The importance of having many multicultural experiences (in the form of expatriate assignments, group work, or study abroad) cannot be overstated. These experiences provide individuals with knowledge about overall differences in behavioral styles and personalities, allowing them to be more creative in multicultural settings. Without multicultural experiences, individuals would be unable to integrate the cultural knowledge necessary for engagement in culturally intelligent behaviors. Our model suggests, however, that simply creating more opportunities for multicultural learning may not always lead to the development of multicultural intelligence. Consider again the example of study-abroad programs. Although studying abroad can certainly be an enriching experience, often upon arrival in a new country with a very unfamiliar culture, individuals may undergo a shock experience, feeling confused, anxious, or even threatened by their surroundings. To manage the shock experience, some students may resort to abstract cultural reasoning for reducing informational uncertainty in their environment and rely on cultural stereotypes to restore a sense of order and predictability.

Let us return to cross-cultural negotiation as another example. While it can certainly be difficult to conduct negotiations when the people involved come from different organizations, the stakes are raised even higher when they come from completely different cultures.

Now, the already complicated task of social navigation becomes coupled with additional obstacles: language barriers, national traditions, and cultural beliefs. In these situations, the negotiators may also resort to abstract cultural reasoning and apply stereotypes of the outgroup culture indiscriminately to guide their judgments. Engaging in such processes would likely compromise the possibility of a win-win solution to the negotiations.

As stated previously, however, there exist certain groups of people that take to multicultural experiences better than others. Individuals high in openness to experience, for example, are not only well equipped to effectively deal with cultural differences, but are also able to appreciate those differences and learn something from them. This means, when working or studying abroad, high-openness individuals remain relatively free of the pressure and anxiety induced by culture shock, and can instead focus on learning from the experience at hand.

It is important to emphasize that, although individuals differ in their chronic levels of openness to experience, situational factors can increase the need for firm answers and subsequently lower their level of openness. For example, when individuals need to complete a task under time pressure, they are less willing to consider alternatives and instead adhere strongly to conventional wisdom for getting results. These individuals tend to adopt the interpretive frame in their native culture to grasp experiences (Chiu et al., 2000) and resist ideas from foreign cultures (Leung & Chiu, in press-b). Similarly, when individuals encounter a lot of uncertainty in their life, they will also become less open-minded and refuse to consider ideas from foreign cultures (Leung & Chiu, in press-b). Thus, one way organizations can ensure that more of their employees will benefit from multicultural experiences is to reduce the salience of these situational factors in the environment.

Although our analysis focuses on acting competently across national cultures, the theoretical framework proposed in this chapter also provides a way to impact multicultural experiences across other types of cultures, for example, professional cultures (Banerjee & Chiu, 2007). Professional cultures, like national cultures, require the fine art of negotiation. Such an instance exists at the interface between the engineers and marketers in a product development firm. In this situation, negotiation involves boundary spanning (Tushman & Scanlan, 1981), or the recoding of information between two diverse units. A negotiator or boundary spanner must convert words into a second semantic space while retaining the meanings held in the first. In a particular job, one might need to address multiple boundary situations (cultural, functional, organizational, and hierarchical) in order to create and manage the knowledge gained through those interactions.

Our model may prove useful in answering other empirical questions. For example, although much work has been done to parse the effects of multicultural collaborations, few studies have examined these effects within the context of academia. One study that has examined these effects found that authors who collaborated with individuals outside their own department produced more creative work than those who did not (Cheng, Sanchez-Burks, & Lee, 2007). This result is consistent with the propositions of our model, specifically with regard to the differential effects of multicultural experiences on creativity and cognitive flexibility.

Another area of science that has remained untouched is that of organizational social planning. Social planning focuses on how the events and activities leading up to a negotiation affect the building of relational capital among its participating members (see Lin, 1999 for more on relational capital). Studies we are currently conducting examine individual differences in social planning ability, and the ways in which this ability reflects CQ levels. This new area of psychological research should prove to be not only complementary to the extant literature on negotiation but also beneficial to many organizations engaging in cross-cultural business ventures.

CONCLUSION

Attempts to reconcile the effects of multicultural experiences have left many researchers facing a theoretical double-edged sword. On one hand, multicultural experiences broaden peoples' worldview and allow them to become more creative through the integration of new knowledge; however, on the other hand, multicultural experiences, particularly experiences with a highly unfamiliar culture, can be a source of stress and conflict, doing more harm than good to those who participate in them.

In this chapter, we have argued that the psychological uncertainty stemming from multicultural exposure is an inevitable phenomenon. Whether its effects on the development of metacognitive CQ are positive or negative, however, is determined by the level of openness to experience. With this factor as our keystone, we proposed a model of how metacognitive CQ develops by way of dynamic interactions between experiential input and personality factors. We believe this model is capable of not only reconciling the differential effects associated with multicultural experiences, but also providing the field with a theoretical understanding of the ways these effects are parlayed into CQ and subsequent organizational performance.

REFERENCES

Adler, N. (2002). Multicultural teams. In N. Adler (Ed.), *International dimensions of organizational behavior* (4th ed.) (pp. 133–163). Cincinnati, OH: Southwestern.

Anderson, P., Lawton, L., Rexeisen, R., & Hubbard, A. (2006). Short-term study abroad and intercultural sensitivity: A pilot study. *International Journal of Intercultural Relations, 30,* 457–469.

Ang, S., Van Dyne, L., & Koh, C. (2006). Personality correlates of the four-factor model of cultural intelligence. *Group and Organization Management, 31,* 100–123.

Ang, S., Van Dyne, L., Koh, C., Ng, K.Y., Templer, K.J., Tay, C., & Chandrasekar, N.A. (2007). Cultural intelligence: Its measurement and effects on cultural judgment and decision making, cultural adaptation, and task performance. *Management and Organization Review, 3,* 335–371.

Banerjee, P., & Chiu, C-Y. (2007). Professional biculturalism: A new perspective of the R & D and marketing interface. Working paper, University of Illinois at Urbana-Champaign.

Benet-Martínez, V., Lee, F., & Leu, J. (2006). Biculturalism and cognitive complexity: Expertise in cultural representations. *Journal of Cross-Cultural Psychology, 37,* 386–407.

Benet-Martínez, V., Leu, J., Lee, F., & Morris, M. (2002). Negotiating biculturalism: Cultural frame-switching in biculturals with "oppositional" vs. "compatible" cultural identities. *Journal of Cross-Cultural Psychology, 33,* 492–516.

Chao, M.M., & Chiu, C-Y. (2007). Experiencing an unfamiliar cultural promotes abstract thinking. Working paper, University of Illinois at Urbana-Champaign.

Chao, M., Chen, J., Roisman, G.I., & Hong, Y-Y. (2007). Essentializing race: Implications for bicultural individual's cognition and physiological reactivity. *Psychological Science, 18,* 341–348.

Chao, M.M., Zhang, Z-X., & Chiu, C-Y. (2006a). Individual and collective responsibility attribution across cultures. Working paper, University of Illinois at Urbana-Champaign.

Chao, M.M., Zhang, Z-X., & Chiu, C-Y. (2006b). Normative judgments on foreign soil: The role of need for cognitive closure. Working paper, University of Illinois at Urbana-Champaign.

Cheng, C., Chiu, C-Y., Hong, Y., & Cheung, J.S. (2001). Discriminative facility and its role in the perceived quality of interactional experiences. *Journal of Personality, 69,* 765–786.

Cheng, C., Sanchez-Burks, J., & Lee, F. (2007). Identity integration and individual creativity. Paper presented at the Annual Meeting of the Academy of Management, Philadelphia, PA.

Chiu, C-Y., & Hong, Y. (2005). Cultural competence: Dynamic processes. In A. Elliot & C.S. Dweck (Eds.), *Handbook of motivation and competence* (pp. 489–505). New York: Guilford.

Chiu, C-Y., Hong, Y., Mischel, W., & Shoda, Y. (1995). Discriminative facility in social competence. *Social Cognition, 13,* 49–70.

Chiu, C-Y., Morris, M., Hong, Y., & Menon, T. (2000). Motivated cultural cognition: The impact of implicit cultural theories on dispositional attribution varies as a function of need for closure. *Journal of Personality and Social Psychology, 78,* 247–259.

Cox, T.H., Lobel, S.A., & McLeod, P.L. (1991). Effects of ethnic group cultural differences on cooperative and competitive behavior on a group task. *Academy of Management Journal, 34,* 827–847.

Earley, P.C., & Ang, S. (2003). *Cultural intelligence: Individual interactions across cultures.* Palo Alto, CA: Stanford University Press.

Fu, H-Y., Chiu, C-Y., Morris, M.W., & Young, M. (2007). Spontaneous inferences from cultural cues: Varying responses of cultural insiders and outsiders. *Journal of Cross-Cultural Psychology, 38,* 58–75.

George, J., & Zhou, J. (2001). When openness to experience and conscientiousness are related to creative behavior: An interactional approach. *Journal of Applied Psychology, 86,* 513–524.

Gibson, D., & Zhong, M. (2005). Intercultural communication competence in the healthcare context. *International Journal of Intercultural Relations, 29,* 621–634.

Guimerà, R., Uzzi, B., Spiro, J., & Amaral, L.A.N. (2005). Team assembly mechanisms determine collaboration network structure and team performance. *Science, 308,* 697–702.

Hofstede, W.K.B., de Raad, B., & Goldberg, L.R. (1992). Integration of the Big-Five and circumplex approaches to trait structure. *Journal of Personality and Social Psychology, 63,* 146–163.

Hong, Y., Morris, M., Chiu, C-Y., & Benet-Martínez, V. (2000). Multicultural minds: A dynamic constructivist approach to culture and cognition. *American Psychologist, 55,* 709–720.

Hong, Y., Wan, C., No, S., & Chiu, C-Y. (2007). Multicultural identities. In S. Kitayama & D. Cohen (Eds.), *Handbook of cultural psychology* (pp. 323–345). New York: Guilford.

Huang, T-J., Chi, S-C., & Lawler, J. (2005). The relationship between expatriates' personality traits and their adjustment to international assignments. *Journal of Human Resource Management, 16,* 1656–1670.

Ip, G.W-M., Chen, J., & Chiu, C-Y. (2006). The relationship of promotion focus, need for cognitive closure, and categorical accessibility in American and Hong Kong Chinese university students. *Journal of Creative Behavior, 40,* 201–215.

Jentsch, F., Hoeft, R., Fiore, S., & Bowers, C. (2004). "A Frenchman, a German, and an Englishman . . .": The impact of cultural heterogeneity on teams. In E. Salas (Series Ed.) & M. Kaplan (Vol. Ed.), *Advances in human performance and cognitive engineering research. Volume 4. Cultural ergonomics* (pp. 317–340). Oxford: Elsevier.

Kashima, E.S., & Loh, E. (2006). International students' acculturation: Effects of international, conational, and local ties and need for closure. *International Journal of Intercultural Relations, 30,* 471–485.

Kaye, M., & Taylor, C.K. (1997). Expatriate culture shock in China: A study in the Beijing hotel industry. *Journal of Managerial Psychology, 12,* 496–510.

Kim, B.S.K, Yang, P.H, Atkinson, D.R, Wolfe, M.M., & Hong, S. (2001). Cultural value similarities and differences among Asian American ethnic groups. *Cultural Diversity and Ethnic Minority Psychology, 7,* 343–361.

King, L.A., Walker, L.M., & Broyles, S.J. (1996). Creativity and the five-factor model. *Journal of Research in Personality, 30,* 189–203.

Kosic, A., Kruglanski, A.W., Pierro, A., & Mannetti, L. (2004). The social cognitions of immigrants' acculturation: Effects of the need for closure and reference group at entry. *Journal of Personality and Social Psychology, 86,* 796–813.

Kruglanski, A.W., Pierro, A., Mannetti, L., & DeGrada, E. (2005). Groups as epistemic providers: Need for closure and the unfolding of group centrism. *Psychological Review, 113,* 84–100.

Kruglanski, A.W., & Webster, D.M. (1996). Motivated closing of the mind: "Seizing" and "freezing." *Psychological Review, 103,* 263–283.

Leung, A.K-Y., & Chiu, C-Y. (in press-a). Multicultural experiences, idea receptiveness, and creativity. *Journal of Cross-Cultural Psychology.* .

Leung, A.K-Y., & Chiu, C-Y. (in press-b). Interactive effects of multicultural experiences and openness to experience on creativity. *Creativity Research Journal.*

Lin, N. (1999). Building a network theory of social capital. *Connections, 22,* 28–51.

Magala, S. (2006). *Cross-cultural competence.* London: Taylor & Francis.

Masgoret, A-M. (2006). Examining the role of language attitudes and motivation on the sociocultural adjustment and the job performance of sojourners in Spain. *International Journal of Intercultural Relations, 30,* 311–331.

Maznevski, M. (1994). Understanding our differences: Performance in decision-making groups with diverse members. *Human Relations, 47,* 531–552.

McCrae, R.R., & Costa, P.T., Jr. (1997). Personality trait structure as a human universal. *American Psychologist, 52,* 509–516.

Ricks, D. (1999). *Blunders in international business* (3rd ed.). Oxford: Blackwell Publishing.

Ross, M., Xun, W.Q.E., & Wilson, A.E. (2002). Language and the bicultural self. *Personality and Social Psychology Bulletin, 28,* 1040–1050.

Schuster, C.P., Zimmerman, R.O., Schertzer, C.B., & Beamish, P.W. (1998). Assessing the impact of executive MBA international travel courses. *Journal of Marketing Education, 20,* 121–132.

Sui, J., Zhu, Y., & Chiu, C-Y. (2007). Bicultural mind, self-construal, and recognition memory: Cultural priming effects on self- and mother-reference effect. *Journal of Experimental Social Psychology, 43,* 818–824.

Sussman, N.M. (2000). The dynamic nature of cultural identity throughout cultural transitions: Why home is not so sweet? *Personality and Social Psychology Review, 4,* 355–373.

Ting-Toomey, S. (2001). *Managing intercultural conflict effectively.* Thousand Oaks, CA:. Sage Publications.

Tushman, M.L., & Scanlan, T.J. (1981). Boundary spanning individuals: Their role in information transfer and their antecedents. *Academy of Management Journal, 24,* 289–305.

van der Zee, K., Atsma, N., & Brodbeck, F. (2004). The influence of social identity and personality on outcomes of cultural diversity in teams. *Journal of Cross-Cultural Psychology, 35,* 283–303.

Ward, C., Bochner, S., & Furnham, A. (2001). *The psychology of culture shock.* London: Routledge.

Wong, R.Y-M., & Hong, Y. (2005). Dynamic influences of culture on cooperation in the prisoner's dilemma. *Psychological Science, 16,* 429–434.

CHAPTER 21

Social Axioms and Cultural Intelligence
Working Across Cultural Boundaries

KWOK LEUNG AND FULI LI

The world is truly shrinking, as globalizing forces make it commonplace for people of diverse cultural backgrounds to work under the same roof. Migration has also led to ethnic diversity in many countries. While intercultural contact has become a frequent event in many corners of the world, academic research lags behind this social reality. Gelfand, Erez, and Aycan (2007) recently noted that the comparative perspective has dominated the field of cross-cultural organizational psychology. While the literature on cultural similarities and differences in the workplace is extensive, we know relatively little about the dynamics of intercultural contact. It is well documented that such dynamics have major impact on work outcomes in culturally diverse work teams (e.g., Earley & Gibson, 2002).

The framework of cultural intelligence (CQ) was introduced to address this gap (Ang & Van Dyne, 2008; Earley & Ang, 2003). Based on a broad view of intelligence (Sternberg, 1986), CQ refers to the capability to interact efficiently with people of diverse cultural backgrounds and function well in culturally diverse settings. Following well-established frameworks of intelligence that distinguish among metacognitive, cognitive, motivational, and behavioral factors (Sternberg, 1986), CQ is also mapped by these four domains. In short, metacognitive CQ refers to the mental capability to acquire and understand cultural knowledge; cognitive CQ refers to the extent of general knowledge and knowledge structures about culture; motivational CQ refers to the capability to channel energy toward learning about and functioning in culturally diverse situations; and behavioral CQ refers to the capability to behave properly in culturally diverse situations. For evidence in support of this framework, see Ang, Van Dyne, Koh, Ng, Templer, Tay, and Chandrasekar (2007) and Ang & Van Dyne (2008).

The CQ framework represents an important step forward in understanding the processes behind intercultural contact. The major objectives of this chapter are to explore the relationships between CQ and social axioms, a pan-cultural framework of worldviews, and to identify future directions that are inspired by the integration of these two frameworks.

SOCIAL AXIOMS: A PAN-CULTURAL FRAMEWORK OF WORLDVIEWS

The Social Axioms Framework

There is a long tradition of mapping cultures with value dimensions, such as those of Hofstede (1980) and of the more recent GLOBE project, to identify cultural dimensions by means of values and leadership behaviors (House, Hanges, Javidan, Dorfman, & Gupta, 2004). To go beyond value constructs, Leung et al. (2002) have proposed the use of general beliefs, or social axioms, to characterize culture. Social axioms are general and context-free, and may be regarded as "generalized expectancies," a concept proposed by Rotter (1966) to describe locus of control. Leung et al. use the term *social axioms* to label these general beliefs because social axioms represent basic premises that are endorsed and relied upon to help make sense of the individual's life space and to guide actions. Social axioms have been defined by Leung and Bond (2007, p. 198) as follows:

> Social axioms are generalized beliefs about people, social groups, social institutions, the physical environment, or the spiritual world as well as about categories of events and phenomena in the social world. These generalized beliefs are encoded in the form of an assertion about the relationship between two entities or concepts.

To define a comprehensive set of social axioms, Leung and colleagues (2002) drew from the psychological literature, which is mostly Euro-American in origin, and interviewed informants and analyzed cultural sources from Hong Kong and Venezuela. Social axioms follow the structure of "A is related to B," and the relationship may be causal or correlational. An example of one such axiom is, "powerful people tend to exploit others."

Leung and colleagues constructed a Social Axioms Survey with 182 items. Exploratory factor analysis of the data collected from Hong Kong and Venezuela suggested a five-factor model as optimal for these two cultural groups. This five-factor model was subsequently confirmed in three more countries: the United States, Japan, and Germany. To establish the universality of the five-factor structure, Leung and Bond (2004) orchestrated a global project involving 40 national/cultural groups. Again, the five-factor model emerged from a meta-analytic procedure that did not assume any structure in the data, both for the 40 sets of student data as well as the 13 sets of adult data collected. This structure was subsequently confirmed by multilevel factor analysis, a more stringent statistical technique (Cheung, Leung, & Au, 2006). The final structure adopted for the student samples contains 39 items, which optimize cross-cultural equivalence across the 40 cultural groups in the sample.

Factor one is labeled *social cynicism,* because the items suggest a negative view of human nature, a bias against some social groups, a mistrust of social institutions, and a belief that people have a tendency to ignore ethical standards. The second factor is labeled *social complexity,* because the items suggest that there are multiple ways to solve a problem, and that people's behavior may vary across situations. The third factor is labeled *reward for application,* because the items suggest that the investment of effort, knowledge, careful planning and other resources will lead to positive outcomes. The fourth factor is labeled *religiosity,* and the items assert the existence of a supernatural being and the beneficial social functions of religious institutions and practices. The fifth factor is labeled *fate control,* because the items suggest that life events are predetermined by external forces, but that there are ways in which people can influence these forces. In contrast to reward for application, the interventions do not emphasize the exertion of effort.

A number of individual-level studies have reported meaningful relationships between the five axiom dimensions and a wide spectrum of variables (for a review, see Leung & Bond, 2004). For instance, Singelis, Hubbard, Her, and An (2003) found that social cynicism correlated negatively with interpersonal trust; social complexity correlated positively with cognitive flexibility; reward for application was related to trying harder the next time when unsuccessful; religiosity correlated positively with traditional Christian beliefs; fate control correlated positively with external locus of control. Most recently, Leung, Au, Huang, Kurman, Niit, and Niit (2007) found generally low correlations between the five axiom dimensions and the ten value types of Schwartz (1992) across several cultural groups, supporting the distinctiveness of axioms from values.

Social Axioms as Adaptive Responses to the Environment

Leung and Bond (2004) have adopted a functionalist perspective on social axioms by assuming that the axioms are pivotal to human survival and adaptation. In evolutionary psychology, it has been argued that competence in two broad domains—social and problem-solving—is needed to explore and survive the social and physical world (Keller, 1997). In the social domain, the ability to deceive others and to detect deception has been documented extensively among primates and humans (e.g., Humphrey, 1983; Whiten & Byrne, 1997). Given that gullibility is dangerous for survival, Leung and Bond proposed that the dimension of social cynicism represents a response to the need to be vigilant about potential exploitation and deceits in a world that is sometimes benign and sometimes malicious.

In the problem-solving domain, Leung and Bond (2004) proposed at least three fundamental issues that need to be considered for overcoming problems encountered in social life. The first issue is concerned with whether or not the problems encountered are generally solvable. The dimension of fate control is related to the perception of the solvability of problems, and high fate control is associated with the belief that life events are determined by fate, but at the same time people can find ways to alter the decree of fate to improve their outcomes. This notion resembles the construct of secondary control, which focuses on accommodating existing realities to maximize well-being (Weisz, Rothbaum, & Blackburn, 1984).

The second issue is whether or not effort will lead to rewards, and the dimension of reward for application is related to this assessment. If the relationship between the exertion of effort and success is seen as weak, there is no point trying, a logic that forms the basis of expectancy model (Vroom, 1964).

The third issue is the perceived complexity of problems and the existence of multiple, equally effective solutions. The dimension of social complexity represents a general judgment about whether the social world is complex and pluralistic, and whether a "best solution" exists. This judgment affects how a problem is approached and how much time is spent searching for more alternatives versus perfecting a chosen solution.

Finally, humans need to seek meaning in their existence (e.g., Williams, 1997), and spiritual activities provide perhaps the most important source of meaning for many people throughout the world. Leung and Bond (2004) proposed that the dimension of religiosity reflects the importance of meaning for human existence, and religion as a major source of meaning in diverse cultures of the world.

Social Axioms and Cultural Intelligence

CQ is assumed to be influenced by personal attributes (Ng & Earley, 2006) and social axioms represent important types of personal attributes. Research on social axioms and CQ is nascent, and therefore research on the relationship between the two is lacking, as a result we have drawn upon indirect research findings to speculate about this relationships.

In the social axioms project (Leung & Bond, 2004), "citizen" means of axiom dimensions for a cultural group can be obtained by aggregating the responses of the respondents from the group. In other words, cultural means can be obtained for the five axiom dimensions for a given cultural group, which makes it possible to relate them to diverse country-level indexes of adjustment and reactions to difficulties across a wide range of cultural groups. Our analysis is at the culture level, with cultural group as the unit of analysis. In addition, a number of studies have examined the relationship between social axioms and adjustment-related variables at the individual level. These findings provided the basis for our development of propositions about the relationship between social axioms and CQ.

Social Cynicism

Leung and Bond (2004) reported that people from cultures higher in social cynicism reported lower satisfaction in the workplace and with life in general, lower hedonic balance (positive affect minus negative affect), more in-group disagreement, and less probability of endorsing achievement via conformity. At the individual level, Bond, Leung, Au, Tong, and Chemonges-Nielson (2004) found that social cynicism was related negatively to the use of the collaborative and compromising styles in resolving a conflict. Fu and colleagues (2004) found that social cynicism was related to the use of assertive and relationship-based influence strategies. Singelis et al. (2003) found that social cynicism correlated negatively with social desirability, interpersonal trust, and cognitive flexibility. Finally, Neto (2006) found that social cynicism was positively correlated with ageism and loneliness, and negatively correlated with self-esteem.

These results seem to suggest that because of a malevolent view of the world and the worry of exploitation, people high in social cynicism often adopt a detached, guarded, and distrustful style in conducting their social lives. Their constant concern with potential exploitation seems to result in unpleasant interactions with others and negative affect.

We propose that social cynicism is likely to relate to low CQ because people high in social cynicism may not trust members from other cultural groups and are less likely to engage in behaviors that facilitate intercultural interaction. In the cross-cultural competency literature, it is widely acknowledged that flexibility is an important personal attribute contributing to cross-cultural competence (Johnson, Lenartowicz, & Apud, 2006). People high in social cynicism are unlikely to display a cooperative, flexible interpersonal style, which may lead to unpleasant incidents and even conflict across cultural boundaries.

We further expect that social cynicism is negatively related to all four components of CQ. People high in social cynicism are preoccupied with guarding their self-interest and are detached from others. They are unlikely to invest cognitive resources in acquiring and understanding cultural knowledge, and as a result their general knowledge and knowledge structures about other cultures should be low. Because they lack trust in people and are not keen to be cooperative, they are unlikely to be motivated to learn about other cultures and how to effectively interact with members from other cultures. Finally, their lack of flexibility is unlikely to help them behave properly in culturally diverse situations.

Reward for Application

Leung and Bond (2004) found that people from cultures higher in reward for application reported less alcohol consumption and less tolerance for divorce. Bond et al. (2004) found that reward for application was related to the conflict style of accommodation. Fu et al. (2004) found that reward for application was related to the use of persuasive strategy in influencing others. Neto (2006) found that reward for application was correlated with mastery. Finally, Safdar, Lewis, and Daneshpour (2006) found that reward for application was related to the active coping style.

These results seem to suggest that because reward for application involves a belief in the positive consequences of the exertion of effort, people who endorse it are willing to confront difficulties, both physical and interpersonal. They are also able to tolerate difficulties in the process of overcoming them. Thus, we propose that reward for application is positively related to CQ. It is interesting to speculate which component of CQ is most strongly related to reward for application. Zhou, Leung, and Bond (2007) presented some evidence that reward for application is related to the exertion of effort, but there is no evidence that it is linked to effectiveness and achievement. In other words, reward for application promotes "working hard," but not necessarily "working smart." Thus, reward for application may not be related to the metacognitive component of CQ, but it should be positively related to the other three components. People high in reward for application are willing to exert effort to learn about other cultures, which should result in high cognitive and motivational CQ. In addition, these people are also willing to work on and tolerate difficulties, which should help them behave properly in culturally diverse situations.

Social Complexity

Bond et al. (2004) found that social complexity was related to the conflict style of compromise and of collaboration as well as the coping style of problem solving. Singelis et al. (2003) found that social complexity was related to cognitive flexibility. Neto (2006) found that social complexity was positively correlated to mastery and self-esteem, and negatively with ageism. Social complexity was also found to relate to openness, a Big Five personality dimension (Chen, Fok, Bond, & Matsumoto, 2006).

These results seem to suggest that social complexity is related to an open-minded, pluralistic style in dealing with problems and interacting with others. Given that openness, a Big Five personality dimension, is related to all components of CQ (Ang, Van Dyne, & Koh, 2006), we expect a positive relationship between social complexity and CQ. Specifically, social complexity should show a positive relationship with metacognitive CQ, because people high in social complexity are willing to explore diverse strategies in learning about other cultures. As a result, they should also be able to master cultural knowledge and hence have good cognitive CQ. Their pluralistic approach to interpersonal relationships should help them behave appropriately in culturally diverse situations. It is unclear, however, whether social complexity is related to motivational CQ. It is possible that people high in social complexity are curious about other cultures and hence are motivated to learn about them. It is also possible these people are just open-minded and pluralistic, and they may not be particularly keen to learn about other cultures. These two possibilities need to be evaluated in future research.

Religiosity

People from cultures higher in religiosity reported less alcohol consumption, higher hedonic balance (positive affect minus negative affect), and higher agreeableness, one of the Big Five personality dimensions. Hui, Bond, and Ng (2007) found that religiosity was negatively related to death anxiety. Fu et al. (2004) found that religiosity was related to the use of the relationship-based and assertive strategies in influencing others. Bond et al. (2004) reported that religiosity was related to both the accommodating conflict style and the competitive or dominant conflict style.

These results suggest that people high in religiosity are easygoing and happy, but also assertive, probably because of their emphasis on firm principles and rules. Consistent with this conclusion, Leung et al. (2007) found that religiosity was related to the values of benevolence and tradition. Tradition involves rules, and people high in religiosity are motivated to comply with them, which may result in an unyielding stance.

We expect that religiosity is positively related to CQ. Ang et al. (2006) found that agreeableness, a Big Five personality dimension, was related to behavioral CQ, suggesting that there should be a positive relationship between religiosity and behavioral CQ. However, given that people high in religiosity may sometimes be assertive and strict in following traditional conventions, they may not be flexible in intercultural contact. Thus, the relationship between religiosity and behavioral CQ may not be strong. It is not clear whether religiosity will show any relationship with the other three components of CQ.

Fate Control

People from cultures that are higher in fate control have an elevated likelihood of death from heart diseases and suicide, and report lower job satisfaction. Bond et al. (2004) found that fate control was related to the coping style of distancing, a tendency to avoid thinking about difficulties, and to the wishful thinking coping style, which involves fantasizing and daydreaming. Hui, Bond, and Ng (2007) found that fate control was positively related to death anxiety.

Fate control also involves a belief in proactive intervention for improving one's fate. Singelis et al. (2003) found that fate control was related to having a lucky number and reading horoscopes, activities that aim at improving an individual's fate. Fu et al. (2004) found that fate control was related to the use of the assertive strategy in influencing others, supporting the argument that fate control is more than just passive acceptance of undesirable events. Finally, Zhou et al. (2007) found that children from cultures that are high in fate control showed high academic achievements.

These results seem to suggest that fate control may be related to passivity in domains that are seen as unalterable, but it may also promote active intervention in domains in which fate is seen as playing a significant role. In the absence of prior research, it is difficult to predict the way people high in fate control would view a culturally diverse situation. If they view it as unalterable, they may be passive and accept any outcome, which would result in a negative correlation between fate control and CQ. However, if they view the situation as amenable to influence, they might take proactive action to improve their intercultural effectiveness. It is also possible that the passive and proactive tendencies of fate control would cancel each other out, giving rise to a null relationship between fate control and CQ. These possibilities need to be explored in future research.

Direct Effects of Social Axioms on Intercultural Effectiveness

We have argued that social axioms should be related to CQ in some meaningful ways. The question can be raised whether social axioms are related to intercultural effectiveness independent of their relationships with CQ. In other words, social axioms may exert direct effects on intercultural effectiveness in addition to indirect effects mediated by CQ.

Given that social axioms are broad, context-free constructs, we expect that CQ is unable to fully mediate the effects of social axioms on intercultural effectiveness. Social cynicism is related to a wide range of negative variables, and we expect that it is also related to low intercultural effectiveness and adjustment independent of the effects of CQ. The main reason is that social cynicism is related to an unyielding interpersonal style and focuses attention on negative events. Reward for application should be related to intercultural effectiveness and adjustment independent of CQ because of its emphasis on striving and tolerance of difficulties. Social complexity should be related to intercultural effectiveness and adjustment independent of CQ because of its emphasis on pluralistic attitudes toward issues. Finally, the effects of fate control and religiosity are difficult to predict, because both dimensions involve elements that may facilitate or hinder intercultural effectiveness and adjustment. Fate control may involve a passive attitude toward problems, but it may also promote proactive intervention under some circumstances. Religiosity involves an agreeable interpersonal style, but it may also involve an unyielding approach that is based on firm principles. In any event, the direct relationships between social axioms and intercultural effectiveness provide fertile ground for future research.

Knowledge of Social Axioms and Cultural Intelligence

Viewing social axioms as antecedents, we have explored the relationships between social axioms and CQ. It is also possible that social axioms may be related to CQ via a different mechanism. Kurman and Ronen-Eilon (2004) surveyed two immigrant groups in Israel, one from the former Soviet Union and the other from Ethiopia. These two groups were asked to report their social axioms as well as to estimate the axiom profile of average Israelis, which was determined by a random sample of Israelis. An Israeli group was also asked to estimate the axiom profile of average Israelis. As expected, Israelis provided more accurate estimations of the axiom profile of average Israelis. More interestingly, for the two immigrant groups, a more accurate estimation of the profile of average Israelis was related to better psychological and interpersonal adjustment as well as functional adaptation (living comfortably in Israel). The only exception to this pattern was social cynicism, and knowledge about the cynicism level in Israel was related to worse adaptation. One explanation for this finding is that if the immigrant groups perceived average Israelis as cynical, they would make less effort to interact with them effectively, resulting in poorer adaptation.

Kurman and Ronen-Eilon (2004) also contrasted the effects of the veridicality of the perception of the axiom profile of average Israelis and the adoption of this profile on the adaptation of the immigrants. Interestingly, axiom knowledge was found to be predictive of both social and functional adaptation, whereas axiom adoption only predicted social adaptation. In other words, accurate knowledge about the axiom profile of average Israelis is more important for adaptation than having a personal axiom profile that is similar to that of average Israelis.

The findings of Kurman and Ronen-Eilon (2004) are indeed intriguing and raise many questions about social axioms and adjustment of immigrants. For example, why is it that knowledge about the axiom profile of a host culture helps the adjustment of immigrants? What are the processes involved? While these questions should be explored in future research, we note that in CQ the cognitive component is concerned with knowledge about other cultures. It seems useful to add an important knowledge domain under the rubric of the cognitive component, namely, the understanding of the axiom profiles of other cultural groups. Again, many interesting research questions can be raised along this line of thinking. Why is it that some people process better knowledge of the axiom profile of other cultural groups? Should the axiom profiles of cultural groups be included in intercultural training? In a nutshell, many exciting research topics can be pursued when we view axiom knowledge as an integral part of the cognitive component of CQ.

CONCLUSION

Intercultural contact is crucial in many domains, from business to the joint effort to tackle environmental crises. It is important to understand the dynamics behind effective intercultural interaction and the factors that promote it. The framework of CQ provides a novel perspective on these issues and effective guidelines for improving intercultural contact.

In this chapter, we have considered the relationships between social axioms and CQ and argue that social axioms represent important types of personal attributes that influence CQ. Overall, we propose that CQ is a proximal cause of intercultural effectiveness, and social axioms are distal causes and exert part of their effects on intercultural effectiveness through the mediation of CQ. Many research questions can be raised with regard to the interplay of social axioms and CQ, and we have made a number of predictions for verification in future research. We hope that our chapter has provided the impetus to integrate these two broad frameworks in future research and shed new light on intercultural effectiveness and adjustment.

ACKNOWLEDGMENT

This chapter is supported by a grant provided by the Hong Kong Research Grants Council (CityU 1466/05H).

REFERENCES

Ang, S., & Van Dyne, L. (2008). Conceptualization of cultural intelligence: Definition, distinctiveness, and nomological network. In S. Ang & L.Van Dyne (Eds.), *Handbook on cultural intelligence* (pp. 3–15). New York: M.E. Sharpe.

Ang, S., Van Dyne, L., & Koh, C. (2006). Personality correlates of the four-factor model of cultural intelligence. *Group and Organization Management, 31,* 100–123.

Ang, S., Van Dyne, L., Koh, C., Ng, K.Y., Templer, K.J., Tay, C., & Chandrasekar, N.A. (2007). Cultural intelligence: Its measurement and effects on cultural judgment and decision making, cultural adaptation, and task performance. *Management and Organization Review, 3,* 335–371.

Bond, M.H., Leung, K., Au, A., Tong, K.K., & Chemonges-Nielson, Z. (2004). Combining social axioms with values in predicting social behaviors. *European Journal of Personality, 18,* 177–191.

Chen, S.X., Fok, H.K., Bond, M.H., & Matsumoto, D. (2006). Personality and beliefs about the world revisited: Expanding the nomological network of social axioms. *Personality and Individual Differences, 41,* 201–211.

Cheung, M.W.L., Leung, K., & Au, K. (2006). Evaluating multilevel models in cross-cultural research: An illustration with social axioms. *Journal of Cross-Cultural Psychology, 37,* 522–541.

Earley, P.C., & Ang, S. (2003). *Cultural intelligence: Individual interactions across cultures.* Palo Alto, CA: Stanford University Press.

Earley, P.C., & Gibson, C.B. (2002). *Multinational work teams: A new perspective.* Mahwah, NJ: Lawrence Erlbaum Associates.

Fu, P.P., Kennedy, J., Tata, J., Yukl, G., Bond, M.H., Peng, T.K., Srinivas, E.S., Howell, J.P., Prieto, L., Koopman, P., Boonstra, J.J., Pasa, S., Lacassagne, M.F., Higashide, H., & Cheosakul, A. (2004). The impact of societal cultural values and individual social beliefs on the perceived effectiveness of managerial influence strategies: A meso approach. *Journal of International Business Studies, 35,* 284–305.

Gelfand, M.J., Erez, M.E., & Aycan, Z. (2007). Cross-cultural organizational behavior. *Annual Review of Psychology, 58,* 479–514.

Hofstede, G. (1980). *Culture's consequences: International differences in work-related values.* Beverly Hills, CA: Sage.

House, R.J., Hanges, P.J., Javidan, M., Dorfman, P., & Gupta V. (2004). *GLOBE, cultures, leadership, and organizations: GLOBE study of 62 societies.* Newbury Park, CA: Sage.

Hui, V.K., Bond, M.H., & Ng, T.S.W. (2007). General beliefs about the world as defensive mechanisms against death anxiety. *Omega: Journal of Death and Dying, 54,* 199–214.

Humphrey, N.K. (1983). The adaptiveness of mentalism. *Behavioral and Brain Sciences, 6,* 343–390.

Johnson, J.P., Lenartowicz, T., & Apud, S. (2006). Cross-cultural competence in international business: Toward a definition and a model. *Journal of International Business Studies, 37,* 525–543.

Keller, H. (1997). Evolutional approaches. In J.W. Berry, Y.H. Poortinger, & J. Pandey (Eds.), *Handbook of cross-cultural psychology. Volume 1* (pp. 215–255). Boston, MA: Allyn & Bacon.

Kurman, J., & Ronen-Eilon, C. (2004). Lack of knowledge of a culture's social axioms and adaptation difficulties among immigrants. *Journal of Cross-Cultural Psychology, 35,* 192–208.

Leung, K., Au, A., Huang, X., Kurman, J., Niit, T., & Niit, K.K. (2007). Social axioms and values: A cross-cultural examination. *European Journal of Personality, 21,* 91–111.

Leung, K., & Bond, M.H. (2004). Social axioms: A model for social beliefs in multi-cultural perspective. *Advances in Experimental Social Psychology, 36,* 119–197.

Leung, K., & Bond, M.H. (2007). Psycho-logic and eco-logic: Insights from social axiom dimensions. In F. van de Vijver, D. van Hemert & Y.P. Poortinga (Eds.), *Individuals and cultures in multilevel analysis* (pp. 197–219). Mahwah, NJ: Lawrence Erlbaum Associates.

Leung, K., Bond, M.H., Reimel de Carrasquel, S., Muñoz, C., Hernández, M., Murakami, F., Yamaguchi, S., Bierbrauer, G., & Singelis, T.M. (2002). Social axioms: The search for universal dimensions of general beliefs about how the world functions. *Journal of Cross-Cultural Psychology, 33,* 286–302.

Neto, F. (2006). Dimensions and correlates of social axioms among a Portuguese sample. *Individual Differences Research, 4,* 340–351.

Ng, K.Y., & Earley, P.C. (2006). Culture + intelligence: Old constructs, new frontiers. *Group and Organization Management, 31,* 4–19.

Rotter, J.B. (1966). Generalized expectancies for internal versus external control of reinforcement. *Psychological Monographs, 80,* 1–28.

Safdar, S., Lewis, J.R., & Daneshpour, M. (2006). Social axioms in Iran and Canada: Intercultural contact, coping and adjustment. *Asian Journal of Social Psychology, 9,* 123–131.

Schwartz, S.H. (1992). Universals in the content and structure of values: Theory and empirical tests in 20 countries. *Advances in Experimental Social Psychology, 25,* 1–65.

Singelis, T.M., Hubbard, C., Her, P., & An, S. (2003). Convergent validation of the Social Axioms Survey. *Personality and Individual Differences, 24,* 269–282.

Sternberg, R.J. (1986). A framework for understanding conceptions of intelligence. In R.J. Sternberg & D.K. Detterman (Eds.), *What is intelligence? Contemporary viewpoints on its nature and definition* (pp. 3–15). Norwood, NJ: Ablex.

Vroom, V.H. (1964). *Work and motivation.* New York: John Wiley & Sons.

Weisz, J.R., Rothbaum, F.M., & Blackburn, T.C. (1984). Standing out and standing in: The psychology of control in America and Japan. *American Psychologist, 39,* 955–969.

Whiten, A., & Byrne, R.W. (1997). *Machiavellian intelligence II: Extensions and evaluations.* Cambridge: Cambridge University Press.

Williams, K.D. (1997). Social ostracism. In R.M. Kowalski (Ed.), *Aversive interpersonal behaviors* (pp. 133–170). New York: Plenum Press.

Zhou, F., Leung, K., & Bond, M.H. (2007). Social axioms and achievement across cultures: The influence of reward for application and fate control. Working paper, City University of Hong Kong, Hong Kong.

CHAPTER 22

Intercultural Competence Development and Triple-Loop Cultural Learning

Toward a Theory of Intercultural Sensitivity

DHARM P.S. BHAWUK, KEITH H. SAKUDA, AND VIJAYAN P. MUNUSAMY

Modern global assignments require individuals to seamlessly transition from one cultural context to the next (Bhawuk, 1990; Bhawuk & Brislin, 1992; Earley & Mosakowski, 2000) as "cultural chameleons" (Earley & Peterson, 2004). However, just as a chameleon sitting on a soccer ball may change its colors to black and white without understanding the game of soccer, individuals may not realize the true nature of their social environment. Researchers and practitioners have long recognized this and have investigated the competencies (Dinges, 1983; Dinges & Baldwin, 1996; Dinges & Liberman, 1989), skills (Bhawuk & Brislin, 1992; Cushner, 1989), and personality traits (Detweiler, 1975, 1978, 1980) that help predict effectiveness in intercultural interactions. Concepts such as intercultural sensitivity (Bennett, 1986; Bhawuk, 1989; Bhawuk & Brislin, 1992; Cushner, 1989), intercultural development (Hammer, 1998), intercultural effectiveness (Elmer, 1987), cross-cultural adaptability (Kelley & Meyers, 1992), intercultural competence (Chen & Starosta, 1996), cultural intelligence (Earley & Ang, 2003), intercultural consciousness (Landreman, 2003), and intercultural maturity (King & Baxter Magolda, 2005) have furthered our understanding of intercultural effectiveness. Though these constructs differ in their definitions and assessments, they broadly fall under the domain of intercultural expertise development, and at the root of this development is the role of learning.

What one should know in intercultural interaction has been examined and advocated extensively (e.g., cultural values), but how an individual can learn during the interaction has not been fully conceptualized in the literature of intercultural expertise development. Understanding how individuals learn is important, as modern global assignments now involve constant travel from country to country. Though one country may be designated as the official assignment, international managers may simply use that country as a station for countless trips to other countries to conduct business. As a result, the realities of global business have forced a premium on the ability to learn how to learn about different cultures.

In this chapter we attempt to synthesize learning theories with intercultural expertise development to provide a model of how individuals can learn and grow in intercultural environments. We do this by discussing the models of expertise development and then synthesizing them with the construct of intercultural sensitivity (Bhawuk, 1989; Bhawuk & Brislin, 1992; Bhawuk & Sakuda, in press). While many aspects of intercultural sensitivity appear to mirror many of the personality traits and skills found in other indicators of cross-cultural success, intercultural sensitivity differs by placing a premium on the development of interest, sensitivity, and respect at the expense of more immediate priorities of accomplishing task-related goals. While our model parallels the metacognitive aspect of cultural intelligence (CQ), which is defined as the capability of an individual to acquire and understand cultural knowledge, including knowledge of and control over individual thought processes relating to culture (Ang, Van Dyne, Koh, Ng, Templer, Tay, & Chandrasekar, 2007), it also cuts across the emotional and behavioral aspects of intercultural interaction. Building on the model of change management at the individual level, we present a triple-loop cultural learning model of intercultural sensitivity, and present a video metaphor to further explain the model. Synthesizing the learning process, we propose a theory of intercultural sensitivity and conclude with a discussion of intercultural sensitivity in light of CQ and the intercultural development model.

MODELS OF CROSS-CULTURAL EXPERTISE DEVELOPMENT

Berry and Ward (2006) argued that the conceptualization and theorizing of CQ can greatly benefit from the vast literature on intercultural training. Specifically, they cited the role of culture assimilators in developing metacognitive strategies. Earlier, Bhawuk (1998) had developed a model of intercultural expertise development that synthesized the role of theory in developing metacognitive strategies. In this model, he suggested that people move in phases, from "layperson," to "novice," to "expert," and finally to "advanced expert." A layperson is one who has knowledge of only his or her own culture, and is at the cognitive stage of learning. A novice is likely to have spent some time living in another culture, thus developing some intercultural skills or expertise. Experts are those who can organize cognitions about cultural differences meaningfully around a theory, and are typically at the associative or proceduralization stage of learning. Advanced experts are those who not only understand cultural differences but also can enact different cultural behaviors smoothly and are at the autonomous stage of learning.

The model of intercultural expertise development also fits well with the model of cross-cultural competence development in which people move from "unconscious incompetence," to "conscious incompetence," to "conscious competence," to "unconscious competence" (Howell, 1982). We are all experts at the unconscious competence level in our own culture, and by fiat become unconsciously incompetent in other cultures, i.e., we do not even know what we don't know. By paying attention to our mistakes in interacting with people from other cultures, we become consciously incompetent, and by intending to modify our behaviors and making an effort to learn new behaviors we become consciously competent. Practicing the behavior leads to its acquisition at the level of unconscious competence. Unconscious incompetence corresponds to the layperson, conscious incompetence to the novice stage, conscious competence to the expert stage, and unconscious competence to the advanced expert level of expertise development.

DISCONFIRMED EXPECTATION AND LEARNING HOW-TO-LEARN

Disconfirmed expectation refers to situations in which sojourners expect a certain behavior from the host nationals, but experience a different one (Bhawuk, 2002; Brislin & Bhawuk, 1999). On the positive side, disconfirmed expectations offer the opportunity to learn by providing concrete examples of how intercultural differences may impact the individual's life. Encountering a disconfirmed expectation creates what Vygotsky calls critical space, in which the individual either chooses to ignore the situation as an aberration or reflect on the situation and learn. For the motivated sojourner, disconfirmed expectations offer the opportunity to go from concrete experience to reflective observation and then to abstract conceptualization and active experimentation (Kolb, 1976; Hugh-Weiner, 1986).

In an intercultural setting, failure to engage in reflective observation may lead to the attribution that an individual's intercultural counterpart is not a nice person or that the host culture is not a good culture. Learning does not occur and the individual may continue to act the same way in the future as they have acted in such situations in the past. However, if reflective observation is practiced, the individual may learn about cultural differences and gain a perspective of the host culture.

If we further develop abstract conceptualization, we acquire theoretical insights, which help us organize cultural experiences coherently into categories and theories. This leads to culture general understanding, and we develop an understanding of *etics,* or universals, and *emics,* or cultural representations of those etics. Active experimentation completes the cycle in that the learner is now testing theories and learned ideas. Through practice, the individual grows beyond a "nice-talk-interculturalist" to become a sophisticated intercultural practitioner (Bhawuk, in press).

TRIPLE-LOOP CULTURAL LEARNING MODEL

It has long been recognized that intercultural sensitivity is necessary for effective intercultural relations (Bhawuk, 1989; Bhawuk & Brislin, 1992; Cushner, 1989). It has been described as the essence of intercultural effectiveness and defined as possessing the temperament to be "interested in other cultures, be sensitive enough to notice cultural differences, and then also be willing to modify behavior as an indication of respect for the people of other cultures" (Bhawuk & Brislin, 1992, p. 416). In this section we trace the mental thought processes involved in intercultural encounters, and present a new triple-loop cultural learning model as a basis for developing intercultural sensitivity.

In monocultural settings the mind interprets the world through a three-step process. Step 1 involves scanning the environment to gather information from the immediate surroundings. The mind dedicates its energy to maximizing the flow of sensory inputs into the brain, and only the simplest cognitive processes are active in deciphering social phenomena. In step 2, the mind compares the information collected in step 1 against its operating norms, or cultural baseline, which is grounded in the individual's native culture. Based on these expectations, which carry components of cultural values, beliefs, and social expectations, the mind deciphers and interprets the environment to process the social situation. In step 3, the mind builds upon step 2 to produce a set of strategies for interacting with the social environment. From the produced set of strategies, one will be selected and performed as a situation-appropriate response. This three-step process is derived from cybernetics, and is analogous to single-loop learning in management literature (Argyris & Schon, 1978; Morgan, 1997). In Figure 22.1, it is described as Loop 1.

When confronted with an unfamiliar intercultural situation, the mind will initially follow its single-loop process to generate and perform an appropriate response behavior. This is likely to lead to a disconfirmed expectation and cognitive dissonance (Festinger, 1957). This stressor may either lead to abandonment of the intercultural encounter or motivate individuals to challenge their intercultural competence, as responding to a disconfirmed expectation forces the mind to operate in a more complex double-loop process.

Once the inappropriateness of the single-loop process is realized, those who are interculturally sensitive initiate a recursive mental loop by questioning the appropriateness of their cultural baseline. They recognize that their lack of experience with the other culture may be obscuring their understanding of the situation, and that the disconfirmed expectation may be related to culture. Step 1 is repeated to account for the possibility that an inappropriate cultural baseline has been used and to account for the new social stimuli (usually negative) generated from the first attempt at performing a situation-appropriate behavior.

The reassessment of step 1 forces a second learned cognitive subcomponent to step 2 to assess the validity of the native cultural baseline for the situation. If the cultural baseline is deemed invalid, a new cultural baseline must be imported to replace the original cultural baseline. Imported cultural baselines are often generated from past experiences with other cultures. Those lacking prior intercultural experiences are incapable of importing new cultural baselines and must proceed through intercultural social information processing with a faulty set of operating norms.

Once an appropriate cultural baseline has been imported, it serves as the basis for attributing social information and for developing a new set of response strategies. If the new cultural baseline is appropriate, then the intercultural interaction is perceived from a similar cultural perspective. If the cultural baseline is inappropriate, then a disconfirmed expectation will be encountered and high levels of intercultural sensitivity will be needed to sustain the motivation to repeat the process using a different imported cultural baseline. Once appropriate operating norms have been found, the individual can proceed to step 3 and attempt to bridge cultural differences by producing a culturally appropriate set of interacting strategies. One of these strategies will be selected and performed as a situation-appropriate response.

Figure 22.1 **Triple-Loop Cultural Learning**

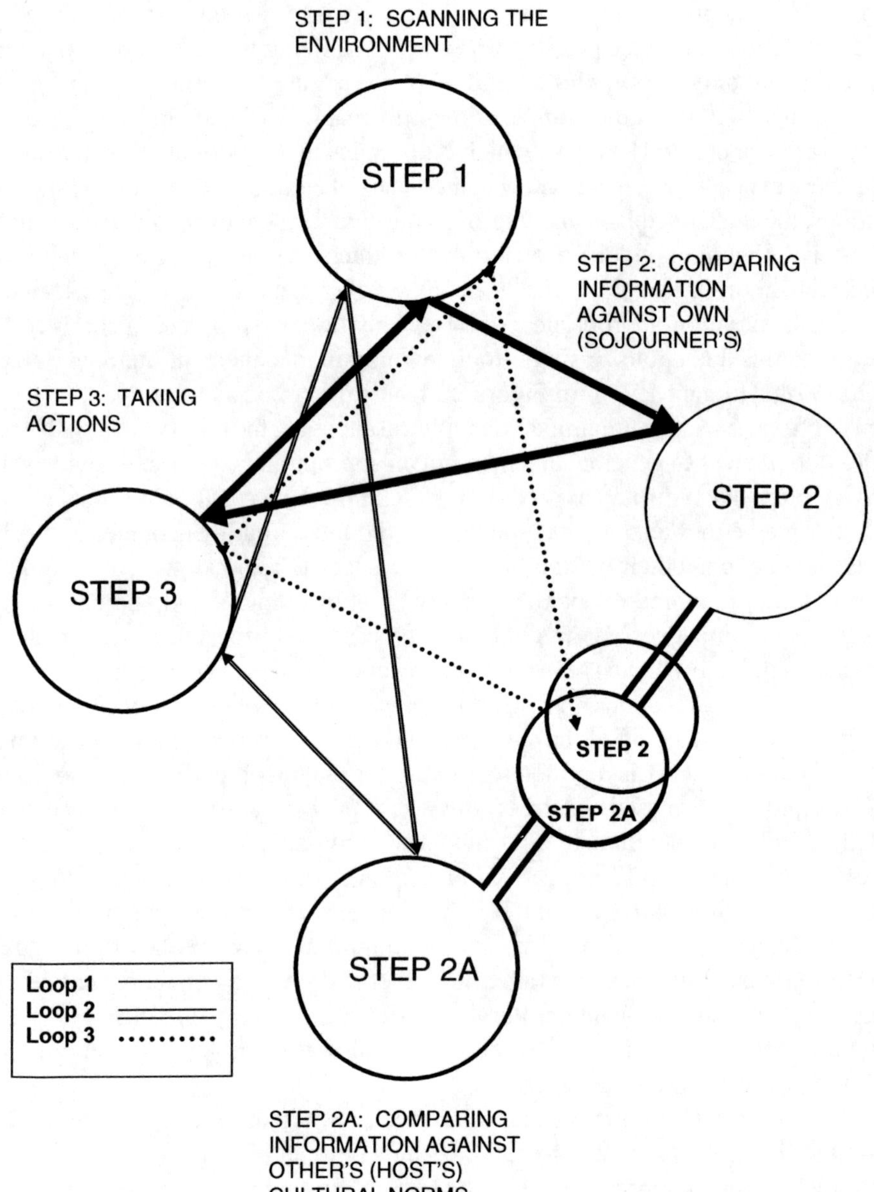

The recursive double-loop process of intercultural sensitivity serves as the basis for creating isomorphic attributions, the process of attributing the actions of another by adopting their cultural perspective. It is also dependent on the realization of a disconfirmed expectation. Disconfirmed expectations serve as a feedback device to evaluate the effectiveness of the selected response strategy. Intercultural situations are often clouded in uncertainty, and more often than not the enacted behavior is not completely appropriate.

An individual may need to probe a social situation with multiple cycles of the double-loop process to determine appropriate behaviors.

As the initiator of isomorphic attributions, the double-loop process of intercultural sensitivity is well-suited for the majority of interpersonal interactions across cultures. It is particularly appropriate for situations where one partner chooses to adopt the cultural baseline of another. This often occurs in situations with a power hierarchy, such as host-guests, supervisor-subordinate, or client and service provider. Another scenario for double-loop intercultural sensitivity is when a person has more intercultural experience and chooses to adopt their counterpart's cultural baseline to foster smoother communication.

Despite the effectiveness of the double-loop process, there are situations where the two parties may choose not to appoint one cultural baseline over the other. These situations often occur when the parties wish to promote equality in the relationship or are simultaneously competing to project an impression of superiority or power over the other. Long-term friendships are an example of the former, while diplomatic negotiations are an example of the latter. Under those situations, intercultural partners may engage in the recursive triple-loop of intercultural sensitivity.

The triple-loop builds upon the double-loop process by creating a distinctly original cultural baseline specific to the intercultural relationship. It seeks to transcend the boundaries of a single culture through the synthesis and convergence of cultural baselines. As outlined in Figure 22.1, the cultural baseline adopted during the triple loop is comprised of the mutually created operating norms adopted from the represented cultural baselines.

A recent phenomenon that has attracted the attention of cross-cultural researchers is the proliferation of intercultural teams in multicultural contexts. Most intercultural encounters involve only two cultural baselines, but intercultural teams in multicultural contexts potentially involve as many different cultures as there are members of the team. In these situations, the triple-loop model of intercultural sensitivity allows for the team to create its own distinct cultural baseline from the aggregate expectations, values, and beliefs of the team. Variation among team members' personal cultural baselines is inevitable, but mutual humility to adopt shared cultural perspectives allows the team to function as a unit. Visualizing triple-loop intercultural sensitivity in multicultural contexts would require adding an additional dimension to Figure 22.1. Step 2-2A would exist as the intersection of all the cultural baselines of members of the multicultural team, with each team member following their own triple-loop mental process.

While the recursive looping models of intercultural sensitivity provide direction for forming isomorphic attributions or transcultural perspectives, it is important to remember that intercultural sensitivity is more than just the ability to adopt the mindset of an intercultural partner. It is also the ability to switch quickly and seamlessly back to the individual's home culture. Expatriates who "go native" become so immersed in their new culture that they abandon their home culture. This is not a demonstration of intercultural sensitivity because the inability to switch back to the home culture makes one incapable of navigating cultural differences. The true essence of intercultural sensitivity is learning to change and adapt to the intercultural requirements of the moment while preserving the flexibility to return to one's home culture.

CULTURAL LEARNING: A VIDEO METAPHOR

Intercultural sensitivity is a process that can be nicely captured using a video metaphor. The first step in the intercultural mental process is to consciously and continuously suspend the attribution process, i.e., to consciously "pause." This pause can take place at multiple times during an intercultural interaction and is necessary because intercultural sensitivity requires suspending cultural attributions and taking the perspective of the cultures involved in the interaction. Scholars have argued that people tend to make quick but stable inferences based on their senses (Argyris & Schon, 1978), and perspective-taking is only possible if the individual's own cultural (stable) perspectives are paused. *Pause* here applies to pausing before interaction, pausing during interaction, and pausing after interaction. Pausing is important because it allows the individual to think before an interaction (e.g., learning cross-cultural differences), suspend judgment during the interaction especially when it did not meet prior expectations (e.g., active probing), and reflect on behavior after the interaction (e.g., debriefing). Depending on the individual's ability, the pause can decrease in terms of duration and frequency over time, but it will never cease.

The second step in the intercultural mental process is to question attributions, expectations, and behaviors. Using the video metaphor, the individual must "rewind" and reflect on behavior in terms of upbringing, cultural norms, organizational culture (e.g., standard operating procedures), and identity. For example, a quick response to a simple mathematical question of 1 + 1 = 2. But, behind this answer, there are few assumptions that go unnoticed. For instance, we assume that 1 is an integer. What if 1 is actually 1.4 but rounded to 1? If we allow one decimal point, then the answer would be rounded up to 3 (1.4 + 1.4 = 2.8 → 3). Hence, the standards that are applied impact the decision. In the "rewind" stage, learning focuses on cultural standards. By rewinding, individuals would be able to make sense of why they behave the way they do, or find out the reason for the behavior.

The third step involves making sense of new cultural standards. Using the video metaphor, the "forward" button is engaged. Being able to understand the cultural reasons for behavior, the individual can now move forward by making sense of the new cultural information and acting accordingly. This is the stage where new cultural standards are understood. Going back to the mathematical example, this is the stage where calculation occurs based on the new operating rules.

The fourth step is about internalizing what has been learned and achieving cognitive consonance. Using the video metaphor, this is the "recording" stage. Once an individual has made sense of new cultural information and the appropriate behavior, learning can be internalized. This is an important stage. Organizational theorists have argued that "people quickly lose track of the data that caused them to draw the inference" (Dixon, 1996, p.8) and hence the recording stage is vital for future retrieval. This would constitute the third loop of learning discussed earlier and is where the individual learns from both cultures (knowing), makes sense of the information (understanding), and acts accordingly (doing).

The fifth step is to modify action and act accordingly. To use the video metaphor, the play button is engaged, and a new cultural behavior is practiced. As individuals act, their actions reinforce the previous stages of pausing, rewinding, forwarding, and recording. Mistakes may still be made, but these mistakes are narrowed down through "recursive behaviors" and are also used to modify the attribution process. The whole process of pause, rewind, forward, record, and play is repeated whenever it is necessary. Aptly put by Dixon (1996, p. 19), "Perspective-taking is more than just being able to play back others' argument in order to check with them for accuracy. It is the ability to comprehend and voice how the situation appears from another's standpoint. Perspective-taking is the opposite of egocentrism, in which the individual is locked into a single view of the situation and is unaware of the limitations of that view or that other viable views may exist."

TOWARD A THEORY OF INTERCULTURAL SENSITIVITY

People are socialized to be ethnocentric (Triandis, 1990). It is natural for all of us to be socialized to value our own cultural practices and to think ethnocentrically that our way is the best way. Accepting this simple fact endows the individual with the humility needed to progress in an intercultural journey. Intercultural encounters provide an opportunity to gain cultural humility as the individual learns new ways of doing the same behavior, hopefully leading toward intercultural sensitivity.

This first step toward developing intercultural sensitivity is the *acknowledgement* of another culture as a way of living differently from the individual's own culture. It is similar to going from unconscious incompetence to conscious incompetence following the skill acquisition paradigm of Howell (1982). The naivete is broken, and the individual learns to become conscious of another culture in which people act differently. The other cultural practices may still be rejected by ethnocentrically judging them as inferior. Or, the individual can choose to be more flexible in judgment and move toward acquiring ways of acting and thinking from the perspective of the other culture. This leads us to the second step, which is accepting the other culture as a valid way of being and doing. It does not mean that individuals must stop practicing their own cultural behaviors, but that they should be willing to accept the practices of the other culture in their own right as valid and not inferior. At this point the individual is still in a cognitive stage of learning, but has taken the first mental step toward accepting other ways of doing and being. This is an early phase of intercultural sensitivity development and a necessary first step toward acquiring intercultural competence. Without crossing the cognitive barrier from acknowledgement to acceptance, it is not possible to acquire intercultural competence.

The challenge of moving from acknowledgement to acceptance can also be explained by theoretical ideas captured by the process of false-consensus effect (Krueger & Clement, 1994; Krueger & Zeigler, 1993; Mullen et al., 1985; Ross, Greene, & House, 1977). People who agree with a position believe that a large percentage of the population agrees with their position, whereas people who disagree with a position believe that a small percentage of the population disagrees with their position. Since we are all ethnocentric, we have a tendency to view our personal cultural values and practices as useful and effective and mistakenly believe that others share our views. Moving toward acceptance requires correcting this process.

Acceptance of cultural differences requires more than just recognizing that people are different from one another. There must be recognition and acceptance of the fact that differences occur beyond the unit of analysis of the individual. Social identity theory (Tajfel, 1982) suggests that humans have an innate tendency to classify and identify themselves as members of social groups. Often these groups are based on demographic features, such as ethnicity, age, or socioeconomic parameters, but inherent in the groupings is the realization that members of each group share more than just surface-level features. Membership in these groups often marks shared values, attitudes, and behaviors, but in some societies (e.g., in the United States) the pressure toward political correctness has created a seemingly distorted belief that member affiliation does not coincide with any mutual similarities other than demographic. Rather, similarities among group members are coincidental and differences between groups are a result of individual differences manifested at the group level. These societal pressures have resulted in the principle that all interpersonal differences are individual differences and every individual must be treated as an individual. Intercultural sensitivity requires a rejection of that notion and an acceptance that differences across groups are often attributable to cultural differences.

Once cultural differences have been recognized and accepted, the next step is for a person to have the *intention* (Fishbein & Ajzen, 1975; Triandis, 1980) to modify his or her behavior in view of the challenges evoked by the cultural differences. Intention being the best predictor of human behavior (Fishbein & Ajzen, 1975), it seems necessary that an individual has the intention to change behavior to go beyond acceptance. Often, cultural differences strike at the core of our values systems. Overcoming natural tendencies grounded in home cultural perspectives may sound easy, but in reality may be quite difficult. Initial feelings of discomfort may be masked, but suppressing visceral reactions from striking differences in core values or beliefs can be nearly impossible. Even after the initial shock of a cultural difference is weathered, one may still need to confront longer-lasting repercussions. Also, since cultural behaviors are habitual, intention to modify behavior must be weighed against strength of old habits (Triandis, 1980).

Tolerance and self-reflection are essential tools to inspire intention to bridge cultural differences. Tolerance builds upon acceptance by receiving a cultural difference into the immediate surroundings. Instead of simply accepting the existence of a cultural difference, a tolerant person agrees to allow a difference to impact his or her life. For example, there is nearly universal acceptance that religious differences exist not as functions of individual differences but as part of the world's tapestry of different cultures. However, despite this acceptance, many people do not exhibit the tolerance to interact with those from different religious backgrounds.

Discomfort may still exist in the midst of tolerance. In those cases, self-reflection offers a path to move away from discomfort toward understanding. Asking questions of oneself to understand why one feels discomfort opens a window to investigate the inner self. Further exploration can be done by seeking knowledge about the differences between the encountered culture and one's own culture. Tolerance and self-reflection reveal a personal willingness to engage in informed compromise over a cultural difference. Once such willingness is offered, a personal strategy can be laid out to effect personal change to accommodate the difference.

The fourth step in developing intercultural sensitivity requires *learning other cultural practices,* which is a necessary behavioral exercise that involves both cognitive and affective dimensions. For example, there are tremendous differences in cultural practices regarding the amount of contact permitted between people of opposite sexes. A person moving from a noncontact culture to a contact culture will face a great deal of emotional strain in learning to properly interact with members of the opposite sex. This affective response is a result of the conflict between two ways of performing a task or behavior. When individuals override behaviors mastered in their own culture, arousal of strong emotion is natural and similar to cognitive dissonance (Cooper & Fazio, 1984; Festinger, 1957; Festinger & Carlsmith, 1959). Controlling this affect requires consciously managing emotions while learning new cultural behaviors.

According to Howell's (1982) paradigm, this conscious management of affect is moving from *conscious incompetence* to *conscious competence.* Positive reinforcement comes from host culture nationals, and slowly but definitely the joy of learning allows the dissonance to fade. It is often the case that many learned cultural behaviors continue to cause discomfort, and a conscious effort must be made to perform the behavior while hiding emotion. This is the fifth step toward developing intercultural sensitivity. Often, cultural behaviors do not change when they fall in the domain of the individual's private life, but those that fall in the public domain or in the workplace do need to be learned despite the discomfort (Bhawuk, 2005).

As in all socially desirable behaviors, it is possible to fake intercultural sensitivity by knowing the appropriate behaviors of another culture. For example, it is difficult to decipher based on behavior whether an individual is performing an organizational citizen behavior or performing a political behavior to please a superior (Ferris, Bhawuk, Fedor, & Judge, 1995). Because of the risks associated with insincerity, it is in the best interest of the individual and the organization to be *authentic* in intercultural interactions. This is an important characteristic of intercultural sensitivity. An interculturally sensitive person is likely to genuinely enjoy adopting ideas and practices from other cultures, and thus enjoy the personal growth and interpersonal harmony. Borrowing a concept from positive psychology (Snyder & Lopez, 2005), we posit that intercultural sensitivity offers an optimistic new direction in cross-cultural adjustment that is grounded in the positive construct of authenticity (Harter, 2005).

Intercultural sensitivity requires us to go beyond a simplistic monocultural perspective of being authentic to a much more challenging and trying concept where the maxim "know thyself" is contrasted with knowing the other. On the surface, a call for authenticity in interpersonal interactions seems almost trite. Idealistic concepts such as authenticity seem out of place in the competitive world of business, and most practitioners would support the notion of authenticity as beneficial, but not necessarily cost-effective or practical for business success. Only recently has research begun to uncover value and merits for authenticity in interpersonal interactions (Swann & Pelham, 2005). It is through this emerging movement in positive psychology that intercultural sensitivity may provide direction and understanding for an increasingly intercultural world.

It is virtually impossible for any person to learn all the cultural practices of a different culture. This is why it is appropriate to view the development of intercultural sensitivity as a lifelong journey. This journey means the accumulation and the amplification of personal growth to bring the joy of learning new concepts, ideas, and behaviors. The reward for undertaking the journey is not always extrinsic or of practical consequence or value, but often intrinsic to the person. The development of intercultural sensitivity is likely to make a person more humane, more tolerant and accepting of differences, and above all, open to dialogue with people with different ideas. Those on the journey of intercultural sensitivity are likely to contribute to better intercultural understanding, a harmonious world, and peace.

DISCUSSION

The constructs of intercultural sensitivity and CQ are similar in several ways. Both view cross-cultural competence as developmental and trainable and focus on the ability to understand and make sense of cultural cues. By placing an emphasis on learning both declarative and procedural knowledge, CQ and intercultural sensitivity can be developed through training techniques such as role-play and experiential learning (Tan & Yong, 2003). They are also similar in that both capture the three domains of cognition, motivation, and behavior. As new cultural behaviors or experiences are encountered, sojourners must metacognitively synthesize their cognitive processes, maintain control over their emotions, and perform situation-specific and culturally appropriate behaviors.

Despite their similarities, CQ and intercultural sensitivity differ in several ways. CQ is often seen as a new facet of a multidimensional perspective of intelligence, making it a skill or developable tool. Intercultural sensitivity, being progressive/regressive, contextual, and variable within a person, is more of a process. Its constant need for commitment and refinement, as well as its fragile and transient nature, require that it be honed and perfected for each encounter. Whereas the skill-based nature of CQ makes it more functional, the process nature of intercultural sensitivity requires more of a commitment to a set way of developing authentic intercultural relationships.

Unlike other cross-cultural competency measures that focus on the completion of objective tasks and assignments, intercultural sensitivity stops short of defining success through goals external to the individual. Rather, it suggests that developing higher levels of intercultural sensitivity is a goal worthy of its own merits. Echoing Kant's categorical imperative, the process of intercultural sensitivity seeks to be an "end," rather than a means to an end. Other cross-cultural constructs are content to provide moral-free guidance and direction, but intercultural sensitivity recognizes that the humanistic potential vested in every intercultural encounter far exceeds the financial benefits that may accrue to the participants.

To conclude, the theoretical foundations of intercultural sensitivity are based on six attributes of intercultural understanding and acceptance that lead to the unifying goal of interpersonal harmony across cultures. We can simplify these six attributes to an acronym of 6 As: *acknowledgement, acceptance, aim* (intention to act), *action* (learning cultural behaviors), *authenticity,* and *accumulation* (lifelong journey). Our notion of intercultural sensitivity resonates with Perry's (1981) work on ethical growth. He described the highest form of committed relativism as the stage at which we accept that, "This is how life will be. I must be wholehearted while tentative, fight for my values yet respect others, believe my deepest values right yet be ready to learn. I see that I shall be retracing this whole journey over and over—but, I hope, more wisely." This statement captures the spirit of intercultural sensitivity by urging all to follow the wisdom of self-truth while embracing others with respect and dignity.

REFERENCES

Ang, S., Van Dyne, L., Koh, C., Ng, K.Y., Templer, K.J., Tay, C., & Chandrasekar, N.A. (2007). Cultural intelligence: Its measurement and effects on cultural judgment and decision making, cultural adaptation, and task performance. *Management and Organization Review, 3,* 335–371.

Argyris, C., & Schon, D.A. (1978). *Organizational learning: A theory of action perspective.* Reading, MA: Addison-Wesley.

Bennett, M.J. (1986). A developmental approach to training for intercultural sensitivity. *International Journal of Intercultural Relations, 10,* 179–196.

Berry, J.W. & Ward, C. (2006). Redefining interactions across cultures and organizations. *Group and Organization Management, 31,* 64–77.

Bhawuk, D.P.S. (1989). Measurement of cross-cultural sensitivity developed by living abroad. Unpublished master's thesis, University of Hawaii at Manoa, Honolulu.

Bhawuk, D.P.S. (1990). Cross-cultural orientation programs. In R.W. Brislin (Ed.), *Applied cross-cultural psychology* (pp. 325–346). Newbury Park, CA: Sage.

Bhawuk, D.P.S. (1998). The role of culture theory in cross-cultural training: A multimethod study of culture-specific, culture-general, and culture theory-based assimilators. *Journal of Cross-Cultural Psychology, 29,* 630–655.

Bhawuk, D.P.S. (2002). *A synthesis of social expectancy, action theory, and learning theories in cross-cultural training: Toward a theory of disconfirmed expectations.* Paper presented at the Academy of Management Meeting, Denver, Colorado, 2002.

Bhawuk, D.P.S. (2005). The dynamics of uneven acculturation: Role of intention, functional culture, and overtness of behavior. Paper presented in the Symposium on Acculturation at the Fourth Biennial Conference on Intercultural Research, Kent State, May 4–7, 2005.

Bhawuk, D.P.S. (in press). Intercultural training for the global workplace: Review, synthesis, and theoretical explorations. In R.S. Bhagat & R. Steers (Eds.), *Handbook of culture, organization, and work.* Cambridge: Cambridge University Press.

Bhawuk, D.P.S., & Brislin, R.W. (1992). The measurement of intercultural sensitivity using the concepts of individualism and collectivism. *International Journal of Intercultural Relations, 16,* 413–436.

Bhawuk, D.P.S., & Sakuda, K.H. (in press). Intercultural sensitivity for global managers. In Michael A. Moodian (Ed.), *Contemporary leadership and intercultural competence: Understanding and utilizing cultural diversity to build successful organizations.* Thousand Oaks, CA: Sage.

Brislin, R.W., & Bhawuk, D.P.S. (1999). Cross-cultural training: Research and innovations. In J. Adamopoulos & Y. Kashima (Eds.), *Social psychology and cultural context* (pp. 205–216). Thousand Oaks, CA: Sage.

Chen, G.M., & Starosta, W.J. (1996). Intercultural communication competence: A synthesis. In B.R. Burleson (Ed.), *Emphasis communication yearbook 19* (pp. 353–383). Newbury Park, CA: Sage.

Cooper, J., & Fazio, R.H. (1984). A new look at dissonance theory. In L. Berkowitz (Ed.), *Advances in experimental social psychology. Volume 17* (pp. 229–266). New York: Academic Press.

Cushner, K. (1989). Assessing the impact of a culture-general assimilator. *International Journal of Intercultural Relations, 13,* 125–146.

Detweiler, R. (1975). On inferring the intentions of a person from another culture. *Journal of Personality, 43,* 591–611.

Detweiler, R. (1978). Culture, category width, and attributions: A model building approach to the reasons for cultural effects. *Journal of Cross-Cultural Psychology, 9,* 259–284.

Detweiler, R. (1980). Intercultural interaction and the categorization process: A conceptual analysis and behavioral outcome. *International Journal of Intercultural Relations, 4,* 275–295.

Dinges, N.G. (1983). Intercultural competence. In D. Landis & R.W. Brislin (Eds.), *Handbook of intercultural training. Volume 1. Issues in theory and design* (pp. 176–202). New York: Pergamon Press.

Dinges, N.G., & Baldwin, K.D. (1996). Intercultural competence: A research perspective. In D. Landis & R.S. Bhagat (Eds.), *Handbook of intercultural training* (pp. 106–123). Thousand Oaks, CA: Sage.

Dinges, N.G., & Liberman, D.A. (1989). Intercultural communication competence: Coping with stressful situation. *International Journal of Intercultural Relations, 13,* 371–385.

Dixon, N. (1996). *Perspectives on dialogue: Making talk developmental for individuals and organizations.* Greensboro, NC: Center for Creative Leadership.

Earley, P.C., & Ang, S. (2003). *Cultural intelligence: Individual interactions across cultures.* Palo Alto, CA: Stanford University Press.

Earley, P.C., & Mosakowski, E. (2000). Creating hybrid team cultures: An empirical test of transnational team functioning. *Academy of Management Journal, 43,* 26–49.

Earley, P.C., & Peterson, R.S. (2004). The elusive cultural chameleon: Cultural intelligence as a new approach to intercultural training for the global manager. *Academy of Management Learning & Education, 3,* 100–115.

Elmer, M.I. (1987). *Intercultural effectiveness: Development of an intercultural competency scale.* Unpublished doctoral dissertation, Michigan State University, East Lansing, MI.

Ferris, G.R., Bhawuk, D.P.S., Fedor, D.B., & Judge, T.A. (1995). Organizational politics and citizenship: Attributions of intentionality and construct definition. In M.J. Martenko (Ed.), *Advances in attribution theory: An organizational perspective* (pp. 231–252). Delray Beach, FL: St. Lucie Press.

Festinger, L. (1957). *A theory of cognitive dissonance.* Palo Alto, CA: Stanford University Press.

Festinger, L., & Carlsmith, J.M. (1959). Cognitive consequences of forced compliance. *Journal of Abnormal and Social Psychology, 58,* 203–211.

Fishbein, M., & Ajzen, I. (1975). *Belief, attitude, intention, and behavior: An introduction to theory and research.* Reading, MA: Addison-Wesley.

Hammer, M.R. (1998). A measure of intercultural sensitivity: The Intercultural Development Inventory. In S.M. Fowler & M.G. Mumford (Eds), *The intercultural sourcebook. Volume 2* (pp. 61–72). Yarmouth, ME: Intercultural Press.

Harter, S. (2005). Authenticity. In C.R. Snyder & S.J. Lopez (Eds.), *Handbook of positive psychology* (pp. 382–394). Oxford: Oxford University Press.

Howell, W.S. (1982). *The empathic communicator.* University of Minnesota: Wadsworth Publishing Company.

Hugh-Weiner, G. (1986). The "learning how to learn" approach to cross-cultural orientation. *International Journal of Intercultural Relations, 10,* 485–505.

Kelley, C., & Meyers, J. (1992). *The cross-cultural adaptability inventory.* Minneapolis, MN: NCS Assessments.

King, P.M., & Baxter Magolda, M.B. (2005). A developmental model of intercultural maturity. *Journal of College Student Development, 46,* 571–592.

Kolb, D.A. (1976). Management and the learning process. *California Management Review, 18,* 21–31.

Krueger, J., & Clement, R.W. (1994). The truly false consensus effect: An ineradicable and egocentric bias in social perception. *Journal of Personality and Social Psychology, 67,* 596–610.

Krueger, J., & Zeigler, J.S. (1993). Social categorization and the truly false consensus effect. *Journal of Personality and Social Psychology, 65,* 670–680.

Landreman, L. (2003). A multidimensional model of intercultural consciousness: A reconceptualization of multicultural competence. Paper presented at the Annual Meeting of the Association for the Study of Higher Education, Portland, OR, November 2003.

Morgan, G. (1997). *Images of organization.* Thousand Oaks, CA: Sage.

Mullen, B., Atkins, J.L., Champion, D.S., Edwards, C., Hardy, D., Story, J.E., & Venderklok, M. (1985). The false consensus effect: A meta-analysis of 115 hypothesis tests. *Journal of Experimental Social Psychology, 21,* 263–283.

Perry, W.G., Jr. (1981). Cognitive and ethical growth: The making of meaning. In A. Chickering & Associates (Eds.), *The modern American college* (pp. 76–116). San Francisco, CA: Jossey-Bass.

Ross, L., Greene, D., & House, P. (1977). The "False Consensus Effect": An egocentric bias in social perception and attribution processes. *Journal of Experimental Social Psychology, 13,* 279–301.

Snyder, C.R., & Lopez, S.J. (2005). *Handbook of positive psychology.* Oxford: Oxford University Press.

Swann, W.B., & Pelham, B.W. (2005). The truth about illusions: Authenticity and positivity in social relationships. In C.R Snyder & S.J. Lopez (Eds.), *Handbook of positive psychology* (pp. 366–381). Oxford: Oxford University Press.

Tajfel, H. (1982). *Social identity and intergroup relations.* New York: Cambridge University Press.

Tan, J.S., & Yong, R. (2003). *Training and developing cultural intelligence.* In P.C. Earley & S. Ang (Eds), *Cultural intelligence* (pp. 258–303). Palo Alto, CA: Stanford University Press.

Triandis, H.C. (1980). Values, attitudes, and interpersonal behavior. In H.E. Howe & M.M. Page (Eds.), *Nebraska symposium on motivation* (pp. 195–206). Lincoln, NE: University of Nebraska Press.

Triandis, H.C. (1990). Theoretical concepts of use to practitioners. In R.W. Brislin (Ed.), *Applied cross-cultural psychology* (pp. 34–55). Thousand Oaks, CA: Sage.

CHAPTER 23

Contextualizing Cultural Intelligence

The Case of Global Managers

MADDY JANSSENS AND TINEKE CAPPELLEN

As today's workplace has become more global and diverse, the concept of cultural intelligence (CQ) has been introduced to understand why some individuals are more effective than others in dealing with situations that are culturally diverse. According to Earley and Ang (2003), CQ refers to an individual's capability to deal effectively in situations characterized by cultural diversity, and is a multifactor construct with cognitive (metacognitive and cognitive), motivational, and behavioral dimensions.

This study aims to contribute to this new research area by exploring CQ for a specific, but increasingly relevant type of international work (e.g., global managers). Working internationally has long been narrowed down to expatriation, in which individuals are relocated into a different cultural context. However, recent international management literature has argued that organizations can no longer afford to transfer people on a permanent basis to deliver certain services to parts of the organization. Rather, organizations increasingly rely on alternative types of international mobility such as global managers, awareness-building assignments, commuting assignments, extended business traveling (Collings, Scullion & Morley, 2007), and SWAT teams—an idea adapted from "special weapons and tactics" units by Roberts, Kossek, and Ozeki (1998) to describe highly mobile teams of experts, deployed on a short-term basis, to troubleshoot, solve very specific problems, or complete clearly defined projects. These new types of workforce management are organizational responses to more complex global realities, characterized by speed, flexibility, and heightened economic interdependencies (Kedia & Mukherji, 1999). They reflect alternative ways of coordinating an organization's activities across national, functional, and business borders (Pucik & Saba, 1998) and methods for getting the right skills or people to where the work is on an as-needed basis (Roberts et al., 1998). Often, these alternative types of international work imply new ways of working across cultures. For instance, commuters interact with foreign colleagues on a recurrent weekly schedule. Or in virtual assignments, managers rely on information technology to interact with their foreign colleagues. As each new type of international work creates its own challenges to cross-cultural interaction, the question arises as to what extent they ask for a particular type of CQ.

In this chapter, we focus on one specific type of international work, global management, as we assume that this work requires a particular type of CQ. Relying on previous definitions (Adler & Bartholomew, 1992; Bartlett & Ghoshal, 1992; Pucik & Saba, 1998), we consider a global manager to be different from the traditional expatriate manager. The global manager is someone who is assigned to a position with a cross-border responsibility rather than a local responsibility, must understand business from a worldwide rather than a countrywide perspective, needs to balance between local and potentially contradictory demands in the global environment rather than aligning a local demand with those from headquarters, and must be able to work with multiple cultures simultaneously rather than with one culture at a time (Cappellen & Janssens, 2005). Such international work implies not only an increase in the variety and frequency of cross-cultural interaction but also a change in the very nature of cross-cultural interaction (Adler & Bartholomew, 1992). However, no empirical research yet exists that examines cultural capabilities for this type of work in more detail.

Through a qualitative study of in-depth interviews with global managers of three international companies, we explore how these experienced and successful managers deal with cultural diversity. Relying on their accounts, we identify their cognitive (metacognitive and cognitive), motivational, and behavioral dimensions of CQ (Earley & Ang, 2003). By focusing on a specific sample of global managers, this chapter is an extension and application of Earley and Ang's conceptualization of CQ (2003), which reflects appropriate cross-cultural capabilities for the complex reality in which global managers operate.

We begin by presenting our empirical study. Relying on both the literature on global management and our interviews, we then discuss global managers' international work, aiming to understand its specificity and consequently the type of cross-cultural interactions. After presenting our findings, we discuss how the cultural ability of the global managers under study refers to the different dimensions of CQ. We conclude by reflecting on broader theoretical implications and future research on CQ as well as practical implications.

EMPIRICAL STUDY

To explore the concept of CQ in the case of global managers, we draw on the results of a larger research study of 45 successful global managers. This chapter relies on data generated by 38 of these global managers who explained in depth how they experience cross-cultural interactions in their work and how they deal with cultural diversity.

The global managers under study were working for three different companies, all operating in a transnational environment. Such an environment was chosen because it pressures organizations to balance global and local forces (Ghoshal & Nohria, 1993). As organizations in transnational environments, such as the automobile industry or computer industry, are challenged to coordinate the complex pressures of integration and responsiveness (Bartlett & Ghoshal, 1992), they are more likely to install alternative types of international mobility. It is in such environments that the task of global managers is to establish worldwide coordination through equilibrating competing forces rather than predisposing decisions in favor of one dimension at the expense of others (Prahalad & Doz, 1987). The three companies under study were headquartered in Belgium: Pharma Corporation, operating in the pharmaceutical industry, View Corporation, and Vision Corporation, both operating in the visualization industry.

We drew on the results of interviews with 38 managers who, at the time of the interview, had global responsibility: 9 in Pharma Corporation, 14 in View Corporation, and 15 in Vision Corporation. We considered them to be successful global managers as they fulfilled more than one global management position within the same company and also showed continued willingness to work globally. These two criteria follow the criteria of successful expatriation (e.g. Black, 1990; Caligiuri, 1997), which suggests that the company positively evaluates the managers' performance and individuals are psychologically comfortable with working with other cultures. Because the managers are successful, we assumed that their accounts of how they deal with cultural differences represent effective behaviors, and consequently provide us with relevant insights on global managers' CQ.

The interviewees were primarily male, except for 6 women participating in the study. The majority of this group, 34, were Belgian, but Indian, Luxembourg, French, and Dutch nationalities also occurred in our sample. The average age of the interviewees was 40.5 years with an average tenure of 8.5 years at the current organization and an average international experience (including expatriate, inpatriate, or commuting assignments) of 10.8 years of which 10 years represented global management experience. Because of our focus on their global responsibility, interviewees held positions within all possible functional domains: research and development, human resources, sales and purchasing, finance, operations, and marketing. The interviews were conducted in 2005 and 2006 at the interviewees' offices. The length of the interviews ranged from one to two hours. The interviews were conducted in Dutch or English and were tape-recorded and fully transcribed.

The data were analyzed through template analysis (King, 1999), starting from a template of four higher-order codes that represent the four dimensions of CQ while inductively searching for subcodes that reflect indicators of each of these dimensions in the specific context of global managers' work reality. We found that encompassing categories of data refer to indicators in the Cultural Intelligence Scale (Ang, Van Dyne, Koh, Ng, Templer, Tay, & Chandrasekar, 2007), while other categories reflect capabilities that are specifically relevant to global managers.

GLOBAL MANAGERS AND THEIR CROSS-CULTURAL INTERACTIONS

To understand the specificity of global managers' cross-cultural interactions, we present in this section the nature of their international work. Relying on the literature on global managers (e.g., Adler & Bartholomew, 1992; Kedia & Mukherji, 1999; Roberts et al., 1998) as well as our interviews, we identified two aspects as crucial in their international work: flexibility and worldwide coordination.

First, the global economic context implies an increasing challenge for organizations to work on a flexible and global basis in terms of workforce management. The right skills must be sited where they are needed, regardless of geographical location (Roberts et al., 1998). This requires organizations to make the distinction between when it is necessary to physically move a person to a particular location and when the person's skills can be delivered through other means. Consequently, permanent transfers such as expatriate assignments are only used when necessary, relying when possible on the use of highly mobile global managers. In one of the interviews, when asked about their international flexibility, a global purchasing director at Pharma Corporation told us:

> My position was called the international division, so I have been traveling quite a lot. Traveling a lot meant a minimum of, I would say in the very beginning, a couple of weeks a year to a full five months a year, so five months being away. So it means in total much more than five months. Most of my time was abroad, like when I was in Japan, I used to go minimum six times per year to Japan, so in operation two or three weeks. But officially, I was not a resident of Japan.

The consequence of this flexible deployment is that global managers spend shorter periods of time in any single country, often moving from one location to another. They use their cross-cultural skills on regular multicountry business trips and in daily interaction with foreign colleagues and clients worldwide, rather than just during foreign assignments (Adler & Bartholomew, 1992). Such short-term, frequent cross-cultural interactions may prevent the aspirant culturally intelligent manager from gaining in-depth knowledge of foreign cultures and learning the fundamental principles of interaction within them. Furthermore, one can ask the question whether country-specific knowledge based on a large amount of contact with people from a single country is even relevant to the global manager (Earley & Peterson, 2004).

In the cases where their physical presence is not indispensable, new technologies can be used for people to interact across borders through teleconferencing or videoconferencing. Global managers do not work exclusively face-to-face; they use virtual tools to communicate in an efficient way, reducing the need for international business trips. A worldwide marketing director at View Corporation told us how she alternates business trips with virtual tools:

> So am I still working internationally? Sure, even more, but I try to condense it. So I try to say to people, "look, what can we already discuss at this point, in videoconference, or conference call. I am certainly going to come over there, but only in a later stage."

So, flexibility is also reflected in the variety of communication tools that global managers need to rely on when interacting cross-culturally. The lack of face-to-face contact that goes along with communication technologies may have implications for CQ. For instance, Earley and Ang (2003) stress the importance of verbal as well as nonverbal behavior in

CQ, arguing that people with high CQ should be able to control their physical display sufficiently so that nonverbal behavior conveys what verbal behavior produces. As global managers rely heavily on communication technologies, the question arises as to how their virtual interaction impacts how they deal effectively with other cultures.

Second, the economic interdependencies in a global context challenge organizations to coordinate their activities worldwide. Such coordination requires a global mindset in which competing forces are equilibrated rather than one dimension being favored at the expense of the others (Prahalad & Doz, 1987). Thinking globally means extending concepts and models from one-to-one relationships to holding multiple realities and relationships in mind simultaneously, and then acting skillfully on this more complex reality (Lane, DiStefano & Maznevski, 1997). Thinking globally refers to the ability to balance different complex forces in pursuit of a unique strategy that blends them (Bartlett & Ghoshal, 1989). Global managers who are responsible for such worldwide coordination are therefore working with people from many cultures simultaneously (Adler & Bartholomew, 1992). They no longer have the luxury of dealing with each country's issues on a separate, and therefore sequential, basis. Rather, they need to consider multiple cultural issues at the same time or at least within a very short time frame. When talking about his daily tasks, a worldwide chemical engineer at Pharma Corporation told us that he works with multiple cultures at the same time:

> I am working internationally because I have many contacts with colleagues that are outside of Belgium. I just got a phone call today from India, yesterday, I had a videoconference with Switzerland, and last week, I was in the United States and in the United States, I had to deal with some Japanese problems.

In addition, worldwide coordination means that information, knowledge, and experience must increasingly be distributed across national, functional, and business borders (Pucik & Saba, 1998). Consequently, organizations are increasingly structured along "centers of excellence" (Galbraith, 2000), and authority and expertise no longer reside exclusively at headquarters (Roberts et al., 1998). This implies that global managers need to interact with foreign colleagues as equals, rather than from within clearly defined hierarchies of structural or cultural dominance and subordination (Adler & Bartholomew, 1992). It is no longer the case that foreigners must adapt to the headquarters' culture; all managers need to make adaptations and all managers need to help to create a synergistic way of working that transcends any one national culture. Although headquartered in Belgium, a worldwide human resources manager at View Corporation told us how they distance themselves from being the center of the world:

> So Belgium, although we are headquartered here, it is not the center of the world. . . . It is not because we are the largest part globally, based here, that this needs to weigh on the decision making. So we are still a very strong Belgian company, . . . but it means that everything with regard to internal communication . . . needs to be in English.

The coordination aspect of global managers' work implies a specific nature of cross-cultural interactions, working simultaneously and on equal basis with people from different cultural backgrounds. As the concept of CQ does not explicitly deal with the challenge of working simultaneously with different cultures, the question arises whether the nature of global managers' cross-cultural interactions requires a specific type of CQ.

CQ OF GLOBAL MANAGERS

In this section, we present the ways in which the interviewed global managers deal with cultural differences. For each of the different CQ dimensions, we first present the elements that correspond to the indicators suggested by Ang and colleagues (2007), followed by new insights on how global managers deal with cultural differences given the specificity of their international work. Within our sample, 28 out of 38 global managers confirmed at least one CQ indicator and 24 out of 38 reported at least one different CQ indicator. We start with the cognitive dimension of CQ, followed by the behavioral, metacognitive, and motivational dimensions of CQ.

Cognitive CQ

Cognitive CQ is an individual's knowledge of specific norms, practices, and conventions in different cultural settings (Ang et al., 2007; Earley & Ang, 2003). This dimension of CQ represents an individual's ability to assess the similarities and differences in cultural situations in ways that allow him or her to produce culturally appropriate behavior.

Global managers in our study agreed on the relevance of cultural knowledge for their cross-cultural work, as "you need to know what is allowed and what is not" in a specific culture. According to them, knowledge is important because "one needs to understand why somebody acts the way he does" and, already referring to behavioral CQ, because "you need to react differently, negotiate differently and so on." Consistent with the Cultural Intelligence Scale of Ang and colleagues (2007), global managers indicated the importance of language because "if you don't speak it, it would be difficult to say what a culture is really like." However, language knowledge does not only encompass a cognitive element, it also impacts the relationship with locals. For instance, one global manager stated, "even though you speak only half of it, the effort builds bridges and makes you get on more easily." In a similar vein, having some historical knowledge is argued to be a sign of respect for the other culture. As a global manager of View Corporation told us, "what I also do, for example, is when you go to a country, you try to know something of its history, to a certain extent I try to know something, out of respect for the people there, for my customers."

Whereas cultural knowledge is considered to be important, some interviewees (n = 7) further explained how they focused primarily on knowledge of managerial styles and behaviors, and less on religious beliefs, marriage systems, and arts and crafts (Ang et al., 2007). They referred to knowledge regarding the importance of hierarchy, relationships in doing business, negotiation styles, direct versus indirect communication, and so on.

For example, a global product manager from Vision Corporation recounted how German, American, and Japanese cultures differ in terms of how confrontational one can be:

> . . . the attitude of really wanting to know how these people function and how they like to be dealt with, how they like to work and then being able to adjust yourself to it. In my experience, this always leads to the best results. For example, Germans always say for themselves what they think and they like you to do the same. Whether this is good or bad, it doesn't matter. It's just that, when you need to deliver some bad news, just do it. Say, I have some bad news, this and that, but I suggest this and that as a solution. With Americans, for example, you need to handle this in a completely different way. To them, everything is always great and okay, even when things are going bad, you need to give it a turn. You really can't be as confrontational as with Germans for instance. The Japanese, they don't know the word no. So when they ask you something and you would like to say no, you need to know that saying no doesn't really fit their culture. It's probably more yes, but . . .

However, while global managers in general pointed to their need to gain knowledge of cultures, some global managers in our sample (n = 8) questioned the ability to acquire in-depth cultural knowledge. In the first instance, they referred to the lack of time they have to do so, given their frequent travels and short visits. For example, one global manager told us, "if you fly in and out, most of the time they are short visits, the cultural awareness is of course important, but not stimulated." Moreover, a few global managers openly questioned the ability to gain full understanding of other cultures. They argued "one can imagine how one behaves in other cultures, but in the end, it is still always a surprise." A worldwide marketing director from View Corporation reported it as follows:

> Because as a foreigner, I cannot understand all of them. They tell me something and they think I understand. It's not about the language, it's about the way to look at life. I think I understand, but in reality, I don't understand. Many people say something and they mean something, and sometimes, all of the time, I need somebody to translate it, what they mean. Not what they say, but what they mean. And they will express it in a different way, depending on the culture.

When asked further about the way they then deal with cultural differences, they argued that "some general leads" can already facilitate working with other cultures. We will discuss their behaviors and tactics more in-depth when presenting new insights regarding the behavioral and metacognitive dimensions.

Behavioral Dimension

The behavioral dimension of CQ reflects an individual's flexibility in exhibiting appropriate behavior when interacting with people who differ in cultural background (Ang et al., 2007; Earley & Ang, 2003).

Global managers in our sample considered flexibility in behavior to be important for success in the global work environment. They very often referred to openness toward other cultures in terms of "not imposing your own way or will but adjusting to the local culture" as a basic attitude. Consistent with Ang and colleagues' (2007) indicators, they pointed to changes in verbal behaviors. For instance, one global manager described being flexible in terms of having meetings in which "in the United States, you can say in relatively simple words what you think; but in the United Kingdom, even in the same language, you have to say it in a more diplomatic way."

In addition however, global managers in our study emphasized the need to adjust their management style while working with other cultures (n = 6). Just as they stressed cultural knowledge of management behaviors, they argued the importance of adopting a different style when working in different cultural environments. They deal differently with hierarchy, convince customers in a different way, or stimulate creativity in another way. A worldwide sales manager in Pharma Corporation called himself a "chameleon" when telling us about his flexibility in exhibiting appropriate management behavior:

> If you are entering into a meeting room typically in the United States, and people, you know, exchange a couple of jokes and then jump on you as if they want to tear you apart, I feel comfortable to go on this level of rapid fire exchange and those kind of things. And usually, it helps managing the situation. But by the same token, if you are, in a completely other extreme, an old Japanese company and you sit on a couch instead of in a meeting room and it takes an hour to go around the table before you even address anything, . . . I don't feel impatient. . . .

Besides emphasizing the need to adjust their management style, some global managers expressed behavioral tactics that until now were not considered expressions of CQ. When global managers who questioned the ability to acquire in-depth cultural knowledge were asked how they tried to work effectively with other cultures, they referred to three types of behavior: (1) they take a personal rather than a cultural approach; (2) they focus on cultural artifacts rather than on underlying values and assumptions; and (3) they rely on local informants rather than gaining the cultural knowledge themselves.

First, when working with a multitude of cultures in a rather short time frame, some global managers reported that they take a very personal approach in their international work (n = 3), such as "having good contacts with people I work with" or "knowing very little of India, but knowing the people who work there by name." They stressed the importance of establishing good interpersonal relationships through knowing each other on a personal level. A second behavioral tactic referred to focusing on the cultural artifacts rather than trying to understand the underlying values and assumptions of cultures (n = 3). Some global managers explicitly argued that they are flexible in exhibiting appropriate behavior but only regarding more "superficial" things. For example, a business unit vice president of View Corporation reported how he is unable to understand all cultures, but adjusts to some of the cultural artifacts:

> So you need to eat with sticks in China and eat burgers with a lot of mustard in the States and drink large glasses of beer . . . I do not try to unravel all these cultures, because I don't think it makes sense. For example, in America, you need to attend a baseball game once, you cannot understand . . . how it is being performed, you cannot imagine. But I don't put a lot of effort in it, I have some colleagues who try to unravel all these things, the American culture . . . I'm not. Just let yourself go with the flow, walk with them, talk to them, yell with them, and then it will work.

In a similar vein, one respondent recounted that he surfs the Internet before traveling to a foreign country. He searches for information or recent events in that country that serve as "conversation openers" when he is meeting new people. Again, this global manager is not so much concerned about exhibiting appropriate behavior based on in-depth cultural knowledge but more about "showing openness and empathy" through expressing an interest in the country. Finally, global managers reported that they rely on local informants to express appropriate behaviors (n = 4). Rather than gaining in-depth cultural knowledge, they find local individuals whom they can trust to interpret cultural behaviors. A worldwide sales and marketing director from View Corporation expressed this as follows:

> And also, I very often find one person in every region whom I trust. One local person whom I can call, who speaks good English and who can, let's say, give me the view of the local people. That's extremely important, because as a foreigner, I cannot understand all of them.

Next to these behavioral tactics related to the inability of knowing cultures, our data revealed some other indicators of behavioral CQ that are related to global managers' specific task of worldwide coordination. Very often mentioned is the behavior of listening (n = 7). Many global managers stressed that "what I do is, I listen a lot; and I try not to impose my view on the people." The reason for this behavior is linked to their task of worldwide coordination. For example, one global manager expressed that "defining your marketing strategy from Europe without involvement of the Americans is suicide. If you really want to work in a global way, then you need to involve people of other cultures in your decision-making process and this means really listening to people." A quality engineer described his listening behavior as a crucial element of his reflective behavior:

> Being open, listening, not giving a reaction immediately, and then, how should I call it? Zooming in and zooming out . . . zooming in to empathize, to familiarize with certain elements and then taking a much broader perspective. And that's a reflection I make in my work daily, a lot, when I'm working on certain things, most of the time it's on processes and then I will always check with Karlsruhe and India, because when we do it like this, it is okay for all three of them or if not, we need to adjust the flavor.

Another, related behavioral indicator that is often mentioned was "taking time" (n = 4). Global managers argued that to be able to take into account local differences, they "need a lot of time," to "be careful" and "avoid the pressure of time." For instance, a business improvement manager in Pharma Corporation described her strategy as follows:

> What I try to do so that I can work with everybody is to be very open, and to welcome them. I speak a lot with them over the phone, and then I always try to say things in a nice tone of voice, and not to be under pressure of time, but take time with them, to let them speak. I also always ask for their input, their feedback, thank them for what they do and tell them that if they want to change something or think about something, they can let me know.

Finally, one global manager mentioned a particular flexibility in exhibiting appropriate behavior that was related to virtual communication. Besides working face-to-face, a lot of cross-cultural interactions in global work take place through e-mail, teleconferencing, and videoconferencing. Talking about the different communication tools, one of our interviewees, a worldwide accounting manager in View Corporation, stressed the importance of selecting the right communication channel, especially when it concerns sensitive topics:

> I try to understand how things fit and when there are remarks, also when I think that something is sensitive . . . a lot of communication runs through e-mail. When I feel that there is something rather strange, I call, because that is a lot easier. That's a huge disadvantage about e-mail, everything is immediately written, on paper, and also it sounds so definite and comes across rude. So, I will try to phone them as much as possible, talk. That's then the only thing I can do.

Metacognitive Dimension

The metacognitive dimension of CQ refers to an individual's cultural consciousness and awareness during interactions with those who have different cultural backgrounds (Ang et al., 2007; Earley & Ang, 2003). It is a critical aspect of CQ because much of what is required when interacting in a new culture is the ability to put together parts into a coherent picture, even if one does not initially know what the result will be (Earley & Peterson, 2004).

Global managers in our study acknowledged the relevance of this dimension, referring especially to consciousness about cultural differences. As they have contact with different cultures simultaneously or in a very short sequential way, our interviewees expressed the need to be aware of "what happens on all sides and being open to small things you see and the things you can see in between the lines." They further indicated that awareness of differences was important because "as long as you know, you first of all won't get annoyed and then second you try to adjust."

Our data expands this notion of being conscious of cultural differences and knowledge, as a few global managers in our study expressed another metacognitive element, i.e., being conscious about integrating different perspectives (n = 2). They argued that part of their international work is to search for compromises or combinations of different approaches. They are aware that "you cannot work in four ways at the same time. You need somehow to find a good compromise." A crisis manager in Vision Corporation expressed his view on this constant search as follows:

> You need to adjust. You cannot impose your method, your way of thinking or whatever on them; you need to integrate anyhow to get something accomplished. And that is the case for China, Japan, Taiwan, the United States, they need to have the feeling that you are one of them or at least that you understand them and that you will defend, this is a heavy word, them at headquarters.

Finally, another indicator of metacognitive CQ that emerged from the data is "being conscious about one's own frame of reference" (n = 2). Rather than being conscious about putting parts together into a coherent picture of the other culture, the global managers in our study pointed to the need to "detach yourself from your own framework, so not taking your own culture as the norm or basis of what counts on a worldwide scale." Again, this suggests that global managers, because of the nature of their international work, cannot be oriented toward building in-depth cultural knowledge of other cultures. As they need to work with many cultures at the same time, they can only be aware that they don't know and focus on "distancing oneself from their own framework."

Motivational Dimension

Finally, the motivational dimension of CQ reflects the ability and motivation to use cultural knowledge and produce a culturally appropriate response (Earley & Ang, 2003). It refers to an individual's drive and interest to learn and function in situations characterized by cultural difference.

Global managers in our study pointed out that the joy of interacting with people from different cultures is an important motivational element. Most respondents find working across cultures extremely "fascinating," "enriching," even, as one global manager put it, the "icing on the cake," because "you get to know a lot of new things, you meet lots of people too, you handle them differently." Most global managers in our study like it because "it just opens your mind to different people, to different mindsets, different mentalities." According to a worldwide sales director in View Corporation, working across cultures fits his personality:

> I may be an exception to that, but I find traveling, for me, for my personality, it is something I like. When I travel, I always ask them, off the record of course, to book me a hotel in the town center, where I can enjoy a little exploration after work. Not much, but just to feel how these people live. I like that a lot, so I also frequently visit local restaurants and so on, so I have this interest.

The global managers in our sample also often mentioned confidence in their ability to deal with cultural differences. Talking about their interactions with people from sometimes completely different cultures, most interviewees felt very comfortable doing so. For some of them, this ability came from their interest and experience as "you observe, you inform, from people who are experienced in how you should deal with it and how you can adjust yourself to it, and then you just do it." For others, their confidence in working across cultures was built during their childhood as they were raised in two or more cultures.

Besides enjoying other cultures and feeling confident in dealing with them, our data suggest an expansion of motivational CQ. Throughout the interviews, our respondents expressed a motivation to work internationally because they "like to experience the world as my working space" (n = 5). It's not only the joy of interacting and living with people from other cultures but also the joy of *working* with many different cultures and different views. Global managers seem to be motivated by "knowing the world and needing to react to all those impulses which is a neverending learning process," which is a critical aspect of their coordination task. A global research and development manager at Pharma Corporation expressed it as follows:

> It is unbelievable to see how you can behave in one environment and having things done in another environment, it will never work. And the way, actually, you deal with people to make it work in a different environment, is one of the most challenging things like switching from discussing a project with our U.S. colleagues and then discussing the same project with our Japanese colleagues. I mean, it's so different to really make it work; it is that challenge I like.

DISCUSSION

Interviewing 38 global managers, our study suggests that the specificity of their cross-cultural interactions requires a particular set of capabilities that extend the current universal construct of CQ (Earley & Ang, 2003). While our data support the four dimensions of cognitive, behavioral, metacognitive, and motivational CQ, they also suggest that global managers require a particular type of CQ because of their short-term and frequent contact, variety in communication tools, and the nature of their cross-cultural interactions.

Short-Term, Frequent Contact

First, our findings suggest that global managers' short-term but highly frequent cross-cultural interactions have important implications for the cognitive, behavioral, and meta-cognitive dimensions of CQ. First, in terms of cognitive CQ, some global managers in our study questioned their ability to gain in-depth cultural knowledge. Second, rather than relying on a purely cognitive basis, global managers in our study turned to behavioral tactics such as taking a very personal approach or acquiring knowledge on a few cultural artifacts to compensate for a limited cognition. Finally, global managers in this study also reported on their experience of distancing themselves from their own frame of reference, pointing to another indicator of metacognitive CQ.

This extension of CQ because of the short-term, frequent cross-cultural interactions of global managers corresponds to the notion of mindfulness. According to Thomas (2006), mindfulness is a linking process between knowledge and behavioral ability in which people are aware of their own assumptions, ideas, and emotions and their selective perception, attribution, and categorization. Compensating for the inability to gain more general in-depth cultural knowledge, mindfulness implies an enhanced attention to the particular current experience or present reality and its context while creating new mental maps of other peoples' personality and cultural background as a basis for immediate action (Thomas & Inkson, 2004). From this perspective, culturally intelligent global managers are able to approach a situation with an open mind, focusing their attention on personal and context-specific details (Thomas, 2006).

Variety in Communication Tools

Our study also points to the consequences for CQ if working across cultures occurs through a variety of communication tools. Due to the nature of their international work, global managers cannot rely only on face-to-face contacts, but make use of a variety of communication tools such as e-mail, teleconferencing, and videoconferencing. Such reliance on a variety of communication tools extends the dimension of behavioral CQ, pointing to the ability to select the right communication channel for the task at hand.

Earlier studies on computer-mediated communication have examined the effects of virtual communication tools, indicating for example that people need to use rich channels for uncertain and equivocal communication (Daft & Lengel, 1984, 1986). Face-to-face communication for example is found to be the richest communication channel, preferred by people working on complex or "un-analyzable" problems, whereas a poor medium such as e-mail is preferred when parties need to edit, store, forward, or print large amounts of text, allowing for more exchange of content in a single unit of time (Hinds & Kiesler, 1995). Therefore, culturally intelligent global managers are able to use this variety of tools strategically, selecting the communication tool corresponding to the characteristics of the message being sent.

Nature of Cross-Cultural Interactions

Finally, the findings suggest that the nature of global managers' cross-cultural interactions—interacting simultaneously with foreign colleagues across multiple cultures on an equal basis—extends the behavioral, motivational, and metacognitive dimensions of CQ. In terms of behavioral CQ, global managers reported relying on behaviors such as listening and taking time to successfully deal with their task of worldwide coordination. Further, our study suggests that the motivational dimension of CQ for global manages also encompasses a motivation to consider the world as one's working space. Finally, the need for global managers to be conscious about the integration of different perspectives in this study reflects an extension of metacognitive CQ.

Being culturally intelligent when working simultaneously with multiple cultures corresponds to the fusion approach proposed by Janssens and Brett (2006). Focusing on global teams, these authors argue that creative and realistic solutions are produced if cultural differences can coexist and be combined such that the distinct qualities of each culture are respected and preserved. In this line of thought, culturally intelligent global managers ensure that foreign colleagues can maintain their cultural way of working, searching for synergistic solutions when working across cultural boundaries (Adler & Bartholomew, 1992).

CONCLUSION

This empirical study extends our understanding of CQ with regard to one new type of international work: the global manager. It shows that global managers' specific types of cross-cultural interactions require particular cultural capabilities, pointing to additional indicators of cognitive, motivational, behavioral, and metacognitive dimensions of CQ. To conclude, we reflect on the limitations, possible avenues for future research, and practice implications generated by this study.

The main limitation of this study is related to the possibility of respondents' bias. When asking someone how he or she behaves in a culturally different situation, the answer may be one of espoused theory (Argyris & Schön, 1974), which reflects the theory of action that he or she gives allegiance to and communicates upon request. However, this might be very different from the theory-in-use. Interpretations of the results therefore must be made carefully. Future research may address this concern by complementing questions on behaviors with observations that might raise the accuracy of the represented theory-in-use (Argyris & Schön, 1974).

Another possible avenue for future research is to examine other types of international work and its corresponding type of CQ. Whereas earlier work considered CQ as a universal construct (Earley & Ang, 2003), this study showed that future research may benefit from considering the specific nature of international work as it may generate particular cross-cultural interactions. Future studies may therefore want to replicate this study for other types of international work, such as virtual teams or commuting assignments. Having identified specific cultural capabilities for different types of international mobility, further research may relate the specifics of CQ to other issues in international work such as selection and training. For instance, they may examine the validity of selection tests that include CQ for specific types of international work.

This study offers a number of insights for developing organizational training programs that support global managers in their CQ. First, instead of offering training on country-specific knowledge, organizations may benefit from developing a training program on mindfulness, in which global managers apprehend how to counterbalance their lack of in-depth cultural knowledge by distancing themselves from their own frame of reference and/or by negotiating reality, learning new ways of seeing and doing in a specific context (Friedman & Berthoin Antal, 2005). Second, organizations can increase global managers' ability to effectively communicate across cultures by offering training on different virtual communication tools. Knowing the advantages and disadvantages of a range of communication tools will help global managers to assess which tools are most appropriate for which purpose. And finally, the skill of combining different cultural perspectives into a creative and realistic acceptable solution can be developed by offering global managers negotiation training, focusing on achieving integrative outcomes (Brett, 2007). So, developing global managers' CQ requires a move from traditional cross-cultural training to training to become a mindful global manager, effective virtual communicator, and integrative negotiator.

REFERENCES

Adler, N.J., & Bartholomew, S. (1992). Managing globally competent people. *Academy of Management Executive, 6,* 52–65.

Ang, S., Van Dyne, L., Koh, C., Ng, K., Templer, K.J., Tay, C., & Chandrasekar, N.A. (2007). Cultural intelligence: Its measurement and effects on cultural judgment and decision making, cultural adaptation, and task performance. *Management and Organization Review, 3,* 335–371.

Argyris, C., & Schön, D. (1974). *Theory in practice.* San Francisco, CA: Jossey-Bass.

Bartlett, C.A., & Ghoshal, S. (1989). *Managing across borders: The transnational solution.* Boston, MA: The Harvard Business School Press.

Bartlett, C.A., & Ghoshal, S. (1992). What is a global manager? *Harvard Business Review, 70,* 124–132.

Black, J.S. (1990). Locus of control, social support, stress and adjustment in international transfers. *Asia Pacific Journal of Management, 7,* 1–29.

Brett, J.M. (2007). *Negotiating globally* (2nd ed.). San Francisco, CA: Jossey-Bass.

Caligiuri, P.M. (1997). Assessing expatriate success: Beyond just being there. In Z. Aycan (Ed.), *Expatriate management: Theory and practice* (pp. 117–140). Greenwich, CT: JAI Press.

Cappellen, T., & Janssens, M. (2005). Career paths of global managers: Towards future research. *Journal of World Business, 40,* 348–360.

Collings, D.G., Scullion, H., & Morley, M.J. (2007). Changing patterns of global staffing in the multinational enterprise: Challenges to the conventional expatriate assignment and emerging alternatives. *Journal of World Business, 42,* 198–213.

Daft, R.L., & Lengel, R.H. (1984). Information richness: A new approach to managerial behavior and organization design. In B. Straw & L.L. Cummings (Eds.), *Research in organizational behavior* (pp. 191–233). Greenwich, CT: JAI Press.

Daft, R.L., & Lengel, R.H. (1986). Organizational information requirements, media richness and structural design. *Management Science, 32,* 554–571.

Earley, P.C., & Ang, S. (2003). *Cultural intelligence: Individual interactions across cultures.* Palo Alto, CA: Stanford University Press.

Earley, P.C., & Peterson, R.S. (2004). The elusive cultural chameleon: Cultural intelligence as a new approach to intercultural training for the global manager. *Academy of Management Learning & Education, 3,* 100–116.

Friedman, V.J., & Berthoin Antal, A. (2005). Negotiating reality. A theory of action approach to intercultural competence. *Management Learning, 36,* 69–86.

Galbraith, J.R. (2000). *Designing the global corporation.* San Francisco, CA: Jossey-Bass.

Ghoshal, S., & Nohria, N. (1993). Horses for courses: Organizational forms for multinational corporations. *Sloan Management Review, 34,* 23–35.

Hinds, P., & Kiesler, S. (1995). Communication across boundaries: Work, structure, and use of communication technologies in a large organization. *Organization Science, 6,* 373–393.

Janssens, M., & Brett, J.M. (2006). Cultural intelligence in global teams: A fusion model of collaboration. *Group and Organization Management, 31,* 124–153.

Kedia, B.L. & Mukherji, A. (1999). Global managers: Developing a mindset for global competitiveness, *Journal of World Business,* 34, 230–251.

King, N. (1999). Template analysis. In G. Symon & C. Cassell (Eds.), *Qualitative methods and analysis in organizational research* (pp. 118–134). London: Sage.

Lane, H.W., Distefano J.J., & Maznevski, M.L. (1997). *International management behavior* (3rd ed.). Cambridge, MA: Blackwell.

Prahalad, C.K., & Doz, Y.L. (1987). *The multinational mission: Balancing local demands and global vision.* New York: The Free Press.

Pucik, V., & Saba, T. (1998). Selecting and developing the global versus the expatriate manager: A review of the state-of-the-art. *Human Resource Planning, 21,* 40–53.

Roberts, K., Kossek, E.E., & Ozeki, C. (1998). Managing the global workforce: Challenges and strategies. *Academy of Management Executive, 12,* 93–106.

Thomas, D.C. (2006). Domain and development of cultural intelligence. The importance of mindfulness. *Group and Organization Management, 31,* 78–99.

Thomas, D.C., & Inkson, K. (2004). *Cultural intelligence: People skills for global business.* San Francisco, CA: Berrett-Koehler Publishers.

PART VI

COMMENTARY

CHAPTER 24

Thinking Intelligently About Cultural Intelligence
The Road Ahead

MICHELE J. GELFAND, LYNN IMAI, AND RYAN FEHR

To scholars and practitioners alike, cultural competencies have long been a topic of interest across a wide range of disciplines, from the familiar fields of cross-cultural management and organizational psychology to the more far-reaching areas of education, health, and counseling. Under the rubric of cultural competencies, many constructs have been discussed in the literature including *flexibility* (Arthur & Bennett, 1995; Gullahorn & Gullahorn, 1963; Hanvey, 1976; Ruben & Kealey, 1979; Smith, 1966; Torbiörn, 1982), *cultural sensitivity* (Hawes & Kealey, 1981), *cultural empathy* (Hannigan, 1990), *intercultural sensitivity* (Bhawuk & Brislin, 1992; Hammer, Bennett, & Wiseman, 2003), *bicultural competence* (LaFromboise, Coleman, & Gerton, 1993), *extracultural openness* (Arthur & Bennett, 1995), *global mindset* (Gupta & Govindarajan, 2002), and *multicultural personality* (van der Zee & van Oudenhoven, 2000). The importance of cultural competence cannot be underestimated. In a world of global opportunities and global threats, there is a great theoretical and practical need to develop cultural competencies within many spheres of life—political, educational, organizational, military, and the like—and across many levels of analysis, including individual, group, organizational, and national.

Yet, despite years of scholarship across multiple disciplines, progress in understanding cultural competencies has been limited theoretically, methodologically, and practically. The literature can perhaps be characterized as suffering from the *jingle and jangle fallacy* (Kelley, 1927), where constructs with the same meaning are labeled differently while constructs with different meanings are labeled similarly. For example, terms such as *cultural sensitivity* and *cultural empathy* (Hawes & Kealey, 1981) both refer to an ability to empathize with the feelings, thoughts, and behaviors of people from different cultures (van Oudenhoven & van der Zee, 2002). Furthermore, under the label of *flexibility,* some authors emphasize the ability to adjust behavior in new cultural settings (e.g., Shaffer, Harrison, Gregersen, Black, & Ferzandi, 2006; van der Zee & van Oudenhoven, 2000), while others have a wider conceptualization including tolerance for ambiguity, the willingness to change, and the ability to deal with stress (e.g., Arthur & Bennett, 1995). Accordingly, there is much confusion and misunderstanding about what exactly cultural competence entails, with no overarching theoretical framework to tie the numerous constructs together and little consensus regarding the operationalization of cultural competence (Chapter 18; Ridley, Baker, & Hill, 2001). Mired in such confusion, the practical utility of cultural competencies is undoubtedly compromised.

It is within this scientific context that the current volume on cultural intelligence (CQ) takes off on its scientific road. Through its many novel and innovative theoretical and empirical chapters, this volume clearly illustrates the promise of CQ to revolutionize and transform the cultural competency literature. A relatively "young" construct on the scientific block, CQ has begun to demonstrate its theoretical elegance, empirical potential, and practical importance in a remarkably short period of time. In short, this volume represents the state of the science and, more generally, the field's collective intelligence about the construct of CQ. As a young field, however, there are a number of growing pains that can also be identified in this volume that provide some critical challenges as well as opportunities for the future study of CQ. In this commentary, we highlight the key contributions that the chapters collectively make to the study of CQ as well as emerging quandaries, questions, and controversies that should be considered on the road ahead.

KEY CONTRIBUTIONS OF THE CQ CONSTRUCT

The CQ construct facilitates theoretical progress in the literature in a number of important ways. First, the CQ construct offers *parsimony* (otherwise known as Ockham's razor principle), or the scientific goal of choosing the simplest theory among a set of otherwise equivalent theories in explaining a given phenomenon. CQ, in attempting to explain effective cultural adaptation, is parsimonious because it focuses on a small number of facets (i.e., metacognitive, cognitive, motivational, behavioral) at a higher, abstract level of generality rather than focusing on a larger number of dimensions at a more specific level. Furthermore, the CQ construct offers *theoretical synthesis and coherence* because it captures the multifaceted nature of cultural competence in a cohesive manner. In this regard, by providing a unified theoretical framework, CQ integrates previously disconnected phenomena. For example, while many cultural competency constructs have focused on one or two of the metacognitive, cognitive, motivational, and behavioral dimensions, they have rarely considered all four dimensions simultaneously, and never as a unified construct.

While the CQ construct is comprehensive, at the same time it also offers *theoretical precision.* With its explicit focus on cognition, motivation, and behavior, CQ is explicit on what it *is* and what it is *not* within its construct space (e.g., CQ is not values nor is it personality). At the same time, the CQ construct serves as a useful benchmark in delineating what other cultural competency constructs are and are not, allowing for some cleanup of the construct confusion that plagues the cultural competency literature, akin to what the Big Five did to the personality literature in the early 1990s. Moreover, while the CQ construct helps to reorganize existing constructs, it also identifies *missing cultural competencies* that have thus far received little attention in the literature. For example, the metacognitive facet with its focus on higher-level cognition (planning, monitoring, and adjusting) involved in strategic cultural learning is particularly important given its hierarchical role relative to cognition, motivation, and behavior.

CQ serves a useful function by connecting research *across disciplinary borders* through a common intellectual frame, helping to unite previously disconnected literatures. Even within this handbook, scholars are applying CQ to an array of disciplines beyond management, including counseling psychology (Chapter 16), communication sciences (Chapter 15), and religious studies (Chapter 17). Even within the field of management, the CQ construct helps to integrate across a broad number of research topics including the literatures on individual differences/personality, intelligence, expatriation, teams, training, the self, and identity, among other topics.

CQ also breaks new ground by linking cultural competencies to the extant literature on intelligence. First, CQ broadens the extant intelligence literature by addressing how individuals adapt to a new kind of environment that has not been addressed in the literature before—the increasingly common environment of diversity that comes with globalization. The CQ construct also expands on the intelligence literature by shifting focus from culture-specific interpersonal types of intelligence (e.g., social intelligence, emotional intelligence) to a culture-free construct. Second, drawing on the framework of *intelligence per se* for cultural competencies opens up a wide range of possible phenomena to be studied that may be relevant to cultural adaptation. For instance, through its connection to the intelligence literature, heretofore neglected cognitive processes, such as declarative knowledge, procedural knowledge, analogical reasoning, pattern recognition, external scanning, as well as self-awareness (see Earley & Ang, 2003), become highly relevant to issues of cultural adaptation.

INNOVATIVE MODELS OF CQ

As numerous chapters in this volume attest, there are many exciting conceptual and empirical developments that are collectively mapping the antecedents and consequences of CQ (Chapters 1 and 2). Highlighting the notion that CQ is a dynamic construct (Chapter 11, Bell & Harrison, 1996; Shaffer et al., 2006), authors in this volume tackle the important question of how people develop their CQ in the first place. At the individual level of analysis, a number of individual difference variables have been shown or theorized to relate to CQ, including need for control (Chapter 8), openness to experience (Chapter 9), global identity (Chapter 11), language ability (Chapter 3), contextualized knowledge (Chapter 20), and multicultural personality (Chapter 10), although the causality of these relationships is unclear.

Numerous situational factors have been identified as precursors of CQ, most notably general international experiences (Chapter 3), nonwork experiences (Chapter 4), and multicultural experiences within a culturally diverse group (Chapter 20). Notably, numerous scholars in this volume have focused on more complex interactions between situational and personality variables that predict CQ. For example, several chapters highlight the notion that international experiences need not always help to develop CQ uniformly; rather they do so particularly among individuals who are high in openness (Chapter 20) and/or have a low need for control (Chapter 8). Others discuss situational moderators of international experiences. Tarique and Takeuchi make the interesting and counterintuitive point that international experiences are stronger predictors of CQ when they are *shorter* rather than longer in duration. Finally, throughout this volume, exciting predictions are also offered regarding the influence of higher-level factors on the development of CQ. Shokef and Erez examined how a global work environment enhances CQ, while Leung and Li (Chapter 21) proposed that culture level variables such as social complexity and social cynicism are critical in enhancing and attenuating CQ, respectively. Clearly, there are multilevel antecedents of CQ.

This volume also illustrates that CQ is related to a number of important outcomes. CQ has been shown and/or hypothesized to relate to a number of affective outcomes, including adjustment (Chapters 2, 5, and 10), well-being (Chapter 2), burnout (Chapter 8), and retention (Chapter 7). CQ has also been linked to performance outcomes, including individual decision-making effectiveness (Chapter 2), adaptive performance (Chapter 9), expatriate performance (Chapter 5), and multinational team integration (Chapter 12). CQ likely has important effects at the organizational level, as illustrated in Mannor's theoretical analysis of top managers' CQ. Particularly intriguing is the link between CQ and executive information processing, including scanning breadth and quality and quantity of information search, quality of investment decisions, and, ultimately, better ability to expand internationally and develop international joint ventures with host national companies.

We would also note that it is very encouraging that, as with antecedents of CQ, scholars in this volume have begun to focus on more complex interactions between CQ and other situational and personality variables in predicting outcomes. For example, Shaffer and Miller highlight the importance of the job context as a moderator of CQ effects, noting that CQ will weaken the negative link between role novelty and role conflict and performance while strengthening the positive link between role clarity and role discretion and performance. Rockstuhl and Ng (Chapter 13) suggest that CQ interacts with team level factors (e.g., diversity), such that CQ moderates the negative link between diversity and interpersonal trust. At a more macro level, Kim et al. make the interesting prediction that CQ is more important for outcomes when cultural distance between the host and home country is larger rather than smaller. In all, this volume clearly shows that we need to examine CQ in conjunction with other factors in order to have a comprehensive understanding of its effects.

Finally, this volume has sought to connect the antecedents and consequences dots through CQ. For example, highlighting the role of CQ as a malleable adaptation, several authors in this volume illustrate that CQ mediates the relationship between individual difference variables and both affective and performance outcomes. Oolders and colleagues demonstrated the mediating effects of CQ in the relationship between openness to experience and performance. Similarly, Ward and Fischer found CQ to mediate the multicultural personality-adjustment link, while Shaffer and Miller theorized that CQ mediates the effects of international experience and language ability on expatriate performance. In all, this research is extremely helpful in that it helps to elucidate the causal pathway through which personality and other individual differences influence individual outcomes.

Taken as a whole, this volume makes significant progress in illustrating the promise of the CQ construct, its antecedents, and its consequences. CQ, a relatively new construct, has taken off quickly and in a decidedly short period of time. Now that the CQ construct is gaining momentum, it is time to examine the implicit and potential controversies and hurdles that warrant attention in future theorizing and research. As Weinberg (1989) noted, "Probably no psychological concept has engendered more controversy than intelligence" (p. 98), as evidenced in numerous debates about general intelligence (Sternberg & Kaufman, 1998) and more recently emotional intelligence (Zeidner, Matthews, & Roberts, 2004). CQ, as another form of intelligence, will likewise benefit from further critical discussions at the level of the construct, methods, and models.

TO FACET OR NOT TO FACET: CLARIFYING THE UTILITY OF CQ FACETS

We have noted that the multidimensional nature of CQ—the facets of metacognitive, cognitive, motivational, and behavioral CQ—serves a number of valuable scientific functions, most notably, providing a theoretical and coherent synthesis heretofore not available in the multicultural competency literature. Yet this volume also illustrates that we are still in a very embryonic state regarding theorizing and research on the facets. First, although factor analyses have confirmed the four separate factors of CQ, it is not clear whether all factors are necessarily part of the intelligence construct. For example, should self-efficacy regarding intercultural interactions (i.e., motivational CQ) necessarily be conceptualized as part of the intelligence construct? Intuitively it seems plausible for a culturally competent person to lack motivation just as a person with high IQ could lack motivation.

At present, theorizing on the facets can be imprecise, inconsistent, and/or contradictory. For example, some research programs focus on overall CQ and others focus on the facet level, raising the question of what the facets add, and when it is critical to theorize on their effects. Inconsistency can also be found regarding the predictors and outcomes of CQ facets (e.g., an identical antecedent being theorized to lead to different facets across different studies, or different facets being proposed to lead to an identical outcome across different studies). For example, international experience was hypothesized to lead to the development of behavioral CQ and not cognitive CQ in Chapter 3 yet to the development of cognitive CQ but not behavioral CQ in Chapter 8. Some authors proposed that motivational and behavioral CQ lead to interaction adjustment among expatriates (Chapter 2), whereas others propose that cognitive CQ is relevant to interaction adjustment (Chapter 7). Inconsistency is not problematic per se, when it identifies competing theories; yet we would suggest that inconsistency, if not attended to, can cause a literature to emerge in a potentially chaotic and confusing fashion, and that the different CQ facets present risks of this nature.

Importantly, although CQ facets were originally purported to act in concert in influencing behavior (Chapter 1; Earley & Ang, 2003), very little research has examined how the dimensions *interact* in predicting outcomes. For example, what is the psychological and social impact of having low cognitive and metacognitive CQ but high motivational CQ? Likewise, what is the impact of having high cognitive and metacognitive CQ but low motivational CQ? Uncovering distinct CQ facet profiles might provide a more nuanced look at facets that is not captured when looking at them in isolation. Focusing on the facets in combination also naturally raises the question of whether some facets are more "basic" than others, and at least whether *some* level must be present in order for others to exert their effects. In all, more precise and comprehensive theorizing is needed on the facets comprising CQ in the road ahead.

PEERING INTO THE CQ BOX: ON THE NEED TO SPECIFY THE MECHANISMS OF CQ EFFECTS

Future research must examine the black box of both the antecedents and consequences of CQ. To date, little is known about the processes through which CQ is developed or the processes through which CQ exerts its effects, although there are some notable exceptions. Tarique and Takeuchi (Chapter 4), for example, provided a particularly compelling temporal framework, describing how individuals develop their CQ by attending to, retaining, and reproducing the knowledge, skills, and abilities (KSAs) they discover in new cultural settings. Additional process models such as these will prove useful in articulating the emergence of CQ. Moreover, specifying the causal relationship between CQ antecedents is also an important research priority. As this volume attests, there are many potential individual difference and situational factors that can be related to the development of CQ (e.g., need for control, openness to experience, language ability, international experiences), yet the causal relationship between these constructs remains largely unexplored, raising the proverbial CQ chicken-and-egg question. Indeed, as Shokef and Erez (Chapter 11) showed in their insightful longitundinal analysis of global identity and CQ, many of the relationships between the proposed antecedents and CQ are very likely reciprocal in nature. Many of the relationships between CQ and outcomes discussed throughout this volume (adjustment, performance, retention) might also be reciprocal, necessitating the development of more dynamic models of CQ.

Likewise, little is known regarding the precise mechanisms through which CQ exerts its effects on outcomes. It is tempting to theorize that CQ affects outcomes because people are more knowledgeable about other cultures, yet this risks the promulgation of quasi-tautological reasoning. A critical question, then, is what precisely are high CQ individuals doing on their international assignments that is in turn affecting a wide range of positive outcomes? Future research must examine the multiple mediators—psychological, interpersonal, and even organizational—that are helping to translate high CQ into higher affective and job outcomes. For example, do individuals with high CQ develop more realistic expectations, which in turn translate into less psychological distress and more adjustment? Are high-CQ individuals better able to become central in local social networks, affording them more tangible and intangible resources that help them to perform their jobs better? Are high-CQ individuals better able to negotiate with their home organizations in terms of their expectations, provisions of resources, time frames, and so on? Opening the CQ black box and addressing these questions will benefit from longitudinal and social network analyses, and process-oriented methods, including the use of experiential sampling methods. Supplementing quantitative analyses of CQ with qualitative methods, as several authors in this volume have cogently advocated (e.g., Chapters 15 and 23), is also a must for future CQ research.

PLAYING DEVIL'S ADVOCATE: CQ AND THE POSITIVE HALO EFFECT

This volume clearly attests to the value of CQ in explaining outcomes above and beyond other cultural competencies, and in showing the importance of CQ for a host of positive outcomes, such as higher adjustment, performance, and lower turnover. Yet in seeking to show the universal positive value of CQ as a construct, we need to be mindful of not throwing the baby out with the bathwater, or, in other words, of continuing to examine other cultural competencies and other forms of intelligence in substantive ways. Put simply, by focusing exclusively on differentiating itself from general and emotional intelligence and existing cultural competencies, CQ research might not be fully exploiting the interactive potential of these constructs. Côté and Miners (2006), for instance, found that emotional intelligence (EQ) can compensate for low IQ, exhibiting its strongest effects on job performance when IQ is low, and it is possible that a similar relationship exists between CQ and other intelligences. Alternatively, it is possible that CQ's effects are partially contingent on other intelligences, such that a certain minimum IQ or EQ is needed for a high CQ to be fully realized. To truly understand CQ, a simultaneous consideration of all intelligences is critical, rather than simply using other intelligences as variables to statistically control in the CQ equation.

It is equally important to integrate CQ with theory on constructs in the cultural competency literature such as intercultural sensitivity, ethnocentrism, cultural flexibility, global mindset, and multicultural personality. It would be useful, for instance, to integrate the temporal development of intercultural sensitivity proposed by Bhawuk, Sakuda, and Munusamy (Chapter 22) with theory on the temporal development of CQ. Likewise, it would seem an oversimplification to suggest that CQ is simply superior to all other cultural competencies. Rather, it would seem best to develop an understanding of the theoretical relationships among the various cultural competencies, and understand *when* some predict while others do not. In all, we must therefore be careful not to focus on CQ at the expense of other previously established constructs in the intelligence and cultural competency literatures.

We would also argue that we should be mindful of the positive halo that currently exists around CQ. Implicit throughout this volume is the notion that CQ is invariably associated with positive values such as tolerance, broad-mindedness, and cooperation, and accordingly, there seems to be a general assumption in the literature that high CQ will always lead to positive outcomes. Yet with the exception of the motivational component of CQ, we see no a priori reason why high CQ (e.g., high cultural knowledge and the ability to adapt to others) will necessarily result in prosocial behavior, raising the question as to whether there is a "dark side" to CQ. For example, are there conditions under which high CQ individuals might take advantage of their extensive cultural knowledge and behavioral flexibility to try to take advantage of low CQ individuals in competitive business contexts? Warriors and generals, for example, have long noted the benefits of having an in-depth understanding of an enemy before engaging in battle. As Sun Tzu said in *The Art of War,* "If you know the enemy and know yourself, your victory will not stand in doubt." Just as Sun Tzu had less than kind intentions for his enemies, it is possible that individuals could use their cultural knowledge for similarly one-sided gains. Put simply, CQ might make it easier to keep your cross-cultural friends close, and your cross-cultural enemies even closer.

Likewise, throughout this volume, the question of whether high CQ has any psychological downside has received little attention. Inasmuch as culture serves as a "system of meaning" that brings certainty and predictability in navigating everyday interactions, an individual with an overly broad and in-depth conceptualization of culture may suffer from not having any "absolutes." Whether it is about personal values or what is considered morally right and wrong, it may be possible that an individual with an extremely high level of CQ might suffer from confusion as a result of an extremely relativistic worldview. Having extremely high levels of CQ across multiple cultures may decrease an individual's basic sense of belongingness, to the extent that he or she cannot help but to feel like a perpetual "participant observer" who sees even their own societal culture from an outsider's perspective. In other words, consciously knowing too much about cultural realities relative to other people who experience culture as an unconscious, invisible part of life, may lead to a certain sense of alienation. In all, future research should examine both positive and potentially negative effects of CQ.

THE MULTILEVEL NATURE OF CQ

Although CQ itself is a construct at the individual level, it is inherently a multilevel phenomenon, requiring research attention at the individual, team, organizational, and national levels of analysis. Much research on CQ, as this volume shows, however, has been largely limited to the individual level of analysis, and thus, the next wave of research on the construct should begin to start tackling the multilevel terrain in which CQ processes exist. For example, individuals high or low in CQ do not exist in a vacuous CQ context; they often have to interact with others who also vary in CQ, raising the question of the impact of the dyadic or team composition of CQ on individual as well as group-level outcomes. For example, is high CQ sufficient for an expatriate to develop an informal tie with a host national, or does the host national (alter) also need to have high CQ? Within dyadic contexts, do both individuals need to have high CQ in order to achieve high dyadic outcomes? For example, within the realm of dyadic negotiation, what are the implications of minimum CQ (lowest level of CQ in the dyad), maximum CQ (highest level of CQ in the dyad), the dyad mean CQ, as well as the dyad difference in CQ, for individual and dyad-level negotiation outcomes? Similarly, as Gibson and Dibble (Chapter 14) aptly note, CQ is likely critical in helping teams externally adjust, raising the question of what the necessary and sufficient composition of CQ is for team effectiveness. Likely, the nature of the task will be a critical driver of CQ composition effects. Gaining high, joint outcomes in negotiation by sequencing cooperative behaviors, for example, is a highly conjunctive task (Steiner, 1972) in which contributions from both negotiators are required for high performance. It is possible in this case that the dyad's ability to attain high performance is a function of the lowest level of CQ within the dyad, or in other words, the "weakest link." Put simply, even if one negotiator possesses high CQ, as long as the other negotiator has low CQ and does not contribute to the joint activity of reciprocating cooperative behaviors, the dyad may still suffer as a result (see Imai & Gelfand, 2007 for a discussion). Thus, compositional models of CQ across multiple types of tasks and contexts will be important to develop in future research on CQ.

As with any construct involving individuals nested in teams, organizations, and cultures, multilevel models of the antecedents and consequences of CQ are in need of development. This includes an examination of both (1) the predictors of CQ across levels of analysis, and (2) cross-level moderators of the effects of CQ on individual level outcomes. For example, the development of CQ might fruitfully be examined through mixed determinant models (Kozlowski & Klein, 2000), wherein CQ has antecedents that exist simultaneously at multiple levels of analysis (e.g., societal culture, industry, organizational culture, work culture, and individual differences). Likewise, much of the extant research on CQ has examined single-level models of CQ as it relates to outcomes, but cross-level direct models and cross-level moderating models will provide a more comprehensive approach to CQ–outcome relationships. For example, it is possible to suggest that culture-level values (e.g., intellectual autonomy, Schwartz, 1994) and culture-level diversity will both predict an individual's CQ (e.g., an intercept-as-outcomes model) and strengthen the impact of CQ on the individual's sense of belongingness and the quality of the individual's social interactions (e.g., a slopes-as-outcomes model).

Finally, as some authors in this volume have suggested, conceptual and empirical work must be done to assess the meaningfulness and dimensionality of CQ at higher levels of analysis. Can teams have high or low CQ (Chapter 11)? Are there "culturally intelligent organizations" that, through their values, assumptions, policies, and procedures, create cultural adaptation at the organizational level? Likewise, do attraction-selection-attrition processes apply to CQ and the emergence of CQ at higher levels? For example, does CQ influence applicants' attraction to multicultural organizations and employees' willingness to apply for cross-cultural or overseas assignments (self-selection processes)? On the other hand, organizations interested in being culturally intelligent might also hire and place employees on the basis of their CQ as inferred through interviews and other selection techniques. Moving up a level, are nations more or less culturally intelligent, as suggested by Leung and Li (Chapter 21)? In this era of globalization, are there societal advantages, such as higher economic outcomes and lower international conflict in countries with high levels of CQ? At the same time, we must consider the possibility that some cultures are more "culturally competent" than others while also recognizing that CQ might not be universally important, for example, in contexts that are highly homogenous or wherein the ecology requires the development of other types of intelligences, e.g., practical or social intelligence (see Sternberg, Chapter 19). More generally, when moving across levels, it will be important to not assume the construct is isomorphic, and to specify the emergence and meaning of the construct at the team, organization, and national levels.

ON THE NEED FOR METHODOLOGICAL DIVERSITY

The CQ scale (Chapter 2; Ang, Van Dyne, Koh, Ng, Templer, Tay, & Chandrasekar, 2007)—by far the most utilized scale as seen throughout this volume—has shown great promise for the study of CQ. Yet future research would benefit from having methodological diversity in assessing such a complex construct, as has been done for other intelligence constructs. Most notably, the use of self-reported CQ surveys brings the usual disadvantages and assumptions associated with self-report methods. For example, the use of the scale assumes that individuals can accurately assess their own CQ levels, yet, there is abundant evidence that people are overconfident in assessment of their own skills and abilities (Dunning, Heath, & Suls, 2004), particularly those who have low competence (Kruger & Dunning, 1999). Put simply, people who know more realize to a greater extent how much they do not know; thus, it is entirely possible for highly culturally intelligent individuals to rate themselves lower than less culturally intelligent individuals.

Indeed, Bhawuk et al.'s (Chapter 22) discussion of individuals progressing from unconscious incompetence to conscious incompetence further suggests that more competence can bring forth the conscious realization of one's relative lack of knowledge and skills. Furthermore, while individuals are rating themselves on the CQS, it is unclear which reference group they have in mind. An undergraduate student with the experience of studying abroad may think of him- or herself as having high CQ relative to other undergraduate students, whereas a global manager who has higher CQ in reality than the undergraduate student may still rate him- or herself as having lower CQ, if the reference group in mind involves other global managers with extensive international experience. As with other culture scales, social comparison effects are also likely to apply to CQ ratings (see Peng Nisbett, & Wong, 1997).

Thus, increasing the diversity with which we measure CQ will help obviate a number of biases associated with self-reports. Numerous possibilities exist. Van Dyne, Ang, and Koh (Chapter 2) illustrate the value of observer ratings of CQ, which were consistent with self-ratings and predicted self-rated adjustment (see Appendix C). Future measurement of CQ should focus on objective tests of knowledge and ability (Chapter 10). In addition to asking individuals to rate their cultural knowledge, objective tests of facts pertaining to legal and economic systems, art, religion, language, and so on across cultures can be assessed. Implicit measures of cultural knowledge, such as the spontaneous cultural inferences task, which uses priming techniques to assess level of cultural expertise (Fu, Chiu, Morris, & Young, 2007), will be useful for future CQ research (Chapter 18). With this technique, individuals are presented with culture-related sentences (e.g., "Tai chi is good for one's health"), and then presented a culture probe word that represents core cultural values (e.g., filial piety). Individuals are then asked to respond if that culture probe word was present in the previous sentence as quickly as possible. For those with extensive cultural expertise, because the culture-related sentence activates their network of cultural representation in the mind, it takes longer to reject the probe word compared to cultural novices.

Cognitive mapping techniques and network scaling could also be developed to assess the complexity of ways in which cultural knowledge is represented in the mind. That is, those with more complex representations of culture should be able to describe certain cultures in more integrated, differentiated, and abstract manners; they should also be able to articulate a greater number of nontrivial ideas pertaining to the culture. In developing new measures of CQ, it will also be useful to turn to related disciplines within psychology. For example, physiological and neurological research would be useful to integrate with CQ in that previous research has shown that perceptions of culture influence physiological reactions to cultural situations (Chao, Chen, Roisman, & Hong, 2007) and that culture itself can even affect neural activation patterns (Goh et al., 2007). Beyond the cognitive sciences, it also might prove useful to link CQ to developmental psychology. Just as specific predictors of CQ such as language ability have been found to be most malleable early in life, it is possible that CQ would be influenced most strongly by cultural experiences that occur during a critical period before a single pattern of cultural expectations becomes deeply entrenched.

CONCLUSION

In conclusion, this volume attests to the promise that CQ has for numerous disciplines. The CQ construct offers parsimony, theoretical coherence, and precision that is unprecedented in the cultural competency literature. Research has already identified important antecedents, consequences, and moderators of CQ effects. The future of CQ is bright, and is undoubtedly filled with numerous exciting theoretical, empirical, and methodological possibilities that have great practical importance in the global village in which we live.

REFERENCES

Ang, S., Van Dyne, L., Koh, C., Ng, K.Y., Templer, K.J., Tay, C., & Chandrasekar, N.A. (2007). Cultural intelligence: Its measurement and effects on cultural judgment and decision making, cultural adaptation, and task performance. *Management and Organization Review, 3,* 335–371.

Arthur, W., & Bennett, W. (1995). The international assignee: The relative importance of factors perceived to contribute to success. *Personnel Psychology, 48,* 99–114.

Bell, M.P., & Harrison, D.A. (1996). Using intra-national diversity for international assignments: A model of bicultural competence and expatriate adjustment. *Human Resource Management Review, 6,* 47–74.

Bhawuk, D., & Brislin, R.W. (1992). The measurement of intercultural sensitivity using the concepts of individualism and collectivism. *International Journal of Intercultural Relations, 16,* 413–36.

Chao, M.M., Chen, J., Roisman, G.I., & Hong, Y. (2007). Essentializing race: Implications for bicultural individuals' cognition and physiological reactivity. *Psychological Science, 18*(4), 341–348.

Cote, S., & Miners, C.T.H. (2006). Emotional intelligence, cognitive intelligence, and job performance. *Administrative Science Quarterly, 51*(1), 1–28.

Dunning, D., Heath, C., & Suls, J.M. (2004). Flawed self-assessment: Implications for health, education, and the workplace. *Psychological Science in the Public Interest, 5,* 69–106.

Earley, P.C., & Ang, S. (2003). *Cultural intelligence: Individual interactions across cultures.* Palo Alto, CA: Stanford University Press.

Fu, J.H., Chiu, C.Y., Morris, M.W., & Young, M.J. (2007). Spontaneous inferences from cultural cues: Varying responses of cultural insiders and outsiders. *Journal of Cross-Cultural Psychology, 38,* 58–75.

Goh, J.O., Chee, M.W., Tan, J.C., Venkatraman, V., Hebrank, A., Leshikar, E.D. et al. (2007). Age and culture modulate object processing and object-science binding in the ventral visual area. *Cognitive, Affective, & Behavioral Neuroscience, 7*(1), 44–52.

Gullahorn, J., & Gullahorn, J. (1963). An extension of the U-curve hypothesis. *Journal of Social Issues, 19,* 33–47.

Gupta, A.K., & Govindarajan, V. (2002). Cultivating a global mindset. *Academy of Management Executive, 16,* 116–126.

Hammer, M.R., Bennett, M.J., & Wiseman, R. (2003). Measuring intercultural sensitivity: The intercultural development inventory. *International Journal of Intercultural Relations, 27,* 421–443.

Hannigan, T.P. (1990). Traits, attitudes, and skills that are related to intercultural effectiveness and their implications for cross-cultural training: A review of the literature. *International Journal of Intercultural Relations, 14,* 89–111.

Hanvey, R.G. (1976). Cross-cultural awareness. In E.C. Smith, & L.F. Luce (Eds.), *Towards internationalism: Readings in cross-cultural communication* (pp. 44–56). Rowley, MA: Newbury House Publishers.

Hawes, F., & Kealey, D. (1981). An empirical study of Canadian technical assistance: Adaptation and effectiveness on overseas assignment. *International Journal of Intercultural Relations, 4,* 239–258.

Imai, L., & Gelfand, M.J. (2007). Culturally intelligent negotiators: The impact of CQ on intercultural negotiation effectiveness. In *Academy of Management Best Paper Proceedings* CD-ROM. Washington D.C.: Academy of Management.

Kelley, T.L. (1927). *Interpretation of educational measurements.* New York: World Book.

Kozlowski, S.W.J., & Klein, K.J. (2000). A multilevel approach to theory and research in organizations: Contextual, temporal, and emergent processes. In K.J. Klein & S.W.J. Kozlowski (Eds), *Multilevel theory, research, and methods in organizations: Foundations, extensions, and new directions* (pp. 3–90). San Francisco, CA: Jossey-Bass.

Kruger, J., & Dunning, D. (1999). Unskilled and unaware of it: How difficulties in recognizing one's own incompetence lead to inflated self-assessments. *Journal of Personality and Social Psychology, 77,* 1121–1134.

LaFromboise, T., Coleman, H.L., & Gerton, J. (1993). Psychological impact of biculturalism: Evidence and theory. *Psychological Bulletin, 114,* 395–412.

Peng, K., Nisbett, R.E., & Wong, N.Y.C. (1997). Validity problems comparing values across cultures and possible solutions. *Psychological Methods, 2*(4), 329–344.

Ridley, C.R., Baker, D.M., & Hill, C.L. (2001). Critical issues concerning cultural competence. *The Counseling Psychologist, 29,* 822–832.

Ruben, I., & Kealey, D.J. (1979). Behavioral assessment of communication competency and the prediction of cross-cultural adaptation. *International Journal of Intercultural Relations, 3,* 15–17.

Schwartz, S.H. (1994). Beyond individualism/collectivism: New cultural dimensions of values. In U. Kim, H.C. Triandis, C. Kâgitçibasi, S. Choi, & G. Yoon (Eds.) *Individualism and collectivism: Theory, method, and applications* (pp. 85–119), Thousand Oaks, CA: Sage.

Shaffer, M.A., Harrison, D.A., Gregersen, H., Black, J.S., & Ferzandi, L.A. (2006). You can take it with you: Individual differences and expatriate effectiveness. *Journal of Applied Psychology, 91,* 109–125.

Smith, M.B. (1966). Explorations in competence: A study of peace corps teachers in Ghana. *American Psychologist, 21,* 555–566.

Steiner, I.D. (1972). *Group processes and productivity* New York: Academic Press.
Sternberg, R.J., & Kaufman, J.C. (1998). Human abilities. *Annual Review of Psychology, 49,* 479–502.
Torbiorn, I. (1982). *Living abroad: Personal adjustment and personnel policy in the overseas setting.* New York: John Wiley & Sons.
Tzu, Sun. *The art of war,* trans. L. Giles. Available at http://classics.mit.edu/Tzu/artwar.html (accessed on 18 February 2008).
van der Zee, K.I., & van Oudenhoven, J.P. (2000). The Multicultural Personality Questionnaire: A multidimensional instrument of multicultural effectiveness. *European Journal of Personality, 14,* 291–309.
van Oudenhoven, J.P., & van der Zee, K.I. (2002). Predicting multicultural effectiveness of international students: The Multicultural Personality Questionnaire. *International Journal of Intercultural Relations, 26,* 679–694.
Weinberg, R. A. (1989). Intelligence and IQ: Landmark issues and great debates. *American Psychologist,* 44, 98–104.
Zeidner, M., Matthews, G., & Roberts, R.D. (2004). Emotional intelligence in the workplace: A critical review. *Applied Psychology: An International Review, 53,* 371–399.

APPENDIX A

Cultural Intelligence Scale (CQS) Self-Report

Read each statement and select the response that best describes your capabilities. Select the answer that BEST describes you AS YOU REALLY ARE (1 = strongly disagree; 7 = strongly agree)

CQ Factor	Questionnaire Items
Metacognitive CQ:	
MC1	I am conscious of the cultural knowledge I use when interacting with people with different cultural backgrounds.
MC2	I adjust my cultural knowledge as I interact with people from a culture that is unfamiliar to me.
MC3	I am conscious of the cultural knowledge I apply to cross-cultural interactions.
MC4	I check the accuracy of my cultural knowledge as I interact with people from different cultures.
Cognitive CQ:	
COG1	I know the legal and economic systems of other cultures.
COG2	I know the rules (e.g., vocabulary, grammar) of other languages.
COG3	I know the cultural values and religious beliefs of other cultures.
COG4	I know the marriage systems of other cultures.
COG5	I know the arts and crafts of other cultures.
COG6	I know the rules for expressing nonverbal behaviors in other cultures.
Motivational CQ:	
MOT1	I enjoy interacting with people from different cultures.
MOT2	I am confident that I can socialize with locals in a culture that is unfamiliar to me.
MOT3	I am sure I can deal with the stresses of adjusting to a culture that is new to me.
MOT4	I enjoy living in cultures that are unfamiliar to me.
MOT5	I am confident that I can get accustomed to the shopping conditions in a different culture.
Behavioral CQ:	
BEH1	I change my verbal behavior (e.g., accent, tone) when a cross-cultural interaction requires it.
BEH2	I use pause and silence differently to suit different cross-cultural situations.
BEH3	I vary the rate of my speaking when a cross-cultural situation requires it.
BEH4	I change my nonverbal behavior when a cross-cultural situation requires it.
BEH5	I alter my facial expressions when a cross-cultural interaction requires it.

For updated information on Cultural Intelligence, please see www.culturalq.com.

APPENDIX B

Cultural Intelligence Scale (CQS) Observer Report

Read each statement and select the response that best describes this person's capabilities. Select the answer that BEST describes this person as he/she REALLY IS (1 = strongly disagree; 7 = strongly agree)

CQ Factor	Questionnaire Items
Metacognitive CQ:	
MC1	This person is conscious of the cultural knowledge he/she uses when interacting with people with different cultural backgrounds.
MC2	This person adjusts his/her cultural knowledge as he/she interacts with people from a culture that is unfamiliar.
MC3	This person is conscious of the cultural knowledge he/she applies to cross-cultural interactions.
MC4	This person checks the accuracy of his/her cultural knowledge as he/she interacts with people from different cultures.
Cognitive CQ:	
COG1	This person knows the legal and economic systems of other cultures.
COG2	This person knows the rules (e.g., vocabulary, grammar) of other languages.
COG3	This person knows the cultural values and religious beliefs of other cultures.
COG4	This person knows the marriage systems of other cultures.
COG5	This person knows the arts and crafts of other cultures.
COG6	This person knows the rules for expressing nonverbal behaviors in other cultures.
Motivational CQ:	
MOT1	This person enjoys interacting with people from different cultures.
MOT2	This person is confident that he/she can socialize with locals in a culture that is unfamiliar.
MOT3	This person is sure he/she can deal with the stresses of adjusting to a culture that is new.
MOT4	This person enjoys living in cultures that are unfamiliar.
MOT5	This person is confident that he/she can get accustomed to the shopping conditions in a different culture.
Behavioral CQ:	
BEH1	This person changes his/her verbal behavior (e.g., accent, tone) when a cross-cultural interaction requires it.
BEH2	This person uses pause and silence differently to suit different cross-cultural situations.
BEH3	This person varies the rate of his/her speaking when a cross-cultural situation requires it.
BEH4	This person changes his/her nonverbal behavior when a cross-cultural situation requires it.
BEH5	This person alters his/her facial expressions when a cross-cultural interaction requires it.

For updated information on Cultural Intelligence, please see www.culturalq.com.

APPENDIX C

Mini-CQS—A Short Version of the Cultural Intelligence Scale

Read each statement and select the response that best describes your capabilities. Select the answer that BEST describes you AS YOU REALLY ARE (1 = strongly disagree; 7 = strongly agree).[a]

Questionnaire Items
I enjoy interacting with people from different cultures.
I am sure I can deal with the stresses of adjusting to a culture that is new to me.
I know the cultural values and religious beliefs of other cultures.
I know the legal and economic systems of other cultures.
I know the rules (e.g., vocabulary, grammar) of other languages.
I am conscious of the cultural knowledge I use when interacting with people with different cultural backgrounds.
I check the accuracy of my cultural knowledge as I interact with people from different cultures.
I change my verbal behavior (e.g., accent, tone) when a cross-cultural interaction requires it.
I change my non-verbal behavior when a cross-cultural situation requires it.

[a]This nine-item version of the CQS was designed to assess overall CQ.

For updated information on Cultural Intelligence, please see www.culturalq.com.

About the Editors and Contributors

Soon Ang is Goh Tjoei Kok Chair Professor of management at Nanyang Business School, Nanyang Technological University, Singapore. She received her PhD from the University of Minnesota and specializes in three distinct areas: cultural intelligence, global leadership, and outsourcing. She serves on the editorial boards for several journals, including *Management Science, Decision Sciences, Organization Sciences, Applied Psychology,* and *Information Systems Research,* and has published in *Academy of Management Journal, Journal of Applied Psychology, Organization Science, Management Science,* and *Social Forces,* among others. She has pioneered and co-authored two books on cultural intelligence (published by Stanford University Press). She has developed globally validated assessment tools for cultural intelligence. She was recently awarded the prestigious Distinguished International Alumni Award by the University of Minnesota for her academic leadership and scholarship record.

Preeta M. Banerjee is assistant professor of strategy at the International Business School, Brandeis University. Her research focuses on technology and innovation management in entrepreneurial firms. She is also an affiliate of the Biology, Business, Economics, and Law program at the Institute for Genomic Biology, University of Illinois at Urbana-Champaign. Before completing her PhD at the Wharton Business School, Banerjee worked in several Silicon Valley consultancy firms. She received her Bachelor of Science degree in Computational Biology and Business at Carnegie Mellon University.

Thomas M. Begley is the Dean of the School of Business at University College Dublin. He most recently held the Governor Hugh L. Carey Chair in Organizational Behavior at UCD. His research focuses on organizational change, cross-cultural management, and team development. He has published in the *Journal of Applied Psychology, Journal of International Business Studies, Journal of Organizational Behavior, Organizational Dynamics, Sloan Management Review,* and *Journal of Managerial Psychology,* among others.

Dharm P.S. Bhawuk, a citizen of Nepal, is professor of management and culture and community psychology at Shidler College of Business, University of Hawaii at Manoa.

He received his PhD from the University of Illinois at Urbana-Champaign. Dr. Bhawuk's research interests include cross-cultural training, intercultural sensitivity, diversity in the workplace, individualism and collectivism, and indigenous psychology and management. He has published more than 50 chapters and articles, and co-edited the book *Asian Contributions to Cross-Cultural Psychology* (Sage 1996).

Tineke Cappellen is a doctoral student at the Research Centre for Organization Studies, Katholieke Universiteit Leuven, Belgium. She holds master's degrees in political science and managerial economics, also from K.U. Leuven, and a master's degree in human resource management from the University of Antwerp Management School. Currently, she is preparing a PhD on global managers, their career correlates, and cultural intelligence.

Gilad Chen is an associate professor of management and organization at the Robert H. Smith School of Business, University of Maryland. His research focuses on work motivation, teams and leadership, and cross-cultural adaptation. His research has won numerous research awards and has appeared in the *Academy of Management Journal, Journal of Applied Psychology, Journal of Organizational Behavior, Personnel Psychology, Organizational Research Methods, Research in Organizational Behavior,* among other journals.

Oleksandr S. Chernyshenko is an associate professor at the Nanyang Business School, Nanyang Technological University, Singapore. He received his PhD in industrial and organizational psychology from the University of Illinois at Urbana-Champaign. Before joining Nanyang Business School, he was a senior lecturer in psychology at the University of Canterbury. His research focuses on applications of psychometric methods in the areas of personality, performance management, and job attitudes.

Audrey Chia is an associate professor of management and organization at the NUS Business School, National University of Singapore. She received her PhD from the University of Texas at Austin. Her research and teaching interests include leadership, change management, social and ethical issues in management, and work-family issues.

Chi-yue Chiu is a professor of psychology at the University of Illinois at Urbana-Champaign. He received his PhD in social-personality psychology from Columbia University. His current research focuses on cultures as knowledge traditions, and the social, cognitive, and motivational processes that mediate the construction and evolution of social consensus. He is also interested in the dynamic interactions of cultural identification and cultural traditions, and the implications of such interactions on cultural competence and intercultural relations.

Rebekah Dibble is a doctoral student in organization and management at the Paul Merage School of Business, University of California, Irvine. After completing her MBA she spent three years working with teams, coaching team leaders, and designing and leading change initiatives. Her current research interests are focused on adjustment and resilience in global teams and collaborations, social and cognitive determinants of reference group formation, and the impact of national culture and government on organizations.

Detelin S. Elenkov is an associate professor in management at University of Tennessee, Knoxville. He received his PhD from the Massachusetts Institute of Technology. His research interests span areas ranging from cross-cultural management and environmental scanning to leadership and multiple intelligences. He has published numerous books, book chapters, and articles in academic journals, including *Academy of Management Journal, Strategic Management Journal, California Management Review, Journal of Management, Journal of International Management,* and *Journal of World Business.*

Miriam Erez is the Mendes France professor of management and economics, faculty of industrial engineering and management, at Technion–Israel Institute of Technology, Haifa, Israel. Her research focuses on work motivation, cross-cultural organizational behavior, and innovation in organizations. Erez is the former editor of *Applied Psychology: An International Review* (1997–2003), and the recipient of the 2002 Distinguished Scientific Award of the International Association of Administrative Professionals and the 2005 Israel Prize in Management Sciences for her contribution toward integrating psychology and management.

Ryan Fehr is a doctoral student in industrial/organizational psychology at the University of Maryland. His research interests include cultural competence, expatriation, social networks, and creativity. He is a National Science Foundation graduate research fellow, and has recently co-authored an article on the future of cross-cultural organizational behavior, forthcoming in the *Journal of Organizational Behavior.*

Ronald Fischer is senior lecturer and research fellow with the Centre for Applied Cross-Cultural Research at Victoria University of Wellington, New Zealand. His research interests are cross-cultural research methods, and cultural differences in psychological functioning, particularly in work settings. Currently, he coordinates a 15-country project on the effects of cultural norms and organizational practices on organizational citizenship behavior. He received the 2007 Early Career Award from the International Academy for Intercultural Research.

Jane E. Flaherty is an organizational change consultant specializing in strategic planning, operational and process design, and transformation implementation. Her passion for helping global organizations maximize the value of their diverse workforce has been a driving force in her research and the growth of her consulting practice. Jane earned her master's of science in organization development from Pepperdine University. She resides in San Francisco with her husband, Matt, and their daughter, Emma.

Michele J. Gelfand is a professor of organizational psychology at the University of Maryland, College Park. Her research interests include cross-cultural social/organizational psychology; cultural influences on conflict, negotiation, justice, revenge, and leadership; discrimination and sexual harassment; and theory and method in culture. She has published in *Annual Review of Psychology, Academy of Management Review, Academy of Management Journal, Journal of Applied Psychology, Journal of Personality and Social Psychology,* and *Organizational Behavior and Human Decision Processes.*

Cristina B. Gibson, is a professor of organization and management at the Paul Merage School of Business, University of California, Irvine. Her research interests include collective cognition, interaction, and effectiveness in teams; the impact of culture on work behavior; and international management. Cristina's research has appeared in journals such as *Administrative Science Quarterly, Academy of Management Journal, Academy of Management Review,* and *Journal of International Business Studies.*

Michael Goh is an associate professor, program coordinator, and training director in the counseling and student personnel psychology program at the University of Minnesota. His teaching, research, and service are focused on improving access to mental health services for ethnically diverse, new immigrant, and international populations. His current research program includes: cultural intelligence and cultural competence in mental health practice, multicultural master therapists, and help-seeking behavior and attitudes across cultures and countries.

Lynn Imai is a doctoral candidate in industrial/organizational psychology at the University of Maryland. Her research interest lies in cross-cultural organizational behavior in the context of conflict management. Her upcoming chapter on culture and conflict from an interdisciplinary perspective will appear in the *Handbook of Culture, Organization, and Work,* and her master's thesis on cultural intelligence and intercultural negotiation was recently published in the *Academy of Management Best Paper Proceedings.*

Maddy Janssens is professor of organizational studies at the Research Centre for Organization Studies, Katholieke Universiteit Leuven, Belgium. She received her PhD in psychology from Katholieke Universiteit Leuven, after which she studied at Northwestern University. Janssens was a visiting professor at INSEAD during 1996 and at the Stern School of Business, New York University during 1999. She has published articles in the areas of expatriate management, cross-cultural methodology, global teams, language in international business, and diversity in organizations.

Kwanghyun Kim is a doctoral candidate in management at the Mays Business School at Texas A&M University, and holds a master's degree in human resources and industrial relations from the University of Illinois at Urbana-Champaign. His current research interests include individual differences and motivation within and across cultures, international human resource management, and performance management at both individual and team levels. His research is forthcoming in the *Journal of World Business* and *Industrial Relations.*

Bradley L. Kirkman is the John E. Pearson associate professor of management and Mays research fellow at the Mays Business School, Texas A&M University. He received his PhD in organizational behavior from the Kenan-Flagler Business School at the University of North Carolina at Chapel Hill. His research centers on global virtual teams, work team effectiveness, international management, and organizational justice.

Jennifer Klafehn is a doctoral student in industrial-organizational psychology at the University of Illinois at Urbana-Champaign. Her current research interests include negotiation, conflict resolution, and other related cross-cultural applications to organizational psychology.

Julie M. Koch is a doctoral candidate in the counseling and student personnel psychology program at the University of Minnesota. She has worked as a school counselor and is a certified K–12 school counselor in the state of Texas. Her research interests include school counseling, multicultural counseling, international and immigrant populations, and counselor training and development. She is an active member of the American Psychological Association, American Counseling Association, and American School Counselor Association.

Christine Koh is an associate professor in the division of information technology and operations management at Nanyang Technological University. She received her PhD in business at Nanyang and her research interests include cultural intelligence, cross-cultural issues in managing foreign talent, and outsourcing management. Her papers have been published in *Group and Organization Management, Management and Organization Review, Information Systems Research, MIS Quarterly, Journal of IT Cases and Applications,* and *Journal of Global IT Management.* She is the director of technology and psychometrics at the Center for Leadership and Cultural Intelligence.

Kwok Leung is a Chair Professor of management at City University of Hong Kong. He received his PhD in social and organizational psychology from the University of Illinois, Urbana-Champaign. His research areas include justice and conflict, cross-cultural psychology and research methods, and international business. He is a senior editor of *Management and Organization Review* and a consulting editor of *Journal of International Business Studies,* a fellow of the Academy of Intercultural Research and Association for Psychological Science (U.S.A.), and a member of the Society of Organizational Behavior.

Fuli Li is a doctoral student in the department of management at City University of Hong Kong and in the department of management science at the University of Science and Technology of China. She received her bachelor's degree in administration management from Anhui University, in Hefei, China. Her current research interests include individuals' innovative behavior and team creativity, and effects of information systems adoption on creativity and innovation.

David Livermore is the executive director of the Global Learning Center at Grand Rapids Theological Seminary where he also teaches intercultural studies. He received his PhD from Michigan State University. He has been conducting applied research on cultural intelligence as it relates to the work of nongovernmental and faith-based organizations. He has worked in more than 75 countries and is author of the award-winning book *Serving with Eyes Wide Open: Doing Short Term Missions with Cultural Intelligence* (Baker 2006).

Michael J. Mannor is a doctoral student in the strategic management group of the Eli Broad Graduate School of Management at Michigan State University. His research is primarily focused in the domains of organizational learning and executive leadership. His research has been published or is forthcoming in the *Journal of Applied Psychology, Journal of Organizational Behavior,* the *Academy of Management Best Paper Proceedings,* and several books.

Gloria Miller is a doctoral candidate in business management at the University of Wisconsin–Milwaukee. She is interested in cross-cultural research and cultural intelligence and in teaching organizational behavior and human resource management. She has been a teaching assistant and guest lecturer in these areas. Her past experience includes more than eight years as a human resource manager.

Vijayan P. Munusamy is a senior research associate at the Center for Creative Leadership®–Asia. He started his career as an engineer and made his first "cultural crossing" toward promoting cultural education in Malaysia after observing that many of the conflicts in the workplace and in society are due to cultural misunderstandings. Recognizing research as an important part of cultural education, he made his second "cultural crossing" toward becoming a degree fellow at the East-West Center, Honolulu, Hawaii.

Kok-Yee Ng is an associate professor in management at the Nanyang Technological University. She received her PhD from Michigan State University, with a major in organizational behavior and minor in industrial and organizational psychology. Her research interests are mainly in cross-cultural organizational behavior, focusing on areas such as cultural intelligence, leadership, trust, and teams. She has published in *Academy of Management Journal, Journal of Applied Psychology, Management Science,* and *Organizational Behavior and Human Decision Processes.*

Tania Oolders is an organizational consultant in Wellington, New Zealand. Her career had moved from chemical engineering to radio journalism (with Radio New Zealand) before she completed her master's degree in industrial and organizational psychology at the University of Canterbury.

Joana R.C. Pimentel is a doctoral candidate at the University of Tennessee. Her research interests include multiple intelligences, leadership, empowerment, and change management. She also works as an organizational development consultant for multinational organizations.

Thomas Rockstuhl is a doctoral student in management at the Nanyang Technological University. He received his master's degree in industrial and organizational psychology from the Technical University of Dresden, Germany. His research interests include the behavioral measurement of cultural intelligence, the development of trust in multicultural teams, cross-cultural training, and expatriate adjustment. He has presented his work at conferences such as the Society for Industrial and Organizational Psychology, the Academy of Management, and the Academy of International Business.

Priscilla S. Rogers is an associate professor of business communication at University of Michigan's Ross School of Business, and senior fellow at Nanyang Business School. Recognition for research with the Nanyang faculty includes: "Best Article on Theory of Technical Communication" (National Council Teachers of English) and "Distinguished Publication" (Association for Business Communication). She received the Association's 1999 Outstanding Researcher award. She has worked for diverse companies including Bank of Finland, Cathay Pacific Airways, and Ford Motor Company.

Keith H. Sakuda is a doctoral student in international management specializing in international organization and strategy at Shilder College of Business at the University of Hawaii at Manoa. His research interests include cross-cultural training and intercultural group dynamics. He currently holds an MBA from the University of Hawaii and a graduate certificate from Fujitsu's Japan America Institute of Management Science.

Sandra Sanger is a doctoral student in the counseling and student personnel psychology program at the University of Minnesota. Her research and clinical interests focus on topics in multicultural counseling, suicide, and crisis intervention. She has specific interests in the interpersonal nature of suicide and training issues related to clinical work with suicidal clients.

Margaret Shaffer is the Richard C. Notebaert distinguished chair of international business and global studies at the University of Wisconsin, Milwaukee. She received her PhD from the University of Texas at Arlington. She is an active researcher in expatriation and cross-cultural organizational behavior and has published extensively in journals such as the *Academy of Management Journal, Journal of Applied Psychology,* and the *Journal of International Business Studies.*

Lu M. Shannon is a doctoral candidate in management at the Michael Smurfit Graduate School of Business at University College Dublin. She also holds an MBA from University College Dublin. Her current research interests include the determinants and consequences of cultural intelligence, international human resource management, and intercultural aspects of organizational behavior.

Efrat Shokef is currently a postdoctoral visiting scholar at the Wharton School, University of Pennsylvania. She completed her doctorate at the Faculty of Industrial Engineering and Management, Technion–Israel Institute of Technology. Her research focuses on global identity and global work culture, and their interplay with national culture as expressed in multinational organizations and multicultural teams.

Stephen Stark is an assistant professor of psychology at the University of South Florida. He received his PhD in industrial and organizational psychology from the University of Illinois at Urbana-Champaign. He has published papers on computer adaptive testing, differential item and test functioning (measurement bias), and issues related to faking in personality assessment.

Robert J. Sternberg is Dean of the School of Arts and Sciences, professor of psychology, and adjunct professor of education at Tufts University. He also is honorary professor of psychology at the University of Heidelberg. He is a past president of the American Psychological Association and is currently president of the Eastern Psychological Association as well as president-elect of the International Association for Cognitive Education and Psychology.

Riki Takeuchi is an assistant professor in the department of management of organizations at the School of Business and Management, Hong Kong University of Science and Technology. He received his PhD from the Robert H. Smith School of Business, University of Maryland at College Park. His research interests include expatriate adjustment and international human resource management, strategic human resource management, organizational justice, and organizational citizenship behaviors.

Ibraiz Tarique is an assistant professor at Pace University, New York City. He received his PhD in human resource management from Rutgers University. His academic research interest is in international human resource (HR) management, focusing on international training and development, and global staffing. His applied research interest is in HR education with a focus on examining the career patterns through which individuals are now becoming HR professionals and the approaches that organizations are using to develop future global HR professionals.

Cheryl Tay is assistant professor of management at Nanyang Business School, Nanyang Technological University, Singapore, and the director of program and assessment at the Center for Leadership and Cultural Intelligence. Her research interests include study of cross-cultural, work-life issues and individual differences, e.g., self-efficacy, in cross-boundary and expatriate management. She has published in *Group and Organization Management* and the *Journal of Applied Psychology.*

Linn Van Dyne, professor, Michigan State University, received her PhD from the University of Minnesota. She has two major research programs: proactive employee behaviors involving initiative and cultural intelligence and has published in *Academy of Management Journal*, *Academy of Management Review*, *Journal of Applied Psychology*, *Organizational Behavior and Human Decision Processes*, *Research in Organizational Behavior*, and other outlets. She is associate editor of *Organizational Behavior and Human Decision Processes* and on the editorial boards of *Academy of Management Journal*, *Journal of Applied Psychology*, *Personnel Psychology*, *Journal of Organizational Behavior*, *Academy of Management Perspectives*, *Human Relations*, and *Management and Organization Review*. She is a fellow in the Society of Organizational Behavior.

Colleen Ward received her PhD in psychology from Durham University. She is professor of psychology and director of the center for applied cross-cultural research, Victoria University of Wellington, New Zealand. Her research focuses on cross-cultural transition and adaptation. She is co-author of *The Psychology of Culture Shock* (2001), Royal Society of New Zealand James Cook fellow in social science (2005–2007), president-elect of the International Academy of Intercultural Research, former secretary-general of the International Association for Cross-Cultural Psychology and immediate past president of the Asian Association of Social Psychology.

Mina Westman is an associate professor at the Faculty of Management, Tel Aviv University. Her primary research interests include determinants and consequences of job stress, work-family interchange, crossover in the family and the workplace, the effects of vacation on strain, and the impact of short business trips on the individual, the family, and the organization. Her empirical and conceptual articles have appeared in the *Journal of Applied Psychology*, *Human Relations*, and *Journal of Organizational Behavior*.

Index

Italic page references indicate figures and tables.

D

E

R

S

W

Y

Z

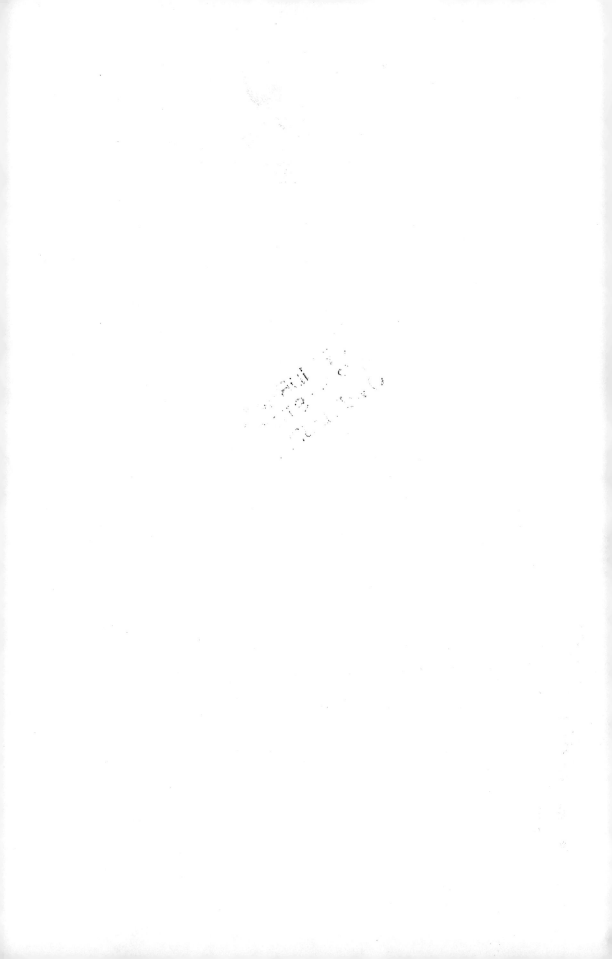